S0-BES-034

BEACON
BIBLE COMMENTARY

Library of Congress
Card Number 64-22906

Printed in the United States of America

BEACON
BIBLE COMMENTARY

In Ten Volumes

Volume IX

GALATIANS
R. E. Howard, B.D., M.A., Th.M.

EPHESIANS
Willard H. Taylor, B.D., M.A., Ph.D.

PHILIPPIANS
John A. Knight, B.D., M.A., Ph.D.

COLOSSIANS
John B. Nielson, B.D., M.A.

I AND II THESSALONIANS
Arnold E. Airhart, B.D., D.D.

I AND II TIMOTHY, TITUS
J. Glenn Gould, M.A., D.D.

PHILEMON
John B. Nielson, B.D., M.A.

BEACON HILL PRESS OF KANSAS CITY
Kansas City, Missouri

BEACON BIBLE COMMENTARY

In Ten Volumes

I. Genesis; Exodus; Leviticus; Numbers; Deuteronomy

II. Joshua; Judges; Ruth; I and II Samuel; I and II Kings; I and II Chronicles; Ezra; Nehemiah; Esther

III. Job; Psalms; Proverbs; Ecclesiastes; Song of Solomon

IV. Isaiah; Jeremiah; Lamentations; Ezekiel; Daniel

V. Hosea; Joel; Amos; Obadiah; Jonah; Micah; Nahum; Habakkuk; Zephaniah; Haggai; Zechariah; Malachi

VI. Matthew Mark; Luke

VII. John; Acts

VIII. Romans; I and II Corinthians

IX. Galatians; Ephesians; Philippians; Colossians; I and II Thessalonians; I and II Timothy; Titus; Philemon

X. Hebrews; James; I and II Peter; I, II, and III John; Jude; Revelation

Preface

"All scripture is given by inspiration of God, and is profitable for doctrine, for reproof, for correction, for instruction in righteousness: that the man of God may be perfect, throughly furnished unto all good works" (II Tim. 3:16-17).

We believe in the plenary inspiration of the Bible. God speaks to men through His Word. He hath spoken unto us by His Son. But without the inscripted Word how would we know the Word which was made flesh? He does speak to us by His Spirit, but the Spirit uses the written Word as the vehicle of His revelation, for He is the true Author of the Holy Scriptures. What the Spirit reveals is in agreement with the Word.

The Christian faith derives from the Bible. It is the Foundation for faith, for salvation, and sanctification. It is the Guide for Christian character and conduct. "Thy word is a lamp unto my feet, and a light unto my path" (Ps. 119:105).

The revelation of God and His will for men is adequate and complete in the Bible. The great task of the Church, therefore, is to communicate the knowledge of the Word, to enlighten the eyes of their understanding, and to awaken and to illuminate the conscience that men may learn "to live soberly, righteously, and godly, in this present world." This leads to the possession of that "inheritance [that is] incorruptible, and undefiled, and that fadeth not away, reserved in heaven."

When we consider the translation and interpretation of the Bible, we admit we are guided by men who are not inspired. Human limitation, as well as the plain fact that no scripture is of private or single interpretation, allows variation in the exegesis and exposition of the Bible.

Beacon Bible Commentary is offered in 10 volumes with becoming modesty. It does not supplant others. Neither does it purport to be exhaustive or final. The task is colossal. Assignments have been made to 40 of the ablest writers available. They are trained men with serious purpose, deep dedication, and supreme devotion. The sponsors and publishers, as well as the contributors, earnestly pray that this new offering among Bible commentaries will be helpful to preachers, teachers, and laymen in discovering the deeper meaning of God's Word and in unfolding its message to all who hear them.

—G. B. Williamson

Acknowledgments

Permission to quote from copyrighted material is gratefully acknowledged as follows:

Abingdon Press: *Abingdon Bible Commentary;* John Knox, *Chapters in a Life of Paul.*

Cambridge University Press: C. F. D. Moule, *The Epistles of Paul the Apostle to the Colossians and to Philemon.*

William B. Eerdmans Publishing Company: E. K. Simpson, *The Pastoral Epistles;* Donald Guthrie, *The Pastoral Epistles;* Francis Foulkes, *The Epistle of Paul to the Ephesians.*

Harper and Row: J. N. D. Kelley, *A Commentary on the Pastoral Epistles;* James S. Stewart, *A Man in Christ.*

Macmillan Company: William Neil, *St. Paul's Epistles to the Thessalonians.*

Oxford University Press: C. K. Barrett, *The Pastoral Epistles.*

Charles Scribner's Sons: D. M. Baillie, *God Was in Christ.*

University of Chicago Press: Edgar Goodspeed, *The Story of the New Testament;* W. F. Arndt and F. W. Gingrich, *A Greek-English Lexicon of the New Testament.*

Westminster Press: William Barclay, *Flesh and Spirit, Letters to the Philippians, Colossians and Thessalonians,* and *Letters to Timothy, Titus and Philemon.*

John Knox Press: *The Layman's Bible Commentary,* Vol. 23.

Fleming H. Revell Co.: F. F. Bruce, *The Epistle to the Ephesians.*

Scripture quotations have been used from the following sources:

The Amplified New Testament. Copyright 1958, The Lockman Foundation, La Habra, California.

The Berkeley Version in Modern English. Copyright 1958, 1959, Zondervan Publishing House.

The Bible: A New Translation, James Moffatt. Copyright 1950, 1952, 1953, 1954, by James A. R. Moffatt. Used by permission of Harper and Row.

The Bible: An American Translation, J. M. Powis Smith, Edgar J. Goodspeed. Copyright 1923, 1927, 1948 by The University of Chicago Press.

New American Standard Version. Copyright 1960, 1962, 1963, The Lockman Foundation, La Habra, California.

The New English Bible. © The Delegates of the Oxford University Press and the Syndics of the Cambridge University Press, 1961.

The New Testament in Modern English. © J. B. Phillips, 1958. Used by permission of The Macmillan Company.

Revised Standard Version of the Holy Bible. Copyrighted 1946 and 1952 by the Division of Christian Education of the National Council of Churches.

The Weymouth New Testament in Modern Speech. Copyright, Harper and Row Publishers.

Charles B. Williams, *The New Testament in the Language of the People.* Copyrighted 1937 by Bruce Humphries, Inc., assigned 1949 to The Moody Bible Institute of Chicago.

The New Testament, R. A. Knox. © 1951, Sheed and Ward.

Living Letters, Kenneth N. Taylor. © 1962, Tyndale House Publishers, Wheaton, Ill.

Quotations and References

Boldface type in the exposition indicates a quotation from the King James Version of the passage under discussion. Readings from others versions are put in quotation marks and the version is indicated.

In scripture references a letter (*a*, *b*, etc.) indicates a clause within a verse. When no book is named, the book under discussion is understood.

Bibliographical data on a work cited by a writer may be found by consulting the first reference to the work by that writer, or by turning to the bibliography.

The bibliographies are not intended to be exhaustive but are included to provide complete publication data for volumes cited in the text.

References to authors in the text, or inclusion of their books in the bibliography, does not constitute an endorsement of their views. All reading in the field of biblical interpretation should be discriminating and thoughtful.

How to Use "Beacon Bible Commentary"

The Bible is a Book to be read, to be understood, to be obeyed, and to be shared with others. *Beacon Bible Commentary* is planned to help at the points of understanding and sharing.

For the most part, the Bible is its own best interpreter. He who reads it with an open mind and receptive spirit will again and again become aware that through its pages God is speaking *to him.* A commentary serves as a valuable resource when the meaning of a passage is not clear even to the thoughtful reader. Also after one has seen his own meaning in a passage from the Bible, it is rewarding to discover what truth others have found in the same place. Sometimes, too, this will correct possible misconceptions the reader may have formed.

Beacon Bible Commentary has been written to be used with your Bible in hand. Most major commentaries print the text of the Bible at the top of the commentary page. The editors decided against this practice, believing that the average user comes to his commentary from his Bible and hence has in mind the passage in which he is interested. He also has his Bible at his elbow for any necessary reference to the text. To have printed the full text of the Bible in a work of this size would have occupied approximately one-third of the space available. The planners decided to give this space to additional resources for the reader. At the same time, writers have woven into their comments sufficient quotations from the passages under discussion that the reader maintains easy and constant thought contact with the words of the Bible. These quoted words are printed in boldface type for quick identification.

Illumination from Related Passages

The Bible is its own best interpreter when a given chapter or a longer section is read to find out what it says. This book is also its own best interpreter when the reader knows what the Bible says in other places about the subject under consideration. The writers and editors of *Beacon Bible Commentary* have constantly striven to give maximum help at this point. Related and carefully chosen cross-references have been included in order that the reader may thus find the Bible interpreted and illustrated by the Bible itself.

Paragraph Treatment

The truth of the Bible is best understood when we grasp the thought of the writer in its sequence and connections. The verse divisions with which we are familiar came into the Bible late (the sixteenth century for the New Testament and the seventeenth century for the Old). They were done hurriedly and sometimes missed the thought pattern of the inspired writers. The same is true of the chapter divisions. Most translations today arrange the words of the sacred writers under our more familiar paragraph structure.

It is under this paragraph arrangement that our commentary writers have approached their task. They have tried always to answer the question, What was the inspired writer saying in this passage? Verse numbers have been retained for easy identification but basic meanings have been outlined and interpreted in the larger and more complete thought forms.

Introductions to Bible Books

The Bible is an open Book to him who reads it thoughtfully. But it opens wider when we gain increased understanding of its human origins. Who wrote this book? Where was it written? When did the writer live? What were the circumstances that caused him to write? Answers to these questions always throw added light on the words of the Scripture.

These answers are given in the Introductions. There also you will find an outline of each book. The Introduction has been written to give an overview of the whole book; to provide you with a dependable road map before you start your trip—and to give you a place of reference when you are uncertain as to which way to turn. Don't ignore the flagman when he waves his warning sign, "See Introduction." At the close of the commentary on each book you will find a bibliography for further study.

Maps and Charts

The Bible was written about people who lived in lands that are foreign and strange to most English-speaking readers. Often better understanding of the Bible depends on better knowledge of Bible geography. When the flagman waves his other sign, "See map," you should turn to the map for a clearer understanding of the locations, distances, and related timing of the experiences of the men with whom God was dealing.

This knowledge of Bible geography will help you to be a better Bible preacher and teacher. Even in the more formal presentation of the sermon it helps the congregation to know that the flight into Egypt was "a journey on foot, some 200 miles to the southwest." In the less formal and smaller groups such as Sunday school classes and prayer meeting Bible study, a large classroom map enables the group to see the locations as well as to hear them mentioned. When you have seen these places on your commentary maps, you are better prepared to share the information with those whom you lead in Bible study.

Charts which list Bible facts in tabular form often make clear historical relationships in the same way that maps help with understanding geography. To see listed in order the kings of Judah or the Resurrection appearances of Jesus often gives clearer understanding of a particular item in the series. These charts are a part of the resources offered in this set.

Beacon Bible Commentary has been written for the newcomer to Bible study and also for those long familiar with the written Word. The writers and editors have probed each chapter, each verse, every clause, phrase, and word in the familiar King James Version. We have probed with the question, What do these words mean? If the answer is not self-evident, we have charged ourselves to give the best explanation known to us. How well we have succeeded the reader must judge, but we invite you to explore the explanation of these words or passages that may puzzle you when you are reading God's written Word.

Exegesis and Exposition

Bible commentators often use these words to describe two ways of making clear the meaning of a passage in the Scriptures. *Exegesis* is a study of the original Greek or Hebrew words to understand what meanings those words had when they were used by men and women in Bible times. To know the meaning of the separate words, as well as their grammatical relationship to each other, is one way to understand more clearly what the inspired writer meant to say. You will often find this kind of enriching help in the commentary. But word studies alone do not always give true meaning.

Exposition is a commentator's effort to point out the meaning of a passage as it is affected by any one of several facts known to the writer but perhaps not familiar to the reader. These facts may be (1) the context (the surrounding verses or chapters), (2) the historical background, (3) the related teachings from other parts of the Bible, (4) the significance of these messages from God as they relate to universal facts of human life, (5) the relevance of these truths to unique contemporary human situations. The commentator thus seeks to explain the full meaning of a Bible passage in the light of his own best understanding of God, man, and the world in which we live.

Some commentaries separate the exegesis from this broader basis of explanation. In *Beacon Bible Commentary* writers have combined the exegesis and exposition. Accurate word studies are indispensable to a correct understanding of the Bible. But such careful studies are today so thoroughly reflected in a number of modern English translations that they are often not necessary except to enhance the understanding of the theological meaning of a passage. The writers and editors seek to reflect a true and accurate exegesis at every point, but specific exegetical discussions are introduced chiefly to throw added light on the meaning of a passage, rather than to engage in scholarly discussion.

The Bible is a practical Book. We believe that God inspired holy men of old to declare these truths in order that the readers might better understand and do the will of God. *Beacon Bible Commentary* has been undertaken only for the purpose of helping men to find more effectively God's will for them as revealed in the Scripture—to find that will and to act upon that knowledge.

Helps for Bible Preaching and Teaching

We have said that the Bible is a Book to be shared. Christian preachers and teachers since the first century have sought to convey the gospel message by reading and explaining selected passages of Scripture. *Beacon Bible Commentary* seeks to encourage this kind of expository preaching and teaching. The set contains more than a thousand brief expository outlines that have been used by outstanding Bible teachers and preachers. Both writers and editors have assisted in contributing or selecting these homiletical suggestions. It is hoped that the outlines will suggest ways in which the reader will want to try to open the Word of God to his class or congregation. Some of these analyses of preachable passages have been contributed by our contemporaries. When the outlines have appeared in print, authors and references are given in order that the reader may go to the original source for further help.

In the Bible we find truth of the highest order. Here is given to us, by divine inspiration, the will of God for our lives. Here we have sure guidance in all things necessary to our relationships to God and under Him to our fellowman. Because these eternal truths come to us in human language and through human minds, they need to be put into fresh words as languages change and as thought patterns are modified. In *Beacon Bible Commentary* we have sought to help make the Bible a more effective Lamp to the paths of men who journey in the twentieth century.

A. F. Harper

Table of Contents

VOLUME IX

GALATIANS

Introduction 19
Commentary 26
Bibliography 125

EPHESIANS

Introduction 129
Commentary 139
Bibliography 273

PHILIPPIANS

Introduction 279
Commentary 286
Bibliography 354

COLOSSIANS

Introduction 359
Commentary 363
Bibliography 429

I AND II THESSALONIANS

Introduction 433
Commentary 439
Bibliography 536

I AND II TIMOTHY AND TITUS

Introduction 541
Commentary 551
Bibliography 694

PHILEMON

Introduction 699
Commentary 702
Bibliography 709

MAPS AND CHARTS 710

Abbreviations and Explanations

The Books of the Bible

Gen.	Job	Jonah	I or II Cor.
Exod.	Ps.	Mic.	Gal.
Lev.	Prov.	Nah.	Eph.
Num.	Eccles.	Hab.	Phil.
Deut.	Song of Sol.	Zeph.	Col.
Josh.	Isa.	Hag.	I or II Thess.
Judg.	Jer.	Zech.	I or II Tim.
Ruth	Lam.	Mal.	Titus
I or II Sam.	Ezek.	Matt.	Philem.
I or II Kings	Dan.	Mark	Heb.
I or II Chron.	Hos.	Luke	Jas.
Ezra	Joel	John	I or II Pet.
Neh.	Amos	Acts	I, II, or III John
Esther	Obad.	Rom.	Jude
			Rev.

Vulg.	The Vulgate
LXX	The Septuagint
ASV	American Standard Revised Version
RSV	Revised Standard Version
Amp. NT	Amplified New Testament
NASB	New American Standard Bible
NEB	New English Bible
IB	Interpreter's Bible
IDB	The Interpreter's Dictionary of the Bible
NBC	The New Bible Commentary
NBD	The New Bible Dictionary
EGT	Expositor's Greek Testament
BBC	Beacon Bible Commentary

c.	chapter	OT	Old Testament
cc.	chapters	NT	New Testament
v.	verse	Heb.	Hebrew
vv.	verses	Gk.	Greek

The Epistle to the

GALATIANS

R. E. Howard

Introduction

A. Authorship

There is no fact of New Testament studies more widely attested than the Pauline authorship of Galatians. The few who have rejected its genuineness have denied the existence of any first-century Christian literature and even of a first-century Apostle Paul. In contrast, this letter has been accepted by the most liberal critics as a norm for first-century authenticity.[1] Thus, "the letter to the Galatians was written, as it claims to have been, by Paul, the Christian apostle of the first century."[2]

B. Date

No evidence is available which determines with certainty when and where Paul wrote this Epistle. However, there are some references in the letter that assist in fixing the date within certain broad limits.[3] The account of the Jerusalem Council (2:1-10; cf. Acts 15) and the subsequent conflict with Peter at Antioch (11-18) determine the earliest possible date to be during Paul's stay at Antioch, between his first and second missionary journeys—approximately A.D. 48-50. The suggestion of two visits to Galatia before the letter was written[4] would make it necessary for Paul to have written it after his Galatian stop on the second missionary tour[5] (Acts 16:1-5). This stop would have been either after arriving at Corinth or when he returned to Antioch, before his third journey (Acts 18:23). Such a date would be approximately A.D. 50-51.

Another possibility is that Paul wrote the Epistle on his third missionary journey, during this extended stay at Ephesus (Acts 19:1-20), or even later while in Macedonia or Corinth (Acts 20:1-2). This would place the date about A.D. 54 or 55.

[1]Cf. E. D. Burton, *The Epistle to the Galatians* ("The International Critical Commentary," ed. S. R. Driver, A. Plummer, C. A. Briggs; Edinburgh: T. & T. Clark, 1921), pp. lxv-lxxi.

[2]*Ibid.*, p. lxxi.

[3]Cf. *ibid.*, pp. xliv-liii.

[4]Gal. 4:13; cf. Burton's argument that this does not conclusively prove two visits, but does strongly suggest it, *ibid.*, p. xlv.

[5]Acts 18:11. The return visit to the churches on the first journey would not have allowed time for the apostasy to develop (Acts 14:21-25).

The similarity of content in Galatians and Romans has produced the suggestion that they were written at approximately the same time,[6] which would place the date at approximately A.D. 56.[7]

An argument against such a late date is the suddenness of the Galatian apostasy,[8] and also the fact that the controversy with the Judaizers had subsided by this time—thus making the issues in Galatians out-of-date.

It appears that the Galatian letter was written shortly after Paul's final visit, probably from Ephesus, approximately A.D. 54 or 55.

C. Destination

The destination of this Epistle appears to be clearly defined, namely, "unto the churches of Galatia" (1:2). But such a conclusion quickly vanishes when it is realized that the term "Galatia" was used in two different ways in Paul's day. In common usage it referred to a relatively small region in northeastern Asia Minor, comparable to Lycaonia, Pisidia, and Phrygia. The official Roman use of the term designated a large province (see map 1) including adjacent portions of the above-named regions.

The migratory movements of the Celtic[9] tribes make up a large part of the pre-Christian history of southern Europe. After a hit-and-run raid in the fourth century B.C., which climaxed with the sacking of Rome, these restless people invaded Greece in the third century B.C., with more permanent objectives. When they were repulsed at Delphi in 279 B.C., the remnants of the defeated army joined a large group of their kinsmen who had not taken part in the invasion and overran Asia Minor. They were gradually repulsed by the native Asians and by the last half

[6]Cf. J. B. Lightfoot's detailed analysis of this similarity as well as with the Corinthian letters, *Saint Paul's Epistle to the Galatians* (London: Macmillan and Co., 1892), pp. 45-56.

[7]Cf. the date of Romans in William Sanday and Arthur C. Headlam, *The Epistle to the Romans* ("The International Critical Commentary"; New York: Charles Scribner's Sons, 1920), pp. xxxvi-xxxvii.

[8]Gal. 1:6. Cf. Lightfoot's argument that this is not significant, *op. cit.*, pp. 41-43.

[9]The early civilization west of the Rhine River was generally called "Celtic" by the early Greek classical writers, but by New Testament times was called "Galatian" by the Greeks and "Gallic" by the Romans. Modern philologists prefer the term "Celtic." Cf. Lightfoot, *op. cit.*, pp. 1-17, for an excellent summary of this civilization.

of the century were confined to a small area in the interior.[10] Early in the second century B.C. these Celts were conquered by the legions of Rome, but for over 150 years were allowed to govern themselves as a "dependent kingdom."[11] In 25 B.C. this relatively small territory was made a part of a larger Roman province that was given the same name.[12] However the Roman official title was in great part ignored by the populace, and the term "Galatia" was used with reference to the northern territory of the Celts.[13]

Where were the churches to whom this letter was addressed? If they were located in the northern territory dominated by the Celtic migrants, when were these churches founded?[14] There is a clear record of Paul founding churches in the cities of Derbe, Lystra, Iconium, and Antioch during his first missionary journey (Acts 13:13-14; 14:16, 21-24). These are all located in the Roman province of Galatia, but not in the northern territory of the Celtic migrants. At the beginning of his second journey Paul returned to these cities "confirming the churches" (cf. Acts 15:41—16:5). Luke adds that the missionary party "went through the Phrygian and Galatian country" (Acts 16:6, lit.). It has been argued that this is not a summary reference to the verses that precede it, but indicates that Paul journeyed to the north and established churches among the Celtic migrants. During Paul's third missionary journey Luke observes that the missionary party passed "through in order the Galatian country

[10]Burton designates the geographical limits of their region as follows: "a territory somewhat north and east of centre, bounded on the north by Bithynia and Paphlagonia, on the east by Pontus, on the south by Cappadocia and Lycaonia, and on the west by Phrygia, and traversed by the rivers Halys and Sangarius," *op. cit.*, p. xix.

[11]Cf. Burton, *op. cit.*, p. xix.

[12]Burton designates the geographical limits of the Roman province of Galatia as the district described above "and the adjacent portions of Lycaonia, Pisidia, and Phrygia" (*op. cit.*, p. xxi). Lightfoot suggests that Isauria was also included (*op. cit.*, p. 7).

[13]It is particularly significant that these people possessed quick apprehension, and an impressionable mind that craved knowledge; but were also inconstant, quarrelsome, treacherous, unstable, and easily disheartened by failure. Their religion (native) was basically superstitious, passionate, and ritualistic, with a slavish obedience to priestly authority. Cf. the excellent summary of the racial characteristics of the Celts in Lightfoot, *op. cit.*, pp. 14-17.

[14]Cf. the excellent summary of the history of opinion on this question by Burton, *op. cit.*, pp. xxiv-xxv. It is of interest to note that in the ancient Church it was assumed that Paul referred to the northern territory of the Celtic migrants. The "South-Galatia Theory" was not proposed until near the end of the eighteenth century.

and Phrygia[15] confirming the disciples" (Acts 18:23, lit.), which can be understood as a return visit to the Celts.

It is not possible to determine with certainty where the Galatian churches were located. However, the fact that Paul consistently used the proper Roman political divisions,[16] coupled with the known existence of churches in the southern area of the Roman province, would suggest that these known churches in the south were those to whom Paul wrote. At best, the argument for the "North Galatia Theory" is based on supposition and conjecture.[17] The all-important fact is that the question does not have any fundamental bearing on the interpretation of the Epistle.

D. Purpose

For centuries the only bulwark against the tide of pagan libertinism was Jewish legalism. Through the law, which had been received by special revelation, these devout people secured a degree of justification with God. Even among the early Jewish Christians the acceptance of Christ was in no sense considered an alternative or substitute for their holy law (cf. Acts 21:20). When the gospel of Christ was preached to the Gentiles the question quite naturally arose as to the necessity of the law. The Apostle to the Gentiles, inspired by a new revelation, proclaimed that salvation was through grace by faith—without the law! Such a message aroused the strong opposition of many who were convinced that a man could be justified only through keeping the law and who feared that to disregard it would be throwing the door open to pagan practices.

The controversy climaxed in the Jerusalem Council.[18] Following Paul's successful evangelization of the heathen province of Galatia the exponents of the law arrived, insisting that there could be no salvation without it. The apostle violently rejected this conclusion, and in this letter forcibly states his case.

Paul's argument is that a man is justified by grace through faith, on the basis of promise and not law. Further, this salvation by grace through faith brings freedom, which includes *free-*

[15]Burton argues that "Phrygian" probably is a noun and not an adjective (*op. cit.*, p. xxxviii).

[16]In contrast to Luke's mixed usage, cf. Burton, *op. cit.*, pp. xxv-xxix.

[17]Burton states that the Lycaonian people were no less warmhearted and fickle than the Celts (*op. cit.*, p. xlii).

[18]The Jerusalem Council was probably held in A.D. 48 or 49 (cf. Acts 15; Gal. 2:1-10).

dom from the law! To remain under the law not only was to fall short of God's grace, but would actually result in slavery or bondage. The law had fulfilled its temporary function and had now been abrogated. Freedom from sin was inseparable from freedom from the law. Some objected that this would allow and even encourage sin. Paul points out that the Spirit is also received by grace through faith, and His presence provides an adequate moral imperative against evil, which is sadly lacking in the law. However, Paul emphasizes that the believer must live under the discipline of the Spirit, not abusing his freedom, and finding the positive expression of his faith through love.

E. Theology

Paul has often been portrayed as teaching that justification is by faith alone. Actually the concept *alone* is a later theological addition. Paul argues that a man is justified by faith *without the works of the law*. However, having been justified by faith, the believer is to fulfill the just requirements of the law, through love.

The logical implication of justification by faith *alone* is antinomianism, against which Paul vehemently objected with "God forbid." His repeated warning that wrong living excluded men from God's kingdom should leave no doubt as to his attitude (cf. comments on 5:19-21). Paul was greatly concerned for his converts to realize that their new faith provided the only adequate means for ethical conduct, rather than absolving them of that responsibility.

There is a distinction in Paul's thought that it is essential to recognize. It can be described as the contrast of the indicative and imperative. In the Greek of the New Testament it is graphically seen in the use of differing moods. The indicative mood depicts a *simple* assertion, in past, present, or future time—"this is, was or shall be." The imperative mood depicts a *commanding* assertion—"this must be." Thus Paul not only indicates what was already the experience of the Galatians, but also what he was exhorting them to experience. By distinguishing his exhortations from his observations an important insight can be found into the apostle's thought.

It is important to remember that Galatians is not a systematic treatise with the material organized in a logical form or scheme. Instead, it is an impassioned letter that is filled with deep emotion. For instance, in the midst of Paul's reference to his conflict with Peter—which he is using as evidence of the divine authority of his message—he quite naturally goes on to give witness to his personal faith (2:11-21). He also pauses to appeal and admonish his "children" in the midst of a strong argument (4:12-20; 5:1).

Although the followers of Christ today are not besieged by the exponents of Jewish legalism, the basic emphasis of Paul is strikingly fitting. How often—and in how many different forms—has come the suggestion and even insistence that a Christian must have the protection of a legalistic cloak! Paul's warning that such legalism can result only in bondage and that the discipline of the Spirit alone can produce spiritual fruit needs to be heard again today.

F. Procedure

At the beginning of each section a brief synopsis is given so that the paragraph can be viewed in its entirety. An attempt has been made to deal with the technical and critical questions in the footnotes. Unless a specific notation is made, the lexical authority for the comments made on the Greek text is taken from Arndt and Gingrich.[19]

[19]William F. Arndt and F. Wilbur Gingrich, *A Greek-English Lexicon of the New Testament* (Chicago: The University of Chicago Press, 1957).

Outline

I. Paul's Introduction, 1:1-10

  A. The Apostolic Greeting, 1:1-5
  B. The Reason for Writing, 1:6-10

II. Authority—from God and Not Man, 1:11—2:21

  A. A Statement of Paul's Authority, 1:11-12
  B. Paul's Apostolic Authority Substantiated, 1:13—2:21

III. Argument—by Faith and Not Law, 3:1—5:12

  A. The Galatians' Own Experience, 3:1-5
  B. The Example of Abraham, 3:6-9
  C. The Limitations of the Law, 3:10-24
  D. Faith Contrasted with the Law, 3:25—5:1
  E. Circumcision Separates from Christ, 5:2-12

IV. Admonition—by Spirit, Not Flesh, 5:13—6:10

  A. A New Slavery of Love, 5:13-15
  B. Life in the Spirit and Flesh Contrasted, 5:16-26
  C. Practical Examples of Love, 6:1-10

V. Conclusion, 6:11-18

  A. Final Summation, 6:11-17
  B. The Apostolic Benediction, 6:18

Section I *Paul's Introduction*

Galatians 1:1-10

A. The Apostolic Greeting, 1:1-5

Paul, having emphasized his divine commission as an apostle, joins with his traveling companions in greeting the churches in Galatia. This greeting is a salutation of grace and peace from God their Father and the Lord Jesus Christ, whose gift of himself had made possible their rescue from the evil age in which they lived. For this gift they glorified God.

In the Earliest Church an **apostle** (1) held a distinct position of leadership and authority.[1] Although he considered himself the least worthy to be called an apostle, because of his persecution of the Church (cf. I Cor. 15:9), Paul still defended his right to that office (cf. I Cor. 9:1-2; II Cor. 11:5; 12:11-12), and repeatedly assumed the title.[2] Paul states that his apostleship was **not of** (*apo,* from) **men, neither by** (*dia,* through) **man;** it was not from a human source or through a human agency. This was the point where his enemies challenged him and sought to undermine his authority.[3] Thus, with this blunt statement at the outset of his letter, the apostle pointedly denies their basis of disqualifying him. Paul declares what he considers the only source and agency of apostleship, i.e., **by Jesus Christ.** He was directly commissioned by Christ.[4] On the Damascus Road he had met the risen Lord; this was the basis of his claim to the apostolic

[1]When listed with the other offices, that of "apostle" is placed first by Paul (I Cor. 12:28; Eph. 4:11), which would imply that it represented the highest authority. Cf. Rom. 12:4-8, where "apostle" is not included. For a thorough study of the title "apostle" in the New Testament and the Early Church, cf. Burton, *op. cit.,* pp. 365-81.

[2]Cf. Rom. 1:1; 11:13; I Cor. 1:1; II Cor. 1:1; Eph. 1:1; Col. 1:1; cf. also I Pet. 1:1; II Pet. 1:1.

[3]The selection of an apostle in Acts 1:15-26 emphasizes identification with the earthly ministry of Jesus and the instrumentality of the other apostles in the selection.

[4]This is the significance of his being a "called . . . apostle" (Rom. 1:1; I Cor. 1:1) and an apostle "through the will of God" (II Cor. 1:1). God "places" (I Cor. 12:28) and "gives" this office (Eph. 4:11).

office (cf. I Cor. 15:8). His authority came through Christ from **God the Father, who raised him from the dead.** Consequently, anyone challenging his authority would have to answer to God himself.

Certainly every servant of Christ—minister and layman—must have the sense of divine commission. The source and agency of his labors must be higher than human authority. If he be sent only by man, he will fail. Of course the precious assurance that "God has sent me" can be abused; but obstinacy and arrogance only cast a shadow on the reality of the claim. It has often been wondered if in the selection of Matthias (Acts 1:23-26) perhaps the eleven apostles missed God's choice. Time has argued that perhaps Paul was God's intended replacement for Judas.

Paul's reference to the resurrection of Jesus as the basis of his claim to a divine commission highlights the importance of this tenet of faith in the Early Church. Everything they believed was contingent upon the fact that God the Father had raised Jesus Christ from the dead. "If Christ be not raised, your faith is vain; ye are yet in your sins" (I Cor. 15:17). It might be asked: How important is the Resurrection to our faith today?

It is not known with certainty where Paul was staying when he wrote this letter (cf. Introduction). However, in keeping with his usual salutations,[5] he sends it from **all the brethren which are with me** (2). This probably has reference to his traveling missionary companions (cf. Acts 20:4) and not to the members of a church. These fellow laborers were undoubtedly known and respected by the Galatian churches, and the mention of them would lend strength to Paul's message.

One of the unsolved questions of New Testament scholarship is the identification of **the churches of Galatia.** Are they located in the northern district of Asia Minor (the popular and ethnic use) or in the southern part of the province of Galatia (the technical Roman use)? The fact that Paul never refers to cities in northern Galatia is a strong argument in support of the south Galatian theory (cf. Introduction; see map 1).

The apostolic blessing, **Grace be to you and peace from God the Father, and from our Lord Jesus Christ** (3), had already, at this early time, become a standard form. It is part of the

[5]Cf. I Cor. 1:1; II Cor. 1:1; Phil. 1:1; Col. 1:1.

salutation in every one of Paul's letters. Although related ideas can be found in Greek and Hebrew greetings, this salutation reflects the unique Christian concepts of God's favor that provides salvation through Christ and the blessedness that is a result.

Paul does not here specifically state that Christ died for man's sins, but there can be little doubt that this is what is meant, when he observes that He **gave himself for our sins** (4). The Cross and the Resurrection are Paul's primary concern, so that he scarcely mentions the life and ministry of Jesus. Paul's understanding of sin makes the Cross indispensable. A dedicated life—even that of Jesus Christ—is not efficacious to atone for sin. The purpose of giving himself is that He might deliver us from this present evil world. Taking the historical fact of the Cross, Paul makes a personal and practical application—present deliverance. The word **deliver** (*exaireo*) suggests a rescue from a helpless state.[6] Such a rescue is not the universal and automatic consequence of the Cross, but is a provided possibility.[7]

Here is the only instance that Paul speaks of this **world** (lit., age) as being **present** and **evil,** although it is elsewhere clearly implied in his common expression "the age." His figure of speech is graphic. Men are helplessly trapped in the grip of this evil age; but through the Cross, Christ is able to rescue them. Paul does not suggest that it is God's purpose to remove men, but He would rescue them from the power of evil in the world. It is significant that the apostle introduces this thought of deliverance from the power of sin as early as his opening salutation. Normally, after the apostolic blessing the apostle gives an expression of thanksgiving to God followed by a note of commendation for those to whom he is writing. It is distinctly different here. The reference to deliverance from sin, based entirely on the death of Christ, highlights Paul's deepest concern —to refute the proponents of the law. Instead of commending the Galatians, he confesses amazement and wonder at their rejection of the grace of Christ.

As a further statement of the identification of Christ with the Father, the apostle adds that this deliverance was **according to the will of God and our Father.** Christ gave himself and

[6]Cf. Joseph being rescued from his affliction in Egypt (Acts 7:10) and Peter being rescued from prison (Acts 12:11).

[7]The Greek mood is subjunctive, denoting strong possibility.

would deliver men in full accord with the Father's will. Thus Paul can conclude—**to whom be glory for ever and ever. Amen (5).**

B. The Reason for Writing, 1:6-10

1. *Galatian Apostasy* (1:6-7)

In this section Paul is astonished that the Galatians were so quickly deserting the Christ who had called them. They were forsaking Him for a different gospel, which was in reality not a gospel at all. Those who were troubling them only desired to pervert the gospel of Christ. As he had previously told them, whoever preached a gospel other than they had received—be it Paul or an angel from heaven—would be under God's curse. Then Paul asks if his preaching appeals to God or to men, and if by it he seeks to please men.

I marvel that ye are so soon removed[8] **from him that called you (6).** Paul was amazed that they were deserting so quickly.[9] The use of the present tense plainly indicates that the Galatians were in the process of deserting. This explains Paul's urgency, as he sought to turn them back before they were established in error. A move or change involves leaving as well as arriving. In order to take up a different gospel these Galatians had to depart from what they had known and experienced. They were deserting God. It was He who had called them from their heathen darkness to himself—the God who is Light, Life, and Love. Paul's amazement is that they could so quickly turn their backs on Him, and reminds them that God had called them **into the grace of Christ.** Basic to the thought of the apostle is the conviction that all things are from God (the Father) through Christ (the Son).

In a vivid play on words, in the Greek, Paul ironically states that they had turned **unto another** (*heteros*) **gospel: which is not another** (*allos*) **(7).** His opponents were evidently calling their teaching a gospel—claiming that it was superior to what Paul had preached. For a moment the apostle accepts their claim. How-

[8]The term **removed** (*metatithemi*), in the middle voice, as here, carries the significance of "changing one's mind," with the implications of desertion or apostasy.

[9]**So soon** (*tacheos*) can mean rapidity of change or brevity of time since their conversion, with the latter choice made preferable by the context.

ever he calls it a *heteros* gospel—"another of a different kind." It is not an *allos* gospel—"another of the same kind."[10] Paul then points out the specific reasons why this was not another gospel of the kind they had received; in fact, it was no gospel at all. A true gospel is "good news"—specifically the good news of salvation. However, Paul's opponents had come to **trouble** (*tarasso*) **you.** Their purpose was to stir up, disturb, and unsettle the Galatians. Through troubling these new converts they hoped to **pervert** (*metastrepho,* lit., overthrow) **the gospel of Christ.** Thus, theirs was no gospel at all, but only a veiled attempt to destroy the gospel of Christ, which is the "good news" that through Christ there is deliverance from this evil age (cf. v. 4). As Paul will later argue in detail, the result of their message was only bondage and slavery in contrast to the deliverance and freedom the Galatians had found by grace through faith.

2. *Crucial Issue* (1:8-10)

But though we, or an angel from heaven, preach any other gospel unto you than that which we have preached unto you, let him be accursed (8). So convinced was Paul that there was no other gospel that he invoked the curse of God upon himself—or even upon angels from heaven—if they "should preach a gospel at variance with (*para*) what we preached to you."[11] This was not careless speech or mere rhetoric. A person of Paul's heritage and training would have profound respect for solemn vows and curses. To be **accursed** (*anathema*) was fatal.[12] The serious nature of the error being promulgated among the Galatians is underscored by such a statement. Paul had warned them of this

[10]Cf. when Jesus promised "another" (*allos*) Comforter—the same kind (John 14:16). This is the accepted distinction between *heteros* and *allos*—cf. Burton, *op. cit.,* pp. 420-22; R. C. Trench, *Synonyms of the New Testament* (London: Kegan Paul, Trench & Co., 1886), pp. 358-61. There are some, however, who maintain that the terms are identical or interchangeable in meaning—cf. Arndt and Gingrich, *op. cit.,* p. 315.

[11]Burton thus interprets *para* in this and the following verse, arguing that Paul's opponents were not adding constructively to what he taught, nor were they directly contradicting him. They were making additions (the law) that were actually subversive. This is the *heteros* gospel of v. 6 (cf. *op. cit.,* pp. 27-28).

[12]J. Agar Beet says that "it denotes that which is to be destroyed at God's bidding, that on which rests the curse of God" (*A Commentary on St. Paul's Epistle to the Romans* [New York: Thomas Whittaker, n.d.], p. 265). Cf. Rom. 9:3.

error before, perhaps when he first preached to them. So he reminds them, **As we said before, so say I now again** (9). The contrast of **say I now** with **we said before** makes it quite certain that he was not referring to the previous verse.

If any man preach any other gospel unto you than that ye have received, let him be accursed. Verse 9 differs from 8 in that the indefinite pronoun "anyone" (*tis*) is used instead of the definite subject—Paul or an angel. Also, in 8 the possibility is more remote—"if we should"—while here the grammatical construction suggests that such is actually taking place—"if anyone is." Unquestionably Paul is referring to what was then being done in Galatia. He had at first simply used himself as a hypothetical illustration.

In our day of increasing tolerance in religion, Paul's dogmatic denunciation may appear somewhat out of place. Certainly there is a proper respect for the faith of others and we support the guarantee that no one suffer religious persecution. But this does not mean that all roads lead to God. Paul's opposition was not a narrow sectarianism; it was concern about the fundamental means of salvation. He was persuaded that the course the Galatians were taking would lead to spiritual slavery—and who should know better than he, who had lived under the law? He must condemn such theology—decisively. Had not his Master warned that He had come to bring a sword (cf. Matt. 10:34)? Our day needs this voice of certainty and conviction, as well as true tolerance.

Paul's opponents had accused him of accommodating his message so that it would appeal to men and win their favor. So he asks: **Do I now persuade** (*peitho,* appeal to) **men, or God?** (10) Is such a serious condemnation humanly appealing? He then repeats the same question in different terms: **Do I seek to please men?** His answer is an emphatic NO! **For if I yet pleased men, I should not be the servant of Christ.** This assertion must be understood in terms of its context. Paul was being accused by the Jews of rejecting the law to please the Gentiles. Elsewhere the apostle clearly demonstrates the importance and even necessity of pleasing men in order to win them to Christ (cf. I Cor. 10:33). The apostle cannot be considered a radical independent. He was sensitive to the attitudes of men. However, if he allowed himself to be placed in bondage to the opinions of men he could no longer be the free servant of Christ. If he had to decide between pleasing men and God, his choice was not in question.

In 1-10 we see "God's Message to Those Who Forsake Christ." (1) The message comes from **God the Father,** 1, and through a concerned spiritual leader, 4:19; (2) God's greatest concern is our salvation from sin, 4; (3) Have you deserted Christ? 6-7; (4) The seriousness of desertion, 8-9; (5) The road to recovery—**I seek to . . . be the servant of Christ,** 10, also 2:18-20 (A. F. Harper).

Section II *Authority—from God and Not Man*

Galatians 1:11—2:21

A. A Statement of Paul's Authority, 1:11-12

Paul declares to his brethren that the gospel he had preached to them was not a human or man-made message; he had not received it from man, nor had he been taught it. Instead, he had received it through a revelation of Jesus Christ.

At the outset Paul wants them to understand that his authority is from God and not man: **I certify** (*gnorio,* make known to) **you** (11). What he thus asserts in a direct statement he will presently substantiate in detail. By addressing them as **brethren** he indicates that the apostasy of the Galatians was not complete or irrevocable; they were still his fellow Christians. As Paul would emphasize later, **the gospel which** he **preached** was the pronouncement that salvation was by grace through faith and not by works of the law (cf. 3:1—4:31). There is no suggestion in the entire letter that he had any further theological conflicts with his opponents. Of particular significance is the fact that the gospel **is not after man.**[1] This expression has a special significance for Paul, and can even be equated with "fleshly."[2] The apostle's meaning is clear: his gospel was not a merely human message, as he further explains in the next verse.

This message was not human because Paul had not **received it of man** (12), nor was he **taught it.** Neither the source of his gospel nor the method by which he had received it was human. Most Christian teachers, even in Paul's day, had been taught by other men, but not he. Instead the gospel came **by the revelation of Jesus Christ.** This refers not to a general revelation, available to all who would receive it, but to a special and personal revelation to Paul.

The claim that one has a personal revelation makes him chargeable with being both presumptuous and dangerous. It is not difficult to appreciate the concern of Paul's opponents. On the

[1]Cf. Burton on *kata anthropon* (after man) (*op. cit.*, p. 37).

[2]Cf. I Cor. 3:1-4, where *sarkinos, sarkikos* (fleshly), and *anthropon* (man) are parallel.

basis of what would appear to them as a strictly private and personal revelation he was abrogating much of what they considered vital and sacred. Through the ages men have risen to proclaim a message for which they claim special revelation. This is precisely the fallacy of much of the modern concept of "inspiration." Such teachers agree that the Bible is "inspired." But so have other works been inspired—even those of a Shakespeare and a Beethoven. This, of course, destroys the uniqueness of the Scriptures. We recognize that God has inspired and given revelations to men since Bible times. But the revelation of the written Word is unique. In this sense it is terminal and not continuous. Paul's audacious claim was fully substantiated, not by him, but by the Spirit of God. Our task is not to add to the written revelation, but to understand and explain it.

B. Paul's Apostolic Authority Substantiated, 1:13—2:21

1. *Before Conversion Zealous Opposition* (1:13-14)

Paul reminded the Galatians that they had known of his conduct in Judaism—his excessive persecution of the Church and zealous pursuit of the traditions of his forefathers.

These heathen converts in Galatia had most likely **heard** (13) of this period of Paul's life from his own lips, which would be in keeping with his custom of using personal testimony in his preaching. They knew of his **conversation** (conduct) **in time past in the Jews' religion.** The translation of *anastrophe* as **conversation** is one of the unfortunate Elizabethan expressions in the KJV. That the term means the entire manner of life—conduct or behavior—is readily seen in the description that follows. Paul has reference specifically to his conduct in the religion of the Jews—literally, in Judaism. Also, the Galatians were well aware **how that beyond measure** he had **persecuted the church of God, and wasted it.** Paul's persecution of the Christian Church[3] was excessive and extreme. The term **wasted** (*protheo*) is a very strong one, meaning to "destroy" or "pillage"—having the clear implications of the ravages of warfare. Thus the apostle describes his pre-conversion conduct as a personal war against the Church of Christ.

[3]New Testament scholars consider it significant that Paul refers to the Church as a whole—using the singular number—and not to local groups or congregations.

Paul not only demonstrated his zeal by persecuting the Christians and destroying the Church, but at the same time he **profited** (*prokopto,* progressed)[4] **in the Jews' religion above many** of his **equals in** his **own nation** (14). Born of Hebrew parents, he had accepted the strictest interpretation of the law—he was a Pharisee. Even by such stringent standards he could describe himself as "blamelessly righteous" (cf. Phil. 3:5-6), **being more exceedingly zealous of the traditions of my fathers.** His progress in Judaism went far beyond the righteousness of the law—in its strictest sense. He describes himself as a zealot.[5] This was, of course, an essential part of Pharisaism.[6] In this regard he exceeded many of his contemporaries.

Paul's basic argument in this section is that his pre-conversion life demonstrates that he received the authority for his gospel from God and not man. For support of this he points to the facts of his extreme hostility to Christianity (on the negative side) and his superior progress in Pharisaical Judaism (on the positive side). Both are proofs that his acceptance of Christianity could not in any sense be traced to Christian (human) influence or instruction.[7] Only a divine revelation could accomplish it.

2. *After Conversion—No Human Consultation* (1:15-24)

a. Paul in Arabia and Damascus (1:15-17). God had marked Paul at birth to preach to the Gentiles. When God called him—through the revelation of His Son—Paul did not visit the apostles in Jerusalem, but went away in Arabia (perhaps 200 miles south of Damascus, and 100 miles southeast of Jerusalem; see map 2). Only after three years did he visit Peter and James in Jerusalem, and then for only fifteen days. Following this he went into Syria and Cilicia (see map 1). During this time he was unknown to the Judean churches, except through the report that their former persecutor was now preaching the faith he had once destroyed.

[4]*Prokopto* means to "go forward by laborious activity."

[5]Paul is not using the term *zelotes* in its technical sense, referring to a radical political party of his day. His Pharisaical affiliation would prohibit it.

[6]Cf. Jesus' accusations against the Pharisees, Matt. 15:3-9.

[7]Cf. the theory that Paul's zeal was due to an inner struggle against conviction that Christianity was true and right—perhaps a result of his witnessing Stephen's martyrdom.

As observed by Burton,[8] the whole section introduced by **but** (15) is not in contrast to what has gone before. Rather it is an extension of it. Thus, a better translation would be: and **when it pleased God.** The expression **when it pleased God** is a Hebraism that recognizes the divine sovereignty. It is simply another way of saying, "when God willed." It was God who had **separated** Paul **from** his **mother's womb.** This last expression is another familiar Hebraism, which refers to birth. Paul is thus calling attention to the fact that from his birth God had set him apart. **Separated** (*aphorizo*) can mean to separate *from,* in the sense of excommunication (cf. Luke 6:22), or to separate *to.* Here the latter meaning is obviously intended and thus amounts practically to an appointment. God had appointed Paul to his special task at birth. Then one day, on the Damascus Road, this appointment was revealed,[9] and God **called** him. The blindly zealous Pharisee was confronted by the risen Christ—and heard the call of God. As noted in 6, Paul viewed the proclamation of the gospel as God calling men to himself. The apostle had heard it from the lips of the resurrected Lord. The call and the appointment were, as are all of God's blessings, **by his grace.**

The details of this revelation are given elsewhere, primarily in the three accounts of Paul's conversion (Acts 9:1-18; 22:4-16; 26:9-18). As evident by his abbreviated reference here, the all-important fact was that the experience was designed to **reveal his Son in me** (16). This became the foundation stone of Paul's ministry, upon which everything else was built. He was rightfully an apostle, because he had seen Christ (cf. I Cor. 9:1; 15:8). Before both countrymen and Roman captors he had only one defense—he had met the risen Lord. Thus his authority to preach the gospel, now under attack, was that he had received it by a revelation of God's Son. What was this revelation? It has been described as a "farce," a "hallucination," a "sign," a "trance," and a "vision." But all such explanations miss the main point—*it was a personal revelation.* God has revealed **his Son in me!** The purpose of the experience was that Paul **might preach him among the heathen.** The term **heathen** (*ethnos*) designates the Gentiles as distinct from the Jews (cf. Acts 9:15; 22:15; 26:16-18).

[8] *Op. cit.*, p. 49.

[9] J. Agar Beet terms this "the historical realization of God's purpose (*op. cit.*, p. 27).

As Paul's experience with Christ became the focal point of his whole life and ministry, so the Christian today needs a comparable point of reference in his spiritual life. To be sure, Paul's experience was unique, but nonetheless, there is a personal experience of confrontation with Christ that provides spiritual reality to the seeking soul today. Not only is this necessary in terms of a call to the appointed minister of Christ, but it is no less essential to every follower of the Saviour. An encounter with the living, risen Lord is the indispensable beginning of every transformed life—the miracle of the new birth. This becomes to the twice-born a point of perspective which brings all that follows into focus. "Once I was blind, but now I see."

Paul substantiates his claim by pointing out that after his conversion and special revelation he **conferred not with flesh and blood.** The word **conferred** (*prosanatithemi*) means to contribute or add something. In this case the apostle is making it clear that no man added to his gospel—it came from God. His activity following his conversion, as well as before, supports this claim.

Neither went I up to Jerusalem to them which were apostles before me (17). The Jews always spoke of going **up to Jerusalem,** and it likewise became the recognized seat of human leadership and authority in the Early Church. It is significant that the new convert, having been specially called, did not consult with the Christian leaders. This strongly supports Paul's claim to a unique authority. The word **before** is important in that it is underscoring Paul's apostleship. He too was an apostle, although others preceded him in that holy calling.

Paul **went into Arabia,** which is in marked contrast to Jerusalem. It was a desert place rather than a thriving metropolis. Here Paul found communion with God rather than communication with men. He does not state the purpose of his trip to Arabia, but it is clearly implied that it was a withdrawal or retreat and not for missionary activity. From the perspective of history we know that Paul needed to rebuild his whole system of thought. This was essential in order for him to minister beyond the borders of Judaism. The earlier apostles had simply added Christ as the expected Messiah to Judaism. Paul was to go further than this. After his period of meditation in Arabia, Paul **returned again unto Damascus.** Here he preached, probably with renewed vigor and insight.

b. Paul's Brief Visit to Jerusalem (1:18-20). **Then after three years I went up to Jerusalem to see Peter** (18).[10] This is the first mention of the city of Damascus, which is predominant in all of the accounts of Paul's conversion in Acts. The fact that he **returned again** to Damascus clearly indicates that he had originally departed from there. The mention of the **three years** has the effect of stating that he delayed consulting with the leaders of the Church for this long period of time. The **three years** most likely represents the total period from his conversion. There is no suggestion that Paul's trip to Jerusalem was for the purpose of obtaining approval or sanction of his gospel. It was simply a visit to meet Peter, the recognized leader of the Church. And it was a brief visit—only **fifteen days** in contrast to the three years that had passed since his conversion. Certainly such a short time would provide little opportunity for instruction or training.

But other of the apostles saw I none, save James the Lord's brother (19). It would be expected, if he were seeking official approval or acceptance, that he would visit all the apostles. This he pointedly denies,[11] stating that the only apostle he saw besides Peter was James, the brother of the Lord. This reference to James is of special importance because he, as the leader of the Jerusalem church, was later identified with the legalistic group that took issue with Paul.

[10]The chronological problem of this passage and the record in Acts (9:19-30; 22:17-21; 26:20) is often mentioned in NT studies. The following chronology would appear to harmonize the main events from the four accounts: After his conversion Paul preached for a short time in Damascus, then went into Arabia for an undetermined period, after which he returned to Damascus. After three years (probably from his conversion) he went to Jerusalem for his brief visit with Peter and James, at which time he did some preaching and witnessing. Then he went to Cilicia (Tarsus), from whence Barnabas brought him to Antioch in Syria.

[11]Paul's emphatic denial here that he visited with any of the other apostles, besides Peter and James, must be harmonized with the report of Luke that Paul had been brought "to the apostles" and was with them, "going in and out of Jerusalem" (Acts 9:27-28). The Acts accounts would certainly suggest that Paul had been with the entire apostolic band. This underscores the different nature of Luke's record and Paul's account. Paul's point (in Galatians) is that he did not submit his gospel to the apostles for their sanction or approval. His fifteen-day visit with Peter and James could not be construed as such. His denial of seeing any of the others could simply mean that he had not visited with others in the same sense as with Peter and James.

Paul's attitude toward the leaders of the Church must not be misunderstood as contempt for human leadership. His whole world had crumbled and only God could rebuild it—in solitary communion. Later, when his gospel was challenged, he could do no other than defend it in this manner. There is every evidence that he deeply respected human leadership and authority (cf. Acts 21:18-26), but he did not hesitate to call any man to account if he compromised the truth of his conscience. This is simply to recognize that the highest human authority is personal conscience. Thus fifteen centuries later Martin Luther, a disciple of Paul, defied Church and empire by declaring: "It is neither safe nor right to act against conscience!"

Paul could therefore assert, **Now the things which I write unto you, behold, before God, I lie not** (20). This solemn statement—calling God as a Witness to the veracity of his words—is a method used by Paul to emphasize the importance of what he was saying (cf. Rom. 9:1; II Cor. 1:23; 11:31; I Thess. 2:5).

c. *Paul in Syria and Cilicia* (1:21-24). The account in Acts (9:28) fills in much of the detail about **afterwards** (21). Paul's years in Syria and Cilicia (see map 1) came after he had openly preached and discussed Christ in Jerusalem and after he had aroused the murderous opposition of his enemies (cf. Acts 9:29; 22:17-20). His Christian brethren sent him to Tarsus for the sake of his personal safety. He evidently made that city his headquarters in Cilicia, after which he was brought to Antioch in Syria (see map 1) by Barnabas (cf. Acts 9:30; 11:25).

The statement that he was **unknown by face unto the churches of Judaea which were in Christ** (22) must not be understood to mean that the Judean Christians had not seen or heard Paul after his conversion. The whole point of his argument was that for this extended period he was not preaching and working in Jerusalem—the earliest center of the Church. The accounts in Acts make it quite plain that Paul had preached and witnessed in Jerusalem before he had returned to Tarsus. However, for this period of approximately eleven years he did not return to Judea.

During this interim the church in Judea **had heard only, That he which persecuted** them **in times past now preacheth the faith which once he destroyed** (23). This must have been thrilling and unbelievable news—**and they glorified God in me** (24).

3. *Paul's Gospel and the Jerusalem Council* (2:1-10)

a. Report by Paul (2:1-2). Fourteen years later Paul, with Barnabas, went to Jerusalem to privately convey his gospel to the leaders of the Church. These prominent men added nothing to Paul's message. Even in spite of some who had spied on Paul, they did not require his colaborer Titus to be circumcised. Instead, they gave their blessing to Paul and Barnabas, recognizing their commission to the Gentiles as comparable to the ministry which the other apostles had to the Jews.

Fourteen years after, Paul **went up again to Jerusalem with Barnabas, and took Titus with** him (1). It is not clear what this **after** refers to. Was it after his conversion or after his previous visit, which followed his conversion by three years? The question has little bearing on the purpose for relating the incident, but it is significantly related to the chronology of Paul's life. The probability is that the fourteen years marks the time between visits to Jerusalem.

Barnabas' association with Paul began when he supported the newly converted Pharisee in his desire to join the disciples at Jerusalem (Acts 9:26-27). Later Barnabas gave Saul the chance to get started in a ministry at Antioch (Acts 12:22-26). We have no detailed information on how Titus became associated with the apostle. It is clear that this Grecian Christian was one of Paul's early converts (Titus 1:4). At the close of the second missionary journey, Titus was already a leader in the young Church. The reference here indicates that he was among the "certain other" workers in Antioch chosen to represent them at this historic conference (Acts 15:1-2).

The trip to the Jerusalem council was **by revelation** (2). This is to emphasize that Paul was under divine direction. When the Judean visitors sought to enforce circumcision in the largely Gentile church at Antioch, Paul and Barnabas strongly resisted them (cf. Acts 15:1-2). The Acts account suggests that the church in Antioch gave Paul and Barnabas the assignment of representing their cause at Jerusalem, but Paul emphasizes here that the directive had a higher source. Human planning and divine guidance are not mutually exclusive (cf. Acts 15:28).

Paul **communicated unto them that gospel which** he preached **among the Gentiles.** The gospel message that Paul placed before[12] them was that Jesus Christ had been crucified, resurrected, and was coming again; and there was righteousness for *all* men through faith in Him without the works of the law. According to Acts 15:4, Paul and his party reported to the whole church at Jerusalem, while here in Galatians it is specifically stated that it was **privately.** This would indicate that the public session was preceded by a private conference, which would certainly be the part of wisdom. See comments on Acts 15:4-12.

To them which were of reputation is a free translation of what appears to be a broken sentence or thought, perhaps due to the anxiety or even agitation in Paul's mind.[13] It reflects his concern that he not say too much—or too little! He was relating the fact that he had gone to the leaders of the Church for clarification of a crucial question; and yet he did not want to imply total submission to their judgment, or deny his own unique and divinely given authority. Thus, he refers to James, Cephas (Peter), and John as those who "seemed to be somewhat" (6) and "seemed to be pillars" (9). They were **of reputation** in the sense that they appeared to be such in the eyes of the Church. Behind Paul's hesitancy was the conviction that the ultimate authority must be from God, not man.

One of Paul's familiar metaphors is that which depicts the Christian life as a race (cf. 5:7; I Cor. 9:24-26; Phil. 2:16). He refers to his life and ministry among the Gentiles as such a race and was concerned **lest by any means I should run, or had run, in vain.** He realized that if the recognized leaders in the Jerusalem church opposed his gospel all the work he had done would be destroyed by their emissaries and he could not hope to accomplish anything in the future. His certainty of the divine origin of his message did not blind him to the practical fatality of division and divergence in the Church.

b. Refusal to Circumcise Titus (2:3-5). In v. 3 is the first actual mention in the letter of the specific question at issue—the enforced circumcision of the Gentile converts. Was it necessary? Paul writes, **But neither Titus, who was with me, being a Greek, was compelled to be circumcised.** The apostle's purpose in relat-

[12]*Anatithemi*, meaning to "place upon" and thus to "place before for consideration."

[13]Cf. Barclay, *The Letters to Galatians and Ephesians* (Philadelphia: The Westminster Press, 1958), p. 16.

ing this entire incident was to show that even there in the Jerusalem church his Greek companion was not compelled to submit to the ceremonial law. This being true, what grounds could his opponents possibly have for insisting on circumcision in the homeland of the Gentiles?

Verses 4 and 5 are parenthetical, calling attention to those who were exerting pressure to enforce circumcision. The pressure came **because of false brethren unawares brought in, who came in privily to spy out our liberty which we have in Christ Jesus, that they might bring us into bondage** (4). The expression **false brethren** suggests that they were fellow believers, but their insistence upon the necessity of the law constituted in Paul's eyes a denial of Christ (cf. comments on 2:21). These men had been **unawares brought in**; i.e., "brought in secretly." Their express purpose was **to spy out**—gain firsthand evidence—of the freedom from the law that these Gentile converts enjoyed in Christ. All this was an attempt to force the law upon them and to enslave them again (cf. comments on 4:1-10). The element of secrecy most certainly relates to their motives. Undoubtedly they posed as Christian brethren and in the confidence of this fellowship observed the freedom of the Gentile converts. They would then take this information and seek to enforce circumcision.

Paul was not daunted by these people or their tactics. He writes: **To whom we gave place by subjection, no, not for an hour; that the truth of the gospel might continue with you** (5). These false brethren now sought before the Jerusalem church to force Paul to conform his gospel to the law. It was against this pressure that Paul states he did not "yield in subjection" (lit.), **no, not for an hour.** Even Titus, in spite of their arguments and demands, was not compelled to be circumcised. This is probably the specific point at which Paul would not yield. The reason he refused to "budge an inch" was because this was a defense of the truth of the gospel that had been preached to his Gentile converts. This message of Christian truth could not continue if he failed. If he submitted to the circumcision of his Gentile converts, the gospel he had preached to them could not be true.

c. *Recognition of Paul's Ministry* (2:6-10). Paul refers again to the "pillar apostles" as those **who seemed to be somewhat** (6). Here he goes into more detail in his depreciation of their importance. **Whatsoever they were** is literally, "Of what kind they formerly were." This undoubtedly refers to the fact that these men had been associated with Jesus in His earthly ministry. Even this fact made no difference to Paul, for a very good reason—**God accepteth no man's person,** literally, "God receives not the face of a man." This simply means that with God the outwardly apparent is not important.

Paul is here dealing with a problem that was rapidly getting out of hand in the Early Church, especially in the Gentile areas. Those who had been with Jesus during His earthly ministry were given a place of distinction that could have dangerous consequences. The Jews had a built-in safeguard against idolatry, but Paul's Gentile converts could easily fall into this trap. With their idolatrous background it was only a short step from the veneration of Jesus' earthly disciples to a cult of divinity. In fact, already Paul's claim to apostleship was being challenged by his enemies at this very point—he had not been one of the original disciples. Thus, while writing to Gentile converts about his relationship with these leaders, he emphatically points out that with God the outward appearance is not the important thing. Authority in the Church comes from God. It comes, not on the basis of one's past outward relationship with Jesus on earth, but in the light of one's present inward experience with Christ. This did not mean that Paul had no respect for these leaders, or even that he did not hold them in high esteem. The fact that he was in Jerusalem for conference demonstrates the opposite. It is instead a reflection of his concern that the true basis of authority be observed.

Not only did the leaders of the Church decline to compel Titus to be circumcised, but **they who seemed to be somewhat**[14] **in conference added nothing.** This is Paul's central purpose for relating the incident. In the defense of his authority as having come from God, he here relates that even the leaders of the Church did not add anything to his message.

Instead they acted **contrariwse, when they saw that the gospel of the uncircumcision was committed unto me, as the gospel**[15] **of the circumcision was unto Peter** (7). Such positive action was based on an important and far-reaching insight. As

[14]As noted by the italics in the KJV, the phrase **to be somewhat** is an editorial addition by the translators, seeking to clarify the meaning.

[15]The words **the gospel** were here added by the KJV translators. They are genuine in the first part of the verse.

Peter was the recognized leader of those who were ministering the gospel in the Jewish world, so they saw that to Paul had been **committed** (lit., entrusted) a similar ministry to the Gentiles.

This recognition of leadership, which Paul calls an **apostleship,** was based upon the clear evidence of the same divine activity[16] in Paul as in Peter. **He that wrought effectually in Peter to the apostleship of the circumcision, the same was mighty in me toward the Gentiles** (8). The same God energized them both.

The happy result of this conference was that **when James, Cephas, and John, who seemed to be pillars, perceived the grace that was given unto me, they gave to me and Barnabas the right hands of fellowship** (9). For the first time Paul identifies the leaders of the Jerusalem church, to whom he had been referring in previous verses. Listing first the name of **James** (the brother of Jesus) suggests that he was the leader of the church—perhaps in administration—while Peter was the leader of the missionary work to the Jews. These men took positive action. Paul and Barnabas were given the recognized pledge of friendship and agreement, **the right hands of fellowship.** In the light of this total and unquestioned approval, how could Paul's authority be questioned?

As a result Paul and Barnabas were sent **unto the heathen, and they unto the circumcision.** There is some question as to whether this division was racial or geographical. There were Gentiles in Palestine and Jews in the Greek-Roman-Asian world. The most obvious answer is that Paul was given unquestioned authority in the territory where he had been working—outside Palestine. This was the real question at issue. However, it also seems obvious that the decision affected directly the requirements to be placed upon Gentile converts, wherever they resided.

The Jerusalem church leaders made only one provision in their approval, that Paul **should remember the poor** (10). This he was **forward** (*spoudazo,* zealous or eager) **to do,** which can be seen by his consequent activity (cf. Rom. 15:31; II Corinthians 8—9).

[16]**Wrought effectually** and **was mighty** translate the verb *energeo.* This is one of Paul's favorite terms to depict the working of the Holy Spirit in man, whether through inner experience (cf. I Cor. 12:6, 11) or outer result (cf. Phil. 2:13). The word "energy" is a direct transliteration. Cf. also Eph. 3:20.

4. *Paul's Gospel Defended and Expounded* (2:11-21)

On a visit to Antioch, Peter had freely eaten with the Gentiles until others from Jerusalem arrived; then he withdrew from them. This so influenced the Jewish brethren at Antioch —and even Barnabas—that they played the hypocrite with Peter. Paul publicly opposed his fellow apostle for this conduct, because it was contrary to the truth of the gospel. He asked Peter how he, a Jew by birth, who at times lived like a Gentile, could compel the Gentiles to live like Jews. Both Peter and Paul, having learned that a man is not justified by the law but only through faith in Christ, had themselves thus believed in Him. Although considered sinners by the Jews, they would actually become sinners in the eyes of God only if they built again that legalistic structure they had once destroyed. Paul testified that he had died to the law in order to live unto God. Having been crucified with Christ, he now lived no longer for self, and the life he lived in the flesh was by faith in Jesus Christ. Thus the grace of God was not nullified.

This episode is another evidence of Paul's authority as an apostle. It was sometime after the Jerusalem Council that **Peter**[17] had **come to Antioch** (11), a church dominated by Gentile Christians. Perhaps he had heard that Jews and Gentiles were sharing a common meal. There Paul had **withstood him to the face.** This public confrontation was justifiable in Paul's mind because Peter **was to be blamed** (lit., stood condemned).

Paul writes of his fellow apostle that before **certain came from James, he did eat with the Gentiles** (12). When Peter arrived at Antioch and observed the common-table fellowship between Jews and Gentiles, he joined them, with no apparent problem of conscience. It is not surprising that Peter should do this after his experience with Cornelius and his subsequent defense before the Jerusalem church.[18] But when Jerusalem

[17]In v. 9, Paul uses Simon's Aramaic name "Cephas." The Greek translation of this was **Peter** (*petros*). The best Greek text has "Cephas" in 11 and 14.

[18]Cf. Acts 10:1—11:18. Although Peter's concern about his visit to Cornelius' home was expressed in terms of that which was "unclean," it involved more than the actual eating of food. Certainly the central issue was fellowship which was typified in Semitic culture by the common table. There is no evidence that the Jerusalem church understood the incident as a new general policy of Jewish-Gentile fellowship. Instead, there is

visitors arrived in Antioch, they were critical of what they observed—perhaps that is why they had come. As a result Peter withdrew and **separated himself.** The literal meaning is that he "gradually drew back,"[19] **fearing them which were of the circumcision.**

In 11-21 we see "Elements of Moral Cowardice." The story of the Jerusalem conference forms the background introduction. (1) Fear of our friends can make us compromise our convictions, 11-12; (2) Personal compromise influences others to do the wrong thing, 13; (3) Honest rebuke is needed and not to be resented, 14-19; (4) Honest dedication and effort to allow Christ to live in us is the effective cure for cowardice, 20-21 (A. F. Harper).

a. Insincerity and Wrong Influence (2:12-19). The serious consequence was that **the other Jews dissembled likewise with him** (13). Paul calls this hypocrisy.[20] The problem was one of basic insincerity—either while participating in the table fellowship or by separation from that fellowship in the interests of the law. Paul concludes that at one time or the other the action was a sham. It will be seen, as Paul proceeds, that it was this duplicity that was the great wrong—not simply the refusal of Jews to share table fellowship with the Gentiles. Perhaps if Peter had refused at the outset to join in such fellowship the issue would never have arisen.

every indication that its significance was simply the recognition that the gospel had been given to the Gentiles as well as the Jews. The decision of the Jerusalem Council further indicates that the two groups would be separate, with the Jews continuing under the law. This presented a critical problem for Paul, because his churches in Macedonia and Achaia, as well as Asia Minor, were in great part made up of both groups. How was Christian fellowship possible if the Jewish believers were separated from their Gentile brethren because of the restrictions of their law? In Antioch the Jewish believers had placed the unity of their Christian fellowship above the limitations of the law.

[19]The term *hypostello* was used in classical Greek to indicate a strategic withdrawal of troops, and suggests a cautious retreat. The imperfect tense can be adequately translated only by adding the word "gradually."

[20]*Synypokrinomai* is the Greek word used. It literally means to "join in pretending or playing a part." The word relates to an actor who plays a part on the stage, and thus has the ethical significance of one who acts out of pretense, sham, or outward show. The word "hypocrisy" is a transliteration of the Greek term (*hypokrisis*).

In the strictest scriptural sense hypocrisy is the direct opposite of sincerity. Hypocrisy is duplicity, and sincerity is purity or singleness of motive. Thus, profession is hypocritical only to the degree that it reflects insincerity. But to the extent that one's words or actions are not sincere he is being hypocritical.

The power of influence, for good or bad, is frightening to the serious-minded person. When **Barnabas also was carried away with their dissimulation,** it must certainly have been a great blow to Paul. It is difficult to imagine one of Barnabas' spiritual stature acting thus, but it underscores the awesome power of influence. Even the great—to say nothing of lesser men—have many times risen or fallen while watching and listening to someone else. One of the greatest responsibilities of leadership is the power of influence, and nothing can cause more damage here than hypocrisy.

There is some question as to **when** Paul **saw** this take place (14). Could he have been present in Antioch and yet have failed to see what was happening before such tragic consequences developed? It is possible that, even though seeing it, Paul hesitated to take drastic action; but this hardly fits his personality. Thus it has been suggested that he was absent from Antioch when the situation was developing and saw it only when he returned. Paul was persuaded that Peter, and the rest of the Jews whom he influenced, **walked not uprightly** (*orthopodeo,* walk straight) **according to the truth of the gospel.**

So Paul confronted **Peter before them all.** His primary concern was to defend the truth of the gospel, but he was also convinced that the hypocrisy should be clearly revealed. To accomplish this it was necessary for him to publicly rebuke Peter, the recognized and highly respected leader of the Church. Such action was indeed a bold step, but Paul was convinced that the enormity of the error justified it. Now, at this later time, he could refer back to it as evidence that he had divine authority for the gospel which he preached.[21]

Paul's challenge to Peter was, **If thou, being a Jew, livest after the manner of Gentiles, and not as do the Jews, why compellest thou the Gentiles to live as do the Jews?** This un-

[21]It is possible that Paul's actual words to Peter end with v. 14. Verses 15-21 would then be his discussion with the Galatians of the principles involved. However it is not difficult to conceive of Paul using the occasion to actually preach a sermon—using Peter as an object lesson.

questionably refers to living according to the customs of the respective groups, with specific emphasis here on eating habits. Although Peter was a Jew, his convictions permitted him to live like a Gentile and not like a Jew, as was vividly illustrated by his conduct before the Jerusalem visitors arrived. By withdrawing himself, and influencing the other Jewish believers to do likewise, the only basis of fellowship would have to be on Jewish terms. Thus Peter's actions had the practical effect of compelling the Gentiles to live like the Jews—under the law.

Peter and Paul were **Jews by nature, and not sinners of the Gentiles** (15). This contrast is basically one of racial origin rather than moral character, although the two are related. The term **sinners** (*hamartoloi*) is used with reference to the Gentiles because it was the typical manner in which the Jews referred to them. Paul is simply pointing out that Peter and he were Jews by birth, and not of Gentile origin.

But even though Jews, and trained to observe the laws of Moses, they had come to know **that a man is not justified by the works of the law, but by the faith of Jesus Christ** (16). This is the thesis that Paul will argue in chapters 3 and 4.[22] His point here is only to observe that this truth had been accepted by both of them. This is the first mention of the important word **law** (*nomos*), and it is used here with its limited meaning of human **works.** This meaning forms the foundation for Paul's rebuke. Peter had submitted to the demands of the law, although he had known and experienced the fact that justification came only by faith in Christ. The closing phrase of the verse is obviously a reference to the Scriptures for support. **For by the works of the law shall no flesh be justified** is an allusion to Ps. 143:2. Following the Septuagint, Paul clarifies the quoted verse and thus gives "a re-exposition in clearer form of a doctrine already taught by the Jewish prophets."[23]

The apostle next observes that **while we seek to be justified by Christ,**[24] **we ourselves also are found**[25] **sinners** (17). This last

[22]Cf. comments on 3:10-14 for the meaning of the term justification.

[23]Burton, *op. cit.*, p. 124.

[24]This is the familiar Pauline formula, *en Christo* (in Christ), which most often depicts the intimate fellowship of the believer with Christ, but here it has a basic causal relation to the previous verse.

[25]The aorist indicative (*eurethemen*) should be translated "were found."

phrase has been interpreted in many different ways.[26] Its meaning here is not the usual scriptural meaning. The term "sinners" has already been used in this context with a clear legalistic meaning (cf. v. 15). Paul had strongly emphasized (v. 16) that Peter and he had been justified by faith in Christ—disregarding the works of the law. Thus, although they were Jews by birth, their Jewish opponents would conclude that they were "sinners" —even as the Gentiles who were outside the scope of the law. There is no suggestion that Paul would deny this premise of his enemies. They were "sinners" in this legalistic sense of departing from the ceremonial law.

The conclusion that such a premise implied was put in the form of a rhetorical question[27]—**Is therefore Christ the minister of sin?** If faith in Christ caused them to become "legalistic sinners," then is not Christ the cause of sin? There is here a crucial change of concepts; **sin** (*hamartia*) is now not a legalistic, but a moral, term. *Hamartia,* in the New Testament, does not mean to violate the law, but to disobey God, which brings guilt and condemnation.[28] Is the man of faith—although a "sinner" in relationship to the law—living under the condemnation and guilt of actual sin? Does Christ **minister** such to him? Paul's answer is emphatic: **God forbid** (*me genoito,* Let it not be).[29] Such a thought was abhorrent to Paul and a travesty on his Lord. Instead of sin, Christ brings forgiveness and peace to the man of faith.

Paul now carries his argument one step further. Turning away from the works of the law did not make him an actual sinner. The opposite is true; **for if I build again the things which I destroyed, I make myself a transgressor** (18). If he were to return to the observances of the law, he would be rebuilding a false structure that he had previously destroyed. The reference is plainly to Peter's actions at Antioch, but Paul graciously states

[26]Cf. the excellent summary in Burton, *op. cit.,* pp. 127-30.

[27]Cf. similar conclusions in Rom. 3:5-6; 5:19; 6:1-2, 15.

[28]For an excellent analysis of the meaning of *hamartia* in the NT, cf. Burton, *op. cit.,* pp. 439-43.

[29]*Me genoito* is a characteristic expression of Paul (found elsewhere only in Luke 20:16). It follows a rhetorical question that expresses the accusations of his opponents. Usually the question is based on a previously stated premise, with which Paul is in agreement (Rom. 3:5-6; 5:19—6:2). It is this pattern that strongly suggests the interpretation of v. 17 as stated above.

it in the first person. By such a return to the law he would make (lit., demonstrate) himself to be transgressor. Paul uses here an unambiguous term for actual transgression (cf. Rom. 2:25, 27). It is significant that a man demonstrates himself a transgressor, instead of this being simply God's pronouncement.

It will be seen in later chapters that the law served a temporary function, which was superseded by the coming of Christ. Thus Paul is speaking of erecting again that which was torn down because it was only temporary. J. Agar Beet aptly likens it to the scaffolding that is temporarily erected to assist in building a permanent structure.[30] In the edifice of the Christian life the temporary scaffolding of duty should give way to the permanent framework of love.

Paul's argument that obedience to the law and not disobedience would show him to be a transgressor would be a paradox to his Jewish readers. But he offers his own experience as proof of the paradox. This is indicated by the use of the personal pronoun.[31] **I through the law am dead to the law** (19). This is not surprising. His death with Christ, which he goes on to discuss in the next verse, results in his death to the law and a discharge from its slavish control (cf. Rom. 7:1-6). By dying *to* something Paul obviously means to have all relationships severed, so that it can no longer exercise influence or control upon him. He is as completely severed from it as one who is dead (cf. comments on 5:24; 6:14). This is much more than a figure of speech.

What is surprising is that it was through the law itself that Paul gained release from the law. This certainly does not mean that the law was the actual means of release, because he makes it clear that release came only through death with Christ (20). What he means is that it was through the works of the law, and the resulting frustration, that he realized the necessity of abandoning it. This is what he alludes to here (v. 16) and describes in detail in Romans 7. Here is the clinching argument: If he returned to the works of the law after he realized the necessity to abandon them, he would be making himself a transgressor.

The positive result is **that I might live unto God.** Having

[30]*Op. cit.*, p. 54.

[31]There is an interesting development in this passage: from the second person (v. 14), to the first person plural (vv. 15-17), to the unemphatic first person singular (v. 18), to the emphatic first person singular (vv. 19-21).

been discharged from the law through death, he was now free to live to God. Thus the most significant objection to legalism is seen. Not only does it fail to deliver from sin, but it is actually a hindrance to the total devotion that should characterize the Christian's life.

b. The New Life in Christ (2:20-21). This new life under God, free from the hindrances of the law, was possible only because Paul had been[32] **crucified with Christ** (20). This is one of his most significant theological concepts. When a man enters into Christ he enters into His death. He dies with Christ.[33] This is more than a figure of speech, describing a psychological separation or deliverance from sin. It means that by faith a man makes Christ's death his own. The *future* result is that he does not face eternal death for his sins.

There is also a *present* benefit. The power of sin is broken in a man's life, because he died to sin with Christ. Of particular significance to the present context is the fact that death with Christ is the *only* way that those enslaved by the law can find freedom (cf. comments on 5:1).

It is imperative that the sinner's death with Christ not be confused with crucifixion of one's essential selfhood or what is often termed self-crucifixion. It is rather the old, inner self, helplessly and hopelessly depraved by sin, that dies. Paul's terminology is strange to modern ways of thinking, yet it depicts a truth that is well known in human experience.

However, the believer does not stay dead. **Nevertheless I live; yet not I, but Christ liveth in me.** The counterpart of death with Christ is always resurrection and a new life in Him. The man of faith walks in "newness of life" (Rom. 6:4), in the "likeness of his resurrection" (Rom. 6:5), and "lives unto God" (Rom. 6:11). He "brings forth fruit unto God" (Rom. 7:4), and serves Him in "newness of spirit" (Rom. 7:6). It is vital to grasp the full impact of this wondrous truth. Death to sin is significant only because it makes the new life possible. Deliverance from sin is the opening of the door to a glorious new life in Christ.

The order of the Greek text is striking as it is literally translated into English: "and I live, no longer I [*ego*], but lives in me, Christ." The KJV is a little more extensive than the original,

[32]The perfect tense should be translated "I have been" and not "I am."

[33]Rom. 6:3; cf. Rom. 6:1-11; Col. 2:12, 20; 3:3. Crucifixion simply denotes the method of death.

and is somewhat misleading. Paul does not say, **Nevertheless I live.** Instead, he says: "And I live no longer I, but Christ lives in me." The emphatic first-person pronoun (*ego*) could simply emphasize the personal aspect of the statement and thus be translated, "And I *myself* no longer live." However, in the light of the phrase that follows, **but Christ liveth in me,** it is much more significant. He is saying, "I live no longer *as I once did,* but in a new way—*no longer I.* Now Christ lives in me—He is the Lord of my new life." Paul lives "no longer I" because in a crisis capitulation he had surrendered his sovereignty—he was "no longer I"! Thus he can write elsewhere—"For to me to live is Christ" (Phil. 1:21). This is also described by Paul as life *under the Spirit* (cf. comments on 5:16-26).

When W. G. Coltman preached on Gal. 2:20 he used the theme "The Victorious Life." He pointed out that this life involves three wonderful secrets: (1) Christ instead of me; (2) Faith instead of feeling; (3) "Now" instead of "then" (*Galatians, the Grace Way of Life,* Dunham Publishing Company).

Between the old life *under sin* and this new way of living, there is the "no-man's-land" of life *under self.* Although the believer has been freed from the grip of sin, he is still lord of his own life. Thus Paul uses his personal example to set forth the ideal that God expected of them. Such a life involves a crisis capitulation, as the believer surrenders his sovereignty to God.[34] This is returning to God what man usurped in the Garden of Eden. Elsewhere it is described graphically in the imagery of a "love slave" presenting himself voluntarily to his master (Rom. 6:19), and as a priest presenting his sacrifice on the altar (Rom. 12:1). The implications of this crisis must be lived out in a lifelong process, which Paul often refers to as walking or marching by the Spirit.

And the life which I now live in the flesh I live by the faith of the Son of God. The new life under the Spirit is lived in the flesh, which here means in the present, earthly body—with all of its limitations, weaknesses, and temptations. It is also lived **by . . . faith.** Paul witnesses that, as he was justified by faith, so he lives the new life of the Spirit by faith in **the Son of God.** All

[34] The *believer's* surrendered sovereignty must not be confused with the *sinner's* death with Christ. Also Paul *never* uses death or crucifixion as a metaphor of destruction of man's God-given selfhood. *In Pauline terms* man's will does not die, but is surrendered or presented to God.

the way the believer's life must be one of total dependence upon Christ, **who loved me, and gave himself for me.** This is the acknowledgment that everything in the Christian's life finds its source in the love of Christ, which caused Him to die for us. There is no other motivation of grace. This emphasis upon love became a veritable creedal confession.[35]

Having given his personal witness, Paul concludes that his life of faith did **not frustrate** (nullify) **the grace of God** (21).

E. W. Martin asks, "What Is Holiness?" In v. 20 he finds three answers: (1) Mortification, **I am crucified with Christ;** cf. also 6:14; Rom. 6:6-7; Heb. 13:12-13; (2) Vitalization, **the life which I now live . . . I live by . . . faith;** cf. Acts 1:18; (3) Manifestation, **Christ liveth in me** (*Preachable Holiness Sermon Outlines*).

The next statement is in Paul's typical style, as he makes the transition in his argument. **For if righteousness come by the law, then Christ is dead in vain.** This could well serve as his text. If a man can obtain righteousness through the works of the law, then Christ died in vain. Having concluded his defense of the divine authority of his gospel, he now turns to the subject of his concern for the Galatian churches.

[35]Cf. Eph. 5:2, 25, where it is found in a more extensive form.

Section III *Argument—by Faith and Not Law*

Galatians 3:1—5:12

A. The Galatians' Own Experience, 3:1-5

Calling the Galatians foolish (senseless), Paul asks who bewitched them, before those eyes the crucified Christ was publicly portrayed. He wanted to know one thing—Had they received the Spirit by works of the law or by the hearing of faith? Did they expect to complete in the flesh what was begun in the Spirit? Was their suffering in vain?

Having defended his message by establishing its divine authority, Paul now turns to the task of refuting the objections of his opponents. He begins by referring to the experience of the Galatian converts themselves. **O foolish** (*anoetoi,* senseless)[1] **Galatians** (1) expresses again Paul's sense of surprise and indignation (cf. 1:6). They were blind to spiritual reality. The only explanation must be that a magician had thrown a spell over them—**who hath bewitched you?**[2] What makes their spiritual blindness so shocking is the fact that Jesus Christ had **been evidently set forth** (*prographo,* publicly portrayed), before their very eyes, as having been crucified.[3] With the clarity of a public proclamation Paul had set before them the truth about Jesus. This vision of the Crucified should have saved them from the fascinating and deadly gaze of the bewitchers, but it had not.

This only would I learn of you (2). The question of whether or not his message—salvation through faith without the works of the law—was true could be easily answered. All that was necessary was to learn (lit., find out) one thing from their own

[1]The term **foolish** has taken on a certain element of sophistication in English literature that softens its meaning. The Greek word means "unintelligent," but in the sense of a failure to use one's power of perception, rather than a natural stupidity. Cf. "stupid" (NEB).

[2]The phrase **that ye should not obey the truth** is not in the earliest MSS, and appears to be an addition taken from 5:7.

[3]The KJV is misleading—Jesus Christ was publicly portrayed but not crucified **among you.** The best Greek text does not have **among you.** Even if the phrase were retained it should go with "publicly portrayed," rather than with **crucified.**

experience. **Received ye the Spirit**[4] **by the works of the law, or by the hearing of faith?** He asks them to look into their own hearts and remember what had happened to them. When Paul had brought the gospel to them they had received the Spirit, and obviously had known it. The question now was, how had they received Him? The alternatives that Paul proposes are the leading antitheses of the Epistle—**the works of the law** (symbolized by circumcision) and **the hearing of faith.**

Paul again refers to their senseless actions. **Are ye so foolish? having begun in the Spirit, are ye now made perfect by the flesh?** (3) The question of the previous verse is quickly answered; they received the Spirit by faith. Paul's opponents could not successfully argue that the works of the law were essential for the *commencement* of the Christian life. So their appeal was that circumcision was essential for its *completion.* Thus Paul asks if that which is begun in the Spirit can be completed in the flesh.[5] Is it possible that the new life that begins with the reception of God's Spirit, working in man's heart, can be brought to its fulfillment by a legalistic rite performed on his body? The answer must be *no.* Paul knew a better path to Christian fulfillment and perfection.

"Holiness in Galatians" is presented under three aspects: (1) The crucifixion of the carnal self, 2:20; (2) The path to perfection, 3:2-3; (3) The fruit of the Spirit, 5:22-23 (Ralph Earle).

Paul next makes another appeal to the experience of the Galatians. **Have ye suffered so many things in vain?** (4) As his converts, they must have suffered in the wake of his intense persecution (cf. Acts 14). So now he asks, was all their suffering in vain? It certainly would be if they now repudiated the gospel that had instigated that persecution. Paul's next expression, **if it be yet in vain,** reflects a reluctance to accept such a conclusion.

The question of v. 5 is similar to that of 2, with some important differences. **He therefore that ministereth** (supplies) **to you the Spirit, and worketh miracles among you, doeth he it by the works of the law, or by the hearing of faith?** (5) The present participles (**ministereth** and **worketh**) clearly indicate that Paul is referring here to the Galatians' present experience. Thus he

[4]Here, as in 4:6, Paul refers to the divine **Spirit.** However, in v. 3 the term *pneuma* begins to take on a "fused" meaning of the Spirit-filled human spirit in contrast to a fleshly-minded human spirit.

[5]Here **flesh** refers to the place where circumcision occurs, "outer man" (present earthly body).

tactfully acknowledges the continuance, at least for the present, of their spiritual life. What was their opinion about the God who daily supplied them with the Spirit and through that Spirit was daily working miracles? Are such ministries through **the works of the law, or by the hearing of faith?**

B. The Example of Abraham, 3:6-9

As Abraham's faith was reckoned **to him for righteousness** (justification, Gen. 15:6), so today the men of faith are the true sons of Abraham. This was foreseen in Scripture as God promised to bless all the Gentiles in Abraham (cf. Gen. 12:3; 18:18).

As the Galatians could see from their own experience that salvation was by faith and not by works of the law, so Paul contends it can also be illustrated by the example of Abraham. The nature of the contention in cc. 3 and 4 strongly suggests that the apostle is replying to previous argument by his opponents, probably based on Genesis 12—17.[6] Undoubtedly they were arguing that anyone who was uncircumcised had broken the covenant and was cut off from God's people (cf. Gen. 17:14). From this very context (Genesis 12—17) Paul calls attention to an important verse which they were obviously ignoring. **Abraham believed God, and it was accounted to him for righteousness** (6). This is a direct quotation from the Septuagint version of Gen. 15:6. When God promised Abraham that He would make of him a great nation (Gen. 12:3), with descendants as numerous as the stars of the heavens (Gen. 15:5), Abraham "had faith in God"[7] (Gen. 15:6), although this promise was a human impossibility (cf. Rom. 4:17-22). His faith was the basis of the covenant that he entered into with God (cf. Gen. 15:8; 17:2), and this faith was "reckoned"[8] **to him for righteousness.**[9] Circumcision was added later

[6]Cf. Burton, *op. cit.*, pp. 153-54.

[7]The Greek term translated **believed** (*pisteuo* is a cognate of the word "faith," *pistis*). Thus it literally means "to have faith in."

[8]This term (*logizomai*) basically means to "calculate" or to "count up," thus having the meaning to "take into account" or "reckon" when God does the reckoning, as here. However, when man does the reckoning (cf. Rom. 6:11) it has the meaning of "regarding" or "considering."

[9]The term **righteousness** (*dikaiosyne*), along with the verb *dikaioo* (**justify**) and the adjective *dikaios* (**righteous**), is one of the most significant in Pauline thought. E. D. Burton states that in this OT passage it "signifies that conduct or attitude of mind which God desires, and which renders man acceptable to him" (*op. cit.*, p. 462).

as the seal of the covenant (Gen. 17:10-14). The important point that Paul is making is that the basis of even Abraham's acceptance with God was faith and not circumcision.

From this Old Testament reference Paul draws a startling conclusion—**Know ye therefore that they which are of faith, the same are the children of Abraham** (7). The Jews argued that the privileged relationship of being "sons[10] of Abraham"[11] necessitated the seal of circumcision, and thus could not be claimed by any uncircumcised person. This Paul rejected, arguing that, if the basis of Abraham's acceptance with God was his faith, then the men of faith today are the true sons of Abraham—exclusive of circumcision.[12] There is here an important distinction. The significant relationship with Abraham is not racial[13] through outward circumcision, but ethical, on the basis of inward faith.

Going further, Paul suggests that this faith relationship between Abraham and his "sons" was foreseen in the promise made by God. **And the scripture, foreseeing that God would justify the heathen through faith, preached before the gospel unto Abraham, saying, In thee shall all nations be blessed** (8). Paul contends that God's promise to Abraham—**In thee shall all nations be blessed** (cf. Gen. 12:3; 18:18)—was actually made in the light of His foreknowledge that one day He would **justify**[14] the "Gentiles"[15] by **faith.** God was proclaiming beforehand these good tidings to Abraham. In answer to the argument of the Jews that the blessings of Abraham were restricted to the circumcised, Paul pointed to the fact that the uncircumcised Gentiles were being blessed—they were being justified by faith! Thus he reasons back that it was with this fact in mind that God,

[10]The Greek term *huioi* is better translated "sons" than **children.**

[11]Paul changed the familiar Jewish expressions "seed of Abraham" (cf. Gen. 5:5, 18) and "blessings of Abraham" (cf. Gen. 12:3; 18:18).

[12]Cf. Rom. 2:28-29; 9:4-8. Cf. also Burton's observation that a familiar Semitic use of the term "son" was with reference to one who walked in another's footsteps or was like him (*op. cit.*, p. 158).

[13]Whether a "Jew" was born such or adopted, circumcision made him a part of the Jewish race (cf. Gen. 17:12-13).

[14]Cf. comments on 3:10-14 for the significance of **justify** (*dikaioo*).

[15]The Greek term *ethnos* literally means "nations" or "people," but in common usage referred to the non-Jewish world and thus signifies "Gentiles" or **heathen.** In the KJV the same word is translated **heathen** and **nations** in this verse.

through foreknowledge and planning, made the original promise to Abraham. This substantiates his contention that the men of faith are the true sons of Abraham.

The argument is summed up by Paul—**So then they which be of faith are blessed with faithful Abraham** (9). This truth is a proper inference[16] from the argument of the previous verses. Those who are men of faith are receiving the blessings that Abraham received as a man of faith. The adjective **faithful** (*pistos*) must here be understood in its active sense of "full of faith" and not in its passive meaning of "trustworthy" or "dependable." It is better translated "believing," but this fails to emphasize its close relationship to **they which be of faith.**

C. The Limitations of the Law, 3:10-24

1. *The Law Brings Curse, Not Justification* (3:10-14)

The Scriptures point out the limitation of the law (***works***) by teaching that it can only bring a curse. Further, the Scriptures plainly state that **the just shall live by faith.** Christ redeemed man from this curse of the law and provided the way of faith by being made himself a curse through hanging on the Cross.

By pointing to the limitations of the law, Paul continues his argument that man's acceptance with God is on the basis of faith. Turning from the specific examples of Abraham and the Galatians themselves, he speaks in more general terms of **as many as are of the works of the law**[17] (10). The emphasis here is not primarily on doing or keeping the law; it is rather on those who are products **of the law.** This is the essence of legalism, wherein a person's character comes out of his obedience to the statutes of the law under which he lives.[18]

Legalists of this sort are under the curse, **for it is written, Cursed is every one that continueth not in all things which are written in the book of the law to do them.** Behind this conclusion there is an unexpressed premise—that no one is able to keep all the law. The passage quoted (Deut. 27:26) is from an

[16]The verse is introduced by *hoste,* which is here used as an "inferential particle" meaning "and so" (C. F. D. Moule, *An Idiom Book of New Testament Greek* [Cambridge, The University Press, 1953], p. 144).

[17]Paul's meaning of **law** (*nomos*) in this whole section (3:10-24) is a legalistic system rather than the divine standard.

[18]By contrast cf. Paul's commendation of the "doers of the law" in Rom. 2:13.

exceedingly broad summary of the law and emphasizes that it is not simply a series of regulations that can be easily kept. The law, in its truest sense, touches all of life, even attitudes and motives. Thus undetected transgressions are revealed as one's insight deepens. Because of this, condemnation rather than justification must be the inevitable result.

It is essential to realize that Paul did not accept this as God's intended manner of dealing with men. He is here simply refuting his opponents on the basis of their own thesis—that men are justified by law. Even by it they stand condemned. If a man insists on approaching God on the basis of law (works), the only possible consequence must be God's curse and judgment.[19]

Not only does the way of law find its logical consequence in a curse, but the Scriptures clearly make faith, and not law, the basis of justification. **But that no man is justified by the law in the sight of God, it is evident: for, The just shall live by faith (11).**

"To justify" and "to make righteous" are translations of the same Greek verb. This term—"righteousness" (*dikaiosyne*)—is one of the most significant concepts in Pauline thought. It has, however, been interpreted in widely divergent ways. There is little question that it refers at times—perhaps primarily—to the new status of the believer, and is thus a *forensic* term depicting God's judicial verdict of acquittal on the sinner. (Cf., e.g., Rom. 3:20-21; 4:3, 5-6; 5:1, 9, 17; Gal. 2:16-17, 21; 3:6, 8, 24.) It is also used many times as an *ethical* term that relates to the moral transformation produced in the life of the believer. Thus, one makes a mistake to insist upon either meaning to the exclusion of the other. In a given context usually one concept is predominant, but the other still exists in the background. In Romans and Galatians, where he is dealing with the controversy over the law, Paul understandably emphasizes the forensic meaning of righteousness. But it is erroneous to suggest—as many have—that this new relationship is void of moral and ethical significance. The "man of faith" is not only acquitted, but the power of sin is broken in his life. The ethical meaning of righteousness seems to be implied in Rom. 6:13, 16, 18-20; 8:10; Eph. 6:14; Phil. 1:11.

[19]Cf. Burton's attempt to designate this as the "curse of the law" as distinct from "God's curse" (*op. cit.*, pp. 164-65). Such a distinction is difficult to establish. God does not choose to deal with man on the basis of law, but if man rejects the way of faith God has no alternative.

The apostle refers to Hab. 2:4 as scriptural support for his argument that men are justified by faith and not by law. The expression **shall live** is added to the basic concept of a man being just or righteous, by faith.[20] This can mean that justification itself is new life, thus equating it with regeneration; or it can refer, as a result of regeneration, to the obtaining of eternal life in heaven as the consequence of faith.[21]

The way of law and the way of faith are direct opposites: **And the law is not of faith** (12). There can be no combining of the two. Undoubtedly Paul's opponents were trying to add their legalistic requirements to the faith of his converts, and he stoutly resisted this. Again Paul refers to the Old Testament for support of his insistence upon the total irreconcilability of faith and law (works)—**but, The man that doeth them shall live in them** (cf. Lev. 18:5). There is no middle ground—a man lives one way or the other.

The absolute antithesis between faith and law is further seen in the fact that **Christ hath redeemed us from the curse of the law** (13). If the law, and its consequent curse (cf. v. 10), placed man in such bondage that it required the death of Christ to provide deliverance,[22] it could never be a supplement to, let alone a substitute for, faith. This is Paul's argument. In the verses to follow (3:25—5:1) he describes in various figures how Christ redeemed men from the bondage of sin and gives to them the freedom of sonship. It is not clear, however, in what sense Christ is **made a curse for us.**[23] Certainly, when Christ died "on behalf of"[24] sinful men, taking upon himself the consequences of their sins (cf. II Cor. 5:21), He came under God's curse and condemnation. Even further, this speaks of the method of His

[20]The translation of the verse in the strict order of the Greek is, "The just man by faith will live."

[21]Cf. an additional possibility of its meaning that the man justified by faith will live a life reflecting this new relationship. Such an interpretation would emphasize the ethical implications of justification with which Paul deals later in detail.

[22]The word "redeem" (*exagorazo*) literally means to "buy back" and in this sense "to deliver." The aorist tense indicates that this refers to the once-for-all act of Christ on the Cross as a provision, the actual possession of which must be realized in personal experience.

[23]Cf. Burton's analysis of the possible meanings (*op. cit.*, p. 172).

[24]The Greek preposition *huper*, used here, can mean both "on behalf of" and "in place of" man (cf. Moule, *op. cit.*, p. 64).

sacrificial death. As Christ hung on the Cross, He became a curse on behalf of lost men, because **it is written, Cursed is every one that hangeth on a tree.**[25] In one sense this is an ironic play on words. As Christ died to deliver men from the curse of the law, the very manner of His dying placed Him under the curse of that law.

All attempts to define Christ's redemptive mission in terms other than a *work He did for man* fail to take into serious consideration this passage—and many like it in Paul's writings (cf. Rom. 5:6-11; II Cor. 5:21; Eph. 2:15). The atonement of Jesus Christ was far more than exemplary—it was representative. He provided salvation for all men.

The grand purpose of Christ's redemptive act supports Paul's argument. He died in order **that the blessing of Abraham might come on the Gentiles** (14). The way of law brought only a curse, but the way of faith **through Jesus Christ** brought **the blessing of Abraham** to all men.

The apostle had already made clear (cf. 3:6-9) that Abraham's **blessing** was justification by faith. A further result of Christ's redemption was **that we might receive the promise of the Spirit through faith**; that is, receive the Holy Spirit, who had been promised. This clearly emphasizes the two great truths: (*a*) that all of the treasures of the Christian life are provided by the death of Christ on the Cross; and (*b*) that they are to be possessed by sinful men *only* through faith. We believe this to be true both of justification and of the gift of the Holy Spirit in entire sanctification. Every significant heresy that has challenged the Christian Church has rejected, ignored, or minimized these fundamental dogmas. The result, whether in the first or the twentieth century, is a curse and not salvation.

2. *The Law Cannot Annul the Earlier Promise* (3:15-18)

The limitation of the law (works) is further seen in the fact that, coming many years later, it cannot annul the covenant of promise which God ratified to Abraham and his seed.

To illustrate that the law cannot be imposed upon the believer as a basis for his relationship with God, Paul turns to a well-established principle in human relations. **Brethren, I speak after the manner of men** (15; cf. comments on 1:11). His argu-

[25]Deut. 21:23 refers to the body of a criminal being hung publicly on a tree after execution.

ment is that, if this principle is self-evident among men, it most certainly should be accepted between men and God. **Though it be but a man's covenant, yet if it be confirmed, no man disannulleth, or addeth thereto.** The illustration is clear. Once a **covenant** (contract) has been ratified, even if it is only between men, it cannot be nullified, or have additions made to it.

Having established this principle, Paul pauses parenthetically to emphasize that **to Abraham and his seed were the promises**[26] **made** (16). He had shown (3:6-9) that the basis of Abraham's relationship with God was faith. Thus the covenant, which guaranteed the promised blessings, was ratified to Abraham and his seed on the terms of faith.

The **seed** of Abraham would quite naturally be understood as his *spiritual* descendants by faith, particularly in the light of the previous argument (3:6-9) and that to come (3:28-29). But a sentence follows which is not needed for the argument and is obviously an afterthought. **He saith not, And to seeds, as of many; but as of one, And to thy seed, which is Christ.** As afterthoughts often do, this raises problems.[27] It is probable that Paul was simply emphasizing that every blessing from God to men is centered in Christ. The apostle repeatedly taught that the promises were made to the men of faith, who were Abraham's spiritual seed. In any case it must be remembered that Paul is dealing with legalists and could simply be using here their own technical and tedious rabbinical methods to refute them.

Returning to his basic argument, Paul applies the principle he had established—**and this I say, that the covenant, that was confirmed before of God in Christ, the law, which was four hundred and thirty years after, cannot disannul, that it should make the promise of none effect** (17). The law could not annul the covenant that God had previously ratified, **four hundred and**

[26]The promise refers both to the blessings and to the covenant that guarantees them. Cf. Gen. 15:18; 17:1-8. Cf. also Gen. 12:2-3; 13:14-17; 15:1, 5 for the stated blessings, which were twofold—an innumerable posterity and the promised land.

[27]In non-biblical Greek, the LXX, and the NT the term **seed** (*sperma* and the comparable Heb. term) in the singular number was often used to refer to groups. The OT passages referred to by Paul (Gen. 13:16; 15:5; 17:7-9) clearly use "seed" with reference to Abraham's descendants (cf. RSV), and in this context (Gal. 3:28-29) believers are described as Abraham's seed (singular). It has been suggested that **Christ** refers to all of the believers as a single body or race designated by its Lord (cf. I Cor. 12:12). For a thorough consideration of the problem cf. Burton (*op. cit.*, pp. 505-10).

thirty years[28] before. To do so would be to abolish the promise of God to Abraham and his seed, which was unthinkable.

The apostle repeats his insistence that there can be no compromise between the two basic principles—justification by works and justification by faith (cf. v. 12). **If the inheritance**[29] **be of the law, it is no more of promise** (18). It can't be both—the later law would destroy the earlier promise. **But God gave it to Abraham by promise.** There was no question in Paul's mind. The promise was by faith and the law had no jurisdiction.

3. *The True Function of the Law* (3:19-24)

In the light of its depreciation by Paul, one could understandably ask, **Wherefore then serveth the law?** (19) If it brings only a curse and cannot annul God's earlier promise, what is its significance? What is its true function? The answer to this question reveals even further the limitations of the law. **It was added because of transgressions** (cf. Rom. 4:15). The inferiority of the law, as compared to faith, is seen in the fact that it is an addition—not in the sense of adding anything to faith (cf. v. 15), but simply as appearing at a later point in history. It was introduced on the human scene **because of** (lit., for the sake of) **transgressions.** The full significance of this will be seen in the verses to follow.

Also, the law was temporary, serving only until **the seed should come to whom the promise was made.** As noted above (v. 16), **the seed** of Abraham refers primarily to Christ and then to those who are in Christ. Paul could not resist pointing to an additional inferior quality of the law. Following the current rabbinic teaching, thus effectively arguing on their own premise, he notes that the law **was ordained** (lit., came through the command) **by angels.** It also came **in** (by) **the hand of a mediator,** Moses, who stood between God and men.

The significance of these observations is seen in the verse that follows—**Now a mediator is not a mediator of one, but God is one** (20). Reportedly three hundred interpretations have

[28]The chronology of the LXX, which Paul follows, is not exactly the same as the Hebrew OT, but this minor discrepancy is not important to his argument.

[29]The blessings promised by God came to be understood as an **inheritance** (cf. II Chron. 6:27), and this term was readily adopted into the Christian vocabulary (cf. Acts 20:32; I Cor. 6:9-10; 15:50).

been proposed in explanation of this difficult verse! Paul's reasoning seems to be that a mediator implies an indirect or second-hand relationship. The law was received in this manner; while, in contrast, the promise was received directly from God.[30]

Paul's devastating argument raises the all-important question, **Is the law then against the promises of God?** (21) Certainly this is the question his opponents would raise. His answer is an indignant **God forbid** (cf. 2:17). He then goes on to point out that his depreciation of the law as the way to righteousness stems from the fact that by his own works man is unable to produce righteous results. **If there had been a law given which could have given life, verily righteousness should have been by the law.** The way of law could not give life. If such were possible, righteousness would come by it and not through faith.

Instead of his argument pitting the law against the promises, it reveals what is the true function of works. Faith and works are not intrinsically in conflict, but when rightly understood are in different spheres. The conflict arises when the law is used for a purpose contrary to God's intent. The function that God intended for the law is found in v. 22: **But the scripture hath concluded all under sin** (cf. Rom. 3:9). **The scripture** has reference to a specific passage, most likely Deut. 27:26. This, as the context makes plain, is a scripture relating to the law. Because men must keep the whole law or be guilty, the law **hath concluded** (lit., shut up) **all under sin.** NEB clarifies the meaning thus: "But Scripture has declared the whole world to be prisoners in subjection to sin, so that faith in Jesus Christ may be the ground on which the promised blessing is given, and given to those who have such faith."

As Paul viewed man under the bondage of sin, because of his abuse of the law, he could still see a positive benefit of this past bondage—**that the promise by faith of Jesus Christ might be given to them that believe.** The law, even though abused, still provided a holding action. The very fact that righteousness was not possible by the law prepared man for the promise through faith in Jesus Christ. Disillusionment paved the way for realization. The failure to find salvation through the law prepared man for the hope of such salvation in Christ. Thus the law filled a

[30]Cf. Barclay's suggestion that the law, received through mediation, implies dependence upon two parties for fulfillment. while the promise depends only upon God (*op. cit.*, p. 32).

vital function. In the following verses Paul explains this positive function in more vivid terms.

But before faith came, we were kept under the law (23). In literal terms, the law "guarded"[31] men. It might be asked: Guarded from what? Historically the law kept Israel from the horrible sinful excesses of heathenism, which was undoubtedly one of the chief concerns of Paul's opponents (cf. "Purpose," Introduction). The conscientious Jew, faced by the demands of the law, had a knowledge of sin. Though this knowledge did not keep him from sinning to some extent, nevertheless it guarded him from heathen profligacy. The law was a constant source of moral restraint through the guilt and condemnation that it provided.

Thus **we were . . . shut up**[32] **unto the faith which should afterwards be revealed.** The law guarded man in this twofold manner: restraining him from the excesses of heathenism, and revealing faith to be his only true source of salvation.

Paul graphically describes this true function of the law by using an illustrative figure that was widely understood in the society of his day. **Wherefore the law was our schoolmaster to bring us unto Christ** (24). The term **schoolmaster** (*paidagogos*) really means "custodian" or "guide," and referred to "the man, usually a slave, whose duty it was to conduct a boy or youth to and from school and to superintend his conduct generally; he was not a 'teacher' (despite the present meaning of the derivative 'pedagogue')."[33] Paul is describing how the law puts a man under a bondage like that of a minor child under the supervision of a slave attendant. In the verses to follow it will be seen that such supervision is no longer necessary to the man of faith.

The important observation here is that the law, shutting man up **under sin** and **unto . . . faith,** served the temporary function of protecting and preparing him for the coming of Christ. Contrary to the argument of Paul's opponents, the law had no permanent function, but served only until **we might be justified by faith.**

[31]**Kept under** (*phoureo*) means "to hold in custody" or "to confine."

[32]The same Greek word (*sunkleio*) is used here as in v. 22 (**concluded**).

[33]Arndt and Gingrich, *op. cit.*, p. 608. The Greek term for "teacher" is *didaskalos*.

D. Faith Contrasted with the Law, 3:25—5:1

1. *Sons Versus Slaves* (3:25—4:11)

Paul next points to the fact that the Galatians were no longer servants (lit., slaves), but sons of God through Christ. In this relationship frustrating earthly distinctions disappeared and the Galatians were all heirs of God's promise to Abraham. But even an heir in his infancy was no better than a slave, being under strict supervision. So they, like infants, were once enslaved by the elements of the world. But God, through His Son, redeemed them from the law's bondage in order that they might receive sonship, which was confirmed by His Spirit crying, "Abba, Father," in their hearts. As God's sons they were also His heirs through Christ. This being so, Paul asks how they who had thus known God could desire to be enslaved again through the observance of "feasts" and "fasts." This backsliding caused Paul to fear that all his work had been in vain.

a. Sons of God by faith in Christ (3:25-29). Paul continues his argument that salvation is by faith and not by law, describing the striking contrast between the two. Against the contention of his opponents, he insists that these two ways are mutually exclusive and cannot complement or supplement each other. To illustrate this fact he points out the dramatic difference between sons and slaves. **But after that faith is come, we are no longer under a schoolmaster** (25). Paul's attitude toward the law was not due to what it had done before Christ came. He rejected the way of salvation by works because it now had no longer a proper function—it had been superseded. After the way of faith came through Christ,[34] men were freed from the bondage of the law.

The glorious truth is that ye (Christians) **are all the children of God by faith in Christ Jesus** (26). Paul here changes from the impersonal first-person pronoun *we* to the more specific second person, ye, and in this way applies what he has to say more directly to the Galatians. It is as if he had said: "Now this applies to you!" Through faith in Christ they had become the

[34]The coming of faith here relates to the objective and historical coming of Christ on His redemptive mission and not as the repeated and subjective experience of individual believers (cf. 4:4-5; 3:23).

sons[35] of God. Thus they should not allow themselves to be placed under the bondage of the law—they were sons and not slaves.

Although the coming of faith was an objective and historical fact, it still must be subjectively and individually experienced. This had taken place in the lives of the Galatians—**For as many of you as have been baptized into Christ have put on Christ** (27). Undoubtedly this refers to the initiatory rite of water baptism, which these earliest Christians viewed as the "formal and visible gate into the Christian life."[36] The reference here to baptism was probably due to its similarity to circumcision. Both were initiatory rites. The Jews argued that circumcision alone would open the door to God's favor. Paul reminded these Galatians that they had been baptized into Christ, and had thereby put on Christ. This is a familiar Pauline figure. The basic metaphor is that of putting on a new garment which, although distinct from a man, becomes a veritable part of him.[37] The figure describes the believer's union with Christ, which is so close and intimate that he lives and moves in Christ, and Christ in him.

There is here no allusion to the mode of baptism, as in Rom. 6:3-4.[38] However, Paul's other references to the rite would strongly suggest that he was thinking in terms of immersion.[39] Of much more significance is the question of the objective efficacy that the Early Church associated with baptism. Paul's problem in Corinth (cf. I Corinthians 10) suggests that

[35]The term *huioi* (children) is more correctly translated as "sons." This becomes even more significant as an entirely different word (*nepioi*) is translated "children" in 4:1, 3.

[36]Beet, *op. cit.*, p. 99. Paul's references to baptism relate to the water rite and are not figurative (Rom. 6:3-4; I Cor. 1:13-17; 12:13; 15:29; Eph. 4:5; Col. 2:12). The one significant exception (I Cor. 10:2) was probably because of an overemphasis there on the magical quality of the rite.

[37]Cf. Rom. 13:14; also Eph. 4:24; Col. 3:10 in the more indefinite sense of the "new man." This figure is closely associated with the more extensive expression—"in Christ."

[38]Contrary to the impression of some, the Greek word *baptizo* does not have the intrinsic meaning of "immersion" (cf. Arndt and Gingrich, *op. cit.*, p. 131).

[39]The writings of the Apostolic Fathers show clearly that all three modes —immersion, effusion, and sprinkling—were in use by the middle of the second century. It is quite plain that immersion was preferred unless one's physical condition dictated otherwise. However the concept of one mode being exclusively necessary on theological grounds is relatively modern.

some looked upon baptism as possessing somewhat the same magical qualities that were found in the Greek mystery religions. However, even apart from this, the extensive relating of salvation to faith would argue strongly that it and not baptism was considered the essential means of salvation. The incident at Philippi reflects the pattern: Believe on the Lord Jesus Christ and then be baptized (Acts 16:31-33). Yet baptism was considered more than a sign or symbol. It was unthinkable in the Early Church that a believer converted at night remain unbaptized—even until morning (Acts 16:33).

As is so often the case, extremes destroy the central reality. Baptism should be required as a witness of one's faith in Christ and even perhaps for church membership, if one is to follow the example of the Early Church. However, to insist upon one exclusive mode, or to emphasize the rite until it becomes "baptismal regeneration," is to miss the spirit of the New Testament.

Having pictured the unity that the believer has with Christ, Paul for the moment turned aside to consider the implications of this unity. Not only were the believer and his Lord united, but all believers were united as one in Christ. **There is neither Jew nor Greek, there is neither bond nor free, there is neither male nor female: for ye are all one in Christ Jesus** (28). It is fortunate that Paul listed the ineradicable distinctions of sex as well as those of race and society. This keeps crystal-clear the fact that his meaning is spiritual. The existence of these earthly distinctions will continue but they can disappear as hindrances to fellowship in the body of Christ, and it is of this that he is speaking. This is Paul's inspired vision of the oneness that exists in Christ because God is no respecter of persons. It must be remembered that Paul is here dealing with the question of preferential standing with God. In Jewish society the Jew, the freeman, and the male were all superior; while the Gentile, the slave, and the female were all inferior. These discriminations were also applied to man's relationship with God. Paul is arguing that in the sight of God all are one and equal as they approach Him on the basis of faith in Christ.

Certainly this does not mean in this day of increasing enlightenment in the area of social and racial concern that the Christian can retreat to his citadel of *spiritual* unity and ignore his responsibilities as a member of society. There is here an inferential truth that men who are of equal value in the eyes of God should not be discriminated against by those who profess to be followers of Christ.

The climaxing implication of the believer's union with Christ is seen in the fact that **if ye be Christ's, then are ye Abraham's seed, and heirs according to the promise** (29). The Judaizers were seeking to undermine the Pauline gospel by claiming that *only through the law* could one be a child of Abraham and receive the consequent inheritance. Paul had argued, contrariwise, that the Galatian Christians were the true seed of Abraham by faith and would thus receive the promise (cf. comments on 3:16). Because they were Christ's they were consequently Abraham's seed and heirs according to God's promise to Abraham. They were sons, and this fact guaranteed the glorious prospect of inheritance.

b. Exalted from Servants to Sons (4:1-7). These Galatians, whom Paul had just described as sons and heirs of God, needed to be reminded of what had taken place in their lives. As a background, Paul alludes to a familiar custom regarding minor children. **Now I say, That the heir, as long as he is a child, differeth nothing from a servant, though he be lord of all; but is under tutors and governors until the time appointed of the father** (1-2). A minor child[40] was placed under the supervision of guardians[41] and stewards[42] until a time that his father had previously appointed. In such a state the child, even if he were an heir apparent, had no more freedom than a servant (slave), though he was lord of all, i.e., legally master of the household.

This illustration points to the slavery of the Jew under the law. However, its primary purpose was to show the Galatians exactly where they stood—**even so we, when we were children** (3). As noted above (3:26), Paul's remarks had become markedly personal to the Galatians. Although here, and in v. 5, he reverts to the more impersonal **we,** he still is speaking specifically to his converts in Galatia. He was using sympathetic identification, perhaps for emphasis or to soften the blow to come. They too had been "infants" at one time. In their case, as Gentiles,

[40]The Greek word *nepios* indicates an "infant." Here the significant thing is that the child is an intellectually and morally immature minor.

[41]Tutor (*epitropos*), meaning one who has general oversight of a minor or an orphan.

[42]Governors (*oikonomos*) means house stewards.

they had not been under the law, but **were in bondage under the elements of the world.**

From the time of the Apostolic Fathers the meaning of Paul's expression **the elements** (*stoicheia*) **of the world** has been debated.[43] In the light of its association with the law here in Galatians[44] and the manner in which it is used in its only other occurrences in the New Testament,[45] it seems clear that this expression relates in some manner to sin among the Gentiles even as the law relates to sin among the Jews. Many of the non-Jews sought salvation through rules, regulations, fasts, feasts, and holy days. These could well be **the elements of the world** which enslaved the Galatians (cf. Col. 2:8-20), even as the Jew was in bondage to sin through the weakness of the law.

In 4-5, Paul gives a more detailed description of the epochal coming of Christ and the coming of faith (cf. 3:19, 23, 25). This event was in the **fulness of time** (4), referring back to "the time appointed of the father" (2). The world was in a state of remarkable preparedness for this coming. When conditions were right, Christ came. This is the faith of the Church regarding His return (cf. Acts 1:7; I Thess. 5:1). **God sent forth his Son.** Here is one phase of the miracle of the Incarnation—the divine, preexistent Son was "given" or **sent.**[46] The other phase of the Incarnation is that this Son, as a baby, was **made of a woman.** Jesus entered into the world by the process of natural birth. As a child in a Jewish home, He was **made under the law.**

Christ came **to redeem them that were under the law** (5; cf. comments on 3:13). The purpose of Christ's redemption was basically positive. The Galatians had been delivered from bondage, in order that they **might receive the adoption of sons.** The concept of man being a son of God is not unique with Paul

[43]The word *stoicheia* has the fundamental meaning of "standing in a row" and thus an "element of a series." The four basic interpretations of the expression are: (1) the physical elements of the universe, (2) the heavenly bodies, (3) spirits or demons—good or bad (even associated with the giving of the law), (4) rudimentary or elementary religious principles. Cf. Burton, *op. cit.*, pp. 510-18, for an excellent brief analysis. Cf. the verb *stoicheo* in 5:25.

[44]To submit to the law was to return to these "weak and beggarly elements" (4:9).

[45]Cf. Col. 2:8, 20, where the "elements" are associated with philosophy, traditions, decrees, injunctions, and teaching of men.

[46]Cf. John 1:4; 3:16-17; I John 4:9-14.

(cf. I John 3:2), but the reception of that relationship through adoption is found only in his writings.[47] The illustration of adoption emphasizes the fact that the convert is receiving blessings which he had not been privileged to enjoy by his former position. Always in the background of Paul's thought is the fact that the Galatians had been outside the covenant, but now through faith are the true heirs of Abraham. This illustration is consistent with the figures of "birth" (cf. John 3:3-9; I Pet. 1:23) and being "made alive" (cf. Eph. 2:5). All depict the new relationship that the believer has with God.

The coming of Christ was an objective and historical fact. It took place so that those in bondage might be freed and receive sonship. However this provision must be personalized in one's own experience as the individual believer exercises faith in Jesus Christ. **And because ye are sons, God sent forth the Spirit of his Son into your hearts** (6; cf. Rom. 8:14-17). The presence of God's Spirit in the believer is the evidence that he is indeed the son of God. Thus, in the believer's heart, the Spirit of God's Son cries: **Abba,**[48] **Father.** This is the filial cry, from a loving son, upon the recognition of a loving Father. Here is the only use of "heart" (*kardia*) in Galatians. It is a term used extensively in the New Testament to represent the inner life of man, and is the arena of divine activity.

The element of personal witness to the believer's heart by the Spirit of God, so ably emphasized by the Wesleys, is a vital part of Christian experience. Salvation is by faith, but such faith has its response.[49] It is wondrously and gloriously personal, God suiting to each soul the manifestation of himself that results in the cry—**Abba, Father.**

Wherefore thou art no more a servant (slave), **but a son** (7). The contrast is complete—between a slave in bondage and a **son** who is an **heir of God through Christ** (cf. Rom. 8:14-17). The slave is governed, subservient, and bound. The **son** receives

[47]*Huiothesia* (**adoption**, sonship) is found only here and in Rom. 8:15; 9:4; Eph. 1:5; and with reference to the redemption of the body in Rom. 8:23.

[48]This is the untranslated Aramaic word for "father," equivalent to *pater*, the translated Greek term that follows it.

[49]Cf. Rom. 8:14-17 and also Hebrews 11. which basically describe the witness to faith.

from his father all the treasures that have been provided for him. Paul is speaking here specifically of the inheritance from Abraham. The express purpose of this argument is to prove to the Galatians that they would receive the blessings promised to Abraham's seed by pursuing the way of faith, and not by turning to the way of law.

c. Backsliding from Sonship to Slavery (4:8-11). Having reminded them of their relationship to God as sons, Paul prepared to raise the all-important question, by referring again to their pre-conversion state—**when ye knew not God** (8). At that time they were undoubtedly quite ignorant of the existence of the true God, to say nothing of knowing Him experientially. In this condition of ignorance they **did service unto them which by nature are no gods.** The Jew, monotheist as he was, refused to acknowledge the existence of any other god than Jehovah. He did, however, recognize spirits and powers on a sub-divine level. Paul is stating that the Gentiles' old heathen idols, purporting to be gods, were impostors. However, the significant fact is that the Galatians had served them as if they were true gods. This devotion brought them only slavery.

But now, after that ye have known God (9) indicates that their present state is in marked contrast to their former one. Their previous ignorance had been replaced by a personal, experiential knowledge[50] of the true God. Then, to emphasize that such knowledge was dependent upon God, and not them, Paul adds, **or rather are known of God.**

Now the question that burned in the apostle's heart could be asked, **How turn ye again to the weak and beggarly elements, whereunto ye desire again to be in bondage?** The use of the present tense[51] indicates that they were in the process of turning. Paul's heart cry was—"How can you do it?" They knew the slavery which once had been their lot. In its place they had found the glorious liberty of the sons of God. In spite of the glowing promises of the Judaizers, to submit themselves to the law was to return again to the enslaving **elements** (cf. 4:3),

[50]The Greek word (*oida*) used here for "know" means primarily to be acquainted with a person, in distinction from *ginosko,* which means to learn or come to understand.

[51]**Turn** and **observe** (vv. 9-10) are in the present tense.

which were weak and poor.[52] It was incredible to Paul that this could be their wish or desire.[53]

The specific part of the law to which the Galatians were turning was the observing of **days, and months, and times, and years** (10). These referred to Jewish festivals and fast days. The likelihood is that the Judaizers had started their attack at this point and the Galatians were already entering into these observances.[54] Such activities would be quite similar to the "elements of the world," under which they had previously been in bondage (cf. 4:3, 9; Col. 2:20-23), and thus would have a point of special appeal.

Perhaps the Galatians did not realize where this path led, but not so the apostle. He declares, **I am afraid of you,** better translated, "I fear for you." This is the true shepherd's heart, as he sees his flock turning down a dangerous path. He fears for their safety and the outcome of their wandering. But there is also another element in Paul's fear: **lest I have bestowed upon you labour in vain.** He had gone to Galatia at no small personal price and had labored there without reservation. Now he fears that all this labor has been in vain, as indeed it would be if they reverted to Judaism.

2. *A Personal Appeal* (4:12-20)

Turning from his line of argument for a moment, Paul makes an appeal to his Galatian converts. He begs them to adopt an attitude like his own toward the ceremonial Jewish law. He then reminds them of the circumstances under which he brought the gospel to them and the affection with which he had been received, although he had had a repulsive affliction. Attention is called to the motivation of his opponents' concern, as compared with his "birth pangs" for them. His only wish was that he could be with them in person, so that the tone of his appeal might be softened.

[52]The KJV fails to indicate a significant word in the Greek text, which speaks of wishing to serve the **elements** *anew* (*anothen*) as slaves. This is the same word used in John 3:3, 7—to be "born anew."

[53]Cf. comments on 5:4 for a brief discussion of the modern teaching on unconditional eternal security in the light of the problem in Galatia.

[54]Burton suggests that at the time of Paul's writing the Galatians had already adopted the feasts and fast days, and were now being urged to submit to circumcision (*op. cit.*, p. 233).

Affectionately calling the Galatians **brethren** (12), he pleads —**I beseech you.** It is more literally translated, "I beg you." No longer was the apostle arguing; he was now imploring. His personal appeal was, **Be as I am; for I am as ye are.** This is specifically a reference to his understanding of the law. He, a born Jew, had chosen the way of faith. They, having once accepted Christian faith, were now ready to disown it for the way of law, which he had rejected.[55] Thus he makes the appeal that they become again what he had become.[56]

The meaning of the obscure remark, **Ye have not injured me at all,** was undoubtedly clear to the Galatians, but is hidden from the modern reader. Phillips interprets it, "I have nothing against you personally."

a. The Memory of His Reception Among the Galatians (4:13-16). The thought of having possibly labored in vain among the Galatians brought flooding back into the apostle's mind the memory of his reception by them. **Ye know how through infirmity of the flesh I preached the gospel unto you** (13). This alludes to the fact that Paul's preaching to them was due to his illness. He either went there or remained there because he was ill. The added clause, **at the first,**[57] identifies this visit as his initial contact with them.

What made this so important to Paul's appeal was their reaction to this unusual situation—**And my temptation which was in my flesh**[58] **ye despised not, nor rejected** (14). His in-

[55]Paul had rejected the law as the basis of salvation; but, as the other first-century converts from Judaism, he continued to keep much of the Jewish ritual (cf. Acts 3:1; 20:16). He also had a deeper evangelistic reason for maintaining his Jewish standing (cf. I Cor. 9:20).

[56]This, and the observations that immediately follow (cf. v. 19), suggest that their drift to apostasy had reached a point of broken relationship with God; they had to become *again* what they had been.

[57]*To proteron* can mean "the first time," implying two visits by Paul, or simply "formerly." Much has been written to the effect that this proves two visits, but Arndt and Gingrich state, "From a lexical point of view it is not possible to establish that Paul wished to differentiate between a later visit and an earlier one" (*op. cit.,* p. 729). Cf. the discussion of possibilities with the same conclusion in Burton, *op. cit.,* pp. 239-41.

[58]The meaning of **flesh** (*sarx*) here and in the previous verse is clearly the present, earthly body.

firmity was so offensive that it was a severe trial[59] to them.[60] They were tempted to treat him with contempt and disdain. Instead, they received him **as an angel of God, even as Christ Jesus.** Their reception had been overwhelming. Instead of despising him, they received (welcomed) him **as an angel**[61] **of God.**

Remembering such a welcome, Paul could rightly now ask, **Where is then the blessedness ye spake of?** (15) Where is the frame of mind in which they had (lit.) "blessed themselves"? The question is rhetorical, implying that it had ceased. So genuine had been their happy reception of him, and his message, that Paul could **bear . . . record, that, if it had been possible, ye would have plucked out your own eyes, and have given them to me.** It has often been assumed that this statement indicates that Paul's illness (cf. v. 13) was one of poor eyesight,[62] but it is quite possible that this is simply a vivid illustration of their willingness to do anything humanly possible for him.[63] In any case Paul was describing their utter selflessness in their willingness to assist him.

In the light of this he asks: **Am I therefore become your enemy?** (16) Once considered the beloved **angel of God,** for whom they would sacrifice their very eyes, now is he an **enemy,** who literally hates them. It must be remembered that this is the view that the Galatians were evidently taking of Paul and does not express the apostle's feelings. He suggests that they have this attitude **because I tell you the truth.** He had done nothing but preach the true gospel to them—truth tested in the crucible of his own experience.

[59]The word **temptation** (*peirasmos*) means both a "trial" and a "temptation."

[60]The KJV suggests it was Paul's trial, but the Greek text makes it clear he is referring to the Galatians' trial.

[61]*Angelos* can mean human messenger or superhuman being.

[62]There have been many suggestions as to Paul's infirmity, sometimes associated with his "thorn in the flesh" (II Cor. 12:7). Some of these are: persecution, temptation to sensuality, spiritual trials (despair and doubt), epilepsy, malaria, fever, and a malady of the eyes. There seems little question that it was repulsive to those who listened to him preach. However, the precise nature of his suffering cannot be determined (cf. Burton, *op. cit.,* pp. 238-39).

[63]Cf. the modern expression, "I'd give my right arm to do this."

b. Not All Religious Zeal Is of God (4:17-20). In contrast to his own frank truthfulness, Paul realizes that the Judaizers **zealously affect** ("make much of," RSV) **you, but not well** (17). Paul's opponents were truly "deeply concerned" about the Galatians, but not for their good. Their interest was for another reason **—yea, they would exclude you.** It is not stated what the Judaizers sought to exclude the Galatians from, but it can be safely concluded that they did not want these converts to remain under the influence of Paul. The purpose was **that ye might affect** (have zeal for) **them.** Paul's opponents sought to separate his converts from him and tie the Galatians to themselves.

The apostle recognizes that **it is good to be zealously affected always in a good thing, and not only when I am present with you** (18). This is a difficult verse to interpret, but in the light of the previous statements it seems that Paul is saying it is good for these Galatians to have someone concerned about them. The RSV translates the verse: "For a good purpose it is always good to be made much of, and not only when I am present with you."

In 19-20, Paul expresses the depth of his concern for the Galatians, in contrast to the superficial interest of his opponents. He addresses them affectionately as **my little children** (19). This is a familiar Pauline expression.[64] He likens his deep concern for them to a woman in birth pangs—**of whom I travail in birth again until Christ be formed in you.** The language graphically reveals his deep concern and the figure strikes a responsive note in the heart of every mother. Only supreme love brings such involvement. The term **formed** (*morphoo*) is particularly revealing; it extends the figure of "Christ in you" (Col. 1:27) to the newly forming embryo in the womb.[65] The key word is **again.** This was the second time that Paul had gone through this agony of spiritual parenthood. The expression indicates the extent of the Galatian apostasy.

This personal appeal is closed with an earnest **desire to be present with you now, and to change my voice** (20). When is a concerned loved one's presence more appreciated—and needed— than at childbirth? This yearning moved the heart of the apostle.

[64]He most often uses the expression in reference to an individual (cf. I Cor. 4:17; I Tim. 1:2) but also for groups (I Cor. 4:14; II Cor. 6:13).

[65]This is a mixed metaphor (cf. Rom. 7:1-6)—Paul suffers the labor and the Galatians have the birth. It does not, however, destroy the truth illustrated: soul agony for renewed birth.

Written words can be cold and even misleading. He wanted to assure them of his loving concern. Nothing could do that like his presence; but obviously this was impossible. There was also in Paul's desire the element of uncertainty: **for I stand in doubt of you.** This doubt was the uneasiness of being perplexed and baffled. NEB has, "I am at my wits' end about you." How could this situation have come to pass in his beloved Galatians?

3. *Freedom Versus Slavery* (4:21—5:1)

Returning now to his basic argument, the apostle uses an illustrative allegory, based on the story of the two sons of Abraham and their mothers. Ishmael, born of a slave-maid (Hagar), according to the flesh, was cast out for having persecuted his brother. Isaac, born of a free woman (Sarah), through the promise, became heir of all. These two mothers are symbolic of the two covenants. The old covenant, originating at Mount Sinai and now centered in Jerusalem, is (like Hagar) in slavery with her children. The new covenant, coming from Jerusalem above, is (like Sarah) the mother of the children of promise, who are free. Even Isaiah rejoiced and sang of this new day (54:1). Paul then exhorts his Galatian converts to stand firm in the freedom to which Christ had freed them, not allowing themselves to be burdened again with the yoke of bondage.

a. The Two Covenants (4:21-26). In an abrupt manner—undoubtedly for emphasis—Paul asks: **Tell me, ye that desire to be under the law, do ye not hear the law?** (21) The word **desire** suggests that Paul was torn by doubt and uncertainty (cf. 4:20), fluctuating between hope and almost despair for them. It is impossible to determine exactly the extent of their acceptance of the law. Here Paul suggests the worst—that they really wanted the way of the law. He therefore demands[66] that they hear what the law has to say. He intimates that the Judaizers had not told them all there was to know. Now he would illustrate his argument from the record of the law.

For it is written, that Abraham had two sons, the one by a bondmaid, the other by a freewoman (22). The familiar incident of the two sons of Abraham, Ishmael and Isaac (cf. Genesis 16; 21), is of primary importance because the central appeal of the Judaizers was related to being the seed and heirs of Abra-

[66]The form of the question suggests such insistence.

ham. Paul says, "Let us examine the record!" There is a vital difference between the two boys: Ishmael was the son of a **bond-maid** (maid-slave),[67] and Isaac the son of a **freewoman.**

Paul saw in this the spiritual significance that **he who was of the bondwoman was born after the flesh; but he of the free-woman was by promise** (23). Ishmael was born simply through physical conception,[68] but Isaac was the child of promise. Although his birth took place through natural means, the advanced age of Abraham and Sarah (together with Sarah's lifelong barrenness) made Isaac the miracle child promised by God and received by faith (cf. Heb. 11:11-12).

As Paul views these facts of Jewish history, he concludes that they **are an allegory** (24). He is not suggesting that this was the original meaning of the scripture, but rather that this is a legitimate spiritual meaning that can be used to illustrate the argument he has been making.[69]

Allegorical argument was quite common in this period.[70] As suggested above (3:16, 20), Paul used rabbinic methods, due both to his desire to meet his opponents on their grounds and also as a result of his own training. Two points should be made clear. The drawing of spiritual applications did not in any way indicate Paul's doubt of the historical truth of the incident, as is so often the case today.[71] Further, this **allegory** is actually an illustration used in support of an argument already extensively presented. It had, therefore, a confirmatory function.

First Paul notes that **these are the two covenants.** The use of the verb **are** in this passage is best understood as "represent" or "stand for." Thus, "these two mothers represent two covenants." Hagar, bringing forth her son into slavery, is likened to the old covenant of Mount Sinai, that could result only in slave-

[67]The word *paidiske* literally means a "girl," but in biblical literature always indicates a slave girl.

[68]The meaning of **after the flesh** (*kata sarka*) is related to racial lineage. Cf. Rom. 1:3; 4:1; 9:3, 5; I Cor. 10:18; Eph. 2:11.

[69]Cf. Burton's excellent discussion of the significance of such allegorical argument (*op. cit.*, pp. 254-56).

[70]Cf. the use of scripture allegorically by Philo, a leading Jewish theologian (pre-NT period), in Hebrews (NT), and by Origen, a Christian theologian (post-NT period).

[71]There is no evidence that Paul questioned the historical validity and scriptural authority of Genesis.

ry.[72] This is Paul's basic contrast—between the freedom of faith and the slavery of law (works).

In v. 25 the apostle proceeds to apply the allegory in more detail—**for this Agar is mount Sinai in Arabia.** There is some question as to the correct Greek text,[73] but it seems clear that Paul is simply saying that in the allegory Hagar represents Mount Sinai in Arabia. Hagar and Mount Sinai **answereth to Jerusalem which now is** means that these two symbolize the Jewish legal system of Paul's day, which had its center in Jerusalem. He thus concludes that Jerusalem is in slavery to the law, with **her children,** the Jews, even as were Hagar and her son.

By contrast, **Jerusalem which is above is free, which is the mother of us all** (26). The mother of us who are free—living by faith—is the Jerusalem above. The Jewish community (living by law) is mothered by Jerusalem in Palestine, but the Christian community (living by faith) is mothered by the eternal Jerusalem. Paul thinks in terms of the believer living the heavenly life now.[74]

b. Thanksgiving for the Way of Faith (4:27-28). Paul pictures Isaiah rejoicing and singing about this day of realization: **For it is written, Rejoice, thou barren that bearest not; break forth and cry, thou that travailest not: for the desolate hath many more children than she which hath an husband** (27). In this verse (Isa. 54:1) the prophet foresees the day when those presently **barren** and **desolate** (in the Babylonian captivity) shall have many more children than those **which hath an husband** (Judah before the Exile). This glorious vision (cf. Isa. 52:7-12) was never fulfilled in Old Testament times, and is seen by Paul to have its meaning in the spiritual children being born in the early Christian era.

This he specifically states in 28. **Now we** (you),[75] **brethren,**

[72]Ishmael was born before Isaac and 430 years before Mount Sinai, but here Paul is simply illustrating the contrast between "works" (natural conception) and "faith" (divine promise); he is not dealing with the time schedule.

[73]Some important early MSS leave out "Hagar," thus reading: "For Sinai is a mountain in Arabia."

[74]Cf. Phil. 3:20; Col. 3:1-3. For a similar contrast of Mount Sinai and the heavenly Jerusalem cf. Heb. 12:18-29.

[75]The Greek pronoun is in the second person (you). These Galatian Gentiles were true children of God's promise to Abraham.

as Isaac was, are the children of promise. At this point Paul comes back to his allegory. These Galatians, even as Isaac, were not born through merely natural processes, but were indeed the children of promise.

c. The Inherent Conflict Between the Flesh and Faith (4: 29-31). In 29 a further point of application is seen by the apostle: **But as then he that was born after the flesh persecuted him that was born after the Spirit, even so it is now.** The historical reference could be to the conflict between the two individual sons,[76] or to the well-known enmity between their posterity. Observing this, Paul remarks that even so, in his day, those born according to the flesh (cf. comments on 4:23) were persecuting the ones who were **born after the Spirit.**[77] He does not here give the details of the persecution (cf. 3:4; I Thess. 2:15-16).

Returning again to his allegory, he asks: **What saith the scripture?** (30) Although this question is in the context of his allegory, this is not Paul's typical use of the Scriptures (cf. 4:27). It does however reflect Paul's total acceptance of their authority. His enemies sought to discredit him at this point.

The Bible, and especially the New Testament, is God's *Message* to man—admittedly received through human channels. It must first be understood in the context of the specific historical situation that called forth its appearance. Thus, such questions as why, when, and to whom any specific part of it was written are indispensable. But the reader must go beyond this if the Bible is to serve God's purpose. The application of that Message must be sought. This precisely is the miracle of Scripture. It does have an application and fulfillment for the reader that makes it unique. The Message that thus comes to men today has the power of divine authority—this is God's Message for them. It cannot be rejected, ignored, or modified without eternal loss to those who treat it thus.

Continuing his allegory, Paul notes that the Scripture said—

[76]Cf. Gen. 21:9. The KJV and ASV read **mocking**, but the RSV and the ASV margin read "playing." The LXX, which Paul followed, can be translated "laughed at." It would seem that the element of mockery was present to some degree to call forth the radical consequences.

[77]This is an excellent example of the Pauline style in which he intimates what is yet to come. With either "uncontrollable anticipation" or "planned intent" he plants the seed of his forthcoming ideas (cf. comments on 5:13—6:10).

Cast out the bondwoman and her son (30). Thus the apostle indicates the inescapable conclusion that the expulsion of Hagar and Ishmael, as representatives of those living under law, points to the rejection of all of Abraham's children according to the flesh.[78] This allegory is not a full picture of Paul's anti-legalism. His conclusion is not based only upon an allegory; the whole problem had been painstakingly examined from every angle by the apostle (cf. 3:10-24). There is a reason for the drastic action described here: **for the son of the bondwoman shall not be heir with the son of the freewoman.** There can be no dividing of the inheritance. Paul is simply giving a dramatic illustration of the irreconcilable conflict between salvation by works and salvation by faith. Those who are true sons—by faith—are heirs of all (cf. 3:25—4:11).

Paul concludes the allegory by stating in concise form its main point: **So then, brethren, we**[79] **are not children of the bondwoman, but of the free** (31). He had been contrasting the way of faith and the way of law. Thus he concludes that we **are not children** of the law but rather free children of faith. The allegory is thus a confirming illustration of the truth he had already convincingly argued.

d. The Freedom of Faith (5:1). There is difference of opinion regarding the relevant context of 5:1. Does it sum up what has preceded, either the immediate allegory or the entire argument of cc. 3—4, or does it serve as the pivotal transition to the closing exhortations of the Epistle? It will be treated here as a *summation* of the argument that Paul has made, namely, that the law brings slavery and faith brings freedom. There is no doubt that it is "an epitome of the contention of the whole letter."[80]

Paul admonishes the Galatians to **stand fast therefore in the liberty wherewith Christ hath made us free** (1). Using the imperative mood (see Intro.), the apostle commands: "Stand firm!" He could command such action as the consequence of

[78]Cf. Romans 9—11 for a more detailed treatment of this question revealing Paul's deep compassion for his people.

[79]Here the pronoun is first person plural as Paul identifies himself with the Galatians (cf. 4:28).

[80]Burton, *op. cit.*, p. 270. Burton contends that this verse opens the "Hortatory Portion" of the Epistle (*ibid.*, p. 270), while Beet associates it with the foregoing section (*op. cit.*, p. 138).

his argument. They were to stand firm with the "freedom[81] with which Christ had freed[82] them." There can be no doubt that this refers to freedom from the slavery of the law (cf. 4:5, 26, 31). This freedom was a liberation from the power and grip of sin which had enslaved them through the law (cf. 3:19—4:11; Rom. 7:7-25). The next phrase makes this unmistakably clear: **and be not entangled again with the yoke of bondage.** For these Galatians to turn to the law, as they were being urged to do by the Judaizers, would mean that they would be **entangled** (lit., burdened or weighted down) **again.**[83] This **yoke of bondage** would mean the end of their freedom in Christ.

E. Circumcision Separates from Christ, 5:2-12

Paul concludes his argument of the entire Epistle by describing the inescapable results of the Galatians' submitting to the law. He names circumcision for the first time as the crux of the problem in Galatia. Acceptance of this requirement removes all the benefits of Christ and places upon the Galatians the burden of the whole law. Those thus sinning would sever themselves from Christ and fall from grace. By contrast, those living by faith have through the Spirit the hope of righteousness. Actually, circumcision or uncircumcision is not the issue with Paul. Rather, the decisive factor is faith operating through love. Paul then asks who had torn up the racecourse on which they were running so well. This action certainly could not have been the work of Christ, who had called them. It was rather an example of the way that evil spreads—"A little leaven leaveneth the whole lump." The apostle expresses confidence that the Galatians will heed his concern and closes with the wish that their troublers would leave them and join the ranks of their mutilated heathen neighbors.

1. *A Warning Against Circumcision* (5:2-4)

Paul puts behind this closing summation of his argument all the power of his personal influence: **Behold, I Paul say unto you** (2). The inescapable consequence of this false doctrine is that,

[81]The term *eleutheria* can be translated "freedom" or "liberty," but "freedom" has more identification with the context.

[82]The comparable verb form, *eleutheroo.*

[83]Cf. the significance of "again" in comments on 4:9.

if ye be circumcised, Christ shall profit you nothing (lit., be of no use to you). **If ye be** (present subjunctive) clearly defines future possibility. This suggests the status of the Galatian converts. Obviously they had adopted at least some of the Jewish festivals (cf. 4:9-10), and were at the moment seriously contemplating submitting to circumcision. There is no evidence that the Judaizers, up to this time, had sought to enforce any other part of the law (e.g., laws concerning food).

Paul warns that if they allow themselves to be circumcised they will forfeit the benefits of their relationship with Christ. Obviously the Judaizers had assured the Galatians that they would not affect their Christian faith through the acceptance of the law as represented by circumcision. This Paul had repeatedly disproved in the foregoing argument.

And the consequence of such action is not just its futility: **I testify again to every man that is circumcised, that he is a debtor to do the whole law.** Paul had plainly told them this before (3:10), but he repeats for emphasis. The man who takes up any part of the law—in this case circumcision—is obligated to keep it all. Evidently Paul's opponents had also failed to make this plain to the Galatians.

What Paul had said repeatedly he states again in unmistakable terms: **Christ is become of no effect unto you, whosoever of you are justified by the law; ye are fallen from grace** (4). This, in capsule form, is his contention throughout his entire argument. All the other points climax in this. To the Galatians,[84] seeking to be or thinking they are justified[85] by law, Paul has a stern warning. With such, Christ has nothing more to do![86] Further, they have lost God's grace.[87] In the strongest language

[84]The second-person pronoun **unto you** makes it more direct.

[85]The Greek present passive tense is literally "**are** (being) **justified.**" This must be understood as hypothetical, in harmony with the context. Paul has clearly stated that no one can be justified by law (cf. 2:16; 3:11).

[86]*Katargeo,* translated in the KJV is **become of none effect,** is a very strong word. In the active voice it means "to abolish" or "wipe out," and in the passive voice (as here) it means "to be released from association with" or "to have nothing more to do with." The aorist tense indicates that such estrangement is climactic (cf. Arndt and Gingrich, *op. cit.,* p. 418).

[87]**Fallen** (*ekpipto*) literally means to "fall off or from" and has the significance of consequently perishing (cf. petals falling from a flower). In nautical terms it means to "drift off course" or "run aground on rocks." In a figurative sense it means "to lose" something or someone (cf. Arndt and Gingrich, *op. cit.,* p. 243).

possible, Paul stated the consequences of seeking to be justified through the law. They would lose God's grace because Christ would have nothing more to do with them. It is important to see that this loss was due to the fact that they had abandoned God's grace and not because God had taken it away. The two ways are absolutely incompatible. The apostasy of turning to the law is fatal (cf. Heb. 10:26-31).

There was in Galatia the possibility of apostasy. The Galatians had experienced grace and were now turning from God. Since New Testament times it has been beyond comprehension how those who have "tasted of the heavenly gift, and were made partakers of the Holy Ghost, and have tasted the good word of God, and the powers of the world to come" (Heb. 6:4-5), could return to the old life of sin. This question has been so acute that some have developed a theology that denies its possibility. They say that any who return permanently to the life of sin never had found new life in Christ, and all who have found such life will inevitably come back to their Father and home. Others, more boldly, insist that, once a man becomes the child of God, his choices and decisions cannot alter this new relationship. But neither Scripture nor human experience substantiates such a teaching.

This false theology is built on a minimizing of the power of man's Satanic adversary, and on a gross misunderstanding of the power of God. One of the most sublime truths of the New Testament revelation is that of God's self-limitation. He will not transgress or abuse human freedom. The same God who will not save a man against his will, will not keep a man saved against his will. This is the key to sustaining grace. As long as a soul desires and wills to love and serve God, he is secure. But when a man chooses to return to the slavery of sin and Satan, God Almighty will respect that decision.

2. *Righteousness Is by Faith* (5:5-6)

In v. 5, Paul presents the greatest possible contrast to salvation by works. **We through the Spirit wait for the hope of righteousness by faith.** The **we,** referring to those who with himself turn not away from Christ, is in contradistinction to "you" of the previous verse. Paul emphasizes that he, and those following him, are living **through** (by means of)[88] **the Spirit.** Although it is unstated, those who are under the law live by means of the "flesh"[89]—their reliance is upon the flesh instead of the Spirit. Men of faith **wait for** (lit., eagerly await) **the hope of** the **righteousness** that is theirs **by faith.** Elsewhere Paul makes it plain that this hope is the anticipated resurrection, with all of its promise.[90]

The apostle's use of **righteousness** (*dikaiosyne*) here is clearly the inclusive concept; he includes both the righteousness of God's justification and the ethics of changed lives. The next verse, and the intensive ethical exhortation that follows, plainly indicate an emphasis on moral character as well as forensic standing.

Paul's opponents insisted that circumcision was essential to the Galatian converts because it alone made one an heir of Abraham. In the foregoing argument this had been decisively disproved. Now the apostle could declare that to the man **in Jesus Christ neither circumcision availeth any thing, nor uncircumcision** (6). This does not mean that it made no difference if a believer were circumcised, thus adding works to his faith. Such would repudiate his faith. Rather, it meant that this Jewish rite had no value for bringing a man to Christ. For salvation, uncircumcision had no value either. Such distinctions were lost in Christ. The true values in God's sight were not material, racial, or social but spiritual (cf. I Cor. 13:13; II Cor. 4:18). This was revolutionary. Many, even in the early Christian Church, were unconvinced and afraid of this position (cf. comments on 2:7-10).

But Paul did not stop there. What did have value—eternal value—was **faith which worketh through love.** Probably this verse is the most inclusive and extensive single statement on the nature of New Testament salvation that Paul ever made. Salvation is not faith alone. Such an assertion is a travesty on the thought of the apostle (cf. Introduction). True faith expresses

[88] Burton sees this as a "dative of means"—*pneumati,* **through the Spirit** (*op. cit.,* p. 278). Cf. comment on 5:16-26 for the meaning of **Spirit.**

[89] Cf. the meaning of "flesh" (*sarx*) in comments on 5:16-26.

[90] Cf. Rom. 8:19, 23, 25, where **wait** (*apekdechomai*) is also used. Certainly **righteousness** is not the content of hope, because it is already possessed by faith. Instead, the genitive form of *dikaiosyne* has an instrumental function: hope is *by* righteousness (cf. C. F. D. Moule, *op. cit.,* p. 44).

itself[91] through love. Here is Paul's first mention in this letter of the all-important term **love** (*agape*). It is introduced here, probably because he had been accused of removing from life the dynamic for ethical conduct. Instead of eliminating the moral nerve center, he was, in fact, providing it. Faith expresses itself in love, through the power of the Spirit. The substantiation of this is seen in his closing admonition (5:13—6:10).

3. *The Dangers of the Galatian Heresy* (5:7-9)

Turning back to the situation in Galatia, Paul writes: **Ye did run well; who did hinder you that ye should not obey the truth?** (7) Using one of his familiar metaphors of the Christian life, the athletic contests (cf. 2:2; Rom. 9:16; I Cor. 9:24-26), he wants to know who broke up the race[92] when they were doing so well. The specific hindrance was to be unpersuaded[93] or to **not obey the truth.** Paul well knew the answer to his rhetorical question, but he wanted it made crystal-clear. **This persuasion cometh not of him that calleth you** (8). The God who had called them (cf. 1:6) was not a party to this rejection of faith and acceptance of law. Rather than God persuading them to take the step they had taken, it was a few Judaizers in Galatia who were threatening to corrupt the entire Christian community.

In v. 9, Paul quotes a proverb, undoubtedly well-known to them, **A little leaven leaveneth the whole lump.** In the New Testament, leaven usually represents evil. The proverb is equivalent to our own: One rotten apple will spoil a bushel. Wherever men congregate, a misguided, noisy minority can influence a large assembly. Freedom of speech is a precious and inviolate right, but men of every day need to distinguish between claim and proof. Our great danger is that mentioned by Jesus, "Ye do err, not knowing the scriptures, nor the power of God" (Matt. 22:29). But why not apply the proverb positively? A little

[91]**Worketh** (*energeo*), which we transliterate "energy," means to "operate" or "work," but the clause "expresses itself" more accurately reflects the middle voice used here. However, in the NT—and especially in Paul—there are always the overtones of the operation of the Spirit (cf. 2:8; Eph. 3:20).

[92]Burton suggests that this can mean going onto the racetrack (getting in the way) or even breaking up the road (*op. cit.*, p. 282).

[93]**Obey** (*peitho*) is the common Greek word for "persuade," but in the passive voice can mean "obey." However, lack of persuasion precedes disobedience.

spiritual leaven can leaven a whole church, community, country, and world. Dare we have such faith?

4. *Paul's Confidence and Concern* (5:10-12)

The apostle's next expression refers back to vv. 7-8. He had spoken there of the Galatians' persuasion. Now he adds: **I have confidence in you through the Lord** (10). He too had a persuasion.[94] He had confidence in these converts **that ye will be none otherwise minded.** Paul trusts that when they receive this letter they will think no differently than he does. This is the greatest expression in the entire letter (cf. comments 4:11) of his confidence in the satisfactory outcome of the controversy.

Paul turns next to those who were disturbing the Galatians: **he that troubleth you shall bear his judgment, whosoever he be.** Paul's opponents would suffer the tragic consequences that he had shown to be the lot of those who took the way of law rather than the way of faith. The phrase **whosoever he be** could indicate either (*a*) that Paul did not know his adversaries or (*b*) that judgment would be theirs regardless of who they were.

Verse 11 suggests that Paul's opponents had assured the Galatians that under certain circumstances Paul himself still approved of the circumcision they were advocating. In answer the apostle asks: **Brethren, if I yet preach circumcision, why do I yet suffer persecution?** (11) Paul, of course, had preached circumcision in his pre-Christian days. There were remarks that he made and incidents that occurred (cf. Acts 16:3; I Cor. 7:18) that could be so interpreted. The convincing argument that he was not still preaching this doctrine was the fact that he was now being persecuted for rejecting circumcision.

The "scandal"[95] of the Cross, among Jews, was the denial of circumcision. For Paul to promote, or permit, circumcision under the threat of persecution would be to remove that scandal—**then is the offence of the cross ceased.** Such was unthinkable to the apostle.

So deeply disturbed was Paul by the intent of his enemies in Galatia that he declares: **I would they were even cut off which**

[94]**Confidence** is the same Greek word used in vv. 7-8 (*peitho*); but in the perfect tense, as here, it means "to trust in" or "put one's confidence in."

[95]This is a transliteration of the Greek word for **offence** (*skandalon*).

trouble you (12). The apostle had reached the unbelievable place (for a Jew) where he looked upon the proposed circumcision of his converts as nothing but mutilation of their bodies. Thus, in the desperation of a deep concern he expressed the wish that those who insisted upon circumcision would go on and undergo emasculation of themselves.[96]

This brings to a close Paul's argument that salvation is by faith and not by law (works). Coupled with his similar teaching in Romans, it has become the foundation of the essential doctrine of justification by faith. This truth has been central in evangelical Protestantism since the days of Luther and the Reformation.

The remainder of the letter is in an entirely different mood, as Paul concerns himself with admonition instead of argument.

[96]This probably refers to the practice of emasculation by the priests of Cybele, with which the Galatians would be acquainted. If so, this is more than a crude physical reference. Paul may have been saying that it would be better for the Christian Church if these Judaizers were out-and-out heathen, because then the Galatians would pay no attention to them. Cf. the discussion in Burton, *op. cit.*, p. 289. Cf. also Phil. 3:2.

Section IV *Admonition—by Spirit, Not Flesh*

Galatians 5:13—6:10

A. A New Slavery of Love, 5:13-15

Paul here concisely states the basis for the ethical conduct to which he is about to admonish the Galatians. The freedom to which they had been called was not to be abused as a base of operations for the flesh. Rather, they were to serve one another as love slaves. The whole law finds its fulfillment in one word, namely, "Thou shalt love thy neighbour as thyself" (Lev. 19:18). But if they continued fighting among themselves, as wild animals, they would be destroyed.

1. *The Nature of Christian Liberty* (5:13)

Paul now turns to a new task.[1] He here points out the moral implications of the Christian faith. **For, brethren, ye have been called unto liberty** (13). This has reference to freedom from the law and the consequent freedom from sin. To such freedom they were **called** by God. Painstakingly Paul had argued that this was an indispensable part of their newfound faith in Christ. His insistence on this freedom quite naturally caused his opponents to fear that he had destroyed the only bulwark against the tide of pagan immorality (cf. Introduction). Their fear was that the Gentiles not only would lack an essential restraint but would misunderstand this freedom. The term **only** is not used to restrict what had been stated, but rather to call attention to something of additional importance.[2]

To quiet the unnecessary fears of his enemies and to properly guide his converts, Paul exhorts that they should **use not liberty for an occasion to the flesh.** This, obviously, would be an abuse

[1]This would appear to mark the decisive change in Paul's mood, rather than 5:1, where the imperative "Stand firm" is the logical climax of his entire argument (3:1—5:12) and not the commencement of his ethical exhortations.

[2]Cf. 1:23; 2:10 and Phil. 1:27 for similar examples.

of their freedom of faith—but exactly what does it mean? As noted above (cf. comments on 5:1), the believers' freedom resulted in a release from the compulsive grip and power of sin. They are no longer controlled by the sinful flesh—forced to live *by* it! However, the abuse of their freedom would provide an **occasion** (opportunity)[3] for sin to regain its control over them (see comments on 5:16-25).

In typical fashion, Paul saw the safeguard against such an abuse of freedom, not in its denial through the compulsive slavery of legalism, but in a new voluntary slavery of love—**by love serve one another.** Here is the imperative mood (cf. Intro.) stated in clear, positive terms. They were admonished voluntarily to enslave themselves[4] to each other. Here is a vital and revealing paradox! They were free, yet to remain free they must enslave themselves again (cf. Rom. 6:15-22; I Cor. 9:19). This is Paul's constant concern. How will you use your freedom? How will you live your new life? (See comments on 2:20.)

This new slavery was possible through[5] **love** (*agape*). The context reveals that the significance of *agape* is "clearly that of benevolence, desire for the well-being of others, leading to efforts on their behalf."[6] The man in Christ is "liberated to love."[7] This certainly harmonizes with Paul's consistent teaching.[8] When coupled with 15, it becomes clear that the threatened abuse of their freedom was in the area of personal relationships.

Thus Paul strongly denied that his rejection of works eliminated the dynamic for moral and ethical conduct—instead it provided such a dynamic. True faith finds its expression in love. This is further seen in the important fact that *agape* is not mere human sentiment; it is the love of God that has been poured out in the believer's heart (cf. Rom. 5:5). *Agape* is the fruit of

[3]**Occasion** (*aphorme*), used only by Paul, is a military term meaning "the starting-point or base of operations for an expedition, then generally the resources needed to carry through an undertaking; in our literature occasion, pretext, opportunity" (Arndt & Gingrich, *op. cit.*, p. 127).

[4]**Serve** (*douleuo*) is the word Paul repeatedly used to mean "serve as a slave." Cf. also Mark 9:35; 10:45, where the term *diakonos*, meaning "servant" or "helper," is used in a comparable manner.

[5]The meaning of *dia* with the genitive case is "through" and not **by** (cf. Moule, *op. cit.*, p. 54).

[6]Burton, *op. cit.*, p. 293.

[7]Stauffer, "Love," *Bible Key Words*, I, 54.

[8]Cf. the treatment of *agape* in comments on 5:22.

the Spirit. Thus the real alternative to the regimentation of legalism is the discipline of the human spirit by submission to the guidance of the Holy Spirit.

This slavery of love as related to men is the continuing aspect of the new life under the Spirit which began in the believer's "capitulation to Christ."[9] In I Thess. 3:12-13, Paul clearly identifies such a love walk with holiness. As the Lord "makes" the believers to increase and abound in this love for one another, and toward all men, the result is the establishment of their hearts blameless in holiness (*hagiosune*).[10]

Paul's concern for the right use of freedom reflects one of the most critical needs in the Church today. How often men find new life in Christ and the freedom it brings but still are not living under the Spirit (cf. comments on 5:16-26)! Instead they remain in a no-man's-land, living under self. They are in constant danger of abusing their freedom and losing that new life. As Paul so well knew, there is only one solution to this problem of sin; that is to voluntarily enter the new slavery of love through the crisis of capitulation. To do so is to truly begin life under the Spirit.

2. *Love Fulfills the Law* (5:14-15)

As support for the striking imperative "to serve one another" as slaves through love, Paul declares that **all the law is fulfilled in one word, even in this; Thou shalt love thy neighbour as thyself (14)**. At first glance this appears to contradict all that he had laboriously argued with reference to works of righteousness. If the law had only a temporary function which was abrogated by the coming of Christ, why should the believer be concerned about fulfilling the law?

There is no doubt that Paul uses "law" (*nomos*) in two different ways, but this must not be construed to mean that the term intrinsically has contradictory meanings. In Romans and Galatians where Paul is combating the Judaizers, he uses the term in the sense in which his opponents used it, namely, "a legal-

[9]For the distinction between the commencement (crisis) and the continuing (process) of the new life "under the Spirit," cf. comments on 2:20.

[10]Cf. the entire context (I Thess. 3:12—4:10), where this basic concept is developed. Cf. also Romans 6, where the *crisis* "presentation" (aorist imperative of *paristemi*) of oneself to God and one's members as "weapons" to righteousness (v. 13) would be *unto* "sanctification" (v. 19—*hagiasmos*) and bring "fruit" unto "sanctification" (v. 22).

istic system." When Paul uses the word in this manner, which can be termed polemic, it is necessary to understand it as an effort to find salvation through good deeds—works of righteousness. To such works of law the believer is dead (cf. Rom. 7:4, 6). On the other hand, Paul's understanding of law, in its basic sense as the divine standard, has binding requirements on all men. These requirements, however, can be met or fulfilled only through Christ (cf. Rom. 8:4). The love (*agape*) that Paul admonishes the Galatians to express is not human; it is rather the love of God and the fruit of the Spirit.

Thus the whole[11] law with all of its requirements is fulfilled through the love of God (Christ), as it is expressed in the believer's life. In many newer translations, the word **fulfilled** is replaced by "summed up."[12] The reason for this is the parallel passage in Rom. 13:9: "If there be any other commandment, it is briefly comprehended [*anakephalaioo,* summed up] in this saying, namely, Thou shalt love thy neighbour as thyself." In the Romans passage it should be noted, however, that it is the commandments, some of which Paul had just listed, that are "summed up" in the "great commandment." Even in this context (Rom. 13:8-10), he makes it clear that love is the fulfillment (*pleroo* and *pleroma*) of the law. Thus, even though the commandments are *summed up* in the great commandment, the whole law is **fulfilled** in love. This simply means that all of the requirements of the law of God are fully obeyed through love. It is clear that the Christian is not excused from the requirements of the law. God cannot smile on those who do what He forbids. However, such obedience is not the *means* of obtaining salvation, but the *result* of the gift of His grace—the Holy Spirit.

The **one word** is easily recognized as a quotation from Lev. 19:18 (LXX), which Paul used in Rom. 13:9, and Jesus referred to as the second great commandment.[13] James calls it the "royal law" (Jas. 2:8). There is no better commentary on it than Luke 10:27-37; Romans 12—15; and I Corinthians 13.

The ever-practical Paul applies the principle of love to what

[11]**All** (*pas*) is better translated "whole" or "entire," "as a whole is in contrast to its individual parts" (Arndt and Gingrich, *op. cit.,* p. 638).

[12]Cf. Phillips, NEB, Moffatt, *Living Letters,* Berkeley. The Amplified NT uses "complied with" following Vincent (*op. cit.,* IV, 163). The ASV and RSV use "fulfilled," as does the KJV. The Greek word is *pleroo.*

[13]Matt. 22:39; cf. Matt. 19:19; Mark 12:31; Luke 10:27.

was obviously the urgent problem in Galatia: **But if ye bite and devour one another, take heed that ye be not consumed one of another** (15). Evidently the Judaizers had not convinced all of Paul's converts. The result was grievous strife. Paul describes it as wild animals in deadly combat. The order and tenses of the terms used are climactic: **bite, devour,** and **consumed** point to complete and utter devastation.[14] This undoubtedly hurt Paul more than all else—to see his beloved converts destroying each other. There is certainly no sadder picture in any church in any day. The only adequate remedy is love that causes one to serve rather than to consume his fellowman.

B. Life in the Spirit and Flesh Contrasted, 5:16-26

1. *The Opposition of Spirit and Flesh* (5:16-18)

In this section Paul admonishes the Galatian believers to walk by the Spirit and thus the desires of the flesh would not be fulfilled. He shows that the desires of the Spirit and the flesh directly oppose each other. However, the person who is led by the Spirit is no longer under the law, which leads to the slavery of the flesh.

As suggested in v. 13, the love service into which the Galatian believers were admonished to enter was not mere human affection or sentiment. It was divine love. To achieve this kind of love it was necessary to live in a vital relationship with God, described in this context as living by **the Spirit.** Paul therefore gives a new, but related, imperative: **This I say then, Walk in the Spirit** (16). The word **walk** (*peripateo*) is a common New Testament term. In the Synoptic Gospels it is used exclusively in a literal sense; in the Gospel of John, Revelation, and Acts it usually has the literal meaning. In Paul, however, it is always used in a figurative sense, meaning "to live" or "to conduct oneself." In order to live such a life of love, they must live by[15]

[14]The "biting" and "devouring" (present tense) climaxes in the result of being "consumed" (aorist tense).

[15]In the Greek there is no preposition here (also in vv. 18, 25), as often is the case (cf. Col. 2:6—*en,* "in"). The dative construction can be interpreted as locative or instrumental (cf. A. T. Robertson and W. H. Davis, *A New Short Grammar of the Greek Testament,* Harper & Brothers, 1931, pp. 235-45). Thus the Spirit is either the location in which the believer is to live or the *instrument* (means) by which he is to live. The context strongly suggests the latter. (Cf. comments on 5:18, 25). "By" is used in the ASV, RSV, NEB, Amplified NT, and Vincent (*op. cit.,* IV, 164).

the Spirit. In this context **Spirit** (*pneuma*) refers neither to the human spirit nor the divine Spirit considered independent of each other, but to the divine Spirit as He indwells the human spirit. The believer's inner man is thus to be under the motivating, empowering force of the Holy Spirit. This is in diametric contrast to his former life, which was motivated by the desires of the flesh.

This continuing new life under the Spirit is made possible by the crisis presentation of oneself to God (see comments on 2:20). Before a man can live in such a relationship he must first enter it. Here is Paul's twofold concern.

The apostle chose to state the negative consequence of walking by the Spirit: **and ye shall not fulfil the lust of the flesh.** As the man of faith lives and walks by the Spirit, two things happen. (*a*) The **lust** (desire)[16] **of the** (sinful) **flesh** is not fulfilled.[17] This is because he does not live according to the flesh. The fulfilled desires of the flesh are graphically described (19-21) as "the works of the flesh." (*b*) The second thing that happens as a believer walks by the Spirit is the positive result. The fruit of the Spirit (starting with love) is borne in the believer's life. The context (v. 15) suggests that the immediate problem was lack of this fruitage of love between the Galatian brethren.

As substantiation of his claim, Paul emphasizes the complete opposition of the flesh and Spirit. **The flesh lusteth against the Spirit, and the Spirit against the flesh: and these are contrary the one to the other** (17). The KJV accurately translates the verb form that Paul uses, **The flesh lusteth** (desires) **against the Spirit.** This is often understood and translated as a noun, e.g., "The desires of the flesh are against the Spirit."[18] If, as often happens, the verb has the force of a noun, it simply describes two conflicting ways of life. This is certainly in harmony with the other main passage, where the Spirit is contrasted with the flesh.[19]

[16]**Lust** (*epithumia*) means desire of any kind with no moral implications, but when related to the flesh clearly implies desires of a wrong kind.

[17]**Fulfil** (*teleo*) here means to "fulfill" (perform) or "finish."

[18]RSV; cf. also Amp. NT, E. D. Burton (*op. cit.*, p. 300), J. Agar Beet (*op. cit.*, p. 156).

[19]Rom. 8:1-13. There is little question that the two are opposites here (**flesh** and **Spirit**). Romans 8, rather than Romans 7, is the comparable passage to Galatians 5. Romans 7 depicts a struggle within man, but NT scholars disagree as to the spiritual status of the one in the struggle.

Paul uses v. 17 to substantiate his declaration in the previous verse.[20] The desires of the flesh will not be fulfilled if the believer walks by the Spirit, because life by the Spirit is completely opposite to the way of life by the flesh. The desires of the flesh will not be fulfilled if the believer walks by the Spirit, because they represent two contrasting ways of living; they are completely antithetical.

Too often this verse, taken completely out of context is used to teach the "two-nature theory," which pictures the believer as forever torn between two equally powerful forces. The result is that he lives two lives—serving God with his higher (or new) nature and serving sin with his lower (or old) nature (flesh). Such a bifurcation does serious violence to the thought of Paul. Most significantly, it ignores the context; such a view would actually disprove Paul's claim rather than substantiate it. Further, it ignores Paul's clear teaching that the power of the sinful flesh is broken through the Cross. The flesh, as an instrument of sin, is eradicated (cf. comments on 5:24).[21]

Before Paul moves on to contrast the "works of the flesh" with the "fruit of the Spirit," he adds the important observation **that ye cannot do the things that ye would.** The Greek does not say **ye cannot do,** but "ye might not do."[22] The opposition of the Spirit to the flesh is such that it results[23] in a vital safeguard for the man walking by the Spirit. He does not need to do what he of himself might wish.[24] It is not that he is incapable of following his own desires, but rather that he has the power not to follow them when they are contrary to the will of God. This simply means that the desires of the Spirit supersede the desires of the flesh when a man walks by the Spirit.

Having *defined* the contrast, Paul returns to his theme, but in slightly different terms, before *describing* that contrast. **But if ye be led of the Spirit, ye are not under the law** (18). The

[20]This is the significance of *for* (*gar;* cf. Burton, *op. cit.,* p. 300).

[21]Cf. Barclay's use of this term, *Flesh and Spirit* (Abingdon Press, Nashville, 1962), p. 20.

[22]The present subjunctive of *poieo,* "to do or make." The KJV translation could well be due to an association of this opposition with the struggle in Rom. 7:14-25, which suggests inability (cf. Vincent, *op. cit.,* IV, 164).

[23]It can be result or purpose (cf. Burton, *op. cit.,* p. 302; and Moule, *op. cit.,* p. 142).

[24]*Thelo* (**would**) means basically "to wish," and is here to be identified with the "desires of the flesh."

expression **led of the Spirit** is parallel to **walk in the Spirit** (16).[25] However, the term **led** emphasizes the submission of the believer to the Spirit. The phrase **ye are not under the law** is reminiscent of Rom. 6:14, where, in the midst of a vivid description of deliverance from sin through death with Christ, Paul makes the same observation, and adds: "but [ye are] under grace." The strict alternatives are constantly in Paul's mind. The life under the Spirit, with its victory over the flesh, is in direct antithesis to the life under the law, which these converts were considering.

The man in Christ today does not face the same threat of bondage to law, but the strict alternatives of a life under the Spirit and under sin are no less real. Life under the Spirit is the only safeguard against a life under sin.

2. *The Works of the Flesh* (5:19-21)

The contrast between the Spirit and the flesh is further seen in the manifestation of the works of the flesh. After enumerating them Paul forewarns the Galatian believers that those who do such things are excluded from God's kingdom.

When a man lives according to the passions and desires of the flesh (cf. 5:16-17, 24), certain results are inevitable. Paul calls these results **works of the flesh** (19),[26] a term that is significant as compared to the "fruit" of the Spirit. Such **works** are openly **manifest**—plainly recognizable for all to see what they really are.

a. Sexual Immorality (5:19). The first three **works** relate to sexual gratification, and suggest a climax of depravity. Paul begins here because of the moral climate of his world. Every imaginable form of immorality was commonly and openly practiced by rulers, aristocracy, philosophers, poets, priests, and worshipers—with no sense of shame or remorse. It was the accepted way of life.[27] It is little wonder that this was a problem with which Paul greatly concerned himself as he dealt with his converts from paganism. He would countenance no compromise; immorality could have no place in the Christian life.

[25]The same dative construction is used (cf. comments on 5:16).

[26]Cf. "things of the flesh" in Rom. 8:5; cf. also Eph. 5:3-5; Col. 3:5-9.

[27]Cf. the brief but vivid and documented description in Barclay, *Flesh and Spirit*, pp. 24-27.

Fornication (*porneia*) has the basic meaning of prostitution, but actually relates to any illicit sexual intercourse and thus would include adultery.[28] It also includes unnatural vice or incest, such as homosexuality. **Uncleanness** (*akatharsia*) is moral impurity, of body or mind, that is repulsive to responsible men and separates one from a holy God.[29] The term **lasciviousness** (*aselgeia*) is of more doubtful etymology, but Paul's use clearly ties it to immorality.[30] It is wanton conduct, shameless flouting of the standards of public decency or even self-respect without regard to the rights of others.[31] Barclay relates the three terms significantly: "*Porneia* indicates sin within a specific area of life, the area of sexual relationships; *akatharsia* indicates a general defilement of the whole personality, tainting every sphere of life; *aselgeia* indicates a love of sin so reckless and so audacious that a man has ceased to care what God or man thinks of his actions."[32]

To thinking men the moral laxity that is sweeping our world is a cause for alarm. History clearly reveals that it is the certain harbinger of a collapsing civilization. The most serious sign is the advocating of free love and the removal of moral restraint and inhibitions by educators. The final step will be its acceptance by religious leaders—and there are suggestions of that now present![33] The Christian answer for our day is no different than in Paul's time; it is not a dead legalism, but a dynamic discipline through the Spirit.

b. False Doctrines (5:20*ab*). The second group of evil "works" relates to practices of heathen religions, which were also problems among Paul's converts from paganism. **Idolatry**

[28]Adultery (*moicheia*) is found only in a few of the latest MSS and is therefore omitted in modern translations.

[29]Cf. its use with *porneia* in II Cor. 12:21; Eph. 5:3; Col. 3:5. Also with other terms in Rom. 1:24; Eph. 4:19; I Thess. 2:3.

[30]Cf. with both of former terms (II Cor. 12:21) and with "uncleanness" and "greediness" (Eph. 4:19). Cf. also Rom. 13:13, where it is used with "chambering" (*koite*)—literally, a bed of illicit sexual intercourse.

[31]Cf. Lightfoot's view that "a man may be *akathartos* and hide his sin, he does not become *aselges* until he shocks public decency" (*op. cit.*, p. 210). Burton disputes this and says the essential element of *aselgeia* is *unrestrained* conduct and not public action (cf. *op. cit.*, p. 306).

[32]*Flesh and Spirit*, p. 31.

[33]Cf. the sobering article entitled: "Sex in the U.S.: Mores and Morality," *Time*, Vol. 83, No. 4, Jan. 24, 1964, pp. 54-59.

(20; *eidololatria*)[34] is the worship of both the image and the god it represents. Herein lies its subtle danger. Originally no idol was meant to be worshiped. The image was provided to localize and visualize and thus make it easier to worship the god of which it was a representation.[35] The basic evil in idolatry is that the creation is worshiped instead of the Creator (cf. Rom. 1:19-23). In this sense "idolatry" is no less a problem in our day, even though it is clothed in sophistication.[36] "Whenever any *thing* in the world begins to hold the principal place in our hearts and minds and aims, then that thing has become an idol, for that thing has usurped the place which belongs to God."[37]

It is not a coincidence that idolatry is associated with immorality in Paul's mind. Prostitution was a basic part of many heathen religions. There is a clear precedent for the condemnation of the two, in association with each other, in the Old Testament.[38]

The practice of **witchcraft** (*pharmakeia*) is the use of sorcery or magic in religion. The word originally meant the use of drugs, which was later turned to evil ends (cf. poison).[39] This kind of witchcraft became one means of a broader practice of magic, which through superstitition was closely tied to religion. This problem has long plagued the Christian Church, and in some places a shocking amount of it was "Christianized" rather than eliminated.

c. *Unchristian Human Relationships* (5:20c-21). The next eight "works of the flesh" are at the heart of the vice list. All eight of them have to do with interhuman relations, which points to the fact that this loomed uppermost in Paul's concern.

Hatred (*echthrai*), best translated "enmity," was an accepted and approved attitude of life in the apostle's day. With open enmity between racial and cultural groups—e.g., Greeks vs. Barbarians, and Jews vs. Gentiles—it is little wonder that

[34]Cf. Burton, *op. cit.*, p. 306.

[35]Cf. the excellent treatment of this in Barclay, particularly the evolution of emperor worship (pp. 33-34).

[36]Cf. Barclay's identification of the modern "status symbols" as its most graphic manifestation (*ibid.*, pp. 34-35).

[37]*Ibid.*, p. 35.

[38]Cf. Barclay's observation of the basic relationship of immorality and idolatry (*ibid.*, pp. 35-36).

[39]Cf. the transliteration of the term in "pharmacy."

these attitudes often characterized relationships between individuals. All of this is contrary to the Christian ethic, and is traced by Paul to its true source. "The mind of the flesh is enmity against God" (Rom. 8:7, lit.), and naturally results in enmity to men. Such hatred produces **variance** or strife (*eris*). Enmity (*echthra*) is an attitude of mind towards other people; and strife (*eris*) is the outcome in actual life of that state of mind.[40] Enmity and strife have a crucial interrelation which works in both directions. Enmity results in strife, and strife causes enmity. Paul made it clear that strife, so characteristic of the pagan world (cf. Rom. 1:29), was diametrically opposite to the unity God intended to exist in the Christian fellowship. Thus he strongly condemned its appearance in the church.[41] This was such an important matter that three additional terms are used to deal with the same fundamental issue of divisive elements in the body of Christ.

In both the New Testament and the Septuagint **emulations** (*zelos*) has two distinct meanings. It is used by Paul to mean zeal, enthusiasm, or ardor in the pursuit of a cause or task.[42] In secular Greek *zelos* often depicted a noble virtue (cf. II Cor. 11:2), providing impetus to emulate that which was admired in the accomplishments or possessions of others. However, such concentration on the good fortune of others can degenerate into a begrudging resentment, making *zelos* similar to envy (*phthanos*, 21). Thus emulation (*zelos*) is not intrinsically evil. When one is faced with the success and accomplishments of others, he can be inspired to climb to new heights himself, or he can resent such good fortune in others with a bitter jealousy. This is the second meaning of *zelos* found in the New Testament.[43] It means "jealousy," with an evil connotation. Jealousy is obviously its meaning in this passage.

One of the most complex "works of the flesh" is **wrath** (*thymoi*). In the Septuagint it has a "wide range of meaning, including wrath human and divine, wrath devilish and beastly, wrath noble and destructive."[44] However Paul and other New

[40]Barclay, *Flesh and Spirit*, p. 42.

[41]Cf. Rom. 13:13; I Cor. 1:11; 3:3.

[42]Cf. Rom. 10:2; II Cor. 7:7, 11; 9:2; Phil. 3:6.

[43]Cf. Rom. 13:13; I Cor. 3:3; II Cor. 11:2. The KJV translates it as "envy," but this confuses it with *phthanos* (21).

[44]Barclay, *Flesh and Spirit*, p. 51.

Testament writers use the term primarily with reference to man.[45] Reflecting a distinction found in secular Greek, *thymos* emphasizes the violent and brief aspects of wrath—"explosive temper, or flashing anger"; it is thus distinct from the more inveterate wrath (*orge*). In fact, *thymos* is "rage" that is a veritable "temporary insanity," reflecting a sinful hostility that clearly is a defense mechanism of the flesh. It has often been observed that temper is necessary for a well-balanced personality; thus there is no doubt that anger has both good and bad connotations.[46] But in the New Testament, helpful temper is always *orge,* never *thymos. "Thymos* is something that must be banished from the Christian life . . . the New Testament is quite clear that such displays of temper are sinful manifestations that a man is still in the grip of his own lower nature (flesh)."[47]

The next three "works of the flesh" describe in more detail the **variance** (*eris,* 21) considered above, and are best understood in relation to each other. **Strife** (*eritheiai*) is translated in a wide variety of ways,[48] which reflects an uncertainty as to its meaning. Barclay concludes: "In Paul the word clearly denotes the spirit of personal ambition and rivalry which issues in partisanship which sets party above the church."[49] Selfish personal ambition is deplorable in positions of public trust and responsibility, but it is no less than tragic in the church.[50]

Closely related are **seditions** (*dichostasiai*), best translated as "divisions." Rivalry, motivated by self-interests, can result only in divisions that destroy the unity of the church. Paul is not speaking here of differences based on sincere convictions; he is concerned about divisions that are caused by wrong motives which can be traced to the sinful flesh. Honest differences are

[45]The only exception in Paul's Epistles is Rom. 2:8, which is comparable to its meaning (often coupled with *orge*) in Rev. 12:12; 14:8, 10. In Revelation there is the mixed metaphor in which "the wine of harlotry, with which Babylon intoxicates the nations, becomes the wine of God's wrath for them" (Arndt and Gingrich, *op. cit.,* p. 366).

[46]Cf. Matt. 5:22; Mark 3:5; Eph. 4:26, 31. The basic distinction is righteous anger caused by wrongs to others and carnal anger caused by injuries to us.

[47]Barclay, *Flesh and Spirit,* pp. 52-53.

[48]Cf. Barclay's brief but inclusive analysis (*ibid.,* p. 53).

[49]*Ibid.,* p. 55. Burton's conclusion that *eritheia* basically means "self-seeking" harmonizes with this interpretation (*op. cit.,* pp. 305, 309).

[50]Cf. Rom. 2:8; II Cor. 12:20; Phil. 1:17; 2:3.

not incompatible with harmonious fellowship, because a vital part of freedom and love is respect for the opinions of others even when they conflict with ours. However it does behoove every believer to examine his heart constantly lest prejudice be mistaken for principle and stubbornness for dedication.

What is true of the individual applies no less to the church. Theological and ecclesiastical differences, based on convictions, must be distinguished from divisions that are motivated by corporate self-seeking. Too often, when the church would minister to a society torn by class, party, and racial divisions, she can be quite properly challenged—"Physician, first heal thyself!"

A further step, in the destructive path of divisiveness, is **heresies** (*haireseis*). The English transliteration (heresy) carries with it more of the idea of unorthodoxy than does the Greek term. The original word basically depicts a group that is united by the same beliefs or conduct. Thus it does not intrinsically have a bad connotation.[51] However Paul uses it with reference to the divisive elements in the church, who formed themselves into groups or sects.[52] Such cliques fragmented the church and "a fragmented church is not a church at all!"[53] Quite naturally these exclusive groups considered themselves right and all others wrong. Paul condemned such sectarianism as "works of the flesh."

Envyings (*phthonos*, 21) is a totally evil concept. Unlike **emulations** (*zelos*, 20), it has no possibilities for good. Envy produces bitter resentment, and often an effort to deprive others of their good fortune or success (cf. Rom. 1:29; Phil. 1:15).

Clearly reflected in these "works of the flesh" having to do with interhuman relations is Paul's concern for the unity and harmony of the Christian fellowship. No man lives, or dies, unto himself. Sin is a two-edged sword, with honed edges of personal responsibility and social consequences. The greatest evil of anger, enmity, jealousy, envy, and even rivalry, is what they do to the church. Such personal fleshly attitudes produce strife, divisions, and cliques.

These facts speak of the impossibility of superficial unity. Such evils cannot be swept under the carpet of compromise or

[51]Cf. "party" or "sect" in Acts 5:17; 15:5.

[52]Cf. I Cor. 11:19, where Paul condemned such sects at the love feast and Lord's Supper.

[53]Barclay, *Flesh and Spirit*, p. 59.

pretense. Men who "live by the flesh" cannot "dwell together in unity." There is a "more excellent way," to which Paul turns his attention shortly.

Paul closes his list of "works of the flesh" with two terms[54] whose meanings are quite obvious—**drunkenness** (*methai*) and **revelling** (*komai*). The Scriptures, and surprisingly the world of Paul's day, recognized that **drunkenness** was shameful and degrading. It certainly has no place in the life of the Christian. Although **revelling** was used in secular Greek to mean simply a celebration, in the New Testament it depicts excesses that can best be described as debauchery. Such actions contradicted a Christian testimony.

This list is by no means all-inclusive, and was not intended by Paul to be the exhaustive basis of a Christian code of rules. The phrase **and such like** shows that the writer intended it to be representative in principle of evils that result from living by the flesh. It is tragic, and frightening, to realize that without exception these "works of the flesh" are perversions of what is in itself potentially good. They come from legitimate desires that are illegitimately satisfied. Thus they always remain possible pitfalls even to the man of faith. Satan is a cunning foe and sin is deceptive. The Christian needs frequently to examine his heart and life in the light of Bible teachings and under the guidance of the Spirit.

Paul had evidently warned the Galatians on an earlier occasion (cf. 1:9; 4:13) of the consequences of such living. He reminds them of this and states that the present letter is a repeated forewarning—before the evil happened.[55] **Of the which I tell you before, as I have also told you in time past, that they which do[56] such things shall not inherit the kingdom of God.** The **kingdom of God,** from which a man living by the flesh will be excluded, is the Christian hope of eternal life spent with Christ both here and beyond this world. Such is the believer's "inheritance";[57] it is salvation in its fullest sense.

[54]The term **murders** (*phonoi*) is in only a few late manuscripts and is therefore not included in most modern translations.

[55]Cf. II Cor. 13:2 for a similar construction and warning.

[56]*Prasso,* **do,** although it literally means "to practice," is used interchangeably with *poieo* (to do—cf. Rom. 7:15-21). There is no scriptural basis for the interpretation that Paul means *only* those who habitually practice such evils.

[57]Cf. 3:18; also Eph. 1:11, 14, 18.

This solemn warning had been repeatedly enunciated by Paul to other churches also.[58] The believer is not excused from ethical responsibility any more than is the Jew (cf. Romans 2). There was obviously a point of serious misunderstanding here which unfortunately has continued to this day. Instead of ethical indifference, the man in Christ has for the first time the resources to live as God expects him to.

The reason for Paul's vehement objection to the Galatians' turning to the law was that it would, in fact, be a returning to the flesh. To do so was to cut oneself off from Christ. God does not have a double standard, nor does He view the believer through colored glasses, ignoring his conduct and accepting instead the perfect work of Christ. Every man who lives by the flesh, thus producing its works, is excluded from the kingdom of God (cf. comments on 5:4).

3. *The Fruit of the Spirit* (5:22-23)

The contrast between the flesh and the Spirit is brought to a fitting climax as Paul lists **the fruit of the Spirit** (22). At the heart of his admonition there is an appeal that the believer might be attracted by the **fruit** as well as repulsed by the "works." Although Paul accepted the prevailing view of the Early Church, that the presence and activity of the Spirit were evidenced by supernatural gifts,[59] he recognized that these were not necessarily an evidence of moral character. Thus he placed a higher value on the **fruit of the Spirit,** which directly relates to ethical and moral qualities.[60]

From verses 22-23, Alexander Maclaren discusses "The Fruit of the Spirit." He points out: (1) The threefold elements of character; (2) The unity of the fruit; (3) The culture of the tree; (4) This is the only worthy fruit.

Paul's choice of the term **fruit** is significant, as contrasted with "works." "A work is something which man produces for himself; a fruit is something which is produced by a power which he does not possess. Man cannot *make* a fruit."[61] It has often been

[58] Cf. I Cor. 6:9-10; Eph. 5:5-6; Col. 3:5-6.

[59] The Greek term is *charisma,* which literally means "free gift"; cf. Rom. 1:11; 5:15-16.

[60] Cf. I Cor. 12:31; 13:1-13; 14:1. Cf. also Paul's ethical concern in Rom. 12:9-21; 13:8-10; Eph. 5:1-10; Phil. 1:8-11.

[61] Barclay, *Flesh and Spirit,* p. 21.

noted that **fruit** is singular. Although it does suggest the unity of Christian virtues, too much emphasis should not be placed on this point, because Paul consistently uses the singular form when the term has a figurative meaning.[62]

a. Love (5:22). Paul is saying that these fruits are the result of the divine Spirit *working through* the human spirit. The apostle's list necessarily begins with **love** (*agape*)[63] because it is greater than all other virtues (cf. I Cor. 13:13) and is the outer cloak that binds them together in completeness (cf. Col. 3:14). Indeed, there is a sense in which Christian love is an all-inclusive category and uniquely the source of the other fruit, even as a tree trunk bearing branches, or a prism as it reflects the various colors of light.[64] From this perspective the fruits that follow are *love in action* and descriptive expressions of *agape.*

Love (*agape*) is a distinctly Christian term, created out of necessity to depict adequately the gospel of the new creature.[65] Further, *agape* is used primarily of the love men have, or should have, for one another,[66] which is a reflection of God's love for them. They are to draw their pattern from Him. Barclay's definition is concise, yet encompassing: "*Agape* is unconquerable benevolence, undefeatable goodwill."[67] As such it is a sharing concern and a caring identification with the needs of others. This concern is all-embracing even though recipients are undeserving; it results in the transformation of both the loved and the loving. *Agape* is sometimes misunderstood and confused with what is the accepted concept of love today. But there is a difference. Rather than being an impulsive sentiment that one falls into, *agape* is the response of the whole person involving will, feeling,

[62]Cf. Rom. 1:13; Eph. 5:9; Phil. 1:11, 22.

[63]It is impossible to define this term adequately within the limits prescribed here. Barclay's twelve-page analysis is superb (*Flesh and Spirit,* pp. 63-76). Cf. also Burton, *op. cit.,* pp. 519-21.

[64]Cf. the manifestations of *agape* (I Cor. 13:4-8) with the various fruits of the Spirit.

[65]The noun (*agape*), used first in the LXX (only occasionally), is found extensively in the NT. The verb (*agapao*), though used occasionally in secular Greek, finds its full meaning in the Bible, especially the NT (cf. Burton, pp. 519-21; Vincent, IV, 166-69).

[66]*Agape* is used of the love of God (and Christ) for men, but only rarely of man's love for God (in Paul only in II Thess. 3:5—cf. *agapao* in Rom. 8:28; I Cor. 2:9; 8:3; Eph. 6:24).

[67]*Flesh and Spirit,* p. 65.

and intellect. It is not weak and harmfully permissive, but strong and disciplining.

Agape can perhaps best be defined by what it does as well as by what it is.[68] This kind of love must act with outgoing generosity and forgiveness. It fulfills the law (v. 14), providing an atmosphere that characterizes and motivates the entire Christian life (cf. Eph. 5:2). It enables the truth—which often hurts—to be spoken as an appeal and not an offense (cf. Eph. 4:15). It is the cord that unites the body of Christ (cf. Col. 2:2), keeping liberty from becoming license (v. 13) and building up the people of God (cf. I Cor. 8:1; Eph. 4:16), as they live together in forbearance (cf. Eph. 4:2; Rom. 14:15).

It is little wonder Paul concludes that *agape* should be the believer's "pursuit."[69] He should be satisfied with no lesser prize. Yet this is not something of his own doing. Understandably the "more excellent way" (cf. I Cor. 12:31) is not an easy road. Well might one ask: "Who then can be saved?" How appropriate is the answer: "With men it is impossible, but not with God, for with God all things are possible" (Mark 10:27)! This is perhaps the most significant fact about *agape*. In Christian usage it came to represent a divine quality. Not only does God love us, but He loves through us (v. 13), "because God's love has been poured into our hearts through the Holy Spirit, which has been given to us" (Rom. 5:5, RSV). **Love is the fruit of the Spirit.**

b. *Joy and Peace* (5:22). The next two fruits of the Spirit have a vital relationship to each other. **Joy** (*chara*) is the gladness or happiness that radiates from the life of the believer—an outward expression of the inward **peace.** As such it is seen and known to others. This is the atmosphere of the New Testament.[70] Actually, a basically unhappy Christian is a contradiction.[71] The kingdom of God is characterized by **joy,** along with righteousness and **peace** (cf. Rom. 14:17).

The familiar form of greeting in secular Greek was "rejoice" (*chairein*). Though it probably had no more specific meaning than the modern "How are you?" it must have had a new

[68]Cf. I Corinthians 13, which basically describes what love does.

[69]Cf. I Cor. 14:1. The Greek term *dioko* means to pursue as a hunter.

[70]Barclay calls the NT a "book of joy," observing that *chara* and *chairein* are found over 130 times in it (*Flesh and Spirit,* pp. 76-83).

[71]Unhappiness must not be confused with sorrow or grief. The NT Christian has joy in his sorrow (cf. II Cor. 6:10).

significance to the rejoicing men of faith. Although not the distinctively Christian greeting, it was occasionally used in the New Testament.[72] Barclay captures the spirit of such a greeting as: "Joy be with you."[73]

Joy adds lustre to all the Christian virtues, and illuminates every experience of life, but nowhere is its glow more brightly seen than in adversities. One of the first lessons a new Christian must learn is that joy is not dependent upon circumstances; instead, trials are to be transformed by joy. It is not enough to endure or even to overcome trials, for no triumph is complete without joy (cf. Col. 1:11). Thus it is no surprise that joy and affliction are often found together as the man of faith joyfully suffers for Jesus' sake.[74]

Such Christian joy is not superficial effervescence, but rather, wells up from the deep, inner springs of the Spirit-filled life. It is a **fruit of the Spirit!** Joy is the outward manifestation of inward **peace** (*eirene*). This peace is not simply the absence of trouble, anxiety, and worry. Rather, it is the serenity that results from living in a right relationship with God, men, and oneself. Through faith in Christ man finds peace with God (cf. Rom. 5:1), and this new relationship becomes the foundation for peaceful living in the other two dimensions.

The distinctively Christian greeting included peace—"grace to you and peace."[75] Although **peace** is clearly the gift of the "God of peace,"[76] yet this must not be misunderstood. It is no easy matter to live at peace—especially with some people! Thus Paul must exhort: "If possible, as far as it lies with you, live at peace with all men" (Rom. 12:18, NEB).[77] The believer must pursue the prize of peace (cf. I Pet. 3:11; Heb. 12:14) but it will be found only as he walks by the Spirit, for peace is the fruit of a Spirit-filled life.

c. *Long-suffering* (5:22). Patience (*makrothumia*) is surely a fruit that makes a man like God. As few other terms are, this one is predicated of God and of man as God would have him be.

[72]Cf. the greeting at the birth and resurrection of Jesus (Matt. 28:9; Luke 1:28); cf. also Acts 15:23; II Cor. 13:11.

[73]*Flesh and Spirit,* p. 77.

[74]Cf. Acts 5:41; 13:50-52.

[75]This is found at the opening of all of Paul's letters.

[76]Cf. Rom. 15:33; II Cor. 13:11.

[77]The Greek term "live at peace" is *eireneuo* (lit., keep the peace).

As God is patient with men, so they are to be patient with Him, as well as with their fellowmen; for circumstances and events are actually in the hands of God.[78]

This vital scriptural virtue must not be confused with a mere placid disposition, being unperturbed by any and all disturbances. Such a mode of life is more a native personality characteristic than a quality of spirit. **Longsuffering** is exactly what it suggests, suffering long without going to pieces. Its primary essence is perseverance—never giving up—bearing with people and circumstances. As God has been long-suffering with us (cf. I Tim. 1:12-16), so we are to be with our fellowmen (Eph. 4:2), never admitting defeat however unreasonable and difficult men may be (cf. I Thess. 5:4). It is this kind of patience that reflects truly Christian love (*agape;* cf. I Cor. 13:4). Such patient love is not our own achievement. It is the work of God in men's hearts, for it is a **fruit of the Spirit.**

d. Gentleness (5:22). Men are not to be long-suffering in a moral vacuum. The man of faith is to express **gentleness** (*chrestotes*), perhaps better translated "kindness." In the New Testament the goodness of God is not an awesome moral quality that would repulse man; it is kindness accompanied by forbearance (Rom. 2:4). But when imposed upon, this gentleness can include severity (Rom. 11:22). God's kindness is intended to lead to repentance, so that it can be expressed in forgiveness (cf. Rom. 2:4). This kindness in man is best seen in our forgiveness of others as Christ has forgiven us (cf. Eph. 4:32). Here is the greatest goodness to be found in man—yet few are by nature forgiving. It is **the fruit of the Spirit.**

e. Goodness (5:22). The next fruit is **goodness** (*agathosyne*). It is closely akin to **gentleness;** but of all the fruit listed by Paul, **goodness** lends itself least to precise definition. Barclay's conclusion is that it probably means an openhearted generosity that is undeserved, rather than a begrudging or even niggardly justice meted out solely as it is deserved and earned.[79] Such generosity certainly gives added meaning to the "kindness that forgives," and is indeed a **fruit of the Spirit.**

f. Faith (5:22). Undoubtedly the most misunderstood fruit

[78]The general term for patience with circumstances is *hypomone* (endurance—cf. Rom. 2:7; II Cor. 1:6; I Thess. 1:3).

[79]*Flesh and Spirit,* p. 107.

is **faith** (*pistis*). Here is one of the rare instances when the Greek term is more ambiguous than its English counterpart. Throughout the New Testament *pistis* relates primarily to the believer's complete dependence upon the work of Christ. However, these fruits of the Spirit are *ethical* virtues dealing chiefly with interhuman relations.[80] *Pistis* does, in a few instances, have the ethical meaning of "faithfulness," which is obviously how it is to be understood here.[81] As such it depicts loyalty, trustworthiness, and dependability. As with **goodness** man's pattern for faithfulness is no less than God himself (cf. Rom. 3:3). As God is faithful,[82] so His stewards are expected to be (cf. I Cor. 4:2).

Faithfulness is not only to be found in holding true to God under test and duress, but also in being loyal to one's fellowmen. Paul's commendation of his "faithful" colaborers (I Cor. 4:17; Eph. 6:21) and the "faithful saints" (Eph. 1:1; Col. 1:2) certainly embraces such dependability in human relations. Quite properly, faithfulness represents the highest level of responsibility between husband and wife (cf. I Tim. 3:11). "No church and no marriage can stand unless they are based on loyalty."[83] Such is more than a human virtue, for it is a **fruit of the Spirit!**

g. Meekness (5:23). This "fruit" is one of the most difficult to define, primarily because it is veritably impossible to translate **meekness** (*prautes*) by a single English term. *Meek* certainly does not have the modern connotations of "spiritless" or "spineless." **Meekness** is a blending of strength and gentleness.[84] "It is when we have *prautes* that we treat all men with perfect courtesy, that we can rebuke without rancour, that we can argue without intolerance, that we can face the truth without resentment, that we can be angry and yet sin not, that we can be gentle and yet not weak."[85]

Certainly **meekness** is to be associated with true humility (cf. Matt. 11:29; Col. 3:12), the opposite of pride and arrogance. This is the finest type of strength, and it calls forth exaltation

[80]Cf. I Cor. 13:13, where faith—used in its general sense—is associated with the ethical virtue of love.

[81]Cf. ASV, RSV, NEB.

[82]Cf. I Cor. 1:9; I Thess. 5:24; II Thess. 3:3.

[83]Barclay, *Flesh and Spirit*, p. 110.

[84]Barclay interestingly observes that Aristotle views every virtue as a mean between two extremes (*ibid.*, p. 120).

[85]*Ibid.*, p. 121.

from God. **Meekness** is predicated of Moses (Num. 12:3), who magnificently harmonized strength and gentleness in his difficult role. However, the supreme example is found in Him who was greater than Moses, Jesus Christ. Meekness is the very essence of the character of the One able both to cleanse the Temple and to forgive an adulterous wretch. It is this "yoke" that the disciple is invited to bear (cf. Matt. 11:19), for this is supremely the badge of Christlikeness. It is possessed only as a fruit of the Spirit.

h. Temperance (5:23). The final fruit is **temperance** (*egkrateia*), better translated "self-control." Although this depicts the restraint of all the passions and desires of man (I Cor. 9:25), it also had specific application to being sexually continent (I Cor. 7:9). This is understandable in the world of that day, as in ours. Moral purity was a distinctly Christian virtue, and tends to become so again. It is God's purpose that His children live in the world but remain unblemished by its moral depravity. This is possible as a man walks by the Spirit, for self-control is a fruit of the Spirit. This self-control—or better, Spirit-control—reaches into all areas of daily living.

With an apparent touch of irony, Paul closes his list of the fruits with the observation that **against such there is no law.** At best this is a classic understatement that serves to affirm emphatically his contention that all the law is fulfilled in love and its related virtues. His analysis of love in action dramatically portrays that this is the only way in which God's will for man is fulfilled in its total essence and spirit. It is no less true in the twentieth century. A life of love under the discipline of the Spirit is the only adequate alternative to legalism and to a self-destructive life without restraints.

Paul's primary concern for the unity and harmony of the church finds positive fulfillment here. There will be no strife, division, sects, anger, enmity, jealousy, or envy when men live at peace with one another in kindness, generosity, faithfulness, and meekness. The uniquely Christian virtue of self-control is the answer not only to the triad of moral depravity (v. 19), but also to drunkenness and revellings.

It cannot be stated too forcibly that such a life lies beyond the power and strength of man; it is found only as the fruit of the Spirit. Yet it is available to every man who is truly in Christ. The evils of the world have no power against the man whose heart is totally captured by the Master. He lives in a different world—of the Spirit!

In 16-25 we see "Life in the Spirit," centered in the admonition, **Walk in the Spirit,** 16. (1) This life requires a great religious decision; we must make a choice between a life guided and empowered by the Holy Spirit or a life guided by our own carnal desires, 16-17, 24-25; (2) Life in the Spirit keeps us from the evils of immorality, heresy, and hatred, 18-21; (3) The Holy Spirit in our lives nurtures the growth of every Christlike attitude, 22-23 (A. F. Harper).

4. *Walking by the Spirit* (5:24-26)

Paul here reminded the Galatians that they had crucified the flesh with its propensities and desires. Having new life, as a result, they should live under the Spirit's discipline. This would preclude vanity and envy from arising among them.

Having vividly contrasted the results of living by the flesh and by the Spirit, Paul now focuses his attention on **they that are Christ's** (24).[86] The possessive genitive leaves no question as to Paul's meaning—those who belong to Christ. Such are the men of faith, who are in Christ Jesus.

a. Crucifixion of the Flesh (5:24). Paul makes it clear that those who are truly in Christ **have crucified the flesh.** This metaphor of crucifixion has vital significance for Paul, and is not simply a figure of speech. It depicts the believer's identification, by faith, with the death of Christ.[87] As a direct result the flesh ceases to be an instrument of sin against which man is helpless. The Cross destroys sin in the flesh (cf. Rom. 8:3). No longer is the flesh an irresistible or compulsive force for evil in man. Thus Paul can state that the believer is "not in the flesh," in the sense of being a debtor to live according to it.

It is particularly significant that the crucifixion of the flesh has *happened* to the man in Christ—it is a past fact of experience. This observation by Paul certainly disproves the theology which teaches that the flesh remains unchanged in the believer. What a travesty on the gospel when the Cross is made nothing more than sin's competitor, and is even doomed to defeat in the compe-

[86]The preferred Greek text adds "Jesus."

[87]In the strictest sense it is the inner man that is crucified (dies) with Christ and lives again now (cf. 2:20; Rom. 6:2-12; Col. 2:12; 3:8). The whole man is consequently freed from the compulsive power of sin (cf. Rom. 6:6).

tition! Such a mistaken idea results from a failure to give serious consideration to the crucifixion of the flesh. Jesus died, not to reconcile men to sin, but to deliver them.

The specific manner in which the power of the flesh is destroyed is seen in Paul's observation that it was crucified **with the affections and lusts.** Actually, man's original **affections** (propensities)[88] and **lusts** (desires) are morally neutral.[89] Their character is determined by what influences them.[90] Thus the evil of human desires and propensities arises when these neutral drives are being satisfied in a fleshly way, i.e., contrary to the will of God.

Through the Cross man is freed from the power of the flesh; he no longer lives by it. This does not mean that his propensities and desires are destroyed. Rather, it means that he no longer finds satisfaction and fulfillment in living contrary to the will of God. It is in this sense that the flesh with its propensities and desires has been crucified.

b. Life in the Spirit (5:25-26). Transformed believers are not only new and free men, but we are also spiritual men **if we live in the Spirit** (25). Thus Paul assumes a major premise: The indwelling Spirit of God is essential to the new *life* of the man of faith (cf. Rom. 6:4; 8:9). The believer is described as being alive by[91] the Spirit. Paul uses *pneuma* in a unique manner, almost fusing the divine and human into one concept, which depicts the divine Spirit working through the human spirit (the new inner man).

The life in the Spirit is stated in the indicative mood (see Intro.) and is a description of a *present* experience. It is used by Paul as the basis for a vigorous imperative,[92] **let us also walk in the Spirit.** Since the man of faith has a new quality of existence, he must actively live by the Spirit. To dramatize this, Paul intro-

[88]*Pathemata* is used twelve times in the NT to mean suffering (cf. Rom. 8:18), but only here and in Rom. 7:5 to indicate a "disposition" or "propensity" (cf. Burton, *op. cit.*, pp. 320-21).

[89]Cf. Burton, *op. cit.*, p. 321.

[90]Cf. 5:17, where the desires are influenced by both flesh and Spirit; also Rom. 7:5, where the propensities are influenced by sin. Every "work of the flesh" is a perversion of what is potentially good.

[91]The dative case is best translated here as "by."

[92]The hortatory subjunctive is used (*stoichomen*), which has the same basic function as an imperative, although less of a direct command (cf. Moule, *op. cit.*, pp. 22, 136). Cf. the imperative in v. 16.

duced a vivid metaphor, using the word *stoicheo,* a military term meaning "to march."[93] This figure graphically describes the new dimension of disciplined living under the Spirit.

Paul's central thesis is that the way to gain victory is not simply to deny or reject temptation, for this only leaves a moral vacuum. Instead, he was the one who originally accentuated the positive. The man living by the Spirit walks under discipline. He is so captivated by his new affection that the temptations of the flesh are powerless. The old slavery to sin is escaped by entering a new slavery.

But Paul's primary concern was not the solution of the problem of sin—overcoming the flesh. This was only a door that opened into a wondrous new world—the glorious new life in the Spirit that produces the rich fruit described in 22-23.

Paul's emphasis in Galatians is on the continuing life by the Spirit—living or walking. But such a life must be commenced, which necessitates a vital, crisis capitulation of oneself to God (cf. 2:20).

Paul uses the hortatory subjunctive again to introduce another pivotal verse: **Let us not be desirous of vain glory, provoking one another, envying one another** (26). It points back, providing a concluding application to his exhortation to walk by the Spirit. Such would preclude the believer from becoming[94] "vain-glorious"—literally glorying in things that are of little value. Burton suggests that the Galatians were having the same problem with liberty and the law of love that was found in Corinth.[95] Paul had warned the Galatians about using their liberty as an occasion for the flesh (v. 13). The apostle's emphasis on the Spirit and its fruit, especially love, supports Burton's thesis.

When one is vainglorious (obviously ambitious to get ahead of others), he tends to provoke or tempt others to be envious. The harmony of the fellowship is thus ruptured.

This verse not only points back to the apostle's exhortation

[93]The word means literally to "be drawn up in line," and thus suggests a "formation" and "marching." Derived from it is the idea of living by a rule.

[94]The expression **desirous** is more suggestive than the Greek term (*ginomai*), which simply means "to become." Perhaps the emphasis on desires in the context is the reason for this translation being used here.

[95]*Op. cit.,* p. 323. Cf. I Corinthians 8.

(25) but it also points forward, serving as an introduction to the practical applications of love with which Paul closes his letter.

In 5:25—6:5 we see "Ways to Walk" in Christian relationships. (1) Don't compare your lot with others, or try to get ahead at the expense of others, 5:26; (2) Try always to be understanding and forgiving, 6:1, 3; (3) Help a neighbor who is in need, 6:2; (4) Be self-reliant under God; avoid self-pity; avoid the attitude that others owe you something, 6:4-5 (A. F. Harper).

C. Practical Examples of Love, 6:1-10

1. *Restoring the Fallen* (6:1-5)

Paul admonishes the spiritual brethren to restore any of their number who might be overtaken by sin. This should be done in a spirit of meekness, because they too are subject to testing. This sharing of another's burden fulfills Christ's law of love. Every man should seek to have a true estimate of himself, having passed the test of God's requirements. This and not another's failure is the only proper basis for rejoicing. Each man is responsible for his own life.

a. Restore in a Spirit of Humility (6:1). The clearest evidence that people are living by the Spirit is the presence of love (*agape*), actively manifesting itself in a community of concern. One practical expression of it is to be seen in the restoration of those who have fallen. So Paul writes: **Brethren, if a man be overtaken in a fault** (1). This does not speak of discovering sin in the life of another; it means, rather, if a man is caught unawares by sin in himself. God does not intend for this to happen; and it need not if a man avails himself of the resources Paul had just described.[96] Yet if spiritual failure[97] happens, those **which are spiritual** (those living by the Spirit; cf. I Cor. 3:1) have a decisive responsibility. They are **to restore such an one,** lovingly help him to repair the damage.[98] The present tense

[96]Cf. I John 2:1, where the use of spiritual resources should result in victorious living, yet provision is made for failure—in this case the advocacy of Jesus Christ.

[97]*Paraptoma* (**fault**) is best translated "transgression" (cf. Rom. 5:15). It depicts sin and not simply a fault.

[98]**Restore** (*katartidzo*)—literally to "repair" or "mend." It alludes to the fact that the basic problem in Galatia was division and strife.

indicates that this restoration is a process, rather than a momentary act. It cannot always be accomplished, but one must try. It is a delicate as well as a difficult responsibility and can be done only **in the spirit of meekness.** This attitude, which is a blending of strength and gentleness, is nowhere more needed than here; it is the only spirit in which restoration is possible. The objective is a healthy recovery. "Correction can be given in a way which entirely discourages a man and which drives him to depression and to despair; or correction can be given in a way which sets a man upon his feet with the determination to do better and with the hope of doing better."[99]

At the same time the spiritual man has in himself reason enough to be meek—**considering thyself, lest thou also be tempted.** This does not mean simply to "think about," but rather to "take heed" or even "take warning" (cf. Rom. 16:17). Paul pointedly addresses himself to the individual conscience, **thyself.**[100] Any man may well find himself in the same place of temptation or testing.[101] The term **tempted** (*peiradzo*) is used in at least two different ways in the New Testament. At times it describes conditions that come upon a man unexpectedly over which he has little control. In these circumstances he is promised victory (cf. I Cor. 10:13). However, at other times—as in this case—man is responsible for being in the situation (cf. Matt. 6:13; Luke 22:40, 46; I Cor. 7:5). In such cases a man has already at least partially yielded to the temptation, so it is practically tantamount to sinning. This is exactly the point here. Paul is not speaking about the possibility of being tempted or tried, but of sin. While trying to restore one who has fallen, it is a healthy attitude to remember: "There am I but for the grace of God."

b. Evidence of Obeying Christ's Commands (6:2). To help restore a fallen brother is a tangible way to **bear . . . one another's burdens** (2). The term **burdens** (*bare*) depicts a heavy load of any kind, but here specifically refers to sharing the heartache and shame of one who has spiritually failed. This is a part of the imperative of love, and to obey this command is to **fulfil the law**

[99]Barclay, *Flesh and Spirit*, p. 117.

[100]The plural number (**brethren**) is changed to the singular (**thyself**).

[101]*Peiradzo* basically means to "try" or "test." The idea of "tempt"—specifically solicitation to evil—is a more limited meaning than the basic term.

of Christ. Paul has stated earlier that love fulfills the law; he here adds that this is **the law of Christ.** The apostle undoubtedly means the law as interpreted by Christ (cf. comments on 5:14).

Without question the greatest evidence of divine love that can be seen in the world is a group of people who lovingly **bear . . . one another's burdens**—sharing pain as well as pleasure (cf. John 13:35). This cannot be counterfeited. All merely human motivation fails, dissolved by the acids of jealousy and distrust.

True love must be reciprocal—the opening of our hearts to give and receive. Sometimes it is harder to receive love than give it, and it is particularly difficult for those with personality temperaments that are naturally independent. Yet even this must become a point of spiritual discipline. There is no other way to fulfill the law of Christ save through a sharing of love.

The success of Alcoholics Anonymous demonstrates the therapy of shared suffering, as the helped and helpless alike find healing through mutual dependence. Even more so, in the Christian fellowship, shared love proves to be blessedly redemptive.

c. *Attitudes That Hinder Restoration* (6:3). Paul warns against **a man** thinking **himself to be something** (3). It is dangerously easy for one to build up a strong case for himself when he sees fault in another. But for one to find comfort or satisfaction by measuring himself against another's failures only identifies him as one who **deceiveth himself.** No one else is fooled, only the self-satisfied man.

This verse must not be construed to teach the worthlessness of all men for all time—that a man is **nothing,** and he who thinks he is **something** is deceived. This is not Paul's intent, as is clearly seen in v. 4. Instead, Paul is depreciating any self-estimate that is based upon comparison with others, especially those who have fallen in sin (cf. II Cor. 10:12).

d. *Personal Responsibility* (6:4-5). **Let every man prove his own work** (4) means, "Let a man examine 'his own conduct'" (NEB), or the work of God in himself. Paul is not contrasting human works and divine grace, but is referring to what a man can demonstrate in his own life. It is still "God which worketh in you" (Phil. 2:13). Paul's emphasis is on what a man sees in himself, and not what he sees in others.

If he thus proves his own work, **then shall he have rejoicing in himself alone.** As noted in several modern translations, the meaning of **rejoicing** (*kauchema*) is not boasting, but exultation or even gratitude.[102] A man can rightfully be blessed when he has been put to the test and proved true.

This line of argument brings Paul to the fact of individual responsibility; **every man shall bear his own burden** (5). Thus the apostle has moved from the Christian's social obligations (v. 2) to a man's responsibility for his own soul. The Christian emphasis is found in the interplay of social and individual responsibility and not in either one to the exclusion of the other. In the Christian fellowship the burdens of others are shared in love, but there is also a load[103] that is peculiarly a man's own.

2. *Doing Good to All* (6:6-10)

The believer, as he is taught, is obliged to share with his teachers. Men should not be deceived, thinking that they can evade the consequences of their choices. God cannot be outwitted. A man will reap what he has sown—if it has been to the flesh, then corruption; but if to the Spirit, then life eternal. This should encourage those doing good, for the harvest of goodness will come if they do not give up. Thus, as opportunity is given, the Christian should do good to all men, and particularly to those of the family of faith.

a. The Support of Teachers (6:6). Not only is Christian love seen as a caring identification with those who have fallen into sin, but it is also manifested in a more extensive sharing in the fellowship.[104] This can be seen practically in the believer's relationship to his teachers—**Let him that is taught in the word communicate unto him that teacheth** (6). The word **communicate** (*koinoneo*) means "to share" or "participate," even as a

[102]Cf. NEB, Phillips, Berkeley.

[103]Paul here uses another term for **burden** (*phortion*), which can mean a light or heavy load (cf. Acts 27:10); **burden** (*bare*, v. 2) means a "heavy weight." However it is not certain that Paul intended any difference in meaning.

[104]Burton thinks v. 6 marks Paul's turning from the specific problems in Galatia to general principles of moral and spiritual instruction (*op. cit.*, p. 334). But the fact that Paul returns (11-17) to the very pointed Galatian situation would argue against this. Certainly v. 6 should not be totally isolated from what goes before and after (cf. NEB).

partner.[105] Thus the man of faith, having received instruction in the gospel from his teachers,[106] was under obligation to share with them **all good things.** This is interpreted to mean primarily material and financial support.[107] They were to share their possessions in return for what had been given to them (cf. Rom. 15:27).

b. The Certainty of Harvest (6:7-10). In 7, Paul abruptly says: **Be not deceived; God is not mocked.** Evidently the believers who failed to support their teachers properly (6) thought that such negligence was inconsequential and unnoticed by God. Paul assures them that such action does not outwit[108] God. They are only deceiving themselves.

God has written a law into the constitution of the universe which can be verified in a thousand ways: **Whatsoever a man soweth, that shall he also reap.**[109] The nature of the harvest is determined by the planting. It has been said: "A man is free to choose, but is not free to choose the consequences of his choice." It is a sobering fact that even divine forgiveness does not fully alter this law. How often a child of God grieves over the continuing harvest from lost opportunities, harmful influences, selfish decisions, or the dissipations of yesterday!

In 6-10 we see some of the "Laws of Life's Harvest." The key thought is, **Be not deceived; God is not mocked: for whatsoever a man soweth, that shall he also reap,** 7. (1) It pays for Christians to invest material wealth in spiritual enterprises, 6; (2) Sowing to the flesh means decay and death, 8*a*; (3) Sowing for God means eternal life, 8*b*; (4) Don't stop doing good—God is on that side, 9-10 (A. F. Harper).

The general principle, just enunciated, can be specifically

[105]The noun *koinonia* is the common word for "fellowship" and is one of the most descriptive terms of the Early Church, particularly designating their "communion" and "sharing."

[106]Itinerant teachers early became a vital office in the Church. They were comparable to "prophets," "evangelists," "pastors," etc. (Cf. Eph. 4:11.) Cf. comments on 1:1 for their relation to "apostles."

[107]Cf. Burton, *op. cit.*, pp. 338-39. It could conceivably also mean sharing spiritual responsibilities (cf. Vincent, *op. cit.*, IV, 174).

[108]*Mukterizo* literally means to "turn up the nose" or "ridicule." But the meaning here is to "evade" or "outwit" God.

[109]The figure of sowing and reaping to illustrate conduct and its results is found in Greek philosophy (cf. Burton, *op. cit.*, p. 341), in the OT (Job 4:8), and elsewhere in the NT (Luke 19:21).

illustrated. **For he that soweth to his flesh shall of the flesh reap corruption** (8). Although Paul refers to the same general contrast of flesh and Spirit that was considered in the previous chapter (cf. 5:16-26),[110] his emphasis here is slightly modified by use of the metaphor of sowing and reaping. Basically, he is referring to the harvest of the end time as it is related to the present-day sowing. To sow to the flesh means to live by the flesh, thus satisfying and fulfilling one's desires and propensities in ways not approved by God (see comments on 5:24). Such a life can only bring a final harvest of **corruption.** In addition to **corruption** (*phthoran*) the word means "ruin, destruction, disillusionment, deterioration,"[111] There will be no results of value —only total loss.

However the certainty of harvest does not apply to evil only. It is equally true of the good. The man who **soweth to the Spirit** is he who satisfies his desires and propensities by living in the Spirit. He will reap the glorious harvest of eternal life.

Paul uses this general principle of the certainty of harvest as a means of encouragement: **And let us not be weary in well doing** (9). The term **well doing** is literally doing good. In the context it includes those who restore the fallen and generally share the burdens of others. More broadly, it is doing what one knows is right, no matter how difficult or demanding. In the widest sense it is obeying God, and living by the Spirit. All who do this should not lose heart,[112] **for in due season we shall reap.** The phrase **in due season** means "in its own time" (cf. Eccles. 3:1-8; 8:6).

What a source of blessing and encouragement this promise has been! The whole constitution of the universe lies behind it. The Heavenly Father sees and knows. Few things are more difficult than waiting, but this ordeal is transformed by the assurance that harvest will come.

[110]The argument that this terminology is to be sharply distinguished from 5:16-26, with flesh representing here man's physical body in contrast to his spiritual nature (cf. Burton, *op. cit.*, pp. 339-43), is difficult to substantiate and certainly is not required by the context. This would introduce a completely new set of concepts with the same terms used, and is most confusing and unlikely.

[111]Arndt and Gingrich, *op. cit.*, p. 865.

[112]**Be weary** (*engkakeo*) means physical weariness or mental discouragement.

There is only one proviso—**if we faint not.** This means to give up. Men fail because they quit and not because they are overcome.

Thus, **as we have therefore opportunity, let us do good unto all men** (10). Assured that the harvest will surely come, the believer is encouraged to show forth his faith by doing good at the right time.[113] There is a sowing season as well as a reaping season (cf. Eccles. 3:2*b*). This is sometimes forgotten, but seed prematurely or belatedly sown cannot bring a full harvest.

The apostle adds a final point of emphasis—**especially unto them who are of the household of faith.** This would indicate that Paul's primary concern here is the physical rather than the spiritual needs of men. Christians would have a special obligation to assist their brethren who were suffering physical and material deprivation, particularly if such was due to religious prejudice. It is very possible Paul had in mind the material needs of the itinerant teachers (cf. 6:6).

[113]Opportunity is the word for "time" (*kairos*), which is translated "season" in v. 9.

Section V *Conclusion*

Galatians 6:11-18

A. Final Summation, 6:11-17

Paul closes the Epistle with large letters from his own hand. He notes that his opponents sought to circumcise the Galatians only for the sake of outward appearances, in order to appear orthodox, and to escape persecution for the Cross. Even these Judaizers themselves did not keep the law, desiring others to submit to the rite of circumcision so they could have the satisfaction of glorying in their flesh. In striking contrast, Paul takes glory only in the Cross, by which the world was crucified unto him, and he unto the world. Neither circumcision nor uncircumcision have value, but being a new creation. To those who live by this standard there are peace and mercy, for they are the true people of God. Paul asks freedom from further troubling because his body bears the brand marks of Christ.

1. *Paul's Signature* (6:11)

As he brought his Epistle to a close, Paul took up the pen himself and wrote—**You see how large a letter I have written unto you with mine own hand** (11). The wording of the KJV suggests that he is referring to a long letter. But he is rather calling attention to the large letters he is using to pen his own closing words. NEB translates, "You see these big letters? I am now writing to you in my own hand." This was for the express purpose of emphasis, as he makes a brief summation of his arguments against his opponents, adding a clinching accusation. It would be comparable to boldface type in a book today, with the added authentication of the writer's signature.

2. *An Open Accusation* (6:12-13)

What Paul had cautiously implied (cf. 4:17-18; 5:11), he now states clearly: his opponents were utterly insincere. **As many as desire to make a fair shew in the flesh, they constrain you to be circumcised; only lest they should suffer persecution for the cross of Christ** (12). They sought to compel the Galatians to be circumcised for ulterior motives. In this way they would maintain their good standing in the Jewish community at the expense of Paul's converts. He classifies such selfishness as being in the flesh. In these references to circumcision, the flesh of his converts is certainly in the background of Paul's mind, but in both instances the apostle's use of "flesh" refers to the whole way of living, which he had warned them against. Phillips interprets **a fair shew in the flesh** as "a pleasing front to the world." NEB translates **that they may glory in your flesh (13)** as "in order to boast of your having submitted to that outward rite."

Even more seriously, the Judaizers are accused of seeking to escape persecution for the Cross by enforcing circumcision on the Galatians. This was their only motive, and it clearly indicates that they were Jewish Christians. They were facing persecution from their fellow Jews, which they hoped would be offset by success in bringing the Gentile converts under Jewish law. There is no evidence that such a ruse had been successful; it probably had not been.

The Cross affords no compromise. It has a stigma that must be accepted (cf. 17). How often, through the centuries, men have attempted to temper it, but to no avail! It is still "the old rugged Cross," that cannot be successfully camouflaged or counterfeited.

The insincerity of the Judaizers is further demonstrated in the assertion, **Neither they themselves who are circumcised keep the law (13)**. As translated in the KJV, it would appear that this refers to the Judaizers themselves. This is in line with what Paul rhetorically asserts in Rom. 2:17-24. However the present participle, "being circumcised," may indicate that Paul means the converts of these teachers.[1] Having won converts, they did not require them to keep the whole law (cf. 5:3), proving that they were not motivated by a zeal for the law, as they undoubtedly claimed. Instead, they **desire to have you circumcised, that they may glory in your flesh.** Here **glory** (*kauchaomai*) approximates the English term "boast," but still with the underlying thought of "exultation" (cf. comments on 6:4).

Paul could not have made a more devastating accusation—undoubtedly based on abundant evidence known to the Galatians. Few attitudes are more repulsive. An opponent can be

[1]Cf. Burton's convincing argument (*op. cit.*, pp. 352-53).

respected, no matter how different his position, if one is convinced of his sincerity. When this is not so, it is difficult to avoid contempt.

3. *The Glory of Jesus Christ* (6:14-16)

How inspiring the contrast of v. 14! **But God forbid that I should glory, save in the cross of our Lord Jesus Christ.** Using his unique exclamation, **God forbid** (cf. comments on 2:17), Paul confesses his refusal to **glory** in anything but the Cross. The direct antithesis to his opponents is striking. What they seek to escape at the price of insincerity is the apostle's only basis of exultation.[2]

He has good reason for his glorying, because it is the Cross **by whom the world is crucified unto me.** It was the Cross that had revolutionized his whole life. As noted above (cf. comments on 5:24, n. 87), it was the inner man that died with Christ, but as a result the world can be described as crucified to him. The **world** to which Paul here refers was not a life of outbroken sin, but rather it was his Jewish heritage, circumcision, and Pharisaical righteousness. This "world was once to him a living and vast and tremendous reality. Upon its smile hung all his hopes: its frown was ruin. Consequently he was the world's servant and slave, and the world was his absolute and imperious and cruel lord. This service was hopeless and degrading bondage. But now, through the death of Christ upon the cross, it had utterly and forever passed away."[3]

However, in the deepest sense, the change had taken place in him and not in the world. He testifies, I was crucified **unto the world.** Every man who is not in Christ has his world—that for which he lives and slaves, and perhaps is willing to die. When Christ frees one from this bondage, those looking on can never quite understand, but that is because they do not know the inner joy of him who belongs to Christ. Is it any wonder that this becomes the believer's only glory?

Paul next repeats his unequivocal conviction (cf. comments on 5:6) that **in Christ Jesus[4] neither circumcision availeth any**

[2]Cf. Rom. 5:2-3, 11; I Cor. 1:18-31 for a description of what Paul means by glorying in the Cross.

[3]Beet, *op. cit.*, 176.

[4]The phrase **in Christ Jesus** is not in the earliest MSS but the meaning is in full harmony with Paul's teaching.

thing nor uncircumcision (15). The pride of the Jew (circumcision) and of the Gentile (uncircumcision) alike were of no value; this kind of pride is totally useless in terms of salvation. Only one thing has worth, being **a new creature.** Here is the greatest miracle known to us—the miracle of the "new creation."[5] Through the power of the Cross, God creates a new man.[6]

As Paul always makes clear, the "new man" must live and walk in the will of God (cf. Col. 2:6). This is the climactic emphasis of his admonition (cf. 5:13-26; especially 25). **As many as walk** (*stoicheo,* march) **according to this rule, peace be on them** (16; cf. comments on 5:25). In this case it is living according to the "measuring rule" (cf. II Cor. 10:13-16), which is by the Spirit (cf. 5:25). Upon all such people of God he breathes his apostolic benediction of **peace** (cf. comments on 1:3; 5:22) **and mercy** (cf. I Tim. 1:2; II Tim. 1:2).

The last phrase of 16 is unusual—**and upon the Israel of God.** There is some question as to whether this refers to those of Jewish heritage alone or is a new name for the Christian Church.[7] The latter is more likely because, in the light of what had gone on before, Paul would hardly be expected to separate the Jewish Christians for a special blessing. There is evidence that "new Israel" became a favorite name for the Church in the apostolic age (cf. comments on 3:8; Rom. 2:28-29; 9:6-8).

4. *The Marks of the Lord Jesus* (6:17)

Having made his point, Paul rested his case—**From henceforth let no man trouble me (17)**. The apostle had exhausted himself in the service of Christ and in substance asks that in the future he be spared the abuse and distress heaped upon him by his opponents. The justification for his request is: **I bear in my body the marks of the Lord Jesus.** The figure alludes to the prevalent practice of branding slaves, indicating to whom they belonged.[8] Paul often identified himself as the slave of Jesus Christ; for him it was a favorite figure. The wounds and scars of the battle (cf. II Cor. 11:23-33) were his badge; **the marks** (lit., stigma) **of the Lord Jesus** were indelibly etched on his body. They

[5]As in II Cor. 5:17, *kaine ktisis* is best translated "new creation."

[6]Cf. Rom. 6:4-6, 11; Gal. 2:19-20; Col. 3:10.

[7]Cf. the discussion in Burton, *op. cit.*, p. 358.

[8]Soldiers were also branded, identifying the general under whom they served.

marked him as a slave in deed and not simply in word; but he bore his identification joyfully.

B. The Apostolic Benediction, 6:18

All that remained was to bid farewell, which Paul did in typical apostolic fashion: **The grace of our Lord Jesus Christ be with your spirit.** This was no idle word, but rather a sincere prayer. No one knew better than he that they needed such grace every hour. It could be theirs "in the Spirit." With deep significance Paul's final word to these whom he had of necessity dealt with severely was **brethren.**[9] Although he often used the term, only here does it close a benediction, giving an assurance of his deep and abiding love. With the writer, all who read this letter can add, **Amen!**

[9]The KJV has the term **brethren** out of proper position. In the Greek it comes last.

Bibliography

I. COMMENTARIES

BARCLAY, WILLIAM. *Flesh and Spirit* (An Examination of Galatians 5:19-23). Nashville: Abingdon Press, 1962.

———. *The Letters to Galatians and Ephesians.* "The Daily Study Bible." Philadelphia: Westminster Press, 1958.

BEET, JOSEPH AGAR. *A Commentary on St. Paul's Epistle to the Galatians.* London: Hodder and Stoughton, 1885.

BURTON, ERNEST DE WITT. *The Epistle to the Galatians.* "The International Critical Commentary," ed. S. R. DRIVER, A. PLUMMER, G. A. BRIGGS. Edinburgh: T. & T. Clark, 1921.

LIGHTFOOT, J. B. *Saint Paul's Epistle to the Galatians.* London: Macmillan and Co., 1892.

VINCENT, MARVIN R. *Word Studies in the New Testament,* Vol. IV. Grand Rapids: Wm. B. Eerdmans Publishing Co., 1957 (reprint).

II. OTHER BOOKS

ARNDT, W. F., and GINGRICH, F. W. *A Greek-English Lexicon of the New Testament and Other Early Christian Literature.* Chicago: University of Chicago Press, 1957.

MOULE, C. F. D. *An Idiom Book of New Testament Greek.* Cambridge: The University Press, 1953.

NIELSON, JOHN. *In Christ.* Kansas City: Beacon Hill Press, 1960.

ROBERTSON, A. T., and DAVIS, W. HERSEY. *A New Short Grammar of the Greek Testament.* New York: Harper & Brothers Publishers, 1931.

ROBINSON, H. WHEELER. *The Christian Doctrine of Man.* Edinburgh: T. & T. Clark, 1911.

TRENCH, RICHARD C. *Synonyms of the New Testament.* London: Kegan Paul, Trench & Co., 1886.

WOOD, A. SKEVINGTON. *Life by the Spirit.* Grand Rapids: Zondervan Publishing House, 1963.

III. ARTICLES

JAMISON, LELAND. "Dikaiosyne in the Usage of Paul." *Journal of Bible and Religion,* Vol. XXI, No. 1 (Jan., 1953).

SCHRENK, G. *"Righteousness." Bible Key Words,* Vol. IV. Tr. from *Theologisches Worterbuch zum Neuen Testament.* Adam and Charles Black, 1935.

STAUFFER, ETHELBERT. "Love" (The Apostolic Age). *Bible Key Words,* Vol. I. Tr. from *Theologisches Worterbuch zum Neuen Testament* (edited by G. KITTEL). Adam and Charles Black, 1933.

The Epistle to the

EPHESIANS

Willard H. Taylor

Introduction

Every man who has given himself to a study in depth of Ephesians has come to acclaim it the grandest Epistle of the Apostle Paul. More than any other letter, Ephesians speaks in personal and practical terms to the Christian everywhere. Such has been the reaction of the Church throughout the Christian era. John Chrysostom (345-407) wrote in his *Preamble to the Homilies,* "This Epistle is full to the brim of thoughts and doctrines sublime and momentous. For the things which scarcely anywhere else he utters, there he makes manifest."

Samuel Taylor Coleridge described Ephesians as "the divinest composition of man." A. S. Peake spoke of it as "the quintessence of Paulinism." F. R. Barry once commented that Ephesians is "at once the most 'modern' in many ways of all the books of the New Testament and the richest record of Christian experience." The renowned Edgar J. Goodspeed spoke of this Epistle as "a great rhapsody on the worth of Christian salvation." Many hymns of the Christian Church, among which is "The Church's One Foundation," were inspired by this sublime Epistle. F. F. Bruce characterizes it as "the coping-stone on the massive structure of Paul's teaching."

A. Authorship

In two places in the Epistle the writer identifies himself: (1) "Paul, an apostle of Jesus Christ by the will of God" (1:1); (2) "For this cause I Paul, the prisoner of Jesus Christ for you Gentiles" (3:1). That these references are authentic is substantiated by the fact that the Church fathers assigned the Epistle to Paul of Tarsus as early as the second century. Ephesians was known to Ignatius of Antioch as Pauline before his martyrdom about A.D. 115. Bishop Polycarp of Smyrna, as well as the authors of the *Epistle of Barnabas* and the *Shepherd of Hermas,* give evidence of attributing Ephesians to the Apostle Paul. Marcion, the noted heretic, rejected the Old Testament but favored the writings of Paul. In A.D. 144 he issued a list of approved Christian books, in which were ten of Paul's letters, including Ephesians. Surprising, however, is the fact that he referred to the letter as "The Epistle to the Laodiceans." He no doubt took his cue from Col. 4:16, in which there is a reference to such a letter.

Pauline authorship is further sustained by other Christian leaders of the second century, including Irenaeus of Lyons,

Clement of Alexandria, and Tertullian of Carthage. The famous Muratorian Canon (*ca.* A.D. 190) lists Ephesians as one of the authoritative Christian books. Justifiably, therefore, a large segment of scholarship concludes that the whole Early Church viewed it as genuinely Pauline.

Nevertheless, during the latter part of the nineteenth century a number of critics attacked the authenticity of the Epistle, claiming that Paul was not the author but that a learned follower of Paul composed it. The main arguments against Pauline authorship involve the lack of personal greetings to the recipients, the duplication in varying degree of 75 of the 155 verses of Ephesians in Colossians, the employment of many new words, the allusions to gnostic ideas, and the absence of strong emphasis upon Paul's central doctrine of "justification by faith."[1]

However, a long list of illustrious scholars insist that the Epistle is the direct fruit of Paul's pen.[2] Donald Guthrie's able defense is sufficient here. He writes:

> When all the objections are carefully considered it will be seen that the weight of evidence is inadequate to overthrow the overwhelming external attestation to Pauline authorship, and the epistle's own claims. . . . To maintain that the Paulinist out of his sheer love for Paul and through his own self-effacement composed the letter, attributed it to Paul and found an astonishing and immediate readiness on the part of the Church to recognize it as such is considerably less credible than the simple alternative of regarding it as Paul's own work.[3]

Moreover, the majesty of this Epistle would compel us to assert, if it is not composed by Paul, the assumed author "must have been the apostle's equal, if not his superior, in mental stature and spiritual insight." After all the evidence is sifted, the Pauline authorship still maintains a strong position among students of the apostle.

B. Recipients

To whom was this letter written? This question on the surface may not appear to be important, but an examination of the references to the recipients exposes the problem.

[1]For the most widespread view of the non-Pauline authorship among American scholars cf. Edgar J. Goodspeed, *The Meaning of Ephesians* (Chicago: University of Chicago Press, 1933). For an excellent discussion of the arguments pro and con, cf. Donald Guthrie, *New Testament Introduction: The Pauline Epistles* (Chicago: Inter-Varsity Press, 1961).

[2]B. F. Westcott, J. Armitage Robinson, E. F. Scott, C. H. Dodd, F. F. Bruce, A. H. McNeile, and T. Henshaw, among others.

[3]*Op. cit.*, pp. 127-28.

(1) The title, which has been attached to the Epistle from the earliest centuries, is "To the Ephesians" (Gk., *pros Ephesious*). The oldest manuscript of Ephesians, the Chester Beatty Papyrus (P 46), which is dated about A.D. 200, plus the two outstanding fourth-century codices, Sinaiticus and Vaticanus, employ this title. The witness of the Early Church on this matter is almost universal. The Muratorian Fragment, Irenaeus, Clement of Alexandria, and Tertullian refer to it as the Epistle "To the Ephesians." Tertullian comments that Marcion (*ca.* 150) listed the epistle as "To the Laodicians," but does not include one "To the Ephesians." Adolph Harnack, the famous teacher of Berlin, claimed that the letter was addressed originally to Laodicea, but the name was dropped from the latter because of the bad reputation the church developed at a later time.[4]

(2) The early character of the title would seem to settle the question of the destination of the letter, except that the earliest and best manuscripts do not possess the phrase *in Ephesus* (Gk., *en Epheso*) in 1:1. The Chester Beatty Papyrus, as well as Sinaiticus and Vaticanus, omit this phrase. Origen, the great biblical scholar of the third century, remarks that the words "at Ephesus" were not in the manuscripts that he knew. Also, Basil and Jerome of the fourth century indicate that the best manuscripts available to them lacked this phrase.

(3) Several facts arising out of this apparent conflict between title and address must be kept in mind in seeking a resolution of it. First, titles were probably added to the books of the New Testament at the time they were gathered together, perhaps sometime during the second century. Second, a scribe in seeking a title for this letter might have taken a clue from II Tim. 4:12, where Paul writes, "Tychicus [who carried the Colossian Epistle] have I sent to Ephesus." Third, it is quite out of character for Paul not to address the recipients of his correspondence directly and intimately. According to Acts 19—20 the apostle had lived and worked three years in Ephesus. It seems incredible that he would not have mentioned in this Epistle some of the individuals whom he knew personally at Ephesus. A perusal of the letter reveals that many of his readers were not well known to him (1:15; 3:2; 4:20-21). The conclusion to which these facts lead is that the letter was not written primarily for the church at Ephesus.

[4]Cf. Rev. 3:14-22.

(4) Of the suggestions concerning the recipients of the Epistle, three merit passing consideration. First, Paul addressed the letter originally to a particular congregation, but the salutation and personal greetings were omitted later so that the Epistle could be used more generally. In due time, however, the letter became identified with Ephesus. This view, needless to say, fails to take into consideration the fact, easily verified from his other writings, that the apostle consistently involves personal matters in his correspondence. For this same reason Marcion's assignment of the letter to the church at Laodicea receives little consideration from scholars.

Second, Paul addressed the Epistle to the whole Christian world[5] and not to a particular congregation. It has been conjectured that the introductory greeting might have read originally, "To the saints who are also faithful in Christ Jesus." But grammatically, this proposal breaks down. Furthermore, parallel usage in Romans, II Corinthians, and Philippians militates against the absence of a place name. Such passages as 1:15 and 6:21 seem to suggest that Paul had particular readers in mind.

Third, Paul addressed this Epistle to a number of churches. Originally, a blank space was left at the place where "at Ephesus" appears, in order that a name might be inserted. In other words, Ephesians is a circular letter. In support of this view are several facts. The general thought of the Epistle is applicable to people in different situations, thereby accounting for the lack of personal greetings such as we find in Paul's other letters. It must be remembered that Paul had labored for three years in Ephesus; yet according to 3:2 and 4:21, some doubt is introduced that Paul himself had brought the readers to Christ. Marcion's designation of it as the letter "to the Laodiceans" would be a natural error if he possessed a copy of the original in which this name had been inserted.

How did the letter circulate? Perhaps Tychicus or some other messenger carried the Epistle from place to place and inserted the name of the particular church to which he was reading it. Also, several copies of the letter might have been created, each one bearing the name of a particular church. The former view appears to be more feasible. It is a fair conclusion to say that Paul addressed this Epistle to the churches of the western part of the province of Asia, among which would be Ephesus,

[5]Franke W. Beare, "The Epistle to the Ephesians" (Exegesis), *The Interpreter's Bible,* ed. George R. Buttrick, *et al.,* X (New York: Abingdon-Cokesbury Press, 1953), 602

Colossae, Laodicea, Pergamum, and Philadelphia. Perhaps Ephesus received it first and then it circulated throughout the rest of the region. Since it began its circulation at Ephesus, and also since Ephesus was the chief city of the area, the letter eventually became associated with the Ephesian congregation.

C. The Place and Occasion of Writing

Three explicit notes in the Epistle indicate that Paul was a prisoner at the time of its writing. In 3:1 and 4:1 the apostle speaks of himself as a "prisoner." In 6:20 he writes of himself as "an ambassador in bonds."[6] Where was Paul when he wrote this letter? Our primary source on this matter is the Book of Acts, which records three imprisonments: (1) Philippi (Acts 16:19-34); (2) Caesarea (Acts 25); and (3) Rome (Acts 28:16 ff.). Since the Philippian imprisonment was only for a single night, it can readily be dismissed as the place from which the letter was sent. While the Caesarean imprisonment was lengthier —more than two years (Acts 24:26-27)—it cannot be sustained as the location of the composition of the letter. The "Prison Epistles" indicate that Paul expected a speedy release (cf. Philem. 22; Phil. 2:24). But the general attitude of the Palestinian Jews toward Paul during his Caesarean imprisonment would give little hope of an early dismissal. Also if Paul had been contemplating an appeal to Caesar, knowing that it would necessitate a trip to Rome, he would not have intimated an early release.

Some commentators have alleged that the imprisonment to which Paul refers in these Epistles is one which he experienced at Ephesus.[7] The theory is predicated primarily on I Cor. 15:32, in which Paul asserts that he "fought with beasts at Ephesus." A second source is II Cor. 11:23, in which the apostle suggests numerous imprisonments. While other internal evidence is mustered in support of this position, there is no explicit biblical record that Paul was ever in prison at Ephesus. The reference to a match with beasts must be taken as a metaphor of the intense opposition he faced from evil men. In all likelihood his Roman citizenship and his influential friends in Ephesus would have saved him from imprisonment there.

The most reasonable view is that the Epistle to the Ephesians, as well as Philippians, Colossians, and Philemon, was written

[6]Cf. comments on passages in the other "Prison Epistles": Phil. 1:7, 13-14, 17; Col. 4:2-3, 18; Philem. 1, 9.

[7]The most definitive statement of this hypothesis is given by G. S. Duncan, *The Ephesian Ministry* (London: Hodder and Stoughton, 1929).

while Paul was a prisoner in Rome. The references to "the praetorian guard" (Phil. 1:13, NASB) and to the saints "that are of Caesar's household" (Phil. 4:22) most certainly suggest a Roman setting. Moreover, Paul lived in comparative freedom in Rome while his trial was pending (Acts 28:30). For two years he occupied his own house and thus was able to give attention to any necessary correspondence with his churches in the Aegean area.

If the Roman theory as to the place of writing is correct, what is the sequence of composition of the "Prison Epistles"? Usually the order is conceived to be the following: Onesimus, the runaway slave of Philemon of Colossae, appeared in Rome and came under the influence of Paul. After his conversion he was sent back to his master in company with Tychicus, a native of the province of Asia, who carried the letter to Philemon. In the little letter Paul appeals for leniency for Onesimus. Prior to Onesimus' and Tychicus' departure, Epaphras, one of Paul's colleagues who probably founded the church at Colossae, apparently arrived from that city with some word concerning the spiritual condition of the church there. Thus Paul took advantage of the anticipated trip of Onesimus and Tychicus to Colossae to address a letter to that church (Col. 4:7-9). The completion of the Epistle to the Colossians also provoked Paul to dictate one for all the churches in western Asia. This letter, known as the Epistle to the Ephesians, was also delivered by Tychicus (Eph. 6:21).

The similarity of language and ideas of Colossians and Ephesians supports the view that they were composed together. Ephesians is an expansion of several ideas which are only embryonic in Colossians. By checking cross-references to Colossians, the student of Ephesians will discover the striking linguistic and conceptual similarity between these two Epistles. In this commentary, occasionally, and particularly where the likeness is important, the reference to the Colossian letter has been noted.

D. The Theme of the Epistle

Bruce laments the fact that Paul's thought has been so exclusively identified with the doctrine of justification by faith that the insights of Colossians and Ephesians have been "overlooked, or felt to be un-Pauline."[8] Unquestionably, Galatians

[8]F. F. Bruce, *The Epistle to the Ephesians* (New York: Fleming H. Revell Co., 1961), p. 15.

and Romans, out of which has come the emphasis upon the key teaching of justification by faith, are pivotal Epistles. They occupy a distinctive position as far as the apostle's message is concerned. In Ephesians, however, we possess the most succinct statement of Paul's central doctrine: "For by grace are ye saved through faith; and that not of yourselves: it is the gift of God: not of works, lest any man should boast. For we are his workmanship, created in Christ Jesus unto good works, which God hath before ordained that we should walk in them" (2:8-10). Thus, equally important for an understanding of Paul's thought are the insights of the Ephesian letter.

Ephesians, along with Colossians, introduces us to the apostle's concern with unity. Von Soden has commented that Ephesians is "above all a hymn of unity." Paul seeks to demonstrate that the redemptive plan of God involves essentially the unity of man and the cosmos with himself. At the heart of the order of things there exists a deep rift. Man and God are tragically alienated. Likewise the world in which man lives is disunited, naturally, morally, and socially. Discord is the most characteristic trait of man himself and the world around him. For Paul, Christ is God's answer to this disharmony. The apostle makes his point explicit in 1:10: "That in the dispensation of the fulness of times he [God] might gather together in one all things in Christ, both which are in heaven, and which are on earth." More specifically, with regard to the profound separation of Jew and Gentile, "the mystery of Christ" is that "the Gentiles should be fellowheirs, and of the same body, and partakers of his promise in Christ by the gospel," thus bringing unity. This is all "according to the eternal purpose which he purposed in Christ Jesus our Lord" (2:11-18; 3:1-13).

According to Ephesians, Christ's work of unity begins experientially with the newness of life which man, touched by the grace of God, enjoys. The weighty little phrase "in Christ" is thematic. Paul writes in 1:3: "Blessed be the God and Father of our Lord Jesus Christ, who hath blessed us with all spiritual blessings in heavenly places *in Christ*." To be "in Christ" has many dimensions, among which are adoption (1:5), forgiveness of sins (1:7), sealing with the Holy Spirit (1:13), resurrection from spiritual deadness (2:1-6), reconciliation unto God (2:13-18), putting on of the robe of righteousness (4:22-24), the experience of holiness (3:14-21), and sensitive ethical and social living (cc. 5—6).

As an instrument of reconciliation and unity, God creates the Church, which is Christ's body. Through the Church, God unites Jews and Gentiles, thereby removing the history-long enmity. Christ reconciles them both "unto God in one body by the cross, having slain the enmity thereby" (2:16). Jews and Gentiles become in Christ "one new man, so making peace" (2:15). Gentiles who were once "far off are made nigh by the blood of Christ" (2:13) and together with the Jews enjoy "access by one Spirit unto the Father" (2:18). The Church as the body of Christ witnesses to the fact that cleavages, be they ever so deep, can be removed. These are the "cleavages of nation, race, color, class, religion and culture which engender bitter hostility and threaten our world with annihilation."[9] When the Church is really the Church, she is a unit like a household, a commonwealth of citizens with equal rights, and indeed a holy temple in which the Holy Spirit dwells (2:19-22).

The Church—in the Pauline sense of the Church universal—is always a unity, possessing one Spirit, holding fast to a single creed, and growing in likeness to her Head, Christ, by the ministry of her charismatic leaders (4:1-16). Morever, subjected to her Lord, the Church is led to the experience of sanctification, for which Christ died with the expectation "that he might present it to himself a glorious church, not having spot, or wrinkle, or any such thing; but that it should be holy and without blemish" (5:22-33).

[9] *Ibid.*, p. 17.

Outline

I. Salutation, 1:1-2
   A. The Writer, 1:1*a*
   B. The Recipients, 1:1*b*
   C. The Benediction, 1:2

II. A Hymn of Salvation, 1:3-14
   A. The Source of Salvation Blessings, 1:3
   B. Salvation Enacted Before Time, 1:4-6
   C. Salvation Realized in Time, 1:7-14

III. Prayer and Praise for Divine Enlightenment, 1:15—2:10
   A. The Inspiration of the Prayer, 1:15-16
   B. The Essence of the Petition, 1:17
   C. The Rewards of Enlightenment, 1:18-19
   D. Evidences of God's Power, 1:20—2:10

IV. Spiritual Unity of Mankind in Christ, 2:11-22
   A. Former Alienation from Christ, 2:11-12
   B. Reconciliation of Gentiles and Jews, 2:13-18
   C. Metaphors of Unity, 2:19-22

V. Prayer for Spiritual Fulfillment, 3:1-21
   A. Paul's Stewardship of the Mystery, 3:1-13
   B. Paul's Prayer for Spiritual Fulfillment, 3:14-19
   C. Doxology, 3:20-21

VI. The Unity of the Church, 4:1-16
   A. The Plea for Unity, 4:1-3
   B. The Great Unities, 4:4-6
   C. The Diversity in Unity, 4:7-16

VII. The Old Life and the New, 4:17-32
   A. Life Without Christ, 4:17-19
   B. Life with Christ, 4:20-24
   C. Special New-Life Injunctions, 4:25-32

VIII. Living as the Beloved, 5:1-21
   A. Walking in Love, 5:1-7
   B. Walking in Light, 5:8-14
   C. Walking in Wisdom, 5:15-21

IX. Christian Relationships, 5:22—6:9
   A. Husbands-Wives, 5:22-33
   B. Parents-Children, 6:1-4
   C. Masters-Slaves, 6:5-9

X. The Christian Warfare, 6:10-20
   A. The Preparation of the Christian, 6:10-13
   B. The Armor of God, 6:14-17
   C. The Prayer for All Saints, 6:18-20

XI. Final Greetings, 6:21-24
   A. Commendation of Tychicus, 6:21-22
   B. Benediction, 6:23-24

Section I *Salutation*

Ephesians 1:1-2

A. The Writer, 1:1*a*

The letters of the Apostle Paul begin with the greeting formula common to first-century correspondence. Paul's salutations are usually composed of three parts—the writer, the recipients, and the benedictory word. In most instances Paul follows this threefold greeting, with some amplification in keeping with his relationship to the people addressed. However, what is most significant in this Ephesian introductory word is that the relationship to God in Christ governs the description of the writer and the readers.

Paul describes himself as **an apostle of Jesus Christ by the will of God** (cf. I Cor. 1:1; II Cor. 1:1; II Tim. 1:1). The term **apostle** derives from the Greek *apostolos,* and literally means "sent one." In this basic sense it is used of Christian missionaries in general, such as Barnabas (Acts 14:14), Epaphroditus (Phil. 2:25), Timothy and Silvanus (I Thess. 2:6; the Gk. for "messenger" is *apostolos*). All of God's workmen have an apostolic relationship and responsibility; that is to say, they are "sent on a mission" for God. However, Paul is thinking in more restrictive terms in writing of his own apostleship. He considers himself as a part of the original company of twelve who were specially related to the Master. In keeping with their unique experience, Paul was directly and personally commissioned by Christ to preach the gospel (Acts 26:15-19; Gal. 1:11-17).

Paul describes his apostleship as a creation **by the will of God,** or better, "through the will of God." His apostolic authority is not to be attributed to any action by the Early Church, nor to a pronouncement of the twelve who preceded him.[1] His divine commission as an apostle came at the time of his encounter with the risen Christ on the Damascus Road, and was simultaneous with his conversion. Commenting on the phrase **by the will of God,** R. W. Dale writes that Paul means the divine will was "the strong yet gracious force which placed him

[1]The apostle deals pointedly with this issue in Gal. 1:1, 11-24.

in the apostleship, and which sustained him in all his apostolic labors and sufferings."[2]

B. The Recipients, 1:1*b*

The persons who are to receive this Epistle are characterized as **saints** (*hagioi*) and **faithful** (*pistoi*). The phrase **at Ephesus** is exceedingly difficult to defend since the Chester Beatty Papyrus (P 46) of the third century and the MSS Vaticanus and Sinaiticus, of the fourth century, do not have it.[3]

In what sense are these Christians **saints?** Are they simply a people "set apart" by God for service and so may be deemed "holy"? Or is this word descriptive of the character of the recipients as a morally holy people? Both interpretations are proper and relevant. No man is a saint by personal effort; sainthood comes by the consecrating act of God. However, the soul that is "set apart" by God's grace has been made "holy" because he has knowingly and willingly surrendered his life to God. The sanctity he manifests is not merely a matter of standing with God; it is also a reality of his inner spirit as he lives in dynamic relationship with God through Christ. These people are saints to the extent that the grace of God is operating in their lives. Some of the Ephesian Christians may not enjoy the blessings of full salvation, but they live apart from sin and are growing in their relationship to God. Paul no doubt hopes that their continued life in Christ will lead them to that experience of the wholly sanctified.

These people are also called the **faithful in Christ.** In the original language, the word **faithful** may mean (1) "believers" or "those who have faith," and (2) "faithful ones" or "those who show fidelity." Francis Foulkes rightly concludes, "Here both ideas may be included; they are believers and their calling is to faithfulness."[4] The act of believing issues in fidelity.

The saintly and faithful recipients of this Epistle not only believe **in Christ Jesus**; they also live in Him. The fellowship which they enjoy as a community has been created by Christ as

[2]*Lectures on Ephesians* (London: Hodder and Stoughton, 1887), p. 13.

[3]See Introduction, "Recipients."

[4]*The Epistle of Paul to the Ephesians* ("The Tyndale New Testament Commentaries"; Grand Rapids: Wm. B. Eerdmans Publishing Co., 1963), p. 43.

they have given themselves to Him. As once they were, like all men, "in Adam" (Rom. 5:12-21; I Cor. 15:21-22), alienated from God, they are now **in Christ Jesus** and are reconciled to God.

Paul's gospel might well be characterized as the call to the experience of being "in Christ" (*en Christo*). Stewart observes, "The heart of Paul's religion is union with Christ. . . . Everything that religion meant for Paul is focused for us in such great words as these: 'I live, yet not I, but Christ liveth in me' (Gal. 2:20). 'There is, therefore, now no condemnation to them which are in Christ Jesus' (Rom. 8:1). 'He that is joined unto the Lord is one spirit' (I Cor. 6:17)."[5]

C. The Benediction, 1:2

Combining the common Greek greeting, **grace** (*charis*), and the Jewish greeting, **peace** (*shalom*), Paul expresses more than a passing word of goodwill. Indeed, he pronounces a blessing. The twelve apostles were sent out by the Master with His prerogatives of blessing or rejecting people, depending on their response to the gospel (Matt. 10:11-15). In a similar fashion Paul's words are benedictory in that they carry the power of God with them. They mediate the divine assurance. **Grace** encompasses all the providential acts of God on behalf of undeserving men to initiate and to sustain a saving relationship with Him. **Peace**, the twin gift, is a state of deep satisfaction and settledness. It is divinely created in the hearts and minds of men who have responded to the redemptive overtures of God through His Son, Christ Jesus.

God our Father is the Provider of our salvation, whereas the **Lord Jesus Christ** is the Mediator of it. These initial gifts of **grace** and **peace** can grow as we yield ourselves to God, whose only purpose is to have a people who are maturing in their love for Him.

[5]James S. Stewart, *A Man in Christ* (New York: Harper and Row, n.d.), p. 147.

Section II *A Hymn of Salvation*

Ephesians 1:3-14

No passage in the Pauline writings is weightier in salvation truth than this one. Each verse is laden with majestic insights into God's mighty deeds of salvation for every member of Adam's race. In one long sentence embracing all these verses, the apostle touches upon every facet of saving experience. Any attempt at exposition demands a careful examination of each successive phrase, which flows out of the preceding one and gives birth to the following one.

B. F. Westcott categorizes this passage as "a Psalm of praise for the redemption and consummation of created things, fulfilled in Christ through the Spirit according to the eternal purpose of God."[1] The use of the word **blessed** (*eulogeo,* 1:3) and the triple refrain **to the praise of his glory** (1:6, 12, 14) are the clues to understanding the passage. Dale Moody also has suggested that the structure is doxological and that forms of liturgical prayer constitute a basis of it.[2] The Trinitarian character of these prayers is identifiable: (1) the work of the Father, 3-6; (2) the work of the Son, 7-12; (3) the work of the Holy Spirit, 13-14.[3] This threefold organization is even more impressive in the original language than in our English translations. Recognizing the basic "praise" character of the passage, Moody discusses it with Trinitarian divisions in mind.

A much more explicit designation of the passage is that suggested by John Wick Bowman. He calls it "A Hymn of Salvation."[4] It seems that the apostle bursts into a doxology as he contemplates what lies behind all that has happened in his life and in the lives of his readers. The passage relates therefore to salvation history. It denotes how God laid the plans for man's

[1]*Saint Paul's Epistle to the Ephesians* (Grand Rapids: Wm. B. Eerdmans Publishing Co., 1950 [reprint], p. 4.

[2]*Christ and the Church* (Grand Rapids: Wm. B. Eerdmans Publishing Co., 1963), p. 16.

[3]Cf. the structure of I Pet. 1:3-12.

[4]"The Epistle to the Ephesians," *Interpretation,* VIII (April, 1954), 195.

redemption and how those plans are being fulfilled and actualized in the hearts and lives of these first-century Christians and will be realized also in the lives of all responsive men.

The most helpful division of the passage is: (1) The source of salvation blessings, 3; (2) Salvation enacted before time, 4-6; (3) Salvation realized in time, 7-14.

A. The Source of Salvation Blessings, 1:3

Paul begins by praising God for the spiritual benefits which accrue to him and his fellow Christians because of their relationship to Christ. **Blessed** is the Greek *eulogetos,* which is a compound word composed of *eu,* meaning "well," and *logetos,* meaning "speaking." Literally, the Greek bears the idea of "speaking well" or "eulogizing." In effect the apostle says, "We eulogize God; we speak good words about Him." Essentially God alone is worthy to be blessed because He is genuine and constant in character and action. He alone is truly praiseworthy because there is no mixture in His motives and intentions. Most important is the fact that God is **the Father of our Lord Jesus Christ,** who has made known to us the nature of God. The Supreme One is not an austere, arbitrary judge but the Eternal Father, loving, merciful, and tender in spirit like Christ.[5]

We bless God because He has blessed us. Our praise springs from the gracious disposition of the Heavenly Father toward us. The clause **who hath blessed** in the original language is an aorist participle and thus suggests punctiliar action in the past when the blessings about to be mentioned were received. Paul is referring to the occasions when God spoke words of forgiveness and cleansing to our hearts. While our words at times might have little or no effect upon existing circumstances, God's words are always creative and they bring into being what His will desires. The Word of God can fashion worlds, and that is glorious. But there is more. The creation of a spiritually new son through the announcement of forgiveness exceeds our comprehension. It is sheer miracle.

1. *Spiritual Blessings* (1:3*a*)

With all spiritual blessings is singular in the Greek: "with every spiritual blessing." Paul does not intend to distinguish basically between material gifts and spiritual benefits, though

[5]Cf. John 1:18; Rom. 15:6; Heb. 1:1-3; I Pet. 1:3; Rev. 1:6.

this difference is implied. Rather, he intends "to attribute them to the Spirit of God."[6] The true appreciation of material, physical, and intellectual blessings is dependent on, and proceeds from, the enjoyment of the life of the Spirit.

The phrase **in heavenly places** is peculiar to this Epistle (1:20; 2:6; 3:10; 6:12). A parallel idea is found in Phil. 3:20, where the apostle asserts, "For our conversation [manner of life] is in heaven." In Ephesians this phrase (*en tois epouraniois;* lit., in the heavenlies) refers to the realm or sphere (1) where the risen Christ sits supreme over every other authority (1:20); (2) where spiritually resurrected believers enjoy fellowship with Christ (2:6); (3) "where principalities and powers see the many-hued wisdom of God exhibited through the church" (3:10)[7]; and (4) where the fully armed Christian wrestles against spiritual wickedness (6:12). Quite obviously, the apostle does not conceive "the heavenlies" to be a celestial order as opposed to an earthly sphere. Rather, he thinks of spiritual dimensions as opposed to the material within the experience of men. As Martin has commented, "It is the realm of spiritual experience—not a physical locality but a region of spiritual realities and experiences."[8] The designation **in heavenly places** is not a misnomer because the inner life of the man in Christ has been invaded by the power of heaven. He possesses eternal life and he is in the kingdom of Heaven. Thus in spirit he is lifted above the earthly, the worldly, and the temporal. Temporally, the Christian is *in* the world, but not *of* the world (cf. John 17:13-16).

2. *In Christ* (1:3*b*)

In the lengthy sentence which follows v. 3 the phrase **in Christ** (*en Christo*) and the related phrases "in him" and "in

[6]Dale, *op. cit.,* p. 28.

[7]F. F. Bruce, *The Epistle to the Ephesians* (New York: Fleming H. Revell Co., 1961), p. 27.

[8]W. G. M. Martin, "The Epistle to the Ephesians"; *The New Bible Commentary,* ed. F. Davidson (Grand Rapids: Wm. B. Eerdmans Publishing Co., 1953), p. 1017. Cf. Francis Beare, "The Epistle to the Ephesians" (Exegesis), *The Interpreter's Bible,* ed. George A. Buttrick, *et al.,* X (New York: Abingdon-Cokesbury, 1953), 634: "in the invisible world, in the sphere of the eternal." Cf. J. Armitage Robinson, *St. Paul's Epistle to the Ephesians* (rev. ed.; London: Macmillan & Co., 1903), p. 21: "The heavenly sphere, then, is the sphere of spiritual activities: that immaterial region . . . which lies behind the world of sense. In it great forces are at work."

whom" appear eleven times—approximately thirty times in the whole Epistle. This phrase is unquestionably the keynote of the letter and, to some degree, of Paul's understanding of the Christian faith.[9]

By Paul's employment of the preposition **in** we are not to assume that he expresses a quasi-physical or metaphysical union with Christ. The relationship between the Christian and his Lord is mystical in nature. The mysticism, however, is not that of the pagan mystery cults, which led their initiates to believe that they were semi-deified by surrendering to their gods. Neither is Paul espousing a form of pantheism, in which the person is fully absorbed into Deity, and so loses his individuality.

A deep consciousness of oneness of spirit and purpose resulting from submission to God's will is more nearly what the apostle intends by the phrase **in Christ.** This is the "union of persons," as suggested by Wahlstrom.[10] Our best human analogy is the sharing of life and becoming dependent upon another, as in the case of a genuine marriage. Here a man and a woman become "one flesh"; that is, live according to a common life pattern. There is no more creative human relationship either physically or spiritually. Likewise, for the Christian man the new life **in Christ** is unexcelled in bringing meaning and hope to life. If there is any mysticism in this relationship, it is that which faith engenders. It comes as a man (1) acknowledges the character and rights of God and (2) responds obediently to the righteous demands and will of God. These are revealed to him in the life, ministry, and death of Christ, the Object of his faith. In this relationship, we contribute trust and obedience while Christ administers grace and peace.

James S. Stewart speaks of the potential enrichment in "the permeation of one personality by another which makes spiritual religion possible. It is this that promotes the mystical union. But seeing that personality as it is in Christ has far greater resources, both of self-impartation and of receptiveness, than it has anywhere on the purely human level, it follows that there can exist between Christians and their Lord a degree of intimacy and unity unparalleled and unique."[11]

[9]Cf. I Cor. 12:2; II Cor. 5:17; Gal. 2:20.

[10]*The New Life in Christ* (Philadelphia: Muhlenberg Press, 1950), pp. 89-95.

[11]*Op. cit.*, p. 166.

B. Salvation Enacted Before Time, 1:4-6

The blessings which accrue to God's people are not accidental; they result from the purposes which were established in the mind and spirit of God **before the foundation of the world** (4).[12] Paul has no intention in employing this phrase other than to state that the choice of God is eternal, "a determination of the Divine Mind before all time."[13] Our salvation is not an afterthought, but the fulfillment of the glorious will of God the Father. Robinson comments, ". . . in eternity it is not new; though in time it appears as new."[14]

This purpose is that of election to a **holy** and blameless life which rests upon predestination to sonship (4-5). The phrase **he hath chosen us** (*exelexato*) is in the middle voice and thus literally should be translated, "He chose us for himself." As Westcott states, Paul wishes to emphasize "the relation of the person to the special purpose of him who chooses. The 'chosen' are regarded not as they stand to others who are not chosen, but as they stand to the counsel of God who works through them."[15]

1. *Election to Salvation* (1:4)

Election is a basic affirmation of the Bible. (*a*) It emphasizes the truth that the initiative in bringing about man's redemption is taken by God and not by man. Jesus expressed it in the words of John 15:16: "You did not choose Me, but I chose you" (NASB). (*b*) The election or choice of God is not arbitrary, so that some are destined to salvation and others to perdition, without regard to the disposition of the individual man. The extension of salvation is to all men, as the Bible abundantly declares (John 3:16; Rom. 10:13). The elect are constituted, not by absolute decree, but by acceptance of the conditions of God's call.

Commenting on this Ephesian phrase, Wesley identifies the **chosen** as "both Jews and Gentiles, whom He foreknew as be-

[12]This is the only occurrence of this expression in Paul's letters, but it appears also in John 17:24; I Pet. 1:20. Cf. similar ideas in Matt. 13:35; Luke 11:50; Heb. 4:3; Rev. 13:8.

[13]S. D. F. Salmond, "Ephesians," *The Expositor's Greek Testament*, ed. W. Robertson Nicoll (London: Hodder and Stoughton, n.d.), III, 249.

[14]*Op. cit.*, p. 26.

[15]*Op. cit.*, p. 8.

lieving in Christ, I Pet. 1:2."[16] While assuming the foreknowledge of God, it must not be deduced that His foreknowledge is causative and that man therefore is without freedom. Implicit in this issue is a paradox, the solution for which is to be found "in Christian experience rather than in intellectual and logical terms."[17] Dale writes: "There is not a touch of speculation in this glorious passage."[18] A man knows at the time of his conversion that he has made "a choice between Christ and not-Christ," but as he reflects more and more on his experience he realizes that "even those very first stirrings in his own heart which led him to choose Christ were the work of the Holy Spirit."[19]

(*c*) Those who respond to the gospel in faith are designated the elect, the chosen, or the *ecclesia* (called-out ones). They are the Church. Martin comments: "This new people, the Christian Church, is not the result of a hasty, temporal expedient, but is a part of God's eternal purpose equally with the people of Israel."[20]

(*d*) **In him** (*en auto*) refers to Christ and means that Christ in His redemptive mission is the sphere in which election is fulfilled and realized. Christ is the provisional realization of the choice of God. R. W. Dale notes, "We are all among the non-elect until we are in Him. But once in Christ we are caught in the currents of the eternal purposes of the Divine love."[21]

(*e*) The ethical purpose of God's choice is **that we should be holy and without blame before him in love. Holy** (*hagios*) expresses the positive experiential purpose of God's choice. More than ceremonial holiness is meant here; that is, more than a mere difference stemming from a divine separation. **Holy** expresses the inner, moral difference which prevails when God's grace is operative in the heart. This fact is abundantly indicated in the second word describing the result of the choice, namely, blameless (*amomos*). This is taken from the sacrificial system

[16]John Wesley, *Explanatory Notes upon the New Testament* (London: Epworth Press, 1950 [reprint], p. 702.

[17]N. H. Snaith, "Choose, Chosen, Elect, Election," *Theological Wordbook of the Bible,* ed. Alan Richardson (London: SCM Press, 1950), p. 44.

[18]Cf. his discussion on this issue, *op. cit.,* pp. 25-33. Also, A. M. Hunter, *Interpreting Paul's Gospel* (London: SCM Press, 1954), pp. 136-38.

[19]Snaith, *op. cit.,* p. 44.

[20]*Op. cit.,* p. 1017.

[21]*Op. cit.,* pp. 31-32.

in which sacrifices were expected to be without blemish (Lev. 1:3, 10). However, *amomos* carries an ethical sense in the New Testament. It is used of the offering of Christ (Heb. 9:14; I Pet. 1:10) and can justifiably be understood in this Ephesian context as referring to Christian living. The man in Christ can be without blemish "not merely by human standards but *before Him* who is Witness of all that a man does, and thinks, and says."[22] **Holy** refers to the inner spiritual quality, whereas **without blame** refers to the outer conduct of the life.

The phrase **in love** has perplexed translators with regard to its position in the text. Is it to be included at the end of v. 4 or added to v. 5? Its position determines whether the reference is to man's love or Gods' love. The KJV relates the phrase to 4, while the RSV and others throw it forward to the next verse: "In love He predestined us to adoption as sons" (NASB). To put the phrase with the emphasis on predestination would certainly do no violence to the general tenor of the passage. However, to do so seems redundant because v. 5 ends with an equivalent idea, "according to the good pleasure of his will." Numerous commentators—among whom are Robinson, Salmond, J. B. Lightfoot, and Foulkes—prefer to keep it with 4. They contend that "it is Paul's usual, if not constant, habit to place *en agape after* the clause it qualifies (Eph. iv. 2, 15, 16; v. 2; Col. ii. 2; I Thess. v. 13)."[23] Robinson thus concludes: "Love is the response for which the divine grace looks; and the proof that it is not bestowed in vain."[24] The phrase defines holiness and blamelessness, which are "the end and object of God's election of us, as having their truth and perfection in the supreme Christian grace of love."[25]

2. *Adoption by God* (1:5)

A second facet of man's redemption is expressed in 5, **Having predestinated us unto adoption of children by Jesus Christ to himself, according to the good pleasure of his will.** The expression **having predestinated** (*proorisas*) literally means "having marked out beforehand." It parallels the idea of election, suggesting once again the fact that God's plan had been decided on

[22]Foulkes, *op. cit.*, p. 47. Cf. Rom. 1:9; II Cor. 4:2; Gal. 1:20; I Thess. 2:5.

[23]Salmond, *op. cit.*, III, 251.

[24]*Op. cit.*, p. 27.

[25]Salmond, *op. cit.*, III, 251.

from eternity. Paul here specifies the means by which it is achieved, namely, **the adoption of children by Jesus Christ.** Men were created for fellowship with God as His sons (Gen. 1:26; Acts 17:28), but sin severed that relationship and rendered man a stranger to the divine household. God therefore determined that **by Jesus Christ** restoration to sonship would be granted to those who accept the Eternal Son.

Adoption (*uiothesia*) is an idea peculiar to the Pauline writings, appearing five times (Rom. 8:15, 23; 9:4; Gal. 4:5; Eph. 1:5). It appears to have been taken from the Roman custom rather than from Jewish practices.[26] Adoption in the sense of legal transference of a child from one family to another had no place in Jewish law, but it was quite possible under Roman jurisprudence, though not without considerable formal ceremony. Westcott notes that *son* (*uios*), which forms part of the word for **adoption,** is to be distinguished from *child* (*teknon*). The former suggests the idea of privilege and not of nature.[27] Our sonship, for Paul, therefore does not rest in the natural relation in which men stand to God as having been created by Him, but in a new relationship through grace actualized in the work of Christ. In this spiritual sense adoption for Paul means the acceptance into the family of those who do not by nature belong to it.[28]

Election and predestination, which result in our adoption as sons and thus provide the basis for holy and blameless living, expose "the superlative majesty of God's grace and glory and wisdom and power."[29] They are according to the good pleasure of His will (cf. 1:9). *Eudokia,* translated in the KJV as **good pleasure,** expresses the idea of goodwill or "kind intention" (NASB). The **will** or wish of God in bringing us to sonship is not due to any merit we possess but arises from "His own pure goodness,

[26]Cf. Barclay's lengthy discussion of this subject, *The Letters to the Galatians and Ephesians* (Philadelphia: The Westminster Press, 1958), pp. 91-92. Cf. D. J. Theron, "Adoption in the Pauline Corpus," *The Evangelical Quarterly,* 28 (1956), pp. 6 ff. The author concludes that Jewish rather than Graeco-Roman practices provide the basis for Paul's idea, perhaps referring to Israel's deliverance from Egyptian bondage.

[27]*Op. cit.,* p. 9.

[28]Cf. Paul's explicit statement of this relationship in Gal. 4:4-7.

[29]F. F. Bruce, *op. cit.,* p. 30.

originating only and wholly in the freedom of his own thoughts and loving counsel."[30]

3. *God's Supreme Purpose* (1:6)

Furthermore, the adoption of men as sons of God leads **to the praise of the glory of his grace** (6). This refrain appears again in 12 and 14. The purpose of man's life is to praise God (Isa. 43:21; Matt. 5:16; I Cor. 4:5) and the hope of the fulfillment of the eternal purpose of God for us provides the basis for it. **Glory** is the splendor which relates to God's character as Redeemer. When God succeeds in adopting a son, the divine **glory** breaks through, and consequently the hearts of men are lifted in **praise.** Westcott comments, "The glory of this grace is the manifestation of its power as men are enabled to perceive it. Each fresh manifestation calls out a fresh acknowledgment of its surpassing excellence."[31]

Grace, classically defined as "the unmerited favor of God,"[32] is qualified by the apostle in the appended clause, **wherein he hath made us accepted in the beloved.** The expression **made us accepted** is expressed by the verb *charitoo,*[33] which is derived from the noun for grace (*charis*). Paul is saying that God has "treated us graciously" or "visited us with grace"[34] in the Beloved. Objectively the verb expresses the notion of bestowal of favor. The context, in which God's gift of salvation is central, supports the RSV translation: "which he freely bestowed upon us." **Beloved** is a recognized Messianic title.[35] Paul indicates that it is "in the gift of the Son that the gift of grace becomes ours."[36] Two points must be clear: (1) the incorporation of the believer *in Christ* is the supreme expression of God's grace;

[30]Salmond, *op. cit.,* III, 252.

[31]*Op. cit.,* p. 10.

[32]For a discerning discussion of **grace,** see N. H. Snaith, "Grace," *Theological Wordbook of the Bible,* ed. Alan Richardson (London: SCM Press, 1950), pp. 100-102.

[33]This is a rare verb. In the NT it is found only here and in Luke 1:28.

[34]Bruce, *op. cit.,* p. 30.

[35]Cf. G. Johnston, "Beloved," *Interpreter's Dictionary of the Bible,* hereafter referred to as IDB (New York: Abingdon Press, 1962), I, 378; also, V. Taylor, *The Names of Jesus* (London: Macmillan and Co., 1954), pp. 159-60.

[36]Salmond, *op. cit.,* p. 253.

(2) there is no way that men may know the redeeming grace of God apart from Christ.

C. Salvation Realized in Time, 1:7-14

For the apostle the eternal purpose of God was and is being fulfilled in mankind's history. Paul explains that what God has done and is now doing corresponds exactly to His will (1:5, 9, 11). This will was not motivated by outside factors; it was formulated out of His love and mercy. It is assumed that sin entered into the ways of created man and thus God actualized His purpose to redeem His creatures through "the beloved." The spiritual prospects of believing men as delineated by the writer in this passage range the entire spectrum of human need—freedom, newness, understanding, acceptance, security, and hope.

1. *Redemption Through Christ's Blood* (1:7*a*)

The key word here is **redemption** (*apolytrosis*). It is a substantive for the verb *apolytroo,* which means in classical Greek "to release on ransom." It was so used in speaking of the "*buying back* a slave or captive, *making* him *free* by payment of a ransom."[37] In the Septuagint (Greek version of the Old Testament), *apolytrosis* is employed only once (Dan. 4:30), and in this instance it refers to Nebuchadnezzar's recovery from madness. The passage there does not include the notion of ransom. The verb *lutroo,* which means "to release on ransom," is employed in the Septuagint to express the deliverance of the people of Israel from bondage in Egypt (Exod. 6:6; 15:13; Deut. 7:8). Once again the idea of ransom is not germane to the expression. These facts have led some scholars to assert that *apolytrosis* is weakened in meaning to the point of simply denoting deliverance without the ransom aspect. While the word carried the general meaning of "deliverance," Paul uses it in a modified sense to mean "deliverance with a price."[38]

Other Pauline passages also emphasize the matter of cost.

[37]William F. Arndt and F. Wilbur Gingrich, *A Greek-English Lexicon of the New Testament* (Chicago: University of Chicago Press, 1957), p. 95.

[38]Cf. Leon Morris, *The Apostolic Preaching of the Cross* (Grand Rapids: Eerdmans Publishing Co., 1955), pp. 37-48; James Denney, "Romans," *The Expositor's Greek Testament,* ed. W. Robertson Nicoll (3rd. ed.; London: Hodder and Stoughton, 1908), II, 610; William Sanday and Arthur C. Headlam, *The Epistle to the Romans* ("The International Critical Commentary," 5th ed.; New York: Charles Scribner's Sons, 1899), p. 86.

Some carry a metaphor from the slave market (I Cor. 6:20; 7:23; I Tim. 2:6), and others bear a metaphor from the sacrificial system (Rom. 3:24; Titus 2:14). Three New Testament verses besides the one under discussion state the price involved. Heb. 9:15 speaks of the death of Christ, whereas Rom. 3:25 and I Pet. 1:19 indicate that it is the blood of Christ. **Through his blood** cannot be construed to mean only "a life liberated"[39] and made available for men. Basically the phrase conveys the fact of an atoning death.[40] Herein lies the "price of immeasurable costliness."

Unregenerate humanity is in spiritual bondage, sold under sin, and there is no freedom from this hopeless captivity apart from Christ. The gospel is the word of deliverance. Christ crushes the despot, sin, and sets the enslaved man free through the purchase price of His own death. He died like the sacrificial victims of the Old Testament for purposes of purification, expiation, and the creation of a new relationship between man and his Maker. His death redeems and thus brings deliverance because it lifts man out of the bondage of his guilt and restores him to the kingdom of God, the true homeland of his soul.

2. *The Forgiveness of Sins* (1:7b-8)

The phrase **forgiveness of sins** is parallel to the previous one, which speaks of our **redemption through his blood.** Experientially, our consciousness of redemption is that of having been forgiven of our sins.

Paul's usual term for forgiveness is *charizomai,* which literally means "show favor" or "give freely." Being closely related to *charis* (grace), this verb expresses the idea of God being "gracious toward us." Vincent Taylor comments that it means "setting aside through love of barriers in the way of fellowship."[41]

It is against the background of *charizomai* that we must view the word **forgiveness** (*aphesis*) in 7. Employed only twice elsewhere by Paul (Rom. 4:7; Col. 1:14), *aphesis* denotes "remission," "letting go," "not exacting payment," or "setting aside." God is the Determiner as to what constitutes sin, and it is God who causes the guilt which man experiences when he sins.

[39]Westcott, C. H. Dodd, Vincent Taylor, P. T. Forsyth.

[40]J. Moffatt, J. Denney, J. Armitage Robinson, Leon Morris.

[41]*Forgiveness and Reconciliation* (London: Macmillan and Co., 1956), p. 6.

In His forgiveness, God graciously ceases to demand of the penitent soul the rightful punishment which sin merits. Furthermore, guilt, the one thing which no man can of himself remove from his life, is swept away miraculously by God's mercy and love. Dale writes, "But when God forgives He actually remits our sin. Our responsibility for it ceases. The guilt of it is no longer ours. That He should be able to give us this release is infinitely more wonderful than that He should be able to kindle the fires of the sun and to control, through age after age, the courses of the stars."[42] This does not mean that God makes light of sin, as if to say, "Oh, never mind; it is of no consequence." That would be immoral. As James S. Stewart rhetorically queries, "Is it making light of it, if every single act of forgiveness has—as Paul and John and the writer of the Hebrews all proclaim—the blood of the Lord upon it?"[43]

Trespasses translates the plural of *paraptoma,* which literally is a "false step" or "deviation," and so "a misdeed." Essentially, **trespasses** indicates that one's life is persistently conducted outside the divinely planned boundaries of life. In forgiveness God does not exact payment for our failures to walk the path which He laid out for us. Rather, He remembers them no more.

The appended phrase, **according to the riches of his grace,**[44] follows most naturally from Paul's concept of forgiveness. What God performs in the believing heart is in conformity with (*kata*) His grace; it is in keeping with what He did at Calvary in Christ when He removed the barriers to free acceptance of His creatures. His grace has resourcefulness and wealth that assuredly encompass our pardon and restoration. Foulkes comments, "And God's giving is not merely out of those *riches* but *according to* their measure."[45]

Abounded (8) is a favorite word of the apostle (II Cor. 9:8; Eph. 3:20). It expresses the overwhelming efficacy of God's giving. Two of the gifts which the believer receives as a consequence of the lavish operation of the divine grace are **wisdom**

[42] *Op. cit.,* p. 63.

[43] *A Faith to Proclaim* (New York: Charles Scribner's Sons, 1953), p. 70. This quotation is taken from one of the profoundest passages on forgiveness to be found in contemporary writing.

[44] Six times in this Epistle, Paul speaks of the riches of God—1:7, 18; 2:4, 7; 3:8, 16.

[45] *Op. cit.,* p. 50; cf. Phil. 4:19.

(*sophia*) and **prudence** (*phronesis*).[46] These gifts are intended to open the eyes of men to God's purpose. Robinson distinguishes between **wisdom** and **prudence** as follows: "Wisdom is the knowledge which sees into the heart of things, which knows them as they really are. Prudence is the understanding which leads to right action."[47] **Wisdom** is thus not to be equated with intelligence or academic acumen. It more nearly approximates our word "insight." **Prudence** might well be translated "wise conduct." Barclay comments, "Christ gives to men the ability to see the great ultimate truths of eternity and to solve the problems of each moment of time."[48]

3. *The Knowledge of His Will* (1:9-10)

These two verses explain what the apostle has declared with regard to God's gifts of wisdom and prudence. **Having made known** might well be translated "in that He made known." It is the knowledge of God's will concerning the goal and purpose of life that makes men wise and prudent. Paul is not speaking of acquired knowledge. This knowledge about which he writes is a "given"; it comes by special illumination from God.

The truth that is revealed is called **the mystery.** Current use of the word "mystery" has nothing to do with Paul's use. By it we mean something strange, puzzling, for which a clue is needed for its unraveling. Paul, on the other hand, employed **mystery** to convey the idea of a hidden secret which had been revealed. Traditionally Christians have defined **the mystery** as "the open secret." Mackay calls it "God's unveiled secret."[49]

[46]Some debate prevails as to whether **in all wisdom and prudence** should modify **abounded** or **having made known.** Westcott, Salmond, KJV, Phillips, Beare favor the former, whereas Goodspeed, RSV, NASB favor the latter. Salmond's discussion (EGT, III, 256-58) is excellent. He concludes that Paul intends to indicate the two gifts of **wisdom** and **prudence** which flow out of God's grace and not necessarily "to define the way in which God made known the 'mystery of His will.' . . . Further, it is the grace of God which is magnified in the paragraph and that not in respect of other qualities in God Himself, but in respect of what it does for us" (p. 257).

[47]*Op. cit.*, p. 30. Note what he has to say regarding Paul's use of wisdom in I Corinthians.

[48]*Op. cit.*, p. 96.

[49]*God's Order: The Ephesian Letter and This Present Time* (New York: The Macmillan Co., 1953), p. 59. Cf. also his discussion of the use of **mystery** current in Paul's day, pp. 59-60.

What is this "open secret"? Paul does not tell us immediately, but as we move along in the Epistle more and more of it is unfolded. The **mystery** was not the gospel *per se;* that is, simply the fact that God wishes to redeem us. Rather it included "God's purpose with respect to its limits and sphere."[50] The clause **according to his good pleasure which he hath purposed in himself** denotes that God's redemptive action was not the result of any external pressure, but was brought about by His own "gracious purpose."[51]

Verse 10 describes the all-inclusive dimension of the **mystery;** namely, God will **gather together in one all things in Christ.** As Bruce says, "This is the grand purpose of God which embraces all lesser aspects of His purpose within itself—the establishment of a new order, a new creation, of which Christ is the acknowledged head."[52] The Greek word for **gather together** (*anakephalaioo*) literally means "to bring to a head." It was used to indicate the addition of a series of numbers, that is, to add up a sum. This verb was also employed in rhetoric to refer to a summary at the end of an essay. Generally it indicated any kind of summarizing or gathering together, even the knotting together of a group of threads or cords.[53] The verb is in the middle voice and thus indicates a reflexive action. Paul seems to be declaring that God proposed to reunite unto himself all things in Christ. The harmony which God originally intended to prevail has been destroyed by sin, but now in Christ Jesus He launches a move to restore it.[54]

The word translated **dispensation** (*oikonomia*) literally means "stewardship" or "administration." Since neither of these words seems to fit the context, other meanings have been suggested, such as "arrangement" and "plan." Apparently Paul intends to speak of the plan of operation for bringing God's purpose to pass. Francis Beare suggests the following translation:

[50]W. G. Blaikie, "Ephesians," *The Pulpit Commentary,* ed. H. D. M. Spence and Joseph S. Exell (London: Funk and Wagnalls Co., 1913), p. 13.

[51]Westcott, *op. cit.,* p. 13.

[52]*Op. cit.,* p. 32.

[53]E. F. Scott, *The Epistle to the Colossians, to Philemon and to the Ephesians* ("Moffatt New Testament Commentary"; New York: Harper and Brothers, n.d.), p. 145.

[54]J. B. Lightfoot, *Notes on the Epistles of St. Paul* (London: The Macmillan Co., 1895), p. 322.

"... **with a** view to giving it [God's purpose] effect."[55] This plan of operation relates to **the fulness of times.** The word **times** in this instance is not *chronos,* which expresses duration in minutes, months, years. Paul here uses *kairos,* which is qualitative or epochal time. "Kairological" time is like that which is expressed in the cliché, "I am having the time of my life," or in the expression, "I have lived for this moment." In salvation history, from creation until the advent of Christ, there had been epochal events in which God worked to prepare men for deliverance. Now that "the full measure of their appointed course, with all their lessons of preparation and discipline,"[56] have been accomplished, God's gracious purpose to unite all things has been revealed in Christ. The times of previous redemptive events, such as the Exodus, are summed up in Christ.

Furthermore, as Perry notes, "The time of Jesus Christ is not merely a fulfillment of prophetic messianic time, and of Exodus time, it is the fulfillment of all times, including the time of creation, for indeed until He came the whole creation was 'groaning in travail together' (Romans 8:22), waiting for the revelation of Jesus Christ."[57] Indeed, a new time has come for Christians in Christ, and they view history with a new understanding. They know that **all things . . . both which are in heaven, and which are on earth** will be brought under God's rulership. Alien and discordant elements will be subjected and harmonized.

4. *An Inheritance* (1:11-12)

Speaking of his own people, the Jews, Paul declares, **We have obtained an inheritance.** The verb *kleroo* means basically to "choose by lot." The idea of "lot," however, disappeared in time and "the thought is essentially that which recurs often in the Old Testament when Israel is spoken of as God's portion."[58] This being the case, a better rendering would be, "We were made a heritage" (NEB, Bruce). The obvious thought is that Israel was the specially chosen portion of God, not for her personal

[55]*Op. cit.,* p. 619.

[56]Westcott, *op. cit.,* p. 13. For an enlightening discussion of *chronos* and *kairos,* cf. Edmund Perry, "The Biblical Viewpoint," *Journal of Bible and Religion,* XXVII (April, 1959), 127-32.

[57]*Op. cit.,* p. 131.

[58]Foulkes, *op. cit.,* p. 54; see Deut. 4:20; 9:29; 32:9-10; Zech. 2:12.

privilege, but for salvation purposes.[59] It was through the old Israel in the old order that the counsel of God was wrought out; so now through the new Israel in the new order the plan of God is being fulfilled. Paul makes it plain that the inheritance was related to Christ, and thus Jews too must come to Christ in order to share this inheritance.

Four aspects of this choice receive brief, yet pointed attention. (1) The heritage of God was not an incidental thing but was predestinated by God himself (11*b*). From all eternity God determined to have a people of His own. (2) "Whatever God has purposed is sure of fulfillment; He is described here as the One 'who worketh all things after the counsel of his will.'"[60] While God does not act capriciously and arbitrarily, He does move effectively toward His goal despite the numerous barriers erected by the sinful actions of men. (3) The choice of Israel as an instrument for God's salvation was to the end that she live **to the praise of his glory** (12*a*; cf. 6, 14). (4) There were some pious Jews of the Old Testament times "who cherished a hope in the Christ of promise and prophecy before the appearance of Christ in history."[61] That Jews are meant is indicated by a more precise translation of the clause **who first trusted in Christ.** The Greek says: "who hoped before in the Christ" (the Messiah).

5. *Sealed with the Holy Spirit* (1:13-14)

In 13 the apostle turns to the Gentiles. In so doing he asserts the unity of Jew and non-Jew in Christ. The Gentile Christians' personal spiritual history occurred in three stages. First, they heard **the word of truth, the gospel of your salvation** (13; cf. Col. 1:5). **Truth** in Paul's thought is equivalent to saving facts. What the Gentiles heard was not a dissertation on man and God.

[59]Cf. Rom. 9:3-5.

[60]Bruce, *op. cit.*, p. 34. Cf. Salmond, *op. cit.*, III, 264, for distinction between **counsel** (*boule*) and **will** (*thelema*). He feels that here *boule* involves the ideas of intelligence and deliberation, while *thelema* would simply be volition. The point is that God does not act arbitrarily, but with reason.

[61]Salmond, *op. cit.*, III, p. 265. He goes on to say, however: "Hence it appears simplest . . . to regard Paul as speaking in this clause specially of those who like himself had once been Jews, who had the Messianic prophecies and looked for the Messiah, and by God's grace had been led to see that in Christ they had found the Messiah" (*ibid.*, p. 266). For the view that Paul has in mind the priority in time of the Jews in receiving Christ, cf. Bruce, *op. cit.*, pp. 34-35.

Rather, they had heard the word that God in Christ Jesus had provided redemption from sin—for them. This was **gospel,** good news.[62] Hearing such truth demands action. One cannot act neutrally with regard to it; we must obey or disobey (Gal. 5:7).

Second, they **believed** in Christ. While the phrase **in whom** (13*d*) must be related to the act of sealing, yet the whole context emphasizes that it is faith in Christ which brought about their salvation. After hearing comes believing. This is more than mere trust; it is obediently responding to the demands of God to repent of one's sins and commit one's life to Him. Note that faith has an object, Christ. As Christians keep Christ in view, there is no such thing as "blind faith." We know what Christ is like, and we trust Him. All of life—both the good experiences and the bad—is lived with Christ in view.

Third, **they were sealed with that holy Spirit of promise** (cf. 4:30; II Cor. 1:22). "The sealing followed the believing, and is not coincident with it."[63] This fact is made clear by the aorist participle, "having believed," which normally signifies action antecedent to that of the main verb. **Sealed** comes from the verb *sphragizo,* which in turn is derived from the noun *sphragis,* meaning "seal," "signet," or "the mark made by a seal" (cf. I Cor. 9:2; Gal. 6:17). In New Testament times letters, contracts, and official papers were first fastened with a blob of warm wax and then the signer pressed his identification into it.

At least two thoughts concerning the ministry of the Spirit in the believer's heart are intended by this metaphor. (1) To be sealed means to be attested, or declared genuine. Wesley says that the sealing seems to imply "a full impression of the image of God on their souls."[64] Such an experience would result in a truly Godlike quality of spirit. (2) To be sealed by the Holy Spirit means to be possessed or owned entirely and unequivocally by the Spirit. Ralph Earle comments, "When a person surrenders himself completely to Christ, to belong wholly to Him and no longer to be his own property, then he is 'sealed' with the Holy Spirit as a sign that he belongs no more to himself, but to God."[65]

[62]Cf. "the gospel of the grace of God" (Acts 20:24); "the gospel of God" (I Thess. 2:9).

[63]John Eadie, *Commentary on the Epistle to the Ephesians* (Grand Rapids: Zondervan Publishing House, n.d.), p. 66.

[64]*Notes,* p. 704.

[65]"Gleanings from the Greek New Testament," *Preacher's Magazine,* XXXVII (August, 1962), 9.

Two additional truths concerning the Holy Spirit are briefly expressed. (1) The Holy Spirit is the **Spirit of promise.** The sweep of biblical history is seen here. It was to Abraham and his seed that the promises were made (Gal. 3:16). But, as Robinson notes, the ultimate purpose of God was that the blessing of Abraham should come upon the Gentiles in their reception of "the promise of the Spirit through faith" (Gal. 3:14).[66] The coming of the Holy Spirit was announced by Ezekiel (36:26 ff., 37:1-14), by Joel (2:28 ff.), and by our Lord (Luke 24:49). On the Day of Pentecost, Peter affirmed that the promised Holy Spirit had come (Acts 2:17, 33, 39). Thus, in the descent and indwelling of the Holy Spirit the purposes of God as related to the ancient promises are fulfilled. R. W. Dale, commenting on Peter's words on the Day of Pentecost (Acts 2:38), reminds us that both remission of sins and the gift of the Holy Spirit come from "the infinite grace of Christ" by faith.[67]

(2) The Holy Spirit is **the earnest of our inheritance** (14).[68] **Earnest** (*arrabon*) is derived from a Semitic root and might be translated "guarantee" (RSV), "advance installment" (Goodspeed), or "pledge" (NASB). The primary emphasis is on our future state of blessedness. The deposit or partial payment is in itself a guarantee that the full amount will be paid later. As Lightfoot observes, "The thing given is related to the things assured—the present to the hereafter—as a part to the whole. It is the same in kind."[69] More specifically, "The actual spiritual life of the Christian is the same in kind as his future glorified life; the kingdom of heaven is a present kingdom; the believer is already seated on the right hand of God. . . . Nevertheless the present gift of the Spirit is only a *small fraction* of the future endowment."[70] A similar idea is expressed in Rom. 8:23, where the Spirit is called "the firstfruits." The Holy Spirit therefore is that active Divine Power which, when we possess Him, brings to our lives the assurance of full deliverance and enjoyment of fellowship with God in the world to come. Being filled with the Spirit is a foretaste of the inexpressible joy and peace into which we shall enter one day.[71]

[66]*Op. cit.*, p. 35.

[67]*Op. cit.*, p. 127.

[68]Only other instances of **earnest** in the NT are II Cor. 1:22; 5:5.

[69]*Op. cit.*, p. 323.

[70]*Ibid.*, p. 324.

[71]Barclay, *op. cit.*, p. 102.

On the phrase **the redemption of the purchased possession,** see comments above on v. 11. The reference is not to our acquisition of the inheritance[72] but to God's possession of His redeemed children.[73] Foulkes comments, "God will take completely from alien hands that which is His own. The object redeemed is God's own 'peculiar people.' "[74]

And so the hymn of grace and salvation closes with the familiar refrain, **unto the praise of his glory** (cf. 6, 12).

[72]E. F. Scott, Goodspeed, Moffatt, RSV.

[73]Westcott, Robinson, Wesley, NASB, *et al.;* cf. Titus 2:14; I Pet. 2:9; see also Exod. 19:5; Mal. 3:17.

[74]*Op. cit.,* p. 57; cf. Westcott's theory that the statement includes all created things, *op. cit.,* pp. 17-18; and Bruce's dual concept of the inheritance as both ours in Christ and God's in us, *op. cit.,* p. 38.

Section III Prayer and Praise for Divine Enlightenment

Ephesians 1:15—2:10

A. The Inspiration for the Prayer, 1:15-16

The apostle now moves quickly from praise to God to prayer for his readers. The occasions for his praises are the spiritual blessings accruing to men, both Jew and Gentile, through the fulfillment of the divine purpose in Christ Jesus. **Wherefore** is the translation of *dia touto,* which refers back to what he has just written and might better be rendered "for this reason" (RSV, cf. Rom. 5:12; II Cor. 4:1). The thought of how greatly God had blessed these believers and Paul himself,[1] as well as the report that the apostle had received concerning their present spiritual state, inspired him to pray for them. Apparently the gospel was bearing fruit among these Gentile Christians, but how much cannot be determined, since the apostle does not express the same degree of thanksgiving for them as he did for other groups which he had not visited before he wrote.[2] Nevertheless, he speaks of their **faith in the Lord Jesus**[3] and their **love unto all the saints.** While many ancient manuscripts omit the phrase **your love,** it is so typically Pauline that no violence is done to the thought by including it.[4] Faith which has

[1]"The connection of the thought is as follows: Just because we Christians are so abundantly blessed and because you also have become partakers of this blessing" (G. Stoeckhardt, *Commentary on St. Paul's Letter to the Ephesians,* translated by Martin S. Sommer [St. Louis: Concordia Publishing House, 1952], p. 100).

[2]Cf. Rom. 1:8; Col. 1:3-9. Some scholars take this verse as indicating that Paul did not establish this church and had never visited it. The expression **after I heard of your faith** certainly strongly favors the view that the Epistle was not written originally for Ephesus; he surely knew the Ephesians personally.

[3]Westcott observes, "The use of *ho kurios Jesous* [the Lord Jesus] is significant. The confession 'kurios Jesous' was the earliest Christian creed: I Cor. xii.3; Rom. x.9." (*op. cit.,* p. 21).

[4]Omitted by Chester Beatty Papyrus (P 46); Codices Sinaiticus, Alexandrinus, Vaticanus; cf., however, Rom. 1:8; II Thess. 1:3; Philem. 5; Col. 1:4-5.

its basis in Christ promotes confidence in one's fellowmen, and thus generates a love which binds Christian men together.

Foulkes among others notes two features of the apostle's prayer life (16). First, it is constant: **I . . . cease not to give thanks.** Paul was practicing what he preached, for he exhorted his converts to "pray without ceasing" (I Thess. 5:17; cf. Rom. 12:12; Eph. 6:18; Col. 4:2). Second, it is accompanied by thanksgiving. Likewise, in several passages in his correspondence with churches, the apostle taught that gratitude should be "the unfailing accompaniment of intercession" (Eph. 5:19 ff.; Phil. 4:6; Col. 3:15-17; 4:2; I Thess. 5:18).[5] Phillips paraphrases, "I thank God continually for you and I never give up praying for you." **Making mention** is rendered "remembering" in RSV, but Beare thinks that it is better to render it "asking." The phrase, according to Beare, seems "to have been extended in usage to include the thought of intercession. Such a sense is required by the following clause . . . which is certainly the object of a request, not the matter of a recollection."[6]

When we recall what Paul has written concerning his soul burden for his churches, we cannot help but exclaim with Bruce: "What an intercessor he must have been."[7] Through the help of the Holy Spirit in intercession, Paul sought a great sense of unity among his youthful churches. It is through mutual intercessory prayer that Christians today can enjoy such unity.

B. The Essence of the Petition, 1:17

When Paul prays, he comes with great confidence because he approaches **the God of our Lord Jesus Christ, the Father of glory.** The first phrase bears a note of assurance because the One to whom Paul offers his petition is "the God whom He [Christ] acknowledges and at the same time reveals."[8] God gave bountifully to His Son; why would He not give generously to all those who are "in Christ"? The second phrase, **the Father**

[5]*Op. cit.*, p. 59.

[6]*Op. cit.*, X, 627; Robinson translates the phrase "interceding" (*op. cit.*, p. 149).

[7]*Op. cit.*, p. 38.

[8]Westcott, *op. cit.*, p. 22; cf. Salmond, *op. cit.*, III, 273, on the question of Christ's deity: "In respect of His mission, His mediation, His official work and relations, He has God as *His* God, whose commission He bears and whose redeeming purpose He is to fulfill."

of glory ("all-glorious Father," NEB), adds to the confidence with which the prayer can be made because God is "the sum and source of all perfections" (cf. Jas. 1:17).[9] Blaikie summarizes, "Being also the 'Father of glory,' and having glorified Jesus, even after his suffering, with the glory which he had with him before the world began, he might well be asked and expected to glorify his people."[10]

The essence of the petition is that God **may give unto you the spirit of wisdom and revelation.** In the Greek the gift is "a spirit," thus not referring specifically to the personal Spirit of God.[11] Robinson says, "With the article [the], very generally, the word indicates the personal Holy Spirit; while without it, some special manifestation or bestowal of the Holy Spirit is signified."[12] Notwithstanding, such a gift of spiritual illumination comes from the Spirit. It is a "capacity of apprehending the revealed—of perceiving the drift and meaning of what God makes known, so that it may be a real revelation to us."[13] This experience cannot be enjoyed apart from Him who is described by Isaiah as "the spirit of wisdom and understanding, the spirit of counsel and might, the spirit of knowledge and of the fear of the Lord" (Isa. 11:2; cf. John 14:26; 16:13). The phrase **in the knowledge of him** (God) designates the substance of the wisdom and revelation. Beare comments that "the sum of knowledge of the Christian believer is the knowledge of God, which always means the knowledge of him *as* God, living and true, and the source of all life and truth—a personal knowledge which involves communion, adoration, and obedience in love."[14] **Knowledge** (*epignosis*) is to be distinguished from *gnosis,* also translated "knowledge." Lightfoot observes, "The compound *epignosis* is an advance upon *gnosis,* denoting a larger and more thorough knowledge."[15] This fuller knowledge is that which

[9]Beare, *op. cit.,* X, 628; note that Jas. 2:1 speaks of "our Lord Jesus Christ of glory," indicating that the Son likewise possesses the glory. Cf. Westcott, *op. cit.,* pp. 187-89, on *he doxa.*

[10]*Op. cit.,* p. 6.

[11]Note that **spirit** is not capitalized in either KJV or the modern translations.

[12]*Op. cit.,* p. 39.

[13]Blaikie, *op. cit.,* p. 6.

[14]*Op. cit.,* X, 628-29.

[15]J. B. Lightfoot, *Notes on the Epistles of St. Paul* (London: Macmillan Co., 1895), p. 138.

results from experiential intimacy. It is more than academic and theoretical knowledge; it is personal.

Dale helps us to relate this request of the apostle to the religious experience of the readers.[16] The fact that they are Christians signifies that they had already received divine illumination. But Paul prays that "the Divine Spirit who dwelt in them would make their vision clearer, keener, stronger, that the Divine power and love and greatness might be revealed to them far more fully."[17] Furthermore, with regard to our conversion, "the great *revelation* was made in Christ."[18] But "when the Spirit of God illuminates the mind, we see the meaning of what Christ said and of what Christ did. We simply find what was in the Christian revelation from the beginning."[19] The Spirit-filled man therefore possesses deep insight into the things of God (I Cor. 2: 10-16).

C. The Rewards of Enlightenment, 1:18-19

The clause **the eyes of your understanding being enlightened** has a parallel meaning to the previous verse regarding the spirit of wisdom and revelation. It is another way of describing the gift, which results in "inward illumination."[20] **Understanding** is *kardia* (heart; cf. RSV, NASB). In Hebrew thought, the heart does not refer to the emotions, but to the will. The heart is "the moral understanding, the essential inward being; it is the sphere of good and evil, of sinful resolve and of repentance, of communion with God and of rejection of God."[21] An intriguing parallel from an extra-biblical writing exposes the apostle's meaning here. In II Esdras 14:19-22, Ezra is pictured as being commissioned to write the Holy Scriptures. He asks the Lord to send the Holy Spirit into him (v. 22). To this petition the Lord replies, "And you shall come here, and I will light in your heart the lamp of understanding, which shall not be put out until what you are about to write is finished."[22] Moral and

[16]*Op. cit.*, pp. 133-42.

[17]*Ibid.*, p. 133.

[18]*Ibid.*, p. 137.

[19]*Ibid.*, p. 142.

[20]Beare, *op. cit.*, X, 629.

[21]*Ibid.*, cf. Ps. 51:10, 17; Matt. 5:8; Rom. 10:10.

[22]*The Apocrypha of the Old Testament,* RSV, ed., Bruce M. Metzger (New York, Oxford University Press, 1965), pp. 56-57.

spiritual comprehension is far more important than mere intellectual clearness. Note the opposite state of "blindness of the heart" in 4:18.

The rewards of this illumination are three: (1) **what is the hope of his calling,** (2) **what** (are) **the riches of the glory of his inheritance in the saints,** and (3) **what is the exceeding greatness of his power to us-ward.** A crescendo of emphasis prevails as Paul exalts God. Here we see **his calling,** which looks back to God's gracious choice of His people in Christ Jesus (v. 4) and looks forward "to the hope of ultimate consummation when God's purpose is achieved in His people and they are glorified with Christ."[23] Next is **his inheritance.** It is **the saints** who constitute God's heritage (cf. 14; Col. 1:12); His own possession, the Church, reflects His "abounding glory" (cf. Rom. 9:23; Eph. 3:16; Col. 1:27). **His power** (*dynamis*) operates now in the believer. This immeasurable greatness is like the **working** (*energeia*) of the strength (*kratos*) of His might (*ischys*)[24] in the resurrection, ascension, and lordship of Christ.

Westcott points out that the three aspects of the prayer correspond with the experiences of life.[25]

"We can face the sorrows and sadnesses of personal and social history 'in the hope of God's calling.' We can rejoice in the possession of capacities and needs to which our present circumstances bring no satisfaction when we look to 'the wealth of the glory of God's inheritance in the saints.' We can overcome the discouragements of constant failures and weaknesses by the remembrance of the power of God shown in the raising of Christ."[26]

D. Evidences of God's Power, 1:20—2:10

In a typical Pauline reaction the thought of God's power revealed in Christ leads to an amazing list of illustrations of this manifestation (20-23). Also, Paul moves on to demonstrate how this power is mediated through Christ to the Christians (2:1-10). In so doing, he temporarily leaves behind the central concern of his prayer as stated in 17-18.

[23]Bruce, *op. cit.*, p. 40.

[24]Cf. difference between these four words, Merrill C. Tenney, *The Reality of the Resurrection* (New York: Harper & Row, 1963), p. 73.

[25]*Op. cit.*, p. 24.

[26]*Ibid.*

1. *The Manifestation in Christ* (1:20-23)

a. His Resurrection (1:20*ab*). The measure of God's life-giving power was expressed **when he raised him** (Christ) **from the dead.** Throughout the New Testament one recurring note regarding Jesus is that He was resurrected by God.[27] Indeed, as some scholars have insisted, the Resurrection is "a true starting-place for the study of the making and the meaning of the New Testament."[28] Bruce reminds us that the death of Christ is the chief demonstration of the love of God (Rom. 5:8), but the Resurrection is the chief demonstration of the power of God.[29] Paul will shortly come to say, The power that raised Jesus is "the power that worketh in us" (3:20). Markus Barth comments, "To the author of Ephesians, to speak of God means to speak of the might and the grace of God; of that God who reveals himself by raising the dead. If we kept silent about the resurrection, we would not be speaking of God."[30]

b. His Exaltation (1:20*c*-22*a*). The infinite and majestic power of God was manifested in Christ's ascension and exaltation. After calling Christ from the grave, God **set him at his own right hand.**[31] The seat at the **right hand** of an Oriental king was always reserved for his prime minister or first officer, symbolizing not only honor and dignity, but delegated power. In Christ's case, it means that He was invested with sovereign lordship and universal dominion. **In the heavenly places** would be in the realms where God is at work. (See comments on v. 3.) Christ had been placed **far above all** (every) **principality, and power, and might, and dominion.** Our Lord is above every created power both friendly and hostile, human and spiritual, that now exercises authority in the world. Christ is enthroned above them all, not only because He created them (Col. 1:16), but because through His humiliation He provided redemption. The clause **and every name that is named** might be paraphrased, "Whatever

[27]Acts 2:24, 32; 3:15; 4:10; 10:40; 13:33-37; 17:31; Rom. 1:4; II Cor. 13:4.

[28]Michael Ramsay, *The Resurrection of Christ* (2nd ed.; London: Geoffrey Bles, 1946), p. 7; cf. also Floyd V. Filson, *Jesus Christ, the Risen Lord* (New York: Abingdon Press, 1956), p. 25.

[29]*Op. cit.*, p. 41.

[30]*The Broken Wall* (London: Collins, 1960), pp. 47-48.

[31]Peter on the Day of Pentecost speaks of the exaltation in connection with the Resurrection (Acts 2:33; cf. also Rom. 8:34; Col. 3:1; Heb. 1:3; 8:1; I Pet. 3:22).

else anyone likes to call them."[32] No name can eclipse His name; neither can any name be given equal glory.

Christ's dominion is not temporal but eternal. Therefore powers **in this world** (this age) and **in that which is to come** cannot and will not overcome His sovereignty.[33]

The corollary to Christ's exaltation is His subordination of all else: God **hath put all things under his feet** (22). These words are taken from Ps. 8:6, which speaks of the glory of man as the crown of creation, possessing dominion over all creatures. As in Heb. 2:6-9, the words are here applied to Christ, the Second Adam, who has broken the deadly power of the Fall. By His redemptive work He has won the sovereignty which is rightfully His as Head of the new creation. In Beare's words, He thus "fulfills the destiny for which man was created."[34] Therefore, as Mackay reminds us, "the course of history and the destiny of the universe are both in the hands of Jesus Christ."[35] Paul's matchless Christological passage in Phil. 2:9-11 uniquely recapitulates the thoughts found in this passage.

c. *His Headship* (1:22*b*-23). The "crown rights" of Christ extend not only to principalities and powers (Col. 2:10), but also to the new community which has been called into existence by His life, death, resurrection, and exaltation. God **gave him to be the head over all things to the church** (22). The phrasing is awkward here, but the apparent intention of the apostle is to say that the Redeemer is given to the Church in the capacity of universal headship and thus is her Head, too.[36] As a Gift from God to the Church, Christ presides over the believing community in all things (5:23; Col. 1:18). The union between Christ and His people likewise affirms that the Church has a mediated authority and power. When the Church obediently and faithfully evangelizes in the name of her Lord, she possesses His rulership in the world (cf. Matt. 28:18-20; Mark 3:14 ff.; John 20:21-23). Herein lies both the confidence and the triumph of the Church.

[32]Beare, *op. cit.*, X, 635; Bruce, *op. cit.*, p. 42—"whatever names they may bear"; Robinson, *op. cit.*, p. 41—"every title or dignity that has been or can be given as a designation of majesty."

[33]Cf. Salmond, *op. cit.*, III, 279, on the Jewish concept of two ages; see also 6:12; I Cor. 15:24 ff.

[34]*Op. cit.*, X, 635.

[35]*Op. cit.*, p. 94.

[36]Salmond, *op. cit.*, III, 281.

Beside the function as Ruler, the headship of Christ conveys the concept of vital unity, expressed in the singularly Pauline phrase **his body** (v. 23; 2:16; 4:4, 12, 16; 5:30; Rom. 12:5; I Cor. 10:17; 12:27; Col. 1:24; 2:19). The "body of Christ" (*soma Christou*) does not connote for Paul a mere society or community as we understand these words. It is rather the community of redeemed persons under the headship of Christ. J. A. T. Robinson observes, "But it is of great importance to see that when Paul took the term soma and applied it to the Church, what it must have conveyed to him and his readers was . . . something *not corporate but corporal*."[37] The apostle does not speak of "a body of Christians," but simply of "the body of Christ."[38] The analogy of the human body therefore emphasizes the character of the Church as an organism. Christians form Christ's body.

Several aspects of this profound definition of the nature of the Church need to be noted. First, identification with the believers is more than what we understand as "membership." It is not so much that we join a company as that we are grafted into Christ (John 15). This view makes possible Paul's long discussion in I Corinthians 12 concerning the body and the members. The essential union of Christ with His people derives from the same divine life flowing through each member and from the obedient functioning of the whole group in service to God. Second, the source of this doctrine of the Church is not Greek, Gnostic, nor basically Old Testament, though there is necessarily a relationship between the old and the new covenants. For the essence of this doctrine, Paul probably goes back to our Lord's words at the Last Supper, "This is my body" (Mark 14:22).[39] The sacramental loaf and the body of the Lord are one: "Since there is one bread [loaf], we who are many are one body; for we all partake of the one bread [loaf]."[40]

The phrase **the fulness of him that filleth all in all** is doubtless one of the most difficult in the Epistle. It can be taken in

[37]*The Body* (Naperville, Ill.: Alec R. Allenson, Inc., 1952), p. 50.

[38]T. W. Manson, "The Church, the Body of Christ," *Journal of Theological Studies*, 37 (1936), p. 385.

[39]A. E. J. Rawlinson, "Corpus Christi," *Mysterium Christi*, ed. G. K. A. Bell and A. Deissmann (London: Longmans, 1930), p. 228. Robinson's and Bruce's attachment of this understanding to Paul's conversion experience (seeing Christ in the Christians) is not convincing.

[40]I Cor. 10:17, NASB.

one of three ways. First, the reference is to God. Christ is **the fulness** (*pleroma*) of God who fills **all in all.** Wesley gives substantially this idea when he comments that the sense is "easy and natural, if we refer it to Christ, *who is the fulness* of the Father."[41] Second, if the word *pleroma* is taken in an active sense, i.e., "that which fills up," the reference would suggest that the Church "completes or fills up" Christ. Origen and Chrysostom supported this view. Calvin remarks, "Until he is united to us the Son of God reckons himself in some measure imperfect." The Church, therefore, is "the complement of the head."[42]

Third, the phrase, taken in a passive sense—"that which is filled"—is intended to indicate that Christ is essential to the full being of the Church. Throughout Paul's writings, he speaks of Christians being "filled" with some grace of Christ or of God (Rom. 15:13 ff.; Eph. 5:18; Phil. 1:11; 4:18; Col. 1:9; 4:12). Most crucial in the argument in favor of this interpretation is Col. 2:9-10, which reads: "For in Him all the fulness of deity dwells in bodily form, and in Him you have been made complete, and He is the head over all rule and authority" (NASB).[43] It would seem that Paul's thought is that "the Church is His body intended to express Him in the world; more than that, the Church is intended to be a full expression of Him by being filled by Him whose purpose it is to fill everything there is."[44] Perhaps a reciprocity must be permitted here, so that while Christians are "being filled" by Christ, on the other hand our Lord himself, in some sense, is "being filled" as the Church lives holily in the world and witnesses to men everywhere and in every age.[45] The Church is the receptacle of divine fullness and at the same time the completion of Christ. Commenting on **fulness** (*pleroma*), Lightfoot writes, "It is that plenitude of Divine graces and virtues which is communicated through Christ

[41]*Op. cit.*, p. 706, cf. W. L. Knox, *St. Paul and the Church of the Gentiles* (New York: Macmillan & Co., 1939), p. 186: "that which is filled by him who is always being filled (by God)."

[42]J. Armitage Robinson, *op. cit.*, pp. 42-45; cf. Col. 1:24; cf. Wm. Barclay, *The Mind of St. Paul* (London: Collins, 1958), pp. 248-50; Martin, NBC, p. 1019.

[43]J. A. T. Robinson, Salmond, E. F. Scott, Moffatt, *et al.*, hold to this interpretation.

[44]Foulkes, *op. cit.*, p. 67.

[45]Cf. Westcott, *op. cit.*, p. 28; Barclay, *The Mind of St. Paul*, p. 250.

to the Church as His body. . . . All the Divine graces which reside in Him are imparted to her; His 'fulness' is communicated to her: and thus she may be said to be His *pleroma*."[46]

2. *The Manifestation in the Salvation of Men* (2:1-10)

Paul backtracks now to pick up the train of thought which was introduced in 1:19, in which he asserts that he prays that they might come to see what is the exceeding greatness of God's power. Christ's resurrection, exaltation, and headship of the Church are manifestations of this power. In 2:1-10 the apostle declares that the spiritual renewal of all men, both Jew and Gentile, is part and parcel of the resurrection of Christ, the supreme manifestation of God's might. This theme is succinctly stated in 5: **Even when we were dead in sins,** (God) **hath quickened us together** ("made us alive together"—RSV) **with Christ.** The section divides itself into two divisions: (*a*) the old life of sin (2:1-3); (*b*) the new life in Christ (2:4-10). The contrast between 2:1-3 and 2:4-10 speaks of the mighty power of God.

a. The Old Life of Sin (2:1-3). Paul distinguishes at least five characteristics of the life which his readers once lived apart from God. First, it was a life of spiritual death; they **were dead in trespasses and sins** (1).[47] Spiritual death is "the death of sin,"[48] which is the state of separation from God created by **trespasses** and **sins.** Witness Adam and Eve (Gen. 3:23)! It should be clearly understood that Paul is not just saying that man apart from God is "subject to death or even under the sentence of death; he is *actually dead,* because under the control of a sinful nature."[49] The twin words **trespasses** (*paraptoma*) and **sins** (*hamartiai*) emphasize the total nature of this death. **Trespasses** alludes "to the desires of the flesh, open, gross, and palpable," while **sins** designates more "the desires of the mind, sins of thought and ideas, of purpose and inclination."[50]

[46] *Colossians and Philemon* (London: Macmillan & Co., 1927 [reprint]), p. 263.

[47] The words **hath he quickened** are in italics, indicating that they do not appear in the Greek text. Actually the sentence beginning with 1 and running through 3 is incomplete. Thus, these words have been added by the translators to complete the sentence. Obviously this is what Paul intended to say.

[48] J. A. Robinson, *op. cit.,* p. 48.

[49] Ralph Earle, "Gleanings from the Greek New Testament," *Preacher's Magazine,* XXXVIII (February, 1963), 17.

[50] Eadie, *op. cit.,* p. 119.

The second characteristic of sinners is that they walk **according to the course of this world** (2). The Greek word for **course** is *aion,* which is literally "age." As employed here, it does not bear a chronological sense, but rather "the spiritual character of the times." These people **walked** (conducted their lives) in conformity to the thoughts and pursuits of this present evil and transitory age (cf. Rom. 12:2; I Cor. 7:31; Gal. 1:4). A sixth-century, Palestinian Syriac fragment uses the word *kanona,* which can be translated "rules or canons of operations." Spiritually dead men have forsaken the rules and ways of God for the rules and ways of this world.

Third, these people **walked . . . according to the prince of the power of the air.** This world has a god, the devil. In II Cor. 4:4, Paul speaks of "the god of this world"; by contrast, in I Tim. 1:17 he praises "the King eternal" or "the King of the Ages." The devil exercises his authority in the realm of **the air.** According to Bruce, this means that "he is the leader of those 'spiritual hosts of wickedness in the heavenly places' of whom we are told in Eph. 6:12."[51] Paul's readers once bowed to the transitory god of this world and thus their rewards were as temporary as their god. But Christ brought them liberation from the devil and his cohorts. The term **spirit** refers back to the powers of evil and suggests that inner disobedient disposition which becomes active in the hearts of men when subjected to the evil one. As Foulkes observes, men are "energized" either by God (20) or by the forces of evil; if by evil, they are "rightly called *the children of* disobedience."[52]

Fourth, they, and Paul, too, once lived **in the lusts of our flesh** (3). At this point Paul is constrained to admit that he, though a Jew, was counted among the "sons of disobedience" before He met Jesus. **In the lusts of the flesh** defines "the domain or element in which their life was once spent."[53] It was kept within the confines of the appetites and impulses proper to fallen human nature or springing from it. These people surrendered to the **lusts** (*epithumia,* cravings) of the **flesh** (*sarx*—human nature under the domination of sin). They were **fulfilling** ("indulging," NASB) **the desire** (*thelema,* "wills") **of the flesh and of the mind.** Two sources of evil are exposed here: (1) the

[51]*Op. cit.,* p. 48.

[52]*Op. cit.,* p. 70; cf. Col. 3:6.

[53]Salmond, *op. cit.,* III, 285.

fallen nature of man in general, and (2) "the laboratory of perverted thoughts, impressions, imaginations, volitions, in particular."[54]

Fifth, these persons without God **were by nature the children of wrath.** In their pre-Christian state, unaided by the Spirit of God, the readers, and also Paul, were **by nature** (innately) committed to sin. A law of sinning controlled them and thus they fell under the wrath of God. The phrase **children of wrath** in this instance does not mean "by our birth as children." The fact that every man of Adam's race is born a sinner was recognized in the phrase **by nature. Children of wrath** here simply means "objects of wrath." As Purkiser emphatically states, the wrath of God is "not a reaction of the divine sensibilities and will which may be changed or altered. It is God's unfailing and unceasing antagonism to sin, which must be so long as God is God."[55]

b. The New Life in Christ (2:4-10). For Paul the plight of mankind is never hopeless. Against the dark background of spiritual death the apostle sketches a captivating characterization of the new life in Christ. Three features of this life are here distinguishable.

First, it is a God-initiated life (4-5). In Christ, God historically broke into humankind's tragic situation, and today He breaks into each repentant man's sinful state to bring salvation. Such is the force of Paul's forceful conjunction: **But God.** He always makes a difference. **Even when we were dead in sins,** His love was acting in our behalf (cf. Rom. 5:6, 8). **Mercy** is God's disposition toward sinful men, but **love** is His motive in all that He does for them. **Mercy** is rich (exhaustless), but **love** is great (indescribable and magnanimous). It is "on account of" and not "through" this great love that God chose us and **quickened us together,** "made us alive together" (5). The word **together** does not appear in the text as a single word, but is expressed by the adding of the prefix *syn* to the verb "to quicken." Paul coined this compound verb, doubtless, to emphasize that salvation is the result of union with Christ (cf. Rom. 6:6, 8; Col. 2:12; II Tim. 2:11). The resurrection of Christ is not

[54] *Ibid.*, III, 286.

[55] "Second Thoughts on 'The Wrath,'" *Seminary Tower,* XIV (Fall, 1958), 3.

only the assurance of spiritual regeneration; it is also the means of regeneration. Dead men are raised from spiritual death in and with the risen Christ, all initiated by the love of God (cf. Rom. 6:11). For the discussion of Paul's spontaneous summary of the gospel, **by grace are ye saved,** see comments on v. 8.

Second, the new life in Christ is resurrection life (6-7). As Christians, both Jews and Gentiles, we share not only the resurrection of Christ, but also His exaltation. God **hath raised us up together** (*synegeiro*), **and made us sit together** (*synkathizo*). These verbs are in the aorist tense and express punctiliar and completed action. As Bruce says, ". . . believers are viewed as being already seated there with Christ, by the act and in the purpose of God. Temporally, indeed, we live on earth so long as we remain in this body; but 'in Christ' we are seated with Christ where He is."[56] That is the meaning of **in heavenly places** (see comments on 1:3). The Christian, having been lifted "from the deepest hell to heaven itself" (Calvin), enjoys life and citizenship in heaven (cf. Phil. 3:20). The purpose of this resurrected and exalted life of the new man is **that in the ages to come he might shew the exceeding riches of his grace in his kindness toward us through Christ Jesus** (7). "In the limitless future, as age succeeds age,"[57] spiritually resurrected men will display God's grace. Note the repetition of the praise theme of 1:6, 12, 14.

Third, life in Christ is given to us (8-10). Expanding on the parenthesis of v. 5, Paul presents "one of the great evangelical summaries of the New Testament." **For by grace are ye saved through faith; and that not of yourselves: it is the gift of God** (8). The second part of this verse parallels the first. Our salvation from the bondage of sin, springing out of the grace of God and appropriated through faith, is **the gift of God** (cf. 1:7). Thus, we do not earn by good works (the essence of legalistic religion) the right to deliverance from sin and death. Never![58] Grace means that it all begins and ends with God. Salvation is thus a gift from our Creator. Verse 10 emphasizes this fact: **For we are his workmanship, created in Christ Jesus.** Simpson comments, "We have undone ourselves, but in Him resides our

[56]*Op. cit.*, p. 50.

[57]*Ibid.*, p. 51.

[58]Cf. Rom. 4:5; 11:6.

help. The Creator mends His spoiled *chef d'oeuvre* with his own hands, nor will he 'split the praise of grace.' "[59]

While grace is the origin or source of our salvation, faith is the means or instrument. The demonstrative pronoun **that** in 8 is not to be taken as referring to faith as the gift of God. As Wesley and others suggest, the reference is "to the whole preceding clause, **ye are saved through faith.**"[60] It is salvation itself that is **the gift of God.** Faith raises no claims, lest it too be called a "merit" or "work." If such prevailed, the believing man would have the right to boast or glory in self (cf. Rom. 4:2). Faith is the free, obedient response of man to the divine overtures of salvation. But when faith operates and the sinner possesses the joy of new life, the spontaneous declaration is, "It is all of God!"

Paul reminds us, however, that **works** have a place in God's salvation. When grace operates through faith, a new man is created **unto good works** (10), as God had originally intended. **Good works,** which are in keeping with those elements of the law of God that are retained in Christ, follow the experience of faith. And to the man of faith these **good works** are not human works, but God's works inspired by the ministry of the Spirit in his life. Hence the new life in Christ is a manifestation of the mighty power of God!

[59]E. K. Simpson and F. F. Bruce, *Commentary on the Epistles to the Ephesians and Colossians,* ("New International Commentary on the New Testament," Grand Rapids: Wm. B. Eerdmans Publishing Co., 1957), p. 54. Cf. W. T. Whitely, *The Doctrine of Grace* (New York: Macmillan Co., 1931), pp. 43-44.

[60]Wesley, *op. cit.*, p. 707.

Section IV *Spiritual Unity of Mankind in Christ*

Ephesians 2:11-22

In the second half of chapter two the apostle returns to the experience of his readers as heathen who have been brought into the Christian community. He so frequently involves himself in any discussion of the work of Christ that he becomes identified with the people to whom he writes, as in 2:10. After such a digression Paul here takes up his thoughts which he dropped at the end of v. 2. He reminds his readers of their Christless, hopeless past and of their unity with the people of God now. They have been brought into a Christian fellowship along with Jewish believers. Now out of their Christ-inspired relationships there is being erected an edifice for the indwelling of God's Spirit.

A. Former Alienation from Christ, 2:11-12

Wherefore remember (11) is not a casual appeal on the part of the writer; it involves the very reason why Paul is so greatly concerned that the Church be a united society. It calls to mind what Mackay designates as the Sacred Rift,[1] which existed historically between the Jews and the Gentiles. The Jews were descendants of Abraham and the sign of their acceptance as covenant people was the rite of circumcision. The uncovenanted Gentiles, on the other hand, were despised by the Jews and contemptuously nicknamed the **Uncircumcision.** Instead of the Jews fulfilling their mission to the nations by sharing their knowledge of God, they practiced a hate-breeding and grace-denying separation (cf. Gen. 12:3; Isa. 42:1, 6; 49:6).[2] Paul declares that **circumcision in the flesh** does not necessarily assure circumcision of the heart (cf. Phil. 3:3). He wants his readers to remember the change in their relationship to God which has come about through Christ. Grace has closed the chasm, and what had been God's plan of unity for all men originally is now

[1]*Op. cit.*, p. 40.

[2]Cf. Barclay, *Ephesians*, p. 125, on the contempt of the Jews for the Gentiles.

being realized. Note that **flesh** here means the physical body. In v. 3 it referred to the fallen human nature (see comments there).

Speaking more specifically concerning the Gentile alienation, the apostle enumerates the spiritual tragedies involved in it. First, these people **were without Christ** (12; "separate from Christ," NASB). Before they heard and responded to the word of grace, they had "no part or parcel in the Messianic people,"[3] which means that they possessed no hope of the Messiah or any of the benefits that went with it.[4] Their history was Christless. No greater tragedy can befall a people. Second, they existed as **aliens from the commonwealth of Israel.** The alienation is expressed here by *apallotrioustha*i, which means essentially "excluded from" (cf. NASB) and not simply a lapse from a former attachment. **Commonwealth** (*politeia*) has two senses: (1) state or nation, and (2) citizenship or the rights of a citizen. The first meaning is in keeping with the national exclusiveness of the Jews. The Gentiles were outside the community of God's people except for a few proselytes, and even among proselytes the feeling of being an outsider was not wholly removed.

In our day, the alienation has taken a different form; indeed, it has been reversed and the Christian tends to reject the Jew. We forget the indebtedness of Christians to the Jews for the preservation through the centuries of the promises which have now been fulfilled in Christ. But instead this service to the world ought to arouse in us a love for the Jews. It should lead us to every possible effort to remove the Jewish barrier of rejection of Christ.

Third, they **were strangers from the covenants of promise.** Israel was a covenant community. These covenants were made with Abraham (Gen. 12:2-3; 15:8-21; 17:1-21), with the people under Moses (Exod. 24:1-11), and later were declared to be replaced with that which is "new" (Jer. 31:31-34). They provided the very basis of Israel's existence. God's covenants held promises of blessing if His people faithfully obeyed the terms which He set down. The greatest blessing was the assurance of deliverance through God's Messiah. Because the Gentiles were outside the commonwealth, they were **strangers** (*xenoi*, for-

[3]Bruce, *op. cit.*, p. 53; cf. Rom. 9:5.

[4]Foulkes, *op. cit.*, p. 79.

eigners) or nonparticipants in "the privileges, present or prospective, which were pledged to Israel."[5]

Fourth, as a consequence, these people possessed **no hope** and were **without God.** The moral and spiritual desolation of such Gentiles was therefore complete. They had no hope of "the final triumph of the Divine righteousness and love; for them the final issues of the history of the world were dark, troubled, uncertain; their golden age was in the past and was irrevocably lost, while the golden age of the Jewish people was in the future."[6] Someone has observed that we need an infinite hope, which faith in God alone can give. Westcott notes the pathos of the strange combination of **without God** (*atheoi,* atheists) and **no hope.**[7] They faced nature and life without hope because they had no relationship with the Interpreter of nature and life. Westcott goes on to say that "the Gentiles had, indeed, 'gods many and lords many,' and one God as 'a first Cause' in philosophic theories, but no God loving men and Whom men could love."[8]

B. Reconciliation of Gentiles and Jews, 2:13-18

1. *Nearness Through the Blood of Christ* (2:13)

Once again we come upon one of Paul's dramatic transitions (cf. v. 4). The past of the Gentiles was desolate and forboding, **but now in Christ Jesus** all is changed! The writer's terminology and thought seem to come out of Isa. 57:19: "Peace, peace, to the far and to the near, says the Lord" (RSV; cf. v. 17). The "near" people, in this case, were the Hebrews and the **far off** people were the Gentiles. **Sometimes** means "once." These distant ones, who did not have the hope of the covenants nor the joy of God's presence, are now brought within range of the grace and redemptive power of God. This was accomplished **by the blood of Christ** when He gave "His life, willingly yielded up in death as a sin-offering on behalf of 'the many' (Isa. 53:11-12)."[9] Thus both Jew and Gentile can be brought nearer to God and, as a result, nearer to one another by the sacrifice of Christ. In Christ the great barriers are removed from the life of mankind.

[5]Cf. G. E. Mendenhall "covenant," IDB, I, 714-23.

[6]Dale, *op. cit.,* pp. 206-7.

[7]*Op. cit.,* p. 36; cf. Paul's description of Gentiles in Rom. 1:18 ff.

[8]*Ibid.*

[9]Bruce, *op. cit.,* p. 54; cf. 1:7.

2. *Enmity Abolished Through Peace* (2:14-15)

a. The Broken Wall (2:14). Robinson observes that the apostle takes a third word from the Isaiah verse mentioned above (57:19). Besides "near" and "far," he employs "peace."[10] **For he** (Christ) **is our peace** (14). He not only purchased peace through His passion; He is in himself the very essence of peace. Indeed, He is the righteous, sacrificing Prince of Peace (Isa. 9:6 ff.; Luke 2:14). Thus, as Barth has written, "to confess Jesus Christ is to affirm the abolition and end of division and hostility, the end of separation and segregation, the end of enmity and contempt, and the end of every sort of ghetto!"[11] He **hath made both one** in reality means that He has united *everyone,* for Jew and Gentile comprise all the races of men.

One of the actions of Christ as Peacemaker is that He **hath broken down the middle wall of partition.** To what is the apostle referring? Barth lists four possibilities. (1) The allusion is to the wall between the outer and inner courts of the Temple in Jerusalem which separated the Gentile visitors and the Jewish worshipers (see Chart *A*). This five-foot barrier represented the spiritual division between the Jew and the Gentile. (2) The wall or curtain which hung between the holy place and the holy of holies, symbolizing the separation between God and man (see Chart *A*). Christ's death, of course, rent this curtain in twain (Mark 15:38). (3) The wall might refer to "a function which the Law had assumed after it was 'fenced in,' as the rabbis used to say, by man-made statutes and ordinances." The development of a religion of legalism on the basis of the Holy Torah resulted in making the Law a divisive institution (cf. Rom. 3:31; 7:12; Gal. 3:23 ff.; Col. 2:22 ff.). (4) By the wall Paul might mean "the barrier between God and man, and between man and man, which consists of angels and other principalities and powers, such as are enumerated in Eph. 1:21."[12]

Many commentators hold that **the middle wall of partition** is a metaphor of the division between Jew and Gentile, and the wall of the Temple provided the suggestion.[13] This position is supported by v. 15. Quite obviously the real cause of division

[10] *Op. cit.,* p. 58.

[11] *Op. cit.,* p. 37.

[12] *Op. cit.,* pp. 33-36.

[13] Bruce, Martin (NBC), Wesley, Barclay, J. A. Robinson, *et al.* See Paul's experience in Acts 21:29 ff.

is the "legalized" religion of the Jews. Whatever our theory regarding the meaning of this Pauline term, the gospel truth is clear. Translated into more modern terms, "Jesus Christ has to do [is concerned] with whatever divisions exist between races and nations, between science and morals, natural and legislated laws, primitive and progressive people, outsiders and insiders."[14] Christ has broken down every barrier of the spirit between men.

b. The Abolished Law of Commandments (2:15). The whole system of legal observances constituted a barrier between the Jew and the Gentile. Practices, such as circumcision, special preparation of foods, and preoccupation with ceremonial "cleanness," naturally created and perpetuated a state of animosity between these two groups. This was especially true when the Jews tended to be religiously proud because of their faithful adherence to these laws. The phrase **having abolished** (*katargesas*) has the meaning of "nullifying" or "making invalid." It refers primarily to **the law**, but thus also indirectly to the **enmity**. The whole clause should be taken as follows: "The enmity is removed by the nullifying of the law which occasioned it."[15] **Ordinances** carries with it the notion of "dogmas" or "regulations" and thereby introduces the issue of legalistic religion. Men are always separated and never united when religious hope is presented as residing in acceptance with God through meritorious works. Christ **in his flesh**, that is, in His incarnation, ministry, death, and resurrection, wiped out all such dividing elements between men. Foulkes observes: "The way of approach is now by grace, by a new creative work of God, the same for both Jews and Gentiles."[16]

The second portion of 15 asserts again the purpose of the coming of Christ: "that in Himself He might make the two into one new man, thus establishing peace" (NASB). The Second Adam by His own involvement in the whole of man's life fathered a new humanity. This new creation is **in himself**—in vital union with Jesus Christ. Blaikie reminds us of the extent of the newness: ". . . the Gentile is not turned into a Jew, nor the Jew into a Gentile, but both into one new man, thus removing all grounds of jealousy."[17]

[14]Barth, *op. cit.*, p. 37.
[15]Beare, *op. cit.*, X, 656; cf. Col. 2:14.
[16]*Op. cit.*, p. 83.
[17]*Op. cit.*, p. 64.

3. *Reconciliation of Both to God* (2:16-18).

Paul makes it clear in 16 that the removal of the breach between the two great divisions of mankind results from the reconciliation of both Jew and Gentile to God. **By the cross,** that is, by the atoning work of Christ (cf. 13), God was enabled to forgive the sins of both Jews and Gentiles, thus effecting a new relationship between himself and all mankind. The word for **reconcile** is *apokatallasso* and means literally "to exchange completely." The experience of reconciliation, a predominantly Pauline idea (cf. II Cor. 5:18-20; Col. 1:20), is that of exchanging one set of relationships for another set. Because of sin Paul's readers were once "at odds" with God and with their fellowmen. They were alienated from God, but now they are reconciled to Him, living in harmony with divine purposes and laws. A restoration of fellowship with God has been effected by grace. In such an experience there necessarily is brought about **one body,** which is Christ's Church. By analogy, just as angles equal to a third angle are equal to each other, so men reconciled to God are reconciled to each other. One living organism, in which members of diverse backgrounds and abilities are united, was the object of Christ's work at Calvary. His death, therefore, was verily the "putting to death" of the enmity.

In the statement that Christ **came and preached peace** (17; cf. 1:13; Isa. 57:19), Paul is speaking of the work of the risen Christ in announcing the peace which His death made possible. Westcott observes: "At His first appearance among the disciples He gave a twofold greeting of 'Peace.' "[18] The message of the Church, which is a reiteration of Christ's proclamation, is "the gospel of peace."

In 2:13-18 we see "Christ's Ministry of Peace." (1) Christ is our Peace, 14; (2) Christ makes peace through His death, 15; (3) Christ in His ministry in the Church proclaims peace, 17.

A positive result obtains because of Christ's work. **Through him,** both Jew and Gentile **have access . . . unto the Father** (18). The word **access** (*prosagoge*) can sometimes be translated "introduction." In Oriental times, the individual who introduced persons to a king was called a *prosagoges.* But Christ is more than an Introducer; He is actually the Way to God (cf. John

[18] *Op. cit.,* p. 39; cf. also J. A. Robinson, *op. cit.,* p. 66; cf. John 14:27; 16:33; 20:19-23.

14:6). He has provided therefore the privilege of admission to God's presence. The writer to the Hebrews reminds us that we ought to "come boldly unto the throne of grace" (Heb. 4:16). Beare comments: "Christ brings us into the throne room of the King of Kings; and causes us to know him in the fullness of his glory as the Father."[19] Paul's Trinitarian views come to the surface here. Any understanding of these truths must relate to the facts of Christian experience and worship. In His work on the Cross, Christ breaks open the way to the **Father,** who receives repentant sinners. The Holy **Spirit,** who is the Spirit of Christ, indwells, energizes, and sustains the body of Christ. The reconciled relationship with God is thus maintained. (See comments on 4:4.)

C. Metaphors of Unity, 2:19-22

The apostle here returns to the status of the Gentiles and repeats in the language of 12 that through Christ they are **no more strangers** (*xenoi*)—"foreign visitors with no rights in the community"—**and foreigners** (*paroikoi*)—"aliens enjoying temporary and limited rights as residents."[20] Their relationship to God now as the redeemed of the Lord is not one whit inferior to that of the Jews. Paul employs three figures by which to express the grand unity which prevails in the fellowship of Jewish and Gentile believers.

1. *"Citizens with the Saints"* (19*a*)

In this metaphor, taken from city life, the apostle assures the Gentiles that "their names are engraven on the same civic roll with all whom 'the Lord shall count when he reckoneth up the people.' "[21] The Jews were at one time **the saints,** citizens of the city of God, and the Gentiles were outsiders. This is no longer the situation. The Gentile believers form part of the new Israel (Gal. 6:16), which is composed of all Christians. They share all the rights and privileges of this new people.

2. *"The Household of God"* (19*b*)

This second metaphor, taken from family life, suggests a more intimate relationship. Gentiles are now "God's house-

[19]*Op. cit.,* X, 659.
[20]*Ibid.,* p. 660.
[21]Blaikie, *op. cit.,* p. 67.

mates, full members of His family, on the same basis as the natural children of Abraham who have entered into God's family by 'like precious faith.' "[22] The relationship with believing Jews can be characterized only by words like "kinsmen," "brothers," and "fellow saints." Miraculously and graciously, the Gentiles have been bound in love to the believing Jews.

3. *"An Holy Temple in the Lord"* (20-22).

The use of the word **household** (*oikeioi*) in 19 apparently led to this characterization of the Church. *Oikeioi* is derived from the word meaning house in the sense of dwelling place. Robinson comments, "They are not merely members of the household, but actually a part of the house of God."[23] The Church is **an holy temple** under construction, and is **an habitation of God through the Spirit** (22).

Four aspects of the metaphor are spelled out in these verses. First, **the apostles and prophets** are the foundation stones of the temple (20*a*), having this designation because their function is to proclaim the Word of the Lord. Wesley observes that "the word of God, declared by the apostles and prophets, sustains the faith of all believers."[24] Some scholars see a contradiction in Paul's thought here with his use of this metaphor in I Cor. 3:11. There it is said that Christ is the Foundation. The problem is resolved when we see that he employs the metaphor in different senses. In the Corinthian passage the thought revolves around himself and others as builders. In the relationship here it is clear that Christ is the Foundation on which they build. Paul is emphasizing the various stones used in the building. In this relationship Christ is the **corner stone.** All others are of less significance. However, even though of lesser importance, the apostles, and other ministers in the Church, are foundation stones in God's building.

Second, Christ is the **chief corner stone** of the temple (20*b*-21). The word **chief** should probably not appear here. The lexicons agree that the Greek word means simply "cornerstone." The history of this thought goes back to Christ himself (Mark 12:10). He lifted it from Ps. 118:22, which reads: "The very stone which the builders rejected has become the head of the

[22]Bruce, *op. cit.*, pp. 56-57.

[23]J. A. Robinson, *op. cit.*, p. 67.

[24]*Op. cit.*, p. 709.

corner" (RSV).[25] Two views prevail as to the precise place of this stone in an ancient structure. (1) It was the stone set in the foundation at a corner, not only to bind it together, but to establish the line for the walls.[26] This view is in keeping with I Pet. 2:7 and supports the idea that Christ is the One on whom the building depends. (2) It was the stone placed at "the summit of the edifice as its crown and completion."[27] Bruce seems to favor this interpretation. He writes: "The cornerstone is cut out beforehand, and not only bonds the structure together when at last it is dropped into place, but serves as a 'stone of testing' to show whether the building has been carried out to the architect's specifications."[28] Whichever interpretation is accepted, the intention of the apostle is to affirm that Christ controls the shape and the form of the Church.

Third, the believers in Christ are the living stones which when **fitly framed together groweth unto an holy temple.** Early manuscripts differ as to a phrase here. Some have *pasa he oikodome,* **all the building**; others have *pasa oikodome,* "every building." The second rendering suggests to some commentators a complex of buildings, and thus Paul speaks of the erection of additional edifices related to the main sanctuary. On the other hand, it is more probable that Paul was concerned to show that the Church is still in the process of erection. Thus he employs the metaphor of growth. Mackay comments: "New living stones must continue to be added to the incompleted building, and those there already, and those still to be laid in the sacred structure, must 'grow into an holy temple in the Lord.'"[29] This growth, however, takes place and will result in beauty only as the new members "by the quality of their discipleship in adhering closely to their Lord, contribute to the unity, strength and completeness of the Church."[30]

[25]Cf. Acts 4:11; I Pet. 2:7.

[26]Foulkes, *op. cit.,* p. 87; Salmond, *op. cit.,* III, 300. J. H. Thayer makes this observation: "For as the corner stone holds together two walls, so Christ joins together as Christians, into one body dedicated to God, those who were formerly Jews and Gentiles" (*A Greek-English Lexicon of the New Testament* [New York: American Book Co., 1889], p. 24).

[27]Beare, *op. cit.,* X, 661.

[28]*Op. cit.,* p. 57.

[29]*Op. cit.,* p. 131.

[30]*Ibid.*

Fourth, the temple, into which Gentiles are builded, is **an habitation of God** (22). Under the old order, Tabernacle and Temple existed only to provide a place for the Holy One of Israel.[31] But Paul wrote to the Corinthians: "Know ye not that ye are the temple of God, and that the Spirit of God dwelleth in you?" (I Cor. 3:16) Under the new covenant, God not only calls a people, but He abides with them. Thus, as Mackay affirms: "The Christian Church, when it is truly the Church, is the Home of the Presence."[32]

In 4-22 we see "The Church, God's Habitation." The unity of the Invisible Church is the background theme. (1) The foundation of the Church, 20; (2) The construction of the Church: all-inclusive, 11-19; exclusive, 4-11; symmetrical in design—**fitly framed together**; growing to completion—**groweth into an holy temple in the Lord,** 21; (3) "In Christ" the Church is **the habitation of God through the Spirit,** 22 (G. B. Williamson).

[31]Cf. Solomon's prayer in II Chron. 6:12—7:3.

[32]*Op. cit.*, p. 132. For additional discussion of these metaphors, see Paul S. Minear, *Images of the Church in the New Testament* (Philadelphia: Westminster Press, 1960).

Section V *Prayer for Spiritual Fulfillment*

Ephesians 3:1-21

Boldly and summarily, the apostle has declared the potential unity of mankind through God's work in Christ Jesus. Jews and Gentiles can become one people in the Christian Church, the temple of God, through the Holy Spirit. Paul intends now to offer a prayer for his readers that they might be inwardly strengthened and might enjoy the highest possibilities of the new life in Christ. However, he is interrupted by the thought of the mystery of the call of the Gentiles and his ministry to them (1-13).

For this cause (1, 14) obviously refers back to the preceding description of God's gracious incorporation of the Gentiles in the plan of redemption. Between these twin phrases is the extended parenthesis on the mystery of the gospel. Logically this passage is a digression, but it has high value, for it enlarges upon the central theme of the Epistle—God's purpose was and is to unite all things in Christ (1:9-10). Paul's mission in the world is also set forth here. To him has been entrusted the task of bringing **all men to see what is the fellowship of the mystery, which from the beginning of the world hath been hid in God** (3:9).

A. Paul's Stewardship of the Mystery, 3:1-13

1. *The Revelation of the Mystery* (3:1-6)

In a direct and unapologetic manner Paul calls attention to his current situation as **the prisoner of Jesus Christ for you Gentiles** (1; cf. 4:1; II Tim. 1:8; Philem. 1, 9). This brief note involves three things: (1) The article **the** before **prisoner** is not intended to elevate Paul above others who are suffering for the Lord, but rather to state the class of men to which he now belongs. (2) The originating cause of his prisonership is Christ.[1] (3) The phrase **for you Gentiles** (lit., in behalf of you Gentiles) possibly is a subtle reminder that it was the animosity of the

[1]Cf. Salmond, *op. cit.*, III, 302.

Jews to his Gentile mission which caused his imprisonment (Acts 21—26). The phrase more probably means that the Gentiles' spiritual life is somehow benefited because he is not free. In 13 he states poignantly that his tribulations are their glory.

Verses 2-6 enlarge upon Paul's commission to serve the Gentiles. First, he reminds them **of the dispensation of the grace of God** which was given to him in their behalf (2). The word **dispensation** (*oikonomia*) can refer either to his office or to the act of God in bestowing the office. NEB translates thus: "Surely you have heard how God has assigned the gift of his grace to me for your benefit." Apostleship is sometimes called a grace (*charis*).[2] Hodge comments, "Paul esteemed the office of a messenger of Christ as a manifestation of the undeserved kindness of God towards him, and he always speaks of it with gratitude and humility."[3] The emphasis falls upon the fact that God "dispensed the grace" to Paul. Perhaps the ideas of responsibility and grace coalesce here. Or to put it another way, "Stewardship and grace are virtually equivalent."[4] As Hodge notes, "His office and the grace therewith connected . . . were both an *oikonomia* and a *charis*."[5] In the work of the Lord, ministerial responsibility with inward grace spells triumph for the church.

Second, the mode of Paul's divine appointment was **by revelation** (3). Following the general views expressed in Gal. 1:12, the apostle asserts that a divine communication informed him of the glorious truth of the universality of the gospel. Just as the twelve apostles possessed knowledge of God's gracious purpose that was not founded on hearsay, he also had been instructed directly by God (cf. I Cor. 15:8; Gal. 1:15-17).

Third, the message which Paul is commissioned to declare is **the mystery of Christ** (4-6; cf. Col. 4:3 and comments on 1:9). The clause **as I wrote afore in few words** (3) might have reference to some extinct Pauline letter, but it seems more reasonable to construe it as a reference back to 1:9 ff., and 2:19 ff. Paul assumes that because of his former assertion his readers will understand that he is thoroughly informed in the mystery of Christ as he now makes it clearer to them. Phillips renders v. 4,

[2]Cf. Rom. 12:3; 15:15; I Cor. 3:10; Gal. 2:9.

[3]*A Commentary on the Epistle to the Ephesians* (Grand Rapids: Wm. B. Eerdmans Publishing Co., 1950), p. 159.

[4]Beare, *op. cit.*, X, 665.

[5]*Op. cit.*, pp. 159-60; cf. Col. 1:25.

"What I have written briefly of this above will explain to you my knowledge of the mystery of Christ."

The apostle says that **the mystery** (paradoxically, the open secret) **in other ages was not made known unto the sons of men, but is now revealed** (5). Paul wrote substantially the same truth in Col. 1:26—"Even the mystery which hath been hid from ages and from generations, but now is made manifest to his saints." What was it that was concealed from previous generations? Certainly it was not the salvation of the Gentiles, for there is much in the Old Testament concerning their redemption. As early as the promise to Abraham in Gen. 12:3, the divine intention to save (bless) all men, both Jews and Gentiles, was disclosed. Speaking of the Suffering Servant, Isaiah declared in the eighth century B.C.: "I will also give thee for a light to the Gentiles, that thou mayest be my salvation unto the end of the earth" (Isa. 49:6). Bruce notes that "in Rom. 15:9-12 Paul quotes a string of passages from all three divisions of the Old Testament (the Law, the Prophets and the Writings) in which he finds foreshadowings of the result of his own apostolic ministry among the Gentiles."[6] **The mystery** hitherto unknown was that Gentiles should be joined with Jews in one body, that there should be created "one new man" (2:15), "by the incorporation of Jewish and Gentile believers alike, on the common ground of divine grace, as fellowmembers of the body of Christ . . ."[7] Foulkes takes the **as** in 5 to be "in such measure as" or "with such clarity as" now.[8]

The divine purpose, which was "there in the treasury of the heavenly secrets from eternity,"[9] has now been disclosed to **his holy apostles and prophets.** These men, set apart or "consecrated" (*hagiois*) by God for the reception and declaration of this mystery, were the Twelve (cf. 2:20). But, in a peculiar way, Paul felt the impact of this message and thus became known as "the apostle to the Gentiles." Indeed, the proclamation of this mystery was specially committed to him. Acts 9:15 states: "But the Lord said unto him [Ananias], Go thy way: for he [Saul] is a chosen vessel unto me, to bear my name before the Gentiles,

[6] *Op. cit.*, p. 61.

[7] *Ibid.*

[8] *Op. cit.*, pp. 93-94.

[9] J. A. Robinson, *op. cit.*, p. 77.

and kings, and the children of Israel." **By the Spirit** recalls Jesus' words in John 14: 26; 16: 13.

The apostle now summarizes (6) in a threefold manner "the mystery of Christ," employing three words which are very difficult to translate. Paul was fond of compound words. In this verse he uses three with the prefix *syn,* meaning "together with": *synkleronoma, synsoma,* and *synmetocha.* These emphasize the concept of unity or community.[10] The "open secret" asserts that, first of all, the Gentiles are **fellowheirs** with the Jews; that is to say, they share the same spiritual inheritance. That legacy includes all the benefits of the covenant of grace, which Hodge delineates as "the knowledge of the truth, all church privileges, justification, adoption, and sanctification; the indwelling of the Spirit, and life everlasting."[11] Hodge goes on to comment that this is "an inheritance so great that simply to comprehend it requires divine assistance, and elevates the soul to the confines of heaven."[12]

Moreover, the Gentiles are **of the same body,** "constituent portions of the body of Christ." This is another way of saying that they are as much partakers of Christ as the Jews. The word *synsoma,* by which Paul expresses this idea, must have been coined by him because it does not appear in Greek literature elsewhere. Paul wants to convey the idea that the Gentiles are incorporated into the body of Christ and thereby stand with the Jews on equal ground, as far as sharing Christ's life.

Lastly, the Gentiles are **partakers of his promise** (*synmetocha*). Once they were strangers from the covenants of promise (2: 12), but now they "share on equal terms with Jews the promise of life and salvation (cf. II Tim. 1: 1)."[13] Westcott takes this phrase to be a specific reference to the gift of the Holy Spirit (cf. 1: 13). He sees in the phrasing "an expressive sequence" in the three elements of the full endowment of the Gentiles. "They had a right to all for which Israel looked. They belonged to the same Divine society. They enjoyed the gift by which the new society was distinguished from the old."[14]

[10]Moffatt has translated the three words as "co-heirs, companions, and co-partners."

[11]*Op. cit.,* p. 165; cf. 1: 13-14; Gal. 3: 29; 4: 7.

[12]*Ibid.*

[13]Foulkes, *op. cit.,* p. 94.

[14]*Op. cit.,* pp. 46-47.

The new relationship of the Gentiles is realized **in Christ.** They do not come by way of the Jewish faith nor in any sense do they become "Jews." They hold the same place with Christ as the Jews. As always, **the gospel,** when effectively preached under the anointing of the Holy Spirit, brings about the spiritual birth of men, whether Jew or Gentile, young or old, rich or poor. None is anything before he comes to Christ; all are uniquely Christ's when united to Him.

This comprehensive verse sets forth (1) The nature of the blessings promised by God to all men, **fellowheirs of the same body;** (2) The condition by which enjoyment of these blessings may be realized, being **in Christ;** (3) The means by which that union is effected, **the gospel.**[15]

2. *The Ministry of the Mystery* (3:7-13)

Continuing with the general theme of the mystery of God's grace, Paul speaks of his ministry with regard to it. **Whereof** means "of this gospel" (RSV). Four illuminating aspects of his service are given expression in these verses.

a. Called by God (3:7). Paul's role as a minister (*diakonos,* servant) was not self-chosen, for he declares that he **was made a minister** (7). This office of servanthood was conferred upon the apostle—it was **according to the gift of the grace of God.** In no way did the former persecutor of the Christian believers deserve such a privilege. God in His sovereign, unmerited action laid His hand upon Paul for this mission to the Gentiles. The gift of serving Christ in this manner flowed from the free grace of God. Furthermore, the apostleship to the Gentiles was **by the effectual working of his power.** This ministry would have failed had it not been accompanied with divine enablement. Blaikie comments: "Spiritual office without spiritual power is miserable; but in Paul's case there was the power as well as the office."[16] Natural capacities doubtless accounted for much in the apostle's effectiveness, but that which made his ministry truly persuasive and redemptive was the power of God (cf. I Cor. 3:6-7).

b. Minister and Message (3:8-9). With humble recognition that he is not worthy of this gift because he is **less than the least of all saints** (Christians),[17] Paul asserts that the purpose

[15]Cf. Hodge, *op. cit.,* p. 166.

[16]*Op. cit.,* p. 105.

[17]Cf. similar self-depreciation in I Cor. 15:9; II Cor. 12:11; I Tim. 1:15.

of his ministry is to **preach among the Gentiles the unsearchable riches of Christ.** The nature of these **riches** he explains in 8-12. **Unsearchable** carries the idea of "trackless, inexplorable, not in the sense that any part is inaccessible, but that the whole is too vast to be mapped out and measured."[18] The word **riches** does not convey scarcity but preciousness. The Gentiles are now hearing the glorious truth that the Messiah of the Jews is also their Saviour.[19] They too can enjoy the riches of compassion, forgiveness, sanctification, and guidance which the risen Christ has brought to needy men. Concerning Christ, John 1:16 declares, "Out of his full store we have all received grace upon grace" (NEB).

A corollary purpose of Paul's ministry is theological in character, **to make all . . . see** (*photisai,* to cast light upon) **what is the fellowship of the mystery** (9). The apostle's first task is to evangelize the Gentiles, but at the same time he must **make all . . . see,** i.e., enlighten all mankind as to how the revealed truth meets the needs of men. **The fellowship** (*oikonomia,* dispensation) **of the mystery,** according to Westcott, here means "the apostolic application of the Gospel to the facts of experience."[20] An additional note on the mystery (4-6) is now given. This **mystery** was not a new kind of action on the part of God, nor any divergence from His original plans, forced upon Him by developments in human history. It was **hid in God, who created all things;** i.e., it existed in the heart and mind of Deity "from all ages."[21] The introduction of the creatorship of God may be simply an expression of reverence or a reminder that "none but the creator can be a redeemer."[22] The phrase **by Jesus Christ** does not appear at this point in the best MSS, but cf. Col. 1:16.

c. The Function of the Church (3:10-12). **To the intent** means "in order that." Through the Church, now constituted of Jews and Gentiles redeemed by the blood of Christ, Paul's service involves "the display of God's wisdom before the intelligences of the heavenly order" (10).[23] **The principalities and powers**

[18]Beare, *op. cit.,* X, 669.

[19]*Christou* has the article with it, thus suggesting this Messianic usage.

[20]*Op. cit.,* p. 48.

[21]Bruce, *op. cit.,* p. 64.

[22]Hodge, *op. cit.,* p. 171.

[23]Westcott, *op. cit.,* p. 48.

(*archai* and *exousiai*) cannot here mean any type of earthly rulers because Paul says they are **in heavenly places.** Neither are they to be considered demonic powers, for, as Salmond suggests, the power of God would be more appropriate in dealing with them than the wisdom of God. Salmond concludes: "The *archai* and *exousiai* can only mean *good* angels . . . and these names of *dignity* . . . are appropriate here as suggesting the *greatness* of Paul's commission, and perhaps also . . . the glory put upon the *ecclesia* [church]."[24]

Doubtless these angels of God who rule the spheres have an interest in the scheme of man's redemption (I Pet. 1:12). The apostles and prophets have received the truth regarding God's plans and have communicated it to the Church. The Church in turn mediated the truth to the whole universe. Beare comments, "The powerful rulers of the spheres see the church forming, observe how it gathers into one the hostile segments of humanity, and so learn for the first time **the manifold wisdom of God.**"[25] When the Church fulfills her mission of making known the divine wisdom, Paul's ministry is validated. **Manifold** (*polypoikilos*) appears only here in the New Testament. It means "variegated, of differing colors." Robinson comments that "the metaphor is taken from the intricate beauty of an embroidered pattern."[26] Who can fathom the majesty and diversity of God's wisdom in redeeming the world? In Rom. 11:33, Paul exclaims, "Frankly, I stand amazed at the unfathomable complexity of God's wisdom and God's knowledge. How could man ever understand his reasons for action, or explain his methods of working?" (Phillips) God's plans are perfect in their conformity to His holiness, but at the same time they are enacted in keeping with the capacities of man and the complicated needs of human life. The end result is the redemption of souls.

In typical Pauline literary style, 11 and 12 expand the thought into areas which are not directly germane to the central thesis. The disclosure of the manifold wisdom was **according to the eternal purpose** (lit., according to the purpose of the ages). While the intention had only recently been revealed, it had its origin in eternity. The clause **which he purposed in Christ Jesus**

[24]*Op. cit.*, III, 309; cf. Bruce, *op. cit.*, pp. 64-65.
[25]*Op. cit.*, X, 671.
[26]*Op. cit.*, p. 80.

may be construed as "fulfilled in Christ." Westcott renders it, "which He accomplished in Christ Jesus."[27]

Picking up an idea previously introduced in 2:18, the apostle reinforces it in 12. In our Lord **we have boldness and access** to God the Father. The two words **boldness** (*parresia*) and **access** (*prosagoge*) mean respectively "freedom of address" and "freedom of approach."[28] *Parresia* signified in classical Greek the freedom of speech which was accorded a citizen of a democratic state. In applying the word here, Paul suggests "the liberty of Christian men to approach God directly with no intermediary apart from Christ, who embraces Godhead and Manhood in His one person."[29] See comments on 2:18 for a discussion of *prosagoge*. **Confidence** (*pepoithesis*) is employed in the New Testament only by Paul and then only six times in his letters. According to Salmond, it suggests "the state of mind in which we enjoy these blessings";[30] namely, boldness and freedom. **By the faith of him** does not mean Christ's faith, but our faith in Him.

Verses 11-12 suggest three significant truths. (1) Our open door to God has always been His plan for men, 11. (2) The ground of our boldness and access is Christ. It is in Him that we have this liberty. We cannot come to God through any merit of our own; we must come "on the infinite merit of an infinite Saviour," 12; (3) The indispensables of personal communion with God are freedom of address and freedom of access, 12.

d. The Glory of Suffering (3:13). The **tribulations** sustained by the apostle in the fulfillment of his commission were endured for the benefit of his readers (13). **Wherefore** (*dio*) does not refer back to the great privileges of "boldness" and "access," in 12 but rather to the thought of the whole passage (7-12), "the dignity of the office committed to Paul and its significance for them."[31] It might have appeared to the readers that Paul's imprisonment and trials augured ill for the Christian cause. Such a view was contradictory to his evaluation of sufferings. In Col.

[27]*Op. cit.*, p. 49; cf. also Salmond, *op. cit.*, III, 310; Bruce combines the two possibilities and speaks of Christ as "the center and circumference of this purpose" (*op. cit.*, p. 65).

[28]Cf. 6:19; Heb. 4:16; 10:19.

[29]Bruce, *op. cit.*, p. 65.

[30]*Op. cit.*, III, 310.

[31]*Ibid.*, III, 310-11.

1:24 he writes of his own attitude: "[I] now rejoice in my sufferings for you, and fill up that which is behind of the afflictions of Christ in my flesh for his body's sake, which is the church." Since he did not lose heart, he did not want his readers to become disheartened. Indeed, he sees a deep meaning in his hardships; they are "the glory of those for whom he suffered."[32] They expose both the grandeur of the truth that the readers had embraced and the ministry of the one who proclaimed that truth. If his readers see this interpretation of tribulations, they will rejoice with Paul and not faint.

B. Paul's Prayer for Spiritual Fulfillment, 3:14-19

For this cause signifies the end of the long digression which began with 3:1, where this same phrase appears. The **cause** to which the apostle refers is found in c. 2. This cause is the extension of divine mercy and saving grace to the Gentiles, thus granting them equal privileges with the Jews through Jesus Christ. It provides the basis for the petition of the apostle. Recalling their enjoyment of the reconciliation of the Cross, their peace of a covenant relationship with God, and their incorporation into the household of God leads Paul to prayer. The burden of his intercession is that these new Christians might come to experience all of man's God-given spiritual privileges in their fullness.

1. *The Address of the Prayer* (3:14-15)

Paul's attitude in prayer is expressed in the posture he assumes: **I bow my knees** (14). It was customary for the Jews to stand for prayer with arms outstretched toward heaven (cf. Matt. 6:5; Luke 18:11, 13). That Paul would kneel suggests the intensity and urgency of his petition. As Foulkes comments, to prostrate oneself was "an expression of deep emotion or earnestness, and on this basis we must understand Paul's words here."[33]

Paul's prayer is addressed to **the Father of our Lord Jesus Christ.** On the basis of manuscript evidence, the phrase **of our Lord Jesus Christ** should be omitted from the text. However, Paul so frequently qualifies his use of divine names that one is fully justified in accepting the idea conveyed by the phrase

[32] J. A. Robinson, *op. cit.*, p. 80.

[33] *Op. cit.*, p. 101; cf. also Barclay, *op. cit.*, p. 150. For biblical examples of this posture, see I Kings 8:54; Luke 22:41; Acts 7:60; 9:40; 20:36; 31:5.

(cf. 1:17). Addressing one's entreaty to the Father is in keeping with God's plan for His children. When we are born again, we are adopted into the family of God (1:5). We are thus able to call God "Abba, Father" through the ministry of the Holy Spirit (Rom. 8:14-17; Gal. 4:6). Beare comments, "It belongs to the nature of God as Father that he should hear the prayer of his children and grant their requests (Matt. 7:11).[34] The apostle's manner of address here may be the result of the influence of the Lord's Prayer in the early Christian community.

Paul's description of God as the Father **of whom the whole family in heaven and earth is named** (15) expresses a thought which is not adequately conveyed by our English translation. In the Greek, *patria* (**family**) is a derivative of *pater* (**father**). It has been suggested that a more proper translation of *patria* would be "fatherhood."[35] Thus, a better rendering of this verse is, "from whom all fatherhood in heaven and on earth receives its name."[36] The fatherhood of God is "the source of fellowship and unity in all the orders of finite beings. . . . Every 'family,' every society which is held together by the tie of a common head . . . derives that which gives it a right to the title from the one Father."[37] Martin reminds us that "the Fatherhood of God is not a mere metaphor drawn from human relationships. The very opposite is the case . . . The archetype of all fatherhood is seen in the Godhead, and all other fatherhoods are derived from Him."[38] Prayer becomes a genuine communion when we realize that God is Father in the highest and noblest sense, and He is approachable!

2. *The Power of the Spirit* (3:16-19)

The apostle is concerned throughout this letter that his readers be enlightened about the redemptive work of God in history and in their hearts. Thus this prayer, along with the petition in 1:16-23, emphasizes the need for further illumination. However there is a difference. In the earlier prayer "he begins with the thought of personal enlightenment which leads to a living sense

[34]*Op. cit.*, X, 675.

[35]For a contrary view, see Hodge, *op. cit.*, pp. 179-80; Alfred Martin, "Ephesians," *The Wycliffe Bible Commentary* (Chicago: Moody Press, 1962), p. 1309.

[36]F. F. Bruce, *The Letters of Paul: An Expanded Paraphrase* (Grand Rapids: Wm. B. Eerdmans Publishing Co., 1965), p. 275.

[37]Westcott, *op. cit.*, p. 50.

[38]W. G. M. Martin, *op. cit.*, p. 1023.

of the greatness of the Divine power." In this one he commences "with the thought of personal strengthening which issues in higher knowledge and completer work."[39]

To be strengthened with might by his Spirit (16) is a divinely given experience (cf. Col. 1:11). It is granted by God **according to the riches of his glory,** that is to say, "on the scale of and in the style of . . . the resources of His ever-blessed Nature."[40] The phrase **to be strengthened** is an aorist infinitive (*krataiothenai*), suggesting crisis or punctiliar action. Paul seems to be speaking of that second experience of the Christian in which "the Holy Spirit of Promise, the Lord of Pentecost, the Spirit of Counsel and Might" cleanses and empowers the heart. This is no surface work. It happens **in the inner man,** in "the true and enduring self."[41] The prayer therefore is that the Holy Spirit may touch "the master spring of the whole life," strengthening and vitalizing it for service to God.

That Christ may dwell in your hearts by faith (17) is not to be taken as describing another and higher blessing, but a further explanation of the previous experience of v. 16. Beare, following Westcott, concludes that this aspect of the prayer is a second object of the verb **grant.**[42] However, the absence of the connective "and" supports the view that the strengthening by the Spirit and the indwelling of Christ in the heart are not totally different experiences.[43] Quite obviously, enjoying the presence of the Spirit is tantamount to enjoying the presence of Christ. Once again, we have an aorist infinitive (*katoikesai*) to express the idea of dwelling. Besides connoting decisive and critical action, the word means permanent residence as opposed to temporary sojourn (*paroikein*). Moule comments that Christ's coming is "so deep and great, as to constitute a practically new arrival, and remaining where He so arrives not as a Guest, precariously detained, but as a Master resident in His proper home."[44] **In your hearts** means at the center of the whole personality.

[39]Westcott, *op. cit.,* p. 51.

[40]H. C. G. Moule, *Ephesian Studies* (2nd ed.; London: Pickering and Inglis, Ltd., n.d.), p. 129.

[41]Bruce, *Ephesians,* p. 67; cf. Rom. 7:22.

[42]*Op. cit.,* X, 678.

[43]Foulkes, *op. cit.,* p. 103; cf. Salmond's view that this is the *end* and *effect* of the strengthening, *op. cit.,* III, 314.

[44]*Op. cit.,* p. 130.

And since the abode of Christ is a gift, it must be received **by faith.**

Being strengthened by the Spirit and thus fully indwelt by Christ results in being **rooted and grounded in love.** These biological and architectural metaphors are employed also in 2:21. Cf. also Col. 2:7 ("rooted and built up") and Col. 1:23 ("grounded and settled"). These two participles are in the perfect tense, thus suggesting established relationships. This is not in any static sense, but rather as a whole-souled, growing involvement with Christ. **In love,** an essential correlative of faith, is to be construed with the participles, so that love is "the *soil* in which the life is rooted" and "the *character* of its foundations."[45] Perfect love in the heart makes for growth and stability. Dale summarizes v. 17 as follows: "Love will not be an intermittent impulse, or even a constant force struggling for its rightful supremacy over baser passions; its authority will be secure; it will be the law of their whole nature; it will be the very life of their life."[46]

This profound experience of the Spirit-filled and Christ-indwelt life is needed in order **to comprehend with all saints** (Christians) **the love of Christ** (18-19). Several truths are wrapped up in this verse. *First,* divine realities are not known by intellectual pursuit alone. **May be able** (*exischusete*) is "may have the strength." The verb **comprehend** (*katalabesthai*) means literally "to lay hold of" or "to grasp." As employed here it suggests the difficulty of knowing the deep things of God through our merely human faculties. We need therefore the ministry of the Spirit. This is precisely the truth which the apostle asserts in I Cor. 2:9-10: "But as it is written, Eye hath not seen, nor ear heard, neither have entered into the heart of man, the things which God hath prepared for them that love him, but God hath revealed them unto us by his Spirit: for the Spirit searcheth all things, yea, the deep things of God."

Second, even though the individual Christian is strengthened by the Spirit, he cannot by himself hope to comprehend the full scope of divine truth. The comprehension comes **with all saints** (cf. Col. 1:26). "What must for ever transcend the knowledge of the isolated individual" the whole body of the saints may

[45]Beare, *op. cit.,* X, 679.

[46]*Op. cit.,* p. 250.

know together.[47] Bruce comments, "It is a vain thing for Christian individuals or groups to imagine that they can better attain to the fulness of spiritual maturity if they isolate themselves from their fellow-believers."[48]

Third, the dimensions of the divine love are four: **breadth, and length, and depth, and height.** Commentators through the ages have sought to affix some special significance to each projection of love.[49] However, in all likelihood Paul was simply "trying to express with rhetorical fulness the magnitude of the vision which opens before Christian faith as it seeks to comprehend the ways of God."[50] Here are the wonder and the glory of a life that is "hid with Christ in God" (Col. 3:3).

According to v. 19, the love of Christ which we are to know **passeth knowledge.** How are we to explain such a statement? Wesley observes that Paul corrects himself regarding our knowledge and asserts that it cannot be fully known. It has been suggested, on the other hand, that the apostle realized that he might have trapped himself with this emphasis upon knowledge, which would have been much too Gnostic. He therefore seeks to say that love is greater than knowledge. In keeping with this interpretation, it might be more proper to translate the clause: "the love of Christ, which surpasses knowledge" (RSV, NASB). A much more satisfying solution is offered by Hodge. He suggests that "love of Christ" is Christ's love to us which passes knowledge. Since it is infinite, inhering in an infinite subject, it lies beyond our comprehension. He writes, "This love of Christ, though it surpasses the power of our understanding to comprehend, is still a subject of experimental knowledge. We may know how excellent, how wonderful, how free, how disinterested, how long-suffering, it is, and that it is infinite."[51] He goes on to say that this is the highest and most sanctifying knowledge. "Those who thus know the love of Christ towards them purify themselves even as he is pure."[52]

Climaxing his prayer, Paul petitions that these people **might be filled with all the fulness of God.** He is not requesting that

[47]J. A. Robinson, *op. cit.*, p. 86.

[48]*Ephesians*, p. 68.

[49]Cf. Wesley, *Notes*, p. 711; Barclay, *op. cit.*, p. 155.

[50]Beare, *op. cit.*, X, 679.

[51]*Op. cit.*, pp. 189-90

[52]*Ibid.*

their lives be deified; they are not to be filled with that fullness of which God is full as an infinite Being. Rather, he desires that they enjoy the fullness of grace which God communicates to men through His Son. Wesley takes the phrase **with all the fulness of God** to mean "with all His light, love, wisdom, holiness, power, and glory."[53] The tense of the verb **filled** is aorist and suggests, according to Martin, that "this experience is not looked upon as something gradually acquired, but is thought of as some positive experience of the believer."[54] Perhaps a parallel to this verse is Matt. 5:48—"Be ye therefore perfect, even as your Father which is in heaven is perfect."

C. Doxology, 3:20-21

In his prayer Paul has not asked for small things; he has requested of God that Christians be illuminated, strengthened, and filled by the Spirit. As Dale comments, "It might seem that after a prayer like this the apostle would have paused and wondered whether he had not been asking for what lay beyond all hope."[55] But no, realizing that his highest aspirations put no strain on the divine resources, Paul breaks out into a doxology in which he declares the glory and magnitude of the power of God. In effect, the apostle confidently proclaims, ". . . what God promises He performs; what He commands He enables."[56]

Three truths are expressed in v. 20. First, God **is able to do** all things. Paul could not entertain the idea that God is limited by any power outside of himself. Second, God is able to do **exceeding abundantly above all that we ask or think.** The scope of God's power exceeds the hopes and imaginings of the human heart. The expression **exceeding abundantly** (*huperekperissou*) is of Pauline coinage and is called by Bruce a super-superlative, meaning "superabundantly." God's ability to carry out His purposes lies outside the greatest human powers of comprehension. Third, **according to the power that worketh in us** is intended to assert that there is a relationship between the believer's present enjoyment of divine power in conversion and

[53] *Op. cit.*, p. 711.

[54] *Op. cit.*, p. 1023.

[55] *Op. cit.*, p. 258.

[56] Dwight H. Small, *The High Cost of Holy Living* (Chicago: Covenant Press, 1964), p. 13.

the infinite power of God which is able to do that for which the apostle prayed. Erdman states the truth succinctly: "This 'power that worketh in us' is the measure and means of the limitless ability of God to do for us and in us far more than we ask or receive."[57]

In 16-20 there is reflected "Superabundant Grace." The inwardness of holiness is clearly portrayed. (1) **Strengthened . . . by his Spirit in the inner man,** 16; (2) Christ dwells in the heart **by faith. Rooted and grounded in love.** Dimensions of love comprehended, 17-18; (3) **Filled with all the fulness of God.** Knowing the surpassing **love of Christ,** 19; (4) **The power that worketh in us,** 20 (G. B. Williamson).

Unto him be glory (21) can be taken either as a statement, "Unto Him is the glory," or as an imperative, "Unto Him be the glory." The latter form seems more appropriate. Paul says, in effect, "Let the glory or excellence of God be disclosed **in the church** and in **Christ Jesus"** (*en Christo Jesou*). The modern translations agree in using the phrase "in Christ Jesus" rather than **by Christ Jesus** (RSV, NEB, NASB). Christ and His Church are linked together by Paul. Both demonstrate the glory of God and both bring praise to Him.

Throughout all ages, world without end can be rendered "from generation to generation evermore" (NEB). This linkage of synonym and repetition is the apostle's way of emphasizing "the eternity of praise." Throughout the ages means "one age supervening upon another into the remotest infinity,"[58] Christ and His people, the Church, will display the glory of God—His abounding grace, of which the Church has been the recipient.

In 14-21 we see "The Prayer for Divine Fullness," offered to the universal Father for all the children, 14-15. (1) The aims—(*a*) to be **strengthened with might,** 16, (*b*) **to know the love of Christ,** 19, (*c*) **that ye might be filled with all the fulness of God,** 10; (2) The means—(*a*) **his Spirit,** the indwelling Christ, 16, (*b*) **by faith,** 17; (3) The resources—**according to the riches of his glory,** 16, and **according to the power that worketh in us,** 20 (W. E. McCumber, *Holiness in the Prayers of St. Paul*).

[57]*The Epistle of Paul to the Ephesians* (Philadelphia: Westminster Press, 1931), p. 71.

[58]Bruce, *Ephesians*, p. 71.

Section VI *The Unity of the Church*

Ephesians 4:1-16

Essentially cc. 1—3 have been given to the exposition of God's saving purpose as it relates to the whole of creation and the role of the Church in achieving that objective. With c. 4 the apostle, following the plan of Galatians, Romans, and Colossians, turns from a discussion of the great revealed truths of redemption to ethical exhortation and instruction. However, this division of the Epistle cannot be maintained too rigidly because the doctrinal affirmations are not neglected in cc. 4—6. Indeed, the hortatory strain is interspersed with, and enforced by, reference to these revealed truths. Moreover, new aspects of the doctrines are introduced and explained in support of the conduct to which Paul calls his readers.

The overarching theme of unity comes to refined expression in this section of c. 4, particularly as it relates to the Church. God's answer to the disharmony of this world is Christ. All men become one, with no barriers separating them, as they receive God's gift of newness of life through faith. These united believers constitute the Church, called into being and maintained by Christ. But the Church has a function in the world, namely, to witness to God's love for men and to proclaim the reconciliation that is offered to all. Markus Barth observes: "The Church has its place and function between Christ and the world. She is not the mediator of salvation; she is not the saviour of the world; she is not even a redemptive community. But she knows and makes known the Saviour and salvation."[1] The task of the Church therefore is one of unity. To fulfill her mission in the world the Church must exemplify throughout her membership the power and glory of the grace of God. When she lives worthily, the Church promotes more than just good feeling and mutual respect among men; she ministers Christ to men. As a result, men are transformed and endowed with divine love, the only sure foundation of unity. Each member of the body of Christ must live faithfully with this grand result in view.

[1]*Op. cit.*, p. 142.

A. The Plea for Unity, 4:1-3

1. *The Worthy Walk* (4:1)

Paul repeats the fact that he is now **the prisoner of the Lord** (cf. 3:1). In doing so, he hopes to provoke in his readers serious reflection on their present way of living. He exhorts them to **walk worthy of the vocation** to which they have been called (cf. Phil. 1:27; Col. 1:10; I Thess. 2:12;). **Walk** (*peripateo*) in the New Testament means to "conduct one's life." In this instance the appeal is to live as befits (*axios*) their **vocation** or calling. **The vocation wherewith ye are called** does not refer to the divinely given call to the ministry. As Moody aptly states, "It is a call that comes to all Christians by the sole fact that they are Christians."[2] "Conversion" therefore approximates the idea behind the word "calling." However, as Moule remarks, conversion emphasizes the human side in the great change, whereas "calling . . . draws attention to the divine side, the Voice of prevailing power."[3] The thrust of the verse is simply that they have been graciously invited into a new relationship with God and have not yet entered into all of its benefits. They are under obligation to continue this walk with God and to live out that "call" in such a way as to bring honor to the name of Him to whom they belong by promoting peace among men.

2. *The Four Graces of Unity* (4:2)

The worthy walk, which provides the basis and atmosphere for unity, evidences itself in at least four graces or virtues: **lowliness, meekness, longsuffering,** and **forbearing one another in love.** These graces are not traits of the natural human spirit. Rather, they are gifts of the Holy Spirit to Christ's followers (cf. Gal. 5:22-23), and they emanate from the Redeemer himself. The call to a worthy walk is a call to conduct one's life in conformity to the image of Christ, to live in holiness and righteousness among men.

Lowliness (*tapeinophrosyne*) is "a thankful sense of dependence upon God" and is the opposite of pride and conceit. The stance of humility is that of a man looking upward. Westcott remarks: "The proud man only looks at that which is (or which

[2]*Op. cit.,* p. 87.
[3]*Op. cit.,* p. 174.

he thinks to be) below him; and so he loses the elevating influence of that which is higher."[4] **Meekness** (*praotes*) means more than modesty or weakness. It is that "unresisting, uncomplaining disposition of mind, which enables us to bear without irritation or resentment the faults and injuries of others."[5] Here again, Jesus is the supreme Example. Without contradiction from man, He could say of himself: "I am meek and lowly in heart" (Matt. 11:29). In II Cor. 10:1 the apostle speaks of "the gentleness of Christ." Meekness has been called "the disposition of the lamb."

The third grace is that of **longsuffering** (*makrothymia*). Moule defines it as "the enduring, unweariable 'spirit,' which knows how to outlast pain or provocation in a strength learnt only at the Redeemer's feet."[6] The opposite of this virtue is "the short temper." It is noteworthy that the Vulgate, the Latin Bible, employs the word *longanimitas* to translate *makrothymia.* In the seventeenth century an attempt was made to coin the word "longanimity" much like the word "magnanimity." "Longanimity" would be the disposition of patiently enduring hardship and abuse with the strong hope of improvement (cf. Rom. 2:4; I Pet. 3:20).

Forbearing one another in love is the practical outworking of a patient spirit in which we go on loving and respecting others despite their faults and weaknesses. The main intention of Paul's discussion of these virtues is not to set forth a pattern of behavior toward men in general. He is concerned with the inevitable tensions and conflicts which arise in the Christian community. Beare concludes, "The harmony within the fellowship, which is the harbinger of universal harmony, can be maintained only in the measure that all Christians practice the virtues here mentioned."[7]

3. *The Unity of the Spirit* (4:3)

Christians have a unity-keeping responsibility. Paul reminds his readers that they must walk worthily before the Lord by **endeavouring to keep the unity of the Spirit. Endeavouring** (*spoudazontes*) is a mild translation; a better rendering would be "giving diligence" or "striving earnestly." "Spare no effort"

[4]*Op. cit.*, p. 57.

[5]Hodge, *op. cit.*, p. 200.

[6]*Op. cit.*, pp. 176-77.

[7]*Op. cit.*, X, 684.

is the NEB translation. The exhortation is that they must give serious attention to preserving the oneness of the church. **Spirit** in this instance must not be taken to mean the human spirit or the "concord of spirit" naturally generated in the Christian community, but rather the Holy Spirit.[8] That this unity is a creation of the Holy Spirit is substantiated by Paul's reference to the Spirit in I Cor. 12:13: "For by one Spirit are we all baptized into one body." The gift of the Holy Spirit brings the unity of an integrated personality to the individual heart and also a uniting bond of love to the whole fellowship of believers. The unity is thus at once personal and social, and the Holy Spirit is the originating and sustaining Cause.

Some commentators take the phrase **the bond of peace** as parallel to "in love" in v. 2. More acceptable, however, is the view which takes **of peace** (*eirenes*) as a genitive of equivalence. This permits the interpretation that "peace *is* the bond" which creates unity. As Salmond notes, "The unity . . . will be theirs in so far as they make peace the relation which they maintain one to another, or the bond in which they walk together."[9]

B. The Great Unities, 4:4-6[10]

Paul here lists seven things which are the essence of the Church's oneness. The repetition of the word **one** makes it emphatic, which, for Calvin, means that "*Christ* cannot be divided. *Faith* cannot be rent."[11] Mackay observes that the seven basic unities fall into three groups.[12] First of all, there is **one body, one Spirit, one hope.** The formal connection he sees as follows: "The *one body* is vitalized by the *one Spirit* and moves progressively towards the *one hope*."[13] The second group is composed of **one Lord, one faith, one baptism.** "Loyalty to the *one Lord* gives birth to the *one faith* and is signalized by the one act of *baptism*."[14]

[8]Cf. Salmond, Calvin, Hodge, Beare for a discussion of Paul's use of *pneuma* in this verse.

[9]*Op. cit.*, III, 321; cf. Col. 3:14.

[10]This title is borrowed from John A. Mackay, *op. cit.*, p. 135.

[11]*Commentaries on the Epistles of Paul to the Galatians and Ephesians* (Grand Rapids: Wm. B. Erdmans Publishing Co., 1948 [reprint]), p. 269.

[12]*Op. cit.*, p. 136.

[13]*Ibid.*

[14]*Ibid.*

Last of all is the **one God and Father of all.** Every other unity exists and is sustained because of the gracious action of God.

1. *"One Body"* (4:4)

This is a reference to the Church, the body of Christ, previously mentioned in 1:23 and 2:16. Paul could not tolerate two bodies of Christ, one composed of the Jews and another composed of the Gentiles. Through the power of the Cross, reconciliation with God has been effected for both Jew and Gentile, thus creating the possibility not only of the vertical relationship of peace with God but also the horizontal relationship of peace with all men. **One body** of believers thus has been brought into being (2:16).

2. *"One Spirit"* (4:4)

The reference here is to the Holy Spirit. This is in keeping with an implicit Trinitarian perspective, for the following verses refer to the Father and the Son. Membership in the body of Christ comes by the drawing, regenerating, and indwelling of the Spirit (cf. Rom. 8:9). Foulkes reminds us that "this fact prevents any view of the Church as a mere organization; for the presence of the Spirit constitutes the Church, and is the basis of its unity."[15] In more specific terms, the Spirit is "the special seal of God upon the members of the Community. The most disastrous thing that Christians can do is to 'grieve the Holy Spirit.' For then 'love, joy, peace in the Holy Ghost' disappear, and with them one of the most precious Christian unities."[16]

3. *"One Hope"* (4:4)

Hope has already figured in Paul's presentation of the gospel. Once his readers were "strangers from the covenants of promise, having no hope" (2:12). But now they have an "inheritance" and the possession of the Holy Spirit is a "guarantee" or "foretaste" of its fulfillment (1:12-14). Paul prays that they may come to a fuller understanding of their hope (1:18). The hope of our calling, as well as theirs, is that which possessed us when we responded to the overture of grace. It is the hope of sharing the glory of our Master in the home which has been prepared for us (cf. I John 3:2).

[15]*Op. cit.*, p. 112.

[16]Mackay, *op. cit.*, p. 137.

4. *"One Lord"* (4:5)

We now move to the second trilogy of the sevenfold unity of the Church. The reference to the lordship of Christ is in keeping with the earliest creedal statement of the Church. When men in those days accepted Christ, their confession was that *Jesus is Lord.* Paul writes to the Romans that if men will confess with their mouths "Jesus as Lord" (NASB), and believe in their hearts that God raised Him from the dead, they will be saved (Rom. 10:9).[17] In that passage Paul goes on to say that Christ is Lord of both Jew and Greek (Rom. 10:12). The unity which he emphasizes here in Ephesians is that which results from a common allegiance to the risen Lord. As Master, Christ commands our supreme worship and service, thus shutting out any other loyalties, whether to man or to fabricated, illusory gods.

5. *"One Faith"* (4:5)

Faith (*pistis*) may refer to the act of believing or to that in which one believes. It may denote subjectively the acceptance of Christ as one's personal Saviour, but on the other hand it may mean objectively "the faith which was once delivered to the saints" (Jude 3). Since Paul had just mentioned the lordship of Jesus, he perhaps had in mind the experience of believing in Christ for salvation. The common joy of forgiveness and adoption likewise provides a foundation for unity in the Church. Joy resulting from a common experience breaks down barriers between otherwise alien peoples and binds them into a single social group.

6. *"One Baptism"* (4:5)

Three views prevail as to what Paul intends by this phrase. First, some hold that he is speaking of the rite of water baptism, which served as an initiatory ceremony for admission into the Christian community. All members come into the Church by this experience of being baptized in the name of the Father, the Son, and the Holy Spirit.[18] Second, there are those who believe Paul is referring to Spirit baptism, relating it therefore to the

[17]Cf. Acts 2:36; Rom. 14:9; I Cor. 12:3; Phil. 2:11. For a forceful rebuttal of the theory that the designation of Christ as Lord was a development of the Hellenistic church, see Alan Richardson, *An Introduction to the Theology of the New Testament* (New York: Harper and Bros., 1958), pp. 153-54.

[18]Cf. Blaikie, *op. cit.*, p. 147.

ministry of the Spirit on the Day of Pentecost. This was Christ's baptism, which is to say, *He provided it by sending the Spirit* (cf. Matt. 3:11; Acts 1:5). This view does not assert that water baptism is superseded, but rather emphasizes the fact that it has now received "a richer significance from the saving work of Christ and the bestowal of the Holy Spirit."[19]

The view that interprets the **one baptism** as a Spirit baptism provided by Christ lends support to the Wesleyan interpretation. This third view says that Paul is speaking of "the baptism with the Holy Spirit," which among Wesleyans and others is a second work of grace. The central argument in support of this interpretation is the fact that Paul does not refer to the Lord's Supper in this list of unities. Thus, when speaking of baptism, he does not have a ritual or ceremony in mind.[20] The only true unity of the Church is "the unity of the Spirit" (v. 3).

7. *"One God and Father"* (4:6)

Some commentators see in this list an advance in thought from the Church to Christ to God, "who is One in the highest and most absolute sense."[21] God is the Source of all that tran-
His people. Commenting on this unity, Dale writes, "We all
spires in the Church through Christ and the Spirit. He is **above all**—He is sovereign and supreme. He is **through all**—His power penetrates the whole Church. He is **in all**—His Spirit abides in worship before the same eternal throne and in Christ we are all the children of the same Divine Father."[22]

C. The Diversity in Unity, 4:7-16

1. *The Law of Bestowal of Gifts* (4:7)

The conjunctive **but** leads us into another thought. Salmond says it "sets the *each* over against the *all*, and this in connection with the injunction to keep the unity of the Spirit."[23] The shift is from the unity of the whole to the parts that make up the whole, namely, the individual members. The apostle recognizes

[19]Bruce, *Ephesians*, p. 79.

[20]Ross Price, "The 'One' Baptism," *Herald of Holiness*, L (March 8, 1961), 10-11.

[21]Salmond, *op. cit.*, III, 322.

[22]*Op. cit.*, p. 269.

[23]*Op. cit.*, III, 323.

a lack of uniformity in endowment for service in the Church and this is the source of diversity in the distribution of gifts. Paul had already faced this problem in his correspondence with the Corinthians, to whom he wrote that "there are diversities of gifts, but the same Spirit" (I Cor. 12:4).

Each is given **grace according to the measure of the gift of Christ.** In this context **grace** does not refer to saving grace, but rather to special endowment as illustrated in Paul's mission to the Gentiles (3:7). The law which governs the bestowal is not only the variation in human abilities, but the pleasure of the sovereign God. "Each gets the grace which Christ has to give, and each gets it in the proportion in which the Giver is pleased to bestow it; one having it in larger measure and another in smaller, but each getting it from the same Hand and with the same purpose."[24] The differences are all within the divine plan, and relate to God's saving purpose in giving His Son.

2. *The Source of the Gifts* (4:8-10)

The source of these several gifts is the ascended Lord. To express this idea the apostle quotes Ps. 68:18, which in the original setting pictures the Lord returning triumphantly to His sanctuary after defeating Israel's enemies. From what He has taken as booty, He distributes to His people. Christ is pictured here as the Conqueror laden with spoils, leading a line of prisoners—**he led captivity captive**—and giving gifts to the Church.[25]

In 9 and 10, Paul parenthetically explains the meaning of the Ascension, which was introduced in 8. **Now that he ascended** can be construed: "as to this matter of ascension." Ascension implies a descent—**into the lower parts of the earth.** The **lower parts** must be taken to mean Hades[26] or possibly the grave[27] and not simply a region lower than the heavens. In these verses the apostle covers not only the humiliation but also the exaltation of Christ. The intended impact of his words is that the Giver of gifts is the Sovereign of the universe. Christ is thus exalted **that he might fill all things.**

[24] *Ibid.*

[25] Cf. Hodge, Calvin, Salmond for discussions on the difference between Paul's quotation and the rendering in the psalm.

[26] Beare, *op. cit.*, X, 689.

[27] Moule, *op. cit.*, p. 190.

Taking the Greek word *pleroo* to mean "to fill," some Lutherans have construed this phrase to suggest the omnipresence of Christ's body. Others, taking it as meaning "to fulfill," suggest that Christ fulfills all the prophecies of the old dispensation. Still others render the word "to accomplish or to perfect" and relate the clause to the consummation of Christ's redemptive work. The more reasonable interpretation is that Christ, now that He has descended and ascended, fills the whole universe with His activity as Sovereign and Lord. Barclay concludes his remarks on these verses with this cogent sentence: "To Paul the ascension of Jesus meant not a Christ-deserted, but a Christ-filled world."[28] This means, also, that He fills His Church with His presence. Wesley sees this latter idea in the clause and speaks of Christ filling "the whole Church, with His Spirit, presence, and operations."[29]

3. *The Classification of Gifts* (4:11)

When he wrote these words, Paul apparently had in mind his listing of the ministries in I Cor. 12:28. The Corinthian passage involves a longer list of spiritual gifts (*charismata*), but in this passage Paul is interested in setting forth especially these offices necessary for the expansion and nurture of the Church. Christ gave the Church **apostles:** the chief ministers, the twelve who had seen the risen Lord and received their commissions from Him. The **prophets** stood close to the apostles, and their special endowment was that of an inspired ministry. Foulkes asserts that their primary function was like that of the Old Testament prophets, to "forth-tell" the word of God. However, on occasion they foretold future events, as in Acts 11:28 and 21:9, 11.[30] **Evangelists** were itinerants, who went from place to place to win unbelievers (cf. II Tim. 4:5), in much the same manner as they do today.

It has been suggested that the first three categories apply to the Church universal, whereas the last two apply especially to the local church. **Pastors** are shepherds of a flock of communicants; the Greek word (*poimen*) employed here means literally "shepherd." The task of the **pastors** is to feed the flock and to protect them from spiritual dangers. **Teachers** might refer

[28]*Op. cit.,* p. 178.

[29]*Op. cit.,* p. 713; cf. also Salmond, Hodge, Bruce, Foulkes.

[30]*Op. cit.,* p. 118.

to another function of the pastor. Bruce claims that these terms "denote one and the same class of men."[31] However, it might be that **teachers** represent a class of somewhat lesser responsibility than the **pastors,** but who nevertheless hold a special place in the Church. All five ministries are Spirit-bestowed and given by Christ to His Church.

4. *The Purpose of the Gifts* (4:12-16)

Speaking primarily of the internal life of the Christian community, Paul describes the purpose for which Christ has given the Church these various ministries. At least four dimensions of the divine purpose are distinguishable.

(*a*) First, these ministries are given to edify or build up the body of Christ (12). The three phrases in this verse, each one commencing with the preposition **for** in KJV, give the impression that a threefold purpose is being expressed by the apostle. In the original language, the stress falls upon the last one. The NASB translates the verse as follows: "For the equipping of the saints for the work of service, to the building up of the body of Christ." The object therefore of these special servants is to bring about a **perfecting** (*katartismos,* lit., adapting or equipping) **for the work of the ministry** (*diakonias*). The expectation is that there shall be an active and fruitful labor for the Lord, with the result that the Church will be built up. Souls are won and simultaneously the life of the community is deepened and strengthened by the Church's unified service.

(*b*) Second, these ministerial gifts are given to foster maturity. Verse 13 looks back to the previous one and offers further explanation of the "building up" of the Church. Once again Paul uses three phrases, each introduced with the preposition *eis:* (1) **in the unity of the faith;** (2) **unto a perfect man;** (3) **unto the measure of the stature of the fulness of Christ.** But these are not to be taken as parallel ideas. The first one speaks of the means of maturity, the second of the reality of maturity, and third of the measure of maturity. Thus a better rendering of the verse would be: "So shall we all at last attain to the unity inherent in our faith and our knowledge of the Son of God—to mature manhood, measured by nothing less than the full stature of Christ" (NEB).[32]

[31]*Ephesians,* p. 85.

[32]Cf. Phillips' translation.

The unity of the faith, and of the knowledge of the Son of God constitutes the means of maturing. Unity is a gift of the Spirit (cf. 3) but faith and knowledge are required to receive it. Faith here is response to and trust in the Son of God—God manifested in the flesh, who died on Calvary in our behalf. **Knowledge** (*epignosis*) is here akin to faith, in that it means "understanding, acquaintance, discernment." It is not to be equated with intellectual knowledge but rather with personal relationship. Unity is born out of that intimacy with the Son which grace provides. Paul is not speaking however of the initial experience with Christ. The apostle is concerned about the growth and enlargement of understanding and comprehension of God's purposes and will as revealed in association with Christ. Such growth the members of the Christian Church can and should enjoy in greater measure as they faithfully serve Him.[33]

Unto a perfect man refers to that level of maturity in the Church both collectively and individually in which God's power is fully manifested in holiness and righteousness. Such a state will not be attained in its maximum meaning until hereafter when we shall possess in resurrection perfection the graces of Christ (cf. Phil. 3:7-16).[34]

The stature of the fulness of Christ provides the yardstick for determining Christian maturity. Hodge writes, "The church becomes adult, a perfect man, when it reaches the fulness of Christ."[35] The key to the interpretation of the verse is the phrase **the fulness of Christ.** What is this fullness? Salmond says it is "the sum of the qualities which make Him what He is."[36] When the Church measures up to the full maturity of her Lord, she is perfect. And as she grows toward that maturity she draws nearer to her goal in Christ. We need to remember also that there is no growth in the Church apart from our growth as individual believers. It is we who must press toward **the fulness of Christ.**

(c) These ministries are given to insure stability in the Church in the face of divergent doctrines and the deceit of men

[33]Cf. Bruce, *Ephesians*, p. 87.

[34]For a full and accurate analysis of the meaning of "perfect" in this context see Ralph Earle, "Gleanings from the Greek New Testament," *Preacher's Magazine*, XXXVIII (Dec., 1963), 15-16.

[35]*Op. cit.*, p. 234.

[36]*Op. cit.*, III, 333.

(14). This is a corollary of maturity, as Paul indicates by his introductory clause: **that we henceforth be no more children.** One of the clear evidences of immaturity is the inability to withstand intelligently and spiritually the claims of false doctrines. Paul's words are picturesque. The expression **tossed to and fro** appears only here in the New Testament and is derived from *kludon* (billow or wave). Hence the verb literally means "to be tossed by waves." Immature Christians are like boats tossed in the storm. **Carried about** is taken from *peripher̄o,* which often has the idea of violent swinging about. The NEB translates these two verbs "tossed by the waves and whirled about by every fresh gust of teaching." The task of ministers is to lay a heavy hand on the rudder of the Church, to hold it steady, and to provide doctrinal ballast through a faithful preaching and teaching ministry.

Those who introduce false teachings, to which unstable believers fall prey, are not only deceived themselves, but they **lie in wait to deceive** others. This is an inadequate translation and might better be rendered "makes use of every shifting device to mislead" (Weymouth). They employ **sleight** (lit., dice playing). Metaphorically, it came to mean "trickery" (RSV). The warning of Paul is stated well by Moule: "For alas, there are those around you who not only do lead you astray, but mean to do it, laying deliberate traps, and arranging well-drawn methods, on purpose to guide you away from the Christ they do not love."[37] The only adequate safeguard against the subtlety of heresy is a growing faith and an increasing knowledge of the truth. Ministers must provide the opportunity for such maturation and thus ensure stability in the church.

(*d*) Last, these ministries are given to make possible a growth into Christ. **Speaking the truth** (15) is derived from the verb *aletheuo,* which is generally translated "to speak the truth." But there is more in Paul's thought than articulation. He is thinking in terms of living and acting. Dale comments, "Truth was to be the life of all Christian men. The revelation of God in Christ was to penetrate and inspire their whole activity. Truth was to become incarnate, personal, in them. . . . they were not only to speak, they were to live it."[38] And this living is to be **in love,**

[37]*Op. cit.,* p. 193; cf. Rom. 16:17-18; II Cor. 2:17; 11:13; Gal. 2:4; Col. 2:8.
[38]*Op. cit.,* p. 281.

that is to say, with the motives and disposition which love evokes. Some truth can be harshly confessed and lived, but the Christian community must always express itself in love. The result will be the progressive movement toward the perfection of Christ, the Head of the Church. Note that this is substantially identical to the thought in 13. Moreover, this positive action is the best defense against the effects of error described in 14.

In 16 the apostle returns to the analogy of the body and uses it to emphasize the unity which Christ, the Head, brings to the Church. He visualizes the wonderful, yet complicated structure of the human body with its several parts **fitly joined together and compacted** ("bonded and knit together," NEB).[39] **Joint** in the analogy apparently refers to a ligament by which the various parts of the body are connected. When the body is functioning **according to the effectual working in the measure of each part,** that is to say, when each part is active in keeping with its purpose, harmony prevails and growth is assured. Christ, of course, is the Center and Source of all spiritual life. He imparts "cohesion and the vital power for growth."[40] This growth results in the **edifying** or "building up" of the Church **in love** (cf. 1:4; 3:17; 4:2; 5:2). The upbuilding has to do primarily with internal spiritual development, but when the Church is internally strong she increases numerically.

In summary, Paul sees the unity of the Church in organic and not organizational terms. The real unity lies within and is the result of a healthy organism. The Spirit creates such oneness; it is not the work of men, however clever and personable they might be. When this unity prevails, participated in by each member and encouraged by the faithfulness of gifted ministers, the Church grows in symmetry and beauty, to the amazement of the world of unbelievers.

In 4-16, "The Christian's Ultimate Goal" is suggested by the thought of **the measure of the stature of the fulness of Christ.** (1) The means to this end. Teaching and preaching the Word of God, 11-12; (2) The ideal epitomized, 4-7, 15. A corporate faith and a corporate body, 16. (3) The goal approximated in a stable character, 14. A heart with Christ enthroned. A united Church (G. B. Williamson).

[39]Note the use of these words in 2:21 and Col. 2:2, 18.

[40]Beare, *op. cit.*, X, 695.

Section VII *The Old Life and the New*

Ephesians 4:17-32

The word "walk" figures prominently in cc. 4—6, in which Paul gives practical direction to his readers regarding Christian living. Note its use in 4:1, 17; 5:2, 8, 15. In 4:1 the apostle exhorts Christians to "walk worthy" of the calling wherewith they were called. With 4:17 he introduces a new aspect of the Christian's walk. Couched in negative terms, his injunction is that they are to **walk not as other Gentiles walk.** They must abandon the pagan way of life in every respect, and give themselves to Christ's way of life.

The Christians with whom Paul is corresponding "had been breathing from their childhood the foul atmosphere of a most corrupt form of heathenism; they were breathing it still."[1] It is imperative therefore that through the power of Christ they break away from this lifelong influence. In seeking to incite a sensitivity regarding this matter, Paul describes the old life without Christ and the new life with Him (4:17-24). He then proceeds to offer some specific directives which relate to the new life (4:25-32). In 4:17-24 the apostle not only explores further what he has already presented in 2:1-10, but applies it directly to his Gentile readers. In the former section he includes himself in his description, but in this latter passage he speaks pointedly and consistently to their specific situation and experience.

A. Life Without Christ, 4:17-19

The adverb **therefore** (17) must be taken as resuming the thought begun in 1-3. The long explanation of unity in 4-16 constitutes a digression from the exhortation upon which Paul launched in the first three verses. **This I say . . . and testify** parallels the words "I beseech you" in v. 1. While the two words **say** (*lego*) and **testify** (*martyromai*) are accurately translated in the KJV, their real meaning does not break through in the English. Strong personal and solemn conviction precipitates

[1]Dale, *op. cit.*, p. 296.

Paul's appeal. This mood is somewhat captured by the RSV: "Now this I affirm and testify in the Lord." Bruce's paraphrase reads: "This is what I mean; this is what I urge upon you in the Lord's name."[2] **In the Lord** has been variously construed to mean "by the Lord," or "on the Lord's authority,"[3] by which is meant "in communion with the Lord."[4] Apparently the writer wants to convey the idea that he is identifying himself with the Saviour, and his exhortation is precisely what Christ would give.

The injunction takes a negative form: **walk not as other Gentiles walk.** Conduct yourselves in such a way as to show the real difference that exists between you and your pagan neighbors! The apostle then plunges into a capsule description of the pagan way of life, the life apart from Christ (cf. Rom. 1:21-32).

1. *"The Vanity of Their Mind"* (4:17*d*)

Mind (*nous*) in Hebrew thought includes more than the cognitive faculty; understanding, conscience, and the affections are also comprehended in it. Thus, **mind** refers to all aspects of man's being which enable him to recognize moral values and spiritual truth (cf. Rom. 1:28; 7:23; I Tim. 6:5). **Vanity** (*mataiotes*) bears the meaning of "purposelessness, uselessness, or emptiness." In the context, the word takes on the connotation of futility, delusion, and utter moral failure. Without the illumination of God's Spirit, man's path leads only to that which frustrates, because essentially he is "given over to things devoid of worth or reality."[5] Both personal experience and the history of mankind bear out this evaluation of man's life apart from the Saviour.

2. *"Having the Understanding Darkened"* (4:18*a*)

Paul explains in this sentence what the vanity of 17 involves. For one thing, it includes the darkening of the **understanding** (*dianoia*). This is "the inward darkness caused by unbelief," and is to be contrasted with the inner illumination for which Paul prays in 1:18: "the eyes of your understanding being enlightened." Speaking of the Gentiles in Rom. 1:21, Paul asserts that "their foolish heart was darkened."

[2]*The Letters of Paul*, p. 277.

[3]Bruce comments, "It is *the Lord's* will" (*Ephesians*, p. 90).

[4]Hodge, *op. cit.*, p. 248; Salmond, *op. cit.*, III, 338; NASB, "with."

[5]Salmond, *op. cit.*, III, 339.

3. *"Being Alienated from the Life of God"* (4:18b)

Martin sees a reference to the fall of man in this clause. The present state of man is "the result, not of separation from God simply, but of active alienation."[6] The pagan life represents an infinitely tragic "deviation from the true nature of man." Estrangement from God really means spiritual death because God is the only Source of life for mankind. The Christian answer to this condition is "reconciliation with God" (II Cor. 5:17-21; Col. 1:20-21). John supports Paul in this declaration: "He that hath the Son hath life; and he that hath not the Son of God hath not life" (I John 3:12).

The state of death and futility in which the Gentiles find themselves is not accidental, but is the result of ignorance and the blindness of their hearts. Ignorance (*agnoia*) sometimes means pardonable ignorance, that which is due to circumstances beyond one's control (cf. Acts 17:30). Culpable ignorance is usually expressed by the Greek word *agnosia,* as in I Pet. 2:15. But here *agnoia* seems to carry that connotation. Paul does not intend to suggest that the Gentile spiritual condition carries no guilt. The next phrase, properly rendered "the hardness or callousness of their heart" indicates "a deliberate steeling of the will against every impulse until men become past feeling."[7] **Hardness** (*porosis*) is employed to denote the hardening of the skin or the creating of a callous by constant contact with a foreign substance. Insensitivity to pain results. So incessant sinning brings about a hardening of the heart.

4. *Being Past Feeling* (4:19)

Moral insensibility means shamelessness, haughtiness before God and man, and living without the restraint of conscience. The ultimate result is moral irresponsibility, in which sin runs rampant through the life. Paul speaks of the Gentiles as having **given themselves over** or "abandoned themselves" (NEB) to sin. In Rom. 1:21-28, he declares that God gave them over to their own sinful ways, but here the apostle shows the other side. The tragedy is twofold—the man who abandons God in order to keep his sins, and the ultimate, reluctant act of God when He abandons the man whom He can no longer help. The outcome of this abandonment to the sinful life is now portrayed. **Lascivi-**

[6]W. G. M. Martin, *op. cit.,* p. 1025.

[7]Beare, *op. cit.,* X, 697.

ousness (*aselgeia*) is shameful, wanton sensuality, or simply excess. Bruce translates it "wanton living."[8] This seems to encompass both the idea of sensuality and excessiveness. **Uncleanness with greediness** expresses the manner in which this wantonness is evidenced. The noun for work (*ergasia*) can mean "business" or "the gains of business," so that the clause conveys the idea of making a trade of impurity. More reasonable is the view that takes the phrase **to work** to mean "indulging in" rather than "trading in." Salmond paraphrases the verse as follows: "They gave themselves willfully over to wanton sensuality, in order that they might practice every kind of uncleanness and do that with unbridled greedy desire."[9] The prevalence of immorality in the ancient pagan society was in many cases approved by its attachment to temple practices. In twentieth-century America, sophisticated sensuality is as often promulgated in the name of cultural freedom and maturity. Both are anti-Christian and degrading to society.

B. Life with Christ, 4:20-24

The conjunction **but** (20) functions to introduce the kind of life opposite to that which Paul's readers once knew and which still prevailed among the pagans. This conjunctive serves to distinguish sharply the apostle's description of the old life from the new.

The statement, **ye have not so learned Christ,** is difficult both in grammatical structure and in thought. This is the only instance in which the verb *manthano,* "to learn," is used with a personal object. To *learn Christ* sounds awkward until we recall that the Scriptures speak of "preaching Christ" (I Cor. 1:23). Hodge asserts that this "does not mean merely to preach his doctrines, but to preach Christ himself, to set him forth as the object of supreme love and confidence."[10] Thus to *learn Christ* must mean to know Him experientially as the Son of God and one's personal Saviour. It involves more therefore than an academic acquaintance with His teachings. An equivalent Pauline phrasing of this concept is found in Phil. 3:9-10: "and be found in him . . . that I may know him." This experience of *learning*

[8] *The Letters of Paul,* p. 277.

[9] *Op. cit.,* III, 340.

[10] *Op. cit.,* p. 256.

Christ necessarily includes accepting him as Messiah and adopting His way of living.[11] Blaikie comments, "He that learns Christ appropriates him in the efficacy of his atonement, in the power of his Spirit, in the force of his lessons, and in the spirit of his influence, and finds the whole to be diametrically opposite to the godless world."[12]

Verse 21 is parenthetical, but is not intended to introduce a doubt by its use of **if.** As Salmond suggests, the verse is "a delicate supposition" that Christ was "the subject and the sum of the preaching" which they heard.[13] Furthermore, they had not only **heard him,** but had **been taught by him.** Robinson summarizes the thought: "Christ was the message which had been brought to them, He was the school in which they had been taught, He was the lesson which they had learnt."[14] The clause **as the truth is in Jesus** presents a subtle problem. Why the shift to the name Jesus, which is rarely used alone by the apostle? Perhaps it is a reminder that "the voice of 'the Christ' is heard and his teaching received in the historical 'Jesus.' "[15] During His earthly ministry our Lord said, "I am . . . the truth" (John 14:6). It may be that Paul had in mind a theological thrust against the Gnostics when he added this clause, since they separated the "heavenly Christ" from the man Jesus.

1. *Putting Off the Old Man* (4:22)

Paul here continues the thought which he began in 20. The new fullness of life is to be realized by a threefold experience: (1) Putting off the old man, 22; (2) Being renewed in mind, 23; (3) Putting on the new man, 24.

The grammatical structure linking 20 and 22-24 presents some uncertainties of exegesis, particularly with regard to the interpretation of the phrases **the old man** (*ho palaios anthropos*) and **the new man** (*ho kainos anthropos*). Each of verses 22-24 is introduced with an infinitive, the translation of which can be variable. The KJV appears to translate them in a simple declarative mode with the use of the conjunction **that.** Salmond says of the infinitive, "It has something of the force of the im-

[11]Cf. NASB, Bruce, Phillips.

[12]*Op. cit.*, p. 151.

[13]*Op. cit.*, III, 341.

[14]J. A. Robinson, *op. cit.*, p. 106.

[15]Beare, *op. cit.*, X, 698.

perative, but is not to be taken as the same as the imperative."[16]

An important question is raised as a result of this grammatical problem. Is the apostle simply asserting that when they came to know Christ in saving grace they had at that time put off the old man and put on the new man? Or is he exhorting them to engage in a spiritual activity which is subsequent to that initial experience? Are the putting off, the renewing, and the putting on spiritual exercises to which the newly born must give themselves? The answer is decided by the way one interprets the meaning of the infinitives. In this case the grammatical construction is not decisive. The interpreter therefore must rely on the context and the related teaching of the entire New Testament. Three answers have been projected, the key thought revolving around the two phrases **the old man** and **the new man.**

(*a*) The first view looks upon Paul's statement as relating only to self-discipline following conversion. R. W. Dale is an exponent of this position. Commenting on putting off "the old man," he writes: "But in them there is an 'old man,' a baser nature, a morality formed by the current opinions and prevalent habits of the world; and they have to put it away."[17] He also asserts: "But this complete moral revolution is not accomplished either by one supreme effort of our own will or by any momentary shock of Divine power. It must be carried through in detail by a long, laborious, and sometimes painful process of self-discipline."[18] This view is held by Bruce, Foulkes, Robinson, Hodge, and others who accept the theological position that the principle of sin is only gradually removed through the ministry of the Spirit. To one of the Wesleyan persuasion it is significant that these scholars recognize and affirm the biblical teaching that there is in the converted man a remaining principle of sin, and that it needs to be removed—and can be removed by the work of the Spirit. The most telling argument against the gradual method proposed is the fact that **put off** (*apothesthai*) and **put on** (*endusasthai*) are aorists and thus indicate punctiliar, completed action.

(*b*) A second view, which the writer believes has much to commend it, depends upon accepting the infinitives as simple

[16]EGT, III, 342.
[17]*Op. cit.*, p. 314.
[18]*Ibid.*, p. 311.

declarative assertions. This view sees the old man as "the old, the former, the now past, state of things"[19] which is put off at the time of conversion. Moule takes the aorist infinitives as not suggesting "a *duty* but a *fact*. The 'putting-on' like the 'putting-off,' is viewed . . . as *fait accompli*."[20] The putting off **the old man** is thus "a figurative expression for the abandonment of their former . . . mode of life, which was according to their corrupt nature."[21] Henry E. Brockett, in commenting on **the old man** and **the new man,** likens the believer to "a weaver weaving a pattern into the fabric on the loom. In his unregenerate days he used to weave according to the 'old' pattern, namely, 'the old man.' But now he has 'put off the old man and his deeds,' namely, he has discarded the 'old' pattern, and now he weaves his fabric (his daily life) according to a new pattern altogether, that is, he has 'put on the new man'—according to Christ. The believer is responsible to do the weaving."[22] Though the above statement appears in a passage dealing with the sanctified life, it seems to identify "the old man" with the unregenerate life.

Col. 3:9-10 suggests a parallel experience: "Lie not one to another, seeing that ye have put off the old man with his deeds; and have put on the new man, which is renewed ['being renewed,' NASB] in knowledge after the image of him that created him." (Cf. the interpretation of Nielson, BBC, in comments on Col. 3:8-11.) Furthermore, Paul's declaration in Rom. 6:6 can be thus interpreted. It reads, "Knowing this, that our old self [margin, 'man'] was crucified with him that our body of sin might be done away with that we should no longer be slaves to sin" (NASB). The crucifixion of the old man, the old way of life, is to the end of providing the occasion for God to destroy the body of sin, the carnal mind.[23] In addition, the concept of newness in the Pauline writings often refers to the initial ex-

[19]Moule, *op. cit.*, p. 220.

[20]*Ibid.*, p. 211.

[21]Amos Binney and Daniel Steele, *The People's Commentary* (New York: Eaton and Mains, 1878), p. 527. This commentary asserts that "the old man" is the opposite of "the new creature" of II Cor. 5:17.

[22]*Scriptural Freedom from Sin* (Kansas City, Mo.: Nazarene Publishing House, 1941), p. 100.

[23]For a careful exegesis of this position, cf. Cecil Paul, "A Study of the Sixth Chapter of Romans with Special Reference to the Question of Freedom from Sin," an unpublished B.D. thesis, Nazarene Theological Seminary, 1958. Cf. Binney and Steele, *op. cit.*, p. 408.

perience with Christ. Cf. II Cor. 5:17: "Therefore if any man be in Christ, he is a new creature [lit., creation]: old things are passed away; behold, all things are become new." See also Gal. 6:15; Rom. 6:4; Eph. 2:10.[24]

(c) A third view, which is generally held by holiness scholars, identifies **the old man** with the carnal mind, which is removed in the experience of entire sanctification. W. T. Purkiser classifies the phrase under the general group of terms suggesting the sinful condition of the unsanctified heart. He comments: "He has been 'crucified with him [Christ]' (Rom. 6:6), and is to be 'put off or away,' 'stripped off' as an old suit of clothes."[25] Speaking of the hereditary character of evil, Harry E. Jessop calls attention to Rom. 6:6; Eph. 4:22; Col. 3:9, and asserts: "Here, evidently, is an intruder into our nature. It is declared to be *old,* and there is reason for it. It dates a long way back, being a racial contamination beginning with the fall and consequently passed on as a corrupted birth strain to all who follow."[26] Wesley seems to equate the old man and the carnal nature, which is purged in a second experience. He speaks of **the old man** as "the whole body of sin" and the new man as "universal holiness."[27] William Greathouse, after defining the old man as "the old self-centered, self-seeking, corrupt self," asserts that it is put off in the spiritual death of the self-will. This is followed by "the process" of being **renewed in the spirit of** the **mind** (4:23). Within this process there comes "a crisis moment when we 'put on the new man.' This 'new man' was 'created' once and for all in Christ, who is the Image of God restored to the race. But in the crisis of entire sanctification we 'put on' that Image—*Christ is stamped upon us.*"[28]

[24]Cf. Roy A. Harrisville, *The Concept of Newness in the New Testament* (Minneapolis: Augsburg Publishing House, 1960), pp. 75 ff.

[25]*Sanctification and Its Synonyms* (Kansas City, Mo.: Beacon Hill Press, 1961), p. 58; cf. modified statement, p. 89; cf. Charles E. Brown, *The Meaning of Sanctification* (Anderson, Indiana: The Warner Press, 1945), p. 215.

[26]*The Heritage of Holiness* (Kansas City: Beacon Hill Press, 1950), p. 43; cf. also his *Foundations of Doctrine* (Chicago: Chicago Evangelistic Institute, 1938), p. 13.

[27]*Op. cit.,* p. 715.

[28]"Ephesians," *Search the Scriptures,* edited by Norman R. Oke (Kansas City: Nazarene Publishing House, n.d.), X, 35. Cf. also Greathouse on Rom. 6:1-14 in *Search the Scriptures* and in BBC, Vol. 8.

Generally, those who follow this interpretation hold that (1) the infinitives here have the force of imperatives. Thus, Adam Clarke comments on 4:24 that Paul means, "Get a new nature."[29] Most modern translations give grammatical support to this interpretation when they employ the imperative mood to translate these infinitives. (2) A distinction is also made between the phrases **concerning the former conversation** (conduct), which is taken as the unregenerate way of life, and **the old man** or Adamic nature. (Cf. translations in RSV, NEB, NASB, Moffatt, Goodspeed, C. B. Williams, Berkeley.) The effect is that now the readers who have already turned away from the former sinful life in conversion are exhorted to put off the carnal nature in a second crisis experience.

Put off, as well as **put on,** are metaphors of the act of changing clothes, and suggest here a change of character. **Conversation** means "manner of life." The word translated **which is corrupt** (*phtheiromenon*) is a present participle (lit., being corrupted), but can be translated corrupt or "polluted" (an existing condition) without doing violence to the general thought of the verse.[30] This corruption involves the illusions of wrong desire (cf. Phillips). **The old man** is subject to deceit, and all the while selfishly desires things for himself. But that "acquisitive characteristic, rather than strengthening him, ruins him: it is 'deceit' —by it he becomes more dependent and ceases to live his own life."[31] The old life, dominated by the old self, was lived in frustration. Though the sinful desires of the unredeemed self promised joy and happiness, they could not fulfill the promise.

2. *Renewing the Mind* (4:23)

Be renewed is a present infinitive (*ananeousthai*) derived from the adjective *neos*. It suggests the idea of being new in the sense of young or "that which has not been in existence long." A continuous renewal of the inner life, that is, **the spirit of the mind,** is expected as one puts on the new nature (24). The dynamic character of the new life is denoted here. A parallel Pauline verse is Rom. 12:2: "And continue to be transformed by the renewing of your mind" (lit.). This renewal is not the result of human effort; it is the work of the Holy Spirit upon the

[29]*Op. cit.*, II, 79.

[30]Foulkes, *op. cit.*, p. 130.

[31]Harrisville, *op. cit.*, p. 68.

human spirit. The transformation comes as the individual surrenders himself to the leadership of the Spirit. Harrisville, following other commentators, notes the fact that, since the change is in **the spirit of** the **mind,** Paul is indicating "the radical and fundamental nature of the renewal, i.e., that it affects that part of the human personality which directs the thinking and willing."[32]

3. *Putting On the New Man* (4:24)

Simultaneous with the stripping off of "the old man" is the putting on of **the new man** (*ho kainos anthropos*), **which after God is created in righteousness and true holiness.** The phrase **after God** is explained by Paul's Colossian passage, in which he speaks of the new man as being renewed "after the image of God" (Col. 3:10). The likeness of God is revealed in and mediated through Jesus Christ. When we put on Christ (Rom. 13:14; Gal. 3:27), who is "the new man of all men" (cf. I Cor. 15:45 ff.), the divine nature is made effective in us. Peter speaks of men becoming "partakers of the divine nature" (I Pet. 1:4). The new life which is **created** (aorist tense) is characterized by **righteousness** (*dikaiosyne*) and **holiness** (*hosiotes*). These are complementary qualities of the spirit and are the products of the grace of God operating in the heart. Salmond distinguishes between them: "The former expresses the right conduct of the Christian man distinctively in its bearings on his fellowmen, and the latter the same conduct distinctively in its relation to God."[33] The word **true** is related to both qualities according to the Greek text.

C. Special New-Life Injunctions, 4:25-32

In these eight verses the apostle gives in rapid-fire succession six injunctions which relate to the new nature which they have put on and to the new life in Christ. These are implications and consequences of having "put off . . . the old man." **Wherefore** clearly indicates the relationship, and can be interpreted, "now that you are new men," or, as Westcott renders it, "seeing that Christ is your life."[34] The directives are five in number.

[32]*Ibid.*
[33]*Op. cit.*, III, 344
[34]*Op. cit.*, p. 73.

1. *Lying* (4:25)

The first injunction is that of **putting away lying** (cf. Col. 3:9). A better translation is "falsehood" (NASB). The Greek word is *he pseudos,* a noun which denotes more than the spoken word; it includes all forms of deception. The verb for **putting away** is in the aorist tense and denotes an action that is once for all (lit., having put off the falsehood, keep on speaking truth). The positive exhortation is offered: **speak every man truth with his neighbour** (cf. Zech. 8:16). **Speak** is in the present tense, suggesting that speaking the truth is to be continuous. **Neighbour** in this context can be taken as referring primarily to other members of the Christian community, as suggested by the last clause of this verse. One of the motives which Paul believed should be evident in all Christian behavior is the attempt to keep the unity of the Church. Thus he appends the words, **for we are members one of another.** There is, of course, the more general sense in which all men are interrelated—**members one of another.** This fact of our human situation also calls for speaking the truth.

2. *Anger* (4:26-27)

Be ye angry, and sin not parallels a statement in Ps. 4:4 as translated in the Septuagint, which reads, "Rage and sin not." According to Hodge, the meaning in Psalms is, "Do not sin by raging."[35] But this does not seem to be the apostle's meaning here. He admonishes, in effect: "If you are angry, do not sin." Righteous anger is consistent with the Christlike life, as we see in our Lord's experience of cleansing the Temple (Mark 3:5; John 2:13-17). Foulkes remarks, "The Christian must be sure that his anger is that of righteous indignation, and not just an expression of personal provocation or wounded pride. It must have no sinful motives, nor be allowed to lead to sin in any way."[36] Anger becomes sin whenever it desires, or is willing, to harm someone. Sin is personal and divisive in character, and by its very nature disrupts and breaks personal relationships. When anger has this intention, or when it results in dividing Christian brother from brother, it is sin.

Even righteous anger has its dangers. Therefore Paul counsels: **Let not the sun go down upon your wrath** (*parorgismos,*

[35]*Op. cit.,* p. 269.

[36]*Op. cit.,* p. 133.

lit., paroxysm or excitement). The apostle's advice is to "keep their anger on a short rein."[37] Delay in effecting a subsiding of the feelings will **give place** (*typos;* provide an opportunity) for Satan to sow wrong attitudes in the spirit and serious dissension in the body of Christ (cf. Jas. 4:7). And how adept Satan is at using such open doors!

3. *Thievery* (4:28)

Paul now exhorts his readers, some of whom used to pilfer and plunder, to make sure that every form of dishonest acquisition is removed from the life. It may appear from casual reading that theft was still practiced by these people. Hodge insists that this is not the case. The injunction is addressed to those who possessed reputations for thievery before conversion. They are not now engaged in such activity but are exhorted not to submit to temptations to appropriate what belongs to others.[38] Positive and counteractive measures are recommended by the apostle. **Let him labour** (*kopiato*) has the emphasis of "toil with strong motivation." **With his hands** is interpreted by Moule as "making honest gains by honest pains."[39] The motives for such hard toil are not only the recovery and maintenance of character, but the acquisition of goods which can be distributed **to him that needeth,** thus becoming a contributing, constructive member of society. Phillips renders the verse, "If you used to be a thief you must not only give up stealing, but you must learn to make an honest living, so that you may be able to give to those in need."

4. *Impure Speech* (4:29)

As is common today, Paul's readers had indulged in foul language, a habit which had become so ingrained that possibly traces of it remained among them. **Corrupt** (*sapros*) is a strong word meaning "putrid, vile, morally unwholesome."[40] Such talk, even if only suggestive of previous language, would be most unbecoming to a Christian. A positive injunction is added. A Christian must cultivate the habit of speaking **that which is good,** defined here as that which is "helpful to the occasion" (NEB). **Minister grace unto the hearers** has been translated "which God can use to help other people" (Phillips). Behind Paul's ex-

[37]W. G. M. Martin, *op. cit.*, p. 1026.

[38]*Op. cit.*, p. 272.

[39]*Op. cit.*, p. 233.

[40]Wesley, "stinking in the nostrils of God" (*op. cit.*, p. 716).

hortation seem to be the words of Prov. 15:23: "A word spoken in due season, how good is it!" Purity and truth alone are not sufficient for the Christian's speech. There must be that kind of blessing and helpfulness which characterized the words of Jesus (cf. Luke 4:22; cf. also Col. 3:16; 4:6). Wholesome conversation can be a means of grace along with other Christian sacraments and activities.

5. *Grieving the Spirit* (4:30)

Grieve not the holy Spirit must not be wholly detached from the previous injunction. Malicious, sacrilegious, or impure language which injures others "causes pain to or distresses" (*lypeo*) the Third Person of the Holy Trinity. Hodges comments that the people of God are the temple of God because the Holy Spirit dwells in them (I Cor. 3:16-17). "To pollute, therefore, the souls of believers by suggesting irreligious or impure thoughts to them, is a profanation of the temple of God and an offence to the Holy Ghost."[41] The Holy Spirit, who indwells believers and who gives himself freely to them in love, is deeply wounded whenever such irreverent and destructive talk is permitted. Unholy speech is, however, not the only conduct that grieves the indwelling Spirit. One may also grieve Him by inattention and by all forms of disobedience. **Sealed unto the day of redemption** repeats the thought in 1:13; see comments there.

6. *Bad Temper* (4:31-32)

The cluster of evil characteristics given in 31 are descriptive of the old nature, and those listed in 32 depict the new nature. An internal relationship exists between the four traits mentioned in 31. **Bitterness** (*pikria,* a highly irritated state of mind) leads to **wrath** (*thymos,* fury, as a passing passionate feeling). This in turn produces **anger** (*orge,* wrath as a settled spirit with a desire to retaliate), which provokes finally **clamour** and **evil speaking** (*krauge* and *blasphemia*). Evil feelings deepen to the extent that the carnally captive individual must explode into arguing and harmful speech. **Malice** (*kakia*) refers to "the spring of the faults which have been enumerated."[42] *Kakia* is a generic term which takes in all the others which have been mentioned ("bad feeling of every kind," NEB), and thus suggests depravity.

[41]*Op. cit.,* p. 274.

[42]Westcott, *op. cit.,* p. 75.

In v. 32 the apostle appeals to the example of God in Christ Jesus to enforce the injunction regarding forgiveness. He says that we should treat others in the same way that God has treated us with forgiveness, which involves kindness and compassion.

Surely it is not possible for natural man readily and freely to forgive others, nor to maintain equanimity of spirit in the midst of the aggravating experiences of life. He must come to know Christ intimately, to be so fully united with Him that he has a new nature (24). He must be so entirely given over to God that the ungrieved, indwelling Holy Spirit has full control of his life (30). It takes divine love (*agape*) to live graciously in this world, and to hold the right attitude toward others.

Note should be taken of the fact that Paul is here speaking primarily of the relationships within the Christian community. Love and forgiveness must prevail in the household of faith if men apart from our Lord are to see the possibilities of grace for themselves.

Section VIII *Living as the Beloved*

Ephesians 5:1-21

Usually, interpreters of Ephesians ignore the chapter division here and carry through to 5:2. There is a clear relationship between 4:32 and 5:1-2. The appeal that Paul makes to God's forgiving action in 4:32 is repeated in 5:1 in the exhortation, **Be ye therefore followers of God.** Likewise, the call to **walk in love** (5:2) generalizes the advice in 4:32 to be kind, tenderhearted, and forgiving. Nevertheless, the existing chapter division appears to be proper if we think of Paul as making a fresh appeal to his readers on the basis of their relationship to God as His "beloved children" (1, NASB). He calls them to live a life commensurate with their nature as children of God—those who have been adopted by love into the family of the Heavenly Father and have experienced His redeeming love.

"Living as the Beloved"[1] involves (1) Walking worthy of our calling, 4:1; (2) Walking in a manner different from the Gentiles, 4:17; (3) Walking in love, 5:2; (4) Walking in light, 5:8; (5) Walking in wisdom (5:15).

A. Walking in Love, 5:1-7

To be **followers** (*mimetai,* imitators) **of God** means to **walk in love** (1-2). God is love, and because He acts in keeping with His nature, He acts lovingly toward men. Paul writes in Rom. 5:8: "But God commendeth [demonstrates] his love toward us, in that, while we were yet sinners, Christ died for us." Already in this Epistle the apostle has prayed that they might be "rooted and grounded in love" (3:17), that they speak "the truth in love" (4:15), and that they function within the Christian community to the end that it be built up "in love" (4:16). Now he counsels them to make their whole lives a reflection—indeed, a demonstration—of the love of God. Salmond comments, "The 'imitation' must take effect in the practical, unmistakable form of a loving course of life."[2] **Love** in this instance is not *eros,* the love of

[1]Topic suggested by Markus Barth, *op. cit.,* p. 159.
[2]*Op. cit.,* III, 350.

natural relationships; nor *philia,* the love of friendship; but *agape,* the love of pure self-giving, that asks nothing in return and that wishes only for the well-being of the one to whom it is given.[3] *Agape* is God's love, and He gives it to men most fully in the gift of himself as the Holy Spirit. He thus gives himself that men might "live in love."

1. *The Pattern of Love* (5:1-2)

Dietrich Bonhoeffer, while he was in prison, wrote: "No one knows what love is except in the self-revelation of God. . . . It is only the concrete action and suffering of . . . Jesus Christ which will make it possible to understand what love is." He echoed Paul's thought as given here. Both the reality and the possibility of walking in love are portrayed in Christ. The truth that **Christ also hath loved us** constitutes the starting place of the gospel. But there is more to it than just the fact of love. This love issued in a priceless gift: **and hath given himself for us.** Witnessing to his own experience, Paul writes in Gal. 2:20 of the Son of God, "who loved me, and gave himself for me." Love acts; indeed, it acts profoundly and surprisingly. Christ's gift of himself was both **an offering and a sacrifice** (*prosphoran kai thusian*). Hodge comments that "anything presented to God was a *prosphora,* but *thusia* was something slain. The addition of that term, therefore, determines the nature of the offering."[4] Christ presented himself to die on Calvary for the sins of mankind. He became a Sin Offering that we might be delivered from sin (Rom. 3:25). **For a sweetsmelling savour** ("a fragrant aroma," NASB) is reminiscent of the Old Testament sacrifices, the odor of which ascended to the heavens and pleased God. The sacrifice of our Lord likewise brought profound happiness to the Heavenly Father.

Our love must partake of this love of Christ. If we are to imitate God, we must love men with the same sacrificial love which Christ exemplified. We must be so yielded to Christ's way that we will be willing even to suffer with Him if need be in order to enjoy the approbation of the Father and to be God's people in the world.[5] Mackay touches the heart of the truth here when he remarks that to "copy God" is "to be like a Person,

[3]Cf. William Lillie, *Studies in New Testament Ethics* (Philadelphia: Westminster Press, 1963), pp. 163-81.

[4]*Op. cit.,* p. 278.

[5]Cf. J. A. Robinson, *op. cit.,* p. 114.

to reflect His image" and not simply to be loyal to truth or even "loyal to loyalty."[6]

In 4:20—5:3 we see "The Truth in Jesus." Sanctification is this truth in Jesus, John 17:17, 19. This is sanctification, present, entire, and progressive. (1) **Put off . . . the old man.** By crucifixion unto death, Rom. 6:6-7. By expulsion—resurrection life replacing the former manner of life and corruption of deceitful desires, 22. (2) **Put on the new man**—a renewed mind, Rom. 12:2; II Cor. 5:17. A re-creation after the likeness of God **in righteousness and true holiness, 23-24.** (3) The new man lives in honesty toward **his neighbor**—he loves social righteousness, 25, 28—he has a holy indignation toward sin, 26—he is uncompromising in resistance toward Satan, 29—he has a meek and quiet spirit of love, 31-32; 5:2; (4) The sanctified are **sealed unto the day of redemption** by the Holy Spirit, who must not be grieved, 30 (G. B. Williamson).

2. *The Perversion of Love* (5:3-4)

The apostle now thinks of love's opposite. The grand thought of the pure love of Christ suddenly forces him to see the other side, the contrast to this way of love. He sees "love's perversion"[7] in certain sins. (1) **Fornication** (*porneia*) includes every kind of immorality and sexual perversion.[8] (2) **Uncleanness** (*akatharsia*) simply means immorality ("impurity," NASB), and probably is intended here to emphasize this aspect of the previous word. (3) **Covetousness** (*pleonexia*) is correctly translated here; however, many scholars think that it takes on the connotation of greed, relating back to the two previous words. All such acts have only one purpose and that is to gain selfish personal ends, regardless of the harm to others. Conduct of this kind eventually destroys all possibilities of genuine love. **Saints** (Christians) certainly will not indulge in these love-destroying practices. Indeed, Paul says, "Don't even talk about such things" (Phillips).

(4) **Filthiness** (*aischrotes*) means literally "immoral conduct," though it would do no violence to take it to mean filthy talk (cf. Col. 3:8). (5) **Foolish talking** (*morologia*) is really

[6]*Op. cit.*, p. 170.

[7]Foulkes, *op. cit.*, p. 141.

[8]Cf. Barclay's description of conditions in the Graeco-Roman world in the first century A.D. (*op. cit.*, p. 191).

"silly talk" (NASB), the kind of talk that would come from an intoxicated person. (6) **Jesting** (*eutrapelia*) is construed by Robinson to mean "the lightness of witty talk" that plays "too often on the borderline of impropriety."[9] **Not convenient** means "not fitting" (RSV); the NEB says "these things are out of place." We are not to conclude that this passage depreciates "spontaneous Christian gaiety and a sense of humor, but [it indicates] that Christians are not to indulge in empty frivolity."[10] Most certainly, followers of Christ must not engage in smutty talk. On the contrary, thanksgiving for God's deliverance from all sin ought to be in their hearts constantly and on their lips often.

3. *The Penalty of Perversion* (5:5-7)

In these verses, side by side with two exhortations, Paul speaks of two penalties. The first exhortation is in the form of a warning: **Let no man deceive you with vain words** ("shallow arguments," NEB; 6). Apparently the apostle feels compelled to caution them against individuals who might say that these vices will not affect their community or their personal lives. The second exhortation is a directive that they **be not . . . partakers** (7) with such people, who are among **the children of disobedience** (6*b*; cf. 2:2).

The two penalties for the perversion of love are (*a*) no **inheritance in the kingdom of Christ and of God** (5) and (*b*) liability to **the wrath of God** (6*b*). **These things** would be the evils of vv. 3-5. The use of the Greek present tense (*echei*, **hath**; 5) would suggest that such evildoers do not know the benefits of the Kingdom even now. Without a doubt, they will not share in the Kingdom in the future. The phrase **kingdom of Christ and of God,** found only here in the New Testament, does not denote two kingdoms. While temporally the Kingdom is committed to Christ now, it is nevertheless in essence the kingdom of God (cf. Col. 1:13; I Cor. 15:24 ff.). In missing the Kingdom these perverters of love fall under the heavy hand of the righteous anger of God. Already they are its objects (cf. 2:3), but in that last day they will feel the full fury of it.

[9]*Op. cit.*, p. 116.

[10]Alfred Martin, *op. cit.*, p. 1313.

B. Walking in Light, 5:8-14

1. *The Children of Light* (5:8)

Conducting one's life in love gives a dynamic to life. There is no stronger motive for provoking action. But love must have direction, too. Thus, the apostle calls the beloved to **walk as children of light.** Paul contrasts their spiritual change in striking language:[11] "Once you were darkness, but now you are light in the Lord" (RSV). Formerly they were not only groping in darkness, but they were part of it, and contributors to this darkness of sin. Now they are by grace partakers of the light. According to Mackay, the exhortation here is, "Let the children of the light express their true nature. Let them live in accordance with it."[12] Christ is the Light and He creates **children of light** (John 8:12; I John 1:7). Possessing light or being in the light also suggests God's full grace for holy living. Jesus spoke of having "the whole body full of light" and "having no part dark" (Luke 11:34-36).

2. *The Fruit of Light* (5:9)

The best early manuscripts have "the fruit of light" (*photos*) instead of **the fruit of the Spirit** (cf. RSV, NASB). Apparently a copyist, thinking of Paul's enumeration of the fruit of the Spirit (Gal. 5:22-23), conjectured that a substitution of the word "Spirit" for "light" would aid the reader. The meaning is the same with either reading. The three words, **goodness, righteousness, and truth,** characterizing the fruit do not reflect important differences. Collectively they indicate Paul's attempt to assert "the moral significance of *light,* as against false mystical interpretations, or any boast of 'enlightenment' which was barren of moral effect."[13] An inescapable ethical responsibility to be God-like rests upon those who have received the Light.

3. *The Test of Light* (5:10)

Verse 9 is parenthetical and so 10 naturally completes v. 8. **Proving** (*dokimazo*) can mean either "approve" or "test," as in the act of proving the quality of metals. The sense of testing seems most appropriate. Paul wants his readers to conduct their lives in a morally discriminating way and this requires that they

[11]Cf. the same contrast in I Cor. 6:9-11; I Thess. 5:4-5.

[12]*Op. cit.,* p. 167.

[13]Beare, *op. cit.,* X, 709; cf. parallels in John 3:19-21; I John 1:5-7; 2:8-11.

put all their actions "to the test of acceptability" **unto the Lord,** that is, unto Christ.[14] Correspondence between our actions and the perfect, reasonable will of God—insofar as it is known through the illuminating direction of the Holy Spirit—is absolutely necessary if God's blessing is to rest upon our lives.

4. *The Reproof of Light* (5:11-13)

Paul now speaks specifically to the question of the relationship between the children of light and **the unfruitful works of darkness** (11). Does this expression refer to evil persons or to their evil deeds? The answer seems to be *both.* Paul's language in 8 seems to identify the persons participating in the nature of their deeds, whether darkness (evil) or light (good). Christians are not to have **fellowship** (*synkoinoneite*) with evil, whether it be deeds or persons. This verb has the idea of "communing with." It does not necessarily exclude association with "the children of darkness" in the daily routines of life. Calvin makes this distinction: "We must beware of joining or assisting those who do wrong. In short, we must abstain from giving any consent, or advice, or approbation, or assistance; for in all these ways we have fellowship."[15] While this interpretation might be too severe, it does suggest that Christians must "take no part" (NEB) in their works of darkness. Notice that the **works** are described as **unfruitful.** Foulkes comments that "the Apostle does not set one kind of fruit over against another. It is a matter of fruit or no fruit in the sight of God."[16] If **fellowship** produces nothing of eternal good, then it is not for Christians.

The children of light, on the other hand, must **reprove** or "expose" (RSV) the ways of sinful men. Salmond contends that the verb translated **reprove** (*elengcho*) means oral reproof.[17] The consensus of scholars is that it should be taken to mean that the Christian by his life ("a silent process," E. F. Scott) is to bring to light and thus reprove the deeds of darkness.[18] The example of Jesus, and of Paul himself, would certainly indicate that these two need not (indeed should not) be mutually exclusive. Quite obviously, a redemptive purpose lies behind this

[14]*Ibid.;* cf. Rom. 12:2.

[15]*Op. cit.,* p. 310.

[16]*Op. cit.,* p. 146.

[17]*Op. cit.,* III, 356.

[18]Cf. Beare, Foulkes, Alfred Martin, Phillips, NASB.

exhortation. The hope of Paul is that the doers of these deeds of darkness will repent and turn to Christ because of the light shed upon their lives by Christian acquaintances.

Verse 12 expresses why the works of darkness must be reproved. First is their exceeding sinfulness, **for it is a shame even to speak of those things.** Second is the fact of their hiddenness, for they are accomplished **in secret.** Light's essential nature is that of removing darkness and bringing into view whatever is thus concealed. But **the light** of which Paul speaks not only makes visible what is darkened; it transforms that upon which it shines (13). Concerning this transforming power, A. M. Hunter writes, "Let light play steadily on some dark object and it will change it into its own likeness. So the effect of Christian goodness on pagan society will be first to shame and then to purify it."[19]

5. *The Gift of Light* (5:14)

This verse is a bit of poetry used to conclude Paul's appeal to "walk as children of light" (8). NEB sets it in poetic form thus:

Awake, sleeper,
Rise from the dead,
And Christ will shine upon you.

Perhaps it is an early Christian baptism hymn, sung "to symbolize the emergence of the new Christian from the dark sweep of paganism into the radiance and awakening light of the Christian way."[20] Some say it is a poetic compilation of Old Testament scriptures.[21] In any case it is calculated to praise Christ, the Light of the World, who will give light to all men.

C. Walking in Wisdom, 5:15-21

How to relate this next division of the Epistle to the preceding exhortation is problematical. The word **then** (*oun*) is simply the adverb "therefore." Hodge sees a reference back to 5:10-11. The "children of light" are instructed not to have fellowship with the works of darkness, but rather to live so as to reprove and correct them. "Therefore," Paul commands, see **that ye walk**

[19]"The Letter of Paul to the Ephesians," *Layman's Bible Commentary* (Richmond: John Knox Press, 1959), p. 70.

[20]Barclay, *op. cit.*, p. 196.

[21]Moule, *op. cit.*, p. 261.

circumspectly.[22] A simpler view is that which relates it to the preceding verse. Paul's readers must not live carelessly in the evil environment just because they have received enlightenment from God.[23] In either case the main thrust is upon a mode of life which is directed by wisdom. Paul exhorts, **Walk circumspectly, not as fools, but as wise** (15). **Circumspectly** (*akribos*) can mean "exactly," or "by rule," that is, according to a set norm. However, it can also be rendered "diligently" or "carefully" (cf. NASB, RSV, Moffatt, Goodspeed).

The word wisdom appears twice in the Epistle (1:8, 17). The **wise** (*sophoi*) are not intellectuals, men who possess great academic knowledge. Rather, they are those who have received the light and thus are committed to the truth of God. Essentially, wisdom is a derivative of faith in God. Paul goes on to indicate the various ways by which this wisdom is manifested in one's personal life and in the community of believers.

1. *"Redeeming the Time"* (5:16)

Redeeming (*exagorazomenoi,* buying) does not need to carry the idea of paying a particular price, but rather "making the most of." **Time** (*kairos*) "denotes a critical epoch, a special opportunity, which may soon pass."[24] The most accurate rendering would be "making the most of your opportunity" (cf. Col. 4:5). Service to God lies behind the apostle's thought. As Erdman says, "The wisdom of their walk would thus consist in their careful endeavor to seize upon every fitting season for doing good, and to make their own every possible occasion for the fulfillment of duty."[25] The precious opportunity to witness for Christ must not be allowed to slip out of our hands, **because the days are evil.** The obstacles erected by sin are numerous and formidable; thus we must be prepared to act immediately upon the gracious leading of the Holy Spirit. Phillips renders the verse, "Make the best use of your time, despite all the difficulties of these days."

2. *Understanding the Will of the Lord* (5:17)

All Christian living relates to the will of God. That will has as its central purpose the salvation of all men. These people

[22] *Op. cit.*, p. 298.
[23] Cf. Beare, *op. cit.*, X, 712-13.
[24] Bruce, *Ephesians*, p. 109.
[25] *Op. cit.*, p. 103.

are exhorted not to become **unwise** (*aphrones,* dumb, stupid), by slipping into negligence and inactivity. They are to seek to know the will of the Lord and to follow it in everyday living to the salvation of their own souls and the souls of others. Blaikie remarks, "The will of the Lord is the great rule of the Christian life; to know and in the deeper sense understand this, is to walk wisely and to walk surely."[26]

3. *Being Filled with the Spirit* (5:18)

Behind this exhortation might have been the drunken and debauched ecstasies of the mystery religions, which were induced by the use of intoxicating wine. Paul insists that drunkenness is "the gateway to profligacy" (excess). The Christian must seek to keep a clear mind always. The day-by-day experiences of the Christian man must be that of being **filled with the Spirit.** The verb **filled** is a present imperative and can be translated "be continually filled with the Spirit." But it stands to reason that a Christian cannot *go on being filled* until he has first been filled at some given time, as was true on the Day of Pentecost. Ralph Earle comments, "This is not to be a transitory experience, but an abiding one."[27] The verbs in the present tense which appear in 19-21 suggest that Paul is not here calling his readers to the crisis of being sanctified wholly, but rather to the subsequent life in which the Holy Spirit fills us moment by moment, having already been "sealed with the Holy Spirit of promise" (1:13, NASB; cf. 4:30). Moule paraphrases:

"Let the Holy One, your Sealer and Sanctifier, so surround and possess you that you shall be as it were vessels immersed *in* His pure flood; and then, yielding your hearts without reserve to Him, you shall be vessels not only immersed but open; '*in* Him,' and '*filled*' in Him, as He continually welcomes, continually occupies and hallows all parts of your nature, all departments of your life."[28]

4. *Expressing the Spirit's Joy* (5:19-20)

What a contrast between the results of drunkenness and the filling of the Spirit! It is generally agreed that Paul is not here speaking primarily of worship services, but rather of the normal

[26]*Op. cit.*, p. 210.

[27]"Gleanings from the Greek New Testament," *Nazarene Preacher,* XXXIX (October, 1964), 38.

[28]*Op. cit.*, pp. 274-75.

social intercourse of every day. Spirit-filled men will be heard **speaking to one another** in the language of devotion and praise (19*a*; Col. 3:16). **Psalms** may refer to the Book of Psalms of the Old Testament. **Hymns** probably mean early Christian compositions, some of which appear to have been preserved in the New Testament. Many scholars have accepted the following as hymns or parts of hymns: Phil. 2:5-11; Col. 1:12-18; Titus 2:11-14; I Pet. 3:18-22. The Book of Revelation has several poetic passages which must have been sung in the early years of the Church. **Spiritual songs** may be spontaneous creations expressing joy and praise at a time of special outpouring of the Spirit upon the people.

Erdman takes the clause **singing and making melody in your heart to the Lord** as suggesting a feeling of praise in the heart. He writes, "The silent music of the rejoicing heart is to accompany the praise of anointed lips."[29] The central thrust of both the "outward" and "inward" rejoicing is thanksgiving (20). God has done wonderful things for His people and these He has given through His Son. Thus the praise is to **the Father in the name of our Lord Jesus Christ** (cf. I Cor. 5:4; 6:11; Col. 3:17; II Thess. 3:6). Mercy and grace have been mediated to men through Christ; thus He provides in His atoning work the access to the Father, unto whom gratitude is expressed. How shall we explain the possibility of being thankful to God for all things? As just noted, Paul probably means "for all the blessings that God has given us." If we understand the expression as fully literal, Paul's parallel statement from Phil. 4:6 is helpful, "*in* every thing . . . with thanksgiving." We may be thankful for God's help *in* the midst of circumstances even when we find it hard to be thankful *for* the situation. And further, the man who walks with God can always find some part of any circumstance an occasion *for* thanksgiving (cf. Rom. 8:28).

5. *Submitting to One Another* (5:21)

Paul's concern with unity in the Church breaks through to the surface again. When a genuine spirit of thanksgiving prevails among God's people, there will be a readiness to subject oneself to the others within the community. The essential equality of every member is produced by the common experience of grace

[29]*Op. cit.*, p. 105; cf. Westcott, *op. cit.*, p. 82: "The outward music was to be accompanied by the inward music of the heart."

and forgiveness. This is the basis for mutual submission. Allen interprets Paul's exhortation as "mutual consideration." "It does not mean spineless and cringing yielding to the aggressiveness of others, but is rather the outcome in practice of a strong and sober attitude of respect for one-self and for others."[30] The phrase **the fear of God** is found in the best manuscripts as "the fear of Christ." **Fear** (*phobos*) in this case is not pathological fear, but simply "reverence," as it is frequently interpreted in the Old Testament. Fear of the last judgment is not the background for this behavior. Christians are ready to yield to the demands of the Church because they want the body to be strong and united, knowing full well that they will be held accountable to their Lord for any disharmony. Authoritarianism and independence of spirit eventually destroy unity. Joyful submission to one another, on the other hand, is the highest reverence to the Head of the body, Christ. Such reverence maintains the Church in peace, and therein is her greatest strength.

[30]*The Epistle to the Ephesians,* "The Torch Bible Commentaries" (London: SCM Press, Ltd., 1959), p. 125.

Section IX *Christian Relationships*

Ephesians 5:22—6:9

Through most of this Epistle, Paul has occupied himself with a description of, and exhortations to, the Christian Church. Through Christ all barriers to admission into the divine society have been broken down, so that now both Jew and Gentile can worship and serve God together in covenant love. The duties which necessarily devolve upon each member as he enjoys the life of the Church have been explicitly set forth, all to the end of keeping "the unity of the Spirit in the bond of peace" (4:3). But as Dale remarks, "The true Christian life is not an isolated life. To live always alone, among Divine and eternal things, is a false ideal of moral and religious perfection."[1] Outside the fellowship of believers there is a set of personal relationships or social institutions which existed long before the historical Church and which for every person are largely fixed. For example, each person lives within the framework of the family. In Paul's day this primary social unit involved not only the parent-child and the husband-wife relationships, but also the master-servant associations. What did it mean, then, to live the new life in these common relationships? Would it make any difference when a person had become a Christian? It is to a discussion of Christian living in the family that the apostle now turns.[2]

Two principles control Paul's discourse on the Christian understanding of domestic relations. The first is "the far-reaching precept of mutual subjection," which has already been stated in v. 21, and which in all likelihood led him to discuss these related matters at this point. While in each set of associations the "lesser" person is asked in one way or another to submit to the "greater" (5:22; 6:1, 5), there are exacting responsibilities for the "greater" too. The modern mind sometimes finds this approach to social relations offensive, since unbridled freedom is the god par excellence for man today. In v. 21 the participle translated **submitting yourselves** (*hupotassomenoi*) is in the

[1]*Op. cit.*, p. 349.

[2]The state-citizen question is discussed in Rom. 13:1-7; cf. Col. 3:18—4:1 for another list of "household duties."

present middle voice and so leaves a degree of choice. W. O. Carver has observed that subjection is to be "voluntary, personal, and having full ethical value for the one who subjects himself and for others whom he serves in spiritual surrender."[3]

The second principle is that in each set of relationships "the obligation is based on the connection of the believer with Christ (5:22; 6:1, 5)."[4] It is being "in the Lord" that commits one to this kind of living. This submission to one another is not the same level of commitment as one must make to the Lord. The degree of subordination required in these areas is determined by one's obedience and submission to Christ. Paul believes that if the graces of the Lord flourish in the Christian Church they most certainly ought to be expected to prosper in the closely knit life of the individual family.

A. Husbands-Wives, 5:22-33

Paul starts with the highest of the familial relationships, that of the husband and wife. The other two sets of relations are of relatively lesser importance. The parent-child relationship is a product of the love between a man and a woman, whereas the master-slave relationship is part of the attempt of a man to provide economically for his family. Notwithstanding, both of these social interdependencies bear profound significance in being a Christian in this "first great frontier of human existence."[5] The starting point for the cessation of strife is a holy bond between husband and wife.

1. *The Submission of Wives* (5:22-24)

Every personal relationship has some element of submission in it. In the natural order of things the husband occupies a position of priority. Paul fully recognizes this in calling wives to **submit yourselves** (22; cf. I Cor. 11:2-16; Col. 3:18). Unrelated maritally, male and female by creation are equal, but in the family setting the husband must assume certain divinely ordained prerogatives and the wife must gladly accept this relationship. Bruce writes that it is not that "wives are inferior to their husbands, either naturally or spiritually. But Paul recognizes a

[3]*The Glory of God in the Christian Calling* (Nashville: Broadman Press, 1949), p. 165.

[4]Westcott, *op. cit.*, pp. 82-83.

[5]Mackay, *op. cit.*, p. 188.

divinely ordained hierarchy in the order of creation, and in this order the wife has a place next after husband."[6] Wives must be willing to surrender to their husbands in order that the husband may exercise the authority which is his responsibility. Many modern marriages have been wrecked because wives have been unwilling to recognize this fact as it relates to the husband's labor, location of the home, and discipline of children. This deference by the wife is done **as unto the Lord,** that is, as part of her duty to the Lord. It is assumed that Paul speaks here in terms of Christian families, where this kind of submission should be both feasible and possible.

To bring his appeal within the frame of reference of this letter, Paul introduces the analogy of the headship of Christ as a reinforcement of his assertion that wives should submit to their husbands (23; cf. 1:22). In I Cor. 11:3, Paul wrote: "I want you to understand that the head of every man is Christ, the head of a woman is her husband, and the head of Christ is God" (RSV). In this "ascending chain of relationship" two important ideas are evident. (1) Headship "denotes primarily controlling authority and the right to obedience."[7] (2) Control and obedience take place "within a living organism where the two parts are complementary each to the other."[8] Unity lies at the base of all three relationships mentioned in the Corinthian note, and Paul sees the hope of united families in this understanding of the husband-wife relationship.

Not only is the husband **the head of the wife;** he is also analogously **the saviour of the body.** By strictest interpretation, the last phrase applies in the text primarily to Christ, who is "the deliverer and defender of the Church which is His body."[9] Surely the husband cannot be the saviour of his wife in redemptive terms, but he can be her protector and provider. Any sacrifice and self-giving that create a sense of well-being and security will normally evoke free and loving submission from his wife. Martin concludes, "The husband must find the pattern of his conduct in the conduct of Christ towards His Church."[10]

[6] *Ephesians,* p. 114.

[7] Beare, *op. cit.,* X, 720.

[8] *Ibid.*

[9] Bruce, *Ephesians,* p. 114.

[10] W. G. M. Martin, *op. cit.,* p. 1028.

Verse 24 repeats the responsibility of the **wives** to be subject **to their own husbands,** just as **the church is subject unto Christ.** The little phrase **in every thing** might be offensive to modern woman with her far-reaching freedom in society. What if she has responsibilities outside the home such as would prevail in a chosen career? The answer is a matter of priorities. Foulkes remarks: "She may fulfill any function and any responsibility in society, but if she has accepted before God the responsibility of marriage and of a family, these must be her first concern."[11] As the Church is expected to give first place to her devotion and service to Christ, so the wife must give first place to her functions as wife and mother. The intimate and delicate character of the marital and family relationships permits no equivocation at this point. But when submission takes place within the context of love, it is not grievous nor humiliating, but magnifying.

2. *The Love of Husbands* (5:25-33)

Let not wives think that husbands go scot-free in this relationship. Paul has something to say to the husband too. St. Chrysostom commented: "Hast thou seen the measure of obedience? hear also the measure of love. Wouldst thou that thy wife should obey thee as the Church doth Christ? have care thyself for her, as Christ for the Church."

Love your wives (25), Paul writes to the husbands. Behind this exhortation and endowing it with infinite meaning is the majestic analogy of the Church as the bride of Christ, which was introduced above but is developed to its climax here (cf. 27). The word **love** is a present imperative (*agapate*) and means "continue to love" or "go on loving." The love which brought husband and wife together in marriage must be nurtured and expressed as the years of marriage pass. Throughout the marital years, husbands should love their wives as they did on the day they took them as brides.

Husbands must love their wives, **even as Christ also loved the church.** In this analogy Paul characterizes the love that a husband is to have for his wife. Christ's love for the Church is the supreme example of all loves, and in this instance the love which a husband must demonstrate toward his wife.

a. Christ's Love Was a Self-giving Love (5:25). Christ "gave himself up" for the Church (25*b*, RSV). For Paul, God gave

[11]*Op. cit.*, p. 157.

Christ to mankind, and Christ in turn gave himself for man's deliverance. (Cf. Rom. 5:8.) In Gal. 1:4 he speaks of "our Lord Jesus Christ, who gave himself for our sins." In Titus 2:14 he describes Christ as the One "who gave himself for us." Already the apostle has touched upon this essential truth in 5:2, where he appeals to his readers to "walk in love, as Christ also hath loved us, and hath given himself for us."

In the highly christocentric theology of Paul, Christ is the norm for the whole of life. Here sacrificial, self-giving love constitutes the very essence of Christian living. If "walking in love" is necessary for the whole life, it follows that it is compulsory for this particular relationship in life. The application thus is that, as Christ gave himself up for His Church, a husband must be willing to make any sacrifice, even the sacrifice of his own life, if necessary, for the well-being and happiness of his wife. Moule interprets Paul as saying, "Love your wives, with a love warm always with the first summer of its pure human gladness, but kept high and true meantime by an ideal great as heaven."[12] The supreme affection of Christ involves passion, undying devotion, sensitivity to need, and self-denial. With such love, husbands must love their wives.

b. Christ's Love Was a Sanctifying Love (5:26-27). The object of Christ's great sacrifice of himself in death, provoked by His unsurpassed love, was the sanctification of the Church. In our English translation the thought of Paul does not come through clearly. The two words **sanctify** (*hagiase*) and **cleanse** (*katharisas*) are translated as if they are identical verb forms. **Cleanse,** however, is an aorist participle and indicates action which has taken place prior to the action of the main verb, **sanctify.** This being the case, the most proper translation would be: "that he might sanctify her, having cleansed her" (NASB). In other words, "having cleansed her" refers to the cleansing which takes place in regeneration, whereas **sanctify** denotes the cleansing from inbred sin. Hodge favors this handling of these verbs. He asserts, "The Bible always represents remission of sin or the removal of guilt as preceding sanctification. We are pardoned and reconciled to God, in order that we may be made holy."[13] While he would not accept sanctification as a second crisis ex-

[12]*Op. cit.*, p. 291.
[13]*Op. cit.*, p. 320.

perience, Hodge is explicit as to the distinction between regeneration and sanctification which the aorist participle properly denotes. Since both verb forms are in the punctiliar aorist tense, we are justified in taking them as referring to decisive rather than to gradual experiences. The Bible teaches that both regeneration and sanctification are such crisis experiences.

With the washing of water by the word has its parallel in Titus 3:5, where Paul says that God has saved us "by the washing of regeneration, and renewing of the Holy Ghost." Baptismal regeneration is not intended by the term **washing.** As Bruce says, "To this perversion, needless to say, the New Testament gives no countenance; regeneration is an inward change wrought by the Holy Spirit."[14] However, the symbolism of baptism is used to carry the thought. The cleansing away of the guilt and power of sin in the experience of regeneration is signified and witnessed to publicly in baptism.[15] The symbolism of water as representing spiritual purification or cleansing is found throughout the Bible and we should see this particular reference within that context (cf. Ezek. 16:9; 36:25; I Cor. 6:11; Heb. 10:22). The phrase **by the word** cannot be construed to mean either the baptismal formula or the confession of the recipient of baptism; it refers to the gospel or the word of God. It is also to be attached to the word **sanctify,** rather than to **cleanse.** In keeping with this analysis, the translation would be: "Christ sanctified His Church by the word, having cleansed it with the washing of water." In John 17:17, it is recorded that Christ prayed, "Sanctify them through thy truth: thy word is truth." The word of God is the means or instrument by which the deeper purification beyond conversion is accomplished. This second blessing is administered by the Holy Spirit upon the acceptance by faith of the meritorious death of Christ by the converted Christian.

Paul seems to have moved a great distance from his central concern of the love which husbands must have for their wives. The intrinsic beauty of his analogy of the bride and bridegroom captured his imagination and led his thought in this direction. But essentially he still is speaking to his point. Wives have imperfections; they do not come to their husbands as perfect wives, just as is the case with the Church. Christ's love led Him to pay the supreme price of death in order to sanctify His bride. So the

[14]*Ephesians*, p. 116.

[15]Wesley, *op. cit.*, p. 719; Dale, *op. cit.*, p. 358.

love of the husband must be such as to effect the removal of those traits in the wife which would keep the marital relationship from yielding its God-intended joys. Barclay remarks, "Real love is the great cleanser and purifier of all life."[16]

The sanctification of the Church makes it possible for Christ to **present it to himself a glorious church** (27). The word **present** (*parastese*) is not to be taken here to mean the presenting of an offering, but simply as "setting forth." Christ is "at once the Agent and the End or Object of the presentation."[17] Christ presents the bride **to himself.** Strangely, the preparation of the bride for the wedding is fundamentally the work of the Bridegroom. No external beautification can make her acceptable to Him. Beauty is love's work. In this case, the Bridegroom's sacrificial love refines the relationship with the Church until the bride comes forth in the beauty of holiness. **Glorious** simply means "in keeping with the nature with which He has endowed her," a nature resplendent in its own right. Westcott paraphrases the expression **not having spot, or wrinkle, or any such thing** as "without one trace of defilement or one mark of age."[18] Wesley interprets the first phrase as "impurity from any sin." He explains **wrinkle** as a "deformity from any decay."[19] **Holy and without blemish** repeats the thought in 1:4. This is the great object of the Lord's cleansing ministry. In II Cor. 11:2 the apostle speaks of his own "godly jealousy" over the Church to present her "a pure bride to her husband" (RSV). The ultimate presentation will take place at that final day of Christ's appearing, but even now it is taking place so that men might see His marvelous grace.

In 25-27 we see "A Glorious Church." The Church maintains a threefold relationship: (*a*) to the world, the ecclesia (gathered out); (*b*) within itself, the koinonia (fellowship); (*c*) to Christ as His body, the kerygma (preaching). (1) The Church beloved that it might be sanctified, 25-26. (2) The Church sanctified and cleansed: by **washing of water**—baptism. By the Blood applied, as set forth in the Lord's Supper. **By the word.** All of these vitalized and realized in the presence of the Spirit, 26. (3) The Church presented as the bride of Christ, sub-

[16]*Op. cit.*, p. 206.

[17]Salmond, *op. cit.*, III, 369.

[18]*Op. cit.*, p. 85.

[19]*Op. cit.*, p. 719.

missive, glorious, universal, and victorious, 27 (G. B. Williamson).

c. *Christ's Love Was a Sustaining and Caring Love* (5:28-31). Paul here returns to the husband-wife relationship, but he has not left his analogy. At the end of 29 he adds the phrase, **even as the Lord the church.** Two things are said here by way of the husbands' loving care of their wives. First, they are to love their wives **as their own bodies** (28). The meaning of this phrase is obscure in the English. Love of the physical body is not intended. Husbands should love their wives "as being their own bodies; as part of their total self, not as another being external to them."[20] The unity of relationship is such that **he that loveth his wife loveth himself.** Husband and wife are "complementary parts of one personality."[21]

Second, when the husbands think of their wives as part of themselves, as their **flesh,** instinctively they will sustain, protect, and tenderly care for them (29). They will act in the same way as Christ, who loves and cares for us as **members of his body** (30). The phrases **of his flesh, and of his bones** do not appear in some translations. The best and earliest manuscripts do not have them. It has been conjectured that a scribe added them in anticipation of the next verse, which is a quotation from Gen. 2:24.

The primeval law of marriage, as given in Gen. 2:24, is recalled by the apostle in v. 31. This is not to emphasize that a husband must separate himself from his father and mother when he takes his bride, but rather to reinforce the idea of oneness, as expressed in the clause: **and they two shall be one flesh.** The creation ordinance declares the absolute unity and identity of husband and wife. Numerous attempts have been made to apply this verse mystically and allegorically, especially as regards identity of man with Christ and the Church.[22] But such interpretation should be avoided. The interpretative relationship between the union of Christ with His Church and the union of the husband with his wife is part and parcel of the entire passage. But the analogy must not be taken any further than the emphasis on unity. The union of Christ with His Church is without a doubt

[20]Beare, *op. cit.,* X, 724.

[21]*Ibid.,* p. 725.

[22]Cf. Salmond for a resumé of the history of interpretation, *op. cit.,* III, 372-73.

the highest of relationships and it suggests to Paul the pattern for the marital relationship. In this connection Barclay sees an emphasis upon the "unbreakable" character of love. Commenting on the husband's identification with his wife, he writes, "He is united to her as the members of the body are united to each other. He no more thinks of separating from her than he would of tearing his own body apart."[23]

d. Christ's Love Is a Mystery (5:32-33). The exclamatory statement, **This is a great mystery**, needs clarification. A better translation is given by the NASB: "This mystery is great." The word *mysterion* is employed by Paul in several ways. First, it denotes the eternal secret of God to save all men through Christ, and especially to incorporate the Gentiles into His believing people (cf. 1:9; 3:3-9; 6:19). Second, used in the plural, it denotes divine truths in general (I Cor. 4:1; 13:2; 14:2). Third, used in the singular, it has reference to "some particular deep truth of the divine plan which has been revealed" (cf. Rom. 11:25; I Cor. 15:51). In this third way it is employed here in v. 32.[24] The sense of Paul's statement is, "It is a great truth that is hidden here" (NEB).

But what is the antecedent which evokes this declaration? It is not the reference to the creation ordinance, though that would be most natural. At least that is the way Paul thought his readers might interpret it. So he clarifies himself: **I speak concerning Christ and the church.** Despite the original intention to deal with the husband-wife relationship, Paul finds himself again caught up in the wonders and glories of Christ's union with His Church. To be sure, there is something of mystery in all the relations of life, but the preeminent mystery—the mystery of mysteries—is that of the love and sacrifice of Christ for His redeemed people.

Descending from his lofty heights, the apostle summarizes what he has been saying in the preceding passage. Verse 33 takes us back to verse 22. **In particular** emphasizes the obligation which falls upon each husband to **love his wife even as himself.** The word **reverence** translates a verb which is more literally "fear" (*phobetai*). But wives certainly cannot be their true selves by living in fear of their husbands. In 21, the same idea is used.

[23]*Op. cit.*, p. 207.

[24]Foulkes, *op. cit.*, p. 162.

Christians are exhorted to submit to one another "in the fear of God." Apprehension and dread are not intended by this phrase, but faith, and reverence as understood in Old Testament thought. "The fear of the Lord is the beginning of wisdom" (Prov. 9:10). Thus, the wife is to **reverence her husband** in the sense of respecting him as head of the home and of clinging to him in faith, knowing that he has forsaken "all others" for her. Chrysostom expresses the meaning here with discerning words: "And of what nature is this 'fear'? It is that she should not gainsay thee, or set herself against thee, or love pre-eminence; if fear govern to this extent, it is enough. But if thou lovest her, as thou art commanded, thou wilt achieve more than this; nay, rather, thou wilt achieve this no longer by fear, but love itself will have its own effect."

B. Parents-Children, 6:1-4

A second dimension of the domestic structure now receives Paul's attention, namely, the relationship between parents and children. When there is genuine love in the home, the proper basis for wholesome living for all the members prevails. Nevertheless, duties devolve upon each member.

By including these few verses Paul dignifies the place of the child in the Christian home and community. Such concern was not the attitude of the ancient world. Roman practice gave the father absolute power over his children. He had the right to punish them as his wrath might sinfully dictate, to sell them into slavery if he thought they were too expensive or worthless to him, or under certain conditions, to put them to death. This power of the father over his children extended throughout his lifetime. Child life was cheap, as is revealed in a letter dated 1 B.C. and written by a Roman soldier, Hilarion, from Alexandria, Egypt, to his wife, Alis. He orders her to permit their expected child to live if it is born a male, but to cast it out if it is a female.[25] Turning children loose to fend for themselves was a common practice in that day. Against such devaluation of young human life Jesus spoke when He called the children to himself (Matt. 19:14). Paul stands with Jesus in seeing the infinite value of every child, and His careful delineation of the mutual responsibilities of children and parents supports this fact.

[25]W. H. Davis, *Greek Papyri of the First Century* (New York: Harper and Bros., 1933), p. 1; cf. Barclay's discussion, *op. cit.*, pp. 207 ff.

1. *The Obedience of Children* (6:1-3)

Paul charges: **Children, obey your parents** (1). Martin has noted that "*obedience* is a stronger term than *submission,* which was given as the duty of the wife."[26] The verb generally translated "to obey" (*hupakouo*) is a compound created from the word "to hear" (*akouo*). Thus it has in its background the idea of "listening" or "attending to," hence "obeying." Much disobedience results from the unwillingness of children to listen to the instructions given and to the reasons for those instructions. Moule's paraphase is suggestive: "with the listening ear of unhesitating attention."[27] Children have a moral obligation, to the extent that they are able to conceive it, to keep the lines of communication between themselves and their parents open by being ready to listen and to obey. **In the Lord** parallels phrases found earlier (4:1, 17; 5:22) and defines the sphere within which obedience is to take place. Salmond says it is "a Christian obedience fulfilled in communion with Christ."[28] Apparently Paul is speaking to a situation in which all are Christians and does not specify what the attitude should be when the parental orders are contrary to the law of Christ.

The sanctions for this injunction are two. First, Paul says obedience is **right** (*dikaios*). In the Pauline vocabulary this word means "righteous." So the apostle is not asserting that obedience is simply fitting and orderly, but rather that it is "well pleasing unto the Lord" (Col. 3:20). This meaning of **right** is further enforced by quoting the fifth commandment. Men who are righteous live by God's laws. Children who would be righteous in their relationship with their parents must keep this particular law.

Second, and closely related to the previous appeal, is Paul's declaration that obedience honors one's parents. The apostle quotes Exod. 20:12 and Deut. 5:16—**Honour thy father and mother.** Salmond comments, "*Obedience* is the *duty; honour* is the *disposition* of which the obedience is born."[29] Readiness to obey is not enough; there must be actual obedience, if honor of parents is to be evident. Moreover, an emphasis is made here

[26] Alfred Martin, *op. cit.,* p. 1315.

[27] *Op. cit.,* p. 303.

[28] *Op. cit.,* III, 375

[29] *Ibid.,* III, 375

upon the fact that this is **the first commandment with promise.** In what way this is the **first** (*prote*) commandment with an attached promise has created some difficulties, because the second of the Ten Commandments has a promise, also (Exod. 20:4-6). Probably the best explanation is that Paul here uses **first** to mean "first in importance" for children.[30]

Paul combines elements from Exod. 20:12 and Deut. 5:16 in stating the twofold **promise.** The idea of prosperity, **that it may be well with thee,** is taken from Deuteronomy; whereas long life, **mayest live long on the earth,** is found in Exodus. Is this promise to be dismissed as simply a vestige of Israelite faith, or is it relevant now? Can we properly hold our prosperity and longevity as benefits of obedience? There has been bargain-counter Christianity in our time, and the uses of it are revolting to the Christian Church. But we must not lose sight of the Bible's declaration of rewards. As Theodore Wedel writes, "There simply *are* rewards that come to the godly—nonmaterial, if rightly seen, but no less humanly concrete."[31] Hodge insists that this is "a revelation of a general purpose of God, and makes known what will be the usual course of his providence."[32] However, it may not be carried out in every life. "The general promise is fulfilled to individuals, just so far 'as it shall serve for God's glory, and their own good.' "[33]

2. *The Duty of Fathers* (6:4)

Disobedience of children can destroy the peace of a Christian home, but on the other hand parental insensitivity and harshness can be just as devastating. Thus Paul has a word for the parents, represented here by the father, to whom are given the direction and discipline of the family. The duty of the father is twofold. First, there is a negative responsibility: **provoke not your children to wrath.** The verb here is *parorgizo,* and is found only in Paul's Epistles (Rom. 10:19; Eph. 4:26). Here it means "to irritate" or "to exasperate." Fathers are exhorted not "to excite the bad passions of their children by severity, injustice, partiality, or

[30]Cf. Moody, *op. cit.,* p. 129; for lengthy discussions see Salmond, *op. cit.,* III, 375; Foulkes, *op. cit.,* pp. 164-65.

[31]"The Epistle to the Ephesians" (Exposition), *The Interpreter's Bible,* ed. George A. Buttrick, *et al.,* X (New York: Abingdon-Cokesbury Press, 1953), 731.

[32]*Op. cit.,* p. 359.

[33]*Ibid.*

unreasonable exercise of authority."[34] Discipline in the home is absolutely necessary, but too many rules and regulations, along with the inevitable nagging which such a situation creates, will eventually lead to outright rebellion. Phillips expresses the point succinctly, "Fathers, don't overcorrect your children or make it difficult for them to obey the commandment."

Second, there is a positive responsibility: **bring them up in the nurture and admonition of the Lord.** The two words **nurture** (*paideia*) and **admonition** (*nouthesia*) can be translated "physical punishment" and "rebuke." This translation would give the impression that Paul is exhorting chastisement and oral correction. But the more reasonable explanation is that *paideia* is education in the widest sense, "the whole process of instruction," as it is used in Greek literature generally. Even in this sense, however, disciplinary action is not entirely removed. **Admonition** (*nouthesia*) is simply instruction or teaching. The use of the verb "to bring up" (*ektrepho*), in parallel construction with "to cherish" (*thalpo*), in 5:29, supports this more positive translation of these words. The task of the father is to involve himself in a serious and tender program of training his children in all those areas of life which will bring about personal, social, and spiritual growth. All discipline and instruction must be done in the mind and spirit **of the Lord.** Foulkes comments, *"The nurture and admonition of the Lord* is that which the Lord is able to bring into the life of a child if parents do their work of teaching and training in the Word of the Lord."[35]

C. Masters-Slaves, 6:5-9

Continuing his wise counsels concerning domestic relationships, Paul turns to the most serious social situation of the first century. The world of the apostle's day was a world filled with slavery. It has been estimated that there were sixty million slaves in the Roman Empire. The affluence of the Roman society encouraged the tendency to seek freedom from all daily labor, so that in due time it was beneath the dignity of a Roman citizen to work. This led to a rapid expansion of slavery. Surprising to the twentieth-century reader is the fact that slaves existed at all levels of the social structure. Not only unskilled laborers, but

[34]Hodge, *op. cit.*, p. 359.
[35]*Op. cit.*, p. 166.

many doctors, teachers, secretaries, artists, actors, and individuals related to high-level political positions were also enslaved.

Slavery in the Roman world might result from being captured in war, found guilty of crime, sold by one's father while a child, or hopelessly indebted to a creditor. As a slave a man became the indisputable property of his master. If the master was a kind and considerate person, life for the servant was endurable, and sometimes to be preferred over freedom. In some cases, where a slave was attached to a family, he was considered one of the members of the household and enjoyed many of its privileges. On the other hand, the life of most slaves was grim and tragic. Masters, who held the power of life or death and who at times looked upon slaves as mere property, did not hesitate to mistreat and brutally beat them.[36]

Upon reading Paul's instructions to slaves and masters (cf. also Col. 3:22-25), as well as those of Peter (I Pet. 2:18-25), a Christian in a free society might wonder why Paul did not vigorously attack the system of slavery of his day. As Beare says, "The injunctions . . . do not imply either approval or condemnation of the institution of slavery in itself, but are based upon the matter-of-fact recognition that it constituted the sociological framework within which many members of the Christian community found their lives actually cast."[37]

No command to release slaves is found in Paul's writings. Why? Several reasons have been offered for this lack. (1) Paul expected the near return of the Lord and thus decided there was nothing to be gained by introducing a massive movement to change this social evil (cf. I Thess. 4:13-18). (2) To encourage the emancipation of slaves on a church-wide scale "would have been to confirm the suspicion of many people in authority that the gospel aimed at the subversion of society."[38] (3) The economic status of slaves was such that to offer them freedom would have put them at the mercy of society. To remain legally related to a good master constituted greater protection than to be free. (4) It has been suggested that among the Christians the slave was accorded all the privileges of the Christian fellowship and en-

[36]Cf. A. H. J. Greenidge, *Roman Public Life* (London: Macmillan & Co., 1901), pp. 21-24; Barclay, *op. cit.*, pp. 212-14.

[37]*Op. cit.*, X, 732.

[38]Bruce, *Ephesians*, p. 125.

joyed growth in spiritual things, so that his civil status was in no sense a spiritual hindrance. None of these reasons satisfies us fully, because, as Bruce comments, "slavery under the best conditions is slavery none the less, and it could not survive where the gospel had free course."[39]

What is most significant in this Ephesian passage is the appeal that Paul makes to the slaves and the masters to make this relationship one through which Christ might be seen in their lives. Paul's brief Epistle to Philemon, in which he makes intercession on behalf of Onesimus, the runaway slave, illuminates in a specific manner the instructions given here to both slaves and masters. Onesimus is to be received "not now as a servant, but above a servant, a brother beloved" (Philem. 16).

1. *The Obedience of Slaves* (6:5-8)

In calling slaves to **be obedient** to their **masters,** the apostle uses the same strong word as in speaking to the children (1). This fact indicates Paul's recognition of the stringent character of the institution of slavery. But at the same time it shows his sensitivity to the attitudes required to keep relationships of this kind intact. Readiness to listen, to be teachable, and to comply with order constitute the substance of the call to obedience.

The phrase **masters according to the flesh,** describing the ones to whom slaves are to be obedient, is puzzling to interpreters. Most generally, in Paul's teaching, **according to the flesh** is taken antithetically, standing over against "according to the Spirit." Thinking in these terms Hodge writes of this present use: "It limits the authority of the Master to what is external; the soul being left free."[40] But carried to its final conclusion, this line of reasoning asserts that matters which are **according to the flesh** are under the final jurisdiction of the slave's earthly masters, whereas only matters which are "according to the Spirit" are under Christ's direction. The exhortations of Paul, therefore, would be limited to the duties related to the external and material. A better and more precise way to interpret this phrase is to see that above the temporal order is the spiritual order, which is permanent and finally controlling. Bruce comments, "The slave-master relationship belongs to the passing temporal order . . . In the spiritual realm, Christian slaves and

[39]*Ibid.*

[40]*Op. cit.*, p. 363.

masters alike were fellow-servants of one Lord, Jesus Christ."[41] Christ is the higher Master and He oversees the whole life of the slave. While the slave's first loyalty and obedience must be rendered to his God, yet he recognizes this other authority and seeks to render sincere and generous obedience.[42] In the current struggle of enslaved peoples throughout the world, it is imperative that Christians, in their earnestness to right the wrongs, remember that every corrective action must be inspired by the Spirit of the Lord and bathed in love.

In a series of pithy phrases the apostle characterizes for the slaves what obedience means.

a. "With Fear and Trembling" (6:5). This is a familiar phrase of Paul's. It appears in I Cor. 2:3 with reference to his ministry among the Corinthians; in II Cor. 7:15 with reference to the Corinthians' anticipation of the visit of Titus; and in Phil. 2:12 with reference to the working out of one's salvation. Paul by no means suggests that slaves should cringe before their masters, but simply that they should keep a deep sense of respect and reverence for them. Beare writes, "This is the *fear and trembling* which is inseparable from all serious effort to fulfill the will of God in moral action (Phil. 2:12)."[43] The sense of awe which infuses the life of the Christian as he lives before his Maker reaches even into this relationship.

b. "In Singleness of Your Heart" (6:5). The word **singleness** (*haplotes*) is found only in the New Testament in Pauline writings (Rom. 12:8; I Cor. 8:2; 9:11, 13; 11:3; Col. 3:22). It means literally "one fold" of a piece of paper as against "two folds." A firm, all-inclusive purpose rather than a divided loyalty obviously underlies its sense. Hodge remarks, "The thing enjoined is, therefore, the opposite of double-mindedness."[44] Paul is appealing to the slaves to serve their masters without hypocrisy, but with undivided loyalty as pertains to the responsible task involved. **As unto Christ** means with an obedience regarded as being rendered to Christ himself.

c. "Not with Eyeservice" (6:6). Verse 6 contains a negative explanation of the notion of single-mindedness in 5. **Eyeservice**

[41] *Ephesians*, p. 122.

[42] Cf. Beare, *op. cit.*, X, 733.

[43] *Ibid.*

[44] *Op. cit.*, p. 364.

(*ophthalmodouleian*), a word coined by Paul (Col. 3:22), expresses the practice of appearing very busy and dependable whenever the "boss" is present. Such behavior is deceptive, for it is designed "to save appearances and gain undeserved favor, which is not rendered when the master is absent."[45] To act in this manner is contrary to Christian living, because it makes such persons **menpleasers** (*anthropareskos*) and not **servants** (slaves) **of Christ, doing the will of God from the heart.** Servants of God act with a concern to do the will of God from inner compulsion. **Heart** is here *psyche,* which is understood to be an equivalent of "the inner life." As Christ's slaves, their obedience must spring from the soul. Their love to Christ, rather than external factors, must finally control their service. Barclay's comment is cogent: "The conviction of the Christian workman is that every single piece of work he produces must be good enough to show to God."[46]

d. "With Good Will Doing Service" (6:7-8). The service rendered by a believing slave is to be done with **good will** (*met'eunoias*). The thought is more than "a ready willingness."[47] Disposition is involved in this word, which is found only here in the New Testament. Westcott translates it as "kindly feeling,"[48] and the NEB employs the word "cheerful." An ancient will of a slave master, dated A.D. 157, orders the release of five of his slaves "because of their good will and affection" toward him.[49] Paul could not settle for anything less than Christian love even in this relationship, which would by its very nature evoke strong hostility.

The apostle acknowledges in 8 that conscientious service will not always be rewarded by these earthly masters, but it will not be overlooked by the Lord. Every **good thing** will **receive of the Lord** its just reward. The word translated **receive** (*komisetai*) sometimes bears the idea of "recovering" or "receiving back" (Matt. 25:27; II Cor. 5:10; Col. 3:25). Thus Salmond asserts, "The 'good thing' done is represented as being given back to the doer; the certainty, equity and adequacy of the reward being thus

[45]Salmond, *op. cit.*, III, 378.

[46]*Op. cit.*, p. 215.

[47]Bruce, *Ephesians*, p. 124.

[48]*Op. cit.*, p. 90.

[49]Cf. Beare, *op. cit.*, X, 734.

signified (cf. especially II Cor. 5:10)."[50] The books will be balanced, Paul is saying, and the slaves are to be encouraged by that fact (cf. I Cor. 15:58). The future judgment will be impartial, so that each person will receive back what his deeds merit **whether he be bond or free** (cf. Col. 3:24-25). Westcott's words at this point are sobering: "The Divine judgment lies essentially in each deed of man."[51]

2. *The Forbearance of Masters* (6:9)

In exemplifying Christian grace in all the relationships of the domestic situation, the apostle sees that reciprocity is demanded in slavery too—perhaps especially in slavery. The responsibility devolving upon the masters is presented as both positive and negative in character.

a. They are exhorted to **do the same things** unto the slaves. What are **the same things?** It is unnatural to interpret them as services which the masters owe to their slaves. In all likelihood this phrase refers back to "good will" in v. 7. Christian principles must be observed by the masters. They are to show the same goodwill and consideration which are expected from the slaves. In the treatment of his slaves, a master must remember the word of the Lord, "Therefore all things whatsoever ye would that men should do to you, do ye even so to them" (Matt. 7:12).

b. **Masters** are exhorted also to refrain from **threatenings.** First-century slave owners were not known to be careful in the exercise of their authority, and they thought it was necessary to keep slaves in their places by employing the fear motive. They threatened them with physical and material punishment. **Forbearing** (*aniemi*) means, in this instance, "slackening, releasing, and giving up" the practice of threats.[52] Remove threats from the relationship and imbue it with goodwill and thoughtfulness, based upon Christian appreciation for each person, and the result will be a new basis for the resolution of the slave problem. Moody comments, "Threats destroy personal relations and put people behind a mask of insecurity and fear. Love removes these barriers and creates brotherhood."[53] Depersonalization and tyranny are cut from the same cloth. Tyrannize and you depersonalize.

[50]*Op. cit.*, III, 380.
[51]*Op. cit.*, p. 90.
[52]Salmond, *op. cit.*, III, 380.
[53]*Op. cit.*, p. 133.

Conversely, personal dignity and freedom saturated with love belong together. Christian grace repudiates threats and tyranny; it provides the basis for personal dignity and freedom.[54]

In their moments of temptation to become harsh and tyrannical, masters are to remember (1) that their **Master also is in heaven** and (2) that there is no **respect of persons with him.** Their service will receive reward or punishment just as that of the slaves. God is Master and Judge of all. He is not influenced by social position. Moral facts rather than social status are His only concerns. Faithfulness and kindness will be rewarded, but disloyalty and treachery will be severely punished, whether committed by slave or master.

The only sound basis for life either on the domestic front or the labor front is a heart-to-heart relationship in which mutual love and respect prevail. This necessitates what Paul earlier declared: we must submit ourselves to one another in the fear of God (5:21).

[54]Cf. Mackay's discussion, *op. cit.*, pp. 191-94.

Section X *The Christian Warfare*

Ephesians 6:10-20

Upon first observation, the thought of warfare seems to be out of character in this Epistle. To this point the apostle has been speaking about things which remove strife and produce unity and peace. The blessing of the gospel is that it breaks down walls of hostility between men and binds them into a community of peace (2:14-22). Christ is the Bringer of peace by means of His cross. Moreover, in the section just discussed (5:22—6:9), the apostle's great interest is to remove strife and to promote Christian nurture in the domestic relationships in the early Christian community. As Erdman comments, "If in any of his writings reference to spiritual warfare might be omitted, it would most naturally be in the Epistle to the Ephesians."[1]

However, this sudden shift from "the peaceful scene" of the Christian community to "the field of battle" where forces of evil are pictured as being in a massive attack on the Christians is not without its justification. Paul is dealing "with the unseen as well as with the seen."[2] The forces which threaten the Christians as they move along the path of life are not only those which arise out of the human context, but also the supernatural hosts of wickedness. Christians belong to a spiritual as well as to a natural world and can expect to be assailed by spiritually wicked forces. Human ingenuity and strength are not adequate against such powers; God's people need divine resources if they are to win in this struggle. The instructions of the apostle therefore are designed to assure the Christian of victory in the battle.

A. The Preparation of the Christian, 6:10-13

1. *The Source of Strength* (6:10)

Finally (*tou loipou*) does not bear the idea of "in conclusion" so much as "henceforth." A temporal sense is intended, so that "in the future" would not be a mistranslation.[3] Paul wants his

[1]*Op. cit.*, p. 121.

[2]Westcott, *op. cit.*, p. 92.

[3]Cf. Salmond, Beare, Goodspeed, Westcott; cf. Gal. 6:17.

readers to see that disruptive forces play upon the affairs of their lives, and they should be prepared for thrusts by the enemy against their otherwise peaceful existence. Their hope lies in being **strong in the Lord, and in the power of his might.** It is significant that the verb for **strong** (*endunamousthe*) is a present passive. It suggests, first, that they continue to be strengthened by the Lord, and second, that the source of this strength is outside of themselves. It comes from Christ as one lives in union with Him.

In 1:19, Paul prays that they may be so enlightened that they will comprehend "the exceeding greatness of his power," and realize "the working of his mighty power" through faith. In 3:16 he prays that his readers might "be strengthened with might by the Spirit." At that point Paul is dealing with a deeper experience of the Holy Spirit. In this verse, however, the emphasis falls not upon the acquisition of new power but the use of the strength which Christians now possess through their union with Christ.[4] In the conflict with the demonic powers Christians must draw immediately and continually upon Christ's power if they would know victory. What is true of the individual Christian is also true of the Church, as she seeks to stem the tide of evil in the world.

2. *The Need for God's Armor* (6:11)

Paul implores his readers to **put on the whole armour of God** (cf. Rom. 13:12; II Cor. 6:7; I Thess. 5:8). The Greek term which the phrase **the whole armour** translates is *panoplian.* The word carries the idea of completeness, and we are called to "put on God's panoply." Two divergent views are held with regard to this exhortation. According to the first interpretation, the emphasis falls upon the fact that it is *God's armor* which must be donned.[5] God is pictured in Isa. 59:17 (Septuagint) as wearing armor, and the Christian is invited to wear this same protection when he goes forth to battle. The second interpretation places the emphasis, not upon the fact of the armor being God's, but upon the element of completeness, "the idea being that we need not only a Divine equipment, but that equipment in its *completeness,* without the lack of any single part."[6] Our foe is so formid-

[4]W. G. M. Martin, *op. cit.*, p. 1029.

[5]Cf. Beare, W. G. M. Martin, *et al.*

[6]Salmond, *op. cit.*, III, 382.

able that we must clothe ourselves with all that God provides for our offensive and defensive struggle. Thus, we must "put on God's complete armor" (Phillips).

There seems to be no necessity to make a choice between these views. It is not either/or, but both/and. The armor which is the power of God must be realized in the life of God's people completely if they win in this cosmic conflict. Paul's careful description of the various parts of the armor in 6:14-17 eloquently supports the second view, but we should not overlook the former emphasis.

The purpose for attiring oneself in the armor of God is that there might be defense **against the wiles of the devil. Wiles** (*methodias;* cf. 4:14) might better be rendered "schemes" or "stratagems." The word is found nowhere else in Greek literature but in this letter. Apparently it is intended to convey the idea of deceitful plans or crafty assaults. Included in **the wiles of the devil** are all "the manifold temptations to unbelief, to sin, to conformity with the surrounding pagan world, which beset the Christian at all times."[7] More than a human mind gives birth to the exceedingly subtle attacks upon the Christian. As Bruce comments, Paul himself had had extensive experience with the work of the devil, and so he can say: "We are not ignorant of his devices" (II Cor. 2:11; cf. I Cor. 7:5; II Cor. 11:3, 14; I Thess. 2:18).[8]

In 10-18 we see "The Warfare of the Sanctified." (1) Our relentless foe must be faced and conquered. For this we are to take **the whole armour of God,** 11-13. (2) The defensive armor —(*a*) The girdle of **truth**—an enlightened understanding and a steadfast character; (*b*) **The breastplate of righteousness**—a holy life to absorb criticism and persecution; (*c*) **The shield of faith** to ward off the enemy's vicious attack, 14, 16. (3) The offensive armor. There must be offensive action to win—(*a*) **The sword of the Spirit**—God's Word in hand, the Bible in heart and in mind; (*b*) **Feet shod** for long, arduous marches in obedience to Christ, the Commander; (*c*) **The helmet of salvation** to guide and guard our thoughts that they be for Christ rather than sinful, selfish ends, 15, 17. (4) All of our spiritual equipment is to be strengthened and reinforced by prayer, 18 (G. B. Williamson).

[7]Beare, *op. cit.,* X, 737.

[8]*Ephesians,* p. 127.

3. *The Enemy of the Christian* (6:12-13)

The enemy to be defeated is the devil and the entire host of demonic forces in the universe. Paul makes it clear that the Christian warfare is not carried on against human forces, for he says that we **wrestle not against flesh and blood,** (12). Human strength would be sufficient if this were the case. However, because wicked spiritual forces are arrayed against the Christian, only divine, spiritual resources can resist them. Paul says we are up **against principalities, against powers, against the rulers of the darkness . . . against spiritual wickedness in high places** (cf. 1:21; 2:2; 3:10; Rom. 8:38-39; Col. 1:13). There are various ranks among the hosts of Satan but it is hardly possible to make distinctions between these various orders.[9] Suffice it to say that, no matter how stable the lives of God's people, they are never free from subtle attacks of Satan through agencies of the evil power structure. Phillips' paraphrase of 12 expresses well the thought here: "We are up against organizations and powers that control this dark world, and spiritual agents from the very headquarters of evil."

The apostle believed in the personal character of the powers of evil in the universe. Furthermore, he believed that these forces were organized. Mackay writes: "Here is something quite different from the power of heredity, something more grim and awesome than those judicial, dialectical forces which operate in history, whereby at times history fools man's logic and at other times brings to destruction his titanic pride."[10] He goes on to say that Paul was not thinking of "those demonic powers in contemporary history [dictatorial governments and anti-religious Communism] which arrogate to themselves the status and attributes of Deity."[11] Mackay asserts that if Paul were living today "he would still insist upon the personal character of supernatural evil."[12] The Christian's personal enemy possesses neither omnipotence, omniscience, nor omnipresence, but he is organized throughout the world for the one purpose of defeating the people of God.

In high places is the fifth and last appearance of this phrase which is elsewhere translated "in heavenly places" (1:3, 20; 2:6;

[9]For extensive discussion of these words, cf. Moody, *op. cit.*, pp. 139-41.

[10]*Op. cit.*, p. 195.

[11]*Ibid.*

[12]*Ibid.*

3:10). Here it means the realm of spiritual conflict. The entire verse is a reminder that Christians, even with their glorious personal experiences with Christ and their highest experiences of worship and service, are not immune from attacks of the wicked spiritual hosts.

Paul now repeats his exhortation of 11: **Wherefore take unto you the whole armour of God** (13). **Wherefore** is the apostle's way of catching up and applying what has been previously declared. In effect, he says, "Realizing the concentration and power of your enemies, take up the armor of God." The object of the fully armed soldier is to **withstand in the evil day, and having done all, to stand.** To **withstand** (*antistenai*) introduces a stronger idea than that which is given in 11. A better translation would be "to resist" (NASB, Phillips). **The evil day** has been variously interpreted. Jerome thought it was the day of judgment. Wesley comments that it is "either at the approach of death, or in life."[13] Others think of it as the period immediately preceding the Second Coming. The apocalyptic passages of the New Testament intimate an increase of conflict before the second advent of our Lord (Mark 13; II Thess. 2:3). The use of the article with the Greek word for **day** (*hemera*) suggests a particular day, but some commentators take this simply to be a special time of conflict for the individual Christian, such as is indicated in Ps. 41:1: "The Lord will deliver him in time of trouble."[14] It is quite possible, with Bruce and Westcott, to take the phrase as designating "the present age." In 5:16, Paul asserts that "the days are evil." Bruce concludes, "The age is evil because of the evil forces which, although vanquished by Christ, are still able to exercise control over a world which will not avail itself of the fruits of Christ's victory."[15] The Christian must take up the armor provided by God and, having fastened it securely about him, go out to resist evil in his time.

The apostle's spirit of optimism breaks through with the words **and having done all, to stand.** The phrase **having done all** might better be rendered "having accomplished all things." While it can mean "having finished putting on the armor," prepara-

[13]*Op. cit.*, p. 722.

[14]Cf. Hodge, *op. cit.*, p. 381; Salmond, *op. cit.*, III, 385; Erdman, *op. cit.*, p. 123.

[15]*Ephesians*, p. 129; cf. Westcott, *op. cit.*, p. 95.

tion seems not to be the main idea here, but rather that of successfully resisting the enemy. When the foe has been routed and driven from the field, we can stand victorious and unafraid. To resist effectively means that one will not be dislodged from his position and can hold his post in triumph. Hence, as J. A. Robinson remarks, "the Apostle never contemplates the possibility of defeat."[16]

B. The Armor of God, 6:14-17

By keeping themselves "strong in the Lord," that is, equipping themselves with God's armor, Christians can successfully win the fight against the forces of evil. This is Paul's assurance. Now he turns to describe in detail the "whole armour" (*panoplia*) with which God's man must clothe himself.

Several preliminary facts regarding this description are worth noting. Polybius, who lived between 201 and 120 B.C., spent a lifetime writing history, and became an authority on war tactics. In one of his volumes he gives a full description of the suit which the Roman infantry wore.[17] Paul omits two essential portions of this full dress of the Roman soldier—the greaves (armor for the legs below the knees) and the spear. J. A. Robinson concludes that Paul is thinking not so much of the Roman soldier but more in terms of the Old Testament picture of God the Warrior and transfers elements of it to the Christian. Many of the pieces of the armor are mentioned in Old Testament passages to which Paul might have turned (cf. Isa. 11:4-5; 59:14-17; see also the apocryphal book, The Wisdom of Solomon 5:17 ff.).[18]

Second, in his famous allegory *Pilgrim's Progress,* John Bunyan notes that the armor offered no protection for the back. This suggests that retreat from the battle by the Christian could not be entertained in the apostle's view of the warfare.

Third, the order in which the pieces of armor are described is the order in which the soldier would put them on. Piece by piece Paul mentions the various parts of the military suit and applies each one to some aspect of Christian preparation for victorious living.

[16] *Op. cit.,* p. 133.

[17] *History,* VI, 23.

[18] *Op. cit.,* pp. 133-34; cf. Barclay's view of Paul's being chained to a soldier in Rome, *op. cit.,* pp. 216-17.

1. *The Belt of Truth* (6:14)

Paul's readers are exhorted to stand, **having your loins girt about with truth.** With the free-flowing garments of the East, the first thing for a soldier to do was to fasten the belt about his waist. The belt bound his tunic tightly to his body, thus giving uninhibited movement. The belt also provided a means for carrying his sword in much the same way as military officers attach pistols to their belts today. Other pieces of armor probably were fastened to it. **Truth** (*aletheia*) is not to be taken as the gospel in the objective sense, for that is identified later as the sword. **Truth** here is to be subjectively understood, but it is more than the human virtue of sincerity and honesty in the usual sense. As Hodge defines this **truth,** it is the knowledge of and belief in the revealed word of God.[19] The apostle is thinking in existential terms when he speaks of truth. When a Christian soldier girds himself with truth, in the Pauline sense he appropriates the Word through faith. This gives assurance, stability, and decisiveness to his life and action. Thus he not only has wisdom and understanding, but he is *living* in truth. Herein is his strength in the hour of test. Reason, tradition, creeds, and philosophies may snap under the stress of battle, but the Word of God believed and lived remains intact. For Moule, to be girded with the belt of truth means to be "calm and strong in the reality and simplicity, through grace, of your relations with your King."[20]

2. *"The Breastplate of Righteousness"* (6:14)

In Isa. 59:17, God is pictured as putting on "righteousness as a breastplate, and an helmet of salvation upon his head." **Righteousness** (*dikaiosyne*) is not to be taken as the new status which man has with God through faith in Christ. Rather it is the life of purity and rectitude which the new relationship with God creates. Just as truth has a subjective dimension, so with **righteousness.** Barclay writes, "When a man is clothed in righteousness, he is impregnable. Words are no defence against accusations, but a good life is."[21] The protecting quality of purity and holiness cannot be gainsaid. Dale remarks, "A pure heart resents with disgust and scorn the first approaches of temptation to im-

[19]*Op. cit.*, p. 382.
[20]*Op. cit.*, p. 328.
[21]*Op. cit.*, p. 217.

purity."[22] Moreover, to yield to sin is to make oneself vulnerable. Cowardice and hesitancy are by-products of the unrighteous heart, while bravery and courage flow from right thinking and acting.

3. *The Sandals of the Gospel* (6:15)

The specially designed military sandals were fashioned to protect the feet and to enable the soldier to keep his balance in rough places. Also they afforded ample footing for quick movement. The Christian warrior must have the protection and mobility which come with having the **feet shod with the preparation of the gospel of peace.** The word **preparation** (*etoimasia*) can mean (1) preparation in the sense of making ready, (2) a state of preparedness, (3) foundation or steadfastness, and (4) readiness or preparedness of mind.[23] Paul has in mind this last meaning—the readiness which the gospel of peace creates. Hodge comments, "As the Gospel secures our peace with God, and gives the assurance of his favour, it produces that joyful alacrity of mind which is essential in the spiritual conflict."[24] The **peace** which Paul here writes about is peace with God through salvation. In the background we can discern Isaiah's exclamation: "How beautiful upon the mountains are the feet of him that bringeth good tidings, that publisheth peace; that bringeth good tidings of good, that publisheth salvation; that saith unto Zion, Thy God reigneth!" (52:7; cf. Eph. 2:17)

4. *"The Shield of Faith"* (6:16)

Above all has the sense of "in addition to all the rest." **Shield,** in this instance, is not the small, circular one (*aspis*) sometimes carried by Roman soldiers, but the large, oblong shield (*thyreos*) which was part of the armed suit of the Roman when the battle was severe. It was carved out of wood and was covered with leather to intercept and quench the ignited arrows shot by the enemy. The heavily armed Christian carries a **shield of faith,** which Salmond construes as "*saving* faith—the faith by which comes the Divine forgiveness and the power of a new life."[25] Moule, on the other hand, interprets faith as used here to be

[22] *Op. cit.*, p. 217.

[23] Salmond, *op. cit.*, III, 386.

[24] *Op. cit.*, p. 385.

[25] *Op. cit.*, III, 387.

"reliance altogether on your Lord, that looks wholly outward, Godward."[26] He goes on to say that this is the essence of faith and that is what gives it its saving power. The faith which brings deliverance from sin is the faith that keeps. The faith which is obedient response to the call of God is the faith which goes on trusting God. Mackay's words are penetrating: "A Christian's trust must be in God. He must cherish no doubt regarding the basis of his faith and the truth of his cause. He must be a man of intense conviction who has about him that air of calm decision . . . He knows who he is and to whom he belongs."[27] With such faith "every burning missile the enemy hurls" (Phillips) can be stopped and extinguished. **The wicked,** that is, the devil, need not pierce the soul with his **fiery darts** and thus inflame it to sin.

5. *"The Helmet of Salvation"* (6:17)

Continuing his description and exhortation, Paul urges us to **take the helmet of salvation. Take** (*dexasthe*) should be translated "receive." After putting on the other pieces of armor, the soldier received from the attendant **the helmet,** a more delicate and properly fitted apparel for the protection of this vital part of the body. Likewise he received **the sword.** The timing, however, is not the significant fact in Paul's figure. Rather the salvation which we receive from God is our great protection for every worthwhile value in human life.

It does not seem proper to interpret **the helmet of salvation** as solely the great confidence which we possess that God has power to save.[28] Rather, it symbolizes the protection which participation in God's salvation assures. If a soldier goes into the fray estranged from God, a foreigner and alien, without God, he has no guarantee of protection. But if he has been, and is, a partaker of the grace of God unto salvation, he will be "more than conqueror." God takes care of His own. "If God be for us, who can be against us?" (Rom. 8:31; cf. 8:37-39). And this salvation embraces both the present and future. I Thess. 5:8 speaks of the helmet as "the hope of salvation." Westcott states the point tersely: "The sense of salvation puts life beyond all danger."[29]

[26]*Op. cit.*, p. 329.

[27]*Op. cit.*, p. 197.

[28]Cf. Mackay, *op. cit.*, pp. 197-98.

[29]*Op. cit.*, p. 97.

6. *"The Sword of the Spirit"* (6:17)

The phrase **the sword of the Spirit** has been interpreted in two ways. Goodspeed takes **the sword** to be **the Spirit,** so he translates the exhortation: "Take . . . for your sword the Spirit, which is the voice of God." On the other hand, Beare insists that the phrase has a possessive note, and should be rendered: "the sword which is the property of the Spirit" or "the sword which the Spirit Himself wields."[30] Beare's view supports the interpretation that the sword of the Spirit is "the sword which the Spirit gives." This translation is abundantly supported by the next clause, in which the sword is designated as **the word of God.**

Two views also prevail as to the identification of **the word** (*rhema*). First, it is "that utterance of God appropriate to the occasion which the Spirit, so to speak, puts into the believer's hand to be wielded as a sword."[31] The commentators who take this position refer to the words of Jesus in Matt. 10:19, in which He exhorts His disciples not to take thought what they will speak when they are taken into custody, "for it shall be given you in that same hour what ye shall speak." A second and more acceptable view is that which identifies **the word** with the Holy Scriptures.[32] The very fact that our Lord rebuffed Satan with the Scriptures amply supports this relationship. Furthermore, the fairly consistent association of the Holy Spirit with the Scriptures should not be overlooked (II Tim. 3:16; II Pet. 1:20-21).

All the other pieces of armor mentioned in this list can be classified as defensive in nature, since their purpose is to enable the Christian to stand. But **the sword of the Spirit** is for offensive warfare. Wesley comments: "We are to attack Satan, as well as secure ourselves; the shield in one hand, and the sword in the other. Whoever fights with the powers of hell will need both."[33] The writer to the Hebrews reminds us that "the word of God is quick, and powerful, and sharper than any two-edged sword" (Heb. 4:12). With Gods' Word the Christian can dispel doubts and inflict mortal wounds on temptations.

[30]*Op. cit.*, X, 743; cf. Salmond, Alfred Martin, Hodge, *et al.*

[31]Bruce, *op. cit.*, p. 131.

[32]Cf. Barclay, Hodge, Dale, Blaikie, Foulkes, *et al.*

[33]*Op. cit.*, p. 723.

C. The Prayer for All Saints, 6:18-20

Some commentators look upon prayer as the seventh piece in the Christian's armor, but it is more reasonable to believe that Paul drops the metaphor with the reference to "the sword of the Spirit" at the end of 17. It is true, however, that he still is concerned with the Christian's victory in the struggle. The participle **praying** is connected with all the foregoing commands (10-17). Foulkes suggests that the apostle is saying in effect, "Each piece put on with prayer, and then continue still in *all prayer and supplication.*"[34] The Christian soldier can stand true, successfully resisting his spiritual foes, only as he remains in the spirit of prayer, ready always to lay his needs before the Lord. The more general word for **prayer** is *proseuche,* while **supplication** is from the word *deesis,* which carries the meaning of "entreaty" or "petition."

1. *Pray Always* (6:18)

Always is the translation of the phrase *en panti kairo.* It can be translated "in every time or season." *Kairos* sometimes has the force of a special circumstance and hence in this context could mean "in the time of conflict." More likely, habitual and constant prayer is intended. In I Thess. 5:17, Paul exhorts believers to "pray without ceasing." Our Lord declared that men ought "always pray and never lose heart" (Luke 18:1, Phillips). Constancy in prayer is imperative for victory.

2. *Pray in the Spirit* (6:18)

In the Spirit does not refer to the human spirit with its capacity for devoutness and earnestness, but rather to the Holy Spirit, who is the great Inspirer and Intercessor. He helps us to formulate our petitions in keeping with the will of God (cf. Rom. 8:26-27).

3. *Pray with All Perseverance for All Saints* (6:18)

Watching (*agrypnountes*) bears the military idea of "keeping awake." Christians are to be vigilant in prayer, not permitting themselves to become listless. This is the only way to be prepared. **Perseverance** is related to **supplication with all saints.** Beare comments, "The unsleeping alertness of the Christian is to be shown especially in persevering intercession on behalf of

[34]*Op. cit.*, p. 177.

all his comrades in the fight."[35] Unity in the fight against evil is absolutely necessary. Prayer, therefore, must be unselfish. Erdman remarks, "One fights more valiantly and more gallantly when he remembers that he is not alone."[36] And this is especially true when he realizes that others are "standing with him in prayer."

In 6:10-18 we see "The Christian Life as Real Warfare" or perhaps "Getting the Most out of Life Means Putting the Most into It." Paul suggests some of the key factors—and to all of these we must give serious attention: (1) Determination and steadfastness, 13; (2) Truth, 14; (3) Right conduct, 14; (4) Peace with God and with our fellows, 15; (5) Faith, 15; (6) A personal experience of salvation, 16; (7) Use of the Bible, 16; (8) Prayer, 18; (9) Personal witness and intercession for others, 18 (A. F. Harper).

4. *Pray "for Me"* (6:19-20)

Paul's position in prison, **an ambassador in bonds,** does not move him to request special prayers for his personal well-being and peace, but rather for the furtherance of the gospel. His request is twofold. First, he desires wisdom "that utterance may be given to me in the opening of my mouth" (19*a*, NASB). The apostle is conscious that a great responsibility has devolved upon him to preach the gospel. In doing so he wants to be sure that, when opportunities present themselves, he will speak the right word. He wants to be sure that his word is always God's word. Second, he desires boldness **to make known the mystery of the gospel.** He wants power to declare the truth that God in Christ Jesus has provided salvation for all men, both Jew and Greek. He desires courage to preach this message without flinching before the face of men and without compromising the gospel. He must preach the whole gospel for the whole wide world.[37]

Verse 20 repeats the second request, but introduces the unusual designation of the apostle as **an ambassador in bonds.** Literally, this phrase reads, "an ambassador in a chain" (*presbeuo en halusei*). The word probably refers to a wrist chain by which he is handcuffed to a soldier. Strange but true, the King's leading ambassador is a prisoner. But is he really the prisoner? In

[35]*Op. cit.,* X, 746.

[36]*Op. cit.,* p. 126.

[37]Cf. comments on 3:3-9 for a discussion of the mystery.

speaking of the fact that Paul was chained to a soldier, Bruce poses the question: Which of the two was the prisoner?[38] The facts of the case are that Paul wants so much to preach the gospel at Rome that he feels he can fulfill his ambassadorial duties even though he is chained. He is not seeking sympathy, therefore; he seeks their prayers only that he will be able to **speak boldly** what he knows he **ought to speak,** when opportunity is presented.

[38]*Ephesians,* p. 134.

Section XI Final Greetings

Ephesians 6:21-24

A. Commendation of Tychicus, 6:21-22

The customary list of greetings to individuals in the churches to which Paul wrote is missing in this Epistle. As indicated in the Introduction, this letter was intended as a general one to be circulated among the churches of Asia Minor. Most naturally, any of the church people to whom it would be read would want to know about Paul's circumstances. The apostle writes here that the bearer of the communication, Tychicus, would be prepared to inform them.

1. *The Messenger's Commendation* (6:21)

Tychicus' name appears in several places in Paul's letters, and we learn a little of his background from Acts 20:4. His home was somewhere in Asia and he went with Paul to Jerusalem to deliver to the Christians there the offering which the apostle had collected over several years. Tychicus is mentioned in Col. 4:7-9 as the bearer of the Epistle to the Colossian church and probably the letter to Philemon. It is possible that he delivered the lost letter to the Laodiceans, mentioned in Col. 4:16. His name appears again in II Tim. 4:12 and Titus 3:12. These services to the church show why the apostle calls him **a beloved brother** (*ho agapetos adelphos*) and **faithful minister** (*pistos diakonos*, lit., attendant). The loyalty of Tychicus in serving Paul created a bond of fellowship between them until Paul could call him "a dear brother" and trusted him with this assignment. He could be sent anywhere by Paul, and he would fulfill the task.

2. *The Messenger's Task* (6:21-22)

Tychicus will convey two bits of information. First, he will make known Paul's **affairs**, literally, "the things concerning me" (*ta kat'eme*). He will tell them about the apostle's housing and food and generally how things are going with him. Second, he will give them word about Paul's health. **How I do** (*ti prasso*) might be translated "how I fare,"[1] or "how I am" (NEB). Paul

[1]Salmond, *op. cit.*, III, 392.

says that his messenger will **make known to you all things.** Tychicus will be prepared to give a full report of these matters.

Verse 22, in which Paul uses the words **I have sent,** is written from the standpoint of the readers. This is an epistolary aorist in the Greek. Paul is sending (present tense) Tychicus, but at the time they read the letter he will have been sent (past tense). The message concerning the apostle's circumstances will **comfort** their hearts. They will be strengthened and encouraged in their own situation as they know that God is providentially caring for Paul.

B. Benediction, 6:23-24

In closing this majestic letter, the apostle offers a benedictory prayer in which he mentions "the three great qualities of the Christian life, the three blessings, of which he has said so much in this Epistle."[2] The leading redemptive notes which have carried the theme of unity throughout the letter are sounded once again at the conclusion. Paul well knows that a Christian cannot be much of a Christian if he does not excel in **peace,** in love **with faith,** and in **grace.** But these are not natural human virtues; they are gifts **from God the Father and the Lord Jesus Christ.**

1. *Peace and Faith with Love* (6:23)

Peace (*eirene*) is by no means a simple greeting in which one's welfare is the concern. It is more than mental tranquility and composure. Rather, as understood in the Epistle, it is a new relationship between God and man. Peace in its essential nature is reconciliation. To the degree that Christ lives in the heart, we possess peace. As Paul says in 2:14, "He is our peace." The calm of the soul redeemed is the calm of Christ's indwelling.

Love with faith suggests that love is the primary virtue, which is in accord with Paul's position elsewhere (cf. I Cor. 13:13). But, though love is basic, it should be accompanied by faithfulness. Paul sees two virtues here, but wants a conjunction of them to appear in our Christian lives. Notice this union of faith and love in 1:15. Faith in Christ makes Christians, but it is the love of Christ shed abroad in human hearts that identifies them as Christians. Faith thus manifests itself in love. Paul prays

[2]Foulkes, *op. cit.*, p. 181; cf. 1:2, where two of them are mentioned.

that these qualities may be given **to the brethren.** This word emphasizes again his concern that brotherly love remove all barriers between Jew and Gentile, thus creating and maintaining a united people.

2. *Grace* (6:24)

The final word of this benediction corresponds to the first word of the salutation (cf. 1:2). **Grace,** classically defined as "the unmerited favor of God," has been prominent in this Epistle. Now Paul asks God to continue to show divine favor to his readers. He identifies those persons who are to be so blessed as **all them that love our Lord Jesus Christ in sincerity.** The phrase **in sincerity** (*en aphtharsia*) presents some problems. *Aphtharsia* means literally "incorruption" (Rom. 2:7) and is not usually employed to express moral qualities. But in some instances it means essentially "immortality" (cf. I Cor. 15:42, 50, 53-54). The general Pauline use favors the idea of "imperishableness" or "undecaying" grace.[3]

Sincerity therefore is hardly the proper translation. "Undying love" appears in the RSV, and "love incorruptible" in NASB. Westcott's rendering captures a thought in keeping with what Paul has to say in his earlier prayer that they be "rooted and grounded in love" (3:17). He writes that this is a love which is "free from every element liable to corruption."[4] The love with which the Spirit fills the cleansed heart is insured against corruption because its source is the pure heart of God. Love is as endurable as God himself.

Though the word is not in the oldest Greek manuscripts, the reader can join some devout copyist who added a ringing **Amen** to the message of Ephesians.

[3]Salmond, *op. cit.*, III, 394.

[4]*Op. cit.*, p. 100.

Bibliography

I. COMMENTARIES

ABBOTT, T. K. *A Critical and Exegetical Commentary on the Epistles to the Ephesians and the Colossians.* "International Critical Commentary." Edinburgh: T. & T. Clark, 1897.

ALLAN, JOHN A. *The Epistle to the Ephesians.* "Torch Bible Commentaries." London: SCM Press, Ltd., 1959.

BARCLAY, WILLIAM. *The Letters to the Galatians and Ephesians.* Second Edition. "The Daily Study Bible." Philadelphia: Westminster Press, 1958.

BEARE, FRANCIS W. "Ephesians." (Exegesis). *Interpreter's Bible.* Edited by GEORGE BUTTRICK, *et al.*, Vol. X. New York: Abingdon-Cokesbury Press, 1953.

BLAIKIE, W. G. "Ephesians." *Pulpit Commentary.* Edited by H. D. M. SPENCE and JOSEPH S. EXELL. London: Funk and Wagnalls Co., 1913.

BRUCE, F. F. *The Epistle to the Ephesians.* New York: Fleming H. Revell Co., 1961.

CALVIN, JOHN. *Commentaries on the Epistles of Paul to the Galatians and Ephesians.* Trans. by WILLIAM PRINGLE. Grand Rapids: Wm. B. Eerdmans Publishing Co., 1948 (reprint).

CLARKE, ADAM. *The New Testament of Our Lord and Saviour Jesus Christ,* Vol. II. New York: Abingdon-Cokesbury Press, n.d.

DENNEY, JAMES. "Romans." *Expositor's Greek Testament.* Edited by W. ROBERTSON NICOLL. Third Edition. London: Hodder and Stoughton, 1908.

DUMMELOW, J. R. (ed). *A Commentary on the Holy Bible.* New York: Macmillan Co., 1945.

EADIE, JOHN. *Commentary on the Epistle to the Ephesians.* Grand Rapids: Zondervan Publishing House, 1955 (reprint).

ERDMAN, CHARLES R. *The Epistle of Paul to the Ephesians.* Philadelphia: Westminster Press, 1931.

FOULKES, FRANCIS. *The Epistle of Paul to the Ephesians.* "Tyndale New Testament Commentaries." Grand Rapids: Wm. B. Eerdmans Publishing Co., 1963.

HODGE, CHARLES. *Commentary on the Epistle to the Ephesians.* Grand Rapids: Wm. B. Eerdmans Publishing Co., 1950.

HUNTER, A. M. "The Letter to the Ephesians." *Layman's Bible Commentary.* Richmond: John Knox Press, 1959.

LIGHTFOOT, J. B. *Notes on the Epistles of St. Paul.* London: Macmillan Co., 1895.

———. *St. Paul's Epistles to the Colossians and to Philemon.* London: Macmillan & Co., 1927.

MARTIN, ALFRED. "Ephesians." *Wycliffe Bible Commentary.* Edited by CHARLES F. PFEIFFER and EVERETT F. HARRISON. Chicago: Moody Press, 1962.

MARTIN, W. G. M. "The Epistle to the Ephesians." *The New Bible Commentary*. Edited by F. DAVIDSON. Second Edition. Grand Rapids: Wm. B. Eerdmans Publishing Co., 1953.

MOULE, H. C. G. *Ephesian Studies*. Second Edition. London: Pickering and Inglis, Ltd., n.d.

ROBINSON, J. ARMITAGE. *St. Paul's Epistle to the Ephesians: A Revised Text and Translation with Exposition and Notes*. London: Macmillan Co., 1903.

SALMOND, S. D. F. "Ephesians." *Expositor's Greek Testament*. Edited by W. ROBERTSON NICOLL. London: Hodder and Stoughton, n.d.

SANDAY, WM., and HEADLAM, A. C. *The Epistle to the Romans*. "International Critical Commentary." Fifth Edition. New York: Charles Scribner's Sons, 1899.

SCOTT, E. F. *The Epistles of Paul to the Colossians, to Philemon, and to the Ephesians*. "Moffatt New Testament Commentary." New York: Harper and Bros., n.d.

SIMPSON, E. K., and BRUCE, F. F. *The Epistles of Paul to the Ephesians and to the Colossians*. "New International Commentary on the New Testament." Grand Rapids: Wm. B. Eerdmans Publishing Co., 1957.

STOECKHARDT, G. *Commentary on St. Paul's Letter to the Ephesians*. Trans. by MARTIN S. SOMMER. St. Louis: Concordia Publishing House, 1952.

WEDEL, THEODORE. "The Epistle to the Ephesians" (Exposition). *Interpreter's Bible*. Edited by GEORGE BUTTRICK, *et al.*, Vol. X. New York: Abingdon-Cokesbury Press, 1953.

WESTCOTT, B. F. *St. Paul's Epistle to the Ephesians*. Grand Rapids: Wm. B. Eerdmans Publishing Co., 1950 (reprint).

II. OTHER BOOKS

ABBOTT-SMITH, G. *A Manual Greek Lexicon of the New Testament*. Second Edition. Edinburgh: T. & T. Clark, 1923.

The Apocrypha of the Old Testament. Revised Standard Version. Edited by BRUCE M. MATZGER. New York: Oxford University Press, 1965.

ARNDT, W. F., and GINGRICH, F. W. *A Greek-English Lexicon of the New Testament and Other Early Christian Literature*. Chicago: University of Chicago Press, 1957.

BARCLAY, WILLIAM. *The Mind of St. Paul*. London: Collins, 1958.

BARTH, MARKUS. *The Broken Wall: A Study of the Epistle to the Ephesians*. London: Collins, 1960.

BRUCE, F. F. *The Letters of Paul: An Expanded Paraphrase*. Grand Rapids: Wm. B. Eerdmans Publishing Co., 1965.

CARVER, W. O. *The Glory of God in the Christian Calling*. Nashville: Broadman Press, 1949.

DALE, R. W. *Lectures on Ephesians*. London: Hodder and Stoughton, 1887.

DAVIS, W. H. *Greek Papyri of the First Century*. New York: Harper and Bros., 1933.

DUNCAN, G. S. *The Ephesian Ministry*. London: Hodder and Stoughton, 1929.

FILSON, FLOYD V. *Jesus Christ the Risen Lord*. New York: Abingdon Press, 1956.

GOODSPEED, EDGAR J. *The Meaning of Ephesians.* Chicago: University of Chicago Press, 1933.

GREENIDGE, A. H. J. *Roman Public Life.* London: Macmillan Co., 1901.

GUTHRIE, DONALD. *New Testament Introduction: The Pauline Epistles.* Chicago: Inter-Varsity Press, 1961.

HARRISVILLE, ROY A. *The Concept of Newness in the New Testament.* Minneapolis: Augsburg Publishing House, 1960.

HUNTER, A. M. *Interpreting Paul's Gospel.* London: SCM Press, 1954.

KNOX, W. L. *St. Paul and the Church of the Gentiles.* New York: Macmillan Co., 1939.

LILLIE, WILLIAM. *Studies in New Testament Ethics.* Philadelphia: Westminster Press, 1963.

MACKAY, JOHN A. *God's Order: The Ephesian Letter and This Present Time.* New York: Macmillan Co., 1953.

MINEAR, PAUL S. *Images of the Church in the New Testament.* Philadelphia: Westminster Press, 1960.

MITTEN, C. L. *The Epistle to the Ephesians.* Oxford: Oxford University Press, 1951.

MOODY, DALE. *Christ and the Church.* Grand Rapids: Wm. B. Eerdmans Publishing Co., 1963.

MORRIS, LEON. *The Apostolic Preaching of the Cross.* Grand Rapids: Wm. B. Eerdmans Publishing Co., 1955.

PURKISER, W. T. *Sanctification and Its Synonyms.* Kansas City, Mo.: Beacon Hill Press, 1961.

RAMSAY, MICHAEL. *The Resurrection of Christ.* Second Edition. London: Geoffrey Bles, 1946.

RAWLINSON, A. E. J. "Corpus Christi." *Mysterium Christi.* Edited by G. K. A. BELL and A. DEISSMANN. London: Longmans, 1930.

RICHARDSON, ALAN. *An Introduction to the Theology of the New Testament.* New York: Harper and Bros., 1958.

ROBINSON, J. A. T. *The Body.* Naperville, Illinois: Alec R. Allenson, Inc., 1952.

STEWART, JAMES S. *A Faith to Proclaim.* New York: Charles Scribner's Sons, 1953.

———. *A Man in Christ.* New York: Harper and Row, n.d.

TAYLOR, VINCENT. *Forgiveness and Reconciliation.* London: Macmillan & Co., 1956.

———. *The Names of Jesus.* London: Macmillan & Co., 1954.

TENNEY, MERRILL C. *The Reality of the Resurrection.* New York: Harper and Row, 1963.

WAHLSTROM, ERIC. *The New Life in Christ.* Philadelphia: Muhlenberg Press, 1950.

WESLEY, JOHN. *Explanatory Notes upon the New Testament.* London: Epworth Press, 1950 (reprint).

WHITELY, W. T. (ed.). *The Doctrine of Grace.* New York: Macmillan Co., 1931.

III. ARTICLES

BARNETTE, HENLEE. "One Way of Life: Personal and Social," *Review and Expositor*, LX (Fall, 1963), 414-29.

BOWMAN, JOHN WICK. "The Epistle to the Ephesians," *Interpretation*, VIII (April, 1954), 188-205.

EARLE, RALPH. "Gleanings from the Greek New Testament," *Preacher's Magazine*, XXXVII (August—December, 1962), XXXVIII (January—December, 1963); *Nazarene Preacher*, XXXIX (January—December, 1964), XL (January—April, 1965).

JOHNSTON, G. "Beloved," *Interpreter's Dictionary of the Bible*. New York: Abingdon Press, 1962. I, 378.

MENDENHALL, G. E. "Covenant," *Interpreter's Dictionary of the Bible*. New York: Abingdon Press, 1962. I, 714-23.

PERRY, EDMUND. "The Biblical Viewpoint," *The Journal of Bible and Religion*, XXVII (April, 1959), 127-32.

PRICE, ROSS E. "The 'One' Baptism," *Herald of Holiness*, L (March 8, 1961), 10-11.

PURKISER, W. T. "Second Thoughts on 'The Wrath,'" *Seminary Tower*, XIV (Fall, 1958), 3-4.

SNAITH, N. H. "Choose," "Chosen," "Elect," "Election," "Grace," *Theological Wordbook of the Bible*. Edited by Alan Richardson. London: SCM Press, 1950. pp. 44-43, 100-102.

SUMMERS, RAY. "One Message-Redemption," *Review and Expositor*, LX (Fall, 1963), 380-87.

THERON, D. J. "Adoption in the Pauline Corpus," *Evangelical Quarterly* XXVIII (1956), 6-14.

WARD, WAYNE E. "One Body—The Church," *Review and Expositor*, LX (Fall, 1963), 399-413.

The Epistle to the

PHILIPPIANS

John A. Knight

Introduction

A. City and Church of Philippi

The city of Philippi was named after Philip, the father of Alexander. It was the scene of the battle between Brutus and Octavian, which gave birth to the Roman Empire in 42 B.C. Octavian (Augustus), the head of the new state, rebuilt Philippi and filled it with his own soldiers, making it a military outpost and colony of Rome. The strategic location of the city made this colonization extremely advantageous. It commanded one of the principal routes between Europe and Asia. It was the "chief" or "first" city of Macedonia (Acts 16:12), evidently meaning the farthest eastward from Rome, and the "first" city after entering Macedonia from the east.

The inhabitants of Philippi were Roman citizens and thus granted special privileges, with the right of voting, governed by their own senate and magistrates rather than by the governor of the province. The official language was Latin, though Greek was the language commonly used. The colony was a miniature of the Imperial City, and its citizens were proud of their connection with Rome.

A variety of national types assembled in Philippi—Greek, Roman, Asiatic—representing different phases of philosophy, religion, and superstition. That the inhabitants were religiously zealous is attested by the archaeological finds of the rocks near Philippi, which have been called a "veritable museum of mythology."[1] It was appropriate, and quite likely the desire of the apostle, that the gospel in the empire should begin in such a strategic and cosmopolitan city.

The church at Philippi was established by Paul and his companions in his second missionary journey about A.D. 52. There were only a few Jews in the city, an insufficient number to sustain a synagogue. Thus Paul, unable to follow his normal practice of reasoning in the synagogue, joined a group on the riverside "where prayer was wont to be made" (Acts 16:13). Lydia, a

[1]H. A. A. Kennedy, "The Epistle to the Philippians," *Expositor's Greek Testament*, ed. W. Robertson Nicoll (Grand Rapids: Wm. B. Eerdmans Publishing Co., n.d.), III, 400. Cf. also M. R. Vincent, *Word Studies in the New Testament* (New York: Charles Scribner's Sons, 1914), III, 414.

seller of purple, was converted, as was also a slave girl, whose conversion brought a loss of profit to her masters, resulting in the imprisonment of Paul and Silas. From the prison they prayed and sang praises to God and were set free by an earthquake. The prison keeper, seeing the power of God, was converted, with all his household (Acts 16:33).

From this simple beginning the church was constituted, composed initially of Lydia, the first European convert to Christianity, in whose home the church met (Acts 16:40); then the slave girl, the Philippian jailer, and his family. The charter membership of this congregation indicates the power and universality of the gospel. Lydia, the businesswoman, was Asiatic and somewhat wealthy; the slave girl was a native Greek, and represents the lower segment of society; the jailer was a Roman citizen and from the middle class.[2] In Christ Jesus there is no distinction of male or female, bond or free (Gal. 3:27-28).

Luke may have remained at Philippi after Paul's initial visit to organize the Macedonian churches. This is inferred from the fact that Luke uses the first person ("we") throughout his account of the organization of the church (Acts 16), but uses the third person ("they") in describing the events of Paul's travels between his departure from and return to the city (Acts 20:6),[3] at which time Luke apparently rejoined his traveling missionary companions.

It seems likely that the church at Philippi inherited the persecution centered around Paul (1:7, 28-30). They thereby became attached to the apostle in a very personal way, and were intensely loyal to him. Though the congregation apparently was poor (II Cor. 8:1-2), it was marked by a spirit of fidelity and liberality. At least twice prior to the offering delivered by Epaphroditus (1:25, 30), the church had sent gifts to Paul to supply his needs—in Thessalonica (4:16) and Corinth (II Cor. 11:9).

[2]J. B. Lightfoot, *St. Paul's Epistle to the Philippians* (8th ed.; London: The Macmillan Co., 1888), pp. 53-54. For a summary of the character of all the Macedonian churches, cf. J. B. Lightfoot, *Biblical Essays* (New York: Macmillan Co., 1904), pp. 235-50.

[3]Paul's first visit to Philippi after Acts 16 and 17 was on his way from Ephesus to Corinth about A.D. 56 (I Cor. 16:5). His second occurred on leaving Corinth the following spring, A.D. 57, when he observed Easter at Philippi (Acts 20:1-6). On the first of these visits Paul was suffering bodily illness and apparently anxiety over the Corinthian or Galatian trouble. Philippi (II Cor. 1:8-11; 2:12-13; 7:4-12) may have served as a place of respite for him, thereby deepening his tender relationship to this congregation.

B. Authorship

There is no sufficient reason to doubt the authenticity of this letter. External evidence for Pauline authorship comes in part from Clement of Rome, and from Ignatius, Polycarp, and Diognetus.[4] The internal evidence places the issue almost beyond question. The teaching, language, style, and manner of thought are clearly Pauline.

The only argument advanced against Pauline authorship is based on the reference in 1:1 to "bishops" (*episcopois*) and "deacons" (*diakonois*). These offices, so the theory goes, reflect a later stage in the development of the Church. Thus the letter could not be by Paul. This argument, however, is not convincing, since we know that Paul appointed officials in every church he founded (Acts 14:23; 20:17; Titus 1:5). It is not unreasonable to assume that these titles which later became so prominent in the Church were used at the time of this writing, though without the later organizational significance attached to them.

Though the authorship has not been seriously questioned by reputable scholars, some have doubted the integrity of the Epistle, suggesting that it is a composite of two or more letters. This theory has been advanced in light of the fact that Paul drastically changes his tone from 3:2 to 4:3. It has been said that this portion constitutes a separate and initial letter written shortly after Epaphroditus delivered the gift from the church. On this theory 1:1—3:1 and 4:4-23 were written later and carried by Epaphroditus on his return home. This suggestion seems to be supported by the fact that correspondence between Paul and the Philippians is implied, and also by the express reference of Polycarp to "letters" (plural) by Paul to the church at Philippi.[5]

Such a theory, though reasonable, is not compelling, since Paul's change of tone can be adequately accounted for in a simpler manner. In a highly personal letter such as this one, the writer speaks informally and without definite plan. He moves rapidly and sometimes abruptly from one topic to another. Further, it seems likely that Paul is replying point by point to a letter or letters from the Philippians in which they provoked such a change in mood by raising the question of the Judaizers, or perhaps the backslidings of Gentile converts (3:2). It is not difficult to infer that Paul is using this method in composing the entire letter

[4] Clement's *First Corinthians,* 47:1-2; Ignatius' *Letter to the Smyrneans,* 4:2; 11:3; Polycarp's *Letter to the Philippians,* 3:1-5; *Letter to Diognetus,* 5:1-9.

[5] *Op. cit.,* 3:2.

(cf. 1:12 ff.; 2:3 ff., 27; 4:2, 8, 15). In addition, no argument can be made from Polycarp's reference to "letters" since the plural was sometimes used to describe a single writing. Thus Pauline authorship is virtually beyond dispute, and the evidence is insufficient to cause doubt as to the integrity of the Epistle.

C. Place and Date of Writing

The traditional view has been that Paul was in prison in Rome when he wrote the Epistle. It has been argued by some, however, that he was in Ephesus or Caesarea. Both of the latter theories are objectionable. We cannot be certain that Paul was in prison in Ephesus, though this might be inferred from I Cor. 15:30-32 and II Cor. 1:8-10. Even so, the duration could not have been long, and the Epistle suggests a lengthy captivity. It also implies a relationship of long standing between the apostle and the church at Philippi. If Paul had written from Ephesus, this relationship would have existed only three or four years. Further, Paul refers to the fact that of those with him only Timothy is acting unselfishly in sharing his concern (2:20). Such an event seems unlikely at Ephesus, since some of Paul's close friends were there (Acts 19:31; 20:1). Likewise the Caesarean theory may be dismissed. We know that, in Caesarea, Paul was not in immediate danger of his life. The Caesarean imprisonment would not justify the tone of martyrdom which characterizes Philippians.

Clearly the traditional view is the best. The references to "Caesar's household" (4:22) and the praetorium (1:13) seem most natural in Rome. Also on this view the correspondence presupposed by the Epistle can be accounted for best because of the close and direct connections maintained between Rome and her colonies. If the Roman imprisonment is accepted, the letter was written about A.D. 60-61. This would be during Paul's two-year captivity (Acts 28:16-31), at the beginning of which he was permitted to live in his own hired house (Acts 28:30). The letter apparently was written late in this imprisonment after several exchanges of correspondence passed over the eight hundred miles separating Paul and his readers, and possibly after Paul's prison liberties had been sharply curtailed.[6]

[6]Lightfoot thinks Philippians was written earlier than the other prison Epistles—Philemon, Ephesians, and Colossians—since its language is more similar to Romans, which was written about A.D. 56. Cf. Lightfoot, *Philippians*, pp. 30-46. Such an argument is very tenuous, and at most only indicates that one can continue to maintain style and convictions arrived at much earlier.

D. Character and Purpose

This letter is the spontaneous and affectionate expression of one whose whole "remembrance" of the Philippians is highly cherished (1:3). It is written as friend to friends. With the possible exception of II Corinthians and Philemon, this is the most personal and informal of all the apostle's writings. The personal quality of the letter is seen in the fact that Paul uses the personal pronoun approximately one hundred times, in spite of the fact that Christ, rather than self, is constantly exalted. Its informal character is reflected in Paul's rapid movement from one theme to another (2:18, 19-25, 25-30; 3:1, 2, 3, 4-14, 15). There is also the absence of any reference to himself as an "apostle," a reference which characterizes all his other letters except those to the Thessalonians and Philemon. "Philippians is more peaceful than Galatians, more personal and affectionate than Ephésians, less anxiously controversial than Colossians, more deliberate and symmetrical than Thessalonians, and of course larger in its applications than the personal messages to Timothy, Titus, and Philemon."[7]

The occasion for the letter is the return of Epaphroditus to Philippi. As one of the leaders in the church, he had brought an offering from the Philippians to Paul in prison, with instructions to stay and assist the apostle in Rome (2:25, 30; 4:10-18). In so doing Epaphroditus had fallen dangerously ill. The church had learned of the illness and its concern had been communicated to Paul. Thus he writes to thank the church for her generosity (4:14-16) and to alleviate her anxieties concerning Epaphroditus' welfare, as well as to assure for him, because of his faithfulness, a good reception at home (2:25-30).

On the whole a spirit of unity characterizes the Philippian church, though Paul finds it necessary to admonish two ladies, Euodia and Syntyche, to agree in the Lord (4:2). The primary purpose of the letter is not ethical; nor is it doctrinal, though the apostle prays that the Philippians may grow in "knowledge" and "judgment" (1:9). And yet both doctrinal and moral precepts are evident and warmly intertwined. For example, it is in the context of Paul's reference to small personal dissensions in the church that the classic "kenosis" passage is written (2:3-10). While warning against the Judaizers (or perhaps Gentiles who had fallen away from the faith) and against the notion that per-

[7]H. C. G. Moule, *Philippian Studies* (New York: A. C. Armstrong and Son, 1897), p. 5.

fection is attainable by works (3:2), he at the same time encourages his readers to walk worthily of their true "citizenship," which is in heaven (3:17-21), and to look to the final day of Christ as a runner keeps his eye on the goal (3:13-14). Thus he expertly weaves doctrinal and practical matters into a single and beautiful pattern.

Philippians has been called the "Epistle of Excellent Things," and is a good summary of all Paul had delivered to the churches in his earlier Epistles. He is unwavering in his faithfulness to the "gospel," which is referred to nine times (1:5, 7, 12, 17, 27; 2:22; 4:3, 15). Some twenty times the author uses such terms as "rejoice," "thanksgiving," "content," "praise"—none of which are dependent on outward circumstances. In fact Paul is experiencing, in spite of his own uncertain future, the inner calm and peace denoted by these terms. In this sense the letter may be considered a kind of "spiritual autobiography."

The church at Philippi had been formed by the singing of hymns in prison, and now Paul from another prison *with joy* addresses this church (1:4). No wonder it has been called a "singing letter, a love letter."[8]

Here is a letter of "faith." It embodies the apostle's confidence that, as in the case of the faithful Philippian church, which had such humble origins, small things are not to be despised (1:6). That Paul's labor of faith was rewarded is evident from Polycarp's *Letter to the Philippians,*[9] written some sixty years after Paul's last visit there, in which we learn that the church was still standing firm. The keynote of the letter is "fellowship" (*koinonia,* 1:5). It is worthy of note that "sin," the breaking of fellowship, is not once mentioned. The mutual bonds of love which bind Paul and this Christian community together are no mere human sentiment. He and they are knit together as common members of the body of Christ—members who have been "partners" together in the gospel. No more beautiful picture of the relationship between genuine disciples of Christ is to be found in the New Testament than in this simple and charming letter to the Philippians.

[8]G. Campbell Morgan, *The Unfolding Message of the Bible* (Westwood, New Jersey: Fleming H. Revell Co., 1961), p. 370.

[9]1:2.

Outline

I. The Fellowship of Service, 1:1-2
   A. The Servants, 1:1
   B. The Saints, 1:1
   C. The Salutation, 1:2

II. The Fellowship of the Gospel, 1:3-11
   A. The Prayer of Praise, 1:3-8
   B. The Prayer of Petition, 1:9-11

III. The Fellowship of Adversity, 1:12-26
   A. Values of Adversity, 1:12-18
   B. Triumph over Adversity, 1:19-26

IV. The Fellowship of Obedience, 1:27—2:18
   A. The Gift of Obedience, 1:27-30
   B. The Meaning of Obedience, 2:1-4
   C. The Supreme Example of Obedience, 2:5-11
   D. The Admonition to Obedience, 2:12-18

V. The Fellowship of Concern, 2:19-30
   A. The Responsibility of Concern, 2:19-24
   B. The Reciprocity of Concern, 2:25-28
   C. The Risk of Concern, 2:29-30

VI. The Fellowship of His Sufferings, 3:1-16
   A. Alternative to Christ's Sufferings, 3:1-6
   B. Advantage of Christ's Sufferings, 3:7-10
   C. Aspiration to Christ's Sufferings, 3:11-16

VII. The Fellowship of Purity, 3:17—4:9
   A. A Personal Example, 3:17-19
   B. A Promised Exaltation, 3:20-21
   C. A Persistent Exhortation, 4:1-9

VIII. The Fellowship of Gratitude, 4:10-23
   A. The Basis for Gratitude, 4:10-20
   B. The Benediction of Grace, 4:21-23

Section I *The Fellowship of Service*

Philippians 1:1-2

A. The Servants, 1:1

Paul and Timotheus (1). How appropriate that reference should be made to Timothy! He was Paul's "true child in the faith" (I Tim. 1:2, RSV). Apparently on Paul's first missionary journey Timothy had been won to Christ at Lystra (Acts 14:6-7), and on his second journey Paul had chosen this "disciple" as one of his traveling companions (Acts 16:1-3). Timothy was therefore present with Paul at the founding of the church at Philippi (Acts 16:12 ff.), and had accompanied Paul on his subsequent journey to the city (Acts 20). The Philippians would be glad to be remembered by Timothy, whom no doubt they had come to love for his faithful service among them. Indeed, both Paul and the Philippians think so highly of Timothy, and he of them, that Paul plans to send him back to the congregation as soon as possible (2:19-22).

It has been suggested that Timothy is mentioned here because at a point or two in the letter Paul offers a gentle rebuke and wants his readers to know that the censure has the sanction of his partner.[1] However, such a sanction would hardly be necessary in writing to the Philippians. The reference to Timothy not only speaks highly of him, but also speaks volumes concerning the character of Paul. Timothy is Paul's junior in age, experience, and partnership. It is not easy for the senior member of a team to place his assistant on the same level with himself, and yet Paul has sufficient grace to do so.

Paul does not make reference to young Timothy merely because he may have been his secretary and good taste demanded it. Rather, the reference is a result of their true fellowship as **servants of Jesus Christ**. Paul and Timothy are described, literally, as the "slaves" (*douloi*) of their Lord. Here is the Christian's true relationship to Christ. They are Christ's property, body and soul, at His complete and continuous disposal. They are not

[1]J. Hugh Michael, *The Epistle of Paul to the Philippians* ("The Moffatt N.T. Commentary"; New York: Harper and Bros., 1927), p. 2.

their "own" (I Cor. 6:20) because they have been bought "by the precious blood of Christ" (I Pet. 1:18-19). Even as Jesus' "meat" was to do the will of His Father in heaven (John 4:34), or as a slave exists to do the will of his earthly master, so they exist to do the will of Christ. Christ is their absolute and common Master. They are His "love-slaves" (Exod. 21:1-6), who have freely accepted His sovereignty. To be the slave of Christ is to be free from sin (Rom. 6:16-18, 20, 22). Paul and Timothy consequently share in a unique fellowship. The intimacy of these servants is based not so much on their past experiences together as on their common commitment to Christ and emancipation from unrighteousness.

B. The Saints, 1:1

Saints, literally "holy ones" (*hagiois*), refers to those who have been set apart to the service of Christ, separated and different from the world. They belong to, and are to be like, God. They are His purchased possession and His peculiar property. The term is the equivalent of believers or regenerated ones, and indicates those who have been "washed" from sin and set on the road in love to moral and spiritual maturity (I Cor. 6:9-11; I Pet. 1:2). **Saints . . . at Philippi** means the church or "true Christians" (Phillips) at Philippi. Refusing to make any distinctions, Paul addressess **all** those in the church (1:4, 7-8, 25; 4:21), indicating his love for them regardless of their deserts. **Saints** and **servants of Jesus Christ** are virtually synonymous. Thus there is a close fellowship between Paul and Timothy, the bondslaves, and the believers at Philippi.

Saints expresses the state of the Christians in Christ. One is a saint in biblical usage only because he is "in Christ Jesus." This is one of Paul's favorite phrases, and fairly summarizes his theology. Its meaning stands in contrast to "demon possession" (cf. Mark 1:23; lit., in an unclean spirit, or, according to Phillips, "in the grip of an evil spirit"). To be "in Christ" is to be possessed by Him, to be under His control and influence. It is to be held in the heart of Christ. The phrase should be understood as being in the "power of another."[2] As the spirit of one person can transform the total being of another without violating his freedom or individuality, so the Spirit of Christ can transform into new creatures those who are in Him (II Cor. 5:17) without

[2]Cf. I Cor. 15:22; to be "in Christ" is the opposite of being "in Adam."

denying full freedom or the fulfillment of personality.[3] "In Christ" occurs eight times in this Epistle. In all Paul's letters it is found thirty-four times, "in Christ Jesus" forty-eight times, and "in the Lord" fifty times.[4] When the emphasis rests on the historical Jesus, Paul puts "Jesus" first in any combination; when "Christ" takes precedence, he means the risen Jesus, the eternal Messiah.[5] Thus the saint's true life is the life of the risen Christ within him (John 15:4-5), and the fruit of his life is Christlikeness. In this sense every believer experiences initial sanctification (I Cor. 1:2; 6:11). "It is the Spirit who sanctifies; but He does so inasmuch as He roots us in Christ and builds us up in Christ. Therefore saints are sanctified by, or of, the Spirit; but they are sanctified (or holy) in Christ Jesus."[6] Entire sanctification takes place when the heart is cleansed from all sin and filled with the Holy Spirit (Acts 15:8-9).

This is the first mention in order of time of **bishops and deacons** in the New Testament. **Bishops** (*episkopois*), literally "overseers," refers to spiritual leaders of the local congregation (Acts 20:20). At this stage in the development of the Church local congregations had more than one overseer, or pastor. The use of the term does not reflect an organizational significance which it later acquired. "Bishop" seems to be the same as "elder" or "presbyter." Since Philippi was a Roman colony, the Jewish term "presbyter" would be unfamiliar. No doubt the church chose to call their leaders by names which would be in general use, and Paul is following their accepted practice. **Deacons** (*diakonois*), literally, "those who serve," refers to persons who were apparently responsible for the temporal and material needs of the congregation (Acts 6:1-6; I Tim. 3:8 ff.). It may be that Paul refers to these offices as a means of officially expressing

[3]Robert R. Wicks, "The Epistle to the Philippians" (Exposition), *The Interpreter's Bible,* ed. George A. Buttrick, *et al.,* XI (New York: Abingdon-Cokesbury Press, 1955), 16.

[4]William Barclay, *Letter to the Philippians* ("Daily Study Bible"; Philadelphia: The Westminster Press, 2nd ed., 1959), p. 14. For a slightly varying enumeration cf. Charles R. Erdman, *The Epistle of Paul to the Philippians* (Philadelphia: The Westminster Press, 1932), p. 35.

[5]Francis Davidson, "Letter to the Philippians," *The New Bible Commentary,* ed. F. Davidson (Grand Rapids: Wm. B. Eerdmans Publishing Co., 1960), p. 1034.

[6]Robert Rainy, "Epistle to the Philippians," *An Exposition of the Bible,* VI (Hartford, Conn.: S. S. Scranton Co., 1903), 116.

his spiritual counsel, which he hopes these leaders will carry into practical effect.[7]

C. The Salutation, 1:2

Grace be unto you, and peace (2). This greeting, or blessing to the Christians from Christ, is the common form in Paul's earlier Epistles (Rom. 1:7; I Cor. 1:3; II Cor. 1:2; Gal. 1:3; Eph. 1:2; Col. 1:2; I Thess. 1:1; II Thess. 1:2; Philem. 3). He unites the normal Greek and Latin greeting, "joy" or "prosperity" (*charis*), with the Eastern salutation, "well-being" (Heb., *shalom;* Gk., *eirene*), and transforms them into a rich Christian blessing. Here is an illustration of the fact that God makes all things new. **Grace** (*charis*) expresses the free favor of God, or His undeserved favor toward us (II Cor. 4:15; 12:9). Grace is the gift of God which justifies unto salvation (Rom. 3:24; 11:6; Eph. 2: 8-10). It also refers to the fruit of this divine favor—the dispositions which result from grace. Thus we are admonished to "grow in grace" (II Pet. 3:18). Grace brings the gift of **peace,** which is both reconciliation with God and inner assurance which results from faith in Christ's atonement.[8] The Roman government stationed soldiers at points of tension in the empire in order to maintain order. But it was a strained or forced peace, described by the Latin word *pax.* In contrast to this Paul uses the Greek word *eirene,* denoting peace of mind, arising from reconciliation with God. It indicates an inner peace, rather than an outward cessation of hostility maintained by force.

From God our Father, and from the Lord Jesus Christ. The second **from** (*apo*) is not present in the Greek, suggesting the close union in Paul's mind of the Father and Jesus Christ. God's grace comes from the Father through Christ (Rom. 3:24). **Lord** (*kyrios*), literally, "master," was used in the Septuagint to translate the word for *Jehovah.* Though the title is occasionally used in the New Testament as a title of honor (Matt. 13:27), in the Epistles it is constantly employed of Christ. Thus **Lord** as used by Paul indicates full deity. That Jesus was divine was the faith of the New Testament Church, as expressed in its earliest Christian creed, "Jesus is Lord" (I Cor. 12:3; cf. Phil. 2:6, 9-11).

[7]IB (Exegesis), XI, 16.

[8]B. C. Caffin, "Letter to the Philippians" (Exposition), *The Pulpit Commentary,* ed. H. D. M. Spence and Jos. S. Exell, XX (Grand Rapids: Wm. B. Eerdmans Publishing Co., 1950), 2.

Jesus means "Saviour" (Matt. 1:21). He is the Lord, the Master of Paul and Timothy and the Philippians, because He is their Saviour, or Deliverer. Contrast the experience of the damsel possessed with a spirit of divination at Philippi. She was the slave of those who could not be her saviour, while Paul and his companion were "servants [lit., slaves] of the most high God" (Acts 16:16-17). **Christ** (*christou*) was a proper title meaning "Anointed One" or "Messiah" (Isa. 61:1 ff.). The Anointed One was the Appointed One, God's Vice-regent on earth, the officially accredited Messenger from heaven to earth (Matt. 17:5).

The Holy Spirit is not mentioned because this grace and peace is the Holy Spirit himself dwelling in us, revealing to us the Father, and bringing to our remembrance the teaching of the Son, from whom He comes. The meaning of the salutation is clear: "No peace without grace . . . No grace and peace but from God our Father . . . No grace and peace from God our Father, but in and through the Lord Jesus Christ."[9]

What it means to be "A Man in Christ" is suggested by these first two verses. It involves: (1) Acceptance of Christ as Master, 1*a*; (2) Dedication to saintliness, 1; (3) Reception of the Holy Spirit, 2.

[9]Matthew Henry, *Commentary on the Whole Bible* (New York: Fleming H. Revell Co., n.d.), VI, 723-24.

Section II *The Fellowship of the Gospel*

Philippians 1:3-11

A. The Prayer of Praise, 1:3-8

With thanksgiving and joy (*charas*, 4) Paul offers his praise, **I thank my God** (3), for the Philippians. In the Christian life thanksgiving and joy go together, for "what we have the comfort of, God must have the glory of."[1] **My God** indicates the personal quality of the thanksgiving (cf. Acts 27:23). The fact that Paul is genuinely Christ's "slave" (1) entitles him to refer intimately to his Master. Thanksgiving and joy are qualities of the spirit and not the result of outward circumstances. Joy is deeper than happiness, which is dependent on what happens. Paul's circumstances are unpleasant and yet the joy of the Lord is his strength. His is the joy promised and provided by Christ (John 15:11; 17:13), a true fruit of the Spirit (Gal. 5:22). It is the norm of the Christian life (Col. 1:11).

1. *The Joy of Remembrance* (1:3)

Upon every remembrance of you is literally "on account of the whole remembrance of you." Paul is not expressing thanks for disconnected recollections, but for his total past experience with the Philippians. The unbroken remembrance resulted in unbroken thanksgiving and joy. It has been said that memory is the fine art of forgetting. Paul is the recipient of this noble gift. He has been granted the power to forget the harsh experiences of imprisonment and suffering at Philippi, save as they enriched his relationship to God and to the Philippians. He remembers with gratitude their conversion (Acts 16) and subsequent thoughtfulness on several occasions, even quite recently (4:15-18).

2. *The Joy of Supplication* (1:4)

Paul's love for the Philippians is expressed in genuine intercession to God for their welfare, **always in every prayer of mine for you all making request with joy** (4). He does not pray from

[1]*Ibid.*, VI, 724.

a sense of duty, nor out of an attempt to forget his own circumstances. His prayers are intercessory. The word translated **prayer** is *deesei* and indicates an intense request for a necessary gift (Jas. 5:16). His prayer is for **all** (*panton*) the congregation, because the welfare of each affects all.

3. *The Joy of Participation* (1:5)

In the expression **your fellowship in the gospel from the first day until now** (5), *koinonia* (**fellowship**) literally indicates "participation." It has at least three meanings: (*a*) the fellowship of Christians with one another; (*b*) the fellowship of Christians with Christ or the Holy Spirit; (*c*) the sharing of possessions (Acts 2:42; Rom. 15:26; II Cor. 8:4; 9:13; Heb. 13:16; Philem. 6).[2] Paul may well have had all three meanings in mind. The word speaks of the vital, living relationship of the apostle and the Philippians to Christ, and thus to each other—a relationship that had found expression and enrichment in their offerings to him at various times.

In (*eis*) is used technically in such contexts to indicate destination of money payments.[3] Paul evidently is referring to the Philippians' "participation" with him, and gifts to him, in the spread of the gospel since the first day he preached to them. The gospel is furthered wherever fellowship is created. In fact the work of Christ or the gospel is the only true basis for love and fellowship. This was an inward fellowship which had deepened across the years. The Philippians had first "given themselves" (II Cor. 8:5); then they wanted to see the gospel succeed though it meant suffering and sacrifice. Consequently, they gave of their possessions, becoming "workers together" with Paul for Christ and the gospel. They understood the nature of the Church as being a "workshop, not a dormitory."[4] Thus Paul refers to them as "fellow partakers" (*sugkoinonous,* 7) of God's grace. Because they have shared in the furtherance of the gospel they will participate in the rewards with Paul also. Even in the secular contests, "the crown is not only for him that striveth, but for the trainer, and the attendant, and all that help to prepare the athlete.

[2]E. F. Scott, "The Epistle to the Philippians" (Exegesis), IB, XI, 19-20; also Davidson, NBC, p. 1034.

[3]EGT, III, 419.

[4]Alexander Maclaren, *Expositions of Holy Scripture,* XIV (Grand Rapids: Wm. B. Eerdmans Publishing Co., 1952), 204.

For they that strengthen him . . . may fairly participate in his victory."[5]

4. *The Joy of Assurance* (1:6)

The expression **being confident of this very thing** (6) indicates a firm persuasion, the strong assurance of an intent mind. **He which hath begun a good work in you will perform it** means literally "will go on completing it." The **good work** may refer in part to the cooperation of the Philippians with the apostle, but it cannot be restricted to this meaning. "Fellowship" (*koinonia*) has a broader meaning than the sharing of possessions. The **good work** or "the fellowship in the gospel" must also refer to the fellowship of the Philippians with Christ and with each other. There is no definite article in the Greek, but it should be supplied in the English. "The" **good work,** as in *The New English Bible,* is better, since the chief reference is to the work of salvation.

Consequently, Paul can say it is God who has begun this good work. *Enarxamenos* (began) is also used in Gal. 3:3 to attribute the beginnings of the Christian life in the Galatian Christians to God the Holy Spirit (cf. II Cor. 8:6). In classical Greek *begun* is a word of ritual. The verb from which it comes is *enarchomai,* and was used to describe the ritual at the beginning of a Greek sacrifice. The verb used for completing the sacrifice was *epitelein* (to perfect or consummate). Paul seems to be suggesting that the Christian life is a continuous sacrifice to Christ (Rom. 12:1).[6] **Until the day of Jesus Christ** would be the day of Christ's *parousia* or coming. The phrase suggests the idea of a day of testing. Old Testament prophets spoke of the "day of the Lord" as a time of judgment as well as redemption. Paul is confident that God will advance the Philippians in grace, so that they may be constantly prepared to meet the day of trial.[7] Consequently, for the Christian it will be a day of light and victory (I Thess. 1:10).

[5]St. Chrysostom, "Homilies on the Epistle of St. Paul to the Philippians," Homily I, Philippians 1—2. *Nicene and Post-Nicene Fathers,* ed. Philip Schaff, XIII (Grand Rapids: Wm. B. Eerdmans Publishing Co., 1956), 185.

[6]William Barclay, *Letter to the Philippians* ("Daily Study Bible"; Philadelphia: The Westminster Press, 2nd ed., 1959), pp. 19-20.

[7]J. B. Lightfoot, *St. Paul's Epistle to the Philippians* (London: The Macmillan Co., 8th ed., 1888), p. 84.

Paul's confidence is not based primarily on any empirical evidence, though it is buttressed by his past experience; rather, it is born of a personal relationship to God, on whose character and work the persuasion rests. The biblical doctrine of perseverance is a confidence in God. The Christian confides in the infinitude of the Father's love, the infinitude of the Saviour's merit, and in the infinitude of the Spirit's power.[8] "He is able to guard until that Day what I have entrusted to Him" (II Tim. 1:12, RSV). However, one must not draw any hard and fast doctrine of eternal security from this verse. In fact, Paul admonishes the Philippians lest his work among them be "in vain" (2:14-16; cf. Col. 1:19-23). Yet God will bring to perfection or completion the work He has initiated by His Spirit. He will "evermore put His finishing touches to it."[9] Both the beginning and the ending are His work. He is both the Author and Finisher of our faith (Heb. 12:2).

And every virtue we possess,
And every victory won,
And every thought of holiness,
Are His alone.

—Harriet Auber

5. *The Joy of Christlike Affection* (1:7-8)

Even as it is meet for me to think this of you all (7) may be literally translated "as it is right [*dikaion*] for me to care [*phronein*] as to you all." **Because I have you in my heart** has sometimes been rendered "because you have me in your heart." Though either rendering would accurately describe Paul and the Philippians, the latter, considering the construction, is improbable. "Open my heart," wrote Robert Browning, "and you will see graven on it, 'Italy.'" Such human affection characterizes Paul and the Philippians. The apostle declares, **Both in my bonds, and in the defence and confirmation of the gospel, ye all are partakers of my grace.** Paul is not on trial; the gospel is on trial. His **bonds** (*desmois*) are a **defence and confirmation** of the glad tidings. **Confirmation** (*bebaiosei*) was the obligation under which the seller came to the buyer to guarantee against

[8]R. Finlayson, "Letter to the Philippians" (Homilies), PC, p. 28.

[9]H. C. G. Moule, *Philippian Studies* (New York: A. C. Armstrong and Son, 1897), p. 27.

all claims his right to what he had purchased.[10] Paul's defense then is a guarantee of the gospel, and the Philippians are **partakers** (*sugkoinonous*) of grace and of this confirmation.

For God is my record, how greatly I long after you all in the bowels of Jesus Christ (8). The oldest manuscripts read "Christ Jesus." Some have suggested that the Philippians imagined some lack of cordiality in Paul's reception of their gift, thereby accounting for the strong phrase that God is his **record** (witness). **Bowels** (*splangchnois*) refers to the upper intestine, liver, or lungs. These, so the Greeks believed, were the seat of the emotions and affections. Thus the **bowels of Jesus Christ** indicates the "affection of Christ Jesus." This is a powerful metaphor describing perfect union with Christ. Combined with the genuine human affection toward the Philippians (7) is divine love. Christ is the Source of Paul's life, the Heart of his love. Christ's heart has become his, so that he can love the Philippians with the very love of Christ. "The believer has no yearnings apart from his Lord; his pulse beats with the pulse of Christ; his heart throbs with the heart of Christ"[11] (cf. 2:5 ff.; also Rom. 12:10). Could the transforming power of the gospel be more strikingly revealed than in the union or fellowship of these two unlikely parties—a former devotee of Pharisaism on the one hand, and on the other a group whose total life had been formed by the proud atmosphere of a Roman colony!

B. The Prayer of Petition, 1:9-11

And this I pray (9). Paul has spoken of his prayers for the Philippians (4)—prayers of thanksgiving and praise. Now he states the petition that is included in his prayers for them.

1. *The Nature of the Petition* (1:9)

That your love may abound yet more and more. The word used here is not *eros* or *philia,* types of human love, but *agape,* divine love. **Your love** then means "God's love in you." One in whom the love of God dwells loves those whom God loves (I John 5:20-21). Evidently Paul is referring to love for one another. To the Romans he had once written, "Owe no man any thing but to love one another" (Rom. 13:8). Love is continuous, for it is always owing, always conscious of its debt. It is a possi-

[10]EGT, III, 420.

[11]Lightfoot, *op. cit.*, p. 85.

bility only because God "first loved us." **May abound** (*perisseue*) is the present tense, expressing continuous growth and advancement. "The spiritual prosperity of believers should be measured not so much by the point they have reached, but by the fact and measure of the progress they are making."[12] Literally, *perisseue* can be rendered "may keep on overflowing." Thus Paul is praying "that your love for one another will never be doled out in parsimonious pinches, but will rather tumble forth like some magnificent cascade."[13] To underscore his meaning, he adds the superlatives **more and more.**

Growth and progress in love are not the apostle's only concern, however. Love must grow **in knowledge and . . . judgment** if the Christian is to be well-rounded and symmetrical. **Knowledge** (*epignosis*) suggests a thorough, full understanding of general moral principles. **Judgment** or "discernment" (*aisthesei*) refers to the practical ability to apply the general principles in particular situations. It is a spiritual and moral sense or feeling. Hence, "that ye may not only *know* but *feel* that you are of God, by the Spirit which he has given you; and that your feeling may become more exercised in Divine things, so that it may be increasingly sensible and refined."[14] **All** (*pase*) discernment probably means all kinds of discernment. Did the genuine spirit of love of the Philippians lack discernment, so that they had misunderstandings over insignificant matters (4:2)? The more love grows, the more sensitive the moral sense becomes. It has been said that Venus' glass would sliver into fragments if poison were poured into the cup. Likewise, the growth of the love of God within the Christian makes him increasingly sensitive to all forms of evil. Love is the only basis for discrimination. But love must be nourished by truth. This is why Jesus rebuked Peter, who forbade the Master to die (Matt. 16:21-23). His love was unenlightened.

2. *The Immediate Purpose of the Petition* (1:10)

That ye may approve things that are excellent (10). The word **approve** (*dokimazein*) is the verb used for assaying metals

[12]Robert Rainy, *op. cit.*, VI, 116.

[13]Paul S. Rees, *The Adequate Man* (Westwood, N.J.: Fleming H. Revell Co., 1959), p. 21.

[14]Adam Clarke, *The New Testament of Our Lord and Saviour Jesus Christ* (New York: Abingdon Press, n.d.), II, 490.

to detect any flaw or alloy.[15] **Excellent** (*pheronta*) indicates the superior, the best among things that are good, of which only those of more advanced spiritual maturity are able to detect the superiority. Moffatt translates this clause, "enabling you to have a sense of what is vital." **That ye may be sincere and without offence till the day of Christ. Sincere** and **without offence** correspond to "knowledge" and "judgment" in verse 9. This portion of the prayer is both positive, **that ye may be sincere,** and negative **without offence** (stumbling). **Sincere** in its derivation points to honey without wax, implying unmixed motives or single-mindedness (Jas. 1:8). *Elikrineis* (**sincere** or pure) comes from *eile* (the splendor of the sun) and *krino* (I judge). That which is **sincere** is that which may be examined in the clearest and strongest light, without a single flaw or imperfection being revealed. Paul's language here comes from the practice of holding up cloth against the sun to see if there be any fault. Sincerity is perfect openness to God, and is thus as strong a word as perfection itself. "The soul that is sincere is the soul that is without sin."[16] **Without offence** ("void of offense," ASV) describes the character of the man who walks without stumbling, who overcomes obstacles, though unexpected. It is the image of the traveller who in spite of hindrances arrives in good time at his journey's end.[17] Such a one will be ready "for" (*eis*), not **till** (*archis*), **the day of Christ** (cf. 1:6; Eph. 5:27; Jude 24). The emphasis here seems to be on the readiness for this day, whereas 6 stresses God's continuous work in achieving this state of preparedness.

3. *The Ultimate Aim of the Petition* (1:11)

Being filled with the fruits of righteousness, which are by Jesus Christ, unto the glory and praise of God (11). The oldest manuscripts read "fruit" (singular, *karpon*) of righteousness (cf. Rom. 6:22; Gal. 5:22; Eph. 5:9; Heb. 12:11; Jas. 3:18). The righteousness here pictured is that which is **by Jesus Christ,** in contrast to the righteousness which is by the law (3:9). Without this **righteousness** which is in Christ, no fruit is possible (cf.

[15]A. T. Robertson, *Word Pictures in the New Testament,* IV (New York: Harper and Bros., 1931), 437.

[16]Adam Clarke, *op. cit.,* II, 491.

[17]IB (Exegesis), XI, 27.

John 15:4). **Glory** (*doxan*) is the manifestation of God's power and grace; **praise** (*epainon*) is the recognition by men of these divine attributes. As a tree filled with fruit honors the gardener, so a person with the fruit of righteousness brings **glory and praise** to God.

Verses 9-11 speak of "The Fruit of Righteousness," which includes: (1) A love that is abounding and informed, 9; (2) A capacity for making proper moral distinctions, 10*a*; (3) A motivation which seeks the glory of God, 10*b*.

W. E. McCumber finds in verses 3-11 "The Prayer for Transparent Holiness." The object of Paul's prayer is **your love,** 9. (1) The education of love, 9; (2) The regulation of love, 10*a*; (3) The perfection of love, 10*b*; (4) The manifestation of love, 11*ab*; (5) The consummation of love, **till the day of Christ,** 10*c* (*Holiness in the Prayers of St. Paul*).

Section III The Fellowship of Adversity

Philippians 1:12-26

A. Values of Adversity, 1:12-18

Paul has expressed his praise to God for the Philippians' "fellowship in furtherance of the gospel," and has offered a petition for them. Now he attempts to dissolve their anxieties concerning him, evidently in answer to their inquiries. **But I would ye should understand, brethren** (12). They want to know of his prospects (12), of the possibility of his visiting them (25), of the condition of Epaphroditus (2:26), and of how soon he might send them help (4:10 ff.). They have suffered with him for the sake of the gospel in a common fellowship of adversity (1:7, 28, 30), and are eager to learn of his personal situation and of the state of the gospel in Rome. He assures them that God is bringing good out of evil, glorifying himself, and turning events to the favor of His servants who love Him.

1. *The Advance of the Gospel* (1:12-13)

The things which have happened unto me have fallen out rather unto the furtherance of the gospel. Paul's commitment is so complete that he cannot explain how it is with him without stating how it is with the gospel.[1] Luke tells us what some of the things are which have happened to Paul. He has been guarded constantly but allowed to live in his own hired house, to receive those who come to visit him, and to declare to them the good news of the kingdom of God (Acts 28:16, 30-31). But his imprisonment has not been a restriction of the gospel; **rather** (*mallon*), it has become an occasion for its advancement.

The use of *mallon* suggests that the Philippians may have been expecting bad news. Some have thought it points to a change in Paul's circumstances, particularly when considered in light of the reference to his defense (*apologia,* 7). Thus it has been suggested that Paul had been transferred from his hired lodging (Acts 28:30) into the prison where those on trial were

[1]Karl Barth, *The Epistle to the Philippians* (Richmond: John Knox Press, 1962), p. 26.

held. The Philippians would consequently expect that this stricter custody would mean greater hardships. So the apostle removes the supposition.[2] *Prokopen* (progress, ASV), found also in 25, was used to describe pioneers preparing for an army or other group. It comes from *prokoptein,* meaning to cut away trees and undergrowth. Paul's bonds, then, instead of hindering the progress of the gospel have actually served to clear away obstacles and to increase its propagation (cf. I Tim. 4:15).[3] This is what Paul supremely wants, no matter what happens to him personally.

So that my bonds in Christ are manifest in all the palace (13). Better, "my bonds became manifest in Christ," that is, for Christ's sake, "throughout the whole praetorian guard." *Praitorio* has been given four leading interpretations: (*a*) the Praetorian Guard, meaning soldiers; (*b*) the emperor's palace; (*c*) the barracks of the Praetorian Guard; (*d*) the judicial authorities, or those who hear the prisoners' cases. The last interpretation, if accepted, would square with the reference to "defence" in 7, and is a reasonable possibility.[4] Lightfoot has shown fairly conclusively that *praitorio* cannot be applied to the **palace** (as in the KJV), nor to the soldiers' barracks or the whole Praetorian camp. Instead, it refers to a band of men, a guard, or body of soldiers.[5] Though the interpretation as judicial authorities cannot be excluded, the idea of a body of soldiers seems to be the best. Augustus had ten thousand such men. This interpretation is congruent with Luke's statement that Paul dwelt for a time in his own hired house.

In Eph. 6:20, written from the same prison shortly before Philippians, Paul speaks of being an ambassador in a chain (*halusei;* cf. Acts 28:20). This refers to the chain coupling the guard and the prisoner together. With every change of guards Paul is given a new opportunity to witness for Christ. In his two-year imprisonment scores of guards would have heard the gospel from Paul. He had witnessed in the Philippian prison (Acts 16:25-32); now he witnesses still (4:22). In addition to

[2]EGT, III, 423.

[3]M. R. Vincent, *Word Studies in the New Testament* (New York: Charles Scribner's Sons, 1914) III, 419.

[4]EGT, III, 423-24.

[5]*St. Paul's Epistle to the Philippians,* 8th ed. (London: The Macmillan Co., 1888), pp. 99-104.

this personal witnessing, it is possible that Paul has already officially defended himself and the gospel once (7).

"The word of God is not bound" (II Tim. 2:9), so that he can say the gospel is presented throughout the "whole praetorian guard," **and in all other places.** This translation is clearly inaccurate. Better to read, "and to all the rest" (ASV). This phrase substantiates the conclusion that Paul is not referring to a **palace,** but to a group; probably to those who visit him and to others to whom the Word of the Lord would be subsequently related. His imprisonment then has afforded a fresh opportunity to witness for Christ.

2. *Encouragement of the Romans* (1:14)

And many of the brethren in the Lord, waxing confident by my bonds, are much more bold to speak the word without fear (14). **Many** (*pleionas*) **of the brethren** indicates that some are not thus affected by his bonds. **In the Lord** is best understood if not taken with **brethren,** but with **waxing confident.** The RSV rendering is therefore more accurate: "Most of the brethren have been made confident in the Lord because of my imprisonment." The majority of the Romans have become "more abundantly bold" (ASV) **to speak the word.** The best manuscripts read "Word of God" or "Word of the Lord." **To speak** (*lalein*) denotes the fact, rather than the substance, of speaking.[6] That is, their tendency to silence is actually overcome. Not that they have not been speaking, but they are given new and greater boldness to declare God's Word without fear. Their conquest of fear is not based on the probability of Paul's release, for this is by no means certain, but on his triumphant spirit and his evident success in witnessing. It is his courage that has given new heart to the timid Romans who, possibly through persecutions, had grown discouraged.

3. *Proclamation of Christ* (1:15-18)

Of those who have become more bold to declare the Word of the Lord, **some indeed preach Christ even of envy and strife** (15). They are doing so out of a spirit of *erin,* **strife** or partisanship. Their aim, unlike the apostle's, is not primarily to exalt Christ, but to advance their own particular interests. Paul says they **preach Christ of contention** (16; *eritheias*); better, "out of

[6]Vincent, *op. cit.*, p. 421.

faction." The word originally meant working for pay. In time it came to describe a careerist, one who magnifies himself, or canvasses for office. These then are self-promoters and self-seekers.[7] **Not sincerely;** literally, "not purely" or "not chastely." They are not speaking the whole truth, but only that which serves their purpose. Their motives are mixed, corrupted with selfishness (cf. Jas. 3:14). These, therefore, are not preaching in the truest sense. Consequently, Paul uses *katangellousin,* "to announce," a different word from that normally used to describe preaching. They are making known the facts of the gospel, perhaps of Jesus' life, death, and resurrection, but they are doing so out of jealousy or other unworthy motives. They are orthodox, but have no heart. **Supposing to add affliction to my bonds.** They think they are, literally, "raising up friction" for Paul. They are seeking to make his imprisonment a galling experience, possibly by arousing his enemies against him, thus putting his life in greater peril, or at least by troubling him in spirit. These persons apparently are the insincere ones in 2:21, who are looking "after their own interests, not those of Jesus Christ" (RSV; cf. Matt. 23:15). These are not Judaizers, for Paul in other places declares that they subvert the gospel; here he does not do so. It is possible that they are described in Romans 14.[8] Some have suggested that they are old teachers of the church who are envious of the wide popularity of Paul.[9] Whether that be true, it is a characteristic of human nature that jealousy usually arises within one's own class or profession: doctors are jealous of doctors, ministers of ministers, etc. In any case, their actions stem from something personal against Paul. Their preaching, so they assume, will make Paul's imprisonment unbearable.

But there are others who preach out of a spirit of **love, knowing that I am set for the defence of the gospel** (17). These, in spite of any personal misunderstandings, preach (*kerussousin,* proclaim, 15) out of the highest motives of **love** (*agapes*), not out of partisan and factious ambition (cf. I Corinthians 13). Their aim is the same as that of Paul, who is **set** (*keimai*), appointed, like a soldier posted on guard by his captain, for the **defence**

[7]Barclay, *op. cit.,* p. 38.

[8]D. D. Whedon, *Commentary on the New Testament* (New York: Nelson & Phillips, 1875) IV, 318.

[9]Bernhard Weiss, "The Present Status of the Inquiry Concerning the Genuineness of the Pauline Epistles," *American Journal of Theology,* I, 2 (April, 1897), 388-89.

(*apologian*) of the gospel. The term **gospel** here means all his witnessing and propagandizing for Christ. This seems not to refer primarily to Paul's defense in his own personal trial; if it does at all, these—the personal defense and the defense of the gospel—are equated in the apostle's mind.[10]

What then? notwithstanding, every way, whether in pretence, or in truth, Christ is preached (18). **Notwithstanding** (*plen hoti*) is better rendered "only that" (ASV). This is in fact the only way Paul feels about the matter (cf. I Cor. 1:17). Those who are preaching out of **pretence** (*prophasei,* lit., pretext) are those who are speaking **not sincerely** (16). Their purpose in preaching, though not the substance of their message, is different from that of Paul. Not their message, but their spirit, is faulty. Again Paul, as in 17, uses the word *kataggelletai,* i.e., at least Christ is "announced," if not genuinely "proclaimed." Paul seems to subdue all personal annoyance over the situation, and expresses in rather abrupt language a decisive act of the will: **and I therein do rejoice, yea, and will rejoice.** He will not allow any private grievance to cool his love for the gospel and its advance. The all-absorbing passion of his life is the "furtherance of the gospel." Consequently, he dwells on the good that is being accomplished—Christ is being announced—not on the bad motives of the partisans (4:8). Attention to essentials spares him from any bitterness of soul. The truth of the gospel has captured his love; thus he will endure any blow to himself, rather than allow it to hinder the gospel.

In 12-20, Alexander Maclaren finds "A Prisoner's Triumph." (1) An absorbing purpose which bends all circumstances to its service, 12; (2) The contagion of enthusiasm, 13-14; (3) The wide tolerance of enthusiasm, 15-19; (4) The calm confronting of life and death as equally magnifying Christ, 20-21.

B. Triumph over Adversity (1:19-26)

1. *The Basis of the Triumph* (1:19)

For I know that this shall turn to my salvation (19)—rather "my deliverance." Apparently this is a quotation from Job 13:16 in the Septuagint. Paul seems to be comparing himself with Job. Phil. 2:12-15 is very close to the final injunctions of Moses

[10]Vv. 16 and 17 are reversed in the best MSS with the exception of the opening words of each: *oi men* (16) and *oi de* (17).

to the Israelites (cf. Deuteronomy 31 ff.), and may indicate a comparison with Moses also. If such speculation is justifiable, Paul is encouraging himself in the Lord (cf. I Sam. 30:6) by considering the similar lot of the saints of whom he has read in the Old Testament Scriptures.[11] In so doing he is able to see the uses of adversity.

Does **this** (*touto*) refer to the announcing of Christ, of which Paul has just spoken in 18, or to his total set of circumstances? Probably to both. This **shall turn,** literally, "shall come off," or "eventuate" to his salvation. **Salvation** (*soterian*) means more than his "deliverance" from prison or death, for to him personally it matters not whether he lives or dies (20). *Soteria* was used by prophets and psalmists in the Old Testament to indicate victory in a contest for the right. Paul evidently pictures himself as in a battle, wrestling "not against flesh and blood, but against principalities and powers" (Eph. 6:12), over which the ultimate issue will be victory (cf. 1:27-30). Furthermore his imprisonment will perfect his character to the glory of Christ. He is certain that all things "work together for good to them that love God, to them who are the called according to his purpose" (Rom. 8:28), and that his striving in this situation will be his witness in the day of judgment.

Through your prayer means literally "through your supplication" (cf. comment on v. 4). The fellowship that Paul and the Philippians enjoy makes him constantly aware of the need for the prayers of his fellow Christians. **And the supply of the Spirit of Jesus Christ** means, literally, "bountiful supply" (*epichoregias*) (Gal. 3:5). The word comes from *chorus,* which describes those who were employed as a background in Greek tragedies. The expense of the chorus was to be borne or provided by a person selected by the state, who defrayed expenses of both training and maintenance. Also the word was used to describe the beneficences of wealthy citizens who, giving a banquet, furnished food and entertainment for the evening.[12] Thus Paul's experiences will eventuate to his salvation by the "resources of the Spirit" (Phillips), who will "furnish all that is necessary."[13] He will not only

[11]Michael, *op. cit.,* p. 48.

[12]Vincent, *op. cit.,* p. 679; Rees, *op. cit.,* p. 27.

[13]Clarke, *op. cit.,* II, 492.

initially supply grace, but will continue to dispense sufficient grace as the need arises. The expression **Spirit of Jesus** is found only here in the New Testament. Similar expressions make it clear that the reference is to the Holy Spirit (Acts 5:9; 16:7, ASV; Rom. 8:9; I Cor. 12:4; II Cor. 3:17; Gal. 4:6). Whether the Spirit *is* the supply or *brings* the supply makes little difference. Lightfoot is probably right in saying, "The 'Spirit of Jesus' is both the giver and gift."[14]

It is clear that the basis of the triumph is through the prayers of the Philippians and **the supply of the Spirit of Jesus Christ.** Both are necessary. There is only one preposition here (*dia,* **through**) tieing together **prayer** and **supply.** As their prayers go up, the supply of the Spirit comes down. Their prayers and God's grace are like "two buckets in a well; while one ascends the other descends."

2. *The Hope of the Triumph* (1:20-24)

According to my earnest expectation and my hope (20). **Expectation** (*apokaradokian*) suggests the intense turning away from everything to fix on the object of its desire. It is, literally, "stretching out the head" to see something in the distance; evidently, in the case of Paul, it was the day of Christ. **That in nothing I shall be ashamed** is better translated "should be put to shame" (ASV). Paul had not been ashamed of the gospel before coming to Rome (Rom. 1:14-16), and it is his determined hope that he will not now lack **boldness;** literally, "openness in speaking" (cf. Acts 14:13). He desires that **Christ shall be magnified in my body, whether it be by life, or by death. Christ** is the subject of this clause, which is cast in the passive voice. Meyer suggests the passive is used because the apostle feels he is the organ of God's working.[15] Thus Paul does not say, "I shall magnify Christ," but, **Christ shall be magnified.** His body will be the "theater in which Christ's glory is displayed"[16] (cf. Rom. 12:1; 6:13). **To live is Christ** (21), means, literally, "the living is Christ." Because **to live** is the subject of the sentence, Lightfoot translates: "To me life is Christ."[17] Or it has been rendered,

[14]*Op. cit.*, p. 91.

[15]*Critical and Exegetical Handbook to the Epistles to the Philippians and Colossians and to Philemon* (New York: Funk & Wagnalls, 1889), p. 31.

[16]Quoted by Barclay, *op. cit.*, p. 32.

[17]*Op. cit.*, p. 92.

"Living, I shall live Christ."[18] **To me** does not mean "in my opinion." It is more emphatic, and is tantamount to saying, "The commitment of my life is to Christ." Christ is the Object of Paul's natural life. He is the Beginning and End. In light of the reference to the **body** (20), Paul evidently is speaking of his total physical and practical life of service (cf. Rom. 6:16). That which makes this life meaningful and fruitful is Christ. Such a life is not a human possibility. It is a divine work. Consequently, the reference presupposes the deep and inward life of God in the soul. Thus Paul declares: "I am crucified with Christ: nevertheless I live; yet not I, but Christ lives in me: and the life which I now live in the flesh I live by the faith of the Son of God, who loved me, and gave himself for me" (Gal. 2:20). Paul has completely yielded himself to Christ, who lives in him and for him (cf. II Cor. 4:10, 16; 5:15, 17; Col. 3:3). He is "constrained" by a new force—love (II Cor. 5:14). For him life is lived to the full only in Christ, for "this is life eternal," to "know thee the only true God, and Jesus Christ, whom thou hast sent" (John 17:3). He seems to be saying: "The presence of Christ is the cheer of my life, the spirit of Christ the life of my life, the love of Christ the power of my life, the will of Christ the law of my life; and the glory of Christ the end of my life."[19]

To die is gain. Literally, "to have died"; that is, to die would be advantageous. The Greek tense indicates not that death itself is gain, but rather the state after death. **Gain** (*kerdos*) was used to describe interest on money. Thus to die is to cash in both principal and interest and to have more of Christ than when living.[20] Paul's concept of **gain** is quite in contrast to the vulgar motive of material advantage which characterized the merchants of Philippi, and which first awakened hostility to the preaching of the gospel there (Acts 16:19). J. W. C. Wand translates: "To me indeed life means Christ, and death would bring added advantage."[21] Hamlet in his famous "To be, or not to be" soliloquy, debates whether " 'tis best to live and suffer

[18]D. Thomas (Homilies), PC, XX, 48.

[19]John Eadie, *A Commentary on the Greek Text of the Epistle of Paul to the Philippians* (New York: Robt. Carter and Bros., 1859), p. 51.

[20]A. T. Robertson, *op. cit.*, IV, 440.

[21]*The New Testament Letters* (London: Oxford University Press, 1946), p. 129.

the arrows of fortune or die and risk the chance of accusing dreams." Neither prospect is pleasant. Shakespeare "regards both life and death as evils, and does not know which is the less; St. Paul regards both as blessings and knows not which to prefer."[22] For thirty years the apostle has lived, not for self, material things, or personal advancement, but for Christ. He is prepared to die because he is prepared to live. Right living ensures right dying. "To be all for Christ while I live [is] to find at length He is all for me when I die."[23] The entire verse might be rendered: "To me, living and dying, Christ is gain." Maclaren comments beautifully on this passage: "It matters very little to the servant whether he is out in the cold and wet 'ploughing and tending cattle,' or whether he is waiting on his master at the table. It is service all the same, only it is warmer and lighter in the house than in the field, and it is promotion to be made an indoor servant."[24]

But if I live in the flesh, this is the fruit of my labour: yet what I shall choose I wot not (22). The brokenness of the grammar indicates the apostles' quandary. The ASV puts the meaning clearly, "But if to live in the flesh,—if this shall bring fruit from my work, then what I shall choose I know not." Christ is the Fruit of Paul's labor (Rom. 1:13; 1 Cor. 3:6). Grotius explains **fruit of my labour** as an idiom for "worthwhile." Thus, "if I live in the flesh, this is worth my while."[25] Wand's translation helps clarify the meaning: "So long as physical existence gives an opportunity of fruitful work, I hardly know which to prefer."[26] To **live**, according to Barth's rendering, "means to be reaping harvest."[27] **Wot** (*gnorizo*) is the old English for "know." Some think the word means "declare." If so, the idea is: "If it is better

[22]James Hastings (ed.), *The Great Texts of the Bible* (New York: Scribner's, n.d.), XVII, 272.

[23]Robert Rainy, "Epistle to the Philippians," *An Exposition of the Bible* (Hartford, Conn.: S. S. Scranton Co., 1903), VI, 127.

[24]*Expositions of Holy Scripture* (Grand Rapids: Wm. B. Eerdmans Publishing Co., [reprint] 1952), XIV, 223.

[25]A. R. Fausset, "The Epistle of Paul the Apostle to the Philippians," *A Commentary, Critical & Explanatory, on the Old and New Testaments*, ed. Robert Jamieson, A. R. Fausset, David Brown (Hartford: S. S. Scranton & Co., n.d.), II, 362.

[26]*Op. cit.*, p. 129.

[27]*Op. cit.*, p. 40.

for the Church that I live, then I will not declare my personal choice."

For I am in a strait betwixt two (23). Literally, "I am pressed." *Synechomai* describes a traveller in a narrow pass, walled in on either side—able only to go straight ahead. Moffatt translates: "I am in a dilemma." **Having a desire to depart, and to be with Christ; which is far better.** Literally, "the" desire, suggesting that this is not just one among many desires. **Depart** (*analusai*) is a metaphor drawn from the loosing of tent stakes and ropes for breaking camp (cf. II Cor. 5:1; II Tim. 4:6). Such a metaphor provides an appropriate way for Paul, a tentmaker by trade, to describe the departure from this life. Sometimes it was used to describe the pulling up of anchors and setting sail. Adam Clarke suggests that it was a metaphor drawn from the commander of a vessel, in a foreign port, who wants to set sail for his country, but has not yet had orders from his owner.[28] Barclay points out that it is also the word used for solving problems.[29] The state that follows death will bring solutions to life's deep riddles (I Cor. 13:12). **To depart, and to be with Christ** are simultaneous. That is, the dead come immediately into the presence of the Lord. For the Christian, to be absent from the body is to be present with the Lord (John 14:3; II Cor. 5:8). This experience of being with Christ, Paul describes in superlative terms which are partially obscured by translation. **Far better** has been rendered "very much better" (NASB) and "the best thing for me" (Phillips).

Nevertheless to abide in the flesh is more needful for you (24). Here is the other side of Paul's dilemma. On the one hand he desires to be with Christ; on the other is the recognition of his duty toward the Church. Between these alternatives he maintains a "holy equilibrium." The will of God must be done, though it means subordinating his own desire to his duty toward others. **To abide in** (*epimenein te*) is literally to "remain by," not "in," **the flesh.** It means "to stand fast by" as a soldier refusing to leave his post (cf. v. 17). No man lives to himself. Thus Paul must think of the welfare of his friends at Philippi. He is willing to forego eternal bliss for earthly service. Is not this the "mind of Christ" which he desires so much for the Philippians (2:5-8), and which has characterized the life of the

[28]*Op. cit.*, II, 493.
[29]*Op. cit.*, p. 35.

apostle (Rom. 9:3; I Cor. 10:33)? No truer picture of the Christian's understanding of the relation of this world to the otherworld, of reward and service, could be drawn. Paul's longing is not for death, but for Christ. Death will simply be a doorway into a fuller relationship with Him. In no sense does he consider it an escape from the responsibilities of this temporal existence. The charge that the Christian is so otherworldly as to be concerned only with "pie in the sky by and by" is a caricature based on a misunderstanding of the Christian faith. The good of others must always come first, ahead of any personal desires. Consequently, Paul is willing to continue his service that the Philippians might be "more strengthened, like young fowls, who need their mother until their feathers are set."[30]

3. *The Result of the Triumph* (1:25-26)

And having this confidence, I know that I shall abide and continue with you all (25). The opening of this verse should be read with 24. That is, Paul is confident that his life is advantageous to the Philippians; thus, he is expressing a personal conviction (2:24) rather than a prophecy. He is simply stating his persuasion that God will permit what is best. Literally, he is saying, "I shall remain" (*meno*) **with you all,** and "I shall remain ready to help " (*parameno*) **you all. For your furtherance and joy of faith** is better translated "for your progress [*prokopen;* cf. comment on 12] and joy in the faith" (ASV).

That your rejoicing may be more abundant in Jesus Christ for me by my coming to you again (26) is literally "that your boasting may abound in Christ Jesus in me through my presence again with you." **Rejoicing** or "glorying" (*kauchaomai*) may be used in both a false and a legitimate sense (cf. Rom. 15:17; Eph. 2:9).[31] Thus the Philippians' "glorying" (*kauchema*) must be in Christ, though the object of it rests on Paul. **Coming** (*parousia*) is the word used in secular Greek to describe the ceremonious entry of a king or governor into a city, with all the manifestations of joy which attended it. Paul is assured that if

[30]Chrysostom (Homily IV, 1:22-26), *op. cit.,* p. 199.

[31]John Fletcher says the latter is a "glorying" or "rejoicing" upon personally fulfilling the law of faith. This rejoicing is what Paul calls the "witness of the Spirit" or "the testimony of a good conscience," which, "next to the witness of the Word and Spirit concerning God's mercy and Christ's blood, is the ground of a Christian's conscience." Cf. *The Works of the Rev. John William Fletcher* (New York: Waugh & Mason, 1833), I, 504.

he is permitted to see the Philippians again, their mutual fellowship will cause them to give him a royal welcome.

"A Holy Confidence" is portrayed in verses 12-26. It is based on (1) God's loving providence revealed in past events, 12-18; (2) Christ's continual presence in every given moment, 21; (3) God's ability to turn either death or life in the future to the fulfillment of His purposes, 19-26.

Section IV *The Fellowship of Obedience*

Philippians 1:27—2:18

Paul has relieved the Philippians by discussing his personal situation and that of the gospel in Rome. Now he shifts attention from himself to his readers. Though the affectionate tone remains at least until v. 30, the apostle now strikes a hortative note. A clue to the interpretation of this passage may be found in the apostle's references to obedience—both Christ's obedience (2:8) and that of the Philippians (2:12). A leading virtue of servants and saints (cf. 1) is obedience; in this Paul and his readers share a common fellowship. The counsel which is here offered presupposes such a spirit. Paul expects the Philippians to follow him as he follows Christ.

A. The Gift of Obedience, 1:27-30

1. *Obedience in Conduct* (1:27)

Only let your conversation be as it becometh the gospel of Christ (27). **Conversation** in current usage is too limited in meaning to be an accurate translation. It comes from the Latin word *conversari,* meaning "to conduct oneself." At the time of the King James translation (1611) **conversation** referred to the total life and conduct of an individual, not merely to his manner of speaking. Thus the ASV translates the verse: "Only let your manner of life be worthy of the gospel of Christ."

Even this clarification does not bring out the full meaning of the apostle. The word he uses is *politeuesthe,* which comes from *polites,* "citizen." Its original meaning was to live guided by certain regulations and laws. Philippi was a Roman colony, and some of her inhabitants were citizens of Rome. They were thereby entitled to all the privileges of such citizenship (cf. Introduction); and in the same measure they sustained certain obligations. A Roman colony was a bit of Rome on foreign soil. Her citizens were subject to her laws, not those of the provincial authorities. Though they may never have seen Rome, their first allegiance was to the Imperial City. Literally, Paul is saying to the Philippian Christians, "Conduct yourselves as citizens worthily of the glad tidings of Christ," as well as of the city of Rome. The thought is amplified in 3:20, where Paul states, "For our conversation is in heaven." Moffatt's translation of that verse reads, "For we are a colony of heaven." "As Philippi was to Rome, so is earth to heaven, the colony on the outskirts of the empire, ringed round by boundaries, and separated by sounding seas, but keeping open its communications, and one in citizenship."[1] **Only** (*monon*) is emphatic. Paul is declaring, "By all means let attention to your heavenly citizenship be supreme, no matter what." The imperative is clear in Moffatt's translation: "Only, do lead a life that is worthy of the gospel of Christ." The gospel is not only a message to bring deliverance, but also a guide to be followed.

Stand fast (*stekete*) may be a military metaphor meaning to stand firm, to refuse to retreat in spite of enemy onslaughts (cf. John 1:26; 8:44; II Thess. 2:15). This the Philippians are to do, **that whether I come and see you, or else be absent, I may hear of your affairs, that ye stand fast in one spirit.** Or the metaphor may be drawn from the spectacles of the Roman amphitheatre. In any case they are not to count on his coming to them again. Secondary motives would be insufficient to produce in them a lasting steadfastness and acceptable conduct. They must stand firm because of the character of God and the quality of their devotion rather than because of a desire to produce a good impression on a man, even Paul. In their own particular set of circumstances they are to perform their spiritual duties, and not wait for a more expedient time. **Spirit** (*pneumati*) has been interpreted as the Holy Spirit by some and as the human spirit by others. The divine reference appears preferable since the exact expression (*en heni pneumati*) is used in I Cor. 12:13 and Eph. 2:18, where the references are unquestionably to the Holy Spirit. If the human spirit is referred to, it means that quality in personal relationships which makes fellowship with God a possibility. Even if this interpretation be adopted, it is clear in Paul that a genuine "common spirit" is not a possibility apart from the Holy Spirit.[2]

With one mind is, literally, "with one soul" (*psyche*). *Psyche* is the seat of the affections, desires, and passions. These must

[1]Maclaren, *op. cit.*, XIV, 236.

[2]Michael, *op. cit.*, p. 65.

be brought under the control of the Holy Spirit (Rom. 8:4 ff.). **One mind** seems to be an athletic metaphor indicating teamwork and synchronization. Here it signifies a deep inward unity of purpose that is possible only in the Holy Spirit (cf. Acts 4:32). Paul's concern is that the strife characteristic of the church at Rome will not be manifest among the Philippians. They must strive **together,** not in opposition to each other, in a common cause. They have entered the Kingdom violently, and they must continue to protect and extend it violently (Matt. 11:12). The Roman colonies were sometimes expected to extend their frontiers by aggressive warfare. In the same way the "colony of heaven" which is at Philippi is to "fight the good fight of faith" (I Tim. 6:12), thereby enlarging itself. **Faith** is not here to be personified as though one were to strive either "with" or **for** it in an objective sense. Nor does it mean merely a body of teaching. Rather, it refers to the trust and commitment which come as a result of hearing the gospel. The entire expression suggests the maintenance of a right relationship to the gospel and thus to Christ, and could also well include the winning of converts to the gospel. The Philippians are to keep themselves in such a spirit of love as to be able to fight "side by side like one man for the faith of the gospel" (Moffatt).

2. *Obedience in Conflict* (1:28-30)

Terrified (28, *pturomenoi*) originally applied to a frightened animal, particularly a startled or shying horse. In light of the remaining portion of the verse, the **adversaries** (*antikeimenon*) does not refer to Jewish subverters of the gospel but to pagans. Paul evidently has in mind the opposition which he himself encountered in Philippi. The words are paraphrased by Phillips thus: "and not caring two straws for your enemies." If Paul is comparing himself to Moses giving final injunctions to the Israelites recorded in the last chapters of Deuteronomy (cf. comment on 1:19), he may well be using Moses' language: "do not fear or be in dread of them" (Deut. 31:6, RSV).

Which is to them an evident token of perdition, but to you of salvation, and that of God. The word **which** refers back to the Philippian steadfastness in the faith of the gospel (v. 27). The first clause may be translated literally, "seeing it is a clear demonstration to them of destruction." An **evident token** (*endeixis*) means a "pointing out," a proof based upon the evidence of facts (cf. Rom. 3:25-26; II Cor. 8:24). **Perdition** (*apoleias*) signifies destruction, ruin, or waste (II Thess. 2:3). The phrase **but to you of salvation** is more accurately rendered, "but of your salvation." Both **salvation** (*soterias*) and **perdition** (*apoleias*) refer to final destiny. In what way does Paul think the Philippian fearlessness and steadfastness under pressure will be a demonstration to the pagans of their destruction, and of the Philippians' own salvation? Whatever the answer may be, the token or signal is "from God" (ASV). Lightfoot thinks this expression **of God** suggests a practice of the gladiators, whose destiny depended upon the spectators, who by a signal indicated whether the gladiators were to live or die. Thus they closely watched the sign from the grandstands. But the "Christian gladiator does not anxiously await the signal of life or death from the fickle crowd."[3] He gets his signal from **God,** who gives him a surer sign of deliverance. Such poise on the part of the Christian indicates that God is working in him. This glorious fact becomes a sign to the opponents of their ruin, for they witness a superhuman work in the faithful, and despair, "If God is against us, who can be for us?"[4] Is Paul here thinking of the way God dealt with him as a persecutor of the Church, particularly as he witnessed the triumphant death of the first Christian martyr, Stephen (Acts 7:59-60; 9:5)? The Philippians, too, know a classic example of this way of God with men. One of their number, the former Philippian jailer was convicted and converted by seeing the power of God manifested in the life of Paul and Silas (Acts 16:27-34).

In 27-28 we find "Citizens of Heaven." (1) Keep fresh the sense of belonging to the mother city, 27; (2) Live by the laws of the city, worthy of **the gospel,** 27*a*; (3) Fight for the advance of the dominions of the city, **striving together for the faith of the gospel,** 27; (4) Be sure of victory, **in nothing terrified by your enemies,** 28 (Alexander Maclaren).

For unto you it is given in the behalf of Christ, not only to believe on him, but also to suffer for his sake (29). The word **given** (*echaristhe*) is formed on the stem of the noun *charis,* meaning "grace" or "favor." Thus even as belief in Christ, or absolute saving trust, is a gift of God, so also is suffering for the sake of Christ (cf. Matt. 5:11-12; Eph. 2:8; II Tim. 2:12; John

[3]*Op. cit.,* p. 106.

[4]Michael, *op. cit.,* p. 70.

1:12-13). Suffering is not a mark of God's anger (Acts 5:41; Col. 1:24; I Pet. 4:13). To the Philippians it was the "marriage gift when they were espoused to Christ: the bounty when they enlisted in his service. Becoming one with him they entered into the fellowship of his suffering" (3:10).[5] They are to take heart because their suffering is for "Christ's sake" (II Cor. 8:2).

The Philippians had seen Paul's conflicts with enemies on his first visit to them (Acts 16:12, 19; I Thess. 2:2), and now they have heard that he is engaged in similar conflict. Hence the apostle writes, **having the same conflict which ye saw in me, and now hear to be in me (30). Conflict** (*agona*) seems to be an allusion to the athletic contests. Paul pictures the Christians as athletes in the arena, engaged in a wrestling match against their pagan opponents (Eph. 6:12). The Philippians and Paul, as are all Christians, are in the same conflict. Consequently they are "striving together" in a fellowship of obedience.

B. The Meaning of Obedience, 2:1-4

1. *The Source of Obedience* (2:1-2)

If there be therefore any consolation in Christ, if any comfort of love, if any fellowship of the Spirit, if any bowels and mercies (1). The transitional word **therefore** evidently refers back to 1:27. Paul's use of **if** is rhetorical and in no way expresses doubt. **Consolation** (*paraklesis*) may be better rendered "exhortation," for Paul often used the cognate verb in this sense (cf. Rom. 12:1; 15:30; 16:17; I Cor. 1:10; 4:16; 16:15; Eph. 4:1; Phil. 4:2).[6] It may be significant to note the related word, *Paraclete,* which has been rendered as "The Advocate," "Comforter," or "One who strengthens." The strength to which Paul here refers is **in Christ** (cf. 1:1). **Comfort of love** is, literally, "consolation" or "incentive." For the meaning of **fellowship** (*koinonia*), see comments on 1:5. In the Greek there is no article before **Spirit**, but the modern translators are strong in support of KJV at this point (cf. RSV, NEB, NASB). It is presupposed that this fellowship is a gift of the Holy Spirit. **Bowels and mercies** is better translated "tender affections" and "compassions."

[5]M. R. Vincent, *Word Studies in the New Testament* (New York: Charles Scribner's Sons, 1914), III, 427-28.

[6]Michael, *op. cit.*, p. 76.

The meaning of the verse seems clear: If there is any divine strength or support available "to those who are in Christ Jesus as you are (and there is); if there is any consolation or incentive which springs from your love (and Paul is confident there is); if participation in the Holy Spirit means anything (and it does); if there be in you any affectionate tenderness (and Paul is sure there is),"[7] then, **fulfil ye my joy** (2). Lightfoot puts it, "Fill my cup of gladness to overflowing."[8] This fervent appeal by the apostle has been called a "tautology of earnestness."[9] But it is no selfish plea. Paul loves the Philippians as with the love of Christ (cf. 1:7-8). They share with him in a mutual fellowship. Thus what would complete his joy and love would also be for their good (1:3-4). They are his "joy and crown" (4:1), and yet he will rejoice in them even more if they will **be likeminded, having the same love**; literally, "having the same mind and the same love." Further, they are instructed to be **of one accord, of one mind**; literally, "minding the one thing." The Philippians are to act "together as if but one soul activated them."[10] Paul is calling, not for a unity of judgment, but for a moral unanimity—a oneness of disposition.

2. *The Submission of Obedience* (2:3-4)

Let nothing be done through strife or vainglory (3). In the Greek the clause is incomplete; **let** and **be done** are not in the original. In light of the word *phronountes,* translated **of one mind** in the previous verse, the rendering might better be "thinking nothing in the way of strife."[11] The humility of obedience will not countenance anything that is done "according to faction" (*kata eritheian*) or "groundless conceit" (*kenodoxian*). **But in**

[7]Cf. James Alexander Robertson, "The Epistle to the Philippians," *The Abingdon Bible Commentary,* ed. Carl Eiselen, *et al.* (New York: Abingdon-Cokesbury Press, 1929), p. 1244; also Karl Braune, "The Epistle to the Philippians," *Commentary on the Holy Scriptures,* ed. J. P. Lange, trans. Philip Schaff (Grand Rapids: Zondervan Publishing House, n.d.), p. 31.

[8]*Op. cit.,* p. 107.

[9]EGT, III, p. 28.

[10]Albert Barnes, *Notes on the New Testament, Explanatory and Practical,* ed. Robert Frew (Grand Rapids, Mich.: Baker Book House, 1950), p. 165.

[11]A. R. Fausset, "The Epistle of Paul the Apostle to the Philippians," *A Commentary on the Old and New Testaments,* ed. Jamieson, Fausset, and Brown (Hartford, Conn.: S. S. Scranton and Co., n.d.), II, 363.

lowliness of mind let each esteem other better than themselves. This is no plea for an abject servility, which is often the mask of a false humility. Rather, it is a call for genuine self-appraisal which acknowledges that one has shortcomings unknown to others, and that others possess obvious virtues which one himself does not demonstrate. **Look not every man on his own things, but every man also on the things of others** (4). The verse is an imperative. One is not to fix his eye merely on his own interests, as a runner fixes his eye on the goal alone and nothing else (cf. Rom. 12:10). The phrase **every man** is used twice. Probably in the first usage, and certainly in the second, the Greek is plural. It may then be rendered by "each circle" or "each set."[12] The church at Philippi has not been affected by heresy. Rather, there is a threat to the fellowship on account of the self-preoccupation of certain individuals or parties within the church. A genuine humility will prevent any from insisting even on what he considers to be his own rights (cf. I Cor. 6:7).[13]

From verses 1-4, Alexander Maclaren preached on "A Plea for Unity." He notes: (1) The motives and bonds of Christian unity, 1; (2) The fair ideal which would complete the apostle's joy, 2; (3) The hindrances and helps to being of the same mind (3-4).

C. The Supreme Example of Obedience, 2:5-11

Here is one of the most majestic and profound Christological passages in all of Holy Writ. No man could presume to scale the mountain peaks of revelation in these verses. On reading them one is more inclined to praise than to analyze or theologize about them. Considering the careful construction and balance of clauses, it may well be that they are a poem or hymn used in worship by the Early Church. But one cannot avoid interpretation, and historically these verses have given rise to numerous and sometimes opposing viewpoints. Whatever particular shades of meaning one may find here, Paul's essential message (identical with the thought expressed in II Cor. 8:9) is not difficult to discover if it be remembered that his primary purpose is practical in

[12]H. C. G. Moule, *The Epistle to the Philippians,* "Cambridge Bible," ed. by J. J. S. Perowne (Cambridge: University Press, 1895), p. 63.

[13]F. W. Beare, *A Commentary on the Epistle to the Philippians* ("Harper New Testament Commentaries"; New York: Harper and Brothers, 1959), p. 73.

nature. He is dealing with a problem which threatens to dissolve the unity of the believers at Philippi. Over against the mood of some to assert themselves selfishly, Paul sets the spirit of Christ as the supreme example of obedience.

1. *The Reason for Obedience* (2:5-6)

Let this mind be in you (5) is, literally, "Think [*phroneite*] this in yourselves."[14] "Think" is also used in 1:7 and 2:2. However, as has been shown in comments there, it connotes more than mere thought. It refers primarily to disposition. **Was** in the clause **which was also in Christ Jesus** is not in the original text. Perhaps "is" could be better supplied. Moffatt translates the verse: "Treat one another with the same spirit as you experience in Christ Jesus." It has also been rendered: "Have this mind within your community which ye have also in Christ Jesus."[15] This way of putting it is consistent with the admonition that the Philippians work out their own salvation (12). It serves also as a legitimate warning against the erroneous divorce which some professed Christians make between their religious life and their relationships with their fellows. Here is set forth the absolute impossibility of loving God without at the same time loving one's fellowmen.

The Greeks had two words for **form** (6). One of them referred to mere external appearance, as when a mirage takes the form of water. In this case there is no true equivalence between the appearance and that which it appears to be. The other Greek word suggests that the appearance of the object is the true revelation or expression of the object itself. That is, the form participates in the reality; thus the reality discloses itself in the form.[16] It is the second word (*morphe*) which Paul here employs: **Who, being in the form of God** (cf. Mark 16:12). Christ is the *morphe theou,* i.e., the true and full Expression or Revelation of God. This Revelation cannot be explained by any human categories. It is wholly inexplicable aside from the assertion that the absolute Source of the revelation is God himself. Thus Paul speaks of Christ Jesus as **being,** or "subsisting" (*huparchon*) —not the simple "to be" (*einai*)—**in the form of God.** To put it differently, that which is revealed, namely, God, is prior to the

[14]Vincent, *op. cit.,* III, 430.

[15]EGT, III, p. 434.

[16]IB (Exegesis), XI, 48.

revelation itself. But the Revelation, Christ, the Revealer, is One with God, the Revealed. Because this is so, the revelation of God in Christ is true. Consequently Paul is proclaiming kerygmatically and didactically what the Church later maintained theologically—that God and Jesus Christ are *homoousias,* "of one substance."

Thought it not robbery to be equal with God. Robbery (*harpagmon*) comes from a verb meaning to "snatch," "clutch," or "seize violently." Thus the RSV translates the clause: "did not count equality with God a thing to be grasped."[17] "Equality" seems not to refer to *nature* so much as to *relationship.*[18] It seems reasonable to assume that Christ, being the Revelation of God, might have claimed His right to be recognized as equal with God. But contrary to the accusation of His enemies (John 5:17-18), this is precisely what He refused to do—insist upon His own rights, or usurp the place of God. He refused to seek self-enrichment or self-gratification. Paul may have had in mind the contrast between the first Adam, who selfishly desired to be "as gods" (Gen. 3:5), and Christ, the Second Adam, who unselfishly looked on the "things of others" (4).

2. *The Requirement of Obedience* (2:7-8)

Made himself of no reputation (7) is, literally, "emptied himself." Here is the well-known "kenosis" (*neauton ekenosen*) passage. Bruce has observed that the "diversity of opinion prevailing among interpreters in regard to the meaning of this passage is enough to fill the student with despair, and to afflict him with intellectual paralysis."[19] The practical setting should point in this case to the principle that the simplest interpretation is the best. It seems unnecessary to ask, as many have done: Of what did Christ empty himself? His deity? His nature? His divine prerogatives? His equality? Paul simply says that Christ emptied himself. The verb *kenoun* means "to pour out," with Christ **himself** as the object. Thus Christ emptied himself of himself. At no time did He allow selfish considerations to dominate His spotless life. Verses 7 and 8 have been compared with Isa. 53:12, which

[17]Cf. also Vincent, *op. cit.,* III, 432.

[18]Rees, *op. cit.,* p. 43.

[19]*The Humiliation of Christ* (New York: A. C. Armstrong and Son, 1907), p. 8.

says, "He poured out his soul to death" (RSV).[20] This comparison is particularly striking in light of the reference in 8 to death, and in light of the assertion **and took upon him the form of a servant** (7); literally, "having taken the form of a slave." **Took** (*labon*) is an aorist participle, indicating simultaneous action.[21] The implication is that subsisting in the form (*morphe*) of God and having taken the form (*morphe*) of a servant are simultaneous and not incompatible. The latter is the revelation of the former, and the former is the explanation of the latter. Christ's humanity was no play-acting. By taking the form of a servant **He** revealed the true meaning of service. He did not become an actual slave of any single man—though His service was expressed to individual men (Luke 22:27)—but was the actual **servant** of mankind.[22]

And was made in the likeness of men can be rendered, "He became [*genomenos*] like men" (plural). The reference is to the humanity of Jesus, which had a beginning in time, and should be taken in the sense of Gal. 4:4: "God sent forth his Son, born of a woman"[23] (cf. also Rom. 8:3). Donald Baillie has pointed out perceptively: "The Church has never taught that the human element in Jesus, His manhood, is consubstantial or co-eternal with God, but that it is consubstantial with ourselves and belongs to the order of created things."[24] **Likeness** (*homoiomati*), however, cannot be taken to be anything less than man. Christ's humanity was no mere mask or disguise. He was "really *like* men, as He truly *was* man"; but "He was also *more than man, other than men,* without which fact there would be not resemblance but *mere identity.*"[25] Jesus Christ was truly man, but it was in and through Him that the revelation of God came. This makes Him unique and distinct from man—He is "very man and very God." The only way Paul can express this truth is to speak of His likeness to man.

Fashion (8, *schema*) denotes the way Christ appeared in

[20]Michael, *op. cit.*, pp. 90-91.

[21]John F. Walvoord, *To Live Is Christ: An Exposition of the Epistle of Paul to the Philippians* (Findlay, Ohio: Dunham Publishing Company, 1961), p. 43.

[22]A. T. Robertson, *Paul's Joy in Christ: Studies in Philippians* (Nashville, Tenn.: Broadman Press, rev. ed., 1959), p. 72.

[23]Beare, *op. cit.*, p. 83.

[24]*God Was in Christ* (New York: Scribner's Sons, 1948), p. 150.

[25]Moule, *op. cit.*, p. 67.

men's eyes. Thus Barth translates: "Being found in his being as a man."[26] His contemporaries saw Jesus as they saw other men, subject to human drives and suffering (Heb. 4:15). Compare Isa. 53:2: "He hath no form nor comeliness; and when we shall see him, there is no beauty that we should desire him." A divine miracle is required to see God in this Servant. Faith that He is the full and true Revelation of God comes "not of blood, nor of the will of the flesh, nor of the will of man, but of God" (John 1:13). The confession that He is the Christ springs from a revelation of the "Father which is in heaven" (Matt. 16:16-17). Paul puts it elsewhere, "No man can say that Jesus is the Lord, but by the Holy Ghost" (I Cor. 12:3).

He humbled himself, and became obedient unto death (8). It is not stated explicitly to whom obedience was rendered. The phrase **unto death** means "to the extent of death." Yet Christ subjected himself to it "that through death he might destroy him that had the power of death, that is, the devil; and deliver them who through fear of death were all their lifetime subject to bondage" (Heb. 2:14-15).[27] It must be emphasized that Christ's acts of self-humiliation and obedience to death were voluntary—of himself He laid down His life (John 10:17-18)—while at the same time they were in accord with the will of the Father. **The death of the cross** indicates the climax of Christ's self-abasement, for it was the most ignominious of all the modes of death known in Paul's day. The law of Moses had spoken a curse against it (Deut. 21:23), and the Gentiles reserved it for their most hated enemies and common criminals. Thus the Cross was surrounded by the deepest shame (Heb. 12:2).[28] But by His obedience even unto **the death of the cross,** Christ "hath abolished death, and hath brought life and immortality to light through the gospel" (II Tim. 1:10). Consequently, "the cross of Christ has come to be his crown of glory."[29] (Cf. Rom. 5:19.)

3. *The Reward of Obedience* (2:9-11)

Wherefore (*dio*), or in consequence of His obedience, **God also hath highly exalted him** (9). Jesus not only taught that

[26]*The Epistle to the Philippians* (Richmond: John Knox Press, 1962), p. 64.

[27]Beare, *op. cit.*, p. 84.

[28]Vincent, *op. cit.*, III, 435.

[29]Robertson, *Paul's Joy in Christ*, p. 75.

exaltation follows self-humiliation; He also demonstrated it (cf. Matt. 23:12; Luke 14:11; 18:14). The exaltation of Christ includes His resurrection and ascension.[30] **Given him a name** can mean "freely bestowed upon Him a name." Some manuscripts read "*the* Name," clearly distinguishing it from every other name (Eph. 1:20-21). Lightfoot suggests that the name *Jesus* is not here referred to, as many have shared that name.[31] If a particular name is intended, it is probably "Lord" (cf. 11; also Acts 2:26). In the days of Paul a soldier took his oath in the name of Caesar, indicating Caesar's authority.[32] In similar fashion, the new name of Jesus, i.e., "Lord," indicates His absolute sovereignty.

That at the name of Jesus (10; cf. Isa. 45:23) is better translated "in the name of Jesus," or following Moffatt, "before the name of Jesus." The verse may mean that in this name every prayer of man shall be offered (cf. John 14:13-14; Acts 3:6; Eph. 2:18; 3:14; 5:20). The allusion to **things** or beings **in heaven, in earth,** and **under the earth,** no doubt includes the whole of creation (cf. Rom. 8:22; I Cor. 15:24-28; Eph. 1:20-22). All things, both animate and inanimate, cannot now avoid or gainsay His lordship. The latter part of the clause, **that every tongue should confess that Jesus Christ is Lord** (11), seems to have been the earliest creed of the Church (cf. Rom. 10:9; I Cor. 12:3; 8:6). **Confess** encompasses the idea of thanksgiving, or joyful acknowledgment (cf. Matt. 11:25; Luke 10:21).[33] By an alternate reading of one letter, which is supported by some manuscripts, *exomologesetai* may be rendered "shall confess," making it to be a prophetic utterance.[34] The meaning in this case would be that, though all do not now personally accept the lordship of Christ, at the final day, because He will be their Judge, they will be unable to deny that He is also **Lord, to the glory of God the Father** (cf. Rev. 5:13). Thus Christ's self-surrender continues even in His exaltation (cf. I Cor. 15:28).

According to Paul, then, it is the *Servant* who has become the *Lord.* The practical application which the apostle has in mind for the Philippians is expressed in the words of Jesus: "Whoso-

[30]Braune, *op. cit.,* p. 35.

[31]*Op. cit.,* p. 114.

[32]IB (Exegesis), XI, 50-51.

[33]Vincent, *op. cit.,* III, 436.

[34]Walvoord, *op. cit.,* p. 47.

ever will be chief among you, let him be your servant" (Matt. 20:27).

D. The Admonition to Obedience, 2:12-18

Throughout this entire passage, Paul is thinking of the farewell injunction of Moses to the children of Israel, whom he had led in spite of their murmurings, contestings, and disobediences to the very border of the Promised Land (Deuteronomy 32).[35] The apostle tenderly addresses the Philippians as **my beloved** (found twice in 4:1). Because of the mutual fellowship which they enjoy with him, they **have always obeyed** (12). That is, since he is their spiritual father, they have from the beginning of this relationship recognized his authority over them as coming from God.[36]

1. *The Practicality of Obedience* (2:12)

In view of their past obedience, Paul admonishes the Philippians to **work out your own salvation** (12). The structure of the sentence indicates that the phrases **not as in my presence only, but now much more in my absence** are to be connected with **work out,** and not with **obeyed.** Paul's use of **now** (*nun*) suggests that his absence means more than his bodily separation from them. He has been present to them until now by letter even when he could not give them a spoken message. **My absence** evidently refers to his death, following which the Philippians will not have his guiding admonitions. Consequently they must begin to act for themselves, or work out their own salvation.[37] This working at the continuous task of following Christ's example of obedience is to be **with fear and trembling,** i.e., in the spirit of vigilance, humility, and dependence upon God (I Cor. 2:3; Eph. 6:5), as one would hold something exceedingly precious and rare.

Here is no denial of justification by faith, for it is Christians, not unbelievers, who are being addressed. **Salvation** (*soterion*) is something they already possess.[38] The word which Paul uses for **work out** has the idea of bringing to completion.[39] The Philip-

[35]Beare, *op. cit.*, p. 88.

[36]Barth, *op. cit.*, pp. 69-70.

[37]Michael, *op. cit.*, p. 101.

[38]HDB, XVII, 296-97.

[39]Barclay, *op. cit.*, p. 51.

pians are to work *out* as a *community* in their social relationships what God had worked *in* by faith. In view of verses 14 and 15 (as well as c. 3) it is possible that there is in the beginning stages at Philippi the spirit of self-righteousness, which threatens the unity of the fellowship. Thus each factious group is to **work out** its own salvation and stop comparing selfishly its spiritual progress with the other groups. This interpretation is valid if Paul, as seems likely, is comparing himself to Moses, who gave his parting injunctions to Israel *as a body* (Deut. 31:27).

2. *The Promise of Obedience* (2:13)

The working may be done with assurance, **For it is God which worketh in you both to will and to do of his good pleasure** (13; cf. II Pet. 1:10). **Worketh** (*energon*) and **to do** (*energein*) are from the same verb. It is always used of God's action and of effective action. Thus Lightfoot translates, God "works mightily" in you.[40] Salvation is all of God, both the willing and the doing, from start to finish. In no way does this undercut man's part, which has been clearly affirmed in the previous verse. Paul is suggesting that the genuine Christian attitude is that of giving God all the glory. This some of the Philippians obviously were slow to do. The context indicates that "among you" may be better than **in you,** particularly since **of his good pleasure** means literally "for the sake of the goodwill" (**his** is not in the original). See 1:15, where the same word, *eudokian* (goodwill), is used. Paul is confident that God is working, and will continue to work even after the apostle's death, to promote goodwill at Philippi. If Paul is still comparing himself to Moses, he intends this verse as a promise (cf. Deut. 31:8).

3. *The Purpose of Obedience* (2:14-18)

It is unnecessary to determine whether **murmurings and disputings** (14) has to do with one's relations to his fellows or to God. Clearly each involves the other. **Murmurings** (*goggusmon*) indicates a spirit of discontent and stubbornness, as that which characterized the Israelites in the wilderness (cf. Numbers 16; I Cor. 10:10). **Disputings** (*dialogismon*) means "questionings" or "doubtings" (cf. Rom. 14:1). These are put in the order in which they normally appear. Quite often, though not always, in-

[40] *Op. cit.,* p. 116.

tellectual doubt follows moral revolt against God and broken relationships with our fellows. The Christian must remember that "explanations, if they come at all, come after obedience, not before"[41] (cf. John 7:17). Paul clearly sets forth in the following verses the purpose of obedience.

That ye may be blameless and harmless (15) is better translated, that ye may "become" (*genesthe*) or "show yourselves to be" **blameless** (*amemptoi*) in the eyes of men, and **harmless** (*akeraioi*). The latter term means simple, or absolutely sincere, and unmixed (cf. Matt. 10:16). The word was used of wine that was unmixed with water, or of metal that contained no alloy. Thus it has been rendered "guileless," or "innocent" (Moffatt). For the clause **the sons of God, without rebuke**, "children of God" is more adequate because it points to the character of God's family, and thus to a family likeness (John 1:12). **Without rebuke,** or "without blemish" (*amometa*), alludes to Momus, a carping deity among the Greeks, who did nothing worthwhile himself but found fault with everybody and everything. The Christian is to walk so circumspectly that even a Momus himself may have no occasion to find fault with him.[42] The comparable word *amomos* is related to sacrifices, suggesting a sacrifice that is fit to be offered to God. Barclay says that the words translated **blameless, harmless,** and **without rebuke** have to do with the Christian's relation to the world, to himself, and to God.[43]

The Israelites were a "perverse and wicked generation," who thus failed to carry themselves as children of God (Deut. 32:5). Paul is hopeful that the Philippians in the midst of a similarly **crooked and perverse nation** (untoward and warped generation) may **shine as lights in the world.** The **lights** (*phosteres*) refer to the heavenly bodies—sun, moon, and stars. As these provide light for the physical world, so the light of the Christian is to be poured out on the darkness of the moral and spiritual world. The image may also be that of lighthouses on a seacoast. In either case the Christian is to be a "light bearer" (cf. Matt. 5:14). Though his light is reflected from that "Light, which lighteth every man that cometh into the world" (John 1:9), he is to be an active light giver, **holding forth the word of life** (16). *Epechontes* **(holding forth)** was used in classical Greek to describe

[41]Robertson, *Paul's Joy in Christ*, p. 83.

[42]Matthew Henry, VI, 734.

[43]*Op. cit.*, p. 55.

offering wine to a guest.[44] **Word of life,** consistent with the biblical use, must not only refer to a stated message, but to Jesus Christ, the living Word, who is himself both Light and Life (John 1:4; 8:12; I John 1:1). This **word of life** frees from sin and death (Rom. 8:2). It is Christ himself, the Bread of Life, whom the Christian offers to a hungry world. Where he does so, Christ's servant becomes to those who partake the "savour of life unto life" (II Cor. 2:16).

But, further, Paul has in mind a personal purpose for the obedience of the Philippians, namely, **that I may rejoice in the day of Christ, that I have not run in vain, neither laboured in vain.** Increasingly the apostle is thinking of the final day of Christ (cf. 1:6, 10), usually expressed in Scripture as "the day of the Lord." He hopes for some cause to **rejoice** (*kauchema,* boast) among those at Philippi when he comes to give a final account of his stewardship to God. If they failed, he would have run in vain and labored in vain (cf. Gal. 2:2). Paul speaks as if he were already looking back on his life, as though his labors on behalf of the Philippians were completed. **In vain** (*eis kenon*) was sometimes used of water running to waste, or of the training which appeared fruitless to a defeated athlete, or of a weaver of tent cloth who received no wages because a width of cloth was rejected as badly woven.[45]

But this personal hope is not a selfish one. Paul continues: **Yea, and if I be offered upon the sacrifice and service of your faith, I joy, and rejoice with you all** (17). A literal translation is, "If I am being poured out as a libation . . ." **Offered** (*spendomai*) was sometimes used to denote the fact that, when an animal was about to be slain in sacrifice, wine was poured on it as a solemn act of devoting it to God (cf. Num. 15:5; 28:14).[46] Thus if Paul's dying will in any way complete or perfect the sacrifice of the Philippians' faith, or their deeds of service, he will gladly die (cf. II Cor. 12:15; II Tim. 4:6). Moule frames Paul's thoughts thus: "Labored for you, did I say? Nay, if I have to say also *died, poured out my heart's blood,* it is only joy to me."[47] Paul's martyrdom and the Philippians' life (cf. Rom. 12:1) would together constitute a single mutual offering to God.

[44]Vincent, *op. cit.,* III, 439.

[45]Michael, *op. cit.,* 108-9.

[46]Barnes, *op. cit.,* p. 181.

[47]*Op. cit.* p. 76.

The apostle's next words are a loving imperative: **For the same cause also do ye joy, and rejoice with me** (18). The spirit is similar to that of the brave Athenian mentioned by Plutarch who returned to Athens from the victorious battle of Marathon, bleeding to death with the wounds he had received in the action. Coming directly to the house where the magistrates were assembled, he uttered only, "Take your share of our joy," and immediately dropped dead at their feet.[48]

Clearly set forth in verses 1:27—2:18 are "The Marks of a True Christian." One who is Christlike is characterized by (1) A demeanor which is consistent with Christ's gospel, 27-30; (2) A spirit of selflessness which fosters unity and humility, 2:1-8; (3) An obedience which arises out of godly fear, 2:12-13; (4) A testimony which faithfully declares **the word of life,** 2:15-16.

[48]Philip Doddridge, *The Family Expositor* (Charleston, Mass.: S. Etheridges, from the 8th London ed., 1808), V, 213.

Section V *The Fellowship of Concern*

Philippians 2:19-30

It is indeed remarkable to find within a single chapter one of the most profound Christological passages in all the New Testament and also perhaps the deepest human sentiments reflected in any of Paul's writings. Such was the character of the apostle that he saw no dichotomy between doctrine and discipleship, commitment to God and concern for man. Paul knows that the Philippians are anxious about his welfare, and to relieve their anxiety he is dispatching Epaphroditus to them, even before the outcome of his trial is known. Further, he is deeply interested in their spiritual progress, which is being threatened, and promises soon to send Timothy, through whom he also in turn will receive a report from Philippi. It is this mutual fellowship of concern that provides the background for these verses.

A. The Responsibility of Concern, 2:19-24

Paul had a shepherd's heart, which would not permit him to suppose that his responsibility was discharged as soon as he won new converts to Christ. He continued to share in the concern for their growth and development in the faith. Since he cannot go himself to Philippi, he hopes **in the Lord Jesus to send Timotheus shortly** (19). The expression **in the Lord Jesus** is no idle cliché with the apostle. His whole life from center to circumference is under the control of Jesus Christ (cf. 1:8, 14, 21; 2:24; Rom. 9:1). All his actions are subject to his Master. Thus if the Lord approves his plans, he will send Timothy (cf. Jas. 4:15). Apparently Paul not only has confidence in Timothy's ability to ascertain the situation of the Philippians, but also feels that he can press home the appeals of this letter, thereby helping to improve the condition of the Philippian church. Consequently, Timothy will come **that I also may be of good comfort** (lit., strengthened), **when I know your state** (19). Paul is delighted to send him because he has no (other) **man likeminded** (20). Only here in the New Testament is the word *isopsuchon* (lit., one-souled, or equal-souled) used. The meaning could be that there is no other like Timothy, but more likely that no one else shares Paul's concerns as fully as Timothy.

Three characteristics of the apostle's associate minister from Lystra are given. Paul Rees[1] has put them in a charming alliteration which might be titled "A Man Fitted for Christian Service." (1) He is sympathetic, 20; (2) He is selfless, 21; and (3) He is seasoned, 22.

The Philippians were assured that Timothy **will naturally care for your state. Naturally** (*gnesios*), "genuinely" or "truly," implies kinship and may be understood as "like a brother."[2] The word translated **care** suggests in the original a careful mindfulness, or earnestness of thought. Timothy will not make the journey for any personal honor it may bring him, but only because of a sincere concern for those to whom he is sent. **All** (others) **seek their own, not the things which are Jesus Christ's** (21). **All** (*oi pantes,* lit., one and all) cannot refer to those persons mentioned in 1:14-17. No doubt some in Rome are willing to go to Philippi but are unable or unqualified. However, of those who can go and are competent, Timothy is the only one who is willing to undertake the task.[3]

Finally, ye know the proof of him, that, as a son with the father, he hath served with me in the gospel (22). **Proof** (*dokime*) was used of gold and silver which had been tested and could be accepted as current coin. Timothy's record is known to all and is one of absolute faithfulness. In spite of an evident timidity (II Tim. 1:6-7) and certain physical infirmities (I Tim. 5:23), this young man faithfully stood by Paul in Philippi (Acts 16), in Thessalonica and Beroea (Acts 17:1-14), in Corinth and Ephesus (Acts 18:5; 19:21-22), and even now is with Paul in Rome (Phil. 1:1). He was associated with Paul in the writing of I and II Thessalonians, II Corinthians, and now Philippians. He had earlier been sent as a delegate to Jerusalem (Acts 20:4). In it all he had served cooperatively with Paul "for the furtherance of the gospel," even when it meant occupying a place secondary to the apostle.

Though Paul still has hope that the Lord may allow him to

[1]*The Adequate Man* (Westwood, N.J.: Fleming H. Revell Co., 1959), pp. 56-57.

[2]IB (Exegesis), XI, 68.

[3]Charles Erdman, *The Epistle of Paul to the Philippians* (Philadelphia: The Westminster Press, 1932), pp. 86-87.

come to Philippi (24), he will presently send this young man, **so soon as I shall see how it will go with me** (23). For **shall see** the oldest manuscripts use a word from the verb *aphidein,* meaning to see something from a distance. Thus as soon as Paul can see the final outcome of his trial a little more clearly, he will send Timothy. Until then he cannot spare him, but in his place he will immediately send another.

B. The Reciprocity of Concern, 2:25-28

Yet I supposed (I consider) **it necessary to send to you Epaphroditus** (25). This is the man, mentioned only here in the New Testament, who had conveyed to Paul a gift of money from the Philippian congregation (4:18). Thus Paul speaks of him as **your messenger, and he that ministered to my wants.** The word for **messenger** is *apostolos,* i.e., one sent on an errand. In Christian usage it had come to refer to those closest to Christ. Within this special circle Paul places Epaphroditus. The word translated **minister** is *leitourgos,* which in ancient Greece referred to outstanding philanthropists who out of their resources assumed certain civic responsibilities (cf. also 4:18-19).[4] However, as though this tribute to Epaphroditus were insufficient, Paul refers to him as **my brother, and companion in labour, and fellowsoldier.** Together they have shared in a common will, a common work, and a common warfare.

However, Epaphroditus had become ill, even **nigh unto death** (27). After the Philippians were informed of his sickness, he became **full of heaviness** (26) or "sore troubled" (ASV) lest they should worry about him. Thus **he longed after you all.** If Epaphroditus were in any way involved in the factions at Philippi this clause may have been inserted to indicate his impartial affection for them.[5] If his illness had been accompanied by homesickness, which is likely, Paul finds reason to excuse it; or perhaps his maturer years have made him more charitable than when, long before, he refused to tolerate John Mark's similar plight (Acts 15:38). Nonetheless, **God had mercy on him,** and on Paul also, **lest I should have sorrow upon sorrow** (27). Con-

[4]William Barclay, *Letter to the Philippians* ("Daily Study Bible"; Philadelphia: The Westminster Press, 1959), pp. 61-62.

[5]H. C. G. Moule, *The Epistle to the Philippians,* ed. J. J. S. Perowne ("Cambridge Bible"; Cambridge: University Press, 1895), p. 81.

sequently Paul is sending him back **that, when ye see him again, ye may rejoice, and that I may be the less sorrowful** (28). **I sent him therefore the more carefully** may be translated, "I am the more eager to send him" (RSV). The Philippians were gracious enough to send him to Paul in time of need; and now exercising a reciprocal concern, Paul seeks to relieve the Philippians.

C. The Risk of Concern, 2:29-30

It seems that Epaphroditus had been sent not only to convey a gift but to serve as Paul's personal attendant. Lest the Philippians would suppose that Epaphroditus had not fulfilled his task, Paul seeks to assure his generous reception. **Receive him therefore in the Lord with all gladness; and hold such in reputation** ("high regard," NASB, 29); **because for the work of Christ he was nigh unto death, not regarding his life, to supply your lack of service toward me** (30). Some texts say simply **the work,** omitting **of Christ,** indicating that the work of Christ was being given a technical meaning, as "the Way," or "the Name" (Acts 15:38). **Not regarding** is *paraboleusamenos,* which is from a verb meaning "to venture." It is a word used by gamblers who stake everything on a throw of the dice. The early Christians called those who hazarded their lives for Christ *parabolani,* or "the riskers," as Aquila and Priscilla risked their lives for Paul (Rom. 16:4).[6] Epaphroditus—for the sake of Christ—had been willing to risk his life by becoming associated with a man who was being tried by the government. By so doing he had been able to supply in person what the Philippians themselves, because of distance, were unable to do (cf. Col. 1:24).

[6]Robertson, *op. cit.*, p. 95.

Section VI *The Fellowship of His Sufferings*

Philippians 3:1-16

Clearly the mood of the apostle now changes. This obvious fact has led some to argue that the opening part of verse 1, **Finally, my brethren, rejoice in the Lord,** is inconsistent with most of the chapter, and that verses 1*b* through 19 are part of an old letter. But it is not necessary to conclude thus. Nor is there sufficient reason to assume that Paul is about to finish his letter. **Finally** (*to loipon*)—literally, "as for the rest"—he used elsewhere before the close of his writing was in sight (cf. I Thess. 4:1). Rather, the apostle is coming to a crucial problem which threatens the unity of the church at Philippi; i.e., the problem of works-righteousness. He cautions: **My brethren** (encompassing all parties within the church), let your rejoicing be in the Lord and not in any work of the flesh (cf. Luke 10:20). In this passage Paul issues a severe attack against the legalists who would pervert and minimize the gospel. The only safeguard against their impersonal, lifeless brand of religion is a genuine knowledge of Christ, which shares His resurrection power, and participates in the fellowship of His sufferings (10).

A. Alternative to Christ's Sufferings, 3:1-6

1. *The Alternative Reviewed* (3:1-2)

To write the same things to you, to me indeed is not grievous, but for you it is safe (1). **The same things** may refer to another letter, to his warnings in the previous chapter against dissension, to those things which he had spoken earlier to them orally (Paul had visited Philippi after founding the church there), or to that which immediately follows. Probably a combination of these possibilities is the best solution. In any case his repetition **is not grievous** (lit., irksome) to him; and to the Philippians **it is safe,** or perhaps "certain" (as in Acts 22:30; 25: 26). That is, his repeated admonition will make his views clear and certain to them.

Three times he warns, **Beware of** (lit., have your eye on) **dogs, evil workers,** and **the concision** (2). Although the definite article **the** precedes each of these appellations, they are evidently not three classes but one—the Judaizers—described by words indicating their character, conduct, and creed.[1] The context seems to favor the view that these were converted Jews who were attempting to turn Christianity back to Judaism. Judaizers insisted that salvation comes by the works of the law. Paul describes these Jews **as dogs,** a term which the Jews themselves applied to the Gentiles (Matt. 15:26-27). Thus he reverses the metaphor. In Scripture "dog" is commonly used as a word of contempt, reproach, or dread. The writer may have had in mind the pariah dogs of the East, which, half-wild, feed on leftover garbage. Like them these Judaizers are feeding on the garbage of Jewish and fleshly rites. They are **evil workers,** or "deceitful workers," men who work ostensibly for the gospel, but actually are working for evil (II Cor. 11:13).[2] They are "work-heroes."[3] **Concision** (*katatome*) refers to the mere cutting off of the flesh. Thus these persons are "the incision party" (Moffatt), who by placing confidence in the flesh insist on an empty symbol of physical circumcision apart from faith.

2. *The Alternative Rejected* (3:3-6)

Paul reserves the word **circumcision** (*peritome*) for the genuine believers in Christ. These are the true people of God, for they have known the spiritual circumcision (Rom. 2:25-29; Eph. 2:11; Col. 2:11). They **worship God in the spirit** (better, worship by the Spirit of God), **and rejoice in Christ Jesus, and have no confidence in the flesh** (3, cf. John 4:24). The Christian does not consider circumcision as having value in itself, or make it something other than a mere sign. His faith and hope are in Christ.

Putting himself in the place of the Judaizers for a moment, Paul argues that, if the external privileges of the flesh have merit of themselves, he would have more in which to place his trust than all the rest (4, cf. Gal. 1:14). He had been **circumcised the eighth day** (5), according to the Law (Gen. 17:12; Lev. 12:3;

[1]J. A. Robertson, "The Epistle to the Philippians," *The Abingdon Bible Commentary,* ed. Carl Eiselen, *et al.* (New York: Abingdon-Cokesbury Press, 1929), p. 1246.

[2]"The Epistle of Paul the Apostle to the Philippians," *A Commentary on the Old and New Testaments,* ed. Jamieson, Fausset, and Brown (Hartford, Conn.: S. S. Scranton and Co., n.d.), II, 366.

[3]Karl Barth, *The Epistle to the Philippians* (Richmond: John Knox Press, 1962), p. 92.

Luke 1:59). He is no proselyte to Judaism, for in the case of proselytes, circumcision was not performed until adult age (Acts 16:3). He is **of the stock of Israel;** i.e., descended from the patriarch Jacob. Even the Ishmaelites could hark back to Abraham, and the Edomites could claim Isaac as their father; but only the Israelite could trace his descent to Jacob. Paul is **of the tribe of Benjamin,** from which had come Israel's first king, and which faithfully refused to revolt under Jeroboam (I Kings 12:21). He is **an Hebrew of the Hebrews**—born of Hebrew parents, and one who, unlike many of his countrymen, still can speak the Hebrew language. **As touching the law,** he formerly was **a Pharisee** (5), one who meticulously observed the whole Mosaic law (Acts 23:6; II Cor. 11:22). **Concerning zeal** (6), one of the notable Jewish virtues, he had been found **persecuting the church** (Acts 8:1—9:9; Rom. 10:23); **touching the righteousness which is in the law,** he had omitted nothing and was **blameless,** or "found blameless" (ASV).

In these seven things (5-6) Paul had at one time trusted. This trust has been described as confidence in a rite, confidence in race, confidence in religion, confidence in record, and confidence in personal righteousness.[4] But from bitter experience the apostle testifies that they failed to bring him to a personal knowledge of God. These and all like things of the flesh are the bleak alternatives to the life-giving participation in the sufferings of Christ. To trust in these can only lead to a pseudo-worship of God, and an illegitimate confidence in self (3). Six times in this Epistle, Paul uses the term **confidence** (*pepoithe*). He knows in whom he believes and this knowledge is the basis of his joy.[5] Thus the once-proud Pharisee turns to his conversion, which brought about for him a "transvaluation of all values."

B. Advantage of Christ's Sufferings, 3:7-10

1. *The Gain of a Different Perspective* (3:7-8)

But what things were gain to me, those I counted loss for Christ (7). Paul is here using commercial language. **Gain** (*kerde*) is plural, whereas **loss** (*zemian*) is singular. Prior to his conversion Paul had placed on the credit side of the ledger the

[4]John F. Walvoord, *To Live Is Christ* (Findlay, Ohio: Dunham Publishing Co., 1961), pp. 63-64.

[5]EGT, III, 450.

supposed advantages (vv. 5-6), considering each as having value in itself. It is as though he had often reminded God of these virtues one at a time. Here is the very essence of sin. Man is so full of himself that he has no openness of spirit which can be filled with God. He trusts his intellectual acumen, his humanistic ideals, his personal virtues, his disciplined life, his honesty, yea, even his religious exercises—and holds them up to God as though they merited salvation. In contrast, repentance is to become horrified at one's past. Paul on the Damascus road saw that this native trust in his own achievements merited such horror; it was more of a hindrance than a help. When the apostle found Christ, he transferred these former works from the credit side of the ledger to the debit side, considering all of them together as one great loss (Matt. 16:26). As the seaman throws everything overboard in a storm to save his life, so Paul discarded every vestige of personal merit "on account of Christ."

Yea, doubtless—better, "but, yea, indeed, rather, also" (so as to make absolutely clear his position)—**I count** (present tense) **all things but loss for the excellency of the knowledge of Christ Jesus my Lord** (8). Christ had become his own personal Lord and in relation to the **excellency** (*hyperechon,* incomparableness) **of the knowledge of Christ,** all other things are as nothing. When compared with this highest good, all relative goods are not worthy of the name (cf. Eph. 3:19). **For whom I have suffered the loss of all things.** The clause might be rendered, "I was deprived of all my possessions," pointing to a definite time when Paul was transformed. Perhaps the apostle was thinking of the treatment which he received at the hands of the Jewish authorities. He may have been excommunicated by the Jews, disowned by his family, or had his property confiscated. On the other hand, he may have been thinking more generally of the fact that allegiance to Christ meant the renunciation of all that he had come to prize (cf. Gal. 6:14). **And do** (now) **count them but dung.** The present tense is used, indicating Paul's attitude at the moment. **Dung** (*skybalon*) appears nowhere else in the New Testament. It means "dregs," "chaff," "excrement," or "refuse" that is rejected from tables and left to dogs. The word is much stronger than mere "loss," for it suggests that which is never to be touched again.

2. *The Gain of a Divine Person* (3:8-10)

In contrast to the seven things specifically mentioned as **loss,** Paul lists in verses 8-11 seven things to be gained, all of which center around the person of Christ. The first of these is **that I may win** (lit., gain) **Christ.** The tense indicates both the present and the future. Paul is never satisfied with his present knowledge of Christ but is constantly longing for a deeper fellowship with Him. He has gained Christ but has not exhausted the unsearchable riches in Christ (Eph. 3:8; Col. 2:2 ff.). Paul therefore prays to **be found in him** (9). Michael cites a use of this verb from Epictetus which refers to death. Thus perhaps Paul desires to be **found in Christ** at death, and before Him at the judgment (cf. II Pet. 3:14).[6] But he also desires to be **found** now in Christ, as the manslayer was found in the city of refuge, where he was safe from the avenger of blood (Num. 35:25).

Not having mine own righteousness, which is of the law (9) is better translated "not having any righteousness which can be called mine."[7] Here is Paul's doctrine of justification by faith which he elaborated in Romans and Galatians (Rom. 1:17; 3:24; 4:5; 10:3). **Righteousness** means both a right relationship to God and also union with God. **The faith of Christ** is more accurately "faith in Christ" (RSV). Thus the only **righteousness** which has value is that which comes from God through faith (self-surrender or trust) in Christ.

It is only by having the righteousness of God that one may experience true fellowship with Deity. Therefore Paul prays, **That I may know him** (10). The knowledge here spoken of is not that of mere comprehension (I Thess. 1:4), or that which comes by familiarity (Acts 10:28), or insight which results from a logical analysis of the fact (Eph. 5:17). It is not merely a knowledge *about* Christ, but a personal, experiential knowledge *of* Christ. The Old Testament uses the verb "to know" (Heb. *yada;* Gk. *ginoskein*), indicating the most intimate relationships possible between persons. To know Christ in an intimate way is Paul's supreme desire.

The apostle's next concern is for **the power of his resurrection, and the fellowship of his sufferings.** There is only one article in the Greek, which suggests that the ideas expressed are to be taken as one. Paul is clarifying what he means by knowing Christ. He wants to know Him *in* the power of His resurrection.

[6]*The Epistle of Paul to the Philippians* ("The Moffatt New Testament Commentary"; New York: Harper and Bros., 1927), p. 148.

[7]M. R Vincent, *Word Studies in the New Testament* (New York: Charles Scribner's Sons, 1914), III, 447.

It is Paul's desire that the power which raised Jesus from the dead shall operate in his life (cf. Rom. 6:4; 8:11; Eph. 1:12, 20; 2:5-6; Col. 2:12; 3:1; II Cor. 4:10; 12:10). It is not accidental that the power of the Resurrection is mentioned first, and then Christ's sufferings. Only if one has experienced this power can he then share in the fellowship of Christ's sufferings and live a life that is permeated with a redemptive quality (Col. 1:24). In the clause **being made conformable unto his death** Paul means more than a willingness to die as Christ died, on a cross. The reference is clearly to an inward transformation, a conformity to the spirit of Christ. Thus Moffatt translates, "with my nature transformed to die as He died." John Wesley also caught the meaning and commented: "So as to be dead to all things here below" (cf. Gal. 4:19).[8]

C. Aspiration to Christ's Sufferings, 3:11-16

1. *The Pursuit of Resurrection Perfection* (3:11-14)

If by any means I might attain unto the resurrection of the dead (11). Paul thought that all persons both good and bad would be raised from the dead (Acts 24:15). For "resurrection" there, as usually in his Epistles, Paul used *anastasis.* But here the word translated **resurrection** is *exanastasin,* which occurs only here in the New Testament. Apparently the addition of *ex* (out from) emphasizes the resurrection of Christians. Paul wants to attain or "arrive at" (*katantesoeis*) the **resurrection** of the believers; i.e., the quality of life which will accompany those who are raised in Christ. It expresses the spirit of humility and not of doubt, for the power of Christ's resurrection working in him is the earnest and guarantee of this prospect. But steady progress toward the goal is necessary.

From verse 11 through 17 allusion to the Grecian games is obvious. It is clearly reflected in 12, **Not as though I had already attained. Attained** (*elabon*) is not the same word translated "attained" in 11. There it presents the figure of a pilgrimage—arriving at the journey's end. Here it means to receive a prize (cf. I Cor. 9:24). Paul is denying that he obtained the prize in the moment of conversion, or even later. He must continuously put forth effort to receive it. He has won the prize in Christ, but has

[8]*Explanatory Notes upon the New Testament* (London: Epworth Press, 1941 [reprint]), p. 735.

not as yet fully received it. The clause **either were already perfect** seems to refer to that which is to be **attained.** The words **attained** and **perfect** are here a kind of parallelism. Thus **perfect** here has the sense of being perfected or complete.[9] Paul has not finished his Christian course and thus has not yet received the prize (cf. II Tim. 4:7-8). Therefore he declares: **I follow after, if that I may apprehend that for which also I am apprehended of Christ Jesus.** To apprehend means to seize. Apprehending is achieved when one is in full possession (cf. Mark 9:18; John 8:34; 12:35; I Thess. 5:4).[10] **For which** may be taken in the sense of "for which purpose" or "because." Paul is saying: "I am pursuing the prize, namely, Christ, in order that I may lay hold on Him, or fully possess Him, and thus fulfill the purposes in my life for which He first laid hold on me, and possessed me."

No matter how others may evaluate their own spiritual progress, the apostle humbly confesses, **Brethren I count not myself to have apprehended: but this one thing I do, forgetting those things which are behind, and reaching forth unto those things which are before, I press toward the mark** (13-14). Many manuscripts read, "I count myself not yet to have apprehended." Paul's conversion was the beginning, not the end of the race. The picture is that of a runner leaning or throwing himself forward, stretching himself out with all his energies. He does not look back, nor compare himself with the relative position of others on the track. Chrysostom commented: "For the runner reckons not up how many circuits he hath finished, but how many are left."[11] Remembering in order to praise God for His past blessings is wholesome (Eph. 2:11), but forgetting must be continuous in the life of the Christian. Only thus can there be spiritual progress.

Knowing there is yet ground to be traversed, the apostle declares, **I press toward the mark for the prize of the high calling of God in Christ Jesus** (14). **Press** is the same word as in 12, **I follow after,** and in 6, where it is translated "persecuting." It

[9]Adam Clarke, *The New Testament of Our Lord and Saviour Jesus Christ* (New York: Abingdon-Cokesbury Press, n.d.), VI, 502.

[10]John A. Bengel, *Gnomon of the New Testament,* trans. C. T. Lewis and M. R. Vincent (Philadelphia: Perkinpine and Higgins, 1864), II, 443.

[11]"Homilies on the Epistle of St. Paul to the Philippians," *Nicene and Post-Nicene Fathers,* ed. Philip Schaff (Grand Rapids: Wm. B. Eerdmans Publishing Co., 1956), XIII, 239.

literally means "pursue." Paul is pursuing the prize in Christ with the same singleness of purpose, freedom from encumbering weights, and ceaseless exertion,[12] with which he had earlier pursued the Church. He will not run off on side issues as a dog that jumps every trail and holds to none; he will not encumber his spiritual progress by the load of legalism and external rites; he will not allow himself to become complacent by thinking himself to have attained final perfection.

The meaning of **mark** (*skopon*) is uncertain. It may indicate the goal toward which the runner presses, or the definite aim with which he runs. According to the latter interpretation, the runner was expected to follow a white line indicating his course from the starting place to the goal. If he stepped outside the line he did not run lawfully, and thus was not crowned though he arrived first. **Prize** suggests the crown or trophy (I Cor. 9:24; II Tim. 4:8). **High calling** is literally the "upward calling." The Christian is summoned from above (Heb. 12:2). **This calling is of God in Christ Jesus,** who will say to the faithful at the end of the race, "Well done, good and faithful servant." The prize must not be separated from the high calling, for they are intrinsically bound together. The prize is "promised when the call is issued, and given when the call is fulfilled."[13] Insofar as the promise is certain, one already has the prize, and yet he pursues it. Progress in the life of the Christian is as though one were moving toward a light at the end of a long tunnel. He never has the full light till he has arrived, but he has ever-increasing light as he goes forward (Prov. 4:18).[14]

In 13-14 we see "The Race and the Goal." (1) Make God's aim your aim, **the high calling of God,** 14; (2) Concentrate all effort on this one aim, 13; (3) Pursue this end with a wise forgetfulness, 13; (4) Pursue the aim with an eager reaching forward, 13-14 (a New Year's sermon by Alexander Maclaren).

2. *The Progress of Realized Perfection* (3:15-16)

Telos, from which the adjective **perfect** (*teleios*) comes, literally means "end." To the Greek mind it suggested, on the

[12]Charles Erdman, *The Epistle of Paul to the Philippians* (Philadelphia: The Westminster Press, 1932), p. 110.

[13]Vincent, *op. cit.,* III, 451.

[14]J. N. Darby, *Synopsis of the Books of the Bible* (New York: Loizeaux Brothers, n.d.), IV, 490.

one hand, that which is last, final, or complete; and on the other, that which is accomplishing its purpose or function, mature or full-grown. Both senses are seen in various forms of the word throughout the New Testament. Thus it is used in the sense of "fulfilled" (Luke 22:37; John 19:28), "perfect" or "perfected" (Luke 13:32; John 17:23; II Cor. 12:9; Phil. 3:12; Heb. 2:10; 5:9; 7:19; 9:9; 10:1, 14; 11:40; 12:23; Jas. 2:22; I John 2:5; 4:12, 17-18), "finish" and "finished" (John 5:36; Acts 20:24), and "consecrated" (Heb. 7:28). The adjective *teleios* occurs nineteen times in the New Testament, all of which are translated "perfect" in the Authorized Version, except in I Cor. 14:20, where it is rendered "men," in contrast to "children," and in Heb. 5:14, "of full-age," in contradistinction to a "babe."

Unless Paul was manifestly contradicting himself—an accusation which even from a literary standpoint would be grossly unfair—it must be asserted that the perfection which he disclaims in 12 (verb *teleioo*) is different from that which he now claims in 15, **Let us therefore, as many as be perfect** (adjective *teleios*). The difference in meaning corresponds to the above different uses by the Greeks.

In Acts 20:24 the verb is used to allude to a "race" or a "course." The apostle seems to have a similar picture in mind here, where the word means "fit for the race, strong in faith."[15] To change the metaphor, Paul's reference is to those who are thoroughly instructed and mature (cf. I Cor. 14:20; 2:6; Eph. 4:13; Heb. 5:14), who possess a perfection which belongs to the true Christian who has been advanced by faith beyond the stage of the new convert. This Christian perfection must not be understood to have accrued merely by a process of time or by the keeping of the law. Rather, it is a distinct work of God. Thus the writer of the Hebrews exhorts his readers to allow themselves to be "borne on to perfection" (Heb. 6:1).

The **perfect** in this verse are described as those who wisely "worship God in the spirit . . . and have no confidence in the flesh" (3:3). It points to those who "have entered fully into the spirit and design of the Gospel."[16] This is possible only for those "that are alive from the dead," and have yielded their "members as instruments of righteousness unto God" (Rom. 6:13, 19).

[15]Wesley, *op. cit.*, 3:15.

[16]Clarke, *op. cit.*, VI, 503.

Thus minded, literally, "of this mind," evidently points back to the single-mindedness expressed in 13. Thus this realized perfection—Christian perfection—is equated with wholeness and self-unity, and may be considered as being synonymous with the theological term "entire sanctification" (I Thess. 5:23; contrast Jas. 1:8). The single-minded, the "perfect," will prove themselves so by a "holy discontent" with their spiritual progress, judged in the light of the ultimate goal (Rom. 8:29). Augustine stated that one may be an increasingly "perfect pilgrim," though not yet a "perfect possessor,"[17] in the sense of having received the final prize. Similarly, J. Paul Taylor has observed that Paul "denied perfection as a winner (12), but professed perfection as a runner and included others in that classification (15). . . . The perfection of heart here fits us for the perfection of heaven hereafter."[18]

And if in any thing ye be otherwise minded, God shall reveal even this unto you. Lightfoot graphically states Paul's meaning: "If you are sound at the core, God will remove the superficial blemishes."[19] This may be a gentle rebuke to those in Philippi who would contend over a minor point, or would rate themselves too highly. They are not arrogantly to take it on themselves to set everyone else straight. Those who are truly mature will refuse to judge others, recognizing the difference between a babe in Christ and mature manhood (I Cor. 3:1-2; Eph. 4:11-16). It is true that "normally we judge others in relation to our own level of attainment; somewhat less often we judge with reference to Christ; very rarely indeed do we form our judgments with reference to the progress an individual has made since he became a Christian."[20] Possessing the spirit of Christ is that which is of supreme importance.

Nevertheless, or notwithstanding the minor points of disagreement, **whereto we have already attained, let us walk by the same rule, let us mind the same thing** (16). **Walk** (*stoichein*) is a technical expression, indicating Christian conduct, and means to march together in file and in the same direction. The plea is

[17]Quoted in *Abingdon Bible Commentary,* p. 1247.

[18]*Holiness the Finished Foundation* (Winona Lake, Ind.: Light and Life Press, 1963), p. 94.

[19]*St. Paul's Epistle to the Philippians,* 8th ed. (London: The Macmillan Co., 1888), p. 153.

[20]Ralph A. Gwinn, *The Biblical Expositor,* ed. C. F. H. Henry (Philadelphia: A. J. Holman Company, 1960), III, 318.

for Christian consistency.[21] **Attained** is not the same word used in either 11 or 12. Originally it was employed of arrival beforehand, or rapid arrival, and thus suggests a specific experience at a given time. The oldest manuscripts omit **rule, let us mind the same thing.** But the meaning is clear. Paul is simply saying that, having come thus far, the thing to do is to proceed in "the same path."[22] "Walking" in the light is always a condition for receiving further revelation from God. Consequently, one should not be surprised if the Holy Spirit asks for obedience to what one already knows.

The biblical understanding of perfecting character is seen in 12-16 to include: (1) A candid acknowledgment that there are yet spiritual heights to be attained, 12*a*, 13*a*; (2) A singleness of mind which aspires for ever-increasing growth, 13*b*; (3) An absolute dedication to the realization of one's high calling in Christ, 12*b*, 14.

[21]Davidson, NBC, p. 1041.

[22]Robertson, *Word Pictures in the New Testament*, IV, 456.

Section VII The Fellowship of Purity

Philippians 3:17—4:9

Paul has addressed remarks to the legalists (3:1-16) who, though placing emphasis on law and codes of conduct, have failed to enter into the fellowship of Christ's sufferings. Certain libertines, however, seem to have gone to the opposite extreme and rejected all law, using their pseudo-relationship to Christ as a justification for all kinds of acts. Because freedom from the bondage of the Law does not mean license to sin with impunity, Paul is compelled to attack these antinomians. He does so by a strong plea for purity.

A. A Personal Example, 3:17-19

Brethren, be followers together of me, and mark them which walk, so as ye have us for an ensample (17). **Walk** (*peripatein,* lit., walking about) indicates the ordinary circumstances of daily life. The use of **brethren** serves to mitigate the apostle's bold words. **Followers together** is *summimetai,* "co-imitators," which is not used elsewhere in the New Testament. The prefix *sum* may simply mean "all of you." Thus Lightfoot has suggested: "Vie with each other in imitating me" (cf. I Cor. 11:1).[1] It seems more likely however that, since Paul changes from **me** to **us,** he is saying: "Look at others who follow me, for in so doing you will become an imitator of me."[2] This interpretation is consistent with his admonition to **mark them,** an apparent allusion to the line in the stadium which guided the runner (cf. 14). The meaning is simply, Let other Christians whom you can observe be your line or mark.

But examples must be wisely chosen: **For many walk . . . whose end is destruction, whose God is their belly, and whose glory is in their shame, who mind earthly things** (18-19). Their

[1]*St. Paul's Epistle to the Philippians,* 8th ed. (London: The Macmillan Co., 1888), p. 154.

[2]H. A. W. Meyer, *Critical and Exegetical Handbook to the Epistles to the Philippians and Colossians and to Philemon* (New York: Funk and Wagnalls, 1889), p. 146.

final destiny will be eternal condemnation. Moffatt translates **end** (*apoleia*) as "fate," to indicate the inevitable consequences of allowing liberty to degenerate into license (Rom. 6:1, 12-13, 15, 23; 16:18; Gal. 5:13; Jude 4). **Whose God is their belly** may refer to those who insist on the distinction between ceremonially clean and unclean foods (Rom. 14:14-17; I Cor. 8:8).[3] The chief concern here, however, is with the antinomians. If **belly** refers to the womb, as some have thought, then Paul is referring to gross immoralities which were masked under the name of Christian. The meaning would include material values of every sort which would make an idol out of the gratification of the senses. These persons have inverted the true scale of values so that they can actually glory in their shame. "Fallen man is but man inverted; his love is where his hatred should be, and his hatred where his love should be; his glory where his shame should be, and his shame where his glory."[4] Paul is writing concerning those **of whom I have told you often** (cf. 3:1), **and now tell you even weeping, that they are the enemies of the cross of Christ** (18). They are akin to those who say: "We have fellowship with him," while they "walk in darkness" (I John 1:6), or, "Let us do evil, that good may come" (Rom. 3:8). Although they claim to be friends of Christ, they are not crucified with Him, and thus are the enemies of His cross, which is the symbol of death to self and sin. Nonetheless, according to Paul's example, it is in the spirit of weeping and not harsh censoriousness that one must view inconsistencies in others (cf. Luke 19:41).

B. A Promised Exaltation, 3:20-21

In contrast to those who mind earthly things, the true Christian is lifted above them and enabled to set his affection on things above (Col. 3:2), **for our conversation is in heaven** (20). **Conversation** (*politeuma*) means "commonwealth" or "citizenship." As the Philippians were citizens of Rome with all its rights and responsibilities, though in a foreign territory, so the Christian is now a citizen of the great community of heaven (cf. Eph.

[3]C. Latley, *A Catholic Commentary on Holy Scripture,* ed. Dom. Bernard Orchard (New York: Thomas Nelson & Sons, 1953), p. 1130.

[4]Thomas Manton (d. 1667), "Lectures on James," in *The Bible Work: The New Testament,* ed. J. Glentworth Butler (New York: Funk & Wagnalls Publishers, 1883), II, 461.

2:19). Moffatt translates the verse: "We are a colony of heaven." The verb **is** (*huparchei*) means to subsist. It is the same word which is applied to Christ Jesus in 2:6 (cf. Gal. 4:26; Heb. 11:13, 16; I Pet. 1:1; 2:11). It points to the fact that the Christian's heavenly citizenship is not a result of his own works in any present moment, but is always dependent on the prior grace of God.

The Christian will in the future be highly exalted since from heaven he looks for, or "expects and awaits earnestly," the coming of **the Lord Jesus Christ** (cf. I Cor. 1:7; Heb. 9:28). The **Saviour** will bring about man's *final* salvation and **shall change our vile body** (better, the body of our humiliation), **that it may be fashioned like unto his glorious body** (21); i.e., the "body of His glory" (cf. I Cor. 15:44). The two Greek terms for "form" (cf. 2:6, 8) are both used in this verse. **Shall change** or "transform" (*metaschematisei*) indicates that Christ will change the appearance of the body. It will be a completely new kind of body, like the body of the exalted Christ, which cannot now be fathomed (cf. I John 3:2). And yet its new outward appearance, according to the usage of *summorphon* (**fashioned** or conformed) will be appropriate to its inner spiritual character.[5] "The spirit will then have an organ of expression suited to the holiness of its nature and the happiness of its estate."[6] This exaltation of the heavenly citizens will be accomplished by Christ, for it is wrought **according to the working whereby he is able** (lit., the energy of His being able) **even to subdue** (subject) **all things unto himself (21).**

C. A Persistent Exhortation, 4:1-9

In light of the example and exaltation discussed in 3:17-21, Paul gives a firm but warm exhortation. The first verse probably should be included in the previous chapter. Paul glories in the Philippians: **My brethren, dearly beloved and longed for, my joy and crown** (1). He accepts them as brothers in Christ regardless of their individual spiritual attainments and differences of gifts and graces. Accompanying this brotherly relation there is brotherly love, twice expressed in the tender words **dearly beloved. Longed for** (*epipothetoi*) does not occur elsewhere in

[5]IB (Exegesis), XI, 103.

[6]Paul Rees, *The Adequate Man* (Westwood, N.J.: Fleming H. Revell Co., 1959), p. 94.

the New Testament, and indicates the special fellowship which exists between Paul and the Philippians. His converts at Philippi will be his **crown,** his wreath of victory at the end of the Christian race (cf. I Cor. 9:25; I Thess. 2:19), or his **crown** at the final feast on the ultimate day of reward (cf. 2:16). Thus he exhorts: **So stand fast in the Lord.** In the preceding chapter the apostle uses the metaphor of running. Now he employs a military expression, **stand** (*stekete*), as a soldier in the midst of battle (cf. Eph. 6:10-18). Regarding their love and labors the Philippians must ever be advancing. As to faith and fidelity, they must **stand** immovable.

I beseech Euodias, and beseech Syntyche, that they be of the same mind in the Lord (2). Numerous explanations have been given as to who these persons were. The suggestion has been made that they are simply names representing opposing groups, but the names do not stand in opposition. **Euodias** means "prosperous" or "sweet fragrance"; **Syntyche** means "affable" or "fortunate." In light of the reference to **those women which laboured with me in the gospel** (3), it appears probable that these were two real persons. If so, they may be two of the "women who resorted to the river side, where prayer was wont to be made" (Acts 16:13) when the church at Philippi was begun. Since Paul normally did not allow ladies to preach (I Tim. 2:12), they probably were deaconesses. It is possible that the two were in a lawsuit. Whatever the difficulty, they were admonished **to be of the same mind in the Lord. Mind** (*phroneo*) is used in 1:7; 2:2, 5; 3:15, 16; 4:2, 10. The word means more than to think; it is a disposition. Paul is calling for a moral unity regardless of any intellectual differences which may obtain. The phrase **in the Lord** implies that outside Him there can be no unity. One cannot love man without loving God.

And I intreat thee also, true yokefellow, help (3). *Synzygos,* **yokefellow,** has been interpreted as a proper name, and thus a play on words similar to *Onesimus* (serviceable) in Philemon 11.[7] In any case, this **yokefellow,** whom some have fancied to be Silas, was to be a peacemaker (cf. Matt. 5:9). It is not known who **Clement** was, though Clement of Rome has been suggested. Since the women had **laboured with** him and with Paul, he was well known to the congregation. **Book of life** was a Jewish phrase

[7]J. R. Dummelow (ed.), *A Commentary on the Holy Bible* (New York: The Macmillan Co., 1943), p. 977.

used sometimes to describe the roll of an army. Because these persons are members of the Lord's army and have done battle with Paul against a common enemy, their names are in God's **book of life**—the roll of the redeemed.

Rejoice in the Lord alway: and again I say, Rejoice (4; cf. Ps. 37:4; I Thess. 5:16). **Let your moderation be known unto all men. The Lord is at hand** (5). *Epieikes,* **moderation,** describes restraint of passions, soberness, or that which is suitable. It may mean a good disposition toward other men (cf. Romans 14). In I Tim. 3:3 and Titus 3:2 the word is used with an adjective meaning "disinclined to fight." The idea then is that of forbearance, not insisting on one's rights, but acting with consideration for one another.[8] In things which are nonessential the Philippians are not to run into extremes, but to avoid bigotry and animosity, judging one another with charity.[9] **The Lord is at hand** may be a warning used in the Early Church. If so, Paul is saying, "What is the purpose of the rivalries? Bear with one another that God will bear with you when the Lord comes."[10] The clause, however, has also been viewed as a promise of the Lord's nearness, and interpreted in connection with the following verse.

Be careful (anxious) **for nothing; but in every thing by prayer and supplication with thanksgiving let your requests be made known unto God** (6). Though one may plan for the future (I Tim. 5:8), he is not to be anxious about anything (Matt. 6:25). The secret to this quality of life is prayer and supplication. "Care and prayer . . . are more opposed than fire and water."[11] **Prayer** is general and is based on divine promises, involving devotion or worship. **Supplication** is a special entreaty in times of personal need and appeals to the mercy of God. It breathes with thanksgiving for every event, whether of prosperity or affliction. One prays for forgiveness—it is promised; he supplicates for the recovery of his child—that is mercy which exceeds the bounds of

[8]Cf. J. Hugh Michael, *The Epistle of Paul to the Philippians* ("The Moffatt New Testament Commentary"; New York: Harper and Bros., 1927), p. 196; Jamieson, Fausset, and Brown, *A Commentary on the Old and New Testaments* (Hartford, Conn.; S. S. Scranton and Co., n.d.), II, 368.

[9]Matthew Henry, *Commentary on the Whole Bible* (New York: Fleming H. Revell Co., n.d.), VI, 744.

[10]Lightfoot, *op. cit.,* p. 196.

[11]Bengel, *op. cit.,* II, 447.

grace.[12] These requests are to **be made known unto God** (*pros ton theon*)—better, "in the presence of God." Here perhaps is a subtle reminder of God's continuous presence. In view of the conflict at Philippi, Paul probably is saying, "When others don't treat you kindly, pray. Rather than grow anxious about it, let it be known to God." **And the peace of God, which passeth all understanding, shall keep your hearts and minds through Christ Jesus** (7; lit., in Christ Jesus). Thanksgiving and peace go together (cf. Col. 3:15). Though one does not obtain all he requests, the peace of God keeps the heart, the seat of the will. The heart does not keep the peace of God. **Shall keep** is a military metaphor. God's peace will stand guard over the Philippians, even as Philippi is guarded by a Roman garrison. This protective peace "surpasses every understanding," or is superior to all anxious forethought (cf. Isa. 26:3; John 14:27).[13] The phrase **through** (in) **Christ Jesus** suggests that one cannot be so guarded outside of Him.

Finally, brethren, whatsoever things are true (in thought, disposition, and deed), **honest** (serious or worthy of honor), **just** (right in any given situation), **pure** (chaste, as in I Tim. 5:2, but also domestic purity in general), **lovely** (pleasing, inspiring, or worthy of being loved), **of good report** (winsome or reported with the best construction); **if there be any virtue, and if there be any praise, think on these things** (8). **Virtue** was of central importance in the Greek vocabulary of ethics. Thus Lightfoot interprets Paul as saying, "Whatever value may reside in your old [pre-Christian] conception of virtue,"[14] maintain it. But the apostle gives the Philippians more than subjects for meditation. He calls for obedient action and again cites himself as a pattern: **Those things which ye have both learned, and received, and heard, and seen in me, do: and the God of peace shall be with you** (9). In 7 he portrays the peace of God; here he promises the God of peace, or the "God who gives peace" (cf. I Thess. 5:23; Heb. 13:20).

In 4-9 we see certain elements of "The Peace of God." (1) A joyous restraint, 4-5; (2) The privilege of bringing to God requests which are free from anxiety, 6; (3) A delight in that which is wholesome, 8; (4) A sense of God's nearness, 9.

[12]George Williams, *The Student's Commentary on the Holy Scripture* (Grand Rapids, Michigan: Kregel Publications, 5th ed., 1953), p. 934.

[13]Lightfoot, *op. cit.*, p. 161.

[14]*Ibid.*, p. 162.

Section VIII *The Fellowship of Gratitude*

Philippians 4:10-23

The didactic portion of the letter is complete and Paul turns to a concluding topic, namely, the expression of gratitude for the gift which the church at Philippi has sent to him by Epaphroditus. Because some time has elapsed since Paul received the gift, and also because he has not specifically mentioned it earlier in the letter, some have thought that these verses are part of a previous correspondence from the apostle to the Philippians. But the conclusion is not necessary. It is quite normal to express one's thankfulness at the close of a highly personal letter which moves informally from one topic to another. As for Paul's delay, it may well be that this is his first opportunity to respond. Further, the length of time passed since the arrival of Epaphroditus is unknown. However one views the setting of this passage, the meaning is not difficult to discover.

A. The Basis for Gratitude, 4:10-20

But I rejoiced in the Lord greatly, that now at the last your care of me hath flourished again (10). The figure is of a plant which revives in the spring. Though it was **at the last,** once again the Philippians demonstrated their love for Paul. No clue is given as to why they had not done so sooner. Perhaps they had no one by whom to send the gift, or were in "deep poverty" (II Cor. 8:1-2) and financially unable to do so. Whatever the reason, Paul, in contrast to the apparent spirit of some at Philippi, refuses to be easily offended, and he excuses what one of smaller spirit might have interpreted either as willful or neglectful delay. **Wherein ye were also careful, but ye lacked opportunity. Careful** (*ephroneite*) means thoughtful in the sense of definite concern (cf. 1:7). Paul uses the imperfect tense, which suggests his willingness to believe that the Philippians all along had desired to minister to his needs, but were hindered.

Assuring the Philippians of his own well-being, though until recently they have been unable to contribute to it, Paul states:

Not that I speak in respect of want: for I have learned, in whatsoever state I am, therewith to be content (11). In the original the verse reads, "In the circumstances in which I am," indicating his present prison situation. **Content** (*autarkes*) has no equivalent in English, but should be taken in the sense of "competence."[1] The apostle is adequate for every situation, having learned that circumstances as such neither add to nor detract from his higher happiness.

I know both how to be abased, and I know how to abound: every where and in all things (12). Literally it reads "in everything and in all things," i.e., in each particular event of life and in the sum total of all of life. **Abased** (*tapeinousthai*) was used in classical Greek of a river running low (cf. II Cor. 11:7).[2] Paul knows what it is to have plenty, as an animal with ample fodder (Matt. 5:6), or to be hungry—a possible allusion to his working with his hands.[3] **I am instructed** (*memuemai*) is taken from the language of the pagan cults which initiated candidates into their mysteries. Paul has been faced by every type of experience, both pleasant and unpleasant (II Cor. 11:23 ff.), and he does not value the one above the other.

I can do all things through Christ which strengtheneth me (13) can be translated, "I am strong for all things in the Christ who empowers me." **Christ** is omitted in some manuscripts, but is clearly implied. Because Paul apparently refers to abundance in 12 and 18, it has been suggested that he had come into the inheritance of property, making it possible for him to afford the high cost of his trial. Thus, so runs the suggestion, he can say, "I am equal to everything."[4] But there is no basis for such speculation. The meaning is far more profound. Paul can do **all things** which he is called upon to perform in the line of duty or suffering. The verse should be interpreted as a brief summary of Gal. 2:20 (cf. John 15:5; I Tim. 1:12). At first Paul seems to have been using the language of Stoicism (11-12), which maintained that man can of himself overcome all outward pressures.

[1]Henry Alford, *The Greek Testament* (3rd ed.: London: Rivingtons, Waterloo Place, 1862), III, 192.

[2]James C. Gray and George M. Adams, *Gray and Adams Bible Commentary* (Grand Rapids: Zondervan Publishing Co., n.d.), p. 312.

[3]Cf. Robertson, *Word Pictures*, p. 461.

[4]J. R. Dummelow (ed.), *A Commentary on the Holy Bible* (New York: The Macmillan Co., 1943), p. 978.

But this is not the Christian position. His sufficiency is of Christ, who continuously infuses power (*dynamis*) into him. He can be grateful for any and all circumstances, because they are the occasion for the revelation of Christ's power.

Lest the Philippians should assume that his sufficiency in Christ has made their gift superfluous, the apostle delicately assures them of his genuine appreciation. **Notwithstanding ye have well done, that ye did communicate with** (share) **my affliction (14)**. Their participation in his trouble is one of the many ways that God has used to make him strong. **When I departed from Macedonia** (Acts 17:14, probably twelve years before), which was **the beginning of the gospel** for the Philippians, **no church communicated** (shared) **with me as concerning giving and receiving, but ye only** (15). Here is the language of commerce—credits and debits. Of all the churches under Paul's care only Philippi considered keeping an account with him. They had given material assistance and he had returned the favors with spiritual gifts (cf. I Cor. 9:11; Philem. 19). **For even** (also) **in Thessalonica ye sent once and again** (twice) **unto my necessity** (16). Thessalonica was a luxurious community which Paul had visited after leaving Philippi, approximately one hundred miles distant (see map 1). There Paul had supported himself (I Thess. 2:9; II Thess. 3:7-9), whereas the Thessalonians themselves had contributed little. It was there that the apostle was aided by the neighboring Philippians. Such expressions of generosity could not be soon forgotten.

The gifts, however, are of only secondary importance. **Not because I desire a gift: but I desire fruit that may abound to your account** (17)—literally, "not because I seek after the gift, but I seek after the fruit that abounds to your account." **Fruit** (*karpon*) commonly bore the sense of interest on an investment. For their gifts to Paul (II Cor. 12:14), God added the interest to their credit. This is the apostle's way of saying with Jesus, "It is more blessed to give than to receive" (Acts 20:35; cf. Luke 6:39). He who gives always receives more than he who receives. The Philippians by their generosity have stored up for themselves treasures in heaven.

Referring specifically again to the recent gift, Paul says, **But I have all, and abound: I am full, having received of Epaphroditus the things** (perhaps clothes or other necessary items) **which were sent from you (18)**. **I have** (*apecho*) is a technical expression used in drawing up a receipt (cf. Matt. 6:2, 5, 16; Luke 6:24). The sense, then, is: "Your debt to me is more than paid, for which I give you a receipt." The Philippians' thoughtfulness which was directed to Paul he regards as **an odour of a sweet smell, a sacrifice acceptable, well pleasing to God.** This is an obvious allusion to the pleasant fragrance in the Temple produced by the burning of incense to God (II Cor. 2:15; Heb. 13:16). **My God shall supply all your need according to his riches in glory by Christ Jesus** (19)—literally, "will fill up all your need . . . in Christ Jesus." The gifts of the Philippians are a loan, which has been drawing compound interest. Paul cannot repay it, but his God, whom he serves and who receives the sacrifice, will supply their needs, both material and spiritual (II Cor. 9:8), on his behalf.[5] God will do this **according to his riches** (cf. Eph. 3:16), i.e., not just out of His wealth, but on a scale that is worthy of His wealth.[6] **In glory** has been connected by some expositors with **riches;** by others, with **shall supply.** Probably the latter is better, **glory** then indicating the "element and instrument of the supply."[7] Maclaren's comment is illuminating: "When Paul says 'riches in glory,' he puts them up high above our reach, but when he adds 'in Christ Jesus,' he brings them down amongst us."[8]

Contemplating the unlimited resources of God, Paul breaks forth in rapturous praise: **Now unto God and our Father be glory for ever and ever. Amen** (20). It is perhaps better translated, "Now unto our God and Father be the glory for the countless ages of eternity. Amen." Paul no longer speaks of **my God,** as in 19, but of **our Father,** indicating the common bond between himself and the Philippians.

B. The Benediction of Grace, 4:21-23

It has been conjectured that these last verses were written by the apostle's own hand, rather than dictated to a scribe. One

[5]J. B. Lightfoot, *St. Paul's Epistle to the Philippians,* 8th ed. (London: The Macmillan Co., 1888), p. 167.

[6]J. Hugh Michael, *The Epistle of Paul to the Philippians* ("The Moffatt New Testament Commentary"; New York: Harper and Bros., 1927), p. 226.

[7]M. R. Vincent, *Word Studies in the New Testament* (New York: Charles Scribner's Sons, 1914), III, 460.

[8]*Expositions of Holy Scripture* (Grand Rapids: Wm. B. Eerdmans Publishing Co., 1952 [reprint]), XIV, 73.

would expect in a personal letter such as this to find in the closing salutations a number of names. But, as he sometimes did elsewhere, Paul mentions none (cf. Romans, Colossians, II Timothy). In view of the developing parties at Philippi, it is possible that he omits them to avoid giving distinction to some and not to all. **Salute every saint** (believer) **in Christ Jesus** (21). Some expositors grammatically connect **salute** with **in Christ Jesus,** as in other Epistles, e.g., "I . . . salute you in the Lord" (Rom. 16:22; cf. I Cor. 16:19). But in view of 1:1 it seems better to understand the verse as KJV implies. **The brethren which are with me greet you** (lit., salute you). Not only do Paul's associates (including Timothy and others) send greetings but **all the saints,** evidently meaning the Christians of the Roman church itself, **chiefly they that are of Caesar's household** (22). It is known that **Caesar's household** was a general term for those employed in various types of government service. They resided all over the empire, and many were slaves. The reference may be to the men who guarded Paul—some of whom perhaps he had introduced to Christ. It is conceivable that a few of these are natives of Philippi, and have an interest in their home city. This might explain the use of **chiefly.**

The closing benediction suggests that Paul intends the letter to be read to the assembled congregation. Thus he pronounces a parting blessing, **The grace of our Lord Jesus Christ be with you all. Amen** (23). Instead of **all** (*panton*) some manuscripts read *pneumatos* (singular), "your spirit," perhaps a final but subtle entreaty to unity. The Epistle has turned full circle. It began with "grace" (1:2) and now closes with **grace.** This grace alone could create the fellowship which is shared so tenderly by Paul and his beloved Philippians.

Bibliography

I. COMMENTARIES

ALFORD, HENRY. *The Greek Testament*, Vol. III. Third Edition. London: Rivingtons, Waterloo, Place, 1862

BARCLAY, WILLIAM. *Letter to the Philippians*. Second Edition. "Daily Study Bible." Philadelphia: The Westminster Press, 1959.

BARNES, ALBERT. *Notes on the New Testament:* Philippians. Edited by ROBERT FREW. Grand Rapids: Baker Book House, 1950.

BARTH, KARL. *The Epistle to the Philippians*. Richmond: John Knox Press, 1962.

BEARE, F. W. *A Commentary on the Epistle to the Philippians*. "Harper's New Testament Commentaries." New York: Harper and Bros., 1959.

BENGEL, JOHN A. *Gnomon of the New Testament*, Vol. II. Translated by C. T. LEWIS and M. R. VINCENT. Philadelphia: Perkinpine and Higgins, 1864.

BRAUNE, KARL. "The Epistle to the Philippians." *Commentary on the Holy Scriptures*. Edited by J. P. LANGE. Translated by PHILIP SCHAFF. Grand Rapids: Zondervan Publishing House, n.d.

CAFFIN, B. C. "Letter to the Philippians" (Exposition). *The Pulpit Commentary*. Edited by H. D. M. SPENCE and JOS. S. EXELL, Vol. XX. Grand Rapids: Wm. B. Eerdmans Publishing Co., 1950.

CLARKE, ADAM. *The New Testament of Our Lord and Saviour Jesus Christ*, Vol. II. New York: Abingdon-Cokesbury Press, n.d.

DARBY, J. N. *Synopsis of the Books of the Bible*, Vol. IV. New York: Loizeaux Brothers, n.d.

DAVIDSON, FRANCIS. "Letter to the Philippians." *The New Bible Commentary*. Edited by F. DAVIDSON. Grand Rapids: Wm. B. Eerdmans Publishing Co., 1960.

DODDRIDGE, PHILIP. *The Family Expositor*, Vol. V. Eighth London Edition. Charleston, Mass.: S. Etheridges, 1808.

DUMMELOW, J. R. (ed.). *A Commentary on the Holy Bible*. New York: The Macmillan Co., 1943.

EADIE, JOHN. *A Commentary on the Greek Text of the Epistle of Paul to the Philippians*. New York: Robert Carter and Bros., 1859.

ERDMAN, CHARLES. *The Epistle of Paul to the Philippians*. Philadelphia: The Westminster Press, 1932.

FAUSSET, A. R. "The Epistle of Paul the Apostle to the Philippians," *A Commentary on the Old and New Testaments*, Vol. II, by ROBERT JAMIESON, A. R. FAUSSET, and DAVID BROWN. Hartford, Conn.: S. S. Scranton & Co., n.d.

FINLAYSON, R. "Letter to the Philippians" (Homilies). *The Pulpit Commentary*. Edited by H. D. M. SPENCE and JOS. S. EXELL, Vol. XX. Grand Rapids: Wm. B. Eerdmans Publishing Co., 1950.

GRAY, JAMES C., and ADAMS, GEORGE M. *Gray and Adams Bible Commentary*. Grand Rapids: Zondervan Publishing Co., n.d.

GWINN, RALPH A. "Philippians." *The Biblical Expositor*, Vol. III. Edited by C. F. H. HENRY. Philadelphia: A. J. Holman Co., 1960.

HENRY, MATTHEW. *Commentary on the Whole Bible*, Vol. VI. New York: Fleming H. Revell Co., n.d.

KENNEDY, H. A. A. "The Epistle to the Philippians," *Expositor's Greek Testament*, Vol. III. Edited by W. ROBERTSON NICOLL. Grand Rapids: Wm. B. Eerdmans Publishing Co., n.d.

LATLEY, C. "Philippians." *A Catholic Commentary on Holy Scripture*. Edited by DOM. BERNARD ORCHARD. New York: Thomas Nelson & Sons, 1953.

LIGHTFOOT, J. B. *St. Paul's Epistle to the Philippians*. Eighth Edition. London: The Macmillan Co., 1888.

MACLAREN, ALEXANDER. *Expositions of Holy Scripture*, Vol. XIV. Grand Rapids: Wm. B. Eerdmans Publishing Co., 1952 (reprint).

MEYER, H. A. W. *Critical and Exegetical Handbook to the Epistles to the Philippians and Colossians and to Philemon*. New York: Funk and Wagnalls, 1889.

MICHAEL, J. HUGH. *The Epistle of Paul to the Philippians*. "The Moffatt New Testament Commentary." New York: Harper and Bros., 1927.

MORGAN, G. CAMPBELL. *The Unfolding Message of the Bible*. Westwood, N.J.: Fleming H. Revell Co., 1961.

MOULE, H. C. G. *The Epistle to the Philippians*. Edited by J. J. S. PEROWNE. "Cambridge Bible." Cambridge: University Press, 1895.

RAINY, ROBERT. "Epistle to the Philippians," *An Exposition of the Bible*, Vol. VI. Hartford, Conn.: S. S. Scranton Co., 1903.

ROBERTSON, A. T. *Paul's Joy in Christ: Studies in Philippians*. Revised Edition. Nashville: Broadman Press, 1959.

———. *Word Pictures in the New Testament*, Vol. IV. New York: Harper and Bros., 1931.

ROBERTSON, J. A. "The Epistle to the Philippians," *The Abingdon Bible Commentary*. Edited by CARL EISELEN, *et al.* New York: Abingdon-Cokesbury Press, 1929.

ST. CHRYSOSTOM. "Homilies on the Epistle of St. Paul to the Philippians." *Nicene and Post-Nicene Fathers of the Christian Church*, Vol. XIII. Edited by PHILIP SCHAFF. Grand Rapids: Wm. B. Eerdmans Publishing Co., 1956.

SCOTT, E. F. "The Epistle to the Philippians" (Exegesis). *Interpreter's Bible*. EDITED BY GEORGE A. BUTTRICK, *et al.*, Vol. XI. New York: Abingdon-Cokesbury Press, 1951.

VINCENT, M. R. *Word Studies in the New Testament*, Vol. III. New York: Charles Scribner's Sons, 1914.

WESLEY, JOHN. *Explanatory Notes upon the New Testament*. London: Epworth Press, 1941 (reprint).

WHEDON, D. D. *Commentary on the New Testament*, Vol. IV. New York: Nelson & Phillips, 1875.

WICKS, ROBERT R. "The Epistle to the Philippians" (Exposition). *The Interpreter's Bible*, Vol. XI. Edited by GEORGE A. BUTTRICK, *et al.* New York: Abingdon-Cokesbury Press, 1955.

WILLIAMS, GEORGE. *The Student's Commentary on the Holy Scripture*. Fifth Edition. Grand Rapids: Kregel Publications, 1953.

II. OTHER BOOKS

BAILLIE, D. M. *God Was in Christ.* New York: Scribner's Sons, 1948.

BRUCE, A. B. *The Humiliation of Christ.* New York: George H. Doran Co., n.d.

FLETCHER, JOHN WM. *The Works of the Rev. John William Fletcher,* Vol. I. New York: Waugh & Mason, 1833.

HASTINGS, JAMES (ed.). *The Great Texts of the Bible.* New York: Scribner's Sons, 1913.

REES, PAUL S. *The Adequate Man.* Westwood, N.J.: Fleming H. Revell Co., 1959.

WALVOORD, JOHN F. *To Live Is Christ:* An Exposition of the Epistle of Paul to the Philippians. Findlay, Ohio: Dunham Publishing Co., 1961.

WAND, J. W. C. *The New Testament Letters.* London: Oxford University Press, 1946.

III. ARTICLES

WEISS, BERNHARD. "The Present Status of the Inquiry Concerning the Genuineness of the Pauline Epistles." *American Journal of Theology,* I, 2.

The Epistle to the

COLOSSIANS

John B. Nielson

Introduction

A. Occasion

In writing the Epistle to the Colossians, Paul engages in combat (2:1) with one of the most formidable opponents of his career. This enemy of the Church is a strange blending of Judaistic and Oriental religious practices with Christianity. It is called Gnosticism by later writers. "But a wholesale equation of the Colossian error with the later gnostic systems is certainly a rash assumption."[1]

This subtle heresy, revealed in c. 2 of the Epistle, is not necessarily an attempt to eliminate Christ from religion, but to show Him inadequate as man's Saviour. Christ, in this view, is a created being, greater than man certainly, but less than God, one of many mediators between God and man. Christ is stripped of His essential deity and robbed of His propitiatory work at Calvary. Emphasis is placed on externals in religion—works of righteousness, ritualism, asceticism, abuse of the flesh, angelolatry, etc.—as marks of the Christian way. To Paul, such a view is unthinkable, in view of his own firsthand knowledge (Acts 26:13 ff.). And with one stroke of his brush—"in him dwelleth all the fulness of the Godhead bodily" (2:9)—he puts the whole picture in proper perspective. Christ is All; that is all.

This Gnostic view, however, seriously threatened the church at Colossae. It occasioned the meeting between Pastor Epaphras (1:7-8) and the Apostle Paul to deal with the problem.

B. Authorship

The consensus of Christian scholarship is that Paul is the author of the Epistle; the method and content are Pauline. Some scholars still question the Pauline authorship.[2] However, the Early Church attests its authenticity. And it is included in the most important *P 46* papyrus (the Chester Beatty Papyrus),

[1]C. F. D. Moule, *The Epistles of Paul the Apostle to the Colossians and to Philemon,* "The Cambridge Greek Testament Commentary" (Cambridge: University Press, 1957), p. 33.

[2]Baur, Bultmann, etc.

which was written about A.D. 200.[3] M. Renan says that Colossians should be received unhesitatingly as the work of St. Paul.[4]

C. Date

Paul, at the time of writing, was in prison, it appears (4:10), but free to preach (Acts 28:30-31; Col. 4:18). Demas was still with him (4:14; II Tim. 4:10). It is concluded, then, that the time of writing was near the close of Paul's first imprisonment at Rome, about A.D. 62[5] (perhaps as early as 60).

D. Destination

The letter is addressed to the "saints" (1:2) in Colossae (see map 1), a small town on a small stream in the Lycus Valley in Phrygia, about one hundred miles inland from Ephesus. It is about ten miles south of two more important towns mentioned in the Epistle, Hierapolis on the north bank and Laodicea on the south bank.[6]

The church could have been organized when Paul was at Ephesus (Acts 19:10), and probably met in a house (4:15). However, Epaphras, or Paul, could have established the church earlier (Acts 16:6; 18:23). It is strange to hold the view, as some do, that Paul never visited the Lycus Valley churches (cf. Acts 18:23), especially when Paul was such a tireless worker and traveler and was nearby in Ephesus for two whole years. The wording of Col. 2:1 seems to indicate that Paul did indeed know some of the believers there, while some, it is indicated, he did not know, nor had he seen.

Though the town was small and relatively insignificant, the Christians there and the issues in the church were vitally important. They called forth this superb statement by Paul on Christology. The letter was delivered by Tychicus (4:7-8).

E. Purpose

Paul's "achievement lies in his refusal to confine the Person of Christ to the limits of Messianic Judaism or on the other

[3]C. F. D. Moule, *op. cit.*, p. 38.

[4]H. C. G. Moule, *The Epistles to the Colossians and to Philemon*, "The Cambridge Bible for Schools and Colleges," ed. J. J. S. Perowne (Cambridge: University Press, 1893), p. 95.

[5]A. T. Robertson, *Word Pictures in the New Testament*, IV (New York: Harper and Brothers Publishers, 1931), 470.

[6]H. C. G. Moule, *op. cit.*, p. 95.

hand to leave any room for the extravagant systems of Gnostic theosophy in which the historical Jesus played a merely subsidiary role."[7]

Paul shows the uniqueness of the Christian faith and its inevitable conflict with all other systems of religion and human philosophy. The uniqueness is bound up in the *person* of Christ, and the fruit of faith in Him is ethical righteousness (Col. 3:9). Paul will isolate all pretenders to Christ and His position, and will eliminate the practice of formulating doctrine according to human wisdom rather than according to divine revelation. He will refute those who would add any other requirements but Christ for salvation, all those who would in any way depreciate Jesus Christ. He will do so by declaring that the *divine fullness* dwells in Jesus Christ, that He is *the mystery* that has been revealed, that *all treasures* of wisdom and knowledge are in and through Him, and that *perfection* is in union with Him alone. The Christ of Paul's gospel brings one to "the point of rest instead of being hurried along by the whirl of conflicting opinions."[8]

It is becoming more evident that the problem in the Colossian community is pertinent to our day in a way not felt a generation ago. The world is rapidly opening up to accept the so-called Gnostic notion of Christ, that He fits in with all religions and systems. The Colossian errors are also today's errors. In the face of so many cults the issue becomes again the perennial one: "What think ye of Christ? whose son is he?" (Matt. 22:42) So, once again, each individual must identify Jesus Christ for himself in scriptural terms and understanding. And the Epistle to the Colossians is superbly suited to make that identification possible.

[7]Wilfred Knox, *St. Paul* (New York: D. Appleton Company, 1932), p. 145.

[8]Alexander Maclaren, *The Epistles of St. Paul to the Colossians and Philemon,* "The Expositor's Bible," ed. W. Robertson Nicoll (New York: A. C. Armstrong and Son, 1903), p. 2.

Outline

I. Preparatory Remarks, 1:1-14
   A. Paul's Calling as an Apostle, 1:1-2
   B. Paul's Confidence in the Colossians, 1:3-8
   C. Paul's Concern for Spiritual Development, 1:9-14

II. Paul's Christology, 1:15-29
   A. The Apostle's Concept of Christ, 1:15-20
   B. The Contingency of Saving Grace, 1:21-23
   C. Paul's Commission and Involvement, 1:24-29

III. The Conflict, 2:1-23
   A. Doctrine, 2:1-15
   B. Duty, 2:16-23

IV. The Conclusion, 3:1—4:6
   A. A New Frame of Reference, 3:1-4
   B. A Thorough Renunciation, 3:5-11
   C. Moral Responsibility, 3:12—4:6

V. Farewell, 4:7-18
   A. The Addressers, 4:7-14
   B. The Addressees, 4:15-17
   C. The Signature, 4:18

Section I *Preparatory Remarks*

Colossians 1:1-14

In writing the Epistle to the Colossians, Paul challenges what later writers have called Gnosticism. This false philosophy was a most deadly enemy of Christ and His Church. The first chapter of the letter is preparatory to the later "conflict" that is to be joined (2:1). Paul lays the groundwork here for the conflict, setting the tone, and raising his defenses to justify these polemics. He does so by claiming the highest Authority, God himself, to speak out against this most serious challenge to Christ. He proceeds by declaring his confidence that the initial experience of the Colossian believers resided in Christ alone.

Paul follows these introductory remarks by stating in precise terms the necessity for the conflict, the essential nature and work of the Lord Jesus Christ. And after a serious word of caution, he declares his own vigorous involvement in this just cause.

A. Paul's Calling as an Apostle, 1:1-2

This letter is from a man in Christ to a church in Christ. Epaphras, pastor at Colossae (1:7; 4:12-13), reports to Paul on the spiritual condition of his church. He declares that a formidable heresy has arisen to threaten his people. Steps are taken soon thereafter by the apostle to counter the false teaching. As before, at the Jerusalem Council (Acts 15:12) and at Antioch (Gal. 2:1 ff.), Paul, the apostle of Jesus Christ, will allow nothing to dilute the gospel. He will state the case clearly, concisely, and without fear. As noted in the Introduction, he sends the letter by Tychicus (4:7-8).

1. *Authorization* (1:1)

The letter opens with Paul's familiar greeting. He gives his *name*. That **Paul** is the author was received without question by the Early Church.[1] His name may have been changed from

[1]See Introduction.

Saul to Paul by the early Christian community immediately following his conversion (Acts 13:9). It is suggested, however, that he bore both the Hebrew and Greek forms of the name from birth,[2] necessitated by his early environment in Tarsus, a community of three cultures—Greek, Roman, and Hebrew.[3]

Paul gives his *office,* **an apostle,** an envoy or messenger who meets special qualifications (I Cor. 9:1). Though there are those who, like Barnabas, are included in a general category of messengers of the Lord (Acts 14:14; Phil. 2:25), Paul is a special one, divinely commissioned and sent, perhaps taking the place of Judas as one of the Twelve (Acts 1:20; I Cor. 15:8-9).

He also states his *authority.* He is **an apostle of Jesus Christ.** Though both orders are used in different places, "Christ Jesus" is the correct order of the two words according to the best texts. If so, there is a slight emphasis on the word **Christ** and that, probably, because of the nature of the conflict that ensues. Paul would emphasize the exalted Lord rather than Jesus, as He was known in the days of His flesh. The expression **the will of God** lifts the apostle's authority to the highest level.

Paul's opening words reveal something of his *humility.* He includes **Timotheus our brother,** literally, *the* brother, in his greeting, signifying that one of his converts is his equal in relation to Christ. In pagan religions a slave initiated into a mystery cult was no longer a slave, but a freeman who lived with his former owner.[4] In the Christian community it could be no less. Indeed, a slave who became a believer in Christ was no longer to be treated as a slave, but as a brother beloved (Philem. 16; I Tim. 6:2). Here is the scriptural revelation of essential Christian relationships. Though Paul is a special messenger of the Lord Jesus Christ, an apostle of the highest rank, he is yet merely one among many members of the Christian brotherhood. The phrase "the brother" here means, not the loose brotherhood of man, but the brotherhood of Christian men.[5]

[2]H. C. G. Moule, *op. cit.,* p. 63.

[3]W. J. Conybeare and J. S. Howson, *The Life and Epistles of the Apostle Paul* (New York: Thomas Y. Crowell and Company, Publishers, n.d.), pp. 30-34.

[4]C. F. D. Moule, *op. cit.,* p. 147.

[5]W. H. Griffith Thomas, *Christ Preeminent* (Chicago: The Bible Institute Colportage Assn., 1923), pp. 15-16.

2. *Salutation* (1:2)

The letter is addressed **to the saints and faithful brethren in Christ.** If the adjectival sense of **saints** is taken, they are the holy and trustworthy brothers—and both holy and faithful because they are in Christ. If the causal relation is understood, then these are brothers because they are holy. The first view seems to be the better one. Literally, the Greek says, "to those in Colossae, holy and trustworthy brethren in Christ." **Faithful** may be rendered both "trustworthy" and "trusting." **Brethren** indicates that these persons, too, are Paul's brothers because they are in Christ with him. The relationship is both to Christ and to Paul and Timothy.

These appellations seem calculated to prepare the persons to whom the letter is addressed to receive Paul's message. The Greek word for **to the saints** (*hagiois*) has a moral quality. It indicates not only position in Christ, as some would have it,[6] but moral condition; not merely dedication, but ethical righteousness. The purpose and message of the letter confirm this view. Paul is not calling for cloistered, or man-appointed "saints," but for moral men (cf. 3:5 ff.). The author's purpose is to save the Colossian believers from the errors of asceticism, ritualism, feasts, and human ordinances as the signs of a Christian (2:16 ff.). He points them rather to ethical oneness with Christ (3:1 ff.) as the true sign (3:9). All saints are not necessarily mature. They have problems of growth, but they are to be righteous. As Maclaren says, "Saints are not an eminent sort of Christian, but all Christians are saints, and he who is not a saint is not a Christian."[7] But lest it be thought that Paul suggests that morality in itself is sufficient, he adds the words **in Christ.** "Saints are accepted only by virtue of their being in Christ . . . out of Christ the best saints will appear sinners, and unable to stand before God."[8]

The locale of the church addressed is both **in Christ** and **at Colosse,** two spheres of Christian living. As long as they remain **in Christ,** the saints **at Colosse** will be safe from the error. **At**

[6]Many limit *hagios* (holy) to dedication or commitment. See Thomas, Carson, Lightfoot, and others.

[7]*Op. cit.*, p. 13.

[8]Matthew Henry, *Commentary on the Whole Bible* (New York: Fleming H. Revell Co., n.d.), VI, 748-49.

(lit., in) **Colosse** identifies them. Someone suggests that the phrase magnifies them, for, though inhabitants of so small a village, the message of God is for them also (cf. note 22).

With the phrase **in Christ** we come to the very heart of Paul's religion. It is the formula for his gospel which he preached authoritatively everywhere (Gal. 1:8, 12). This formula grew out of a new relationship that he held with Christ, a two-way relationship that was a vital union—he in Christ and Christ in him (II Cor. 5:17; Col. 1:27). Christ had become for him, through the Damascus experience (Acts 26:15), not a person of the historic past that he could only read about and study, but a living Person with whom he held daily communion. **In Christ** became the heart of his theology and the formula for his religious life. Schmoller says that "the phrase *en Christo* is a formula of such deep significance in Paul's epistles, that it is perhaps better always to find in it the idea of union, fellowship with Christ."[9] The phrase is used by Paul to indicate both the mystery of the Incarnation and the means by which the propitiatory work of Christ at Calvary is realized, potentially, when not yet actually. A. J. Gordon says, "No words of Scripture, if we except those, 'God manifest in the flesh,' hold within themselves a deeper mystery than the simple formula of the Christian life in Christ."[10]

Paul's salutation, **Grace . . . and peace,** is probably drawn from Christian experience rather than from Grecian influences or the blending of the salutations of East and West. He uses Grecian words and phrases, but he fills them full of Christian meaning. These words appear to be related as cause and effect. The grace of God brings **peace.** And peace will never be known in the world today apart from the grace of God—grace **from God our Father** (cf. Luke 2:14).

And the Lord Jesus Christ is omitted in the best manuscripts. No violence, however, is done to the meaning of the text by adding the phrase, because all spiritual blessings come through and in Jesus Christ (14 ff.; 2:10). Also, the words in question are included in the next verse. When these two Persons are joined in the ministry of grace, the deity of Jesus is shown. There is perhaps less need to join the two in this verse, for Paul will reveal Christ in a unique way in the entire letter.

[9]"Galatians," *A Commentary on the Holy Scriptures,* ed. John Peter Lange, trans. Philip Schaff (New York: Charles Scribner's Sons, 1886), p. 49.

[10]*In Christ* (New York: Fleming H. Revell Company, 1880), p. 9.

B. Paul's Confidence in the Colossians, 1:3-8

1. *Their Experience of Christ* (1:3-5*a*)

Paul's confidence in the Christian experience of the Colossian believers is shown in two ways.

a. Appreciation for Them (1:3). He prays in their behalf. **We give thanks** is a characteristic quality of and an essential element in Paul's prayers and exhortations to prayer (1:12; 4:2). Only in Galatians is the word omitted from Paul's salutations.[11] The **we** means at least Paul, Timothy, and Epaphras (4:12-13). On the basis of the Greek text there is a question about the received translation. The Greek has it, "We give thanks . . . always for you praying." Is it "thanks always" or "praying always"? It would seem that either is suitable to Paul's thought. And the cause for thanksgiving is the trilogy of the saints' qualities—faith, love, and hope—which he perceives to be in them.

To God and the Father should read rather, "To God *the* Father," showing more clearly the unique relation of Jesus to the Father.[12]

Praying always for you means that whenever Paul prays he includes them. The substance of his prayers for them is outlined in 1:9-13, and is for the unknown brethren (2:1) as well as for the known ones, for they too are in Christ.

Though Paul is greatly concerned, he is yet encouraged over the report and thanks God for these brethren. Some feel that the words **since we heard,** along with a similar thought in 1:8-9 and 2:1, indicate that Paul never visited Colossae. However, these expressions may mean no more than that Paul was not personally acquainted with *all* the believers there.[13] Be that as it may, Paul bases his subsequent remarks, prayers, and thanksgiving on the trustworthy report of Epaphras, their faithful pastor (7).

b. Recognition of Grace in Them (1:4-5*a*). Here we have Paul's famous trilogy of Christian graces—**faith, love,** and **hope.** Each has its own *object:* faith has for its object the divine Saviour, for that is the force of the order of the words **Christ Jesus;** love expresses itself toward **the saints;** and hope has for its object the treasure **in heaven.** Each has its own *sphere* of activity:

[11]C. F. D. Moule, *op. cit.,* p. 47.

[12]See comments on v. 2.

[13]See Introduction.

faith operates in the atmosphere of the divine; love operates in the community of the holy ones; and hope operates in the realm of promise (1:27*b*). Each has its own *end:* faith to inspire; love to create mutual loyalty; and hope to maintain faithfulness. These three are often united by Paul, but here in an unusual order. In I Corinthians 13, one could say that they are stated in the order of their ethical importance, with Christian love as the outgrowth of faith and hope. Here they are in the order of their logical importance. **Faith in Christ Jesus** is the beginning of **love** for Him and **to all the saints.** Both faith and love spring from hope, for that is the force of the preposition, *dia.* It is literally "because of" or "by" hope that faith and love come. On the other hand, the truth must not be limited by the meaning expressed here. It is also true that hope springs from faith in Christ as a present experience—"Christ in you, the hope of glory" (1:27*b*). The three—**faith, love,** and **hope**—are interlocking segments of a whole, each interpenetrating the other.

The present hope is also future: it is **laid up** (stored or reserved) **in heaven,** literally, "in the heavens" (I Pet. 1:4). The believer stands on the promises which give him **hope.** This **hope** is the basis of his inspiration, **faith,** and the source of his ethics, **love.** This is not "pie in the sky" philosophy; it is present, joyous experience (II Cor. 4:16-18; II Tim. 4:8; Heb. 9:28). Though Christ is "there" (Col. 3:1), He is in a very real sense present in them, and us, now.

2. *Their Knowledge of Christ* (1:5*b*-8)

a. By Divine Initiative (1:5*b*-6). **Whereof** refers to this hope of which **ye heard** from Epaphras—and possibly from Paul himself. **Heard** is aorist tense, indicating a completed act, decision, or crisis; that is, they had believed or accepted. **Before** refers not to their heathen state,[14] but prior to their hearing the false teachers, or before the writing of the letter, or in addition to the letter. In the expression **in the word of the truth of the gospel,** the preposition **in** equals instrument, that is, "through" or "by means of" the preaching. **The gospel** is the truth as opposed to the false teaching Paul is about to expose. This false teaching is devoid of the true Object of faith (Christ), true ethics (divine love), true experience (the indwelling "hope of glory"). Paul

[14]Adam Clarke, *The New Testament of Our Lord and Saviour Jesus Christ* (New York: Abingdon-Cokesbury Press, n.d.) II, 513.

calls the church back to the truth and hints at the argument to come. What is that truth? He will thunder it.

Which is come unto you means literally "is present to you." **In all the world** is a legitimate hyperbole.[15] A more accurate translation would be, "even as in all the world it [the gospel] is bearing fruit and increasing even as in you." It seems unrealistic to suppose that everyone in the world, or even that every city or town, had heard. That would be an early date for all to hear.[16] Rather, the apostle is thankful that the gospel is bearing fruit in them, even as it does in believers in every part of the world wherever it has gone and has been accepted and believed. As Paul says, "If *any* man be in Christ, he is a new creature" (II Cor. 5:17). Ethical righteousness (10) is the fruit of faith in Christ, everywhere the same.[17]

Paul's is a universal religion. We see here his worldwide outlook and ministry. Christianity is basically an evangelistic religion, equally applicable to every man, and it comes to man through divine revelation.

The divine word delivered and believed **bringeth forth fruit;** "it bringeth forth fruit of itself" (present middle), indicating that the gospel freely at work in the believer of itself produces good works. The false teachers might have borrowed this verb from the teachings of Jesus and given it their own meaning. Wilfred Knox says that fruit bearing was a "Gnostic catchword" and Paul is here countering their claims.[18] Nevertheless the Christian fruit is ethical (10; 3:5 ff.); the gospel bears the fruit of holy living wherever it goes. There is excellent manuscript support for adding the words "and is augmenting" to the text of the King James Version (the RSV has "growing").[19] The gospel spreads with the fruit-bearing, because the seed is spread abroad with the fruit. The present middle voice here suggests continuous reproduction. "Paul avers that faith in Christ is itself the seed, alive, and growing. Moreover, it is universally attested"—**in all the world.**[20] This remarkable fact

[15]A. T. Robertson, *op. cit.,* p. 474.

[16]See also Col. 1:23 in this connection.

[17]W. Knox, *op. cit.,* p. 51.

[18]Quoted in C. F. D. Moule, *op. cit.,* p. 51.

[19]E. Eberhard Nestle, *Novum Testamentum Graece* (Stuttgart: Privilegierte Wurttembergische Bibelanstalt, 1936), in loco.

[20]C. F. D. Moule, *op. cit.,* p. 51.

of ethical righteousness in them as the fruit of faith in Christ is confirmed with the words **as it doth also in you.**

Since the day ye heard of it—the gospel of grace is prevenient. They did not seek it out; it came to them. And it works its effects somewhat quickly. **And knew** (aorist indicative) is a strong verb, meaning "saw" or "looked into." They searched out the gospel, finding it true, and thus understood the **grace of God**[21] (Acts 17:11). **The grace of God** is a frequent phrase and speaks of all that is beautiful and Godlike. **In truth** may be taken two ways: the **grace of God** is found to be true, or it is found in the truth, the gospel (II Cor. 4:2; Col. 1:5). Man reaches up to find God in the false religions; but in addition God reaches down to reveal himself in the true. The gospel has universal application and results. No one is favored over another. Carson points out that the Colossians are not inferior because they are in a little town.[22] God works the same all over the world.

b. Through Human Instrumentality (1:7-8). They **learned of Epaphras** (4:12). He is their pastor, perhaps founder.[23] Paul certifies that Epaphras has given them correct teaching. He was an able minister and teacher.

It is pointed out that **also** should be omitted on manuscript evidence.[24] If so, it seems to point to the probability that Epaphras organized and established the church. If added, the **also** implies some other teachers. **Learned** (aorist) indicates an experiential fact, not an unending process always short of conclusive knowledge. Epaphras is an able and faithful preacher. Paul adds that he is **our dear fellowservant**—a slave of Christ, like the apostle himself. A trusting and affectionate relationship exists between these two fellow prisoners (Philem. 23).

Who is for you opens up the recurrent problem of how to interpret the pronouns. Is it "for you" or "for us"?[25] If the former, Epaphras is trustworthy; if the latter, he is a faithful minister in Paul's stead. Manuscript evidence is not decisive for

[21]H. C. G. Moule, *op. cit.*, p. 68; Robertson, *op. cit.*, p. 475.

[22]*The Epistles of Paul to the Colossians and Philemon,* "Tyndale New Testament Commentaries" (Grand Rapids: Wm. B. Eerdmans Publishing Co., 1960), p. 27.

[23]See Introduction.

[24]H. C. G. Moule, *op. cit.*, p. 69.

[25]*Ibid.*, pp. 68-69. In the original MSS there is constant confusion of "you" and "us" (or "we"), because these are almost identical in the Greek.

either, but the meaning is not significantly altered by one's decision.

Paul is confident in Epaphras as a **faithful minister.** The gospel was correctly given. The evidence is the "fruit," in themselves (6). Paul will not allow the false teachers to discredit their pastor.

Epaphras has **declared unto us** shows the pastor reporting a threat to vital religion. Despite the grave apprehension lest some be led astray, the pastor's report is gladsome and wholesome because of their **love in the Spirit.** In v. 9 is the adjectival use of the word "spirit" (*spiritual understanding*); here it is the noun, indicating the Holy Spirit. With this statement the Triune God is revealed. This is the only direct reference to the Holy Spirit in the Epistle. **In the Spirit** is the sphere of the working of love, which is the sum of Christian ethics[26] (Rom. 13:10). Such love opposes asceticism and ritualism. Love, it appears, is the main item in the report and is the essential element in the thought of the apostle concerning them.

C. Paul's Concern for Spiritual Development, 1:9-14

These verses are Paul's intercessory prayer for the enlargement and unfolding of the revelation and experience of the Colossian believers. This prayer is Paul's response to the report and also gives an insight into his character. He is happy over the report concerning the believers, but very much concerned over the threat to their continuance and spiritual development in the light of this subtle heresy lately arisen there.

Here we see "A Prayer for Christians": (1) Spiritual infilling, 9; (2) Ethical response, 10; (3) Divine enablement, 11; (4) Appreciation for divine grace (12-14).

1. *Spiritual Discernment* (1:9).

This cause would be the operation of Christian love in them, of which the apostle had just written. For this, Paul is indeed thankful (3), and now he intercedes for them. **Since the day we heard it** would indicate an extended visit on the part of Epaphras. **To pray** and **to desire** (lit., ask) are present participles revealing constancy and faithfulness (3) on the part of both Paul and his companions.

[26]See comments on 4b, and note 32.

a. The Content. Paul is concerned both with volume, **filled** (aorist passive—no halfway experience[27]), and with substance, **his will. Knowledge** (*epignosis*) becomes a technical term to contrast pagan human wisdom with divine wisdom and knowledge. Pagan wisdom is ritualistic (2:16), visionary (2:18), and legalistic (2:21), while divine knowledge is a revelation, not a deduction or intuition of human origin. This divine knowledge springs from a reciprocal experience—knowing God and known of God, Christ in them and they in Christ (2*a* and 27*b*). To **be filled with the knowledge of his** (God's) **will** is to understand the purpose and end of the "mystery" of the Incarnation and sacrifice of Christ (27). To understand this is the true **knowledge** (*gnosis*).

b. The Method. **In all wisdom and spiritual understanding** is the method of Christian growth. The understanding of the divine revelation is known only by spiritual means (I Cor. 2:12-16). The method of the false teachers is purely mental, human. Christ, God's Son (13-14), not intermediaries (2:18), is the true Way of heavenly knowledge. The revelation is complete in the manifestation of Jesus Christ (2:9). Note the frequent use of the word "all"—*all* wisdom, *all* understanding, pleasing in *all* things, *all* might, *all* patience, *all* long-suffering. Here is a breathtaking view of God's purpose in the revelation of Christ.

2. *A Settled Course of Conduct* (1:10*ab*)

That ye might walk (aorist infinitive) calls for a fixed *purpose* in conduct. Righteousness comes from the infilling spoken of in the previous verse. **Worthy of the Lord** provides the *inspiration* for the believer's conduct. This same note is struck in three other places: 2:6; 3:17; and 3:23. To **walk worthy** (worthily) **of the Lord** is the highest aspiration. In I Thess. 2:12, Paul uses the phrase "worthy of God," and Moule points out in this connection that "the Father and the Son are Persons of the same Order of Being."[28] **Unto all pleasing** is "fully pleasing" (RSV), not to men, but to God (II Cor. 5:9; Col. 3:22; I Thess. 4:1). Here Paul states the *objective* of the Christian life. **Being fruitful in every good work** shows the *quality* of the conduct. The **walk** is ethical righteousness; it is to be consistent, and to involve the

[27]Robertson, *op. cit.*, p. 475.

[28]H. C. G. Moule, *op. cit.*, p. 71.

whole of life. The active voice of the verb indicates that man's will and participation are needed and expected. This is not a supposed or a conferred righteousness, but one that is inspired and imparted (6; 2:6-7) with the incoming Spirit of God.

3. *Divine Enablement* (1:10c-11)

Increasing in (lit., augmented by) **the knowledge of God** points out the *power* for the "worthy walk" to be drawn from the knowledge of God. How important, then, the faithful study of God's Word, and prayer! Such holy practices strengthen one for the holy walk. Paul now enlarges on this thought. **Strengthened with all might** (passive participle) again shows that power to live holy lives comes from God. The Spirit-filled man is sustained by divine grace. He can do anything that God requires, for divine aid is available. The direction of life (10) is a settled decision, even though "the Christian does not receive an initial impetus which must serve him the whole journey."[29] The enablement must be in a continuous drawing on the resources of the divine power (*kratos*). That this is divine power is clear from the fact that the word *kratos* is used only of God.[30] The strengthening is **according to his glorious power.** When all things are done for His pleasure (see comments on 10; 3:20, 22, 23) and glory, then power is released in the life, power like His. Here, then, is the *method* of our strengthening. His power in us contrasts with and overcomes the power of darkness (13) and has supreme sway.

The *end* or goal follows. **Unto** (*eis*) is used to denote that the power may enable one to have **all patience,** which Lightfoot says is closely allied to hope, and is the opposite of cowardice. It is the will to persevere when others have given up. **Longsuffering** contrasts with wrath and revenge, and is coupled with mercy.[31]

With joyfulness does not go with "giving thanks" of the next verse, but stands alone.[32] It is closely associated with endurance and patience in the Christian vocabulary: "If joy is not rooted in the soil of suffering, it is shallow" (Matt. 13:20).[33] Joy also is one of the fruits of doing all for God's glory.

[29]Carson, *op. cit.,* p. 37. (See Robertson, *op. cit.,* p. 476.)

[30]*Ibid.*

[31]H. C. G. Moule, *op. cit.,* p. 54.

[32]Carson, *op. cit.,* pp. 37-38.

[33]H. C. G. Moule, *op. cit.,* p. 55.

4. *A Proper Perspective* (1:12-14)

a. Perspective Toward God, the Father (1:12-13). **Giving thanks** to God keeps all things in proper focus. All comes from Him. What shall we render unto the Lord (Ps. 116:12-18) but to receive His benefits and thank Him for them? Since all is by grace, **giving thanks** is the believer's first word of love to the Heavenly Father. Who is to give thanks? Paul or the Colossians? Both, for the inheritance is equally his and theirs (3; 4:2).

The phrase **unto the Father** without the added word "God" is rare outside the four Gospels.[34] "God" is added in some Greek manuscripts, but not in the better ones, and is therefore not included in this verse.[35] God is here "viewed as the Father of the Son, not *immediately* as '*our* Father' " (13).[36] He is designated "Father" because He is the Source of all.

In the clause **which hath made us meet** (qualified or fit), the pronoun is **us** in some texts but "you" in others. "You" or **us**, it makes no difference; it is God who qualifies. A variant reading is: "who has called [*kalesanti*] us to share." Nonetheless, it is still all of God.

Here we see "The call of God." (1) He enables us to answer the call, 11; (2) He delivers, 13; II Cor. 1:10; (3) The power is available to every man, 28; II Cor. 5:17.

God qualifies us **to be partakers** (lit., to share) in **the inheritance of the saints**, as Israel shared the Promised Land (3:24; Rom. 8:17).[37] **The inheritance** is twofold—a deliverance and a transferal (out of Egypt into Canaan). Note that the inheritance is not only future, but also present.[38] It is a present deliverance, sharing, joy, and endurance. It is a present dwelling place ("Beautiful Canaan Land"), a transferal into **the kingdom of** God's **dear Son** (13), where the saints dwell. **Saints in light** (12) again reveals the moral quality of the righteousness of God's children.[39]

Who hath delivered us (13) refers to the Father particularly (12). The verb (aorist) reveals a decisive, completed act. It is a

[34] *Ibid.*

[35] Nestle, *op. cit.*, in loco.

[36] H. C. G. Moule, *op. cit.*, p. 73.

[37] Adam Clarke, *op. cit.*, p. 515.

[38] C. F. D. Moule, *op. cit.*, p. 57.

[39] See I John (1:7 especially), where light equals ethical likeness to God.

present deliverance from sin and sinning; it is already done. However, the full implications of the mighty deliverance are yet to be fulfilled (Matt. 6:13; 27:43; Rom. 7:24; II Cor. 1:10; I Thess. 1:10; II Tim. 3:11; 4:18).

From the power (domination) **of darkness** brings to mind Paul's conversion experience and his commission (Acts 26:18). He is delivered from the domination of Satan into devotion to Christ, from bondage into freedom, from servitude into sonship, from darkness into light (I Pet. 2:9). Christ never domineers; Satan always does. The passions of sin always dominate the man. The fruits of the Spirit never hold a man under domination; the believer controls them. **Power** equals "the authority of." Both the Garden of Gethsemane and the Cross are in the writer's mind in this verse as well as in Luke 22:53.[40]

And hath translated us is also aorist tense. The transferal is thus a present experience: the action is taken, the locales are changed, the relationships are reversed, the rescue is complete. It is God who has caused this change in position (*metestesen*). Someone has suggested that here is a mass relocation job of whole populations, from the dominion of Satan into the kingdom of Jesus Christ.

His dear Son is literally "the Son of His love." The Father has given a Kingdom to His Son, and by a mighty act has arranged to populate it with redeemed people who will share the inheritance. When the Kingdom is completed and secured, the Son will return it to the Father (cf. I Cor. 15:24-28). Such an inheritance calls for **thanksgiving** (12) on our part.

b. Perspective Toward the Son (1:14). **In whom,** it seems, should refer back to the "Son" (13), though "Father" (12) may be an antecedent also (Acts 20:28). **In** indicates that the redemption is by means of union. The means of **redemption** is more strictly the shed blood of Christ. **We have redemption** is, again, a present experience; delivered now because delivered then—at Calvary. The present tense is used because this experience is "the continued result of the rescue effected in the past."[41] **Redemption** means "emancipation" or a loosing from the powers of the dominion of darkness, from both the guilt and power of sin. It is "a release on payment of a ransom for a slave or debtor

[40]C. F. D. Moule, *op. cit.*, pp. 56-57.
[41]*Ibid.*, p. 56.

(Heb. 9:15), as the inscriptions show."[42] Paul never states to whom the payment is made in order for the redemption to be effected.[43]

Through His blood must be omitted here on manuscript evidence. However, the concept is scriptural and the phrase is actually used in Eph. 1:7 (see also Col. 1:20, 22).

The forgiveness of sins is the redemption. The ethical note is again paramount, forgiveness for falling short of God's glory (*hamartion*). One may be as self-righteous as Paul was in early years with regard to the law (Phil. 3:6), but a deeper righteousness is needed (Matt. 5:20). "There is no trace of a nationalistic Messianism in the New Testament conception; nor yet of fancies about 'escape' into immortality without a corresponding change of character (the kind of escape which may have been promised by the false teachers at Colossae)."[44]

In conclusion, the kingdom of God is moral and spiritual, demanding ethical righteousness on the ground of forgiveness by means of the redemption provided by Christ. The Christian's main objective is to live a life worthy of the Lord. There is an infilling that there may be an outflowing, sustained by a divine supply. It is all of God, to whom alone belongs the praise (3:17).

The following four elements are in Paul's prayer: to know what God wants, to live as a Christian should, to draw on divine resources, and to acknowledge all the while the Source of all. As a river has its source and streams and estuary, so the Christian's walk springs out of the fountain of God's grace in a sustained stream of righteousness (Amos 5:24) into the sea of God's glory and praise. All Christian living streams from God and returns to Him. It is for Paul just as important to encourage the Christian to advance ever upward to his fullest development (Eph. 4:13) and usefulness as it is to win him to Christ initially. Dr. Phineas F. Bresee said, "A sanctified man is at the bottom of the ladder. He is now to learn, to grow, to rise, to be divinely enlarged and transformed."[45]

In 9-14 we find "A Prayer for High Country." (1) A full

[42]Deissmann, quoted in Robertson, *op. cit.*, p. 477.

[43]Luther wrongly suggests the payment is made to Satan.

[44]C. F. D. Moule, *op. cit.*, p. 58.

[45]Quoted in Harry E. Jessop, *Foundations of Doctrine* (Chicago: The Chicago Evangelistic Institute, 1944), p. 69.

knowledge of the things of God, 9; (2) A life worthy of our Lord, 10; (3) Fruitfulness in all areas of our activities, 10; (4) A spirit of patience *with joy,* 11; (4) Thankfulness to God for the wonders of salvation, 12-14 (A. F. Harper).

The Colossian Christians face a formidable foe. A great conflict is on. Truth divinely opposes speculations humanly achieved. Truth available to all mankind opposes human wisdom available to only a favored few. Experience of God challenges speculative knowledge about God. Paul now proceeds with his discussion. Christology comes first.

Section II *Paul's Christology*

Colossians 1:15-29

Here is the foundation for Paul's contention with the so-called Gnostic element at Colossae—the revelation of and about Christ. In His revelation, God communicates *himself,* not just some things *about* himself. The revelation of God in Christ is the central and pivotal point of all genuine theology. Therefore, the open challenge to the person and work of Christ calls for rebuttal. Paul will make clear the supremacy of Christ over all. He will hold his readers to his thesis—Christ—not with mere attack, but with persuasive arguments.

A. The Apostle's Concept of Christ, 1:15-20

Paul has already stated his authority to speak. Addressing himself to a "saved" assembly, delivered from darkness and transferred into the Kingdom of light, he declares in precise terms who Christ is, what He has done for us, and how He has accomplished it. Here is the battleground of New Testament theology: the person, position, power, preeminence, and purpose of Christ. This passage is attacked and repudiated by all false gospels. The trustworthiness of various words and phrases is challenged by some. However, the ideas are clearly Pauline and biblical. The evidence is all in favor of biblical, not Hellenistic, origins for the words and phrases. "Thus on the whole, the difficulties do not seem to warrant the conjecture of interpolation."[1]

Paul is saying, "I have the better gospel—Christ is All." There are no intermediary powers to be reckoned with; there is no lesser salvation than fellowship with God himself. Salvation is available to all, not to just a few initiated ones. It is not for this life only, but also for that which is to come. The false cults are all repudiated here.

If Christ be not God, then perhaps there are powers and thrones that stand between God and man with whom men must reckon. If Christ be not God, perhaps He is merely one among

[1]C. F. D. Moule, *op. cit.*, p. 62.

many such emanations from Deity. If this be so, Christ might be untrustworthy; there might be cause for doubt. The only safe way, then, would be to bow the knee to all known powers (16). But, in unequivocal terms, Paul affirms that these suppositions are all false. One must, and indeed will, bow the knee to no one but Jesus Christ (18; Phil. 2:11-12).

Why does Paul speak here of Christ as Lord of the created universe and the redeemed Church of God? Why does he dwell on Christ's deity, power, preeminence, propitiation? Precisely because there are no other ultimate authorities with whom man must reckon except the Lord Jesus Christ. These are the facts of revelation.

1. *The Head of Creation* (1:15-17)

a. The Person of Christ (1:15). **Who** has for its antecedent "his dear Son" (13), the Jesus of history, of Galilee and Calvary (Matt. 17:5). Man is created in the image of God (Gen. 1:27); Christ *is* **the image of . . . God** (Rom. 1:20; II Cor. 4:4; Col. 3:10; Jas. 3:9; Heb. 1:2-3).[2] God in His essential nature is **invisible** to human view. Therefore His person and character are seen in the Son, who is **the image of the invisible God.** Paul is saying that Jesus Christ is none other than God himself. "Christ is all, and in all" (3:11; I Cor. 15:28). Ellicott says, "The Son is the Father's image in all things save only in being the Father."[3] And Thomas quotes Moule, "A Saviour not quite God is a bridge broken at the farther end."[4]

The firstborn of every creature is better translated "the first-begotten of all creation"—meaning, not the oldest, but the One prior to and supreme over all creation. **Firstborn** is equivalent to "only begotten" and is a Jewish technical term meaning "uncreated" (Ps. 89:27; Heb. 12:23).[5] Indeed, this phrase indicates Christ's unique qualifications as Creator and Saviour. He belongs to eternity; He is not created. He is not, therefore, an intermediary being, but is antecedent to all created things (John 1:1-3). This same word, **firstborn,** is used also in relation to Christ and the Resurrection (18).

[2]See Job 38; Psalms 2.

[3]Quoted in H. C. G. Moule, *op. cit.*, p. 77.

[4]*Op. cit.*, p. 41.

[5]C. T. Wood, *The Life, Letters and Religion of St. Paul* (Edinburgh: T. & T. Clark, 1925), p. 320.

b. The Power of Christ (1:16). Christ is the Source, Agent, End, and Sustainer of all creation. **By him** is literally "in Him," indicating primarily union. "In" many times may indicate instrument or means. However this concept of Christ as the Agent or Means of creation is stated later in the same verse in the phrase **by him.** Here the idea is that Christ has in himself all the ideas and powers of creative activity. The biblical view of creation (Genesis 1; John 1:1-4) opposes the theory of naturalistic, biological evolution. With the emergence of the modern "genetic" theory what shall the evangelical Christian say to the prospect of scientists creating life in a test tube? If it comes about, the Christian will understand that this is a discovery of God's process and not a creation. Man creates nothing; God creates out of nothing (*creatio ex nihilo,* Gen. 1:1). We can only discover how life processes come about.[6] Man's theories are merely his way of viewing the facts of the universe.

All things allows no exceptions—all material and spiritual things and powers are inferior to Christ and are under His will and sway. Whatever supernatural powers there may be, Christ is their reason for being. **Were created** indicates a beginning of these things. Both the Father and the Son, with the Spirit, are active in the creative role (Gen. 1:1-2; John 1:1-3). **In heaven** is literally "in the heavens," and **in earth** is literally "on the earth." **Visible and invisible** again shows that nothing is excepted. **Thrones, dominions** (lordships), **principalities** (magistrates), and **powers** may refer to actual persons as well as to offices, perhaps to fallen beings usurping Christ's place in the minds and loyalties of men (2:10, 15, 18). **By him, and for him** shows that Christ is both the Agent and the End or Goal of creation. It is therefore "in," "by," and "unto" Him that all things are made. He is the first and final Cause of creation (I Corinthians 15; Philippians 2). Someone has pointed out that the value of the individual man (21, 28) is still supreme, even in the context of so vast concepts of space and time.

c. The Priority of Christ (1:17). **He is** (not "He was") **before all things** (cf. John 8:58). He is **before** in position, power, and time. **By him** (lit., in Him) means that when all things are in union with Christ they hold together or are sustained (Heb.

[6]For an interesting article on this subject see: "If Scientists Create Life," by John R. Holum, *Christianity Today,* Vol. VIII, No. 7 (Jan 3, 1964), p. 3.

1:3). When not united to Him they cannot stand. If it is insisted that "in" equals agency here, then all things, even evil powers, continue to persist only by His permissive will until He shall deliver the Kingdom to the Father (I Cor. 15:28). The only satisfactory point of rest in the face of so great a question as to the source and being of all created existence is God. He upholds "all things by the word of his power" (Heb. 1:3).

2. *Head of the Church* (1:18-20)

a. The Preeminence of Christ (1:18). Christ by right of creation takes control and authority over a new society, **the body** of Christ, **the church** (2:19; Eph. 1:22-23). The Church is essentially spiritual. "As represented here, the idea rises above the level of 'visibility,' it transcends human registration and external organization, and has to do supremely with direct spiritual relations between the Lord and the believing company."[7] All the members, a cooperative **body**, are obedient to the **head.** Here is one of the most revealing figures of the essential relationship that exists between Christ and His Church. Ecumenism conceived only in terms of human organization is foredoomed to futility, but unity in Christ is a glorious reality.

Christ is not only Head of the Church universal. But because of Him there are new spiritual persons (II Cor. 5:17) of whom He is Head by virtue of His death and resurrection. This fact is more fully explained in 20 ff. **The beginning, the firstborn** has come up from among the dead. This is the first time such a resurrection has occurred. Christ is therefore preeminent (first) in resurrection as well as in all other things.

Is the meaning **in all things** or "in all respects"? It is not a case of either/or, but of both/and. Christ is first in everything. The issue is rightly put to say that Christ is not just a part of our faith: He "is all" (3:11). Moule points out the idea of Christ's "becoming" the Head (aorist subjunctive) in this sense by virtue of His obedience in the framework of time[8] (Phil. 2:8; Heb. 2:10). He has become the Head by His obedience to the death of the Cross (20). We are told that Christ "*learned* . . . obedience by the things which he suffered" at the hands of His creation (Heb. 5:8). Before the Incarnation, Christ gave obedience to no one and to no thing except the Father. But the *obedience* spoken of

[7]H. C. G. Moule, *op. cit.*, p. 81.

[8]C. F. D. Moule, *op. cit.*, p. 69.

here He learned, not from being the Son, but by suffering.[9] Some would suggest that the "fulness" (19) is completed by the suffering and death. It seems more probable that it is the **preeminence** (headship) which is thus completed.

b. The Personality of Christ (1:19). The full deity of Christ is here again shown. As indicated by the italics in KJV, **the Father** is not in the Greek text. What, then, is the subject of **pleased?** A literal translation would be, "Because in Him all the fullness was pleased to dwell." This verse should be understood in the light of 2:9. It is the fullness of Deity, "the fulness of the Godhead bodily," that is pleased to dwell in the Son, who should "reconcile all things" (20) unto the Father. However it is grammatically correct to understand **Father** as the subject of **pleased.**[10] The fundamental meaning is not significantly altered by either interpretation.

With the word **fulness** Paul seizes on a term that had been preempted by the false teachers to describe their views. For them Christ was only a being in an order of beings greater than man, but less than God, and therefore only one among many mediators. But Paul recaptures the word to reveal Christ as being really and fully Deity, as well as being the only Mediator.[11] **Fulness** (*pleroma*) means that which fills, completes, pervades, or fulfills (Ps. 24:1; I Cor. 10:26). In secular literature the word is used of ships fully manned.[12]

Permanence is the inference from the word **dwell.** Permanent, eternal fullness of Deity in Christ is the only basis for reconciliation—for a transaction at Calvary that makes an atonement for sin. *Pleroma* is used eleven times in Paul's Epistles and is applied to each person of the Trinity.[13]

[9]Robert Jamieson, S. R. Fausset, David Brown, *A Bible Commentary* (New York: Fleming H. Revell Co., n.d.). Vol. II, in loco.

[10]Alfred Barry, *The Epistle to the Ephesians, Philippians, and Colossians,* "Bible Commentary," ed. Charles John Ellicott (London: Cassell and Co., Ltd., n.d.), pp. 101-2. (See Robertson, *op. cit.*, p. 480.)

[11]F. F. Bruce, *Colossians,* "The New International Commentary on the New Testament" (Grand Rapids: Wm. B. Eerdmans Publishing Co., 1957), pp. 206-8.

[12]Liddell and Scott, *Greek-English Lexicon* (abridged) (New York: American Book Company, 1882), in loco.

[13]Thomas, *op. cit.*, p. 48.

c. *The Purpose of Christ* (1:20). In Jesus Christ, Deity is pleased to dwell. In addition, God reconciles all things to himself through the self-sacrifice of Christ. **Having made peace** (aorist) is a once-for-all act. Peace is achieved somehow **through the blood of his cross.** Though the efficacy of the Blood be ridiculed and denied by the scoffers, it is here exalted. The blood of Christ is counted as the blood of God (Acts 20:28) and is the means by which God saves (I Pet. 1:18-19).

We have here, in 19-20, "The Plan of Salvation." (1) *Who* it is that saves; (2) *What* He does to save, 20; (3) *How* He does it, 20; and (4) *Why*—because **it pleased the Father,** 19; John 8:29).

Paul certainly teaches reconciliation by atonement and propitiation by blood sacrifice (Rom. 3:23-26). In this he is in hearty agreement with the rest of the New Testament (Mark 10:45; I Pet. 3:18; I John 2:2). There is redeeming value in the blood of Christ. It is His blood that is the price of redemption. Let us therefore bow down and worship. God has made the peace (21-22); let us be grateful. The Son (13) is the antecedent to this verse. It is significant that Paul introduces and concludes such a magnificent statement on Christology with the reference to redemption and reconciliation through Christ's blood.

By him (agency) **to reconcile all things** does not include devils. The clause includes only those things **in** (lit., upon) **earth** and **in heaven** (the heavens); not those "things under the earth" (Phil. 2:10). **All things,** it seems, refers to both the animate and inanimate (II Pet. 3:13; Rev. 21:1). In Phil. 2:10-11 and I Cor. 15:27-28 not only is reconciliation spoken of but also subjection of all things, even of devils, to His will. Every knee shall bow, willingly or unwillingly, to acknowledge the lordship of Christ. The Father is pleased that reconciliation and redemption shall be in Christ—the sacrifice of himself in the Son.

B. The Contingency of Saving Grace, 1:21-23

The danger of apostasy is cause for cautioning by the apostle. The caution concerns continuance in Christ as a necessity. Presentation to God is conditioned on continuance. There are definite barriers ahead to the fulfillment of the purpose of Christ in the Colossians. There are those who would beguile them (2:4), spoil them (2:8), judge them (2:16), and subject them (2:20). Hence this warning concerning responsibilities and dangers.

1. *The Previous Defilement* (1:21*a*)

The Colossian believers are living witnesses of the grand reconciliation. **Sometime** (once) **alienated** recalls the Fall. They were also once deceived, defrauded, estranged, seduced into slavery (13). It would be a grave error should they allow themselves to be so defrauded again. **And enemies** shows that they had been willing participants in the condition. Their **mind** (inward being) was delivered over to the enemy of God. Here is the essence of our depraved nature; it is injected into man by deception, permeates his whole being, and is consented thereto by the deceived. **By wicked works** the inward, carnal condition is revealed. It expresses itself in rebellious acts against God. This condition is not natural to man. Being subverted and deceived, man has been alienated by a foreign power, and this state issues in wicked works. The estrangement is complete and fatal (Eph. 2:1-3). By a negative approach here the apostle would have all to see again what is to be the fruit of true gospel experience in Christ. It is not ritualistic righteousness, but ethical holiness.

2. *The Present Recovery* (1:21*b*-22)

Yet—in spite of the enmity (Rom. 8:7)—**now** (already) **hath he reconciled** (aorist). This speaks of the once-for-all Calvary act (Heb. 9:26). God's part in the reconciling work is complete and finished. Nothing more can be added to the atonement. It remains now for man to be reconciled to God (II Cor. 5:18-21). What has been done decisively and completely by Christ at Calvary as regards our salvation must now be carried out in day-to-day experience on an individual basis (see comments on 3:5-7). **And you . . . hath he reconciled** shows the Colossian believers to be living witnesses of the grand experience.

Paul now states *the divine method*—**in the body of his flesh** (22). The heresy of Docetism, that Christ only appeared to be a man, has no place in Paul's message. The divine Christ of 15-19 is also really human. The Incarnation is not to be doubted; it is a truly physical body that was nailed to "his cross" (20). In some way propitiation (Rom. 3:24-25) is made by His death (lit., through *the* death). In union with Christ, in identifying oneself with Him through faith, the reconciliation is completed. The reconciling act of Christ is not by His incarnation, but by His dying (II Cor. 5:21). It is all of grace: both God's offer and man's response (Rom. 4:16; Gal. 3:13; Eph. 2:7-9). "Paul is led to interpret the death of Christ as being a vicarious act of expiation, a satisfaction, in some sense, of God's righteous demands. . . . Details in Paul's view of how the death of Christ functioned to make acquittal possible are disputed by students of his letters, but surely it is clear that he regarded the death of Christ as having this effect."[14]

The glorious end of the reconciling work is now lifted up—that we might be **holy, unblameable,** and **unreproveable.** These words establish scriptural holiness. Biblical righteousness and holiness are found in the motive or intention. Paul (Rom. 13:10; Gal. 5:14) agrees with Jesus (Mark 12:28-31). The three words indicate a spiritually perfect condition as well as position; they are practically synonymous. When the motive is pure, when love is the sole guiding principle of conduct, the believer is **unreproveable,** blameless, **holy.** Entire sanctification is "Love Enthroned."

In his sight is literally "before Him," or "right opposite, fronting."[15] The Greek word, *katenopion,* is "altogether an unclassical form."[16] The presentation is here present as well as future. Forgiveness (14), holiness (22), and heaven (22-27) have all been made possible by the reconciliation. Therefore the fundamental concern of mortals should be how we appear in God's sight—now and then.

In 21-22 the apostle outlines "The Glory of Salvation." (1) The grand experience, **now hath he reconciled,** 21; (2) The divine method, **in the body of his flesh,** 22; (3) The glorious end, **to present you holy and unblameable and unreproveable in his sight,** 22 (A. F. Harper).

3. *The Possible Apostasy* (1:23).

Given the reality of their experience in Christ, the Colossian believers are cautioned against dangers along the way to the Celestial City. They yet can be deceived and alienated. Paul calls on them to remember how they were reconciled, and for

[14]John Knox, *Chapters in a Life of Paul* (New York: Abingdon Press, n.d.), pp. 151-52. See J. Glenn Gould, *The Precious Blood of Christ* (Kansas City: Beacon Hill Press, 1951), pp. 91 ff.

[15]Liddell and Scott, *op. cit.,* in loco.

[16]W. J. Hickie, *Greek-English Lexicon* (New York: The Macmillan Co., 1934), in loco.

what purpose, that they may be forewarned, and therefore forearmed.

Their continuance in this reconciled state which makes them suitable for presentation is conditioned on perseverance. No predetermined perseverance can be assumed here in order to support a false hope of security. The tragic possibility of voiding the reconciliation and missing the presentation is the basic reason for writing this letter (cf. Acts 1:17-20). **Continue** equals "abide by" or "persist in." It is God who qualifies (12) the believer for his share in the inheritance of the sanctified (Acts 26:18; Eph. 1:11), but the believer must **continue** believing. Free will is not destroyed at the moment of one's first believing. **In the faith** means both the act of believing and an accurate knowledge of the "word of the truth" (5)—**the faith.**

Grounded speaks of the foundation of faith; the Rock is Christ (I Cor. 3:11; 10:4). **Settled** speaks of contentment; nothing else is needed but Christ (3:11). "God is wholly found in Him," so that we may be contented with Him alone as the Object of faith (2:9).[17] **Not moved away** reveals the awful danger (Gal. 3:1 ff.; Eph. 414). If there can be no falling away, why the warning? How tragic, for one who knew, to be deceived again! **The hope of the gospel** is future (3:24), but it is also present (13-14) and inward (27). If **the hope** is not thus present and inward, it is not future.

The gospel having been stated, Paul would now review its verification (6). This is the gospel **which ye have heard.** The message was given to them clearly and correctly by Epaphras (7). They understood it (6).[18] They heard not only with their ears, but also with their hearts (7-8). The message was correctly received. Further, the gospel is universally applicable, for that is the meaning of **preached to every creature.** Literally speaking, not all have heard, but this is the gospel designed for declaration to all mankind. **Preached** is aorist, indicating the cosmic fact—the Cross (Heb. 9:26). The gospel message has been revealed. It is for all men; but its redemptive virtues toward creatures other than man is pure speculation (2:18; Heb. 2:16-18). **Under heaven** no doubt limits the preaching to responsible beings, namely, men,

[17]John Calvin, *Commentary on the Epistles of Paul the Apostle to the Philippians, Colossians, and Thessalonians,* trans. John Pringle (Edinburgh: 1851), pp. 181-83.

[18]Cf. comments on 1:6.

for that is the meaning of **creature . . . under heaven** (*ktisis*).[19]

Finally, the gospel message is apostolically certified. In the expression **whereof I Paul,** the apostle's name is for emphasis. One must recall Paul's Damascus experience and commission to understand the assurance of **am made a minister** (Acts 26: 15-19). **Am made** is literally "became" (Gal. 1:11, 15-16; 2:7, 9). Paul was divinely sent;[20] the false teachers were self-appointed. He was their **minister** (*diaconos,* deacon, servant); the false teachers were their lords. Paul's ministry is basically preaching (*kerygma*); theirs is ritualistic and priestly. Paul's proclamation is threefold: he is **a minister** of *Christ* (7), of the *gospel* (23), and of the *Church* (25).

C. Paul's Commission and Involvement, 1:24-29

The previous clause, "whereof I Paul am made a minister" (23), belongs, it seems, as much with this paragraph as with the former. Paul here states his third main reason for engaging in conflict with these enemies of his Lord; it is his own personal involvement as a commissioned apostle. Though miles intervene, though many of the Colossians are not known to him personally, Paul is desperately involved in their establishment in Christ and in their final destiny.

1. *The Commission Is Redemptive* (1:24)

Now can indicate time or contrast, or it may be viewed merely as a connective. Paul rejoices, not because of **the sufferings** he endures, but **in** them for the good that they bring. Once Paul would have inflicted such sufferings on others; now he welcomes them in order to win men to Christ. This is a remarkable change (Acts 9:1).

In my sufferings is literally "in *the* sufferings," indicating not only Paul's, but all sufferings for them, such as that of Epaphras (4:12-13), and any others who have had a part in bringing the gospel to them. **For you** reminds us that Paul has been transformed and he loves even Gentiles. He can love those he knows not, as the mother loves the unseen, newborn offspring. May God give us that love for all who are in Christ everywhere.

[19]C. F. D. Moule, *op. cit.,* pp. 73-74. (See Liddell and Scott, in loco.)

[20]Maclaren, *op. cit.,* pp. 114-15. (He emphasizes Paul's dramatic change at the time of his conversion.)

Here is the Christian's source of real and abiding joy—to participate with Christ in His redemptive work. The character of Paul's ministry includes not only preaching, prayer, and joy but also suffering, pain, and conflict.

The clause **and fill up that which is behind of the afflictions of Christ** is controversial. One may discard the interpretations: (1) that Paul is referring to a quota of suffering due the body of Christ's followers; (2) the Roman Catholic doctrine of adding to any lack in the atonement of Christ by the suffering of Christ's followers; (3) that these are afflictions laid on by Christ; or (4) that these are Christ's sufferings in Paul. Rather, the Church, as the mystical body of Christ, suffers because of the union of the believer with Christ. Christ asks Paul at Damascus, "Saul, Saul, why persecutest thou me?" (Acts 26:14) To persecute a Christian is to persecute Christ. All opposition to the Church is affliction heaped on Christ. The believer is thus identified with Christ in a vital sense. Suffering in this world should be expected (I Pet. 2:21; 3:14-18). Carson says that affliction continues as long as there is sin and opposition to Christ and His Church in the world. And, he adds, the Christian takes it, not like the Stoic, but with joy.[21]

It cannot be that the atonement is insufficient; Paul has just shown that it is abundantly adequate (13-14, 20). *Thlipsis* (suffering, affliction) is not used anywhere in the New Testament for Christ's atoning death; Lightfoot adds that this is no "sacrificial act."[22] Moule also confirms the opinion when he states that this passage does not refer to the death of Christ, but to the trials and burdens of life.[23] (Cf. Eph. 3:13.) Paul's ministry is redemptive in the sense that he willingly identifies himself with Christ's cause, suffers for Christ's sake, that he may continue to preach the gospel (Rom. 8:17; Phil. 3:8) and win some (I Cor. 9:21-23). He suffers therefore for the sake of Christ's body.[24]

In my flesh is Paul's physical body. **For his body's sake** refers to Christ's mystical body. The body *in* which Paul suffers is his own; that *for* which he suffers is Christ's. The statement

[21]Quoted in C. F. D. Moule, *op. cit.*, p. 50.

[22]*Ibid.*, p. 51.

[23]H. C. G. Moule, *op. cit.*, p. 90.

[24]F. W. Farrar, *Texts Explained* (New York: George H. Doran Co., 1899), pp. 263-64.

which is the church makes it clear to whom he refers. Persecution is redemptively endured when it is according to Christ's purpose and when it helps to perpetuate the Church.

2. *Responsible for a Commission* (1:25-26)

Paul has been called and charged with a mission. In 23 he is made a minister of the *gospel;* in 27 he is the minister of a Person—Christ; and here he is **a minister** of the Church. His ministry involves a revelation (27), a message (23), and an office (24-25). He is **made a minister**—called, commissioned, made responsible. It is an honor conferred on a human instrument but with a global purpose; and is **according to the dispensation of God** (lit., God's act of dispensing). Paul has a stewardship from God of no mean proportions. He is to make the word of God fully known—for that is the sense of the words, **to fulfill the word of God.** Paul's is the "great commission." His ambition is, as with all God's ministers, to make the gospel manifest as he ought (4:4; Eph. 6:19).

The special word of God that Paul is charged with is **the mystery** (the article is for emphasis). **The mystery** is God's self-revelation—the fact that God was in Christ reconciling the world unto himself (21; II Cor. 5:19). The word is probably taken from Grecian culture, but it is filled with Christian content. Paul does the same with other Greek words such as "grace" and "Lord." He gives them a Christian meaning and usage. **The mystery** of the deity and incarnation of Christ has just been stated (15-19). This **mystery** is that secret something behind the visible act, as in the Lord's Supper and baptism. So here, the secret behind the manifestation of Jesus in history is the mystery of the incarnation of God in Him and His propitiation for our sins on Calvary (I Tim. 3:16; I John 2:2). **The mystery** is further deepened with the pronouncement of a kind of racial incarnation as well as the particular event in Jesus Christ—"Christ in you, the hope of glory" (27). This racial incarnation is Christ living in a new race of redeemed men. In addition Paul adds a thought strange to the Jew, that the Gentile is included in God's redeeming grace (27; Eph. 3:4-6, 9-10). **The mystery** is the relation of Christ to His Church; the *Head* to the *body* (Eph. 5:32). This the angels desire to look into (I Pet. 1:12).

In the statement **hid from ages and from generations** (26) Moule suggests that **from** is a preposition of time; that is, the secret was held until the fullness of time.[25] However, the secret was not only hid *for* ages of time, but *from* **ages and generations** of men. As in the case of the two on the road to Emmaus whose eyes were once "holden" (Luke 24:16) and subsequently "opened" (Luke 24:31), so it is God's will now that the secret shall be kept hid no longer (I Cor. 2:9-16; Eph. 3:9-10). The Spirit's ministry is therefore to bring enlightenment (Col. 1:9). And this is the burden of Paul's prayer for the Colossians. The mystery is **now manifest to his saints,** to those who have believed and consequently see. The revelation is ever more glorious and expanding (2; Eph. 2:1-7).

3. *The Commission Is Revelatory* (1:27-28)

To whom God would make known is literally "to whom God willed to make known." God not only decided *when* to make the mystery known, but *to whom.* The secret is revealed only to those who obey Christ; it is not clear to the world, which is still blinded. The crucial point here is the difference between the possession of the fact and the comprehension of the significance of that fact. Oh, the tragedy of holding "the truth in unrighteousness" (Rom. 1:18-19)! Oh, the responsibility that devolves upon the apostle, as well as the saints everywhere who know the truth! The message is for **every man** (28); the Great Commission is in full force. The revelation is manifest that it may be shared, even with **Gentiles.** God's hope for His investment in the saints (Eph. 1:18) is great. **The riches of the glory of this mystery** are the "treasures" (2:3) found in Christ. Those treasures are to be shared among the Gentiles. Since there is only one God, argues Paul, He must be the God of the Gentiles, or else they have no God. The treasure of the indwelling Christ must be shared with the Gentiles as well as the Jews. Paul, therefore, from the day of his commission by Christ, was trudging the highways of the world preaching "among the Gentiles the unsearchable riches of Christ" (Eph. 3:8; cf. Rom. 9:23-24).

a. A Meaningful Message (1:27*b*). The mystery which Paul is to make known is not just empty ritual as was shared by the false teachers with the few initiated ones; it is an indwelling Presence to share with the whole world.[26] The richness of the glory of the mystery revealed is not alone Christ incarnate in

[25]H. C. G. Moule, *op. cit.,* p. 91.
[26]*Ibid.*

Jesus of Nazareth, but Christ in any man, making him new (cf. II Cor. 5:17). The whole phrase, **Christ in you, the hope of glory** speaks of three blessings: the divine, indwelling Presence in this life, the destiny planned for the saints, and the means for attaining that holy end. Thus the indwelling Christ is the pledge of future glory. Eternity is here—the past, present, and future. It seems difficult for Paul to define **glory** specifically; he is content merely to state it. However, this **glory** is tasted here, but realized fully only in heaven (Rom. 3:23; 8:18).

In Rom. 3:23 the glory of God is shown to be moral purity. Man by sinning falls short of that glory. The work of the indwelling Christ is its restoration. While "in Christ" speaks primarily of our justified relation to God, **Christ in you** speaks primarily of our sanctified condition. As A. B. Simpson said, "The deeper life of sanctification is simply Christ within."[27] And he cites the figures of speech used by Paul in this Epistle (2:7, 11-13; 3:1, 3-4) to express it. Simpson adds, Our "actions are to be determined by our relation to Him."[28]

b. A Novel Method (28*a*). Paul's unique method is shown in the phrase **whom we preach.** Preaching is the distinctive Christian method of spreading the gospel as opposed to the methods for propagating Gnostic-type religions. The gospel method is unique in its simplicity and forthrightness. All highly intricate rituals—forms, rites, robes, hats, rings, signs, assistants, vestments—are foreign to this. How simple is the New Testament method (Rom. 10:8-15)! This statement as to method further separates the true messenger from the false.

Preaching involves **warning** (admonishing) and **teaching** (instruction). This method has its authority in the Word (3:16). **Every man** shows the universality and individuality of the gospel appeal. It is another rejoinder against the exclusiveness of the religion of the false teachers in Colossae, which applies only to the predestined, or circumcised, or initiated. Though the gospel may be limited in its success with men, it is universal in its call. Here is the deathblow to Judaism, predestinarianism, and all Gnostic-type religions which have a limited application. Further, Christian preaching is done **in** (not "with") **all wisdom.**

[27]*All in All or Christ in Colossians* (New York: Christian Alliance Publishing Co., n.d.), p. 18.

[28]*Ibid.*, p. 20.

When Christ is properly known, one has the source of true wisdom (2:3; I Cor. 1:30). He is **wisdom.**

c. A Moral Motive (28*b*). **Present** (*paristemi*) is hardly a sacrificial term, as Moule suggests, in this connection.[29] It is rather a term that suggests demonstration, exhibition, or introduction—"to set before."[30] These are to be Paul's fruits of labor, sheaves to lay at the Master's feet, the accounting of his responsible stewardship. The motive of the apostle is to **present every man perfect in Christ Jesus.** Some commentators see only the idea of maturity in **perfect** (*teleios*), avoiding the ethical connotations. But there is no need to limit the meaning to that which is put into it by pagan mystery religions.[31] It has in the New Testament an ethical meaning as well. Paul wants to present his converts to his Lord as moral men (22), holy men—saints (2). W. E. Sangster says, "The ineradicable pollution of our nature on which some theologians insist finds little support in the letters of the Apostle."[32] And in this letter the whole burden is that there may be an end to sin and sinning. Paul's view steers a middle course between antinomianism and fatalism.

The apostle sees love as the key to perfection (3:14), in agreement with Jesus and John.[33] This Epistle shows man's experience of divine grace to be not only a standing, but a state; not only a position, but a condition; not only imputed righteousness, but imparted righteousness. And this righteousness that is required comes about through union with Christ, for it is **in Christ** that we are perfected.[34] This phrase is a rejoinder against any other requirement but Christ. (**Jesus** is not in the best manuscripts,[35] though its omission does not change the meaning of the passage.) The presentation of men made perfect in Christ is to be made *now* as well as in the hereafter.

[29]C. F. D. Moule, *op. cit.*, p. 85.

[30]Liddell and Scott, *op. cit.*, in loco.

[31]C. F. D. Moule, *op. cit.*, p. 85.

[32]*The Path to Perfection* (New York: Abingdon-Cokesbury Press, 1943), p. 41.

[33]W. T. Purkiser, *Sanctification and Its Synonyms* (Kansas City: Beacon Hill Press, 1962), pp. 66-68.

[34]Jessop, *op. cit.*, pp. 161-62. He quotes Joseph H. Smith at length on this point.

[35]H. C. G. Moule, *op. cit.*, p. 94.

4. *The Commission Is Rigorous* (1:29)

The expression **Whereunto I also labour** (toil till one is weary, exhausted)[36] reveals the energy with which Paul undertakes the great work for the salvation of men. **Also** means not only "and" but "really." Paul is committed to the life-and-death struggle for the truth of God and the souls of men. He does not fight secretly, as do his antagonists; he writes an open letter. He toils, **striving** (*agonizomenos,* agonizing), **according to his** (God's) **working.**[37] The work that Paul is doing is God at work —Christ in him (27). Always Christ works in the world, within the bounds of the Great Commission, in proportion to our labors for Him. We are laborers together with him (II Cor. 5:19-20). **Worketh in me mightily** (with power) reveals the source of Paul's driving force and energy. This struggle at Colossae is not easy. Strong foes are these, even as those at the Jerusalem Council. But Paul is committed and ready. He is certain of his calling (25), certain of his message (27; Gal. 1:8), and certain concerning the power of the gospel by virtue of the indwelling Spirit (29).

We have in this section, then, "God's Plan for Men" (1) The mystery of the gospel—Christ incarnate, 26-27; (2) The ministry of the gospel—"by the foolishness of preaching," 28*a*; (3) The motivation for the gospel—the ultimate perfection of man, 28*d*; (4) The might behind the gospel—the supernatural at work in the minister, 29.

Paul concludes the chapter with the moving thought that "the measure of our power then is Christ's power in us. He whose presence makes the struggle necessary, by His presence strengthens us for it."[38]

[36]Liddell and Scott, *op. cit.,* in loco.

[37]Rev. E. Wayne Stahl: "according to His supernatural activity working in me in power."

[38]Maclaren, *op. cit.,* p. 149.

Section III *The Conflict*

Colossians 2:1-23

Paul has laid the groundwork for his confrontation with the lately emerging heresy in the Colossian church. He has stated his confidence in the Christian experience of the Colossian believers (1:1-8). He has laid open the heart and burden of his prayers for them (1:9-14). He has stated precisely the essential elements of the revelation of the mystery of Christ (1:15-20). And he has shown his own inevitable involvement in this conflict with these enemies of Christ, because of both the commitment he has made to Christ and the subsequent commission he has received. The issues are now to be joined. Light opposes darkness, freedom opposes bondage, morality opposes empty ritual.

In the section of the letter now under consideration the Pauline and the pagan views are held in continuing contrast. The struggle centers on two areas—doctrine and practice. Interspersed are repeated warnings lest believers be seduced and thus deprived of their heritage in Christ. It is well that Paul be concerned, for all the benefits of God's grace towards them are in jeopardy because of Satan's devices.

A. Doctrine, 2:1-15

1. *The Incarnation* (2:1-7)

a. The Doctrine Perceived (2:1-3). The strife in which Paul finds himself involved concerns both those whom he knows at Colossae and **Laodicea,**[1] the neighboring town (see map 1), and those whom he does not know (1). With the words **I would that ye knew,** Paul reassures them of his deep love and concern (Rom. 1:13). Absent of necessity (2:5; 4:10), he must be content with this communication in the hands of trustworthy fellow workers.[2]

[1]See Rev. 3:14 ff. for a description of this church at the end of the century.

[2]See Introduction for the question of Paul's visiting the Lycus Valley churches.

For their souls, as for all those who have not seen his face in any century, Paul is in **great conflict.** The figure may be drawn from the athletic contests or even from military action. The conflict must have been waged first in the secret of his heart in the presence of his Lord. Now it is brought out into the open by means of this letter. Paul's energy and incentive for the strife were not merely human. He had been charged with divine energy (1:29; II Cor. 5:14); united with his Lord in a great "striving" (RSV).

The believers must fully understand the issues and the consequences. The methods of the struggle and the fruits of the life will reveal who is trustworthy, the false teachers or Paul and his companions. Satan's appeal is for fleshly satisfaction through various enticements (4, 23), while Christ's appeal is for ethical righteousness through accepting the truth of the gospel.

The struggle centers around the main doctrines, the Incarnation and the atonement. These are crucial, for on them hinges the fate of man's redemption and salvation.

Faith in the doctrine of the incarnation of God in Jesus Christ has its confirmation in experience. Paul strives therefore for the strengthening of the believers in Christian love. **Comforted** (2) means strengthened, not merely consoled. The word comes from *parakaleo,* "to call to the side of";[3] hence, "advocate." In John 14—16 the word is used to describe the ministry of the Holy Spirit. The strengthening comes from unity—**being knit together** (cf. Eph. 4:16). **Love** is the principle by which ethical conduct is determined and achieved (Gal. 5:14). It is the ethical bond (3:14). **Their hearts** does not limit the extent of Paul's concern to those who have not seen him, but includes all.

The strengthening in love leads to the desired end, the "knowledge of God's mystery, Christ" (RSV); that is the significance of the word **unto** (*eis*). **Riches** equals conviction or insight,[4] which gives **assurance** and **understanding** in **full** measure, and brings about the **acknowledgement of the mystery. Acknowledgement** is "know" in the ASV.[5] Christian love will be the ethical bond leading to the conviction of the truth of the incarnation of God in Christ Jesus. Then follows the step of

[3]Liddell and Scott, *op. cit.,* in loco.

[4]C. F. D. Moule, *op. cit.,* pp. 85-86.

[5]Paul may be striking an evangelistic note here.

faith (acknowledgment) which makes the fact real.[6] In other words, "This wealth of conviction is attained by living in the love of God" (Eph. 3:17-19).[7] NASB translates v. 2, "that their hearts may be encouraged, having been welded together in love, and attaining to all the wealth that comes from the full assurance of understanding, resulting in a true knowledge of God's mystery, that is, Christ Himself."

Here the **mystery of God,** as indicated above, is Christ himself. **And of the Father** is omitted in some manuscripts.[8] If retained, the doctrine of the Incarnation is further amplified. Christ as the Son of God is emphasized. If the phrase is omitted, the mystery still concerns the person of Jesus Christ as revealed in vv. 3 and 9 and in 1:15-19. **In whom** (3), that is, in Jesus Christ, **are hid** all the attributes of Deity. This is the mystery. **Hid** means contained, waiting to be revealed in their time[9] (II Cor. 4:3-4). **All** (no exceptions) divine **treasures of wisdom and knowledge** have their source in Him. He is the way to forgiveness, sanctification, wisdom, God. There are no other sources of power or knowledge beside Christ. Therefore the Gnostic methods of arriving at knowledge apart from Him and through mere human speculation are false. Verse 3 is a stinging rebuke to the claims of the false teachers. True knowledge of the way of salvation is found only in the understanding of Christ as the fullest Revelation of God, even as very God himself. Anything less Paul calls "vain deceit" (8). "Christ is all" (3:11). Paul's argument is, then, that persistence in Christian love strengthens the perception of this mystery.[10] He thus shows the way to the knowledge of the doctrine of the incarnate God, who is Jesus Christ (Gal. 4:4-7; I Tim. 3:16). In Him are stored up all knowledge, as its Source; and all wisdom, which is the means of the application of that knowledge (Rom. 11:33; I Cor. 1:30).

The fact just stated gives meaning to the doctrine of atonement which he will declare later (2:8 ff.).

[6]Marvin R. Vincent, *Word Studies in the New Testament* (Wm. B. Eerdmans Pub. Co., 1946), III, 482.

[7]Maclaren, *op. cit.*, p. 161.

[8]Nestle, *op. cit.*, in loco. See also Alexander Roberts, *Companion to the Revised Version* (New York: Cassell, Petter, Galphin & Co., 1881), pp. 65-67.

[9]Robertson, *op. cit.*, p. 488.

[10]C. F. D. Moule, *op. cit.*, p. 86.

b. The Doctrine Received (2:4-7). The doctrine is more than a concept to be understood; it is the source of a new way of life. Because this is true, Christian life itself is in danger.

(1) *Christian life threatened* (2:4). Evil is potent. The Colossian believers are in danger of being beguiled, literally, enticed, to make a miscalculation. If not by sinning, then by false religion, the Christian life would be destroyed.[11] The little word **lest** (4) should remind us that sin, though a formidable foe, need not overpower us. **And this I say** refers to what has just gone before. Paul restates his great concern for them and his faith in the revelation just declared (I Cor. 2:4 ff.). **Enticing words** indicates the methods of the false teachers as opposed to Paul's method of reasonable persuasion and demonstration. Today, as then, the truth of the Incarnation must not be lost in the wordy arguments of human reasonings.

(2) *Christian life supported* (2:5). Paul is there to help. The phrase **with you in the spirit** indicates that the apostle would have his spiritual presence very real to them (Phil. 1:7; I Thess. 2:17), though he must be absent because a prisoner of Rome (4:10). **Order . . . and stedfastness,** says Moule, are military terms or metaphors.[12] NEB translates, "I . . . rejoice to see your orderly array"; NASB renders it "good discipline." **Stedfastness** (*stereoma,* fidelity) signifies "the solid thing which constituted the basis of their church"[13] (lit., the firm foundation).[14] The firm foundation is their **faith in Christ,** the faith that they exercised at the point of their entrance into saving grace. This point is repeated and expanded in the next verse.

(3) *Christian faith actualized* (6-7). **Received** (6) is aorist, indicating a decisive, once-for-all act. It is **Christ Jesus** who is received, and not only the message about Him. **Lord** "recalls the personal name 'Jehovah' in the Old Testament,"[15] and is here applied to Jesus. The article **the** is used to eliminate all rivals (Acts 2:36; Eph. 3:11); it identifies whom they have received. **So walk** means "so live." What they have begun in a crisis decision they are now to live out in daily conduct. They are to live

[11]*Ibid.,* p. 88.

[12]*Ibid.,* p. 89.

[13]Jamieson, Fausset, and Brown, *op. cit.,* in loco.

[14]Liddell and Scott, *op. cit.,* in loco.

[15]Carson, *op. cit.,* p. 59.

in him, in union with Christ, in a new and heavenly atmosphere. They are now to live up to Christ rather than to live up to mere rules and regulations. Questions of Sabbaths, feasts, and rules pale before the Christ as does the shadow before the sun. When one truly has Christ's mind and spirit, true ethics must follow (1:10; 3:7 ff.; 4:5). Thus the Incarnation has its meaning and purpose fulfilled when believing men are joined to Christ by faith. As Moule says, "The Christian Gospel is essentially an *historical* account of what happened in the past; yet also essentially, it means incorporation *now* in the still living Person of Whom it tells—the contemporary Christ."[16]

Rooted and built up (7) are separate metaphors—the one of a tree, the other of a house. **Rooted** is past tense, a fact completed. **Built up** is present tense, indicating a continuing process of construction and development. The tree properly rooted will produce proper fruit, drawing nourishment from the soul's natural soil, which is Jesus Christ. As illustrated by the second figure, the act which launches one in the holy way is to be worked out, built up stone on stone as a structure, in the daily life. **In the faith** means the body of Christian doctrine; more specifically, the doctrine which Paul had stated above (2-3). This truth is the foundation on which they are to be **stablished.**

As ye have been taught is a further reminder of Paul's confidence in the Colossian pastor, Epaphras (1:7). According to Greek grammar, **abounding** may modify both the life in Christ and **thanksgiving.** Paul often emphasizes thankfulness, and that because our blessings are all of grace. Thanksgiving is the fruit of a thriving life in Christ.

2. *The Atonement* (2:8-15)

Following hard on the mystery of the entrance of Christ into the world is the mystery of His departure and what it means to the world of men. In these two doctrines, the Incarnation and the atonement, the mystery of God in Christ is revealed. The truth here concerns who Christ is and what He has done.

The emergence of Christ into history by means of the Virgin Birth (Isa. 7:10 ff.; Matt. 1:18, 20, 23; Luke 1:26 ff.) has no meaning or purpose if there is no atonement made by Him (Rom. 3:24-25; 6:6-10). Any claim that Christ is our Saviour and Redeemer is invalidated if the manifestation of God in Jesus is

[16]C. F. D. Moule, *op. cit.*, p. 89.

not received. It is at these two points that the gospel receives its greatest assault. It is as true today as it was in the Colossian situation. But the Bible declares these two doctrines clearly and boldly.

a. The Basis of the Doctrine (2:8-10). A caution is stated in the word **beware** (8). We note, then, these truths:

(1) *The caution* (8). **Spoil** probably means "kidnap" rather than "plunder" or "rob."[17] Moule suggests, "carry you off body and soul."[18] Here again is the warning about the possibility of backsliding (1:21). Man is shown to be personally responsible, a partner in his own deception. **Philosophy** when it is human wisdom opposed to revelation leads away from Christ. This is the only verse where the word *philosophia* occurs.[19] **Vain deceit** is "delusive speculation" (NEB). What Paul is about to speak of is not arrived at by mere deep thinking, philosophizing, or extensive learning, but by revelation (Gal. 1:12). The apostle is not opposed to wisdom and knowledge as such, but to human arrogance as the source of it. It is so often true that men want "a Christ according to the system of thought, not a system of thought according to the blessed Christ."[20]

Paul points out two pitfalls here: (*a*) **tradition of men**, or mere human wisdom, which is always inferior to divine revelation (I Pet. 1:18); and (*b*) **rudiments of the world** (*stoikeia*), demonic powers or elemental spirits. Percy says that they are either "notions," or more probably "beings," component parts of a series, opposed to Christianity, sufficiently personal to hold people in subjection.[21] These are influential powers, but not ultimate. They will all finally be subjected to Christ. These "gods" are really no gods at all (Gal. 4:8-9). True worship opposes the traditions of men that climax in ceremonialism, ritual, forms, signs, and special days. Such worship ascribes worth to God alone. "A Christianity making much of forms and ceremonies is a distinct retrogression and descent."[22] It is man's substitute

[17]Liddell and Scott, *op. cit.*, in loco.

[18]H. C. G. Moule, *op. cit.*, p. 142.

[19]Farrar, *op. cit.*, p. 264.

[20]Moule quoted in Thomas, *op. cit.*, pp. 73-74.

[21]Quoted in C. F. D. Moule, *op. cit.*, p. 91. Vincent says that they are "teachings," *op. cit.*, p. 486.

[22]Maclaren, *op. cit.*, p. 193.

for a holy, sin-killing religion. Because such religious practice is according to men, it is not after Christ.[23]

(2) *Christ is God* (9-10). Here we find a restatement of the doctrine of the Incarnation. The antecedent for **in him** is "Christ" (8), in whom **dwelleth** or abide (present tense; now) all the essential elements of Deity. **All the fulness of the Godhead** (*theotetos*) does not mean traits of Deity only, but the very nature of God (1:19; 2:3).[24] This is the only use of *theotetos* in the New Testament.[25] **All** allows no lack. **Bodily** signifies "in human flesh," "really"; not typically or figuratively, but "substantially or personally, by the strictest union, as the soul dwells in the body; so that God and man are one Christ."[26] We can but gaze and sing, "Oh, the wonder of it all!" What an arrogant infallibility it is to declare Christ fallible! Docetism said that He only *appeared* to be a man. Gnosticism emphasized that deity was distributed to many beings, of which Christ was one.[27] But Paul is saying that Jesus Christ is God incarnate. In the Son are the attributes of Deity. The Godhead dwells really in Christ bodily. The true "knowledge" (*gnosis*) is Christ; there is no fuller nor more comprehensive revelation of God than He. For Paul, Christ is not a member of an order of beings superior to men but inferior to God, as the Gnostic-type teachers were saying. Jesus Christ is God manifested in the flesh (I Tim. 3:16).

The outcome of Paul's teaching is man's salvation, **ye are complete** (made full) **in him** (10). The RSV has it, "You have come to fulness of life in him." All that is necessary to salvation comes by Jesus Christ. No one else is needed (I Cor. 1:30). **In him** indicates how that life is given; it is by union with Christ, by faith in Him, and in His way of salvation.

In the expression **the head** we see the preeminence of Christ again lifted up to fortify the teaching of the sufficiency of Christ as our Saviour (1:18). His headship extends not only over the Church, which voluntarily serves Him, but over all forces that are opposed to Him (Phil. 2:10-11). **Principality and power** has

[23] *Ibid.*, p. 194.

[24] Vincent, *op. cit.*, p. 486.

[25] Farrar, *op. cit.*, p. 265.

[26] Clarke, *op. cit.*, in loco.

[27] H. R. Mackintosh, *The Doctrine of the Person of Jesus Christ* (Edinburgh: T. & T. Clark, 1912), p. 73.

been translated "rule and authority" (NASB). When one has Christ, he acknowledges no other authority in the spiritual world.

b. The Benefits of the Doctrine (2:11-13). The benefits of the atonement are shown under two figures and a factual statement.

(1) *The figures* (11-12). Salvation by atonement is illustrated by two figures of speech, **circumcision** (11) and **baptism** (12). **In whom** has Christ (8) for its antecedent and signifies union with Him. **Circumcised** here refers to a spiritual act reminiscent of the physical rite of the Jewish faith. It is but a symbol of the real act—**putting off the body of the sins of the flesh.** "This is an inward purification, which to Paul was the true circumcision"[28] (Deut. 10:16; 30:6). It is a figure of our moral cleansing by the **circumcision** (death) **of Christ** (cf. Isa. 53:8). The figure clearly implies that the experience is a decisive act, not a long process. It is **made without hands,** that is, spiritually performed. The phrase **of the sins** is omitted in some manuscripts[29] although its omission or inclusion does not change the essential meaning of the verse.

It is a mistake to view **body of . . . the flesh** as the human body,[30] as some do.[31] Barclay is not quite correct either when he says, "By the flesh Paul meant that part of human nature which gives a bridgehead to sin."[32] Rather, Paul is saying that "the body of flesh" (RSV) is something contrary to human nature that can be *put off* (3:8-9). Paul is speaking in moral and spiritual terms here. Carson falters further when he states that "putting off the body of the flesh" is repudiating it.[33] Many a slave to sin repudiates his old life but is never able to put it off.

It appears, then, that the "body of flesh" is not any part of the "body of our humiliation," which, according to Scripture, cannot be perfected until the resurrection (I Cor. 15:53-54; Phil. 3:21). It is an evil, viewed as a totality (body), wholly distinct

[28]Bruce, *op. cit.*, pp. 234-35.

[29]Nestle, *op. cit.*, in loco.

[30]Robertson, *op. cit.*, p. 77.

[31]Carson, *op. cit.*, p. 66.

[32]*The Promise of the Spirit* (Philadelphia: The Westminster Press, 1960), p. 87.

[33]*Op. cit.*, p. 66.

from the human body and foreign to it. The ruling principle of that "body," the "flesh," operates in man in opposition to "the law of the Spirit of life" (Rom. 8:2, 7; Eph. 2:16). It can defile the spirit as well as the body of man. The "body of flesh," therefore, should not be confused with either the essential spirit or body of man. It can be put off *now* (in this life), dismissed by the **circumcision** (death) **of Christ** in our behalf. **Circumcision** is a figure of the grace of our sanctification. "In spiritual circumcision, through Christ, the whole, corrupt carnal nature is put away like a garment which is taken off and laid aside."[34] It is clear, however, that what is *put off* in this experience in a decisive act must be *kept off* in daily acts of renunciation (3:5, 8-9).

Salvation by the atonement of Christ is here viewed under the figure of circumcision as a moral change in the heart and life of man by the introduction of a new principle of conduct—"the law of the Spirit of life in Christ Jesus" in place of "the law of sin and death" (Rom. 8:2) or the spirit of enmity against God (Rom. 8:7). Imputed and imparted grace are here taught.

The **circumcision of Christ** is interpreted variously: as Christ's death when He put away man's sin—the act of atonement—or Christ's death when He put off His own physical body, or His own circumcision as a child. Of the three the first is the most meaningful (1:13, 21-22; 2:15).

Buried with him in baptism (12) is another figure of what it means to be delivered from the old life of sin and to enter the new life of salvation. It is a symbol of death and resurrection. This verse parallels the previous one. In baptism one symbolically dies to the old life, is buried, and is raised with Christ to the new life. **Through the faith of** equals "through faith in." **Operation** speaks of the energy and "working" (RSV) of God. Man's faith is inspired by the power that was available to raise Christ from the dead. Satan's powers are seen to be insufficient to hold Christ captive, and the same is true of us.

(2) *The factual statement* (13). **And you** takes us back to 1:21 ff. and points up the personal proof in themselves of the sufficiency of Christ. If they will let love (Christian ethics) operate, they will comprehend ever more fully (2:2) the certainty of salvation (1:27). **Dead in your sins** describes the natural condition of man in relation to God—morally dead though physically alive. **The uncircumcision of your flesh** is another

[34]Vincent, *op. cit.*, p. 488.

way of depicting this depraved condition. It appears, therefore, that Paul is not speaking here of circumcision physically performed, but rather of that faith in Christ which is the means of putting off the old life and beginning the new. It is a transformation from deadness towards God to new life in Christ. **Quickened together with him** shows that union with Christ is the means of new life. If the "Head" is alive, so is the "body." To be united to Christ is life. If **uncircumcision** refers to the act physically performed, then Paul is stating what he has said before (Acts 15; Rom. 2:25, 28-29; Gal. 5:6, 11; 6:15). *That kind* of circumcision is shown to be unnecessary and unavailing for salvation. The evidence of saving grace is in being **quickened,** brought to the new life of ethical righteousness, because of having been **forgiven . . . all trespasses.** The one logically follows the other, as heat goes with the sun, yet they are coincident. The quickening speaks of our sanctification begun, even as forgiveness speaks of our justification. **All trespasses** shows that the forgiveness is complete. Christ is the sufficient Saviour (3:11).

c. *The Battleground of the Doctrine* (2:14-15). The battleground of the atonement is seen in Calvary's cross. The charges against man were nailed with Christ to that rough tree. **The handwriting of ordinances** is a signed bond, an IOU made to God and signed (or admitted) by mankind.[35] All responsible men admit the fact of sin, and consent to the justice of the death penalty for it. The charge is **against us.** The handwriting is law and conscience. The legal bond is **contrary to us.** Paul now states the way in which God will remove the death penalty. **Blotting out** means that the charge is "smeared out" as on wax.[36] "Another way of putting it is that, since Christ died and since we are dead with Him by baptism 'into His death' therefore the 'I. O. U.' is no longer valid; our death (with Christ) releases us from the obligation."[37] Christ is the Propitiation for our debt (Rom. 3:24-25). **Nailing** is aorist, signifying a finished work. Here and in John 20:25 are the only references to nails at the Crucifixion.[38] The question can be raised as to who forgives or blots out the charges, the Father or Christ. The two Persons are used interchangeably as the subjects of the actions taken, so

[35]C. F. D. Moule, *op. cit.*, p. 97.

[36]*Ibid.*

[37]*Ibid.*, p. 98.

[38]*Ibid.*, p. 99.

that it can be said that both the Father and the Son are involved in the Calvary work.

The free pardon is the glorious outcome of the terrible conflict that is described so graphically. **Spoiled** is in the middle voice. What this means is that Christ divested himself of all **principalities and powers.** In His death He submitted himself to them but then triumphed over them. He confronts these demonic forces and shows them to be in total opposition to Him. By submitting to the Cross **he made a shew of them openly.** He publicly reveals their true nature. How they opposed Christ and put Him out of the way is open for all to read (Isaiah 53).

Triumphing over them, our Lord leads them as a victorious general leads his prisoners in a procession of victory.[39] The Cross is the cosmic battleground where Christ defeated all the forces of hell single-handedly (Eph. 2:15-16), showing them up for what they really are—enemies of God and all good. These forces, religious and heathen, thought that they were putting Christ out of the way once for all. But what really happened was that Christ put them out of the way. By His resurrection He broke away and showed himself superior. Therefore, says Paul, why should anyone be bound by these worldly powers, judged by lesser authorities, deceived by proven enemies of Christ? He exhorts all to have the enmity circumcised from their hearts, to surrender to God alone (Rom. 12:1-2).

A question is raised regarding the last phrase of v. 15. Is it **in it** or in *Him* that the victory is won? If **in it,** then Paul is referring to the Cross. If the words mean "in Him," then God triumphed in Christ.[40]

His death is our death, symbolized by baptism. His circumcision (being "cut off," Isa. 53:8) is our circumcision. Christ is personally responsible for our redemption. He conquered all opposing forces at Calvary and at the tomb. This was the decisive cosmic battle between God and all Satanic forces.

In the cross of Christ I glory,
Tow'ring o'er the wrecks of time;
All the light of sacred story
Gathers 'round its head sublime.[41]

[39]Liddell and Scott, *op. cit.,* in loco.

[40]Vincent, *op. cit.,* p. 492.

[41]John Bowring.

B. Duty, 2:16-23

Paul's conflict with the Colossian false teachers not only deals with doctrine, but carries over into the realm of human conduct. As someone has said, for Paul, "doctrine is the seed of duty." His concern with duty here involves two areas, ritual and regulation.

1. *Ritual* (2:16-19)

a. Questions of Calendar (2:16-17). **Therefore** refers back to what has just been stated and leads to the conclusion: **Let no man judge** (pass sentence on) **you.** All other religions involve inferior and unavailing reconciling acts and practices—**in meat, or in drink** (eating), **holyday** (festival or yearly feast day), **new moon** (monthly observance), **the sabbath** (weekly observance) (Num. 28:9).[42] Although the article **the** before **sabbath** is not in the Greek, its use in KJV clarifies the meaning. Paul was resisting the Judaizers who insisted on legalistic Sabbath observance.[43] These were issues on which the enemies of Christ succeeded in effecting His crucifixion (Rom. 14:1 ff.; I Tim. 4:3; Titus 1:14; Heb. 9:10 ff.; 13:9-10).

Which are a shadow (17) is explained by v. 18, and placed in contrast in v. 19. **Shadow** characterizes the ritualistic systems of Judaism. The **shadow** points to the reality, Christ. In the Old Testament only the **shadow** could be seen. In the New Testament the **body** (*soma,* substance), which is **Christ,** is present. Yet we still have those who would be "slaves to shadows"—types, forms, and rituals. The ground of Paul's exhortation here is the work of Christ; calendar questions have no value as means to salvation (Rom. 14:17). Their function is to point to the sacrifice of Christ. How foolish to call shadows reality!

b. Questions of Intermediaries (2:18-19). Verse 18 is difficult to translate. We must "either take our choice of doubtful conjectural emendations, or make the best we can of the text."[44] **Beguile** equals "defraud"; Moule says, "declare you disqualified,"[45] and thus deprive one of his rightful prize or reward. Paul

[42]Jamieson, Fausset, and Brown, *op. cit.,* in loco.

[43]Nestle, *op. cit.,* in loco.

[44]C. F. D. Moule, *op. cit.,* p. 106.

[45]*Ibid.*

is saying, "Do not let the ritualist act as an umpire over you." **Voluntary humility** means self-abasement (23).[46] Wahl says that it is literally "delighting in humility," as the scribes (Mark 12:38).[47] Such an attitude is therefore not of grace, but a human achievement. In the light of v. 23 this mortification is a purely human effort to "weaken the material nature of man . . . and pave the way for celestial vision and the full mystical knowledge."[48] Salvation is thus a human ascent by degrees instead of one step of faith in Christ for what He has done for us. Humility is a vice here; in 3:12 it is a virtue. The motive is the difference.

Worshipping of angels (angelolatry) brings to attention again the futility of imploring intermediary beings in order to reach the throne of God. Such imploring may involve self-abasement and self-torture. But even so, it is a false humility. These practices assume that intermediaries are needed for such lofty privileges. Paul is trying to show that there is immediate access to God. **Intruding into those things which he hath not seen** is translated by the RSV, "taking his stand on visions." **Not** should be omitted on manuscript evidence.[49] However, it seems that the clause may be understood with or without the negative. It could mean taking his stand on things he has not seen or perceived (i.e., on mere guess) or taking his stand on visions or mystical experiences of things that turn out to be opposed to Christ as revealed in Scripture. A. D. Nock translates the clause, "always investigating."[50] The true Christian does not have to see or know everything; he can walk by faith when he cannot see (II Cor. 5:7). The ritualist is concerned primarily (and ultimately) only with what he can see.

Vainly puffed up should be joined with the false "humility" of v. 23. **Fleshly mind** is really "mind of the flesh" (Rom. 8:5-8, 13; Gal. 3:3). It means the materialistic, sensual outlook where values are in externals only. Since it is God who qualifies (1:12), no lesser power should disqualify, the believer from his rightful reward by insisting on access to the throne of God through any other agencies. Christ is sufficient.

[46]Vincent, *op. cit.*, p. 495.

[47]Quoted in Jamieson, Fausset, and Brown, *op. cit.*, in loco.

[48]W. Knox, *op. cit.*, pp. 138-39.

[49]C. F. D. Moule, *op. cit.*, p. 104.

[50]Quoted in C. F. D. Moule, *op. cit.*, p. 105.

Not holding should be "not holding *fast*."[51] "He who does not hold Christ supremely above all others, does not hold Him at all."[52] **The Head** refers back to 1:18. Here, then, is the end result of those who would defraud the believer of his reward; it is to sever **the body** from **the Head. Joints** appear to be the points of union between the members of the body; **bands** are the ligaments, nerves, and tissues by which this same union is maintained and nourished. This is hardly a reference to the ministers and various officers of the church,[53] but a figure of the relation of Christ to His Church and of the members of the Church to each other. **Knit together** means "firmly united" (cf. 2:2; 3:14; Eph. 4:4-6). **With the increase of God** is not literally *of* God but *from* God, the increase that God gives (1:10; 2:7).

"Vain deceit" substitutes mediators, asceticism, and self-punishment—all of which can be **seen** and are temporal—for that which is unseen and eternal. But we are to walk by faith, not by sight; we have immediate access to God by faith (Rom. 5:1; Heb. 11:1).

2. *Regulation* (2:20-23)

Wherefore is omitted in the older manuscripts,[54] but the transition it indicates seems valid. **Dead with Christ** in a spiritual sense means deadness to the world of evil. It does not raise a question of doubt concerning their Christian experience. Paul wants the Colossian believers to put into daily practice what they experienced when they first met Christ, died with Him (12) and were raised to new life in Him (13). The Christian must be taught; he must learn, develop, and grow. The direction of the new life is determined in a moment, but the manner of the new life is a day-by-day process. Christians are to be dead to the **rudiments** (*stoicheia,* the lesser spiritual opposing powers) and their demands which are temporal and external (22). To be **subject to ordinances** (a passive bondage) is **living in the world** of sense and time again and not in the world which is above (3:1). These **ordinances** have their origin in earthly and inferior wisdom. These are man-made doctrines, not divine. The

[51]Liddell and Scott, *op. cit.,* in loco.

[52]Jamieson, Fausset, and Brown, *op. cit.,* in loco.

[53]Masson's view quoted in C. F. D. Moule, *op. cit.,* p. 107.

[54]Nestle, *op. cit.,* in loco.

one who has put his whole trust in Christ does not trust in regulations proposed by lesser powers. Verse 21 should be translated with an ascending emphasis—not, **touch not, taste not, handle not;** but "handle not, nor taste, nor [even] touch."[55] The things that one can touch and handle in ordinances are temporal; they perish in the process of being used, like uranium in producing nuclear power. Such commands are powerless to aid true righteousness. What can? The union of the believer to Christ. Morality is not to be achieved by negatives or regulations, but by being joined to Christ. He alone can be the Standard and Inspiration for ethical conduct. By renouncing human rules that are contrary to the love of Christ one arrives at the highest ethics. This is founded on our love for Christ because of what He has done at Calvary. He loses nothing in ethics who renounces rules for Christ. No license for wrongdoing is offered by accepting a higher inspiration for our moral choices (3:12 ff.; Rom. 6:1).

Some declare that v. 23 is "hopelessly obscure,"[56] but this is going too far. **Will worship** (*ethelothreskia*) carries with it the idea of pretense. The verse therefore seems to indicate that this system with its works, mediators, and self-torture gives a false appearance of **humility.**[57] This way *seems* to deny the sinful **flesh,** but in reality it makes the influence of the **flesh** principle more intense and renders ineffective the strong moral incentive that springs from dying with Christ. Phillips renders the verse: "I know that these regulations look wise with their self-inspired efforts at worship, their policy of self-humbling, and their studied neglect of the body. But in actual practice they do honor, not to God, but to man's own pride."

Goodspeed summarizes this section by stating that Paul refutes the Gnostic error

> that a higher stage of Christian experience could be attained by worship of certain angelic beings and communion with them than by mere faith in Christ. They recognized the value of communion with Christ, but only as an elementary stage in this mystic initiation which they claimed to enjoy. It was only through communion with these beings or principles, they held, that one could rise to an experience of the divine fulness and so achieve the highest reli-

[55]Vincent, *op. cit.*, p. 499, and others.

[56]C. F. D. Moule, *op. cit.*, p. 108.

[57]Vincent, *op. cit.*, p. 499.

> gious development. . . . Their movement threatened . . . to reduce Jesus from his true position to one subordinate to that of the imaginary beings of the Colossian speculations.[58]

All false religions and all false interpretations of Christianity put Christ in this inferior position in their schemes. But for Paul, He is supreme: "Christ is all, and in all" (3:11).

This section beginning, "If ye be dead with Christ" (2:20), has its counterpart in 3:1, "If ye then be risen with Christ." Having finished with the polemical part of his letter, Paul proceeds to state more fully the natural fruit of a correct conception and experience of divine grace, namely, ethical holiness. He states flatly that only the grace of God and not human willpower can stop the practice of the indulgence of **the flesh.** He now proceeds to develop this truth.

[58]*The Story of the New Testament* (Chicago: University of Chicago Press, 1916), pp. 42-43.

Section IV *The Conclusion*

Colossians 3:1—4:6

The area of controversy has been covered. Paul now directs the attention of the Colossian believers to the expected outcome of his message regarding the office and work of Christ. Such a view, he declares, issues in ethical righteousness. The practical duties that follow are summed up in a few principles which he states at appropriate places in the exhortation. He reiterates that true ethics have their spring in Christ alone; that they are derived from being in union with Him (1-4). Such a view (2:9) and experience (2:10-12) of Christ as Paul speaks of put the believer in a new world, and give a new understanding of what life is all about.

A. A New Frame of Reference, 3:1-4

1. *The Things of Christ* (3:1)

If ye then be risen parallels "if ye be dead" in 2:20, which introduces a negative approach to the solution of the problem of sin and ethics. Here the approach is positive. **If** does not suggest doubt, but rather means "since." "Whatever He did, we are regarded by God as having done also."[1] **With Christ** here equals "in Christ," for the relationship is intimate and complete. The believer is mystically risen with Christ, even as he has mystically died and been buried with Him under the figure of baptism (2:12). **Seek those things which are above** becomes the lifelong pursuit of the man in Christ. **Where Christ sitteth** refers to the throne of God. The implication of the Resurrection growing out of the doctrines of the Incarnation and atonement leads to the inescapable conclusion of the deity of Christ. This Jesus is the Christ (Acts 9:5). This understanding comes not from thinking or philosophizing alone, but from experience (2:2) and revelation (Gal. 1:16). The believers have a new perspective of all things by virtue of their relation to their newfound Lord.

[1]Thomas, *op. cit.*, p. 92.

2. *Spiritual Realities* (3:2-3)

Set your affection means to be disposed in a certain way, and refers to the mind, will, spirit.[2] The believer is to hold a mental set toward the ultimate, transcendent things, the **things above. On the earth** applies to the carnal, fleshly world.

Dead calls to mind 2:20 and speaks of the believer's relation to the world here and now. To be **dead** to the world contrasts with being "dead in sins" (2:13). The new **life** (3) is from **Christ.** He is its Source (John 10:18). **Hid** indicates that this life is not knowable to the one who does not believe (II Cor. 4:3-6). However it is a reality to the believer and is realized in a new ethical awareness and power for righteousness. That life, though in a sense hidden, waits to be revealed in a far more glorious way (I Cor. 15:51 ff.; I Thess. 4:13-18; I John 3:2). This life is hidden in "Christ, who is our life." **Christ in God** indicates the essential union of the Father and the Son.

Alexander Maclaren discusses "Risen with Christ," based on verses 1-2. (1) The Christian life is a risen life, 1*a*; (2) The aims of the Christian life—**seek those things which are above,** 1*b*; (3) The discipline of the Christian life—**Set your affection on things above,** 2.

3. *Christ Shall Appear* (3:4)

Christ . . . is our life. He is the Source of it. That life is experienced here and now. **Shall appear** is the only reference to the Second Coming in this brief Epistle. That which is hidden or reserved will be revealed to the whole world in majestic and terrible reality (Matt. 24:27, 31). **With him** has both a mystical (3:1) and an eschatological fulfillment (3:4)—the believer **will appear with him in glory,** that is, in heaven at the end of the age.

B. A Thorough Renunciation, 3:5-11

A mystical theology that has no practical ethical outcome is spurious, says the apostle. Paul's emphasis throughout his Epistles is on holiness of heart and life as the fruit of the believer's relation to Christ. He is not concerned for ceremonial sainthood, but for moral holiness. His doctrine is the seed of ethical duty.[3] Righteousness is the logical outcome of and is dependent upon living contact with the risen Christ (Gal. 2:20). Herein is the

[2]Liddell and Scott, *op. cit.,* in loco.

[3]Maclaren, *op. cit.,* p. 261.

source of the strength to follow Christ as opposed to the Gnostic teaching (2:23).

1. *Renounce Sensual Evil* (3:5-7)

Mortify (5) speaks of a slaying, not the abuse of the body for merit. The evil use of the members of the body for the gratification of self is to cease. The act is crucial, decisive (aorist).[4] The RSV says, "Put to death what is earthly in you." Here then is the practical application of 2:20. Mortification is a turning of the will away from self to God. It is called "death." The members that are to be put to death are viewed as parts of a body of sin called the "old man" (3:9).[5] The sins listed seem to be primarily for the gratification of self and have an inward, sensual direction. They are "the modes in which the members sinfully exert themselves."[6] Phillips lists them as "sexual immorality, dirty-mindedness, uncontrolled passion, evil desire." It seems that not only **covetousness** should be taken as **idolatry** (as some hold),[7] but that all the sins listed are also of the essence of false worship. Anything in the place of God in our lives is **idolatry. Mortify** (imperative) shows that the believer has a vital part in the death of evil practices. The believer's part complements God's work in qualifying us for salvation (1:12). Someone has suggested the figure that the plane is provided but the flight depends very much upon the pilot.

This death to all evil action and desire is consistent because the believer has already died with Christ (3; 2:20). What has been done in a crisis experience of divine grace must now be worked out decisively and continuously in daily life. (See comment on 1:21*b*-22. The aorist tense denotes punctiliar action without regard to time.) The slaying is necessary likewise because of the **wrath of God** (6) toward these sins, the evil use of the members of the body. **Wrath** (*orge*) means, not vindictive evil, but righteous judgment. God is terribly righteous. Maclaren points out that wrath is inevitable if God is holy.[8] **Cometh**

[4]A. S. Peake, "The Epistle to the Colossians," *The Expositor's Greek Testament*, ed. by W. Robertson Nicoll (New York: Hodder and Stoughton, n.d.), III, 537-38.

[5]See note on 3:9.

[6]Vincent, *op. cit.*, p. 502.

[7]Peake, *op. cit.*, p. 538.

[8]*Op. cit.*, pp. 279-80.

(present tense) shows that God is *now* actively opposed to evil-doers.[9] **Children** (lit., sons) **of disobedience** is omitted in some manuscripts and is thought to have been added from the parallel passage in Eph. 5:6. The phrase, however, logically fits here, and probably should be retained as in the ASV.[10] **In the which** (7) might be translated "among whom," referring back to their former associates with whom they walked in fellowship when they **lived** (imperfect, "were living") in sin themselves. **Some time** means "once" or "formerly." The memory of their former life and associates in moral degradation is a further incentive for the slayings.[11] Or the passage might simply mean that "their conduct and their condition agreed."[12]

2. *Put Off Social Evil* (3:8-11)

a. A Stripping (8-9). **Put off** (8; aorist middle) means to strip off completely as when undressing. It complements "mortify" (5), which is also aorist. Both indicate decisiveness. Thus, the "slaying" which ends sin in one decisive blow is now stated under another figure. After the crisis follows the living out of that decision in daily life. That which is earthly must now be "stripped off." With the heart now firmly fixed to its true heavenly lodestar it will proceed continuously toward its projected destiny; it refuses the attraction of other influences that would draw it off its course.

Paul lists a few of the sins that are to be **put off.** They seem to have social direction; that is, against others. Concerning **anger** Lightfoot says, "Stoic thinkers had distinguished *thymon* **(wrath)** as the outburst of *orgen* **(anger)** [; the latter was] the settled and continuing condition."[13] **Malice** (*kakian*) is the intention to do harm, and means evil, trouble, or culpable wickedness. As the others are against man, so **blasphemy** should be understood here as railing or slander against man.[14] This is the primary meaning of the Greek *blasphemia* (cf. NASB, RSV).

[9]*Ibid.*

[10]Nestle, *op. cit.*, in loco, footnotes.

[11]Maclaren, *op. cit.*, pp. 282-83.

[12]Vincent, *op. cit.*, p. 502.

[13]Quoted in C. F. D. Moule, *op. cit.*, p. 118. See William Barclay, *Flesh and Spirit* (Nashville: Abingdon Press, 1962), p. 52.

[14]Peake, *op. cit.*, p. 538.

Filthy communication is suggestive, evil talk.[15] Barclay says of words of this nature that when they are used in the singular they speak of the quality of the deed, when they are in the plural they serve as examples of the deeds.[16]

Lie not (9) is, literally, "lie not to yourself" and suggests that one who lies may come to believe his own falsehoods. To **lie not** is the naturally expected result of the act of renunciation; such is the force of the word **seeing.** One is to put into daily practice what has been done once for all in coming to Christ. The adopted child is now to live in harmony with his new environment and to grow. **Put off** (aorist) equals "disrobe" and once again shows the necessity of man's participation and responsibility in the life of righteousness growing out of faith in Christ.

The old man with his deeds has been variously interpreted. It appears in this instance to refer to the whole of the nature and former life of sin before one has met Christ in saving faith. There are only three instances where this phrase is used (Rom. 6:6; Eph. 4:22; and here). W. T. Purkiser says, "Paul speaks of him only to indicate what disposition is to be made of him."[17] Vincent says that the "old man" is the unrenewed self.[18] Purkiser adds, "It should be recognized that the 'old man' may refer to the whole of the former sinful life as well as the cause or root from which that life springs."[19] J. B. Chapman points out that the **old man** which is to be **put off** should not be equated with the self, as though our human nature should be put off. The self continues to exist after the "dying," but it exists with a new pattern of life.[20] Brockett says that the **old man** is the old pattern of life. He suggests the figure of weaving the fabric of life from an old or a new pattern.[21] He also says that the **old man** is "my sinful state as a child of Adam."[22] If the **old man** is the unrenewed self, then the "new man" (10) is the renewed self.

[15]Other lists: Gal. 5:20; Eph. 4:29-31. [16]*Op. cit.*, p. 23.

[17]*Op. cit.*, p. 58.

[18]*Op. cit.*, p. 503.

[19]*Op. cit.*, p. 89, note 14.

[20]Referred to in Purkiser, *op. cit.*, p. 61.

[21]*Scriptural Freedom from Sin* (Kansas City: Nazarene Publishing House, 1941), p. 100. Cf. the discussion on Rom. 6:6 and Eph. 4:22, BBC.

[22]*Ibid.*, p. 58.

It is confusing to some to read that the self should die or be crucified; and it is poor psychology to equate the self with the old man that is put off. However, in a sense it might be said that the self "dies" to the old life when the former sinful life is put off. Paul elsewhere uses a similar figure when he points out that the wife is dead to the law that binds her to her husband, when the husband dies, even though she goes on living (Rom. 7:1-6).[23] Thus Paul can correctly say that he himself is "crucified with Christ" (Rom. 6:6; Gal. 2:20). He is "dead indeed unto sin," though he is now very much "alive unto God" (Rom. 6:11).

b. Put On the New Nature (10:11). **Put on** (aorist) continues the figure of robing. The **new man** is the "new creature" in Christ Jesus (John 3:3; II Cor. 5:17). It is the **renewed** self, the regenerated, sanctified self. **Renewed** (present participle) speaks not of the "old Adam" gradually being transformed into something better, but rather of the new man, already existing in Christ, progressively actualized in the Christian community. The renewing is a continuing actualization, a renewal, as the physical body is constantly renewed.[24] **Image** recalls man's nature as originally created in the image of God (Gen. 1:26-27). **Created** reminds us of Christ, the Creator (1:16), and the new creation (II Cor. 5:17). Man's re-created self is thus after the image of Christ.

In such a world of new men there can be no caste (11). Only sin disqualifies one for salvation—not race, rites, or culture. Christ is in every believer and he in Christ, whatever his station. National, religious, cultural, and social prejudices all disappear within the thoroughly Christian community (I Cor. 15:28; Eph. 1:23; 4:6). **Scythian** probably refers to a fierce people who savagely invaded Jewry in the seventh century B.C.[25] Their acts of cruelty were almost unthinkable, but even such barbarian foreigners could be transformed by Christ. **Bond nor free** takes on added significance when it is recalled that the messenger, Onesimus, who carried the Colossian letter was a slave. **Christ is all, and in all** (lit., All and in all, Christ) means especially that all those in Christ are equally in Him and He in them. Therefore He is all that matters. In addition, all the universe has its source and continuance in Him.

[23]Purkiser, *op. cit.*, p. 61.

[24]C. F. D. Moule, *op. cit.*, p. 120.

[25]Vincent, *op. cit.*, p. 504.

C. Moral Responsibility, 3:12—4:6

Chapters 1 and 2 referred primarily to God's part in man's reconciliation. Chapter 3 emphasizes man's obligation growing therefrom. Having disposed of the negative responsibility, Paul now speaks concisely of the positive ethical responsibilities of the Christian life.

1. *Personal Ethics* (3:12-17)

"Put on" in v. 10 anticipates **put on** in v. 12, which begins a practical application of the all-inclusive, once-for-all decision. **Elect of God** speaks of "grace" and "covenant" (I Pet. 2:9). The Church is the true Israel (Gal. 3:7), and is called the **elect.** Believers are called **holy and beloved. Holy** again stresses the ethical note, for the new nature must correspond with the new calling[26] (1:2). **Beloved** raises the believer to the heights and privileges of 1:13. **Bowels** (*splangkna*) is literally "compassion," or heart of mercy. **Humbleness of mind** and **meekness** suggest a willingness to accept the will of God in all things (I Thess. 5:18). **Longsuffering** forgoes retaliation. **Forbearing . . . and forgiving** (13) was especially necessary because of the bitterness of the disputes that must have arisen over the issues revealed by this letter.[27] Carson says that **forgiving one another** is a corporate idea here and should be, literally, "forgive yourselves."[28] **As Christ forgave** provides the *reason* for such noble action (Matt. 6:12, 14-15), a guiding *principle* and an *example* in forgiveness. **Charity** (14; love) is the capstone of all the building blocks (2:7) of the moral structure. It is the fundamental ethical principle and the sum of all moral law (Rom. 13:10; Gal. 5:14). It is viewed as **the bond of perfectness** or "girdle" that binds together the "clothing" that has just been "put on." Both the graces and the Christian persons are bound together by love (*agape*—divine love) which is imparted with the indwelling Christ (1:27). Here is "Christian perfection" properly so called.

Thus a thoroughgoing righteousness, looking toward a reconciliation that is worldwide (11) in its potential outreach, follows the divine-human reconciliation. The horizontal relationship

[26]C. F. D. Moule, *op. cit.*, p. 123.

[27]Herman Olshausen, *Biblical Commentary of the New Testament* (New York: Sheldon and Co., 1872), V, 232.

[28]*Op. cit.*, p. 87.

must match the vertical. Christ, indwelling the believer, gives him His mind and spirit in all things. The "old man" of hate and enmity is dead. The love which binds the Church together and to her Christ is primarily directed to the "household" of saints (Rom. 12:13; Gal. 6:10), that is, those within the Christian fellowship. Then it is to be directed toward those "without" (4:5),[29] that is, the world of unbelievers, in order to draw them into the "elect" circle.

Peace of God (15) is, rather, "peace of Christ," which is to **rule,** or be the principle for settling all future disputes of doctrine and practice. **In one body** reminds us that the harmony of the various members that are incorporated mystically into the body of Christ is essential to the fulfillment of its use by Christ as His body. The whole organism responds diligently and obediently to do what the Head dictates. **And be ye thankful** (1:3, 12; 4:2) is the inevitable response of one who has come to know the meaning of grace.

The **word** (16) is the Bible, Christ's words more properly speaking. **Dwell** means "make its home" in the heart and mind. The **word** must have a welcome and permanent dwelling place (see 1:19 on "dwell"). The Christian must know the **word** so well that it remains in the heart and mind, ruling all the actions and presiding over all decisions. That Word is the only basis or qualification for **teaching and admonishing** another. Paul advises according to his own practice (1:28); he preaches only Christ.

Both logically and grammatically, **psalms and hymns and spiritual songs** should go with **singing** rather than with **teaching and admonishing.**[30] If the phrase belongs with **teaching,** then the music should be performed for the edification of others and not for personal pleasure or glory. **With grace** means "gratefully" or with the grace of God, that is, with spiritual understanding (I Cor. 14:26; Eph. 5:19). This can be done **in your hearts** under any circumstance when done **to the Lord.** The realization of the infinite and unmerited grace of God makes our praises possible. Such praise is given in the heart as well as on the lips when true worship exists. **To the Lord** should rather be "to God." These abilities to sing, praise, worship, and speak dis-

[29]See Carson, note 28.
[30]See RSV.

tinguish man from mere animal and help to answer the question, "What is man?" (Heb. 2:6-13)

In 4:12, 15-16 we see some of the basic tools of the trade, so to speak, and are given an insight into the religious services and practices of the Early Church.

Whatsoever ye do (17) is a summarizing principle of Christian ethics. Verse 23 is its twin. Specific rules are minimal in the New Testament economy of grace. Personal and specific ethics may be arrived at from principles and example made known by Christ. He is no respecter of persons in this regard. Note the extent of this principle—it applies to every aspect of conduct—**whatsoever** and **all. Do** (aorist) indicates a *settled course of action* (1:10). **In the name of the Lord Jesus** provides the inspiration for all moral conduct. Some manuscripts add "Christ" here.[31] The works of Christ are fulfilled in the work of the believer. This phrase is much like the phrase "in Christ."[32] Paul continues with the reason—only grace can make **thanks** possible in man, who is naturally rebellious, ungrateful, and helpless to perform true Christian duties. **To God** reminds us of the *Object* of ethics (23). And **by him** (Christ) reveals the *energy* by which the Christian life is lived, and the *channel* (*dia*) through whom all rises to the throne of the Father.

2. *Domestic Responsibilities* (3:18-21)

The "in Christ" formula is put into operation here in human relationships, both personal and social. Christian teachings oppose pagan ideas by pointing up the reciprocal nature of duties,[33] and by relating all to a Person who is the Measure and End of all ethics and duties.[34] All men have equal rights, duties, and responsibilities. God is no respecter of persons (25). "In Christ" provides the motive, conditions, and quality of the deeds to be performed.[35] Paul here singles out a few relationships where the principle is applied—husband and wife, parents and children, master and slave.

[31]Nestle, *op. cit.*, in loco.

[32]Carson, *op. cit.*, p. 91.

[33]C. F. D. Moule, *op. cit.*, p. 127.

[34]E. Stanley Jones, *The Word Became Flesh* (New York: Abingdon Press, 1963), pp. 29-30.

[35]C. F. D. Moule, *op. cit.*, p. 128.

a. Role of the Wife (3:18). Though male and female are one in Christ, it is appropriate for the wife to **submit** to the husband, for Adam was first formed, then Eve. Even the Son is subject to the Father (I Cor. 15:28). Moule says that submission means "loyalty."[36] Such a union as that of huband and wife is fashioned after the heavenly relation of Christ and His Church.[37] **Own** should be omitted on manuscript evidence, though the word is included in the parallel passage in Eph. 5:22. The fidelity and submission of the wife presume love from the husband (19). Verses 18 and 19 set up a working partnership. **As it is fit in the Lord** limits the area of submission;[38] it sets up Christian principles as the guides to domestic decisions.

b. Role of the Husband (3:19). **Love** for the wife is the noblest love (*agape*), that is also due God. **Be not bitter** or harsh is a counsel of regard for the weaker vessel (I Thess. 4:3-5; I Pet. 4:7). Love will exclude bitterness, commands, and selfishness. The new life in Christ transforms the home. Husband and wife relationships are here envisaged as mutually respectful and tranquil.

c. Role of the Children (3:20). Given love and respect in the home, obedience is more likely. **Children** are to **obey their parents.** The word means literally "to listen under" or "to look up to."[39] **Well pleasing unto the Lord** keeps the relationship Christian and provides the motive for obedience. Each pleases the other when each pleases God (1:10); likewise, each pleases God when both seek the good of the other.

d. Role of the Father (3:21). **Fathers** are advised to use restraint and wisdom in discipline so that they do not cause their children to lose heart. **To anger** is omitted in some manuscripts,[40] as reflected in the italics of KJV. **Provoke not** (present imperative) means not to nag as a habit.[41] On the contrary, fathers should lend all responsible encouragement to the growing, developing child.

[36]*Ibid.*

[37]Maclaren, *op. cit.*, p. 337.

[38]Robertson, *op. cit.*, p. 506.

[39]*Ibid.*

[40]Nestle, *op. cit.*, in loco.

[41]Robertson, *op. cit.*, p. 507.

3. *Economic and Social Responsibilities* (3:22—4:1)

The subject of slavery is included here, probably due to the fact that Onesimus, Philemon's runaway slave who was returning as a Christian, carried the letter from the sensitive apostle to the Colossians.

It is suggested that this passage does not condone slavery as such. It is rather a setting forth of Christian economic principles. The **masters** of that day are the employers of today, and the **servants** (slaves) are the hired workers. The master must give a fair and just wage, and the laborer must give a fair and full day's labor. Both employer and employee are responsible to God in this regard (4:1).

It is also suggested that this passage is one of several areas of responsibility clustered around the ethical principles in 17 and 23. Thus this advice on social relationships is an outgrowth of 3:17, and not a section standing alone.

a. Role of the Slave (3:22-25). A slave in Paul's day was a piece of property to be owned, but a Christian slave was a person to be received as a brother (Philem. 16). Here the apostle does not seek to upset immediately the existing social order by any violent action. But he does doom its evil structure by injecting Christian principles into civil society. These principles will work as leaven in the dough, eventually to penetrate the whole of society and to transform it after Christ's way. Therefore **servants** (22) should still, as Christians, **obey** their **masters** (Rom. 13: 1 ff.). Paul nowhere suggests disobedience to civil authority, though his fellow apostles support the principle under some circumstances (Acts 5:29). Paul counsels respect for law and order as the will of God. He advises obedience to civil law, but wherever there are evils, to transform them by orderly means (4:1). **Eyeservice** is perhaps an original word with Paul.[42] It indicates self-seeking and obedience only while the master is looking.[43] Phillips translates **with singleness of heart,** "as a sincere expression of your devotion to the Lord." **Fearing God** is to please Him, and by so doing, to fulfill oneself (1:12). The **reward** (24) is not so much in terms of material things as in terms of God's approval. **Christ** is their **Lord** (Master), for they

[42]C. F. D. Moule, *op. cit.*, p. 130.

[43]Robertson, *op. cit.*

really serve Him when they live according to this teaching (17).

Verse 25 indicates the law of divine retribution. Wrongdoing is punished uniformly—without **respect of persons,** slave and master alike.

b. Role of the Master (4:1). **Masters** are shown also to be **servants** (slaves) of their **Master in heaven.** Therefore they too must be obedient. To **give** to their **servants** (slaves) **that which is just and equal** is really advice to the master to free his slaves. It is to receive them as brothers (Philem. 16). The golden rule comes to mind here (3:13*b*). All masters, even those who are evil, are ultimately responsible to God, the **Master in heaven.**

As the previous section had a principle from which domestic ethics were derived, so this section has a principle for economic ethics in 3:23. All is to be done "as to the Lord." Paul stresses this basis. It is Christ, not rules (Gal. 3:21-28). He is the *Means,* the *Motive,* the *Measure,* and the *Object* of all ethics.

Ethical conduct that has its spring and end in any other principle than the glory of the Lord Jesus Christ is not Christian ethics. The Christian sings, "To God be the glory; great things He hath done."[44] And with Mary in the Magnificat he says, "My soul doth magnify the Lord. For he that is mighty hath done to me great things" (Luke 1:46, 49).

4. *Evangelistic Responsibilities* (4:2-6)

Christianity is a missionary faith, and in order for the **mystery of Christ** (3) to be proclaimed properly, Paul pleads for an opportunity to do so, and sets before the Colossians an example.

a. Opportunity (4:2-4). Once again the apostle joins **prayer** with **thanksgiving** (2; 1:3, 9, 12), and that, because all good comes from God. **Continue** emphasizes the need for the Christian to remain in a constant attitude of communion with God (Rom. 12:12). **Prayer** is also here joined with **watch,** as Jesus exhorted His disciples in the Garden (Matt. 26:41). Thomas beautifully says, "We are not to watch ourselves, which would be depressing; we are not to watch Satan, which would be distracting; we are not to watch our sins, which would be dishearten-

[44]Fanny Crosby.

ing; but we are to keep our gaze fixed on Christ, 'looking off unto Jesus.' "[45]

Thanksgiving must be important, for Paul mentions it often. It is the chief means of developing that proper love and appreciation for Christ and all that He has done for us. It serves to keep ever before us our dependence upon Him.

This call to prayer is really a request by Paul for opportunity to spread the word about Christ (Eph. 6:18-19). He says, **Pray for us** (3). This note is often on his lips, for there are many adversaries (I Cor. 16:9; II Cor. 2:11-12). The expression **that God would open . . . a door** reminds us that, even though the spread of the gospel is under divine direction (Acts 16:7), it is also subject to Satanic hindrances (I Thess. 2:18). Perhaps Paul wishes to be freed from prison if God wills it. However, bound or free, he will still **speak the mystery of Christ.** Paul is no coward. What he really prays for is the removal of any obstacles to the fulfillment of his commission. Verse 4 is a request for ability in preaching (Eph. 6:18-19). Our problem as ministers and Christian teachers was his problem too. It is the problem of making the gospel message clear, for such is the force of **as I ought.**

Under the theme "Continue in Prayer," we see (1) The *need* of prayer, 2; (2) The *value* of prayer, 3; (3) The *purpose* of prayer, 4.

This brief piece on prayer is remarkable in what Paul excludes from his requests. It reveals that his one passion is to be useful to his Lord. To live for Christ is not enough, though that is necessary. His great desire is to be enabled to speak the gospel clearly and convincingly.

b. Example (4:5-6). To preach is also insufficient. The gospel must be lived. Example and influence are important. As v. 1 speaks of the Christian's conduct *within* the Christian community, so v. 5 speaks of the Christian's conduct toward those **without**—outside the Christian community. **Walk in wisdom** (5; cf. 2:6) is to behave with tact. The phrase **toward them that are without** is pregnant with meaning. It reveals Paul's lament, his sense of mission, and his driving impulse. Here is the secret of his drawing and persuasive power on the unbelievers. He makes people

[45]*Op. cit.*, pp. 108-9.

realize that he loves them. Here the soul of the evangelist and the missionary is laid bare.[46]

Redeeming the time (cf. Eph. 5:16) means that no opportunity for witnessing should be passed up. It suggests that timing in this important work is fundamental. The Christian must seize the initiative. And especially appropriate for our day, it should remind us that time is running out for this redemptive work. Paul was evangelizing all the time. In the Colossian situation, where false teaching was rampant, he urged the believers to take advantage of the season to spread the truth—and precisely so "because the days are evil" (Eph. 5:16).

The Christian's **speech** (6) should be graceful (from *charis*, **grace**, which signifies the Greek idea of beauty). Even the ordinary things will be affected by our being in Christ. Our speech must be worthy of Him (3:17, 23). **Seasoned with salt** suggests that our words should be palatable and sensible. **That ye may know how ye ought to answer every man** points up our Christian obligation to be well informed about our faith.

Paul has shown that the fruit of a proper understanding and experience of Christ is ethical holiness. Further, it is seen that righteous living is the evidence of correct teaching (1:7-8). The new life in Christ supplants the old life in sins (II Cor. 5:17). The issues have been joined, the false teachers exposed, and the whole matter is now left to God because of Paul's confidence in the power of truth.

[46]*Ibid.*, p. 110.

Section V Farewell

Colossians 4:7-18

The number and importance of the subjects dealt with in such depth and in so few words in this Epistle are staggering. Paul had outside help—help from above. It is no less apparent in this concluding passage. These verses speak of the close fellowship of the believers. Each one is consumed by the same interests; all are interdependent members of Christ's body. There is deep mutual regard for each other, as indicated by such words as **comfort** (8), **labouring** (12), **beloved** (14).

Paul gives a clear insight into the *spirit* of these men. They are filled with faithfulness (7), love (9), forgiveness (10), prayer and devotion (12), and zeal (13). The list of noble traits is long.

Elements of worship in the Early Church are also revealed. They met in their own homes (15). They sang hymns and gospel songs (3:16). They read the Scriptures (16), offered fervent prayers (12), and ministered to each other within the Christian circle according to their abilities (8, 14).

These were men consumed by a sense of mission and destiny. They are called (17), sent (8), servants (deacons, 12), responsible in redemptive matters (12, 17) even unto imprisonment (10).

Further, the *individual* is not lost in the new spiritual community. The identity and role of each person are preserved. They are pray-ers, physicians, preachers, givers, messengers, servants, and sufferers. Each does his duty with varying intensity (12-13). The types of personality are shown by the characteristics and labors of each. Their relationships are close and continuing (10).

The greetings are noble and affectionate, adapted to each person mentioned. Paul, with honest appraisal and accurate estimate of all (note the reserve in speaking of Demas, v. 14), points up his respect for each individual. One would infer that he has power to evoke the highest loyalty and service from other men.

The letter carries Paul's signature written by his own **hand** (18). There is a simple request, and a final prayer that the highest and best which God has to offer may be theirs.

The apostle makes his appropriate comments by noting the individuals in order; first the messengers, then the fellow Jews who are with him, and finally the Gentiles.

A. The Addressers, 4:7-14

1. *Messengers* (4:7-9)

a. Tychicus (4:7-8). **Tychicus** is the messenger carrying the letter and he will supplement the written message with his own verbal report (Eph. 6:21). He is technically not a deacon,[1] but is mentioned five times in the New Testament (Acts 20:4-5; Eph. 6:21; II Tim. 4:12; Titus 3:12; and here). His mission is twofold, to give a report from Paul and to gain information for the apostle; this seems to be the intent of the words **know your estate** (8). Tychicus is called a **faithful minister and fellowservant in the Lord.** The relationship between Paul and this fellow Christian is determined by their relation to the Lord—they are both in Christ.

b. Onesimus (4:9). **Onesimus** is the slave of Philemon, recently converted and thus **a faithful and beloved brother.** He is returning to his master in company with Tychicus. Paul says to the church at Colossae, He is now **one of you.** The apostle thus vouches for Onesimus' Christian experience and inclusion in the mystical body of Christ. Though a slave, he is a new man in Christ. He, too, has a testimony and a report to make known.

2. *Fellow Jews* (4:10-11)

a. Aristarchus (4:10). **Aristarchus,** captured in the Ephesian uproar (Acts 19:29), is a prisoner with Paul in Rome. Some suggest that he is only a metaphorical prisoner. But this is hardly an acceptable conclusion in light of Acts 27:2, which states that he accompanied Paul to Rome.

b. Mark (4:10). **Marcus** (John Mark), a failure as recorded in Acts 13, is now restored, accepted, and recommended by the apostle.[2] Some must still hold reservations about him, but Paul

[1]C. F. D. Moule, *op. cit.*, p. 136.

[2]Some suggest that this reference argues for an early date for the Colossian Epistle. Demas (14) is still with him at any rate. See Introduction on date.

would dispel them all (II Tim. 4:11). It is not known when or how the Colossians had **received commandments.** They may have been sent personally and orally by a messenger or conveyed in an earlier letter. **Receive him** is better translated, "welcome him." Mark, unlike Demas, represents those fellow workers who will not give up.

c. Jesus (4:11). **Jesus** was a common name among the first-century Jews. It would be natural for a Christian to be hesitant to use this sacred name; hence among his fellow Christians he was **called Justus.** He, Aristarchus, and Mark are the only persons **of the circumcision** (Jews) with Paul. The question is raised why there were so few converted Jews. It may be lamentable that so few were faithful or it may be a cause for rejoicing that so few had been imprisoned. **Fellowworkers unto the kingdom** is better translated "fellow workers for the kingdom of God" (RSV). Paul says that they are a **comfort** to him.

3. *Gentiles* (4:12-14)

a. Epaphras (4:12-13). **Epaphras** is the pastor from Colossae (1:7-8). Here Paul gives his estimate of the man. He penetrates to the heart and mission of Epaphras—**that ye may stand perfect and complete in all the will of God** (12). This is the pastor's prayer for the sanctification of his flock. Here also is an insight into what Paul considers most essential in the ministry (cf. 1:28). Once again the importance of prayer is shown. **Labouring fervently** (lit., agonizing, *agonizomenos*) **for you in prayers** (cf. 2:1) is like the agony of Christ in the Garden.[3] **Perfect** (*teleioi*) in this reference means not only "complete" but it has a moral content also (cf. 1:28). **Complete** (a participle) modifies **the will of God** and calls to mind 2:10.[4] It signifies full assurance (2:2) and entire commitment to the revelation given and to **the will of God** (1:9). **Zeal** (*ponon;* 13) signifies hard labor or pain.[5] Aristarchus had a home mission concern. His ministry included churches in three communities—Colossae, **Laodicea,** and **Hierapolis.**

b. Luke (4:14*a*). **Luke, the beloved physician,** joined the party at Troas (Acts 16:10). This is verified by the fact that

[3]C. F. D. Moule, *op. cit.,* p. 138.

[4]See comments there.

[5]Liddell and Scott, *op. cit.,* in loco.

the author of Acts (Luke) introduces the personal pronoun "we" for the first time at that point. The statement in v. 11 that only Aristarchus, Mark, and Justus are Jews is the chief evidence that Luke was a Gentile.[6] Note that two Gospel writers (Mark and Luke) are with Paul. This intimate association assures accurate information and authoritative human sources for Paul's own writings.[7] Note also that Luke is the only Gentile New Testament writer and that he was with Paul to the end (II Tim. 4:11).

c. *Demas* (4:14*b*). Colossians and Philemon (cf. v. 24) were written prior to the defection of **Demas** and the writing of II Timothy (II Tim. 4:10). At this writing (the Colossian letter) Paul says nothing about Demas, a singular silence suggesting doubt or fear concerning him.

B. The Addressees, 4:15-17

Attention is now directed to the brethren of the Colossian and Laodicean churches.

1. *Nymphas* (4:15-16)

Nymphas was the leader or pastor of the Christian congregation in Laodicea. There are two possible readings for the pronoun describing the place where the church met. It can be either masculine or feminine; that is, **his** or "her" **house.**[8] Since Paul is saluting brethren, the masculine seems to be the more appropriate form. It was a house church where the disciples worshiped (cf. Rom. 16:5; I Cor. 16:19). From v. 16 it is to be noted that the Colossian letter was to be read in both churches. In addition it appears that there was a letter addressed to Laodicea, which has been lost. Some suggest that the letter to the Ephesians is meant here. **From Laodicea** (16) must mean a letter from Paul written to Laodicea; it could hardly be a letter from Laodicea to Paul.[9]

2. *Archippus* (4:17).

Archippus was favored with a special message from Paul. It was a word of caution regarding his **ministry** which had been

[6]C. F. D. Moule, *op. cit.*, p. 137.

[7]*Ibid.*

[8]Nestle, *op. cit.*, in loco.

[9]Carson, *op. cit.*, pp. 101-2.

given **in the Lord** (cf. Philem. 2). Some suggest that Archippus needed this word of exhortation because he was lax.[10] Perhaps **Take heed** (*blepe,* see) is a warning about the devious ways of the Gnostics.

C. Signature, 4:18

The salutation by the hand of Paul probably means that the apostle took the pen from his scribe and in his own handwriting added v. 18. In these closing words Paul reminds the Colossians of his suffering in their behalf. But **remember my bonds** is more than a call for sympathy. It is also a statement of his concern and calling under the Great Commission. It is he, their leader, who is bound. But we must recall that he is bound *to Christ* as well as bound *by Rome.*

Grace, unmerited favor from the Lord, is the sum of the gospel message. It is Paul's final prayer for Colossae.

[10]Jamieson, Fausset, and Brown, *op. cit.,* in loco.

Bibliography

I. COMMENTARIES

BARRY, ALFRED. *The Epistle to the Ephesians, Philippians, and Colossians.* "Bible Commentary." Edited by CHARLES JOHN ELLICOTT. London: Cassell and Co., Ltd., n.d.

BRUCE, F. F. *Colossians.* "The New International Commentary on the New Testament." Grand Rapids: Wm. B. Eerdmans Publishing Co., 1957.

CALVIN, JOHN. *Commentary on the Epistles of Paul the Apostle to the Philippians, Colossians, and Thessalonians.* Translated by JOHN PRINGLE. Edinburgh: T. Constable, 1851.

CARSON, HERBERT M. *The Epistles of Paul to the Colossians and Philemon.* "Tyndale New Testament Commentaries." Grand Rapids: Wm. B. Eerdmans Publishing Co., 1960.

CLARKE, ADAM. *The New Testament of Our Lord and Saviour Jesus Christ,* Vol. II. New York: Abingdon-Cokesbury Press, n.d.

HENRY, MATTHEW. *Commentary on the Whole Bible,* Vol. VI. New York: Fleming H. Revell Co., n.d.

JAMIESON, ROBERT, FAUSSET, S. R., BROWN, DAVID. *A Bible Commentary,* Vol. II. New York: Fleming H. Revell Co., n.d.

MACLAREN, ALEXANDER. *The Epistles of St. Paul to the Colossians and Philemon.* "The Expositor's Bible." Edited by W. ROBERTSON NICOLL. New York: A. C. Armstrong and Son, 1903.

MOULE, C. F. D. *The Epistles of Paul the Apostle to the Colossians and to Philemon.* "The Cambridge Greek Testament Commentary." Cambridge: University Press, 1957.

MOULE, H. C. G. *The Epistles to the Colossians and to Philemon.* "The Cambridge Bible for Schools and Colleges." Cambridge: University Press, 1893.

OLSHAUSEN, HERMAN. *Biblical Commentary on the New Testament,* Vol. V. New York: Sheldon and Co., 1872.

PEAKE, A. S. "The Epistle to the Colossians," *The Expositor's Greek Testament.* Edited by W. ROBERTSON NICOLL, Vol. III. New York: Hodder and Stoughton, n.d.

ROBERTSON, A. T. *Word Pictures in the New Testament,* Vol. IV. New York: Harper and Brothers Publishers, 1931.

SCHMOLLER, OTTO. "Galatians," *Commentary on the Whole Bible.* Edited by JOHN PETER LANGE. Translated by PHILIP SCHAFF. New York: Charles Scribner's Sons, 1886.

VINCENT, MARVIN R. *Word Studies in the New Testament,* Vol. III. Grand Rapids: Wm. B. Eerdmans Publishing Co., 1946.

II. OTHER BOOKS

BARCLAY, WILLIAM. *Flesh and Spirit.* Nashville: Abingdon Press, 1962.

———. *The Promise of the Spirit.* Philadelphia: The Westminster Press, 1960.

Brockett, Henry E. *Scriptural Freedom from Sin.* Kansas City: Nazarene Publishing House, 1941.

Conybeare, W. J., and Howson, J. S. *The Life and Epistles of the Apostle Paul.* New York: Thomas Y. Crowell and Company, Publishers, n.d.

Farrar, F. W. *Texts Explained.* New York: George H. Doran, Co., 1899.

Goodspeed, Edgar J. *The Story of the New Testament.* Chicago: University of Chicago Press, 1916.

Gordon, A. J. *In Christ.* New York: Fleming H. Revell Company, 1880.

Gould, J. Glenn. *The Precious Blood of Christ.* Kansas City: Beacon Hill Press, 1951.

Hickie, W. J. *Greek-English Lexicon.* New York: The Macmillan Co., 1934.

Jessop, Harry E. *Foundations of Doctrine.* Chicago: The Chicago Evangelistic Institute, 1944.

Jones, E. Stanley. *The Word Became Flesh.* New York: Abingdon Press, 1963.

Knox, John. *Chapters in a Life of Paul.* New York: Abingdon Press, n.d.

Knox, Wilfred. *St. Paul.* D. Appleton Company, 1932.

Liddell and Scott. *Greek-English Lexicon.* New York: American Book Company, 1882.

Mackintosh, H. R. *The Doctrine of the Person of Jesus Christ.* Edinburgh: T. & T. Clark, 1912.

Nestle, E. Eberhard. *Novum Testamentum Graece.* Stuttgart: Privilegierte Wurttembergische Bibelanstalt, 1936.

Purkiser, W. T. *Sanctification and Its Synonyms.* Kansas City: Beacon Hill Press, 1962.

Roberts, Alexander. *Companion to the Revised Version.* New York: Cassell, Petter, Galpin and Co., 1881.

Sangster, W. E. *The Path to Perfection.* New York: Abingdon-Cokesbury Press, 1943.

Simpson, A. B. *All in All or Christ in Colossians.* New York: Christian Alliance Publishing Co., n.d.

Thomas, W. H. Griffith. *Christ Preeminent.* Chicago: The Bible Institute Colportage Assn., 1923.

Wood, C. T. *The Life, Letters and Religion of St. Paul.* Edinburgh: T. & T. Clark, 1925.

III. ARTICLES

Holum, John R. "If Scientists Create Life." *Christianity Today,* Vol. VIII, No. 7 (January 3, 1964), p. 3.

The First and Second Epistles to the THESSALONIANS

Arnold E. Airhart

Introduction

A. The City of Thessalonica

For more than twenty centuries Thessalonica (see map 1; the modern name is Salonika) has maintained a position of importance as a center of Greek influence. It was founded in 315 B.C. by the Macedonian king, Cassander, and named after his wife, who was a sister of Alexander the Great. In later Roman times it was made a political capital, and in 42 B.C. was given the status of a "free city" because it had sided with Antony and Octavius in the Second Civil War. As a free city, it appointed its own magistrates, called "politarchs" ("rulers of the city," Acts 17:6).

Thessalonica was located on the Egnatian Road, the great highway which linked East and West. Possessing a famous harbor, it was in Paul's day a strategic converging point of culture and commerce, a great and thriving center. Cicero spoke of it as "placed in the lap of the Empire."[1] In world trade, in Hellenistic culture, in Roman government, in Jewish influence, and subsequently in Christian missionary strategy, it was a key center.

B. The Founding of the Church

When Paul and his companions set sail from Troas across the Aegean Sea and landed in Macedonia, the Christian missionary invasion of Europe had begun (Acts 16:6-12). Leaving Philippi, it would appear from Acts 17:1 that they deliberately selected Thessalonica as a strategic center in which to found a church.[2] The story is told in Acts 17:1-10. Paul preached in the synagogue for three Sabbaths, but it is possible to think that his ministry continued there for several more weeks. Bicknell points out that this is presupposed by Paul's working at his trade (I Thess. 2:9), and by his receiving two gifts from Philippi

[1]Charles R. Erdman, *The Epistles of Paul to the Thessalonians* (Philadelphia: The Westminster Press, 1935), p. 9.

[2]Because Luke ceases at this point to use "we" in his account in Acts, it is usually held that he did not accompany the party to Thessalonica. Silas is mentioned as being there, but Timothy is not. However, from the Epistles it is clear that Timothy was present.

during this period (Phil. 4:16).[3] Further evidence concerning the length of stay in the city is found in the considerable number of converts from heathenism (cf. I Thess. 1:9). Such was Paul's success that the unbelieving Jews were "moved with envy," and caused so much trouble that Paul and Silas had to leave "by night" (Acts 17:10). They left behind them a strong, witnessing, growing church (cf. I Thessalonians 1).

C. Occasion of the First Letter

From Thessalonica the party went to Beroea (see map 1), where another church was begun. There another persecution started, instigated by Thessalonian Jews. Leaving Timothy and Silas behind, Paul journeyed to Athens (Acts 17:10-15). Because of his growing concern for the Thessalonian church, the apostle soon dispatched Timothy back to Thessalonica so that he might minister and bring back word (cf. comments on I Thess. 3:1-2). In the meantime Paul went on to Corinth, where sometime later Timothy and Silas joined him (Acts 18:5), and brought eagerly awaited news. The good report about the continuing success of the strategic missionary church caused the beleaguered apostle to rejoice exceedingly (cf. I Thess. 2:19-20 and 3:7-9). With immense relief of spirit, and in personal affection, he wrote I Thessalonians and sent it by some messenger unknown to us.

D. Place and Date of Writing

Based mainly on Acts 18:5, coupled with the other known facts, it is generally accepted that the first letter was written from Corinth. Paul's stay in that city is one of the fixed points in the Pauline chronology. While in Corinth he was brought before Gallio, the deputy, or governor of Achaia (Acts 18:12-17). Inscribed stones, found at Delphi, contain the names of the emperor Claudius and of Gallio as deputy, and a date, that of the emperor's twenty-sixth acclamation as ruler. Since governors normally held office only one year, or two at the most, it is possible to date Gallio's term in Corinth as beginning about the summer of A.D. 51. Further, since Paul stayed in Corinth for eighteen months (Acts 18:11), he was probably there a short while before Gallio's coming as governor. It is generally assumed from the narrative that he wrote I Thessalonians not long after arriving in Corinth. Thus the generally accepted date of the

[3]*The First and Second Epistles to the Thessalonians* (London: Methuen & Co., Ltd., 1932), p. xiii.

letter is A.D. 50 or possibly 51. Happily, this date serves as a kind of anchor for dating Paul's movements.

E. Purpose of the First Letter

The contents of the letter suggest strongly what information Timothy brought about the church. The letter overflows with expressions of love and encouragement. It came spontaneously out of Paul's heart. There were at least four matters of concern, however. (See extended discussion of these in the commentary.) Opposers were viciously slandering Paul's character and ministry. Because of the converts' recent association with heathen standards, there was some danger of laxity in moral matters. At least, some were tempted. Further, there was misunderstanding regarding the teaching of the Second Coming. Lastly, there appeared to be a growing problem of disrespect for leadership affecting church discipline. As a basic solution, Paul wrote pointedly of the experience of heart holiness, and of growth in Christian grace.

F. Occasion and Date of the Second Letter

Silas and Timothy were with Paul when he wrote the second letter (II Thess. 1:1). Corinth is the only known place, according to the story in Acts, where this was true prior to Paul's return to Macedonia.[4] A comparison of the two letters confirms the generally accepted view that the second letter was also written from Corinth within a short while (possibly a few weeks) after the first.[5] It is fair to assume from the letter's references that a message, either by mouth or by letter, had come back to Paul from Thessalonica following the delivery of the first letter.

G. Purpose of the Second Letter

Two of the problems dealt with in the first letter, moral laxness and the slanders against Paul, are not mentioned in the second. The first letter had doubtless had its proper effect upon those involved (cf. II Thess. 1:3 and 3:1-3).

[4]Leon Morris, *The First and Second Epistles to the Thessalonians* ("The New International Commentary on the New Testament"; Grand Rapids: Wm. B. Eerdmans Publishing Co., 1959), p. 26.

[5]A few scholars argue for the priority of II Thessalonians, reversing the order of the letters. For a good but brief discussion of this see Morris, *op. cit.*, pp. 37-41.

The misunderstandings about the Second Coming continued, however, and had taken a new turn. Paul himself was being represented as teaching a view which he vigorously denied (II Thess. 2:1-3). Besides this, the problem of the discipline of disorderly persons (arising probably out of the erroneous views of the Second Coming) had grown worse rather than better. Paul writes to correct these matters, and while doing so, includes some inspiring passages (see c. 1, and 2:13-17) to encourage the persecuted and the fainthearted.

H. Authorship of the Thessalonian Letters

The Pauline authorship of the first letter is so generally accepted as to call for no discussion here. It is well attested both externally and internally. The external evidence for Paul's authorship of the second letter is likewise, if anything, stronger than for the first.[6] Problems of authorship are found, however, by some scholars, in the contents. These have to do mostly with so-called differences between the two letters in eschatology and in tone. Strangely, some find problems in the opposite fact—a too great similarity in style which is supposed to suggest a forgery. The letter itself claims Paul's authorship, and most scholars think that any internal problems which exist are not such as to discredit the letter's genuineness.[7]

I. The Importance of These Letters

Picturing Paul dictating the first letter in Corinth, Miller writes, "It would have seemed an unimportant thing to an ordinary bystander, but it was an hour filled with tremendous import for that letter is now generally recognized as the oldest Christian writing that survives—that letter was the beginning of the New Testament."[8]

Written barely twenty years after the resurrection of Christ, these letters provide us with an important picture of the Early

[6]Bicknell, *op. cit.*, p. xxvii.

[7]For a full treatment of the question of authorship see Bicknell, *ibid.*, pp. xxiv-xxxviii; James Everett Frame, *A Critical and Exegetical Commentary on the Epistles of St. Paul to the Thessalonians* ("The International Critical Commentary"; Edinburgh: T. & T. Clark, 1912), pp. 28-54, and including a treatment of words and phrases; William Hendriksen, *New Testament Commentary: Exposition of I and II Thessalonians* (Grand Rapids: Baker Book House, 1955), pp. 18-30; and Morris, *op. cit.*, pp. 27-36.

[8]*An Introduction to the New Testament* (Anderson, Indiana: The Warner Press, 1943), p. 160.

Church. The curtain is pulled aside on that church's problems, hopes, fellowship, discipline, and standards.

Here too we see briefly the great doctrines of God, of the deity of Jesus Christ, of the Holy Spirit, of the sanctification of believers, and of the second coming of Christ. The latter two especially are stated with great clarity, but with economy of words. The date of the letters explodes any theory that these doctrines of Christianity required generations of time to evolve.

One of the most intriguing aspects of the study of the Thessalonian letters is that they serve as windows opening into the personality of Paul. Here he bares his heart, his hopes, his humanness. An insight into his methods and work as a missionary-pastor comes as a reward of careful study. To look thoughtfully into the very heart of the great apostle cannot fail to make a reader a better person.

Outline

First Thessalonians

I. Personal Correspondence, 1:1—3:13

- A. Address and Salutation, 1:1
- B. Thanksgiving for Gospel Victories, 1:2-10
  1. Evidence of Christian Values, 1:2-3
  2. Signs of Genuine Conversion, 1:4-10
- C. Recollection Which Strengthens, 2:1-16
  1. The Character of Paul's Ministry, 2:1-12
  2. The Vindication of Paul's Message, 2:13-16
- D. Concern for Steadfastness, 2:17—3:13
  1. Concern Prompts Timothy's Mission, 2:17—3:8
  2. Prayer for Establishment in Holiness, 3:9-13

II. Ethical and Doctrinal Teachings, 4:1—5:28

- A. Guidance in Daily Christian Living, 4:1-12
  1. A Life of Obedience and Purity, 4:1-8
  2. Brotherly Love and Industry, 4:9-12
- B. The Coming of the Lord, 4:13—5:11
  1. The Dead in Christ, 4:13-18
  2. The Living Church, 5:1-11
- C. Exhortation to the Life of Holiness, 5:12-24
  1. Corporate Discipline, 5:12-15
  2. Constant Victory, 5:16-18
  3. Spiritual Discernment, 5:19-22
  4. Sanctifying Grace, 5:23-24
- D. Conclusion and Benediction, 5:25-28

Section I *Personal Correspondence*

I Thessalonians 1:1—3:13

A. Address and Salutation, 1:1

That what will follow is not a treatise but a personal letter is suggested by the opening words, **Paul, and Silvanus, and Timotheus, unto the church of the Thessalonians.** This was the conventional way to begin a letter in the first century: first the name of the sender, then the name of the one addressed, then a greeting.

Of all of Paul's New Testament letters, only in those to the Thessalonians does he call himself simply **Paul** without adding "apostle" or some other title. Perhaps the omission here suggests the warmth of his relationship with the church. It is in keeping with the intimate tone of the letter, although it is clear that Paul wrote in full consciousness of his authority (5:27).

Out of courtesy to his companions and because they had shared with him the Thessalonian ministry, Paul associates Silvanus and Timothy with him in writing the letter. Doubtless the association means the endorsement by the others of the letter's contents, but the letter itself is Paul's. **Paul** is named first; next **Silvanus,** the older of the other two, and Paul's earlier companion (Acts 15:22-41); then **Timotheus** (Timothy), the youngest, who had joined the second missionary expedition en route through Asia (Acts 16:1-3). The great apostle associates himself without affectation with his lesser colleagues. The gospel of Christ does not obliterate ordinary distinctions whether social, official, or of natural endowment. What it does do, through the grace of humility, is to join all ranks in a fellowship of love and labor unmarked by either conscious condescension or servility. Silvanus, called Silas[1] in Acts, was joined also to Paul by the deeper fellowship of their common sufferings.

[1]The tradition which makes Silas and Silvanus two persons is certainly in error. But Silas (Greek contraction) and Silvanus (Latin name) are similar in sound only, not meaning.

Had Paul employed his usual form, he would have written "to the church at (or in) Thessalonica." The form **unto the church of the Thessalonians** appears to direct attention to the local assembly of Christians rather than to their relationship to the Universal Church.

Which is in God the Father and in the Lord Jesus Christ is an expression descriptive and definitive of the true Church. It is a rich New Testament concept. Christians are "in Christ," a dynamic, day-by-day relationship, through vital union with Him.[2] Thus, this isolated local assembly is part of the universal body of Christ (cf. Rom. 12:5). This is in marked contrast with those who are "in darkness" (5:4), or "in the world" (Eph. 2:12).

The whole expression has Trinitarian significance. After the one preposition **in** (the second preposition is not in the Gk. text), Paul naturally associates **God the Father** and **the Lord Jesus Christ,** thus taking the highest possible view of the person of Christ. **Lord** is the usual word for Jehovah in the Septuagint, the Greek translation of the Old Testament. For Gentiles also, the word carried the idea of divinity. The combination of **Lord** with **Jesus** (the human, personal name) and with **Christ** (Messiah, God's anointed, ordained One—the official name) into one title provides the glorious designation of our Saviour. The Christology of this letter, perhaps the earliest of New Testament documents, is clear. This was the faith of the Church from the beginning.

In a way that is distinctive with him, Paul seems to combine the Greek and Hebrew forms of greeting: **Grace be unto you, and peace.** By a slight alteration (*chairein* to *charis*) the common Greek "greeting" becomes the richly meaningful Christian word "grace." **Peace** (*eirene,* Heb. *shalom*) means much more than the absence of strife. It "is the spiritual prosperity enjoyed by the recipients of the divine favour."[3] The greeting is more than a cordial wish. It is also the implicit promise of God's grace, and of His peace through grace[4] to all who will believe.

[2]In this connection see William Barclay, *The Mind of St. Paul* (New York: Harper & Row, Publishers, 1958), chapter xi.

[3]Frame, *op. cit.,* p. 71.

[4]Although the words **from God our Father, and the Lord Jesus Christ** are not supported by the best texts, the concept follows naturally.

B. Thanksgiving for Gospel Victories, 1:2-10

Paul's thanksgiving, **we give thanks to God always for you all** (2) is more than the polite form common in conventional letter writing of that day. It illustrates his warm, personal relationship with his converts, and it exudes deep feeling, joy, and concern. This entire passage is graphic testimony from the primitive missionary church of the utterly transforming force of the gospel in a pagan environment.

1. *Evidence of Christian Values* (1:2-3)

Making mention of you in our prayers is so linked with **remembering without ceasing** as to suggest that prayer was the atmosphere of the Christian leaders' daily lives. The Thessalonians were doubtless prayed for by name, and possibly in the united prayers of the three missionaries.

Here for the first time in his letters Paul introduces the famous trilogy of **faith, hope,** and **love.** In I Corinthians 13, where love is under discussion, it is listed last. Here, where stress is more upon Christ's coming, hope is in the climactic position. (Cf. also 5:8.) Grammatically, however, it is not the famous trilogy which is here prominent, but rather **work,** which is a consequence of **faith; labour,** which is an expression of **love;** and **patience** (steadfastness, endurance), which is a product of Christian **hope.**

Outward evidence of inward and eternal Christian values was to be found by observing the daily lives of these converts: their transformed activities, their loving toil, their endurance under pressure. Conversely, the astonishing effectiveness of their witness (6-10) could be accounted for only as the outflow of divinely implanted qualities. True faith will be evidenced by corresponding works; but mere "good works" which do not spring from faith will lack spiritual fruitage; divinely implanted love will call forth costly exertions;[5] lesser motives will fail under testing. Christian hope will hold men steady under stress; mere human idealism cracks under pressure. (Cf. Col. 1:4-5; Heb. 10:22-24; I Pet. 1:21-22; Rev. 2:2-4.)

Faith is personal response to God's grace: trust in, dependence on, commitment to Christ (cf. Gal. 5:6). The distinctively Christian, high term for **love** (*agape*) is the basis for

[5]*Kopou* (**labour**), meaning costly exertion, is distinguished from *ergou* (**work**), the general term.

Christian action (cf. II Cor. 5:14). New Testament **hope,** no mere sentiment, means certainty with respect to that which is yet future. It affirms divine purpose and victory, and is the foe of all views, fatalistic, cyclical, evolutionary, or otherwise, which enthrone blind force (cf. Rom. 8:24; Heb. 6:11-19). These supreme Christian virtues issue in *action.* Christianity is more than contemplation.

The construction of 3 is difficult. On the whole, it seems best to understand **in the sight of** (lit., before) **God and our Father** as going with **remembering.**[6] Thus RSV translates it, "Remembering before our God and Father your work of faith." Also it seems best to understand **in our Lord Jesus Christ** as directly modifying only **patience of hope.** It is true, of course, that all three attributes named are **in our Lord Jesus Christ,** since the whole life of the Christian is lived in and by Jesus Christ.

2. *Signs of Genuine Conversion* (1:4-10)

In exuberant language Paul recalls the thrilling origin of the Thessalonian church. They are addressed as **brethren beloved . . . of God.** The phrase **of God** should be placed after **beloved,** rather than after **election.** Christian brotherhood is the brotherhood of the twice-born sons of God joined to one another by love and their common life in Christ. It is very real and strong. Such persons have been and are being continually loved by God (cf. Rom. 8:31-39). "Beloved by God" was a term reserved in the Old Testament for Israel and special persons. In Christ, all men may share the privilege.

Of the Thessalonian Christians, Paul affirms: **knowing your election.** This biblical concept has been often misconstrued or distorted. Election means a choice, and in Scripture the elect are those whom God has chosen to be His children and heirs of eternal life. The construction here (4) implies that God's act of election flows from His unchanging love. To this point there is agreement among all who accept the Scriptures as their rule. The cleavage appears at the point of the method and ground of election. For one group it is the secret, eternal counsel of God, His sovereign choice of certain individuals, while passing by

[6]Among versions which indicate a preference, RSV, NEB, Goodspeed, and the *Amplified NT* agree. However, Phillips and Weymouth agree with KJV.

the rest. But the only view consistent with the general tenor of Scripture, as well as with all the passages in question, is that which teaches that election is God's choice unto life, by grace, of all who savingly believe on Jesus Christ. The call is universal, so that while the principle upon which the choice is made is eternally decreed, the election is not arbitrary, but conditional upon the acceptance of the offer of mercy in Christ. The choice is conditional, and therefore the elect are those who are continuing in faith and who are persevering in obedience.[7] (Cf. 2:13-15; II Pet. 1:10.)

Paul does not hesitate to assert knowledge of election to personal salvation. Such assurance is the promise of Scripture. The expression **for** with which 5 begins has really the force of "because," indicating that their election was inferred from the indisputable facts in their experience. Have they faith and love and hope in Jesus Christ? And are these evidenced by **works** such as to turn **from idols**; by **labour**, such **as to serve the living and true God**; and by **patience**, such as **to wait for his Son from heaven** (cf. 9-10)? Personal self-scrutiny should not raise anxious doubts, but rather combat a false trust in the blessing of another day which is only a memory.

Paul now recalls what James Denney calls "the signs of election."[8]

a. The Manner of the Gospel's Coming (5). In their preaching, the missionaries had experienced the sanction of the Holy Spirit, giving spiritual force to their words, and producing in themselves great confidence and boldness. The argument is that the message was shown to be true by evidence inherent in the preaching itself.

Paul can speak of **our gospel** (2:14; II Cor. 4:3; cf. "my gospel," Rom. 2:16; 16:25). It is the gospel of God (2:2, 8-9) or the gospel of Christ (3:2). It is Paul's gospel in the sense of his having personally tested it and also of his being the steward of a sacred trust (2:4). Primitive gospel preaching, the *kerygma,* included salvation through God's grace, proclaimed in the prophets but now realized in the death and resurrection of Jesus Christ, the Messiah.

[7]H. Orton Wiley, *Christian Theology* (Kansas City: Nazarene Publishing House, 1940), II, 335-43.

[8]*The Epistles to the Thessalonians* ("The Expositor's Bible"; London: Hodder and Stoughton, 1892), p. 37.

When preaching is **in word only** (5), that is, in mere human argument or eloquence, the results are also merely human. (Cf. I Cor. 2:1-5, referring to a time very close to this letter.) At Thessalonica the **gospel came . . . also in power,** a spiritual dynamite. The words **and in the Holy Ghost** are explanatory—the power at work was the Holy Spirit. The preached Word has power because it is the Holy Spirit's instrument for performing His gracious work wherever He is not hindered in doing so. Commenting on the Greek construction Moffatt observes that the word translated **much assurance** "must here denote personal conviction and unfaltering confidence on the part of the preachers."[9] The gospel trumpet had sounded with no uncertain sound. God used men at Thessalonica who had already demonstrated their unshakable convictions at Philippi (Acts 16).

The final clause of 5, **what manner of men we were among you,** suggests that the lives of the preachers confirmed their message. This was in contrast with the itinerant teachers of the day who made a living by espousing novel philosophies (cf. 2:1-12).

b. The Manifestation of the Gospel's Power (1:6-10). Evidence of the power of the gospel was further to be found objectively in the change, a miracle of transformation, which took place in the hearers of the Word. The chain of evidence has several links.

First, **And ye became followers** (lit., imitators—our word mimic comes from the same root) **of us, and of the Lord** (6). Conscious of his integrity, Paul does not hesitate to say: "Copy me, my brothers, as I copy Christ himself" (I Cor. 11:1, Phillips). (Cf. I Cor. 4:16; Eph. 5:1.) The life of Christ must be, so to speak, reincarnated in the consistent example of His disciples. The order of words here—first **us** and then **the Lord**—is significant. "We [Christians] are the only Bible the careless world will read."

Significant in this imitation was their joyful obedience to the Word in spite of severe opposition. On this path the Saviour had gone before them! So had Paul and Silas at Philippi. They had suffered mob violence, and the persecution was still going on (cf. 2:14; 3:2-4; II Thess. 1:4).

[9] "The First and Second Epistles to the Thessalonians," *The Expositor's Greek Testament,* ed. W. Robertson Nicoll (Grand Rapids: Wm. B. Eerdmans Publishing Co., 1951), IV, 24.

They had **received** (the term carries the idea of welcomed) **the word in much affliction.** The word **affliction** (*thlipsei*) denotes crushing pressure. The cognate verb was used of crushing grapes in the winepress (cf. Matt. 13:21; 24:21; Rev. 7:14). The paradoxical combination of **affliction** and **joy** is further evidence of election. For such joy is **of the Holy Ghost** (Gal. 5:22). It is not necessary to suppose that they enjoyed their sufferings. Christians however, embracing as they do a different scale of values, see clearly that there will be inevitable cost and opposition in following Christ. When this is accepted joyfully, the mark of genuineness is there (cf. Acts 5:41; I Pet. 4:12-16).

Those who began as imitators soon became examples. Thus does the gospel spread. **So that ye were ensamples** (7, lit., became an example—singular). From *typos* (example) we get our word "type." Of no other church is it said that it became a pattern or a model church. High praise indeed! The church at Thessalonica became a model **to all that believe.** The matter involved was genuineness in faith and experience. The idea seems to be that they had received the authentic stamp so that they in turn could be a "type" for others.[10] What distorted models churches may become who do not copy the Lord but build to their own specifications!

For from you sounded out the word of the Lord (8). The verb here has been associated with loud thunder, or the trumpet, or even echoing reverberations.[11] Phillips has, "You have become a sort of sounding board from which the word of the Lord has rung out." If we recall the trials of Paul in Macedonia and his early anxiety for this church, we can understand his deep satisfaction in its providential and strategic ministry. One senses in this language an exultant, even defiant, note. The worst of circumstances cannot muzzle the Word of the Lord. Rather, they serve to amplify the note of victory! This model church broadcasts or echoes, not its own, but **the word of the Lord,** "the word that Christ inspires."[12]

The extent of the witness was **not only in Macedonia and Achaia** (see map 1), **but also in every place.** The latter expression is probably pardonable hyperbole. Greece had been divided

[10]Archibald Thomas Robertson, *Word Pictures in the New Testament,* (New York: Harper & Brothers Publishers, 1931), IV, 12.

[11]*Ibid.*

[12]Frame, *op. cit.*, p. 85.

since 142 B.C. into these two Roman provinces. Commercially strategic Thessalonica lay astride the traffic between East and West. Barclay observes: "It is impossible to overstress the importance of the arrival of Christianity in Thessalonica. If Christianity was settled in Thessalonica it was bound to spread East along the Egnatian Road until all Asia was conquered, and West until it stormed even the city of Rome. The coming of Christianity to Thessalonica was a crucial day in the making of Christianity into a world religion."[13]

Paul rejoices that **your faith to God-ward** (in God) **is spread abroad.** Nothing advertises the gospel or the church quite like the life-changing conversion of sinners to God. It is pertinent to ask: "Is anything happening in our churches that makes news, because it demands a more-than-human explanation?" From Thessalonica the news was "gossiped" by the streams of travelers until it penetrated far-off places. It illustrates the happy blending of spontaneous witnessing with organized evangelism. Paul adds, **so that we need not to speak any thing.** And in v. 9 he says, **For they themselves shew of us . . .** It may be that Paul's source of information in this connection was travelers who happened to be in Corinth. It is worth noting that Aquila and Priscilla had recently come to Corinth from Rome (Acts 18:2). The travelers **shew** (lit., keep reporting) the news (cf. Phillips). The Thessalonians must have been astonished to hear themselves so described. Our light shines farther than we know.

In the words **shew of** (concerning) **us what manner of entering in we had unto you,** attention is turned back upon Paul and his companions. The implication is that, since the whole account of Paul's coming to Thessalonica is public knowledge, his detractors, the opposing Jews, will be proved false.

The thought of 5 and 6 is now directly resumed: the signs of genuine conversion. The words **how ye turned to God from idols to serve the living and true God** (9) would indicate that the majority of the converts had been won directly from paganism. The story in Acts does not give this detail. "Devout Greeks" (Acts 17:4) would refer to proselytes to Judaism, not to idolaters. Some ancient manuscripts have "and" after "devout," making

[13]*The Daily Study Bible: The Letters to the Philippians, Colossians and Thessalonians* (Edinburgh: The Saint Andrew Press, 1959), p. 213.

"Greeks" a separate class. Further, Paul's work apart from the synagogue (cf. 2:7-12), about which Acts says nothing, was doubtless extensive enough to account for the statement here.[14]

Some writers, among them Morris[15] and Ockenga,[16] note that Paul makes three points in describing the Thessalonians' conversion: (1) They **turned to God from idols;** (2) They began to **serve the living and true God;** (3) They began **to wait for his Son from heaven,** i.e., to live in the light of the coming of Christ.

The word translated **turned** is the characteristic expression in Acts for conversion (Acts 11:21; 14:15; 15:19; 26:18, 20). **To God** and **from idols** express antitheses. In order to face toward God they must turn their backs on idols. A radical change both outwardly and inwardly is meant; a change in conduct—but also in thought, attitude, and will. Destiny is involved. Without true repentance there is no real conversion. Paul did not share the half-admiring attitude of some toward pagan culture. He associated idols with uncleanness and demonism (I Cor. 10: 14-21; II Cor. 6:16-17; cf. Rev. 9:20). Neil states: "Let us have no illusions about what it meant to be a pagan . . . for the ordinary man and woman, bewildered by a multiplicity of temples and shrines to innumerable gods and goddesses, astrology and demonology provided the normal background to life. Eroticism was synonymous with worship. Expediency dictated behaviour. Life was a gamble with fate and ended in extinction."[17] When one remembers that Paul's converts had abandoned as vain the heritage of paganism that had permeated their whole way of life, and that Mount Olympus itself was only some fifty miles distant, the epithet of his persecutors becomes justifiable: "They that have turned the world upside down . . ." (Acts 17:6). But further, conversion involved turning **to God;** that is, facing into the light of personal, moral accountability to the one God, Creator, Redeemer, and Judge. Truly, the word had come "in power, and in the Holy Ghost" (3).

[14]Frame, *op. cit.,* pp. 2-5.

[15]*Op. cit.,* p. 62.

[16]*The Church in God* (Fleming H. Revell Company, 1956), pp. 42-45.

[17]*St. Paul's Epistles to the Thessalonians* ("Torch Bible Commentaries"; New York: The Macmillan Company, 1957), p. 38.

Such repentance issued positively in a twofold way: **to serve** and **to wait** (with a new hope). **To serve** (*douleuein*) suggests total surrender, the service (although loving) of a slave. In the expression **to serve the living and true God** there is contrast with the dead, counterfeit, "nothing" idols (Isaiah 40; I Cor. 8:4; 12:2; Gal. 4:8). God is real to human experience. Trench points out[18] that **true** (*alethinos*) as used of God means that God fulfills not only the promise of His lips but "the wider promise of his name." He concludes, "Whatever that name imports, taken in its highest, deepest, widest sense, whatever according to that he ought to be, *that* he is to the full." (For another application of the expression, note Heb. 3:12.)

The words **and to wait for his Son from heaven** (10) are reminiscent of Titus 2:11-13, a much later Epistle, where again in capsule form Paul strikes the eschatological note. Serving as a faithful steward (cf. Luke 12:36-38) in this world, the Christian awaits in certainty the glory of the next. Tiptoe expectation, facing toward the morning, is his characteristic stance. The expression presupposes preparation and readiness (I John 3:3).

God's Son is identified as **Jesus,** the historical Person, and further as the One **whom he raised from the dead.** The Resurrection, always in the foreground of apostolic preaching, was the supreme proof of Jesus' divine sonship (Rom. 1:4). Here also was the chief argument for the certainty of judgment (Acts 17:31), certifying as it did the defeat of Satan and the ultimate overthrow of evil. He who ascended into heaven will come again **from heaven** (see comments on 4:16).

In Paul's teaching, divine retribution occupied a somewhat complementary relationship to the doctrine of grace (cf. Rom. 1:16-18; 2:1-11; Eph. 5:6-8). Moral law is grounded in the nature of God, involving both love of righteousness and hatred of all unrighteousness. The word for **wrath** is *orge*. In other passages it is used in "wrath of God" (cf. John 3:36; Col. 3:6). Trench, commenting on this word, says it indicates an abiding and settled habit of mind with the purpose of retribution, rather than mere temporary agitation of feeling. It is the necessary complement of God's love. "There is a 'wrath of God' (Matt. 3:7; Rom. 12:19, and often) who would not love good, unless He hated evil, the two being so inseparable, that either He must do

[18]*Synonyms of the New Testament* (Grand Rapids: Wm. B. Eerdmans Publishing Company, 1948 [reprint of 1880 ed.]), pp. 26-30.

both or neither; a wrath also of the merciful Son of Man (Mark 3:5); and a wrath which righteous men not merely may, but as they are righteous, must feel . . ."[19]

It is, then, the personal wrath of God, not an impersonal process by which evil produces disaster. Nor can it be divorced from "feeling" in God without at the same time making His love an unfeeling thing. But God's wrath is without the flaws which characterize that of men.

It is **wrath to come,** an inevitable, approaching "day of wrath" (Rom. 2:5; Rev. 6:17), in terrible contrast with the present day of gracious forbearance. The idea is not exhausted by the day-by-day consequences which are always "coming" because of sin.

From this wrath upon sin it is **Jesus, which delivered us,** (lit., who delivers us, or Jesus, our Deliverer). Vincent says that the verb means literally "to draw to one's self."[20] Jesus is rescuing, drawing from danger, those who are committing themselves, their past, their present, and their future, wholly to Him. The Thessalonian church doubtless had heard from Paul the doctrines of atonement and justification by faith.

C. Recollection Which Strengthens, 2:1-16

In warm, personal language Paul appeals in some detail to memories only suggested in chapter one. His purpose is not mere reminiscence, but defense—justifiable defense of his personal ministry for the sake of truth and the preservation of the church. Obviously, the slanderers were fanatical Jews who, if they could not strike him physically, attempted savage character assassination. The opposition was not inside, as later in the case of Corinth, but outside the congregation.

1. *The Character of Paul's Ministry* (2:1-12)

Besides being a model of defense, this passage is a lovely mirror of truly spiritual pastoral care.

a. Purity of Motives (2:1-8). From the witness of outsiders (1:9), Paul turns again (cf. 1:5) to the witness of the church itself respecting his ministry: **For yourselves, brethren, know**

[19] *Ibid.*, pp. 130-34.

[20] *Word Studies in the New Testament* (Grand Rapids: Wm. B. Eerdmans Publishing Co., 1946), IV, 20.

(1). From lies, slander, and vilification of his person, Paul appeals to the known facts. He stirs up their memory of the life he lived among them. They knew his **entrance in unto you** ("our visit to you," RSV) **was not in vain.** The verb **was** (*gegonen*) is perfect tense, signifying completed action; therefore it may mean literally "has not proved to be" **in vain** (fruitless, NEB). However, Frame[21] and others prefer "empty-handed," suggesting the content and power of the preaching (1:5).

In v. 2, Paul argues that men with base or selfish motives would not, after the persecution at Philippi, have continued so perilous a course from which they could obviously make no selfish profit. High motives are required for men to continue a true, and therefore costly, gospel ministry.

In the words, **But even after that we had suffered before, and were shamefully entreated** (lit., treated insultingly, insolently, or shamefully), Paul expresses both the physical suffering and also the deep hurt of the personal indignities endured **at Philippi** (cf. Acts 16). These indignities, including the affront to his Roman citizenship, had provoked Paul to insist on a public apology from the magistrates (Acts 16:36-39). No one is more keenly sensitive to insolence and injustice than the Christlike man. The words **as ye know** may refer to the marks of the beating still on the bodies of the missionaries when they came to Thessalonica.

We were bold . . . to speak ("had courage . . . to declare," RSV) is an expression used of Paul a number of times in Acts. Far from being intimidated by events, Paul and the others preached with energy and freedom. The courage, Paul insists, was **in our God**; that is, it came from God, in whom they lived. In declaring that he spoke **the gospel of God,** Paul, in refuting the Jews, takes the position of ultimate authority for his message, a position which would not be so well expressed for them by "gospel of Christ" (cf. 8, 13; 1:5). In the expression **with much contention,** the Greek word is *agoni* (from which we get "agony"). Robertson says, "This figure of the athletic games (*agon*) may refer to outward conflict like Phil. 1:30 or inward anxiety (Col. 2:1). He [Paul] had both in Thessalonica."[22] In I Tim. 6:12 the same word is translated "fight" (in both verb and noun forms).

[21]*Op. cit.*, p. 92.

[22]*Op. cit.*, p. 16.

Paul comes now (3) to a direct reply to what must be considered slanderous accusations circulated by implacable enemies at Thessalonica. It would be easy to insinuate that Paul and the others were really no better than any of the cultists who so frequently peddled their deceitful nostrums to the gullible and credulous. There were mysterious Oriental religions and also serious pagan philosophies which competed for a hearing. Was Christianity just another of these? Paul takes the challenge seriously, for repeated lies begin finally to sound plausible, and the seeds of ruinous doubt are sown.

There were three charges, it would seem. **For our exhortation** (appeal) **was not of deceit, nor of uncleanness, nor in guile. Deceit** is literally "error," the idea being that Paul was deluded. **Uncleanness** (cf. 4:7; Rom. 6:19) raises the charge of sensuality or sexual impurity, although Denney[23] feels that the context calls for it to be considered only as impurity of motives. Comparison, however, with the immoral rites of the then current mystery cults makes the lie seem less astonishing. To the pagan mind, religion and morals were not necessarily connected. This slander against Paul was to become a favorite one in later church persecutions. The word translated **guile** (craftiness, trickery) is from a word meaning "to catch with bait" (cf. Eph. 4:14).

Moving from forthright denial to a positive answer (4-6) to these slanders, Paul notes what are probably the most subtle temptations which the minister of the gospel must overcome. For those who serve as leaders, these are searching words.

The accusations in verse 3 are false for three reasons given in 4: (1) **But as we were allowed of God** is literally "but as we have been tested by God." The perfect tense indicates completed testing and thus signifies "stand approved by God." This answers the charge of impurity. (2) **To be put in trust with the gospel** indicates that the gospel originates in God and is theirs as a sacred trust, and therefore is not a delusion. (3) **Even so we speak; not as pleasing men, but God, which trieth our hearts** contradicts flatly the charge that he used guile. **Were allowed** in the first clause and **trieth** in the last are from the same Greek verb meaning "to test," "to prove by testing." Paul is saying that God, who has tested and approved them, is also continually (present tense) testing their hearts. This examination of the

[23]*Op. cit.*, p. 72.

heart (the whole inner life, including motives), this constant scrutiny by Omniscience, is a great comfort to those whose aim is to please God rather than men. Man even at his best "looketh [merely] on the outward appearance"; but God, from whom nothing is hid, "looketh on the heart" (I Sam. 16:7).

We must not think that **pleasing men** and pleasing **God** are opposites in the sense that we welcome men's disapproval as evidence of God's approval. Indeed, to win men to Christ usually requires that we ourselves shall be winsome in our approach. But just here is the subtlety of the temptation to be "menpleasers." How necessary that we be always open to Him who **trieth our hearts!** Paul was much concerned to keep a good conscience (cf. Acts 24:16).

The apostle continues to defend on three more counts the complete sincerity of the missionaries: (1) **For neither at any time used we flattering words** (5). The idea of flattery here is more than the attempt to give pleasure to another person by fair words; it means to try to gain selfish ends by insincere speech. The expression reflects the practices of traveling rhetoricians of that time, and of some public speakers in our day too. It may also reflect the Jewish charge that Paul preached an easy gospel of grace in contradistinction to Jewish legalism. **As ye know** is Paul's appeal again to the established facts. (2) **Nor a cloke of covetousness** is literally "a pretext of greed"; or, to paraphrase, "a disguise to cover up greedy desires." Since the question is one of motives, Paul appeals to God: **God is witness.** (3) **Nor of men sought we glory, neither of you, nor yet of others.** The suggestion is of conduct designed to elicit or extract praise, honor, or expressions of esteem from men. If such expressions come, they might be appreciated in passing, without being fed upon as an end in themselves. The words should not be taken as disapproving hearty expressions of esteem for those who minister.

Self-promotion, self-gain, self-glory—how subtle are these temptations in the life of the Christian worker who is fired with ambition to achieve for Christ and His kingdom! The "pure in heart" may, however, be conscious of purity of motives, as Paul attests.

As proof of the above, Paul reminds them that the missionaries did not insist on certain rights **when we might have been burdensome, as the apostles of Christ** (6). The NEB has, "We might have made our weight felt." Wuest suggests, "We might have stood on our dignity."[24] RSV has, "We might have made demands." There is a question whether the reference here is to the use of authority on the one hand or to the requirement of temporal or financial maintenance on the other. Possibly both ideas are valid, as the three following verses would indicate. Paul, however, is careful always to vindicate the *right* of those who preach the gospel to "live of the gospel" (I Cor. 9:1-15). Since Paul's companions seem to be included in the designation **apostles,** the word *apostoloi* is doubtless used here in its general meaning of "those who are sent," i.e., emissaries, ambassadors, or missionaries, rather than in its more technical reference to the Twelve.

Contrasting positive statements with the preceding denials, Paul declares, **But we were gentle**[25] **among you** (lit., in the midst of you), **even as a nurse cherisheth her children** (7). These are remarkable words, coming from one once known as Saul of Tarsus, the harsh and implacable persecutor. Only from his Lord could he have received and learned this gentleness as a "new creature," indeed, "in Christ" (I Cor. 5:17). The reference to **children** is literally "her own children," and thus may be read, "even as a mother-nurse cherishes (keeps warm, lovingly cares for) her children." The depth of the missionaries' sacrificial love for their converts, and the high standard of their pastoral care, are indicated in words that may seem extravagant to those who are strangers to the love of Christ.

Being affectionately desirous is a single Greek word found only here in the New Testament. Moffatt suggests "yearning for, or over."[26] Frame's rendering is similar, "yearning after."[27] **We were willing to have imparted unto you** (lit., we were well

[24]*Wuest's Expanded Translation of the Greek New Testament: Philippians Through the Revelation* (Grand Rapids: Wm. B. Eerdmans Publishing Company, 1959), III, 48.

[25]Many of the best manuscripts read "babes." The textual problem involves the possibility of an error in copying. "Gentle" is *epioi,* while "babes" is *nepioi,* a difference of one letter. The evidence and arguments on either side are lengthy. Probably because it seems to fit the figure of the verse and make better sense, "gentle" is preferred by ASV, RSV, NEB, Moffatt, and several others. However, Frame, *op. cit.,* p. 100, strongly favors "babes," as do Robertson, *op. cit.,* p. 18, and Morris, *op. cit.,* pp. 76-78. Other than making necessary adjustments to the figurative language involved, the choice affects the meaning only slightly.

[26]*Op. cit.,* p. 27-28.

[27]*Op. cit.,* p. 101.

pleased to impart—not as a possibility but as something done), **not the gospel of God only, but also our own souls** (8). Is it possible, after all, to really share the gospel of the love of God without at the same time giving one's own self also? This heart-and-soul involvement with people is costly; but is there, for the soul winner, an easier way? **Souls** is from *psyche,* which is variously translated "the inner self," "the whole person," "the inmost being," "the life." The secret of all this is hinted at in the expression **because ye were dear unto us** (lit., because you became beloved ones to us). The Thessalonians became *agapetoi,* from *agape,* the distinctive Christian word for divine, self-giving love. There can be no substitute for this tender, God-imparted caring.

b. Purity of Conduct (2:9-12). Paul continues his affectionate appeal to memory by recalling to his readers' minds his toil (9), the marks of his conduct (10), and both the manner (11) and the matter (12) of his exhortation. What has just been said about motives will now be backed up by observable conduct: **For ye remember, brethren, our labour and travail** (9). **Labour** (*kopon*) indicates the kind of work; it was wearisome toil or costly exertion (cf. 1:3, "labour of love"). **Travail** (*mochthon*) indicates the hardship, difficulty, or intensity of the work.

According to Jewish custom and teaching, every boy was required to learn a trade. Paul had learned tent making (Acts 18:3) and this was likely the manual work alluded to here. The expression **labouring night and day** (not through, but during, both nights and days) probably suggests rising early before dawn or working late at night so as to have time available for the preaching and teaching ministry. **We preached unto you the gospel of God** (cf. 3:10 and II Thess. 3:8). The purpose of this painful and strenuous schedule of work was **because we would not be chargeable unto any of you** ("that we might not burden any of you," ASV).

Paul will not insist on "rights" (cf. 6 and comment there) if this in any way limits or hinders the preaching of the gospel. It is the principle enunciated in I Cor. 6:12; 9:12; 10:23. Perhaps it was consideration for the poverty of his converts, although it would seem from Acts 17 that at least some of them could have afforded gifts. At the least, his laboring placed him on a common level with the Thessalonian **brethren**—a not unimportant consideration. Further, it raised common toil to a place of Christian dignity, a position directly in contrast to accepted pagan cultural opinion (cf. II Thess. 3:8-10). Fundamentally, however, Paul wished to remove all grounds for attack on his person and gospel by way of association with the greedy, gift-seeking traveling charlatans of the day. That he did accept gifts from Philippi while at Thessalonica we know (Phil. 4:16). The ministry so signally honored by the Holy Spirit had its roots deep in ethical principle and sacrificial love.

Once again, appeal is made to their knowledge (cf. 2:1, 9, 11)—**ye are witnesses**—and to **God also** (cf. 1:4-5). It is important that conduct should appear right in the eyes of men, but only God's judgment is infallible. The three adverbs summarize the quality of the apostle's conduct: **how holily and justly and unblameably we behaved ourselves among you that believe** (10). There are several Greek words which are translated "holy." Trench suggests[28] that the word used here (*hosios*) indicates reverence for and pious obedience to moral obligations as everlasting ordinances, and as coming from God. Commenting on the adjectival form of these words (*holy, just,* and *blameless*) Frame states: "A man is *hosios* who is in general devoted to God's service; a man is *dikaios* who comes up to a specific standard of righteousness; and a man is *amemptos* who in the light of a given norm is without reproach. All three designations are common in the Septuagint and denote the attitude both to God and to men, the first two being positive, the third negative."[29]

The phrase **you that believe** (you believers) is a synonym for "you Christians." There had been no trace of impropriety or self-seeking in Paul's relation to the converts, as charged by his detractors.

The manner of the missionaries' private pastoral ministry rather than their public preaching seems to be indicated by the words, **As ye know how we exhorted and comforted and charged every one of you** (11). The clause in the Greek with its three participles (exhorting, comforting, charging) does not have a verb to make it a complete sentence. Perhaps, as sometimes happened with Paul, the clause was left grammatically unfinished, as thought and feeling rushed on.

Although the construction is difficult, it seems best to think of the words **every one of you** as relating only to "exhorting."

[28]*Op. cit.,* pp. 328-31.

[29]*Op. cit.,* p. 103.

"Comforting" and "charging" would then be the manner in which the exhortation was applied to each as his special need required. Thus, the NEB supplies the verb "dealt with" and has, "We dealt with you one by one as a father deals with his children, appealing to you by encouragement, as well as by solemn injunctions."

The first of the participles, *parakalountes,* "exhorting" (cf. the related noun *parakleton,* "Comforter," John 14:16), can carry the meanings of exhorting, consoling, encouraging, instructing.[30] The second, *paramythoumenoi,* "comforting," also means addressing for the purpose of persuading, consoling, or encouraging.[31] The third, *martyromenoi,* "charging," carries the idea of declaring solemnly, protesting, beseeching as in God's name, exhorting solemnly.[32]

Changing from the figure of a mother with her children (7), Paul states that he counseled with his converts **as a father doth his children.** This is a favorite figure with Paul (cf. I Cor. 4:14-15), and it no doubt implies affection, understanding, concern, firmness, and discipline. The expression **every one of you** carries in the Greek the clear idea of individual attention (cf. Phillips: "each one of you personally"). Some needed most to be reassured, cheered, and encouraged. Others needed fatherly direction and discipline, or even solemn warning (cf. 5:14; II Tim. 4:2).

The sight of the great apostle so carefully seeking out the individual person provides an important insight into his ministry, and indeed an example for our own. It is a practical commentary on Paul's concern for individual worth in the sight of God, on persons as individual members of Christ's body, and on the Holy Spirit's individual ministry to each Christian man and woman. The concept of the infinite value of every soul came supremely through the gospel of Jesus Christ. The idea was revolutionary in most of Paul's world but was never more relevant than in ours. Within the Church there is no true evangelism or pastoral care which does not follow this example.

The exhortation was to the end **that ye would walk** ("lead a life," RSV) **worthy of God, who hath called** (lit., is calling)

[30]Joseph H. Thayer, *Greek-English Lexicon of the New Testament* (New York: American Book Company, 1889), p. 482.

[31]*Ibid.,* p. 485.

[32]*Ibid.,* p. 392.

you unto his kingdom and glory (12). Here again, as so often in the New Testament, the Christian ethic is related to the nature of God, and dominated by the Christian eschatology (cf. 3:13; 5:23). The Christian walks today in the light of tomorrow's sure hope. To **walk worthy of** is a phrase peculiar to Paul (cf. Eph. 4:1 and Col. 1:10). A person's "walk," as used in many passages, designates his entire conduct or manner of life (4:1, 12; Rom. 6:4; 8:1; Gal. 5:16; Eph. 2:2).

The use of the present tense, "is calling" rather than "called,"[33] suggests that the call of God to salvation in the sense of final glory, although heeded in a crisis of repentance and faith, is yet not a once-for-all event in the past. Just as God is always calling, so believers are always responding (see comment on "delivers" in 1:10). The urgency expressed in 11 is not to be construed as concern for conduct alone, but also for personal salvation.

The **kingdom** is in one sense come, a present possession, but is in another sense coming, a future inheritance. The kingdom or reign of God, through the indwelling Holy Spirit, and the economy of divine grace, is already present in the hearts of believers. It exists where His sovereignty is owned and His will is done. But its consummation and completeness are yet future —at Christ's coming. It is this future aspect which is stressed here. **Glory** signifies splendor, magnificence, brightness. Frame states: "*Doxa* is parallel with *basileia* and suggests not only the radiant splendour of God or of Christ (II Thess. 2:14) but also the majesty of their perfection (cf. Ps. 96:6; Rom. 3:23)."[34]

Verse 12 suggests "The Two Sides of Christian Living": (1) What God does for us, and (2) What we ought do for God. In matchless love He calls us, offering both grace and glory. How shall we respond to this infinite mercy? We may accept His offer and through grace seek to live lives worthy of God. Is it not a paradox? The suggestion seems staggering. Indeed, the whole concept of divine grace finds its corollary in man's utter unworthiness. However, the adverb *axios* (**worthy**, or better, worthily) can mean "suitably."[35] In Rom. 12:1 and II Cor. 5:14-

[33]Some manuscripts have "called," but the major manuscript evidence leads ASV, RSV, NEB, Moffatt, and others to prefer the present tense.

[34]*Op. cit.*, p. 105.

[35]Thayer, *op. cit.*, p. 53.

15, Paul deals with our suitable, fitting, or **worthy** response to God's love.

2. *The Vindication of Paul's Message* (2:13-16)

Continuing the affectionate appeal to memory, the discussion now turns from the character of the apostle's ministry to the vindication of his message. The gist of Paul's appeal in this section, which involves both a defense of his preaching and the encouragement of the converts, is that the word which they welcomed as God's own word was effectually at work in spite of persecutions.

a. The Reception of the Word (2:13). As Paul recalled the Thessalonians' reception of the gospel, he was constantly thankful to God: **For this cause also thank we God without ceasing.** Some scholars think that the **also,** in the sense of "along with you," indicates Paul's reference to the converts' own thankfulness made known to him by a letter. The reference, however, may be simply to Timothy's report (cf. 2:17—3:8 and Acts 18:3). **For this cause** doubtless refers to the preceding account of the apostle's labors, which, happily, were not in vain. Paul thanks God without ceasing **because, when ye received the word of God which ye heard of us, ye received it not as the word of men, but as it is in truth, the word of God.** The apostle is again affirming as in 1:5 and 2:4, against contrary insinuations, that his gospel is the very word of God and no mere philosophy of men. The logic which attests this is that it **effectually worketh** (is working) **in you that believe** (you who are believing).

In the Greek, the two words translated **received** are not the same; the first means simply an outward reception by the mind, while the second means to welcome with approval.[36] The meaning seems to be that when the Thessalonians received or heard the word of God with their ears, they accepted or welcomed it inwardly in their hearts.[37] They did not, as others did in unbelief, consider it to be the mere words of men (cf. Heb. 4:2).

Paul is certainly making a claim to that unction, if not inspiration, by which God speaks with authority and power through His qualified messengers. How important it is to hear this message aright! "Take heed therefore," said Jesus, "how ye hear" (Luke 8:18). As illustrations of this cf. Acts 7:54-57 and

[36]Frame, *op. cit.,* pp. 107-8.

[37]It should be noted that **it** and **as** are supplied (in italics, KJV).

10:44. Solemn responsibility rests upon those who hear the Word of God mediated through Spirit-filled preachers. It is tragically possible to be so preoccupied with the person of the preacher, or so prejudiced by proud and obstinate thoughts, that the Word becomes only words.

Conversely, how important is the character of the preaching! Is it "with authority" or is it "as the scribes"? James Denney says cogently (speaking of the gospel): "But neither does it . . . come to us soliciting our approval; submitting itself, as a system of ideas, to our scrutiny, and courting approbation. It speaks with authority. . . . Its decisive appeal is made to the conscience and the will; and to respond to it is to give up will and conscience to God." And speaking of Paul, he continues, "His theology was the sum of the Divine truth he held, and he *did* preach it—he did not submit it to men as a theme for discussion. *He put it above discussion* [italics mine]. . . . He published it . . . as the word of God, for the obedience of faith."[38]

The Greek word translated **worketh** is a strong one. We derive our word energy from it. It may carry the idea of "setting in operation."[39] The word "is working" only in those who "are believing"; it follows that the operation ceases when faith ceases. As Morris puts it, "We cannot live today on the spiritual capital of yesterday."[40] The energy of the Word is released by faith! God himself is at work through His Word (cf. Heb. 4:12; I Pet. 1:23-25).

The working of the Word within the believers is manifested by the fact of their suffering for Christ's sake and the way in which they had borne their suffering (cf. 1:6).

b. The Outworking of the Word (2:14-16). It is clear that Paul means to suggest that a high honor has been bestowed on the Thessalonians when he says, **For ye, brethren,** (cf. 1:4) **became followers** (lit., imitators) **of the churches of God which in Judaea are in Christ Jesus: for ye also have suffered like things of your own countrymen, even as they have of the Jews** (14). To suffer for Christ's sake, to endure the inevitable antagonism and persecution of the world, is to be found in the holy succession of the true Church from the beginning. Paul sees the persecution as proof of genuineness (cf. John 15:20). He identifies

[38]*Op. cit.*, pp. 84-85.

[39]Robertson, *op. cit.*, p. 21.

[40]*Op. cit.*, p. 89.

the Judean **churches** (lit., assemblies) as Christian by adding **which . . . are in Christ.** The allusion to the Jewish (Judean, see map 2) Christians is probably because they had first suffered for Christ, were the oldest part of the Christian Church, and had endured the fiercest trials. Evidently Paul affectionately thought of them as the mother church. The Thessalonian persecution is ascribed to **your own countrymen,** indicating that the Gentiles had taken up the opposition at first instigated by the Jews (cf. Acts 17:5).

The mention of the persecution by the Jews triggers a "passionate outburst"[41] of condemnation of the Jewish nation's wicked perversity. It is needless to perplex ourselves by reading into these verses ill temper or vindictiveness. Neither are they a moody flash at variance with Paul's usual feeling and attitude. What *is* here is a strong denunciation of sin coupled with prophetic insight into the consequences which are following. The sins of the Jews are cataloged in a series of five expressions (in the Greek they are participial phrases, the participle in the fourth being implied): (1) **Who both killed the Lord Jesus, and their own prophets,** (2) **and have persecuted us;** (3) **and they please not God,** (4) **and are contrary to all men:** (5) **forbidding us to speak to the Gentiles that they might be saved** (15-16).

Although this is written against the background of Paul's recent sufferings at the hands of his Jewish countrymen in Thessalonica, Beroea, and now possibly Corinth, Paul indicates that this attitude has been the trend of the Jewish national history. The rejection of their own prophets reached its awful climax in the crucifixion of Jesus (cf. Matt. 23:29-39; Mark 12:1-12). The listing of this act first would suggest that the whole catalog of sins springs from hostility to Jesus Christ. **Have persecuted us** may be translated "drove us out" or "banished us."[42]

God's plan is to save the world through Jesus Christ, His Son. The Jews displeased Him, and were contrary to all men by hindering, at every turn, God's program to save men. In their outrageous perverseness, exclusiveness, and willful blindness, they not only refused Christ themselves, but tried to prevent the good news of salvation from reaching the Gentiles.

[41]Denney, *op. cit.,* p. 88.

[42]Robertson, *op. cit.,* p. 21.

From all this the result for the Jews is **to fill up their sins alway (16)**. Paul is using the familiar figure of the cup (cf. Isa. 51:17)—here the cup of iniquity. **Alway** (i.e., continually) they have been filling the measure of their sins to the very brim. The cup has been filling up generation by generation; it has now overflowed. Nothing more can be added to make judgment more certain; the inevitable consequence is stated: **for the wrath is come upon them to the uttermost.** On **the wrath** see comments on 1:10. **To the uttermost** (*eis telos*) is translated by RSV and NEB, "at last," and this is also favored by Frame[43] and Robertson.[44] The reference, however, seems to be not to some present or past event of judgment, but rather to the certain climax of a long process. The construction (aorist tense) suggests the prophetic realization of judgment which is still future but already settled.

To rightly assess this passage one should read it along with passages like Romans 2; Phil. 3:1-7; or Romans 9—11. These show not only Paul's keen sense of the Jews' privileges and responsibilities, but also his profound love for his brethren according to the flesh. Perhaps Phillips has caught the mood: "Alas, I fear they are completing the full tale of their sins, and the wrath of God is over their heads."

Exclusiveness, narrow-mindedness, self-centeredness, bigotry, and legalism in religion were not and are not confined to the Jews. These verses warn of the high cost of religion without love.

D. Concern for Steadfastness, 2:17—3:13

Having stirred the memories of the converts with the recollections of the missionaries' ministry among them, Paul moves with v. 17 to discuss his relationship to them since leaving Thessalonica. The pivotal event that has taken place since the missionary party left is Timothy's return visit and his report back to Paul.

1. *Concern Prompts Timothy's Mission* (2:17—3:8)

In this letter which is a classic on the affectionate relationship between the missionary and his converts (or the pastor and

[43]*Op. cit.*, p. 114.
[44]*Op. cit.*, p. 22.

his parish), the climax in feeling is reached in 2:17-20. The historical context has changed from the period of residence to the period of separation. But the psychological context is at first the same: an implied defense against the slanderous attacks on the missionaries' persons and message. The attackers are saying, the reader senses, that Paul's continued absence is proof that he cares little or nothing for the Thessalonians, and that having exploited and duped them, he now gives them not so much as a further thought. This view will at least explain the very strong expressions of feeling in 17-20.

a. Paul's Concern at Separation (2:17-18). **But we, brethren, being taken from you** (*aporphanisthentes,* lit., being orphaned and thus bereaved) **for a short time in presence, not in heart** (cf. Moffatt, "out of sight, not out of mind"), **endeavoured the more abundantly to see your face with great desire** (17). The word translated **desire** indicates strong feeling or passion. "You have been torn," Paul says, "not from our hearts, but only from our presence. And, although the separation has been for only a short time, our affection for you is so great that we are filled with intense desire to see you face-to-face again" (paraphrase).

Wherefore we would have come unto you (RSV, "we wanted to come to you"), **even I Paul, once and again** (according to Frame[45] it means "repeatedly"); **but Satan hindered us** (18). **Hindered** is from a verb used in Gal. 5:7 and I Pet. 3:7. Barclay says, "The word he uses (*egkoptein*) is the technical word for putting up a road-block calculated to stop an expedition on the march. It is Satan's work to throw obstacles into the Christian's way—and it is our work to surmount them, for road-blocks were made to be circumvented."[46]

To attempt to say how Satan hindered the apostle's return would be an exercise in speculation. It is clear that the Bible teaches a diabolical personal power, greater than men, with power to hinder God's work (cf. Eph. 6:11-12). But while Satan might hinder Christian action, he could not defeat the divine purpose for these believers, as the succeeding verses imply. Note that Paul considered the congregation's separation from their pastor's encouragement and instruction to be the work of Satan.

[45] *Op. cit.,* p. 120.

[46] *Letters,* p. 225.

b. Paul's High Hopes (2:19-20). As if to remove any lingering suspicion that others have usurped the Thessalonians' place in his affection, Paul concludes in a burst of feeling: **For what is our hope, or joy, or crown of rejoicing?** (19) **Crown** here is not *diadema,* a royal crown, but *stephanos,* "the crown of victory in the games, of civic worth, of military valour, of nuptial joy, of festal gladness . . . the 'wreath,' in fact, or the 'garland,' . . . but never . . . the emblem and sign of royalty."[47] It is the chaplet awarded to the victor (cf. Jas. 1:12; Rev. 2:10; 3:11). It was a way of celebrating the triumph or honor; thus it meant **rejoicing,** glorying, exulting. Again, as in 1:10, Paul strikes the eschatological note: **Are not even ye in the presence of our Lord Jesus Christ at his coming?** He is referring to no mere earthly honor. He is not motivated simply by hope of reunion in this world, but is living in the light of the great day of Christ's return.[48] (On **Lord Jesus Christ** see comment on 1:1.)

Paul uses four terms to describe what his Thessalonian converts mean to him. In 19 they are his **hope,** his **joy,** his **crown of rejoicing.** Now they are his **glory and joy** (20). The words are full of emotion but are not exaggerations. For some men their hope is wealth, or security, or personal ambition. They have hopes which terminate in this world. The apostle, with a true pastor's heart, has a better hope, which transforms his frequent sufferings. The subjects of his hope are his beloved children in the faith, presented to Christ as trophies of grace (cf. II Cor. 11:2). Their spiritual growth and progress are what make his heart leap for joy (cf. III John 4). They will be the "stars in his crown," the only victor's wreath which he covets. As the glory of the teacher is in producing scholars, so the glory of the Christian is in winning souls (cf. Dan. 12:3; Phil. 2:16). (**Glory** in this passage means the honor which the excellence of one person brings to another.) Even of Christ it is

[47]Trench, *op. cit.,* p. 78.

[48]*Parousia,* "coming," may have a nontechnical meaning (i.e., simply *presence*), and derived from this, "coming," "arrival," or "advent" (Thayer, *op. cit.,* p. 490). It is so used in II Thess. 2:9; I Cor. 16:17; II Cor. 10:10. Quoting Deissmann, Frame (*op. cit.,* p. 123) states that in the Eastern world it is almost technical for the visit of a king. In the NT church the word came early to have the technical meaning of "the second advent of Christ," and is so used here and in 3:13; 4:15; 5:23; II Thess. 2:1, 8; I Cor. 15:23 (cf. Frame, *op. cit.,* p. 123; Morris, *op. cit.,* p. 97). This would be the first such use in the NT.

true (John 17:10). The truth for all is that only this investment in human hearts has final meaning. While Paul is clear that his labors can earn him no merit in the sense of justification, he is likewise certain that his place before Christ at His coming will depend upon the permanence and productiveness of his work (cf. I Cor. 3:11-15).

As Paul retraces in memory the circumstances of Timothy's visit to Thessalonica and the subsequent report, the undertones of defense against his enemies' accusations are not absent, but are submerged by the strong note of concern for the church as it faces severe opposition.

c. *Timothy's Visit* (3:1-2). The chapter division here should be ignored, for there is no break in the thought. **Wherefore when we could no longer forbear** (endure), **we thought it good to be left at Athens alone; and sent Timotheus** (1-2). The problem here is to reconstruct the situation so as to make it agree with Luke's record in Acts. Paul had left Silas and Timothy behind in Beroea, and had been escorted by brethren to Athens (see map 1). On their return to Beroea they carried a request from Paul that Silas and Timothy should join him at once (Acts 17:14-15). From Acts 17:16 and 18:5 it would seem that by the time Silas and Timothy joined him he had gone on to Corinth, inasmuch as these three were reunited there. Luke simply omits any mention of Timothy or Silas being in Athens at all. His condensed story in Acts contains only as much detail as was necessary to his purpose.

Although there are several possible explanations, there is no way to be sure which, if any, of them is the correct one: (*a*) Silas and Timothy could have joined Paul in Athens and from there been dispatched again to Macedonia: Timothy to Thessalonica, and Silas to Beroea or elsewhere. (*b*) Timothy only might have been sent, Silas remaining with Paul. In this case the **we** of v. 1 would become a genuine plural, not an editorial or epistolary "we."[49] This would explain Paul's omission of Silas' name. (*c*) Paul might have sent a message to Beroea

[49]This is Frame's view (*op. cit.*, p. 126) apparently based on the meaning of "we." But this theory would subtract from the situation nearly all the poignant feeling connected with being companionless in the oppressive and difficult environment of Athens, a feeling which seems to be implicit within the wording of the sentence. Neil (*op. cit.*, p. 60) thinks that the total picture indicates that Paul was sick while at Athens.

countermanding his first request and sending Timothy to Thessalonica with a plan to join him later. In this case **to be left at Athens alone** would mean "to continue to be alone." But neither *b* nor *c* seems to fit the plain sense of the words so well as *a*. If we accept *a*, Paul means that Timothy parted from him at Athens, and that he was left without a companion—**alone** (cf. II Tim. 4:11, 16 for comparable poignancy of feeling). As if to stress Paul's deprivation in sending Timothy, as well as the importance attached to the mission, Timothy is described as **our brother, and minister of God, and our fellowlabourer in the gospel of Christ** (2).[50] Although he was the junior member of the party, there is obvious emphasis upon Timothy's status and valued service.

d. Purpose of Timothy's Trip (3:2-4). The purpose of Timothy's mission was **to establish you, and to comfort you concerning your faith: that no man should be moved by these afflictions** (2-3). The verb **to establish** (*sterixai*) carries the idea of buttressing. **To comfort** (*parakalesai*) suggests one called alongside to encourage. Besides this purpose of strengthening the believers, Timothy was also to prevent them from being **moved** (the Gk. sometimes carries the idea of beguiling) in the midst of affliction. On **afflictions** see comments on 1:6. Paul seems to have had in mind the twin perils of discouragement and deception.

As for **afflictions**, the apostle is careful to add, **for yourselves know that we are appointed** (lit., set or destined) **thereunto.** Moffatt has, "Troubles are our lot, you know that well." It was necessary to counteract the Satanic suggestion (used by Satan only when it fits his purpose) that peacefulness and prosperity are evidence of righteousness or true religion, and that conversely pain and trouble indicate God's displeasure. Paul had sought to forearm them for this very test: **For verily, when we were with you, we told you before that we should suffer tribulation** (affliction); **even as it came to pass, and ye know** (4). **Told** is in the imperfect tense, suggesting repeated telling

[50]The variant manuscript readings following the words **our brother** include: "and fellow-worker of God"; "and fellow-worker"; "and minister of God and our fellow-worker"; "and minister and fellow-worker of God." These variations are reflected in the variety of wording in the English translations. For a textual discussion see Frame, *op. cit.*, pp. 126-27; Moffatt, *op. cit.*, p. 31; Morris, *op. cit.*, p. 100 (footnote).

or warning regarding trouble that was at that time just ahead of them. **We,** as the subject of **are appointed** and **should suffer,** doubtless means Christians in general, not just the Thessalonians or the apostles (cf. Matt. 5:10; 16:24; John 16:33; Acts 14:22; II Tim. 3:12; I Pet. 2:21 ff.; 4:12 ff.). Christians are to face trouble, not as an appointment with blind fate, but as something included in God's good and perfect plan.

Christian suffering is not the consequence of a divine penal decree, but is rather the unavoidable result of godliness at work in a wicked world. The cross of Christ is itself an offense and a stumbling block. It is an intolerable rebuke to pride, selfishness, and self-will. To be true to their commission Christians must in love attack the corruption and the false gods of society. Deeper still, they must find their lives' meaning by identifying themselves with Him who could not avoid Gethsemane's bitter cup, and who bore the world's transgressions on the Cross. There is no suggestion here of suffering for suffering's sake. This is no self-induced torture. As Christians, we are destined for holy character and for eternal values; therefore, in a world like this, we are destined also for tribulation. But there is nothing meaningless in such suffering: God uses it in His redemptive purpose, both for His glory and for our spiritual refinement.

e. How Is Your Faith? (3:5) Paul now repeats for emphasis what has already been said in 1 and 2: **For this cause** (because of the persecution, the apostle's loving concern, and the enforced separation), **when I could no longer forbear, I sent** (the **I** is emphatic, "I for my part," and the personal pronoun is changed in this verse from plural to singular) **to know your faith, lest by some means the tempter have tempted you, and our labour be in vain.** The RSV translates it, "for fear that somehow the tempter had tempted you and that our labor would be in vain."

Commentators who espouse a "once in grace, always in grace" view have some problems with this passage. They argue that what Paul sought to learn was whether or not the Thessalonians had originally had true faith and a real conversion, or had merely experienced a spurious, emotional change on the occasion of his preaching the gospel to them. But it is obvious that Paul's knowledge of their election based on evidence derived from the events cited in 1:4-10 was antecedent to his fear lest they should succumb to the tempter (see especially comments on 1:5).

Paul wished to know whether or not their faith, which had been genuine in the beginning, had been extinguished as a result of their temptations. He succeeds in conveying his underlying confidence in them even while expressing the tragic possibility of their spiritual failure, in which case his labor with them would prove to be **in vain.** The purpose of Satan was to destroy the faith of the converts. God uses permitted sufferings to strengthen faith and build holy character; Satan uses the same sufferings to seduce from the path of trust and obedience. In our probation the issue is in doubt only until by our choice and attitude we either humbly receive or willfully frustrate God's sufficient grace.

f. Good News from Thessalonica (3:6-8). The reminiscences which characterize the early part of this letter are coming to a close. **But now when Timotheus came from you unto us** (cf. the correct sense in NEB, "But now Timothy has just arrived"). The letter was written at once upon Timothy's return. The place of reunion was Corinth, where Paul had gone from Athens, if, as is usually done, we take Acts 18:5 as describing the same event. Although Paul does not mention Silas' return here, this is probably because Silas had not been in Thessalonica but in some other part of Macedonia.

The letter again takes on an exuberant tone as Paul recalls how Timothy's tidings changed his anxiety to joyful thanksgiving. As a true pastor with his flock, or a true teacher with his pupils, he had not been able to rest until he had learned of their success and steadfastness. The expression **came from you unto us** suggests that Timothy had in fact become their messenger to Paul, not simply a reporter of his own observations.

Paul had been comforted for two reasons. First, Timothy had **brought us good tidings** (lit., "glad tidings," Robertson[51]) **of your faith and charity** (love). The latter two terms sum up for Paul the life of a Christian in his relations to both God and man (cf. Gal. 5:6). The concept **faith,** mentioned again in 7, is the most definitive term used in describing a Christian. It involves his beliefs, the basic values by which he lives, his profoundest choices, his grasp on God and unseen realities, the hopes he cherishes, the basis and source of his very life in Christ, and his steadfastness in all of this. It is his faith that distinguishes

[51]*Op. cit.*, p. 26.

the Christian from all non-Christians. And it is love (*agape*) which is the universal hallmark of genuine Christian faith (see comments on 1:3). Says Denney, "These two graces of faith and love are the very soul of the Christian life. It is good news to a good man to hear that they exist in any church. It is good news to Christ."[52] The word translated **good tidings** is the one Paul normally reserves for describing the gospel itself. Such was the measure of his joy.

The apostle's second reason for joy was **that ye have good remembrance of us always, desiring greatly to see us, as we also to see you** (6). The Thessalonians held Paul in kindly remembrance. They had all the while (as the construction indicates) reciprocated fully his longing to see them. This fact had double significance. It was a test of their faith, for had they been backsliding in either heart or life they would have preferred Paul's absence. But the joy this news brought to Paul was also a very personal thing, as the verses which follow indicate. It meant a great deal to him to have a place in the hearts of his children in the faith, and in this we see something of the greatness of the man and shepherd of souls (cf. II Cor. 6:11; 12:15; Phil. 1:7).

The coming of Timothy with the **good tidings** had been very timely. **Therefore** (because of the good news), **brethren, we were comforted over you** (lit., encouraged because of you) **in all our afflictions** (see comments on 1:6) **and distress** (*anagkei* in this instance probably signifies physical privation[53] or physical necessity[54]). What is alluded to is not stated specifically in Acts, although the record (Acts 18:1-18) implies that not long after the return of Timothy and Silas the situation in Corinth developed very serious proportions (see vv. 9-10). The pressures on Paul were obviously great, and besides this he was laboring as a tentmaker (v. 3). The coming of Timothy seemed to provide, just when it was most needed, the assurance and courage to vigorously evangelize the great pagan city of Corinth (cf. Acts 18:5). This was accomplished, says Paul, **by your faith;** that is, by Timothy's report concerning their faith.

The next words are a remarkable, and no doubt to some an extravagant, expression. **For now we live, if ye stand fast in**

[52]*Op. cit.*, p. 121.

[53]Frame, *op. cit.*, p. 133.

[54]Robertson, *op. cit.*, p. 26.

the Lord (8). Paul was capable of intense feeling about those to whom he preached. This statement implies that he ranged from a depth of distress not unlike death itself to a height of joy and elation akin to resurrection life. His heart, his very life, was bound up with the spiritual progress of his converts. His was a life lived totally in terms of others, and because of this it had a fullness, richness, and vitality unknown to most men.

There can be no doubt that such full and openhearted living with all its inherent risk of suffering is a basic requirement for success in gospel work. Perhaps it can also be said that this is the price to be paid if the pastor today is to be loved by his people as Paul was loved by the Thessalonians. Paul is saying that the recent good news has been a life-giving transfusion to him. He is also saying, as expressed by the conditional clause, that his continued life is bound up with their continued steadfastness.[55] Perhaps there is here an anticipation of the deficiency in their faith referred to in 10.

2. *Prayer for Establishment in Holiness* (3:9-13)

Verses 12-13 constitute a prayer for a specific grace. This is prefaced by a general statement in 9-11 on Paul's praying for the Thessalonians. Each illuminates the other.

a. Thanksgiving for Present Grace (3:9-10). In the abundance of his joy, Paul acknowledges that the proper expression is neither self-congratulation on the success of his converts nor congratulation of the converts on their steadfastness. The only fitting expression is gratitude to God, by whose grace alone all this is possible. The measure and the proper expression of gratitude are here, as always, a true criterion of a right sense of values. **For what thanks can we render to God again** ("How can we thank our God enough," Phillips) **for you** (i.e., concerning you)? Paul says that his joy is **for your sakes before our God;** and that **night and day** he is **praying exceedingly.** The last word is one of the double compound adverbs of which Paul is fond—*huperekperissou.* To the word **exceedingly** are prefixed in the Greek, not one, but two prepositions giving it the force of "more than out of bounds."[56]

[55]A. J. Mason, *The Epistles to the Colossians, Thessalonians, and Timothy,* "Layman's Handy Commentary," ed. Charles J. Ellicott (Grand Rapids: Zondervan Publishing House, 1957), p. 96.

[56]Robertson, *op. cit.*, p. 26.

It is significant to note how Paul's intense joy over his converts overflows in a cascade of thankful and earnest prayer for them. The prayer has two main petitions: (1) **that we might see your face,** and (2) that we **might perfect that which is lacking in your faith.** The first petition is voiced in 11, and the second in 12-13. Frame comments[57] on the ethical soundness of Paul's intense religious feelings, noting that in his enthusiasm he is yet aware of his converts' moral defects. These defects had doubtless been reported by Timothy, so that Paul's abundant joy, while given full rein, is yet tempered by deep, ethical concern.

b. Prayer for an Added Grace (3:10-13). **Perfect** is from the verb *katartizo*, which means "to render *artios* i.e. fit, sound, complete"[58] and thus "to mend" as in Mark 1:19, or "put in order" or "arrange" (form) as in Heb. 11:3. "This word . . . means generally . . . to 'adjust' differences, 'repair' things out of repair, 'set' bows, 'prepare' dishes, etc.; and here 'make up,' 'make good' that which is lacking to complete faith."[59] Our word *artisan* is derived from it (cf. Eph. 4:12, "the perfecting of the saints"). Both this word and *husteremata,* translated **that which is lacking,** indicate incompleteness or deficiency (cf. NEB, "mend your faith where it falls short"; Moffatt, "supply what is defective in your faith"; Barclay,[60] "fill up the gaps in your faith").

These expressions and the prayer form the transition to the ethical instructions which are to follow and which are thus tactfully introduced.

As so frequently in his letters, Paul bursts into spontaneous, intercessory prayer. The scope of this prayer is breathtaking. The longing to revisit the Thessalonian church is committed to the sovereign, providential control of God (11). The lesson taught is important. The human desire to be with the converts was both beautiful and exemplary, but it was under discipline—subordinated to the will of God, who knows all things. Whether this prayer was answered during the third missionary journey (cf. Acts 20:1-2) or later still, we cannot be sure. But Paul prays for a work of grace to be done in his converts (12-13),

[57]*Op. cit., ad loc.*

[58]Thayer, *op. cit.*, p. 336.

[59]Frame, *op. cit.*, p. 135.

[60]*Letters*, p. 226.

which is not dependent upon the apostle's presence. The work of grace for which he prays is that they may **abound in love,** and be established **unblameable in holiness.**

Now God himself and our Father (RSV, "our God and Father himself"), **and our Lord Jesus Christ,**[61] **direct** (lit., make straight) **our way unto you.** Here again there are Trinitarian implications. **God** the **Father** and the **Lord Jesus** are placed side by side and addressed simultaneously in prayer, implying their oneness. Against those who claim a gradual development in the Church of the concept of Jesus' deity this is doctrinally the more significant in such an early letter as Thessalonians (see comments on 1:1).

And the Lord make you to increase and abound in love—the two Greek verbs are practically synonyms, so that combined they give the idea of superabounding, overflowing love—**one toward another, and toward all men, even as we do toward you** (12). The divine love (*agape*) for which Paul prays is progressive in expression; indeed it is limitless in the possibilities of its growth. It is to be mutually expressed, but to be unselfish and unrestricted in its scope. Paul testifies that all this is exemplified in his own love for them. The prayer is **to the end he may stablish your hearts** (NEB, "make your hearts firm") **unblameable** (see comment on 2:10) **in holiness before God, even our Father, at the coming of our Lord Jesus Christ with all his saints** (13).

The whole emphasis of this prayer is upon the inwardness of personal character. It is implied that the character required to make the Thessalonians ready to stand before Christ at His **coming** is more than a certain blamelessness of outward behavior or service. God's requirement is rather a blamelessness in inward devotement to God, and inward moral purity. Their **hearts,** their whole personalities, inwardly as well as outwardly, must be pure **before God.** Not man's judgment, but God's, will be the standard. The true quality of our love and our motives is known only to Him.

The manner in which this holiness (entire sanctification, cf. 5:23-24) is bestowed is here described as an **increase,** an abounding infusion of the pure love of God which "is shed abroad in our hearts by the Holy Ghost which is given unto us"

[61]Later translations follow the texts which omit Christ.

(Rom. 5:5). It is **the Lord** who will **make you** to **abound in love.** Holiness is a gift of God's grace; not the result of human effort, but the answer to faith in Christ. Since this **love** is from God, it is pure and holy, corresponding with the nature of God. Such love is "the fulfilling of the law" (Rom. 13:10).

This love is the Spirit's instrument for the expulsion of that which is impure and incompatible from the heart; its necessary outcome is full obedience to the will of God. A "holiness" which comes some other way than by a baptism of divine love will be spurious—sanctimonious, censorious, legal. True holiness will be manifested in love for **one . . . another** and for **all men.** Divine love is "the bond of perfectness" (Col. 3:14); it is the energy of all true holiness. It is the means to spiritual stability, since all else is transient.

Here again we note that the Christian ethic is dominated by the Christian hope, just as it is founded on the nature of God. On **the coming** (*parousia*) **of our Lord Jesus Christ** see the footnote referring to 2:19.

Commentators have disagreed as to the meaning of **saints** (*hagioi*; lit., holy ones). Many seek to harmonize the expression **all his saints** with the teaching of 4:13-17, and thus interpret it to mean the resurrected and glorified people of God. Others think the reference is to angels and cite in support such passages as Matt. 16:27; Mark 8:38; II Thess. 1:7; Jude 14. In support of the first view is the fact that Paul himself never uses *hagioi* to refer to angels. There are good arguments on both sides. Perhaps both groups are intended.[62] Thus Moffatt has "all his holy ones"; NEB, "all those who are his own"; Phillips, "all who belong to him."

McCumber finds in this passage (9-13) "The Prayer for Completed Faith." He notes (1) The lack defined, 10; (2) The need supplied, 10, 12; (3) The results expressed, 13.[63]

[62]Cf. Vincent, *op. cit.*, p. 34.

[63]W. E. McCumber, *Holiness in the Prayers of St. Paul* (Kansas City: Beacon Hill Press, 1955), pp. 75-85.

Section II *Ethical and Doctrinal Teachings*

I Thessalonians 4:1—5:28

At this point there is a change in the tone and subject matter of the letter. Paul passes from thanksgiving, defense of his ministry, and reminiscences to practical exhortations on the Christian life. To conclude in this practical way is characteristic of the Pauline letters. In this section the apostle is no doubt dealing with matters on which Timothy's report indicated that instruction was needed. The section contains two passages on practical holiness (4:1-12 and 5:12-24) which are separated by one on doctrine (4:13—5:11). The whole section however, including doctrine, is intensely practical.

A. Guidance in Daily Christian Living, 4:1-12

1. *A Life of Obedience and Purity* (4:1-8)

Furthermore then (lit., for the rest) is an expression marking the transition in subject matter. The double expression **beseech . . . and exhort** (1) indicates the great seriousness of the writer. The apostle does not threaten or command these persecuted Christians. The earnest exhortation matches the fervent prayer which precedes it. God's grace must be matched by human response. The entreaty is **by** (in) **the Lord Jesus.** These ethical requirements follow from union with Christ, and are grounded in and inspired by the authority of Christ. **As ye have received of us** suggests the important place of ethical instruction in the Early Church. It is needful still. **Walk** here stands for the whole manner of living. **Please God** suggests that to glorify God and do His will is the heart of Christian living. The little word **ought** reminds us that the redeemed are men under obligation, and yet the "yoke is easy" and the "burden is light."

Not found in KJV, but derived from the oldest and best manuscripts, immediately following **please God** are the words "just as you are doing" (RSV). Paul is not suggesting that they have been failing in living the Christian life. Indeed, these words are a tactful bit of praise. The emphasis is on achieving, going forward, making faster progress. They are to **abound more**

and more. There is no place to rest in Christian life. To stand still will really mean backsliding. God sets no bounds to progress in grace. The fruit-bearing Christian is purged in order to bring forth "more fruit" (John 15:2). Life is to become "more abundant." The sanctified life is the abounding, fruitful life.

Paul is careful to make clear (2) that the **commandments** ("instructions," RSV) previously given his converts were not on his own authority but **by the Lord Jesus.** The preposition in the phrase may well suggest the whole scope of divine revelation and authority through Jesus Christ. On **commandments,** cf. John 14:15, 21; 15:7, 10, 12; I John 2:4-6; 3:22-24; 5:2-3.) The practice of conscientious obedience to the known will of God is proposed as the minimum foundation for success and growth in the Christian life.

Having established the above principle, Paul proceeds to specific application of it: **For this is the will of God . . . your sanctification** (3). *Hagiasmos,* **sanctification,** is primarily the work of making holy, separating from sin unto God, making morally pure; but it is also the resulting state of holiness.[1] God wishes, says the apostle, to sanctify (to consecrate to himself, and purify inwardly) these Thessalonian converts (cf. 1:7-9) in order that they shall be holy.

This is not, of course, a definition of God's will, but the statement, within the context, of God's purpose for His redeemed children (cf. 1:4; 5:23; also John 17:19; Eph. 5:25-27; Heb. 13:12). **The will of God** may be seen as *precept* (unalterable law or commandment, to which men must submit); as *purpose* (divine wisdom and love seeking their sublime ends); as *power* (divine efficiency working out what is purposed); and as *promise* (utter dependability in the fulfillment of its purpose).

From the general statement of God's plan for human life, Paul proceeds abruptly to the application in a specific instance: **that ye should abstain from fornication** ("shrink from all sexual vice," Amp. NT). "God's plan is to make you holy, and that entails first of all a clean cut with sexual immorality" (Phillips). It may come as a surprise that such instruction should be given to a group like the Thessalonians. Although no slur on their character is implied, such teaching was generally needed among converts from paganism. Neil states: "The fact is that one of the

[1]Thayer, *op. cit.*, p. 6.

most difficult hurdles that any pagan convert had to clear was the Christian attitude to sex. He had been brought up in a world where polygamy, concubinage, homosexuality, and promiscuity were accepted as a matter of course. . . . Many of the religious cults were frankly sexual in character, with phallic rites and sacramental fornication as part of their worship."[2]

It is noteworthy that, along with other matters concerning Gentile practices, fornication is mentioned and forbidden in the directive of the Jerusalem Council (Acts 15:29).

The illegitimate or intemperate satisfaction of sensual appetite remains an area of temptation in all healthy and normal Christians, but the unsanctified Christian is perilously vulnerable to such appeals. There is a resurgent paganism of our own time with its smutty entertainment, pornographic literature, laxity in marriage vows, promiscuity, overall obsession with sex, and general permissiveness in sex relationships. In times like these the New Testament teaching on sexual purity is desperately needed, and the New Testament experience of sanctification, with its full devotion to the will of God, is the real answer. The immoral code of our time is fostered and condoned by such entrenched philosophies as naturalism and evolutionism. Gospel dynamite is required to break up these respectable havens of vice.

Following the negative application of the teaching on sanctification (3), Paul raises two specific matters (4-6). The problem of 4 centers around the word **vessel**, *skeuos*, which literally means "utensil" or "tool." Obviously, Paul here uses it metaphorically. Interpreters and commentators, both ancient and modern, are divided as to whether it signifies "wife" or "body." In favor of "wife" are the parallel uses in Rabbinical literature which could have influenced Paul. Since the lengthy appeal to all the parallel literary uses of the word is rather inconclusive, it would seem that the question should be decided on the grounds of choosing the word which best suits the context. Here again both sides argue strongly on matters of grammar and on what makes the best sense. The solution partly turns upon the meaning of the infinitive *ktosthai*, translated **to possess**. Robertson, for example, says it means "to acquire," "to get," but not "to possess."[3] If so, to think of **vessel** as "body" would be incongruous.

[2]*Letters*, p. 74.
[3]*Op. cit.*, IV, 29.

Moffatt has, "learn to take a wife for himself"; the RSV, "know how to take a wife for himself." John Wesley favored "wife," as do Weymouth and a number of others. However, William Barclay[4] translates, "that each of you should know how to possess [control, manage] his own body." Phillips renders it, "every one of you should learn to control his body"; NEB, "each one of you must learn to gain mastery over his body."

Both Neil[5] and Morris[6] feel that "body" is meant, since to think of a wife as a **vessel** would seem to degrade rather than elevate the view of marriage, and would be out of keeping with the passage and with the spirit of Paul. This interpretation seems most consistent with an ethical and elevated view. The case for "body" does have a precedent in II Cor. 4:7. If one could think of the whole expression as being idiomatic, and of **vessel** as carrying no degrading connotation, then the objection to "wife" would be largely removed.[7]

Sexual purity, self-mastery, and self-discipline, seen as characteristics of the sanctified life, are here under discussion. **In sanctification** means in full consecration of body and spirit, in inward cleansing of depraved passions. **In honour** suggests the resulting reverence for the body, rather than in prostitution of its faculties and appetites. These are lifted up as the way to purity and to the fulfilling of the **will of God** (3). The marriage relationship and all relationships between the sexes are to be in **honour.** Reverence or honor for the body is particularly a Christian concept. (On **honour** cf. Col. 2:23; II Tim. 2:20-21; I Pet. 3:7.)

Paul now contrasts what he has just taught with its opposite. **Not in the lust of concupiscence** (5; "passion of lust," ASV) is in direct contrast with **in sanctification and honour.** Christian holiness would redeem marriage from the degraded level of the **Gentiles** (pagans, heathen) who regarded the body "as an instrument for self-gratification" (Phillips). The Gentiles do so because they are strangers to the revealed and holy law of God. Any

[4]*Op. cit.*, p. 230.

[5]*Op. cit.*, p. 75.

[6]*Op. cit.*, p. 124.

[7]For an interpretation quite different from either of those above, based on the word order and the use of punctuation, see Marvin R. Vincent, *Word Studies in the New Testament* (Grand Rapids: Wm. B. Eerdmans Publishing Co., 1946), IV, 35-36.

revival of sanctity will be accompanied or preceded by respect for the revealed moral law.

Paul now adds the third of the three coordinate clauses which expand the idea of **this . . . the will of God . . . your sanctification** (3). The first is **that ye should abstain** (3); the second begins, **that every one of you** (4); the third clause is, **that no man go beyond** (transgress) **and defraud** (wrong) **his brother in any matter** (6). "In *the* matter" (ASV) is a more exact translation (cf. "this matter," RSV, NEB). The translation **any matter** would open up the discussion to include conduct in general, while the exact translation would indicate "the matter" under discussion, namely, sexual immorality.

A number of influential interpreters have thought that **matter,** *pragma,* should be here thought of as "business." This view suggests that Paul is leaving the question of sexual conduct and is beginning to discuss instead the sin of covetousness, or to put it another way, honesty in business dealings. However, in keeping with a majority of commentators, it seems preferable to think of "the matter" as defined by the context. Nowhere in the New Testament is *pragma* translated "business."

All kinds of immorality and sexual looseness constitute wrongs against innocent people who are, or will become, involved. And such actions are not solely the concern of the immediate partners in sin.

a. God Avenges Those Who Are Wronged (4:6). Having lifted high the Christian standard of personal purity, Paul now reinforces his teaching with a series of solemn sanctions. First: **because that the Lord is the avenger of all such** (6; lit., an Avenger in all these things). The wronged **brother** (person) may be deceived, and the society in which such offenses occur may fail to condemn them or may even condone them, but the judgment of God upon all impurity is sure and terrible. While reckoning in the fullest sense must await the final judgment (and this is likely the primary reference here), there is a recompense exacted upon the bodies and the emotional, moral, and spiritual natures of those who have indulged in immoral conduct. The moral laws of God are written into the constitution of human nature, and the disregard of these laws brings with it a vengeance which is sometimes dramatic, sometimes quiet and stealthy, but always certain (cf. Rom. 1:24-32; Gal. 6:7-8; Eph. 5:5-6).

This whole matter must have been for the Thessalonians a besetting temptation, for Paul states that he had **forewarned** them (lit., told you before) **and testified** (lit., solemnly affirmed) with reference to it.

b. God Calls Men to Holiness (4:7). The second sanction against impurity is the nature of the divine call: **For God hath not called us unto uncleanness, but unto holiness** (7). In this brief but vivid contrast, Paul states the whole sweep of God's high purpose for believers. It is nothing less than holiness, the restoration to man of the moral image of God which has been effaced by sin. "For God called us to holiness, not to impurity" (NEB). The thought returns to that of 3, and to "the will of God," which is here connected with that wonderful day in their lives when in mercy and grace God called them out of a life of sin into fellowship with himself. The call was God's initiative; it was God's love in action. The call was purposeful, and the purpose was nothing less than "the most thorough purity" (Phillips) —holiness of both heart and life. Since the call is mediated by the preaching of the gospel, the Church can have no other message than this. The word (*hagiasmos*) translated **holiness** here is the same word translated "sanctification" in 3 and 4 (cf. comment on the word there). The argument here is that for a Christian to fall short of a life of holiness is for him to deny the divine purpose in saving him in the first place.

c. Do Not Disregard God (4:8). This suggests the third sanction: **He therefore that despiseth** (lit., sets aside and thus "disregards," RSV) **despiseth not man, but God** (8). The verb has no object, but what is meant is quite clear from the context. Negatively, reference is made to the injunctions against sexual impurity; but these are, throughout the passage, set in contrast to the call to holiness, and thus, positively, the reference is to this call. The ethical and spiritual demand for sanctification rests, not in the teaching of a man (the apostle), but in the nature and the will of God.

This third sanction is reinforced by the special characterization of God which follows: **who hath also given**[8] **unto us**[9] **his holy**

[8]The revised translations follow the better texts, which have the present rather than the aorist tense here: "Who gives his Holy Spirit." Thus, the emphasis is on the dynamic, continuing relationship with the Holy Spirit, rather than on the past act of giving.

[9]Revised translations have "you" rather than "us."

Spirit. God dwells in His people in the person of the Holy Spirit. He who **despiseth** sins not against a far-off Deity, but grieves and insults the regenerating and sanctifying Spirit of God. The unusual order of the Greek words translated **his holy Spirit**[10] underlines this truth. The stress on *hagion,* **holy,** is solemn and emphatic: "His Spirit, the holy."[11] *The Amplified New Testament* suggests this: "whose [very] Spirit [Whom] He gives to you [is] holy." Phillips has caught it also: "It is not for nothing that the Spirit God gives us is called the *Holy* Spirit."

The Source of the believer's new life is the Holy Spirit, and in this is seen the utter incompatability of a life of impurity and sin with the life in Christ. Not only is holiness the will of God, but the Holy Spirit, who is at work in the believer's life, is himself the Fountain of true holiness. The peculiar work of the Holy Spirit is to sanctify. If the Spirit's ministry is not rebuffed (cf. 5:19) but rather lovingly received, He will lead unerringly to the entire sanctification of the whole person (cf. 5:23-24).

The message of the foregoing eight verses is peculiarly needed in this hour. To rescue our homes and our nation from the ruin which threatens, the Church must lift high the standard of moral purity to be found only through the sanctifying grace of God in Christ.

2. *Brotherly Love and Industry* (4:9-12)

a. Brotherly Love (4:9-10). With the words **but as touching** (concerning) **brotherly love** (9), Paul begins to deal with another matter which was causing some difficulty in the Thessalonian church. With customary tactfulness he begins in a complimentary manner (9-10) and proceeds then to admonition (10*b*-12).

Brotherly love (*philadelphia*) is in classical Greek the love of the brother by birth, but in the New Testament it always means love of the brother in Christ.[12] Christians are **taught of God to love one another.** The love of this second expression is *agape.* This teaching is not external instruction but the inward implanting of love by the Holy Spirit, whose ministry was mentioned in the preceding verse (cf. I John 3:14-18; 4:7, 20; 5:1-2).

[10]Frame, *op. cit.,* p. 156.

[11]Vincent, *op. cit.,* p. 38.

[12]Frame, *op. cit.,* p. 158.

The Christian Church was a wonder to the heartless, pagan society of Paul's day, which could only exclaim, "Behold how they love one another!" It ought to be thus today. Because love for Christian brothers is an evidence of the new birth, Paul suggests that he need not formally instruct them on this subject. Not only so, but the external expression of this love was not wanting (10*a*). The reference to **the brethren . . . in all Macedonia** suggests a warm fellowship and deeds of loving helpfulness. Here is reflected the mutual concern during persecution, which no doubt characterized these Christians in the capital city in relation to other provincial congregations, as well as to Christian travelers (cf. 1:3; 3:6). In these commendable activities, Paul urges that they shall **increase more and more** ("do better still," NEB). (Cf. comment on the like expression in 4:1.) This is reminiscent of the prayer in 3:12. Where *agape* abounds, *philadelphia* will abound also.

b. A Life of Industry (4:11-12). What condition in the church would have induced Paul to write the rather blunt threefold admonition of 11? It is often conjectured that the problem which is revealed in some detail in II Thess. 3:6-15 was beginning to appear. Perhaps there are hints also in this letter in 5:12-15, 19-20. It is usually supposed—although proof is lacking—that the expectation of the imminent return of the Lord had caused a ferment of excitement in some minds. Idleness was producing restlessness among those who had ceased regular employment, and this state of affairs was in turn producing meddlesome busybodies.

However the case may have been, Paul is underscoring the truth that brotherly love and honest work go hand in hand as Christian evidences. The thirst for sensational religious excitement is sometimes today characteristic of a few loafing busybodies in the church. But true faith will produce tranquility of spirit; proper zeal will motivate to cooperation rather than meddling; and genuine piety will give meaning and worthwhileness to daily work.

Study to be quiet (11) states a kind of paradox. It is literally "be ambitious to be tranquil." RSV has "aspire to live quietly," the opposite of aspiring to be prominently seen and heard. **Do your own business** (be busy with your own things) probably carries the additional meaning of the English idiom, "Mind your own business," i.e., "Don't meddle in other people's affairs."

Failure to **work with your own hands** may have been the root of the difficulty. Denney observes:

> If we cannot be holy at our work, it is not worth taking any trouble to be holy at other times. . . . Perhaps some of us crave leisure, that we may be more free for spiritual work; and think that if we had more time at our disposal, we should be able to render many services to Christ and His cause which are out of our power at the present. But that is extremely doubtful. If experience proves anything, it proves that nothing is worse for most people than to have nothing to do but be religious. . . . The daily life of toil . . . does not rob us of the Christian life; it really puts it within our reach.[13]

Two important considerations are cited (12) which urge upon Christians this kind of living. The first is **that ye may walk honestly** ("that you may command the respect of," NEB) **them that are without** (non-Christians). Says Barclay, "When we Christians prove that our Christianity makes us better workmen, truer friends, kinder men and women, then and only then are we really preaching. The important thing is not words but deeds, not oratory but life."[14] The humblest Christian has opportunity to reflect honor upon the cause of Christ through the consistent and faithful performance of his duties, and nothing can really compensate for the discredit suffered through failure to do so.

The second consideration is **that ye may have lack of nothing.** Grammatically, this expression may be correctly translated either "need of nothing" or "need of no one." In either wording the basic meaning is the same. The idlers are not to depend upon the charity of others. Brotherly love will make people thoughtful of the needs of the poor or unfortunate, but the Christian must not be a parasite or a sponger. A certain reasonable independence in such matters is a Christian virtue.

The economic complexities of our own day, the changing conditions in all kinds of employment, and the problems involving social security place this teaching in quite a different context from that of the first century. These Christian virtues are still the same, however, and the underlying principles may, by a conscientious effort, be applied to modern Christian living. The work of the Kingdom moves forward today through the lives of people who go quietly, dutifully, and lovingly about their

[13]*Op. cit.,* pp. 161-62.
[14]*Letters,* p. 234.

everyday tasks, who serve for Jesus' sake, who do with their might what their hands find to do.

B. The Coming of the Lord, 4:13—5:11

It is evident from the allusions to the second coming of Christ in this letter (1:10; 2:19; 3:13; 5:23) that Paul had preached this doctrine to the Thessalonians. This is in keeping with what we know of apostolic preaching, in which the second coming of the Lord was an integral truth. The *parousia* was a part of the gospel, the good news. It is clear also that problems had arisen which called for more detailed instruction on this subject, instruction which had not been given during the time of the founding of the church. The discussion of two of these questions in the first letter (4:13-18; 5:1-11) and the continuation of the discussion in the second letter, give these Epistles a distinctly eschatological flavor.

1. *The Dead in Christ* (4:13-18).

The Thessalonian Christians, so recently converted from paganism, were apparently deeply troubled (cf. 4:13, 18). When, the Lord having not yet come, some of their number died, the logical question was: What will become of the Christian dead at the Lord's coming? Will they miss the glory of His kingdom and reign?

It is not necessary to make a special case for these Christians based on their belief that Christ would come in their own lifetime. Those who argue that Paul himself first believed that Christ would return during his lifetime and later changed his mind are likewise misreading the expression of the Christian hope in Paul's letters. The imminence of the second coming of Christ has been characteristic of the faith of regenerated believers in all periods of the Church's history. It is so today. It was part of Jesus' own teaching (Matt. 24:36-44; Luke 12:35-40).

The concept of imminence, properly understood, does not demand immediacy, and is not destroyed because the Lord "delayeth his coming" (Matt. 24:48). That such a hope has sometimes been distorted or misconceived by good people is hardly surprising. If the fervent expectancy of the Thessalonian converts seems strange to modern readers, is this not a commentary on the lack of intensity of our own hope? Further, it seems quite unlikely that the Thessalonians were totally ignorant of the doctrine of the resurrection of the dead. Certainly there is no indication that they denied it, as was the case in Corinth somewhat later (cf. I Cor. 15:12). All that is needed to gain some insight into the torn hearts of these bereaved Christians is to imagine in them the absence of understanding, and thus the presence of uncertainty with reference to their departed loved ones at Christ's return.

The purpose of Paul here is to instruct and comfort the Christians at the point of the problem which had so naturally arisen. This is not a detailed description of the Second Advent. It is nevertheless the first, and in fact the only fully explicit, statement in the New Testament of the rapture of the saints. The other passages in question rest for their interpretation in one degree or another on this one. Paul comforts the troubled hearts with the instruction that the deceased Christians will have a full share in the coming Kingdom. They are in no way at a disadvantage when compared with the living Church. All believers, living and dead, are "in Christ," and nothing can separate them from His love and purpose for them (cf. Rom. 8:38-39). The believers' relationship with Christ transcends time and is stronger than death. This glorious doctrine has been an inspiration to Christians through the centuries.

a. The Christian Attitude Toward Death (4:13). Paul uses the expression, **But I would not have you to be ignorant** (13), and similar expressions, to introduce subjects of great importance (cf. Rom. 11:25; I Cor. 10:1; 12:1). He uses a gentle, euphemistic expression for the dead: **them which are asleep.** The present tense may also suggest "those who are [from time to time] falling asleep." Since this figurative language for death is common in both Judaism and pagan Greek writers who have no concept of resurrection, it is impossible to base any doctrinal significance upon it. The ideas which it suggests, such as death without fear or sting (cf. I Cor. 15:55-57), rest, and a future awakening of the body, are certainly at home in the Christian faith. There is no justification for the notion of "soul sleep."

Paul writes so that the Christians will not **sorrow** (RSV, "grieve") **even as others** (cf. "them that are without" in preceding verse) **which have no hope.** Frame thinks that the comparison is an antithesis, and that Paul is indicating, not the manner or degree of grief, but simply that Christians are not to grieve over their dead in Christ.[15] This would require us to understand "to sorrow," or "to grieve," as meaning continued inward grieving. The utter hopelessness of the ordinary pagan in the presence of death (although a few thinkers had risen to a concept of immortality) is seen today in the expressions of modern agnostics. The Christian hope, in sharp contrast, involves confidence in God (cf. Eph. 2:12), being "with Christ" (Phil. 1:23; cf. II Cor. 5:8), and the resurrection of the body.

b. Foundations of the Christian Hope (4:14-15). Paul proceeds to two arguments regarding the destiny of the dead in Christ which bring light and consolation. The first (14) is subjective, based on faith in Christ's resurrection. The second (15) is objective—a revelation from the Lord. The latter is continued in 16 and 17.

The resurrection of **Jesus** (the human name for our Lord links His humanity with ours), an article of faith which is foundational in Christian belief (cf. I Cor. 15:17-19), guarantees the Christian hope. Note that **Jesus died**—that is, He experienced death in its horror without any mitigating influence—while it is said that believers **sleep. If we believe that Jesus died and rose again** ("since we believe"; the Amp. NT thus interprets the import of the conditional clause), then it must follow that **them also which sleep in Jesus will God bring with him.**[16] The argument is compressed, and implied. In order to fully express it, words must be supplied. Christ is alive forevermore in the unseen glory; the Christian dead are in Him, and actively participating with Him; therefore they cannot miss the *parousia,* since God will bring them with Christ when He returns (cf. 3:13).

The word of the Lord (15) is Paul's other argument. This could mean some teaching of Jesus unrecorded in the Gospels, or a revelation from Christ to Paul on this matter. At any rate,

[15]*Op. cit.,* p. 167.

[16]Grammatically, the phrase **in Jesus** (lit., through Jesus) may follow or modify either "sleep" or "bring." RSV has "even so, through Jesus, God will bring with him those who have fallen asleep." A similar construction is followed by Moffatt, Weymouth, Goodspeed, Amp. NT, and others. However, Frame (*op. cit.,* pp. 169-70), following Ellicott, prefers the sense of KJV and ASV. "Bring through Jesus" would suggest Jesus as God's Agent in the resurrection and rapture. "Sleep through Jesus," which is said to be awkward, or perhaps to even indicate martyrdom, would suggest, however, only the mitigation of death for the one "in Christ," or continued union with Christ even in death itself.

it is on Christ's authority that Paul teaches that those alive at Christ's coming will have no advantage over the Christian dead. Paul naturally associates himself (**we**) with those who **are alive and remain unto the coming of the Lord** (cf. I Cor. 15:51). Just as naturally he associates himself with those who will be raised from the dead, in I Cor. 6:14 and II Cor. 4:14. The significant concept of the Second Coming is that of imminence, and more than that should not be read into the passage. Paul lived in continual expectation of the Lord's return, as every Christian should. To say, however, that he dogmatically asserted that he would live to see it is quite another thing, and cannot be substantiated from his writings. The English word **prevent** (ASV, "precede") formerly meant "to come before." The force of the negative is noted in ASV, "shall in no wise precede." (On *parousia* see footnote on 2:19 and cf. comment by Ralph Earle, BBC, Vol. 6, p. 215.)

c. *Our Lord's Appearing* (4:16-18). **For the Lord himself** (16; cf. "this same Jesus," Acts 1:11), not an angel, but the One whom they love and serve, the One who knows His own (II Tim. 2:19), **shall descend from heaven** (cf. John 14:1-3). It is sometimes supposed that the three attendant phenomena, the **shout,** the **voice,** and the **trump,** are three expressions of the same thing;[17] each, however, may be seen as having a distinct meaning. The **shout** ("cry of command," RSV) is a word used in the Greek to denote the cry of a commander to his soldiers in combat, by a charioteer to his horses, or by a ship's master to his oarsmen.[18] It is a loud, authoritative summons, exciting and stimulating. It speaks here of Christ as Victor (cf. John 5:25-29). In the only other place in the Bible where the **archangel** is mentioned (Jude 9), the reference is to Michael. The **trump** ("sound of the trumpet," RSV) **of God** (cf. I Cor. 15:52) characteristically accompanies and denotes in Scripture the importance, solemnity, or majesty of great religious occasions (cf. Exod. 19:16, 19; Joel 2:1; Rev. 1:10). There is nothing in this passage to support the idea of a secret rapture.

At the cry of command, executed perhaps by the archangel, the **dead in Christ** are to be summoned from their graves, and **shall rise first.** The little phrase **the dead in Christ** beautifully

[17]Frame, *op. cit.*, p. 174.

[18]Thayer, *op. cit.*, p. 343.

and compactly presents a precious truth: it is not that in life they *were* in Christ, but that in death they *are* in Christ, and with Christ. The statement that they **shall rise first** has reference to the subsequent catching up of the living (17), and not to a second resurrection of the remaining dead, about which nothing is said. The doctrine of the resurrection Paul treats in some detail in I Corinthians 15.

As the Lord descends, believers ascend **to meet the Lord in the air** (17). Thus we are left to understand that, in the same swift act by which the dead in Christ are raised, those who **are alive and remain** (see comment on 15) are **caught up together with them in the clouds.** The living, then, have no advantage over the dead. **Shall be caught up** is from the Greek verb *harpazo,* which means "to seize on, claim for oneself eagerly, to snatch out or away, to seize and carry off speedily, to catch away."[19] From this we derive the term "rapture." There will be a glad reunion with departed and resurrected loved ones; the living will be **caught up together with them.** In order to accomplish this, the bodies of the living must be changed (cf. Rom. 8:23; I Cor. 15:50-53; Phil. 3:21).

The **clouds** and the **air** here signify simply the lower atmosphere above the earth. There may be some sign of conquest in the expressions however, since the air is said to be the domain of Satan (Eph. 2:2), and clouds are elsewhere associated with the Lord's coming in power (Dan. 7:13; Matt. 24:30).

Paul's concluding statement seems to say that the really important thing about all of this is the glorious truth that "we shall always be with the Lord" (RSV). For the Christian, it is this, after all, which makes heaven meaningful. This is his goal (cf. Phil. 3:7-14). There is little in this passage to satisfy mere curiosity. Paul is silent on a detailed order of events, the fate of unbelievers, the intermediate state, and the judgment.

The curtain of the future has been lifted, and we have seen enough to make our hearts leap with hope and joy. Ultimate triumph for the Christian is certain through Christ. What a word for dark days! Paul exhorts that the teaching be put to a practical, loving (not a speculative) use: **Wherefore comfort one another with these words.** (Cf. 2:11; 3:2; the word **comfort** bears the meaning also of encourage or strengthen.)

[19]*Ibid.,* p. 74.

We may recognize in this passage a bit of Old Testament apocalyptic imagery. In describing so indescribable an event the use of symbols is helpful, but we may take Barclay's warning against a "crude and insensitive literalism,"[20] at least as respects detail involving the physical senses. We should resist however, as a fatal blow to the Christian hope, any view which makes this passage a piece of so-called New Testament mythology. There is more here than the mere symbolism of a "realized eschatology," however much it may be said to teach "spiritual" truth. Unless the language itself is false, the events described are literally promised in time, and thus necessarily in space also. One cannot be comforted by a mythology any more than he can be warmed by a painted fire. We are assured, because this is "the word of the Lord" (15).

Alexander Maclaren finds in this passage "Small Duties and the Great Hope." (1) The duty of Christian love, 9-10; (2) The duty of daily work, 11-12; (3) The descending Lord and the rising saints, 11-18.

2. *The Living Church* (5:1-11)

Although there is a natural sequence from the thought of 4:13-18 to 5:1-11, there is a shift in emphasis. The thought turns from the readers' concern about the dead in Christ to their apparent uncertainty about their own preparedness for Christ's coming. Two false attitudes toward the Second Advent tend to be found among Christians: the one, a restless, speculative preoccupation with signs and dates; and the other, a busy absorption in worldly affairs to the exclusion of the hope.

Paul's antidote for both these tendencies may be summarized under the theme "Preparation for the Second Coming." (1) The unexpectedness of Christ's coming, 1-3; (2) Encouragement and assurance for the troubled, 4-5, 9-11; (3) The personal and moral responsibility of those who look for Christ's return, 6-8.

a. The Unknown Time (5:1-3). The phrase **the times and the seasons** (1; "epochs," NASB) introduces the recurring question of the curious and the anxious: How long before Christ comes? and at what point in history? (Cf. Acts 1:7.) **Times,** from *chronos,* suggests duration, while **seasons,** from *kairos,*

[20]*Letters,* p. 236.

suggests a suitable period. Hendriksen translates it: "the duration-periods and the appropriate seasons."[21] Of this question Paul says, **ye have no need that I write unto you,** no doubt because of previous instruction. The reminder is given, nevertheless, as a cure for restlessness (cf. 4:11). **For yourselves know perfectly** (*akribos* means exactly or accurately) **that the day of the Lord so cometh** (lit., is coming) **as a thief in the night** (2).

One cannot treat adequately, in a few words, the expression **day of the Lord.** For the Jews it was a familiar expression with a rather fixed meaning. It is a frequent theme in the Old Testament prophets, where it is a catastrophic day of judgment on God's enemies, deliverance for God's people, final vindication of God's righteousness, and the beginning of a new era of righteous peace. It is the time between the present evil age and the coming golden age. In the New Testament it is "the day," "that day," "the day of Christ," or **the day of the Lord.** The Old Testament concept is carried over and enriched. In general it may be said that in the New Testament it is a period of time (not a solar day) of unstated duration, which commences with or at least near the time of the return of Christ. It ends with the final consummation of all things (the new heavens and the new earth), and includes in its scope such events as the great tribulation, the resurrection, the judgment, and Christ's reign on earth. Understanding of **the day of the Lord** varies somewhat according to millennial theories and other eschatological questions. But there is general agreement that it is God's day, in contrast to man's day of rebellion. It is **the day** of righteousness in contrast to **the night** of sin. It is a day of terrible alternatives: the sinner's doomsday, the saint's day of glory.

The day will come like **a thief in the night** (cf. Matt. 24:36; Luke 12:39; 21:34), who never announces beforehand his intention, and who strips the unwary of all their treasures.

For when they (i.e., the world, unbelievers) **shall say, Peace and safety** (cf. Matt. 24:37-39; 25:5) is reminiscent of Jer. 6:14. NEB has "while they are talking of peace and security." The idea is of a false security, possibly as to both inward feelings and outward circumstances. The **sudden destruction** (3) of unbelievers does not mean annihilation. Rather it has the

[21]*Op. cit.*, p. 121.

idea of ruin,[22] and is used in II Thess. 1:9, where it means final separation from God. The familiar Oriental simile, **as travail** ("birth-pangs," NASB) **upon a woman with child,** may carry the idea of the inevitability or unavoidability of judgment, or simply that of its suddenness. Morris favors the former,[23] and one commentator speaks of the unbelievers as being "pregnant with their own ruin."[24] Frame, however, confines the idea to suddenness.[25] Paul seems to suggest his own meaning: **they shall not escape.** There is no third alternative in the matter; it is either doom with unbelievers or glory with Christ.

As if suggested by the figure of the **thief in the night** (2), Paul takes up the contrasting metaphors of light and darkness, day and night, watchfulness and sleep, sobriety and drunkenness (4-8), to teach spiritual lessons. These figures are turned several ways to expose more than one facet, but in a general way they indicate those who are saved and those who are lost (cf. Eph. 5:8; Col. 1:13).

b. Encouragement and Assurance (5:4-5). The Thessalonian **brethren** are **not in darkness** (4). The reference is likely to ignorance of the truth as well as to moral and spiritual depravity (cf. II Cor. 6:14). As Christians, enlightened and spiritually transformed by Christ (cf. John 8:12), the coming "day of Christ" will not **overtake** ("surprise," RSV) them **as a thief.**[26]

Those who are **not of the night** (5), and therefore are in the light, are **the children of light, and the children of the day.** This rather Oriental expression suggests that their redeemed natures have an affinity for light (cf. "children of this world," Luke 16:8). By contrast, non-Christians are **of the night,** and **of darkness,** and by implication children of the same. They have an affinity for darkness, and hide from light (John 3:19-21). The Thessalonians, Paul says, **are all the children of light.** The exhortation which follows is not to backsliders, but to encourage

[22]Thayer, *op. cit.,* p. 443.

[23]*Op. cit.,* p. 154.

[24]C. A. Auberlen and C. J. Riggenbach, "The Two Epistles of Paul to the Thessalonians," trans. John Lillie, *Lange's Commentary on the Holy Scriptures* (Grand Rapids: Zondervan Publishing House, 1960), XI, 83.

[25]*Op. cit.,* p. 182.

[26]A number of manuscripts read "thieves." The commentators who prefer this reading (e.g., Frame, *ibid.,* p. 184), feel that it is the thieves who are surprised by the dawn, the reverse of the figure in v. 2.

Christians to sustain this relationship by continued watchfulness. As Christians they belong to a future Kingdom of light where darkness will be forever banished, and although that **day** has not yet come, they are already walking in its light. Those who walk with Christ in the light will not be unprepared for His coming on the day of the Lord. To be a child of light certainly involves openhearted obedience to the truth coupled with trust in Christ (cf. John 12:36; I John 1:6-7).

c. Exhortation to Be Watchful (5:6-8). As he begins the exhortation, Paul tactfully changes to the first person: **Therefore** ("So then," NASB) **let us not sleep, as do others** (cf. 4:13); **but let us watch** ("be alert," NASB) **and be sober** (6). All three of these terms are used metaphorically, and are suggested by the other metaphors of the passage. **Sleep** suggests indifference or indolence. In Eph. 5:14, in a similar context, it connotes spiritual death. **Watch** suggests wide-awake alertness. **Sober** carries the meaning of "calm and collected in spirit, temperate, dispassionate, circumspect."[27] Together they imply that to be a child of the light is more than a formal relationship; there must be ethical connection with the light (note the ethical requirement for preparedness for Christ's coming in 3:13).

Sleep, suggesting careless indifference to Christ's coming, and drunkenness (7), suggesting irresponsible behavior, revelry, sensual indulgence, are the characteristics of the night and the darkness.

Just as in Rom. 13:12, Paul here makes the transition from the above figures to that of armor (8). He has been speaking of watchfulness and sobriety, and this involves defense against the wiles of the devil (Eph. 6:11) and the power of darkness (Col. 1:13). There are wicked and powerful adversaries (Eph. 6:12). Only the defensive armor is mentioned here: **putting on** ("having put on," NASB) **the breastplate of faith and love; and for an helmet, the hope of salvation** (cf. Isa. 59:17; Eph. 6:13 ff., where there is some variance in the description of the armor).

Once again Paul presents his famous triad of virtues (see comments on 1:3). Here again **hope** is mentioned last, as befits the eschatological tone of the passage. This is the armor which is furnished for us by God (cf. Eph. 6:13) but which must be appropriated—put on—by an active obedience. The Christian

[27]Thayer, *op. cit.*, p. 425.

virtues are the gift of God through the Holy Spirit's ministry. The Christian lives by faith, by an active trust in and dependence on Christ. It is a faith which works by love (Gal. 5:6), the principle which regulates his total conduct. He is "saved by hope" (Rom. 8:24), and looks to the future with assurance (cf. Rom. 8:28, 31-32). Thus, in the most vital and vulnerable areas of his life, the Christian may be fully protected.

d. Added Encouragement (5:9-11). The ground of Christian hope and (in the wider context of the whole passage) the antidote for restless uncertainty are found in God's purpose in calling believers (cf. 4:3, 7): **For God hath not appointed us** ("has not destined us," NASB) **to wrath** (see comment on *orge,* The word translated **obtain** carries the idea of personal effort in gaining salvation (cf. Phillips, "that we might secure his salva-
1:10), **but to obtain salvation by our Lord Jesus Christ** (9).
tion"). Thus the sentence contains an interesting tension between the idea of God's purpose and that of man's effort with respect to salvation (cf. Phil. 2:12-13; II Thess. 2:13 ff.). But salvation is by grace without human merit, for it is **by our Lord Jesus Christ.** The effort itself, although of our own choice and free cooperation with grace, is made possible through the indwelling Christ (Col. 1:27). God's purpose is in and through Christ, **who died for us** (10), and rose again. This is the only place in the Thessalonian letters where Christ's atoning death is directly stated, a fact indicating that the doctrine was well known to the Thessalonians. Christ's death is seen as providing for reconciliation and fellowship between God and men (cf. Rom. 14:9).

Alexander Maclaren gives an exposition of verses 9-10 under the topic "Waking and Sleeping." He notes (1) The death which is the foundation of life—**Jesus Christ, who died for us;** (2) The transformation of our lives and deaths affected thereby—**whether we wake or sleep;** (3) The united life of all who live with Christ —**we should live together with him.**

Wake and **sleep** are the same Greek words which are translated "watch" and "sleep" in 6. In that connection they carry the metaphorical meaning of alertness and its opposite, indifference. The context here requires however—and with this nearly all the commentators agree—that we understand a change in the metaphor, making it similar to, but not quite the same as, "sleep" in 4:14. The words now signify, with reference to Christians, those who are alive and those who are dead.

In these verses (8-10) **salvation** is seen in both its positive and negative aspects. In this context it is thought of not so much as God's regenerating act but rather as the final realization of God's full purpose for man. Negatively it is deliverance from **wrath;** positively it is to **live together with,** that is, in personal fellowship with, **Christ.**

Neil sees in 9 and 10 three reasons why the "children of light" can face the Lord's return with assurance: (1) God has called us into His Church; (2) Christ died for us; (3) Christ lives in us.[28]

The entire passage (5:1-10) is a striking study in contrasts. Christians are different from all others: (1) in loyalty they no longer belong to the darkness but to the light; (2) in nature they are the children of light; (3) in conduct and purpose they are watchful and sober; (4) in destiny—not wrath, but salvation.

Paul's words in closing this passage (11) ought to be most instructive to today's Church. The great eschatological truths concerning the Lord's return, heaven, hell, and God's final purpose for His people, are to be means for encouraging and building up the Church: **Wherefore comfort yourselves together** ("encourage one another," RSV), **and edify one another** ("build up one another," NASB), **even as also ye do.** The present tense supports Phillips' rendering, "So go on cheering and strengthening one another." Is it not true that too often these truths are discussed with only academic interest? This world is "too much with us." When the prospect of the Lord's return is a practical aspect of daily living, then this present world—so physically real, so apparently permanent—will slip into proper perspective. What a lovely picture of the church's fellowship and worship we have here also! As members of the church we are to seek opportunities to encourage each other, to build up one another, so that together we may grow in grace and usefulness.

C. Exhortation to the Life of Holiness, 5:12-24

Following the eschatological passage (4:13—5:11), there is a return to the practical exhortations where Paul left them at 4:12. In that passage (4:1-12) the instructions about day-to-day

[28]*Op. cit.*, p. 108.

living grow out of the application to life of God's will for believers, namely, sanctification. In this passage the ethical exhortations seem to build one upon another like the steps of a staircase rising higher until they climax in the triumphant prayer of faith for the entire sanctification of the members of the church (23-24). This is not to suggest that high ethical living is the sanctifying power. The Sanctifier is **the very God of peace** (23). It is rather to suggest that on the human side a full consecration to the life enjoined by these ethical principles is a condition to entire sanctification; and also that only the experience of being wholly sanctified can provide the inward dynamic to meet these high but attainable ethical standards.

In the following verses Paul is no doubt dealing in several more instances with that which was "lacking" (3:10) in their faith, and is still drawing on information supplied by Timothy (cf. 3:6).

1. *Corporate Discipline* (5:12-15)

It is impossible to know exactly what the conditions were which caused Paul to make this plea for church discipline. We may conjecture that some tension had arisen between idlers (see comment on 4:11-12) and the local leadership of the church. In a situation which might, if improperly handled, become inflamed, Paul tactfully appeals: **And we beseech you, brethren** (the designation is disarming), **to know** ("respect," RSV; "appreciate," NASB) **them which labour among you** ("those who are working so hard among you," NEB). Those who **are over you** is literally "those who stand in front of you," or, as Moffatt renders it, "presiding over you." **Labour** here suggests costly effort (cf. 1:3; 2:9). Theirs was no mere honorary office. The three expressions refer to the different functions of the leaders rather than to three kinds of church officers. Early Church organization was relatively uncomplicated (cf. Acts 14:23). These leaders apparently guided the organization, managed the funds, and counseled in spiritual matters. They probably had to get whatever training they enjoyed "on the job." The phrase **in the Lord** suggests the spiritual quality of their leadership and their personal motivation, as well as the kind and limit of the authority exercised. From this and other passages we get an idea of how close-knit these Christian societies were, and how large a place within their fellowship they made for spiritual and moral discipline.

Paul appeals first for the believers to "get to know" (Phillips) their leaders in the sense of appreciating their true worth. He adds to this the further appeal to **esteem them very highly in love for their work's sake** (13). The Greek adverb translated **very highly** is a strong expression; the NEB renders it "highest possible esteem." It is also to be a loving esteem. *Agape* does not depend upon personal like or dislike. Nor is this esteem to be based simply upon respect for the office, but upon a true appreciation of their high task and faithful work. Moffatt's translation, "for the sake of their work," may suggest that this esteem is necessary to success in their task of leadership. At any rate it is true that a relationship of intelligent appreciation, esteem, and love between the church and its leaders is essential to the prosecution of the church's task of world evangelism.

Church leaders are not always, as one suspects might have been the case at Thessalonica, as skilled and tactful as they might be. Some understanding of the burdens of leadership however, mixed with esteem based on Christian love, would resolve most of the friction occasioned by the mistakes and the criticism of such leaders. Robertson remarks: "We need wise leadership today, but still more wise following. An army of captains and colonels never won a battle."[29]

Paul adds, **And be at peace among yourselves.** The loving esteem just mentioned would go far to produce peace. **Among yourselves** in the Greek strongly suggests that the imperative was directed to leaders and followers alike. The responsibility for sanctified relationships rests upon both.

It is quite probable that the three classes referred to as the **unruly, the feebleminded,** and **the weak** (14) correspond to the three groups dealt with in the letter. If so, the **unruly** would be the excited busybodies. **The feebleminded** ("fainthearted," ASV, NASB) would be those who were concerned about the dead in Christ and the soon coming of Christ. **The weak** might be those who were specially tempted to immoral practices.[30]

The significant thing about Paul's admonition, **now we exhort you, brethren,** is that obligation is laid on the whole church. It is not just the leaders who are to warn, encourage, support, and restrain from retaliation (15). The members are to exercise mutual discipline upon each other. Thus we have a

[29]*Op. cit.*, p. 36.

[30]Cf. Frame, *op. cit.*, p. 196.

lovely picture of mutual, loving concern within the fellowship of the church. Paul states these relations as imperatives in 14 and 15; the language is a little stronger than in 12 and 13.

The **unruly** ("disorderly," ASV; "loafers," Moffatt[31]) must be admonished. The noun has a military background, designating those who leave the ranks. Their brethren are not to discuss their failures behind their backs, but to speak to them in love. The **fainthearted** (the word lit. suggests the small-souled) are to be comforted (encouraged). The discouraged need tender treatment. The **weak** are to be supported, kept on their feet. According to Moffatt the verb suggests: cleaving to them, putting your arm around them.[32] Barclay writes: "Instead of letting the weak brother drift away . . . grapple him to the church in such a way that he cannot escape."[33] The three designated types of people need differing kinds of treatment; discernment is necessary. But to this is added, **be patient** (lit. long-tempered) **toward all men.** He who would live by this ideal will *need* patience. It is easier to criticize or ignore or even despise, but this is not love's way (cf. I Cor. 13:4-7). Were it not for the restraining, encouraging, supporting fellowship of the church, thousands would never make heaven their home.

In a pagan society, and under cruel persecution, it would not be surprising if some were tempted to **render evil for evil** (15). Denney says that "revenge is the most natural and instinctive of vices . . . It is the one which can most easily pass itself off as a virtue . . . the last fort which . . . [one] holds against the spirit of the gospel."[34] Paul says it is the duty of the fellowship to see that such a disgrace to the gospel is not permitted (cf. Matt. 5:9). **To follow** after ("seek after," NASB) the **good** doubtless means to earnestly strive to live according to the moral ideal of that love which seeks the highest welfare of all (cf. Rom. 13:10). This applies not only to the brethren but **to all men.**

In 14-24, W. E. McCumber finds "The Prayer for Entire Sanctification." For an introduction he sees: A standard exalted,

[31]*Ibid.*, p. 197, argues for "loafers," i.e., those who refuse to work, comparing with the other three times this word is used in NT (II Thess. 3:6-7, 11).

[32]*Op. cit.*, IV, 41.

[33]*Letters*, p. 240.

[34]*Op. cit.*, pp. 213-14.

14-22; A dynamic furnished, 23-24. His text in 23-24 (1) Points *upward* for encouragement. "The *God* of peace himself." The divine nature necessitates holiness. (2) Points *backward* for encouragement. "The God of *peace* himself." Only the justified have peace with God. Sanctification is a second work of grace. (3) Points *outward* for encouragement. "The God of peace *himself.*" Emphatic contrast to human effort. (*a*) God, the Cleanser: **Sanctify you wholly;** (*b*) God, the Conserver: **Be preserved blameless unto the coming of our Lord Jesus Christ;** (*c*) God, the Caller: **Faithful is he that calleth you** (from *Holiness in the Prayers of St. Paul*).

2. *Constant Victory* (5:16-18)

From matters of discipline Paul turns naturally to the underlying inner spiritual attitudes. Moffatt calls these verses "diamond drops."[35] The beautiful expression of Christian victory is in the form of a triad which is also a unit of thought. The three advices (16, 17, 18) belong together; one builds upon the other, and each involves the other two.

Rejoice evermore ("always," ASV). To persecuted Christians this exhortation seems paradoxical (cf. 3:3; II Cor. 6:10). Yet this is a dominant New Testament theme (Phil. 4:4). It is not circumstance, but sin, which crushes out joy. Paul has cited this joy as a proof of the election of the Thessalonians (cf. comment on 1:6). How can they help but rejoice, even in misfortune, who have forgiveness of sins, the peace of Christ, the love of God, freedom from sin and fear, and the prospect of eternal glory? To be in tune with God is to share in the harmony of eternal gladness (cf. Ps. 4:7).

The idea of harmony with heaven relates naturally to the next exhortation: **Pray without ceasing** ("perseveringly," *Amp. NT;* "never give up prayer," Moffatt). The word **pray** here is a general term which can include all forms of communion. Prayer is much more than addressing God; it is also listening to God, communing with God, consciously depending on God. It is the habit of lifting one's heart to God. The concept here involves a deliberately chosen pattern and habit of life (cf. Rom. 12:12; Eph. 6:8; Col. 4:2). Persevering in prayer is not automatic nor easy, but the joy of the Lord is sustained only through prayer.

[35]*Op. cit.*, p. 41.

In an exposition of 16-18, Alexander Maclaren discusses "Continual Prayer and Its Effects." (1) The duty of continual prayer, 16; (2) The duty of continual rejoicing, 17; (3) The duty of continual thankfulness, 18.

In every thing give thanks. The rejoicing, prayerful heart is thankful of course, but no less is the thankful heart the key to prayer and joy (cf. Phil. 4:6). Gratitude is a lovely Christian virtue, but the significant thing about this command is the phrase **in every thing**, that is, in all circumstances (cf. Eph. 5:20). These include joy and sorrow, sickness and health, gain and loss. Faith in God makes the difference (Rom. 8:28). How often the most unfortunate have the most grateful hearts!

As if to forestall the objection that life on such a level is beyond the reach of Christians, Paul adds, **For this is the will of God in Christ Jesus concerning you** (cf. 4:4). Such a life of victory is the loving wish of the Heavenly Father for His children; such is His purpose. But it is realized only in Jesus Christ: revealed perfectly in His person; provided graciously through His passion; made real personally and practically by His presence.

Barclay sees here "The Three Marks of a Genuine Church": (1) A happy church, 16; (2) A praying church, 17; (3) A thankful church, 18.[36]

3. *Spiritual Discernment* (5:19-22)

As described in chapter one, the Thessalonian church was a working, witnessing body, characterized by such manifestations of the Holy Spirit as joy, zeal, ardor, and enthusiastic activity. Prophesying (20) is here singled out for attention, but no doubt all the *charismata* (gifts of the Spirit) were in some degree manifested. In I Cor. 14:26 we get a glimpse of the free style of worship which sometimes characterized the primitive churches. There was an overflowing enthusiasm among those new creatures in Christ, in whose hearts the Spirit's fire flamed. If they were inexperienced and unwise, and more especially if the enthusiasm were expressed in speech, it could have brought consternation to the older and wiser. We have already noted that there were disagreements between leaders and idlers.

Perhaps because of the unwise zeal of some, there arose the danger of distrust of that freedom in the Spirit which ought to have been cherished. Paul would have them avoid the

[36]*Letters*, p. 240.

extremes of cold indifference on one hand and wild excess on the other. The five exhortations of this passage point the way to the safeguarding of that manifestation of the Spirit in power and liberty without which the church becomes dreary and ineffective. Spiritual churches in our day, pulled toward liturgical experiments on one side or toward emotional excesses on the other, greatly need these inspired advices.

In an implied metaphor, the Holy Spirit is symbolized as fire (cf. Matt. 3:11; Acts 2:3). **Quench not the Spirit** (19; "Never damp the fire of the Spirit," Phillips; "Do not stifle inspiration," NEB; "Do not stifle the utterances of the Spirit," Knox). Frame thinks that what is meant is the repression of the manifestation of the *charismata*.[37] Morris feels the expression is akin to grieving the Holy Spirit (Eph. 4:30) through loafing, immorality, or any other disobedience.[38] Denney's view is broader, involving in a general way the suppression of spiritual fervor in the church's life.[39] Put positively, it is a call to keep the fire of the Spirit burning in our hearts at whatever cost; to keep open the channels of faith, obedient response, and regular devotion.

Despise not prophesyings (20; "prophetic utterances," NASB; "what is spoken in the name of the Lord," Phillips). **Despise** (*exoutheneite*) is literally "count as nothing." Prophecy or prophesying is listed as one of the gifts of the Spirit, but in the New Testament it is generally thought of as "forth-telling" (the lit. meaning of the Gk. word). Thus it usually means Christian preaching, rather than "fore-telling," although the latter meaning is not entirely absent (cf. I Cor. 14:24-25). Since the spurious would be mixed with the real, it would be easy to hold all prophesying in contempt. But God chooses to speak to men through human utterance, and however humble and unskilled the channel, the listener is to look for God's message to himself.

Prove all things (21; "Test everything," RSV; "Examine everything carefully," NASB; "By all means use your judgment," Phillips). The last three exhortations in the passage seem to balance the first two. Christian judgment, good sense, careful examination are required in the life of the Church. This also is

[37]*Op. cit.*, p. 205.

[38]*Op. cit.*, p. 175.

[39]*Op. cit.*, p. 233 ff.

supplied by the Spirit (cf. I Cor. 14:29 and 12:10, where "discerning" is one of the gifts). Erdman writes, "The tests to be applied he does not specify. Elsewhere he indicates that all spiritual gifts are to be exercised in love, that their real purpose must be to edify others, and that those who are moved by the Spirit will admit the lordship of Christ and will endeavor to advance his glory."[40]

Hold fast that which is good (21). When wheat and chaff have been separated, hold on to the wheat. When the counterfeit has been discovered by the ring of the genuine coin, keep what is of value. No man ever became wealthy simply by discarding what is spurious. This is the delusion of the destructive critic.

Abstain from all appearance of evil (22; "from every form of evil," NASB). "*Eidos* . . . naturally means look or appearance . . . But, if so taken, it is not semblance as opposed to reality (Milligan)."[41] The thought is to shun evil wherever it appears. It is a sign of robust spiritual health to have a fear of and a shrinking from all that would grieve our Lord, to obediently separate oneself from whatever the Spirit reveals as wrong. Concomitant with this is a longing for the good (21), a hungering and thirsting after righteousness (Matt. 5:6).

4. *Sanctifying Grace* (5:23-24)

Paul has concluded his instructions. Having set before the believers moral, ethical, and spiritual standards, he turns naturally to prayer for them. The prayer is urgent and fervent. The conjunction with which it begins, **And the very God of peace** ("Now may the God of peace," NASB), connects it with the foregoing ethical section, and suggests that only the God who sanctifies through and through can bring the readers to the actual living of this life. It is significant that in a prayer for sanctification God is addressed as **the very God of peace** ("the God of peace himself," ASV). Peace, in the classic Hebrew sense (see comment on 1:1), includes complete spiritual prosperity or well-being. God is the Source of peace. To experience God's sanctifying grace men must first receive His peace (cf. Rom. 5:1). To be justified is to have peace with God, and to have, in regeneration, the beginning of that sanctification which

[40]*Op. cit.*, p. 66.

[41]Robertson, *op. cit.*, p. 38.

Paul here prays will become entire and complete. Peace *with* God becomes the deeper peace *of* God communicated by the inward harmonizing of the whole person in all his parts and functions. For this Paul is praying.

The verb **sanctify,** from *hagiazo,* means both to separate from things profane and dedicate to God, and also to purify (both externally, and internally by a reformation of the soul).[42] In the New Testament usage, purification is primary. The comprehensiveness of the purification is indicated by the modifier **wholly.** *The Amplified NT,* following Luther, has "through and through." "This word is not found elsewhere in our Greek Bible, but its usage in the few instances known in literature leaves no doubt of its meaning. It is formed from *holos* (all) and *telos* (end), and suggests finality as well as completeness."[43]

It should be noted that **sanctify** is in the Greek aorist tense. In the preceding verses (19-22) Paul uses the present tense, which indicates continuing action for the five verbs involved. But the aorist indicates, not continuing action or process, but an action which takes place and is conceived of as completed. This is not to say that there is no process preceding the sanctifying act, and certainly not to say that the act is such as to preclude a continuing process of growth *in* holiness after the crisis. Paul *is,* however, praying for the purifying action of God in the lives of these believers so that they will say, "The work has been done; we have been, and are now, entirely sanctified."

In addition to this, we recall that the Thessalonian believers as described by the apostle were genuinely born-again, working, witnessing, exemplary brothers in Christ (cf. 1:1, 3-4, 6-10). It becomes evident therefore that Paul is here praying for their entire sanctification as a second work of God's grace, definite in the sense of both time and experience.

As if to emphasize the comprehensiveness of the sanctification, Paul continues, **and I pray God** (the words are supplied in KJV; note italics there) **your whole spirit and soul and body be preserved.** ASV translates it "preserved entire," and NASB "preserved complete." This preservation is to make the Christian **blameless** ("without blame," NASB) **unto** ("at," ASV) **the**

[42]Thayer, *op. cit.,* p. 6.

[43]John W. Bailey, "The First and Second Epistles to the Thessalonians" (Exegesis), *The Interpreter's Bible,* ed. George A. Buttrick, *et al.,* XI (New York: Abingdon-Cokesbury Press, 1955), 314.

coming of our Lord Jesus Christ. The second clause of the prayer is somewhat explanatory of the first. "Whole," *holokleron*, "means complete in all its parts (*holos*, whole, *kleros*, lot or part). There is to be no deficiency in any part."[44] The predicate adjective is taken as modifying all three of the nouns which follow.[45]

Paul is thinking again of the *parousia*. Only the sanctifying act of God will prepare believers for the testing of that day. Paul has in mind also the preserving, stabilizing, keeping grace of holiness. Entire sanctification is not to be deferred until the Lord's coming, as the context makes clear, since the prayer involves preservation until that day. On **blameless**, see the comment on 2:10 (cf. II Pet. 3:14).

A great deal has been written as to whether or not the apostle's expression **spirit and soul and body** is an effort to describe human constitution as essentially threefold, that is, as a trichotomy. But this would not be in keeping with the tono of his teaching on the nature of man in the other Pauline passages. The stress is rather on the whole person. The total being of man is to be sanctified (cf. passages like Mark 12:30). Wiley says:

> While man is composed of a material and an immaterial portion, the latter in exact Scripture terminology is viewed in a two-fold manner. When viewed as the power of animating a physical organism it is called *psyche* or soul; when viewed as a rational and moral agent, this same immaterial portion is known as *pneuma* or spirit. In the usage of St. Paul, the *pneuma* is the man's higher part in relation to spiritual things; the *psyche* is that same higher part in relation to bodily things.[46]

The cleansing is to reach into every part of man's nature: his affections, his will, his imagination, the springs of his motive-life. His body is included as the temple of the Holy Spirit (I Cor. 6:19) and as the vehicle and instrument of personal life (cf. Rom. 6:12-13, 19).

The great scope of the prayer is such that a word of assurance is needed. This sanctification does not rest in man's powers, struggles, achievements, or even his consecration of himself. It is God who **will do it** (24). And this assurance is based upon the character of God. He is **faithful.** He will do what He says

[44]Robertson, *op. cit.*, p. 39.
[45]Frame, *op. cit.*, p. 211.
[46]*Op. cit.*, II, 19.

He will do, and His purpose in calling men is that they may be holy (cf. 2:12; 4:3, 7; II Thess. 2:13-14; Eph. 1:4).

These verses (23-24) then present (1) The imperative, (2) The source, (3) The nature, (4) The extent, (5) The result, and (6) The assurance of entire sanctification.

For the question: "What Is Entire Sanctification?" J. Ottis Sayes finds in 16-24 the following answers: (1) It is the optimistic outlook, 16-18; (2) It is the inward reflection, 19-22; (3) It is the integration of the whole being or personality, 23; (4) It is the culmination of the promise of God in our experience, 24.

D. Conclusion and Benediction, 5:25-28

The letter closes on a warm, personal note: **Brethren, pray for us** (25). The great apostle was ever humbly conscious of his own weakness in himself (cf. I Cor. 2:1-5) and his need for supernatural assistance (cf. Rom. 15:30; Eph. 6:19; Phil. 1:19; Col. 4:3). The request reinforced mutual fellowship and confidence. It serves as a reminder to us to pray habitually for our spiritual leaders.

Greet all the brethren with an holy kiss (26). The customary way to exchange personal greetings in that society was by a kiss. Among Christians it was a **holy kiss** because it symbolized Christian love and oneness in Christ. Within the Church the practice later took on formal, liturgical significance. Paul is saying, "Give my kindest personal greetings to everyone." Phillips gives it a modern setting with, "Give a handshake all round among the brotherhood."

It is significant that Paul says **all the brethren.** He has written frankly about their needs, but **all** are **brethren,** and not even the weakest is to be left out of his fellowship. We may infer from the spirit of this the need for warm expressions of friendship and cordiality among Christians and toward those whom we would win to Christ (cf. Rom. 16:16; I Cor. 16:20; II Cor. 13:12; I Pet. 5:14).

I charge you is a very solemn expression (properly, "I adjure you," ASV) **by the Lord that this epistle be read unto all the holy brethren** (27). Later versions omit **holy,** although some MSS have it. It is likely that the letter would be read at some public gathering of the church. Perhaps Paul feared that some, possibly those who needed it most, would be absent when it was read. As the first of such letters it was important to have it understood that it was for all, not just the leaders or some other select group. Paul was rebutting the accusation that he did not really care for his converts (see comments on chapter 2). Mason has written, "It amounts to a claim to inspiration."[47] We may see in it today a strong exhortation to the reading of the Scriptures in the hearing of those who do not read them for themselves.

Paul ends as he began, with an emphasis on **grace** (see comment on 1:1). It is more than a farewell; it is the supreme benediction. It sums up in a word every blessing, every good thing. Grace alone is sufficient. **The grace of our Lord Jesus Christ be with you. Amen** (28).

[47]*Op. cit.*, p. 122.

Outline

Second Thessalonians

I. Encouragement for the Persecuted, 1:1-12
   A. Address and Salutation, 1:1-2
   B. The Grace of God Demonstrated, 1:3-4
   C. The Judgment of God Anticipated, 1:5-10
   D. Power and Grace of God Supplicated, 1:11-12

II. Instruction to the Troubled, 2:1-17
   A. Lawlessness and the Son of Perdition, 2:1-12
      1. Correction of an Error, 2:1-3
      2. Description of the Man of Sin, 2:4-10
      3. Consequences of Perversity, 2:11-12
   B. Election of Grace and Heirs of Hope, 2:13-17

III. Discipline of the Disorderly, 3:1-18
   A. Prayers and Confidence Mutually Needed, 3:1-5
   B. Work and Quietness Commanded of Idlers, 3:6-12
   C. Firmness and Kindness Required, 3:13-15
   D. Conclusion and Benediction, 3:16-18

Section I *Encouragement for the Persecuted*

II Thessalonians 1:1-12

A. Address and Salutation, 1:1-2

The address and salutation in this letter (1-2) are only slightly different from the opening of the first letter (see comments on I Thess. 1:1). **Silvanus** is elsewhere known as Silas (Acts 15:40); **Timotheus** is better known as Timothy (II Cor. 1:1). **Our Father,** rather than "the Father," describes **God.** The wording here brings to mind the bond of faith which unites the apostles to the persons addressed. Again we note how Paul associates naturally **God our Father** and **the Lord Jesus Christ** as being coequally the Source of **grace** and **peace.** These two words sum up the whole of spiritual good.

B. The Grace of God Demonstrated, 1:3-4

Paul's customary thanksgiving is warm and generous. It is of special interest here for two reasons. The first is the emphasis on the propriety of the apostle's thanksgiving on their behalf. Paul reiterates the high praise of the first letter, mentioning again the three great virtues ("hope" is not named as such immediately, but **patience** is). **We are bound** ("we ought," NASB) **to thank God always for you, brethren, as it is meet** (3; "as is only fitting," NASB). It is frequently supposed that this expression of obligation and fitness is Paul's reply to the protests of the "fainthearted" (cf. I Thess. 5:14) that they were unworthy failures.

The second thing of interest is that Paul is rejoicing over answered prayer: **because that your faith groweth exceedingly** ("is growing abundantly," RSV), **and the charity** (love) **of every one of you all** (KJV is lit.) **toward each other aboundeth** ("grows ever greater," NASB). The picture is of luxuriant growth, like that of a tree or plant. Furthermore, Paul is careful to include all of them in the statement. This is what he prayed for so fervently in I Thess. 3:10 and 12 (cf. comments there).

The verse provides a significant commentary on Christian growth. There were in this church a good deal of ignorance, misunderstanding, and even fanaticism of a sort, all of which was apparently compatible, at this stage at least, with abounding faith and love. Significant also is the fact that such growth took place in a time of tribulation (cf. 4).

It is a great thing in a church when the grace of God in the lives of its members is so evidently demonstrated as to provide a witness that cannot be gainsaid. To thanksgiving Paul adds boasting (in the Lord): **So that we ourselves** (the implied contrast in the expression suggests adding the words, "contrary to your expectations"[1]) **glory in you** ("speak proudly of you," NASB) **in the churches of God** (4). (Cf. I Thess. 2:19-20 and see the comments on these verses.) The particular qualities about which Paul rejoiced were their **patience** ("steadfastness," RSV; cf. I Thess. 1:3) and their **faith.** They were able to hold up or to **endure** because their faith was in God and His promises. The expression **in all your persecutions and tribulations** suggests continued and repeated sufferings which were still going on. **Tribulations** (*thlipsesin*) is the same word translated "affliction" in I Thess. 1:6 (see comment there).

C. The Judgment of God Anticipated, 1:5-10

This subject of persecution and affliction naturally raises the question of justice and fair play. What sense does it all make? Is this a moral universe? (On "afflictions," see the comments on I Thess. 3:3.) Paul proceeds to vindicate **the righteous judgment of God** (5). The Thessalonians' patience and faith in persecution (not simply the persecution itself) **are a manifest token** ("plain indication," NASB) **of the righteous judgment of God** (cf. Phil. 1:28). The **which** of v. 5 refers back to v. 3. Such steadfastness in spite of undeserved suffering and hatred is evidence of a divine power at work ("proof positive of God's equity," Moffatt). God is with them; they belong to Him (cf. the idea of the mark of divine election in I Thess. 1:6). God has a purpose in view: **that ye may be** ("so that ye may be," NASB; the Gk. expresses purpose[2]) **counted worthy** (cf. Luke 20:35). The RSV has "made worthy," but this is not the proper sense. No personal merit accrues from suffering as such, although God uses it in the refining of our souls through grace.

[1]Frame, *op. cit.*, p. 223.

[2]Robertson, *op. cit.*, p. 43.

God purposes to account His children **worthy of the kingdom of God, for which . . .** [they] **also suffer** (cf. Acts 5:41; I Pet. 4:12-16). Since persecution is inevitable (cf. I Thess. 3:3), the Christian should keep his eyes on God's purpose. Future judgment will reveal this. (Cf. the idea of **righteous judgment** in Rom. 3:25-26.) The **kingdom** seems here to be thought of in its future aspect (see comment on I Thess. 2:12).

The moral argument in this passage turns two ways. First, **the righteous judgment of God** is shown in sustaining and justifying His persecuted people now; second, God's **righteous judgment** is shown in punishing the wicked and rewarding the faithful in a future reckoning. Their steadfastness in suffering is seen as proof of their true faith (and also as evidence of the awful moral state of the world). Their suffering for Christ's sake is also a guarantee of future judgment; in a moral universe there must necessarily be a rectifying of life's injustices. It is assumed that the readers will agree with the basic principle of reward and punishment. This is axiomatic if God exists and is righteous. To deny it is to be plunged into moral chaos.

Thus we have in the passage "The Judgment of God." (1) The moral basis of judgment, 5-7*a*; (2) The time and the circumstances of the judgment, 7*b*; (3) The basis and the nature of punishment, 8-9; (4) The basis and the nature of reward, 10.

Paul now proceeds to the second side of the moral argument. **Seeing it is a righteous thing** should be cast in a conditional form as in ASV, "if so be that it is." The thought, however, is of an assumption which is beyond dispute; thus the NASB rendering, "for after all it is only just." **With God** is literally "by the side of God," and so "from God's standpoint."[3] **To recompense** means "to repay" (NASB; cf. I Thess. 3:9, where in a different context the same word is translated "render"). **Tribulation to them that trouble you** is better rendered "affliction to them that afflict you" (ASV; see comment on *thlipsis,* I Thess. 1:6).

Recompense will be not only negative, but positive: **And to you who are troubled** ("afflicted," ASV) **rest** (7). NASB translates this "relief." The Greek word *anesin* means freedom from restraints and tension, "as in the slackening of a taut bow

[3]*Ibid.*

string."[4] The reference is surely to heaven itself. In the nature of the case a Christian cannot be motivated simply by a selfish hope of reward; nevertheless, such holy reward is both comfort and incentive in the Christian life. Conversely, although fear of punishment, by itself, is an insufficient motive to repentance, its presence in men has an altogether salutary effect.

Paul adds **with us,** indicating that there will be a fellowship of rest, as there has been a fellowship of suffering.

The thought shifts now to the time and circumstance of judgment: **when the Lord Jesus shall be revealed** (lit., "at the revelation of the Lord Jesus," ASV). Paul has previously written of the Lord's coming (*parousia,* I Thess. 2:19; 3:13; 4:15; 5:23). Here the term is *apokalypsis* (revelation). The word means literally "an uncovering."[5] It is used for the coming of Christ (cf. Luke 17:30; I Cor. 1:7), for the manifestation or unveiling of things or truths hitherto not seen (cf. Rom. 8:19; Gal. 1:12; Eph. 1:17), and Paul uses it also with reference to the man of sin in 2:8. With reference to Christ's return no temporal distinction between *parousia* and *apokalypsis* can be determined from this passage. Christ, who has been loved and worshipped although unseen, will be unveiled. His work which has hitherto been unseen will be made visible.

The manifestation will be **from heaven** (cf. I Thess. 4:16) **with his mighty angels** (lit., "with the angels of his power," ASV; cf. Jude 14), **in flaming fire** (8; lit., in a fire of flame). The reference to fire seems to indicate primarily the brilliance and majesty of the revelation (cf. Exod. 3:2; Isa. 66:15; Rev. 1:13), although it may also suggest punishment.

Frame suggests that we have in the three phrases a brief description of "The Revelation of Christ." (1) The place, **from heaven,** 7; (2) The attendant retinue, **his mighty angels,** 7; and (3) The manner, **in flaming fire,** 8.[6] The picture is notable for its restraint and brevity.

The expression **taking vengeance** (8) would be repulsive if taken as meaning personal vindictiveness. However, as in I Thess. 4:6, God is the Avenger, the Administrator of moral justice. NEB has "he will do justice."

[4]Morris, *op. cit.,* p. 201 (footnote).

[5]Thayer, *op. cit.,* p. 63.

[6]*Op. cit.,* p. 232.

A number of commentators think that **them that know not God** suggests the heathen, while those **that obey not the gospel of our Lord Jesus Christ** are the Jews. This was Denney's view.[7] Actually, both sins were and are characteristic of people in every society. For **them that know not God,** NEB has, "those who refuse to acknowledge God." Paul stresses elsewhere a willful and culpable ignorance of God (cf. Rom. 1:28; Eph. 4:17-18; I Thess. 4:5). The culminating and most grievous sin of all is the rejection of Christ and of God's gracious invitation in His Son (cf. Mark 12:1-12; Rom. 2:8; 10:16, 21).

The nature of retribution is described and those involved are indicated (9). In the Greek the pronoun **who** is qualitative and suggests "people such as this." They **shall be punished** (lit., will suffer or pay the penalty) **with everlasting destruction.** The word rendered **everlasting** (*aionion*) is literally "age-long." But the coming age is endless. The same word is used in speaking of the everlasting or eternal life of believers. Frame says the word here refers to "the destruction whose consequences are age-long, that is, to Paul and to the N. T. in general, 'eternal' (Mark 3:29; Matt. 25:46; cf. Dan. 12:2)."[8] That this **destruction** is not annihilation is clear from the words which follow and which expand the thought. This punishment means to be banished **from the presence** (lit., as NASB, "away from the presence") **of the Lord, and from the glory of his power** ("might," RSV). The nature of the punishment is unending separation from the face of the Lord, and thus from every good. It is the exact opposite of the estate of the redeemed, whose eternal bliss is found in the presence of Christ. These words are filled with infinite sadness almost too terrible to contemplate. And yet the fate of the wicked is, at the most, only the fulfillment of the choice of those who will not have Christ to reign in their lives.

Denney speaks of the finality of the gospel: "Obey, and you enter into a light in which there is no darkness at all: disobey, and you pass eventually into a darkness in which there is no light at all . . . It is *not* a question of less or more, of sooner or later, of better or worse; what is at stake in our attitude to the gospel is life or death, heaven or hell, the outer darkness or the glory of Christ."[9]

[7]*Op. cit.,* p. 295.

[8]*Op. cit.,* p. 234.

[9]*Op. cit.,* pp. 299-302.

There is a return to the thought of v. 7 in the words, **When he shall come to be glorified in his saints** (lit., holy ones), **and to be admired** ("marvelled at," RSV) **in all them that believe** (10; but the tense is aorist, thus "who have believed," NASB). In the two phrases beginning **to be glorified** and **to be admired,** there is a touch of poetic parallelism. Moffatt suggests that there may be here a quotation from a Christian hymn.[10] At His coming, Christ will be the Center and Focal Point of all. His glory, His attributes, His blessedness will be seen in the persons of the saints, who are also described as **them that believe.** Their characters, like mirrors, will reflect or reproduce His glory. The awe-inspiring revelation will be the cause of thanksgiving and rejoicing. Those who will admire or marvel are not identified; they are, doubtless, all who will behold, human or angelic. All this will take place **in that day,** the day of Christ's coming. These words are placed last, for emphasis.

We should note the mutuality of Christ's relationship to believers. Barclay calls it "the reciprocal glory."[11] Christ is glorified in the believers, whose glory alone is Christ (cf. this idea in John 13:31; 14:13; 17:1, 4, 10, 22; cf. also I Thess. 2:20).

The parenthetical words, **because our testimony among you was believed,** seem to have been inserted as a particular assurance to the fainthearted among the Thessalonians (cf. I Thess. 5:14). It is as if Paul had said, "And when I say 'all,' I mean to include all of you." Again the aorist tense is used, pointing back to the act of believing in the decisive hour which began their Christian careers—careers to be climaxed on the day of glory.

D. Power and Grace of God Supplicated, 1:11-12

The magnificent prospects which Paul has just set forth as the hope of believers are not to be realized except through supernatural help. Thus the apostle passes naturally to prayer. We see again the stress and reliance on intercessory prayer. The missionaries cannot be with their converts, but they can pray for them. **Wherefore** ("To this end," RSV) **also we pray always for you, that our God would count you worthy of this calling** (11). Frame (along with others) holds that the proper transla-

[10] *Op. cit.,* IV, 46.

[11] *Letters,* p. 244.

tion of *axiosei* is "to count, or deem, or reckon worthy," not "to make worthy," as in RSV.[12] In the most fundamental sense the Christian hope is in the merit and worthiness of Another, that is, Christ. This prayer, however, is pointless unless we see in it the clear implication that it is holy character as evidence of saving faith which qualifies men on "that day." Justifying grace and grace for holy living are not separated in experience, but only in thought. **Calling** can refer to the past, or conversion (cf. I Cor. 1:26), and also to future blessedness (cf. Phil. 3:14). Unless it is mere rhetoric, the prayer implies the possibility of the called ones being counted unworthy at the last. Bicknell says, "St. Paul certainly held that believers might fall from grace and prove unworthy of their calling."[13]

Paul now continues with the second petition of the prayer, parallel with the first: **and fulfil all the good pleasure of his goodness.** In agreement with the substance of most of the later translations, NASB has, "fulfill every desire for goodness" (cf. "every good resolve," RSV, Moffatt). Thus the fulfillment is not that of God's pleasure (although there is nothing contrary to this idea), but of the inward purpose or resolve of the Thessalonians themselves for goodness. **Goodness** (*agathosunes*) is listed as the fruit of the Holy Spirit (Gal. 5:22). The desire or resolve for it is implanted by the Spirit. But resolve after uprightness in heart and life is not enough; Paul prays for the realization. With the inwardness of good resolve, Paul couples the outwardness of **the work of faith** (see comment on this phrase on I Thess. 1:3). The prayer is for the completion of every work which faith begins. Only **with power,** the power of divine grace, is fulfillment possible. But God can do it.

Taking verse 11 as a whole, one senses the urgency not only of present holiness of heart, but also of continuous progress and growth in both the inward and outward aspects of the life of holiness.

But now the prayer contemplates an even higher end than the acceptance before God of the readers and the means to that acceptance. The high objective is **that the name of our Lord Jesus Christ**[14] **may be glorified in you, and ye in him** (12). Here

[12]*Op. cit.*, p. 240.

[13]*Op. cit.*, p. 70.

[14]The best texts have only "Lord Jesus," rather than **Lord Jesus Christ.**

again, as in 10, there is expressed the beautiful concept of the reciprocal glory. **Name,** as in Old Testament usage, signifies not just identity but the revealed character of the person. Here it suggests Christ's lordship and condescending grace. It is a wonderful thought that the holy character of the redeemed may add luster to the brightness of our Lord's person, and that because the redeemed are **in him** they too are **glorified** (see comments on v. 10).

The whole tenor of the prayer has stressed the utter dependence of the saints upon the strength of God for steadfastness and growth in the Christian life. All human merit is excluded in the expression **according to the grace of our God and the Lord Jesus Christ.** This grace has its source in the Father's love and is mediated through the Son. It is the Christian's hope not only in the beginning, but in the progress, and until the successful conclusion of his course.

This great prayer looks toward the future with bounding faith and optimism. Paul prays (1) For the fulfillment in the believers of their **calling,** 11 (cf. the "high calling of God in Christ Jesus," Phil. 3:13-14); (2) For the growth in inward grace and outward works which makes all this possible, 11; (3) For that resulting reciprocal glory of Christ and His own which is "the chief end of man," 12; and (4) The prayer acknowledges that for its answer we must rest upon divine **power** and **grace,** 12.

Section II *Instruction to the Troubled*

II Thessalonians 2:1-17

Problems had arisen among the Thessalonian Christians which made it necessary for Paul to take corrective measures in this second Epistle. In the first letter he had instructed them in the comforting and inspiring truth of the Lord's coming and the "gathering together" of all the saints to be with Him. In some way the error was spreading that Paul taught that the day of the Lord was already present. This seems to have produced a ferment of excitement and alarm, as well as a disorderly movement on the part of some who had stopped regular work to await Christ's return. In this passage Paul deals correctively with this matter; in chapter 3 he deals with the disorderly faction.

Farfetched theories, date setting, and fanatical movements have tended, in all periods of the Church's history, to discredit the truth about Christ's return. Those who "love his appearing" (II Tim. 4:8) will not permit these things to obscure the "blessed hope" (Titus 2:13).

It will be helpful, in interpreting what is confessedly one of the difficult New Testament passages, to keep in mind the general background. The little Christian community at Thessalonica is passing through tribulation. There is no assurance of speedy release from suffering. But the message is that God is on the throne; assurance is given that future triumph for Christ and those who are Christ's is certain. Chapter 1 has pointed out that God is a righteous Judge governing a moral universe. Chapter 2 will outline the defeat of evil powers at their very worst, and the fulfillment of God's lofty purpose for the Church.

A. Lawlessness and the Son of Perdition, 2:1-12

1. *Correction of an Error* (2:1-3)

Paul begins with affectionate appeal: **Now we beseech you, brethren, by the coming** ("with regard to the coming," NASB) **of our Lord Jesus Christ.** This is not an adjuration as in KJV and Phillips. The word **by,** which is supplied in the English, wrongly suggests adjuration. **Our gathering together unto him** ("our assembling to meet him," RSV) is a reference to the rapture, discussed in I Thess. 4:13-17 (cf. Matt. 24:31; Mark 13:27).

Concerning the **coming** (*parousia*) of the Lord, Paul appeals for a reasonable rather than a purely emotional approach. He appeals against two conditions: **that ye be not soon shaken in mind** ("do not suddenly lose your heads," NEB), **or be troubled** ("in a constant state of nervous excitement," Frame[1]). The verb which is translated **shaken** can be used of a ship tossed and driven from its moorings.[2] The **troubled** state results from being **shaken in mind.**

The three possible sources of the troubling misinformation regarding the Lord's coming are: **neither by spirit, nor by word, nor by letter as from us** ("as if from us," NASB). Frame thinks (as do others) that the expression "as from us" goes with all three nouns.[3] In such a general statement as this, it is impossible to be sure of the apostle's meaning. He is disclaiming responsibility for the statement **that the day of Christ is at hand** ("has come," RSV; "is already here," Weymouth). **Spirit** has been thought of as a pretended charismatic utterance, or as an inspired but misconstrued statement of Paul. **Word** would be either a pretended or a misconstrued memory of Paul's verbal teaching. **Letter** is understood as a forged (cf. 3:17) or anonymous document, or as I Thessalonians or some other Pauline letter, misunderstood.

At first glance it is difficult to see how anyone could actually think that the day of the Lord had already come. Perhaps the translation **is at hand** in KJV, or "is just at hand" in ASV, was preferred because it blunts the difficulty involved.

Bicknell says: "The answer is that it means that the period designated by the term day had now dawned and the visible appearance of the Lord might be literally a matter of minutes. The despondent felt that they were inwardly unprepared and the idle saw that no motive remained for work."[4] Obviously, when some claimed that the day of the Lord had come, they did not mean that the solemn and glorious events connected with that day had already taken place (see comments on I Thess.

[1]*Op. cit.*, p. 245.

[2]Morris, *op. cit.*, p. 215.

[3]*Op. cit.*, p. 246.

[4]*Op. cit.*, p. 74.

5:2). But rather, if the day had dawned, the end-time events would be momentarily expected.

Paul's rebuttal of this notion is sharp: **Let no man deceive you by any means** ("in any way," RSV). The proof that the day of the Lord has not yet come is that certain necessary evidences of that day are not present. These evidences are, first, **a falling away**, and second, the revealing of **that man of sin . . . the son of perdition.** Beginning with **for . . . except** (3), we have in the original an unfinished statement, a conditional clause without the naming of the thing which is conditioned. This was understood by the readers, but in English some expression like **that day shall not come,** or "it will not be" (ASV), must be added to complete the sense.

The Greek has the definite article, so the subject is *the* **falling away** (*apostasia,* the apostasy). This event has been variously interpreted as referring primarily to a general revolt against God and His rule in the world at large (Frame,[5] Morris,[6] Barclay,[7] Bicknell[8]), to apostasy within the Church itself (Erdman,[9] Ockenga,[10] Hendriksen,[11] Mason[12]). Robertson concludes: "It is not clear whether Paul means revolt of the Jews from God, of Gentiles from God, of Christians from God, or of the apostasy that includes all classes within and without the body of Christians."[13] (Cf. Matt. 24:4-5, 10-13; I Tim. 4:1.)

The apostasy is obviously very closely associated with, although not necessarily simultaneous with, the revelation (*apokalypsis*) of **that man of sin** (see comment on *apokalypsis* in 1:7). The use of the term **revealed** concerning the coming of the **man of sin** suggests a supernatural or mysterious aspect. It implies that he is now hidden and will be suddenly manifested or unveiled.

The oldest manuscripts have "man of lawlessness" (*anomias*) rather than **man of sin** (*hamartias*). The meaning is scarcely changed since sin is lawlessness (I John 3:4). This personage is also **the son of perdition** ("the son of destruction," NASB; "the man doomed to perdition," NEB). Both "man of lawlessness" and **son of perdition** are Hebraisms (see comment on "children of light" in I Thess. 5:5). This man is essentially char-

[5]*Op. cit.,* p. 251. [6]*Op. cit.,* p. 219. [7]*Op. cit.,* p. 245.
[8]*Op. cit.,* p. 74. [9]*Op. cit.,* p. 86. [10]*Op. cit.,* pp. 273 ff.
[11]*Op. cit.,* pp. 169-70. [12]*Op. cit.,* p. 137. [13]*Op. cit.,* p. 49.

acterized by lawlessness and is doomed to destruction. In 8 he is simply called *ho anomos,* "the lawless one."

The methods of harmonizing verse 3 with the eschatological teachings of the first letter are numerous. Some, influenced by a supposed conflict in viewpoint, are disposed to deny (quite unnecessarily) the Pauline authorship of the second letter. The problem centers about the seeming conflict between the imminence and suddenness of Christ's return in the first letter and the suggestion of delay coupled with prior signs in this letter. It may be noted that, according to I Thess. 5:1-11, the day of the Lord comes as a "thief in the night" to those who are "of the night" and "of darkness." The ideas of suddenness and signs often appear together, and are not incompatible. (Cf. also the comment on the meaning of imminence as related to immediacy, I Thessalonians 4.)

Certain dispensational, premillennial views (e.g., a secret pretribulation rapture) may need to be supported by assigning the basic eschatology of the first letter to the rapture (*parousia*) and that of the second letter to the revelation (*apokalypsis*) accompanied by judgment. "Day of the Lord" is sometimes distinguished from **day of Christ** (2). But "day of the Lord" is the preferred reading as evidenced by recent translators. Wuest, in his translation, has "departure" (meaning rapture) instead of **falling away** (3), thus avoiding one problem for a certain theory but posing another.[14] All the above expedients tend to create more problems than they solve. A basic time-distinction between "rapture" and "revelation" cannot be supported by these letters in themselves. When the two letters are approached without a concept that identifies immediacy with imminence, and without a predisposition toward certain dispensational views, the problem of their harmony largely dissolves.

2. *Description of the Man of Sin* (2:4-10)

The man of sin **opposeth and exalteth himself above all that is called God** ("every so-called god," NASB, RSV), **or that is worshipped** ("or object of worship," NASB, RSV); **so that he as God sitteth in the temple of God, shewing himself that he is God** (4; "proclaiming himself to be God," RSV). This man opposes and challenges God, exalts himself above all objects of worship—recklessly and blasphemously claims deity for himself.

[14]*Op. cit.,* p. 62. The arguments are on pp. 57-58.

The language here is doubtless derived in part from Daniel 7 and 8. Daniel's prophecy had had partial fulfillment (perhaps initial fulfillment is better) in events of Jewish history which foreshadowed the coming of the man of sin. About 168 B.C., Antiochus Epiphanes had set up an altar to Zeus in the Temple and had sacrificed swine in the Temple area, precipitating the Maccabean War of independence. In A.D. 40 the Emperor Caligula had attempted to have his statue erected in the Temple. But Paul's description goes far beyond these faint foregleams (cf. also Mark 13:14). The man of sin is commonly identified with the Antichrist of John's Epistles (I John 2:18, 22; 4:3; II John 7) and the beast of Rev. 13:1. Many Protestant scholars of recent centuries have identified "the man of lawlessness" with the pope or the Roman Catholic church as a whole. Earlier writers suggested the emperor Nero, while twentieth-century spokesmen have nominated Kaiser Wilhelm, Mussolini, Hitler, and Stalin. Any would-be world-conqueror will be identified by someone as the man of sin.

The temple of God has been thought to be a rebuilt temple in Jerusalem, or the Church, or even heaven. In agreement with Morris,[15] it seems best to think of it simply as some building which becomes the shrine for this blasphemous worship.

With what may be a mild rebuke, Paul reminds his readers of his previous instruction on this subject. It is quite clear that he is not shifting from his advent teaching in the first letter. **Remember ye not, that, when I was yet with you, I told you** (the imperfect tense might be rendered, I used to tell you) **these things?** (5) Paul can appeal to their previous knowledge, and thus does not need to be as explicit in detail as modern readers could wish he had been. We cannot know all that the Thessalonians had been carefully taught about the man of sin. Doubtless this passage would be less obscure if we did.

Verse 6 is particularly difficult. **And now ye know what withholdeth that he might be revealed in his time.** The RSV renders it, "And you know what is restraining him now so that he may be revealed in his time." Grammatically, **now** may modify either **know** or **withholdeth.** Something, or some power, is restraining the man of sin until the time comes for his revelation. The Thessalonian readers, Paul says, knew the identity of the

[15]*Op. cit.*, p. 224.

restrainer. Modern readers do not know, and therefore they cannot be dogmatic in their interpretation.

For the mystery of iniquity (mystery of lawlessness, best Gk. text) **doth already work** (7). Lawlessness or iniquity operates as a secret, invisible force in society and individuals. It is Satanic and powerful, but providentially restrained. It is a **mystery** both because in its secret workings it is too deep for human comprehension and also because it is to be revealed in due time. This God-defying force will produce the man of sin and the great rebellion (cf. v. 3). The reason that the man of sin has not appeared is stated: **only he who now letteth will let.** NASB translates it, "he who now restrains will do so until he is taken out of the way." In 6 the restrainer is referred to in the neuter gender, and in 7 in the masculine. This may suggest something conceived as abstract from one standpoint and personal from another.[16] Perhaps an impersonal force is thought of as personified.[17] The restrainer has been variously identified by commentators as an angel, Satan himself, the Jewish state, the Roman Empire, and the Holy Spirit. The idea that the Holy Spirit indwelling the Church is meant, and that He **will be taken out of the way** in the rapture of the saints, requires a certain dispensational viewpoint. This is one of the view's chief difficulties. Further, it is hard to account, by this view, for the apostle's veiled language.

Paul had considerable reason to regard Roman law and order in his day as a restrainer of lawlessness (cf. Rom. 13:1-7). He might wish to allude cautiously to its foreseen end. If, in his day, Paul could think of Roman order, personified possibly in the emperor, as the restraining power against utter lawlessness, the concept may be rightly carried over to the idea of civil government in any age. Paul does, in fact, so generalize in Romans 13. Ockenga observes cogently: "The most acceptable view is that this [the restrainer] refers to the Holy Spirit working in common grace through civil government. When civil government collapses and there is a breakdown of restraining law, the result is lawlessness."[18] But if modern readers cannot with certainty identify the restrainer, they can rejoice in the larger truth that God is in sovereign control of His world. He appoints

[16]Robertson, *op. cit.*, p. 51.

[17]Morris, *op. cit.*, p. 226.

[18]*Op. cit.*, p. 289.

the bounds of wickedness. The man of sin will be revealed only **in his time;** i.e., at the appointed time.

With a brevity that omits all the detail which would cater to the curious, but which at once brings to the fore the moral and spiritual message, Paul continues: **And then shall that Wicked** (lit., "that lawless one," NASB) **be revealed, whom the Lord**[19] **shall consume** ("slay," ASV, RSV, NASB).[20] The last part of verse 8 describes how this will be accomplished. **The spirit of his mouth** is better translated "the breath of his mouth" (ASV). **And shall destroy with the brightness of his coming** combines two words which are really synonyms for Christ's advent. **Brightness** (*epiphaneia*) was a word "often used by the Greeks of a glorious manifestation of the gods, and esp. of their advent to help."[21] It here carries the idea of Christ's appearing in brilliance and splendor. For the meaning of **coming** (*parousia*), see the comment on I Thess. 2:19. The glorious presence of Christ is itself enough to snuff out the lawless one who represents wickedness at the pinnacle of reckless power. What a warning to the godless, who presume that God is either powerless or indifferent in the face of sin!

Having assured his readers of the lawless one's doom, Paul resumes direct description of him: **Even him, whose coming** (*parousia*) **is after the working** (*energeian*) **of Satan** ("in accord with the activity of Satan," NASB) **with all power and signs and lying wonders** (9). The parallels with the person and work of Christ are apparent and intentional. The lawless one also has his *parousia.* The three following nouns are all used of Christ's ministry: **power** (*dunamis;* the suggestion is of a supernatural force), **signs** (attesting miracles pointing beyond themselves), and **wonders** ("marvels," Weymouth). In this connection see Acts 2:22; Rom. 15:19; II Cor. 12:12; Heb. 2:4. Grammatically, all three words can be modified by **lying.** They all spring from falsehood and the intention to deceive, but this does not necessarily mean that these **wonders** are mere trickery. This thought is continued in the next verse: **And with all deceivableness of unrighteousness** (10; more lit., deceit of un-

[19]Many later translations, including ASV, RSV, and NEB, follow the MSS which have "Lord Jesus."

[20]The choice between **consume** and "slay" arises from the use of two different words in the Greek MSS.

[21]Thayer, *op. cit.,* p. 245.

righteousness; cf. "all the deception of wickedness," NASB; "unlimited seduction to evil," Amp. NT). **In them that perish** is literally, "in (or for) the perishing." (Cf. the same kind of contrast with "the saved" in I Cor. 1:18; II Cor. 2:15; 4:3.)

With his **signs** and **wonders** the lawless one will entice, persuade, and deceive the perishing ones who are in sharp contrast with the saved. They are deceived and perishing **because they received not the love of the truth, that they might be saved** ("so as to be saved," NASB). Their fault is not ignorance or misunderstanding of the truth, but rather inhospitality toward the truth—a refusal to welcome it (cf. I Thess. 1:6; 2:13). The problem is moral, a matter of choice. The clear implication is "that God had sent them the power to create in them the love of the truth, but that they had wilfully refused to receive it or cooperate with it."[22] It is not only the Truth (the saving truth as embodied in the person of Christ) that is offered to men, but also the gracious ability to appreciate, to embrace, and to love the truth. But in "the perishing," all this is rejected, and what they reject is their only hope of salvation.

In general, there seem to be two opposite tendencies of thought as regards the identity of the man of sin. The first would identify him definitely with the name of some individual or some class of individuals, past or present—Nero (living again), or some other Roman emperor, or the emperors in general; the papacy (see the preface to KJV, or see the Westminster Confession of Faith); or a considerable number of other infamous persons, both historic and contemporary. The second line of interpretation sees in this passage only the symbols of cosmic conflict between the kingdom of God and the kingdom of Satan: theological convictions expressed in symbols which are not reducible to actual space and time. This view despairs of any interpretation which is not "beyond history," past, present, or future.[23]

It is true that in John's Epistles the Antichrist (a later term for the lawless one) is both a tendency and a person, the former seeming to lead up to the latter. There are also many antichrists (Matt. 24:5, 24; Mark 13:22; I John 2:18; II John 7) who more or less approximate the Pauline description of the man of sin. The antichrist tendency or influence is recognizable in forces and

[22]Bicknell, *op. cit.*, p. 78.

[23]Cf. William Neil, *op. cit.*, pp. 132 ff.

movements, past and present, political, social, and religious, which encourage lawlessness and godlessness, either subtly or militantly. Nevertheless, Paul's picture is of an end-time man (not Satan incarnate) consecrated to and controlled by Satan, who will be the final incarnation of rebellion against God, and whose destruction will take place at the second coming of Jesus Christ.

3. *Consequences of Perversity* (2:11-12)

These two verses which close this section underscore again its main theme: God is in control, and He will bend to His purpose the worst that evil can do. Believers need not fear the man of sin. As for his followers, Paul continues: **And for this cause** (11; for this reason) **God shall send** (lit., God sends) **them strong delusion** (lit., an energy of delusion, or "a working of error," ASV), **that they should believe a lie** ("so that they put their faith in an utter fraud," Phillips): **that they all might be damned** (12; "judged," ASV; "condemned," RSV) **who believed not the truth, but had pleasure in unrighteousness.**

There are three stages in the descent of these people into final perdition. First, "because they received not." Having the power to choose and to welcome the truth, they voluntarily reject it. Second, having rejected the truth, they **believe a lie.** They have lost the ability to tell the difference between truth and error. They are described in Isa. 5:20: "Woe unto them that call evil good, and good evil; that put darkness for light, and light for darkness; they put bitter for sweet, and sweet for bitter!" They now approve of, or delight in, wickedness. Third, they suffer the inevitable judgment of God (12).

We see in this God working, not arbitrarily, but through moral law, to accomplish His righteous purposes. The Hebrew thought-pattern is to bypass secondary causes and ascribe all that happens to the direct activity of God (cf. Exod. 9:7, 12; II Chron. 18:22). Our own tendency is often the opposite: to exalt a so-called impersonal law. Of course the moral law is not self-operating; it is God's method with men. The point is that God does not act capriciously in sending a deluding influence upon truth-despisers. The universe is a moral cosmos rather than a moral chaos. The result of willful spurning of light is to come to a state where darkness is no longer distinguishable from light, and thus to come to final ruin. This passage should be compared with Rom. 1:18-32.

The entire section (1-12) offers remarkable insights into the ways of God with men, as well as the character of sin and of the unregenerated human heart. Devotionally, one might roughly outline the passage as follows: (1) The Christian hope, or Christian stability, 1-2; (2) The culmination of evil, or sin unmasked, 3-5; (3) The restraining power, or the divine purpose, 6-7; (4) The final counterfeit, or sin's deceitfulness, 9-11; (5) The Christian's security, or love of the truth, 10*b*; (6) The certain judgment, or the wages of sin, 11-12.

B. Election of Grace and Heirs of Hope, 2:13-17

Paul turns away abruptly from the dark picture which he found it needful to draw in the preceding verses, and returns to the theme of encouragement, using almost the same words as in 1:3. There is deliberate contrast between "them that perish" (10) and **chosen you to salvation** (13); "strong delusion" or "a working of error" (11) and **sanctification of the Spirit** (13); "believe a lie" (11) and **belief of the truth** (13); "that they all might be damned (12) and **to the obtaining of the glory of our Lord Jesus Christ** (14).

It is often observed that here we have Pauline theology in a nutshell. The thought ranges from God's eternal purpose before time to salvation's consummation in the end of time. It is both theoretical and practical. It involves God's grace and man's response.

In order, there are thanksgiving (13-14), exhortation (15), and prayer (16-17). The effect of the paragraph is to produce confidence and assurance in the readers. Nearly all the terms in the passage have been previously used in this and the first letter. For explanation of **But we are bound to give thanks** (13), see comment on 1:3; and for **brethren beloved of the Lord,** see explanation of I Thess. 1:4.

The preceding verses have traced the dreadful picture of the mystery of lawlessness and of the power of evil at work in the world. It is enough to make the heart tremble. But in spite of this Paul engages in thanksgiving **because God hath from the beginning chosen you to salvation** (cf. Rom. 8:28-30; Eph. 1:4; I Thess. 5:9).[24] Salvation is no afterthought with God, nor is He surprised by the forces of evil. God plans, not man's ruin, but

[24]There is a well-attested alternate reading *ap'arches,* **from the beginning,** which involves the change of only one letter. It is *aparchen* (as first-fruits), and is favored by some.

his salvation, and this from the beginning, having foreknown man's plight. Paul rejoices that God has indeed elected men to salvation "before the foundation of the world" (Eph. 1:4). This election is of all those who trust in Christ (see comment on I Thess. 1:4).

The force of this truth upon the Thessalonians is that since they have now trusted in Christ they are caught up in God's eternal purpose and loving provision, and therefore need have no fear. There is no suggestion here of an unconditional election; indeed, the succeeding expressions indicate quite the opposite. Paul is simply saying that, prompted by love, God has taken the eternal initiative in our salvation (cf. John 15:16). He has provided both the gracious invitation and the indispensable means to its acceptance. There is no room for human merit or boasting.

Salvation (13) here involves the widest sweep of the word, although the primary reference is doubtless to final salvation, the end or goal of God's purpose.

God has provided the means of salvation, here presented as twofold: (*a*) **through sanctification** (*en hagiasmoi,* "in sanctification," ASV; see comment on I Thess. 4:3-4, 7) **of the Spirit**[25] and (*b*) **belief of the truth** ("faith in the truth," NASB). There are two sides in the matter of salvation. The initiative and the power are God's; the necessary response is man's. God's grace neither overwhelms nor cancels man's responsibility. Salvation is a moral matter and therefore real choice is involved.

Sanctification is, in its broadest sense, the transforming work which God does in man, involving both the crises of initial renewal and of full cleaning, as well as the process of growth in grace; it is moral and ethical. Man, by freely cooperating with the Spirit, and by means of the gracious ability provided, believes the gospel, and especially trusts in Christ, the Truth (cf. John 17:17). "There is an interrelation of the work of God's Spirit and of the human spirit in salvation. It is not an arbitrary decree which is followed by human submission automatically or all would respond, since it is God's will that every man shall come to the knowledge of the truth, but it depends upon our response to God's Spirit."[26]

[25]*Pneumatos* (spirit) could mean the human spirit, but since sanctification includes the body also (cf. I Thess. 5:23) it is more reasonable to make the word refer here to the Holy Spirit, as the Sanctifier.

[26]Ockenga, *op. cit.,* p. 295-96.

What God planned in His eternal counsel, He offered to the Thessalonians in His providence: **Whereunto he called you** (14; see comment on I Thess. 2:12 and 5:24) **by our gospel** (cf. I Thess. 1:5; "It was his call that you followed when we preached the gospel to you," Phillips). Paul sees himself and his preaching—**our gospel**—as the instrument in God's hands to bring about God's call to salvation. Although salvation is a present reality, the ultimate goal is future glory: **to the obtaining of** ("that you may gain," NASB) **the glory of our Lord Jesus Christ** (see comments on I Thess. 1:10 and 2:12). To belong to Christ is to share His glory (cf. John 17:24; Rom. 8:30).

The concept of the Trinity is implicit in these verses; all three Persons are involved in the work of salvation.

It is clear that our salvation is rooted in love, planned in eternity, initiated in time, and consummated in glory. Essentially, salvation is all of grace since it is originated in God's loving choice, wrought through the power of God's Spirit, bestowed by answering God's call, and perfected in the glory of God's Son.

This then is God's adequate and glorious plan for His people. Paul exhorts the persecuted and fainthearted; **Therefore** ("So then," ASV), **brethren, stand fast** ("stand firm," RSV), **and hold the traditions which ye have been taught, whether by word, or our epistle** (15). There is no ground for a false security, as if their destiny were already fixed, but there *is* cause for assurance as they "stand firm." All that is needed God has provided for His elect, among whom they are numbered (see comments on I Thess. 1:4 ff.).

Traditions (*paradoseis*) refer to what is given or handed over to one. For example, precepts or doctrines handed down by Moses and the prophets, either in writing or orally, are traditions.[27] In I Cor. 11:23 and 15:3, Paul uses the same concept. There the related verb *paredoka* is translated "delivered." It is the origin of **traditions** which establishes their value (cf. Mark 7:8; Col. 2:6-8). Paul's teaching is not self-originated. The reference here to **our epistle** provides interesting light on the concepts of inspiration and canonicity. The reference is probably to I Thessalonians. In the relative absence of written teachings, oral instruction, **by word,** had to suffice. With the formation of

[27]Thayer, *op. cit.*, pp. 481 ff.

the New Testament canon, oral teaching became subject to the apostolic writings.

Hold is a strong expression in the Greek, meaning "have a masterful grip on."[28] Sound doctrine is vital. The Thessalonians are to disregard the voices of theorists and fanatics, and keep to "the word."

Characteristically, Paul concludes this doctrinal section with prayer. **Now our Lord Jesus Christ himself** (see comment on I Thess. 1:1). **Himself** seems to make emphatic that the exhortation of the previous verse can be realized only with divine help. It is **God, even our Father, which hath loved us.** It is He who **hath given us everlasting consolation** ("eternal encouragement," Moffatt) **and good hope through grace** (16). It is God who shall **comfort your hearts, and stablish you** ("encourage and fortify you," NEB) **in every good word and work** (17).[29]

Note that this coupling of Jesus and God the Father in prayer, along with the use of singular Greek verbs (**comfort** and **stablish** in v. 17) governed by the compound subject, implies the highest possible view of the deity of Jesus Christ.

On **hope** and **grace,** see comments on I Thess. 1:1, 3. **Consolation** (16) and **comfort** (17) are from the same word (*parakaleo*) and suggest the work of the Holy Spirit, who is the Comforter. The meaning is encouragement and strengthening more than comfort in the ordinary English sense. This **consolation** (encouragement) is **everlasting** because it originates in God's eternal purpose; it is ever-present, and is unfailing for the future. **Loved us** and **hath given us** bring to mind John 3:16. They suggest the work of Christ in His atoning death as well as the gift of the Spirit to the Church. The Christian hope is **good hope** in contrast with the illusory and unreliable hopes which are based on mere human planning. Paul's confident request for the believers is that God himself will **comfort** their **hearts,** that is, will instill courage into their minds and wills, and **stablish** them—fortify and buttress them against pressure and temptation. The practical outcome of this will be **good . . . work** (faithful Christian living) and **good word** (a ringing Christian testimony).

In this paragraph we find "Encouragement for Christians." (1) God has chosen you, 13-14; (2) **Stand fast,** 15; (3) There is help along the way, 16-17 (A. F. Harper).

[28]Robertson, *op. cit.*, p. 54.

[29]The better texts have the reverse order: "work and word."

Section III *Discipline of the Disorderly*

II Thessalonians 3:1-18

A. Prayers and Confidence Mutually Needed, 3:1-5

With the beginning of chapter 3 there is a change in the letter's content from doctrinal to practical matters. Before giving direct instructions regarding the disorderly element in the church (6-15), Paul tactfully approaches the subject with the appeal and the expression of confidence contained in the first five verses.

Humbly and affectionately, the apostle requests prayer for himself and his companions (see comments on I Thess. 5:25). The request has two specific petitions. In the first, the passion of Paul's soul is laid bare. **Finally, brethren, pray for us, that the word of the Lord may have free course** ("may spread rapidly," NASB), **and be glorified, even as it is with you** (1; "as it did among you," RSV). All three verbs are in the present Greek tense and carry the thought of continuing action. In figurative language the **word of the Lord** (see comment on I Thess. 1:8) is pictured as a runner speeding on to success and triumph (cf. Ps. 147:15; Acts 12:24; 13:48; 19:20). In the idea of the word being **glorified** there may be the thought both of the recognition of its glorious qualities and the manifestation of its power in transforming lives. The success of the gospel in Thessalonica (cf. I Thess. 1:1-10) provides the example. Those who, like the Thessalonians, know God's power in personal experience are best qualified to pray such a prayer.

Here is a large and bold petition which every Christian heart should echo. The great need of our day is that the transforming Word of the Lord may, through the incomparable opportunities which modern media offer, speed on its mission of world evangelism. Preached and taught in the Spirit, and saturated with prayer, the Word of the Lord will triumph now, as then.

The second petition probably should be seen against the background of Paul's difficulties in founding the church in the city of Corinth (cf. Acts 18:1-18). It grows out of the first petition, and is for the sake of the gospel. **And that we may be delivered from unreasonable and wicked** ("evil," ASV) **men: for all men have not faith** (2; "not all have faith," RSV). The root meaning of **unreasonable** (*atopos*) is "out of place." In Luke

23:41 it is rendered "amiss." The idea connotes such words as "perverse" (Weymouth), "wrong-headed" (NEB), "bigoted" (Phillips), or even "outrageous," and "absurd." Everyone whose ministry becomes a threat to the devil's kingdom will, like Paul, experience this kind of irrational and preposterous opposition. Paul asks not necessarily that such opposers shall cease (for he sadly acknowledges that there will be people like this who willfully reject the faith that saves), but rather that he shall be rescued from their devices. Without such supernatural help the Church would be overwhelmed (cf. Matt. 10:16 ff. and Luke 12:32).

The direction of the thought seems to follow an association of ideas and possibly a play on words. The word order in Greek is "for not all have faith" (*pistis*). **Faithful** (*pistos*), however, is **the Lord** (3). The appeal is away from men to the faithfulness of God, a familiar expression with Paul (cf. I Cor. 1:9; 10:13; I Thess. 5:24).

In verse 3, Paul shifts back abruptly from a request for himself to concern for his readers. They needed to be guarded from the evil one, whose strategy included both deception as "an angel of light" (II Cor. 11:14) and the pressure of persecution as "a roaring lion" (I Pet. 5:8).

The appeal to the revealed character of God, in spite of all the outward appearances or circumstances which militate against faith, is one of the basic characteristics of the Thessalonian letters. This is equally true of the teaching on either moral matters or future events. The faithfulness of God—this is the soul's anchor in the storm and in the darkness (cf. the same truth in Isaiah 40). God can be depended on, **who shall stablish you** ("make you stedfast," Weymouth), **and keep you** ("protect you," Moffatt) **from evil.** Several translations have "the evil one." This is because *tou ponerou* can refer either to evil as a principle or to Satan.

Confidence in the Lord's faithfulness leads to an expression of confidence in the readers, who belong to the Lord: **And we have confidence in the Lord touching you** (concerning you), **that ye both do and will do** ("that you are doing and will continue to do," NEB) **the things which we command you** (4). "Confidence in the Lord about you" is an expression which puts rather concisely the divine and human factors involved in the successful work of the Church. Confidence, in this matter, is not in the Lord alone irrespective of human cooperation. Certainly, confidence ought not to be in people alone. Rather, confidence of success is well-founded when men keep themselves in the hands of the Lord, and when the Lord is permitted to work through obedient human channels. The word translated **command** is a strong expression, commonly used of military orders. The same term is used in 6, 10, and 12. Paul is tactfully preparing the readers for the disciplinary measures which will follow.

Characteristically, just before he administers the needed rebuke, the apostle breaks into prayer. How he prayed for his children in the faith! The prayer is about love and patience, qualities particularly needed in the situation to be discussed. **And the Lord direct** ("guide," Weymouth) **your hearts into the love of God, and into the patient waiting for Christ** (5; "the steadfastness of Christ," RSV). The reference of the latter phrase is not to the second coming of Christ, but to Christ's patient or steadfast endurance (cf. Heb. 12:1-3). For a discussion of **direct,** see comments on I Thess. 3:11.

There is stress here on the primacy of the heart life of Christians. The emphatic language suggests that it is important for God to be in control of their hearts (see comments on I Thess. 3:13), and that no lesser matters be allowed to obscure this central issue. **The love of God** in Pauline usage ordinarily means God's love for us, and in this connection would involve assurance of that love. A secondary meaning would be our love to God, growing in quality and expression.

Barclay suggests that here we have "the inward and outward characteristic of the Christian."[1] The inward factor is an awareness of God's love, with the assurance and security which that brings; the outward element is the endurance which Christ can give. "The outward characteristic of the Christian is that when others break he stands erect, and when others collapse he shoulders his burden and goes on. With the love of God in his heart and the strength of Christ in his life a man can face anything."[2]

B. Work and Quietness Commanded of Idlers, 3:6-12

Much space in this letter is given to dealing with the disorderly and idle brethren in the church. This indicates that the

[1]*Letters*, p. 250.

[2]*Ibid.*, p. 251.

problem had grown more serious than at the time of the writing of the first letter, in which relatively little space was given to it (cf. I Thess. 4:11-12; 5:14). Evidently the idlers had failed to heed the first letter. Stronger measures are, therefore, to be taken.

In the name of our Lord Jesus Christ, as here used, means "by the authority of Jesus Christ." Paul thus commands the church, who are addressed as **brethren** (6). The command is authoritative, and yet the appeal is that of a brother to his brethren. The order is **that ye withdraw yourselves from** ("keep away from," RSV) **every brother that walketh disorderly** ("who is living in idleness," RSV). The apostle reminds them that they had not received this kind of teaching from him; it was **not after the tradition which he** (you)[3] **received of us.**

Disorderly (*ataktos*) is the same word translated "unruly" in I Thess. 5:14 (see comment made there). Barclay says, "The word means *to play truant.* It occurs, for instance, in the papyri, in an apprentice's contract in which the father agrees that his son must make good any days on which he absents himself from duty or plays truant."[4] Due perhaps to excitement about the coming of the Lord, the disorderly brethren were loafing, refusing to work, turning from their duties, and accepting no responsibility. This probably led to meddlesome conduct (cf. 11), and even dependence on others for support (cf. 12).

The church is a social fellowship which bears responsibility for the conduct of its members. It cannot be indifferent to these unruly brethren. In order to preserve Christian standards, the disorderly must be made to feel the pressure of Christian sentiment against their irresponsible conduct. The church is to avoid close company with the loafers in order to shame them (cf. 14). Excommunication or total ostracism are not contemplated, but rather a social aloofness which will indicate that a standard has been raised, and that to violate it invites the rebuke of the church. The apostle has stressed the importance of **the tradition** in 2:15 (see comment there).

In order to reinforce the command, Paul appeals first to his own example and that of his companions when in Thessalonica

[3]The best texts have "you," or "they," not **he.** Of modern translations, the majority favor the "you" reading.

[4]*Letters,* p. 252.

(7-9), and then to his instruction given at that time (10). **For yourselves know how ye ought to follow us** ("imitate us," RSV). For comment on a similar expression and on this idea, see discussion of I Thess. 1:6. **For we behaved not ourselves disorderly among you** (7)—certainly that was an understatement! **Neither did we eat any man's bread for naught.** This Hebraism includes the wider idea of obtaining a living; "we did not accept board and lodging from anyone without paying for it" (NEB). Rather we **wrought with labour and travail** ("labor and hardship," NASB; cf. I Thess. 2:9 and comment there) **night and day, that we might not be chargeable** ("might not be a burden," NASB) **to any of you** (8).

The missionaries were careful to avoid the charge that they were parasites or spongers. But on this subject Paul also always guards the apostolic right to support, even though, in the interest of the gospel, he had conscientiously waived his right. **Not because we have not power** ("not because we do not have the right to this," NASB), **but to make ourselves an ensample** ("but in order to offer ourselves as a model for you," NASB). On **ensample** (*typos*), see comment on I Thess. 1:7. On this whole matter of the apostle's labor at Thessalonica and the motives involved, see the comments on I Thess. 2:6, 9. The force of the argument is that Paul the apostle had the right to receive support. Even so while among them he lived independently on the fruit of his toil. How much more should the idle brethren, who have no such right, work to earn their own living!

A further reinforcement of the command to withdraw from the disorderly is the reminder of Paul's previous teaching: **For even when we were with you, this we commanded you, that if any would not work, neither should he eat** (10). The ASV makes clear that it is a refusal to work which is involved, and that the directive concerns such a man: "If any will not work, neither let him eat." Whether Paul is quoting a familiar saying or whether it is original with him cannot be established. Such a rule could not be literally applied except among the poor whose daily bread depended on their own labors, or in a society with some communal arrangement. Perhaps the idlers were asking for support from the church. Perhaps they were actually being fed by the charity of their industrious brethren. If so, it was a false kindness. The loafers needed to be faced with the stern practicalities of life and jolted out of their irresponsible conduct.

It is an interesting comment on Christian charity that Paul could be stern with idlers, but was moved by pity to take an offering for the needy in Judea. If these measures against the disorderly seem unduly severe, it must be remembered that unchecked fanaticism such as this would have destroyed the Thessalonian church. The abiding principle for our own complex society is an emphasis upon shared responsibility, personal dependability, and devotion to duty. These are Christian virtues which are essential to holy character.

Without mentioning names, Paul now openly cites the reason for his forthright statements: **For we hear that there are some which walk among you disorderly** (see comment on verse 6), **working not at all, but are busybodies** (11; "busybodies instead of busy," Moffatt). In the Greek there is a play on words in the latter two phrases: literally, "not working, but working around," i.e., being unprofitably employed. Perhaps under the cloak of religious excitement over the Lord's return, the idlers were excusing their irresponsibility. Quite typically, this idleness led to meddling in other people's lives (cf. I Tim. 5:13). It is not said how Paul had heard, but it was likely by letter or the conversation of travellers. Such conduct may have been common among the pagan Thessalonians (cf. Acts 17:5 ff.). Robertson says, "These theological dead-beats were too pious to work, but perfectly willing to eat at the hands of their neighbours while they piddled and frittered away the time in idleness."[5] There is hardly a more damaging influence in the church than the gossiping tongue of an idle or footloose member.

Now for the first time the idlers are addressed directly, but with conspicuous tact. They are called **them that are such** (12; "such persons," RSV). While Paul uses the word **command** (cf. 6, 10) he tempers it with the expression, **exhort by our Lord Jesus Christ** (see comment on this expression in I Thess. 4:1). The command and the appeal are **that with quietness they work, and eat their own bread** (cf. I Thess. 4:11 and comment there). Someone has remarked that the old maxim applies: "Less noise and more work!" Phillips has, "settle down to work and eat the food they have earned themselves." This appeal for **quietness** (calmness) probably has reference not so much to their meddling as to the restlessness which they were fostering in the church.[6]

[5]*Op. cit.*, p. 60.

[6]Bicknell, *op. cit.*, p. 94.

C. Firmness and Kindness Required, 3:13-15

Having outlined and undergirded the necessary disciplinary action, Paul turns again to address the church as a whole in order to safeguard the entire situation. There are risks in the administration of church discipline, no matter how necessary the action is. One danger is that the spirit of those administering the discipline may be less than Christlike. Another is that the discipline may fail in its purpose, and may drive away rather than save those for whom Christ died.

As a wise leader, Paul writes, **But ye, brethren, be not weary in well doing** (13). To be **weary** means here "to lose courage, to flag, to faint,"[7] "to falter," "to tire."[8] **Well doing** signifies "to do the right,"[9] or "to do the fair or honorable thing."[10] Perhaps Paul is saying, "Whatever the actions of others, do the right thing yourself; don't let people who appear to be religious and yet neglect their duty influence you to neglect yours." Paul may have been tacitly acknowledging that to deal with this situation will be a discouraging and thankless task. He is therefore encouraging the brethren not to lose heart because of the proud or disagreeable attitudes of those whom they are trying to help. Furthermore, they must guard, in their disciplinary action, against harshness, or an uncharitable attitude in themselves.

In spite of oft repeated warnings and teachings contained in this letter and in the first Epistle—as well as in Paul's personal ministry—there is the possibility that some will refuse to obey. Since it cannot be a case of misunderstanding, but of flagrant self-will, the apostle is ready to say his last word on the subject: **And if any man obey not our word by this epistle** ("in this letter," RSV), **note that man** ("mark him well," NEB), **and have no company with him. Have . . . company with** is from a verb meaning "to mix up together." Paul is saying, "Do not associate with him" (NASB), **that he may be ashamed** (14). On the obligation of the church in this matter, see the comment on 6.

Just how is the man to be "marked"? Publicly? By mental notation? It is not stated specifically, but the congregation will identify him as not in good standing. The treatment here is not

[7]Robertson, *loc. cit.* [8]Frame, *op. cit.*, p. 308.

[9]*Ibid.* [10]Robertson, *loc. cit.*

nearly so severe as in the case of the fornicator in I Cor. 5:9-13. There the command is, "Put him out." Here it is, "Don't associate with him." Nevertheless, in a pagan city, to be without Christian companionship would be severe enough! It is evident that to continue in close friendship with one who is willfully violating the doctrines and standards of the church is to appear to place approval upon his conduct, or at the least to fail to disapprove it.

The purpose of this discipline is not mere punishment, but the reformation of the offender. The root idea of the Greek verb rendered **ashamed** is "to have one's thoughts turned in on oneself."[11] Driven, it is hoped, to see himself as others (those who have been patient and long-suffering) see him, the offender will, under the conviction of the Holy Spirit, repent, and be restored to the full fellowship of the brotherhood. This desired end is more easily achieved if he is simply marked in this way, rather than formally excommunicated.

The generous, pastoral heart of Paul speaks in the closing words of the section: **Yet count him not** ("do not look on him," RSV) **as an enemy, but admonish him as a brother** (15). The status of the offender must be protected if he is to be restored. Discipline in which a personal hostility develops has failed already. To see the other person as a brother means that the reproof will not be given by one who stands above and looks down on the offender, but by one who stands on the same level and thus can speak with Christian love. The bonds of true brotherhood in Christ are very real and strong. Such ties are not easily broken. Love is the key to success in the matter of church discipline.

The above fifteen verses may be outlined under the title: "How to Deal with Church Members Who Err." (1) By prayer, 1-2, 5; (2) By optimism and encouragement, 3-4; (3) By personal example, 7-10; (4) By the pressure of majority sentiment, 6, 14; (5) By patient and firm instruction, 12, 15; (6) By persistent love, 15.

D. Conclusion and Benediction, 3:16-18

This letter, containing as it does several rather stormy and stern passages, has a calm and lovely ending. **Now the Lord of peace himself give you peace always** ("at all times," ASV; "con-

[11] *Ibid.*, p. 61.

tinually," NASB). **By all means** may indicate "in all ways" (ASV) or "in every circumstance" (NASB). **The Lord of peace** is Christ (cf. John 14:27; see comment on "God of peace," I Thess. 5:23). Peace is God's gift through grace (see comment on "peace," I Thess. 1:1), and the gift is given only in Christ. It is both peace with God (Rom. 5:1) and the peace of God (Phil. 4:7). In this beautiful prayer Paul sees Christ's peace as completely satisfying. It is continual and adequate; it is not dependent upon changing circumstances. Paul has in mind the needs of the readers, and Christ's peace is the answer. They are suffering persecution and some may be martyred; some are mourning their dead; they are troubled by thoughts of the Lord's return; they are acquainted with the "mystery of iniquity"; some are fainthearted; they have an internal problem of discipline. Knowing these circumstances, Paul prays for Christ's peace. He prays also for the presence and the fellowship of Christ in the midst of the church: **The Lord be with you all** (16). The use of **all** is probably a hint that none are left out of the prayer, not even those who have been or will be censured for idleness (cf. 18).

Paul has doubtless been dictating the letter to a stenographer or amanuensis. It is his custom at the end of the letter (in keeping with the practice of his time) to take the pen from the scribe and write a salutation in his own bold hand: **The salutation of Paul** (17; "I, Paul, write this greeting," NASB) **with mine own hand, which is the token** ("distinguishing mark," NASB) **in every epistle: so I write** ("this is my handwriting," Weymouth). The custom was similar to ours of placing a signature on a typewritten letter. (Cf. I Cor. 16:21; Gal. 6:11; Col. 4:18.) There may be a reference to the possibility of forged letters (cf. 2:2), or to the possibility that the disorderly persons would refuse to admit the letter's genuineness. Whether Paul's handwriting began at verse 16, 17, or 18, or included only verse 17, cannot be known since of course we do not have the original copy of the letter. Reference is made to Paul's other letters, **every epistle.** Only those in our New Testament have, in God's providence, been preserved for us.

This letter ends as does the First Epistle to the Thessalonians, except that here the benediction adds the word **all** (18).[12] Thus the letter begins and ends with the concept of **grace** (see com-

[12]The liturgical **Amen** is not included in the better **texts.**

ments on I Thess. 1:1; 5:28). Just so, through grace the Christian life itself begins, proceeds, and ends.

'Twas grace that taught my heart to fear,
And grace my fears relieved.
How precious did that grace appear
The hour I first believed!

Through many dangers, toils, and snares,
I have already come;
'Tis grace hath brought me safe thus far,
And grace will lead me home.[18]

God's grace, for Paul, is free, universal, all-sufficient, and extended through the atoning merits of Jesus Christ. Like a loving and concerned parent separated from children who are facing perils unknown, Paul, in this benediction, commends to the secure keeping of God his beloved Thessalonians.

[18]John Newton.

Bibliography

I. COMMENTARIES

AUBERLEN, C. A., and RIGGENBACH, C. J. "The Two Epistles of Paul to the Thessalonians." *Lange's Commentary on the Holy Scriptures.* Translated by JOHN LILLIE. Grand Rapids: Zondervan Publishing House, 1960 (reprint).

BAILEY, JOHN W., and CLARKE, JAMES W. "The First and Second Epistles to the Thessalonians." *Interpreter's Bible.* Edited by GEORGE A. BUTTRICK, *et al.*, Vol. XI. New York: Abingdon Press, 1955.

BARCLAY, WILLIAM. *The Letters to the Philippians, Colossians and Thessalonians.* "The Daily Study Bible." Edinburgh: The Saint Andrew Press, 1959.

BICKNELL, E. J. *The First and Second Epistles to the Thessalonians.* "The Westminster Commentaries." London: Methuen & Co., Ltd., 1932.

BUCKLAND, A. R. *St. Paul's First Epistle to the Thessalonians: A Devotional Commentary.* London: The Religious Tract Society, 1906.

CLARKE, ADAM. *The New Testament of Our Lord and Saviour Jesus Christ,* Vol. II. New York: Abingdon-Cokesbury Press, n.d.

DENNEY, JAMES. *The Epistles to the Thessalonians.* "The Expositor's Bible." London: Hodder and Stoughton, 1892.

ERDMAN, CHARLES R. *The Epistles of Paul to the Thessalonians: An Exposition.* Philadelphia: The Westminster Press, 1935.

FRAME, JAMES EVERETT. *A Critical and Exegetical Commentary on the Epistles of St. Paul to the Thessalonians.* "International Critical Commentary." Edinburgh: T. & T. Clark, 1912.

GLOAG, P. J. "I and II Thessalonians" (Exposition). *The Pulpit Commentary,* Vol. 21. Edited by H. D. M. SPENCE and JOSEPH S. EXELL. Grand Rapids: Wm. B. Eerdmans Publishing Company, 1950 (reprint).

HENDRIKSEN, WILLIAM. *New Testament Commentary: Exposition of I and II Thessalonians.* Grand Rapids: Baker Book House, 1955.

HENRY, MATTHEW. *An Exposition of the New Testament.* London: Thomas Nelson, n.d.

MASON, A. J. *The Epistles to the Colossians, Thessalonians, and Timothy.* "Layman's Handy Commentary." Edited by CHARLES J. ELLICOTT. Grand Rapids: Zondervan Publishing House, 1957.

MILLIGAN, GEORGE. *St. Paul's Epistles to the Thessalonians.* Grand Rapids: Wm. B. Eerdmans Publishing Co., 1952 (reprint).

MOFFATT, JAMES. "The First and Second Epistles to the Thessalonians." *The Expositor's Greek Testament.* Edited by W. ROBERTSON NICOLL. Grand Rapids: Wm. B. Eerdmans Publishing Company, 1951.

MORRIS, LEON. *The First and Second Epistles to the Thessalonians.* "The New International Commentary on the New Testament." Grand Rapids: Wm. B. Eerdmans Publishing Co., 1959.

NEIL, WILLIAM. *St. Paul's Epistles to the Thessalonians.* "Torch Bible Commentaries." New York: The Macmillan Company, 1957.

ROBERTSON, ARCHIBALD THOMAS. *Word Pictures in the New Testament,* Vol. IV. New York: Harper & Brothers, 1931.

THE NEW BIBLE COMMENTARY. Edited by F. DAVIDSON. Grand Rapids: Wm. B. Eerdmans Publishing Company, 1953.

VINCENT, MARVIN R. *Word Studies in the New Testament,* Vol. IV. Grand Rapids: Wm. B. Eerdmans Publishing Co., 1946.

WESLEY, JOHN; CLARKE, ADAM; HENRY, MATTHEW; AND OTHERS. *One Volume New Testament Commentary.* Grand Rapids: Baker Book House, 1957.

WESLEY, JOHN. *Explanatory Notes upon the New Testament.* London: Epworth Press, 1941 (reprint).

II. OTHER BOOKS

BARCLAY, WILLIAM. *The Mind of St. Paul.* New York: Harper & Row, Publishers, 1958.

GOODWIN, FRANK J. *A Harmony and Commentary on the Life of St. Paul.* Grand Rapids: Baker Book House, 1951.

MILLER, ADAM W. *An Introduction to the New Testament.* Anderson, Indiana: The Warner Press, 1943.

OCKENGA, HAROLD J. *The Church in God.* Westwood, N.J.: Fleming H. Revell Company, 1956.

RAMSAY, WILLIAM MITCHELL. *St. Paul the Traveller and the Roman Citizen.* London: Hodder and Stoughton, 1920.

THAYER, JOSEPH H. *Greek-English Lexicon of the New Testament.* New York: American Book Company, 1889.

TRENCH, RICHARD C. *Synonyms of the New Testament.* Grand Rapids: Wm. B. Eerdmans Publishing Company, 1948 (reprint).

WILEY, H. ORTON. *Christian Theology.* 3 vols. Kansas City: Nazarene Publishing House, 1940.

WUEST, KENNETH S. *Wuest's Expanded Translation of the Greek New Testament: Philippians Through the Revelation,* Vol. III. Grand Rapids: Wm. B. Eerdmans Publishing Company, 1959.

III. ARTICLES

HENDRIKSEN, WILLIAM. "I Thessalonians." *Christianity Today,* I, No. 17 (May 27, 1957), 27 and 33.

WALVOORD, JOHN F. "II Thessalonians." *Christianity Today,* II, No. 4 (Nov. 25, 1957), 33, 37-38.

The Pastoral Epistles

The First and Second Epistles to

TIMOTHY

The Epistle to

TITUS

J. Glenn Gould

Introduction

A. The "Pastorals"

These writings known as the "Pastorals," comprising the First and Second Epistles to Timothy and the Epistle to Titus, differ considerably from other writings attributed to Paul, due to their unique destination and their predominantly pastoral character. All the other Epistles of Paul, with the exception of the Epistle to Philemon, are addressed to churches and are obviously, in most cases, examples of a chief pastor's work in advising, admonishing, and disciplining the flock over which he has supervision. But the Pastoral Epistles are directed to men who are themselves pastors. These letters are examples of the supervisory work of a chief pastor addressing himself to those who are under-shepherds. This distinction is a basic factor in determining those features of the Pastoral Epistles which have provoked much scholarly discussion and have led to the charge that these letters cannot be the work of Paul.

The designation "Pastoral," despite its obvious appropriateness, has not been applied to these letters from time immemorial, but is of relatively recent origin. To be sure, it was anticipated by St. Thomas Aquinas in the thirteenth century; but not until the early eighteenth century were they referred to as "the Pastorals"; and not until this designation was adopted by the famed commentator Dean Alford, in 1849, did this manner of referring to them become customary.

The designation "the Pastorals" is appropriate within limits. The central concern of the letters is what has come to be called the "cure of souls" as that ministry was being carried on in Ephesus and Crete by Timothy and Titus respectively. Paul is giving advice and warning, exhortation and encouragement to his sons in the gospel who are now his assistants in the care of the churches. Out of the wealth of his knowledge of the faith and his experience in dealing with men and churches of varying types, he gives these younger ministers admonitions and guidance. But the Pastoral Epistles possess the limitation that they are not "manuals of pastoral theology," to use Donald Guthrie's phrase.[1] Most of the topics essential to such a manual are omitted from these letters. They deal vigorously with only a few of the issues faced by a pastor—the issues which were upper-

[1]*New Testament Introduction: the Pauline Epistles* (Chicago: Inter-Varsity Press, 1961), p. 198.

most in importance in these particular churches, and no more. Indeed these letters are designed, in all probability, only to supplement the apostle's oral instruction of these younger ministers. This is a fact which must be borne in mind when reading any of Paul's letters, and especially those directed to churches which Paul himself established. Behind the theological and religious instruction in his Epistles there stands the extensive preaching of the apostle, and back of many of the apparently incomplete discussions of the Epistles there must be assumed a body of coherent teaching imparted by the apostle in oral discourse.

Though the Pastoral Epistles may be limited in the area which is covered, the fact remains that their contents lie squarely in the field of pastoral theology, and the designation "Pastoral" is a fitting one.

B. Authorship

1. *The Traditional View*

The view that St. Paul is the author of these Epistles is not one to be lightly thrust aside. The Epistles claim Pauline authorship; this is clearly stated in the greeting of each letter; and despite the modern tendency to disregard such evidence, the burden of proof still rests with those who would set it aside. On the side of the authenticity of these Epistles is the fact that from the earliest days of the Church they were held to be the work of Paul. Alfred Plummer puts it bluntly in these words: "The evidence respecting the general acceptance of them as St. Paul's is full and positive, and reaches back to the earliest times."[2] It is significant that it was not until the early nineteenth century that the Pauline authorship began to be questioned. Surely Guthrie's point is well taken when he says: "If the grounds of objection [to the Pauline authorship] are as overwhelming as they are claimed [by their proponents] to be, some adequate reason must be given for the extraordinary lack of insight on the part of Christian scholarship over so long a period."[3]

2. *The Attack on Pauline Authorship*

Despite the cogency of the evidence pointing toward the authorship of these letters by Paul, a persistent attempt has been made by some scholars to prove this evidence untrustworthy.

[2]"The Pastoral Epistles," *The Expositor's Bible*, ed. W. Robertson Nicoll (New York: Funk and Wagnalls Co., 1900), p. 5.

[3]*Op. cit.*, p. 202.

The attack on the authenticity of the Pastorals has been carried forward on at least four fronts: (1) the difficulty in fitting them into Paul's career as revealed in the New Testament literature; (2) their alleged incompatibility with the organization of the churches as it is believed to have existed during Paul's lifetime; (3) the doctrinal emphases in the Pastorals which are held to differ radically from the teachings in Paul's other Epistles; and (4) the differences in vocabulary which are held to exist between the Pastorals and Paul's letters to the churches.

a. The first of these is the historical problem: How can these letters be fitted into what we know of Paul's career? Our knowledge of that career rests in large part upon the Acts of the Apostles, with valuable supplementary material derived from Paul's own writings. It must be remembered, however, that the Acts of the Apostles makes no claim to be a biography of Paul. Indeed, Saul of Tarsus (as he was first known in the Acts) is not mentioned until Acts 7:58. The story of his amazing conversion to Christ is related in c. 9; and his full acceptance as a Christian leader does not occur until cc. 11 and 13. No attempt is made to inform the reader as to his childhood and youth. His conspicuous presence on the scene during the balance of the Acts is due solely to the fact that his ministry was the most outstanding of any of the apostles and that Luke, the author of the Acts, was a participant in much of Paul's activity. Luke concludes his account of Paul quite as abruptly as he began it, leaving the apostle at the conclusion of his first Roman imprisonment —an incarceration which ended apparently with his acquittal. There is no evidence in the Acts that Paul's death followed closely upon the events therein related.

The opponents of the Pauline authorship of the Pastorals argue that "it is impossible to fit these epistles into the framework of the Acts history."[4] If there were any evidence that the concluding events related in the Acts coincide with the concluding events of Paul's life, this would indeed be a fatal objection. There is no such evidence, however, and to argue solely from the silence of the Acts as to the final years of the apostle's life is to build an argument on a sandy foundation.

It is quite probable that the apostle was granted acquittal and release from his first imprisonment in Rome and enjoyed some additional years of freedom and Christian leadership. And there is reason to believe that his renewed activity could have

[4]*Ibid.*, p. 203.

included the fulfillment of his cherished desire to visit Spain (Rom. 15:28). As W. J. Lowstuter summarizes the issue: ". . . no valid reason can be given for denying a release and no proof can be cited that actually disproves it. The Pastorals presuppose a release. This allows very reasonably for the various historical references which otherwise prove so hard to manage. Upon release, he could revisit his old churches, renew contact with old work, open new work in Crete, Dalmatia, and Gaul, plan for a winter at Nicopolis, leave a cloak and books at Troas [see map 1] to be sent for in a short time after he had again been thrown into prison, and from a second imprisonment write that his course was finished, his case without hope in imperial courts."[5]

b. The second attack upon the authenticity of the Pastorals fixes upon the ecclesiastical problem: the alleged incompatibility of these Epistles with first-century church organization. It is asserted that the Pastorals reflect a state of advanced organization in the Church which by definition could not possibly have prevailed until the middle years of the second century. The directions given in these Epistles concerning the appointment of bishops and deacons and the qualifications laid down for these offices, the authority which appears to rest with Timothy and Titus in the appointment of such officials, the emphasis upon elders as custodians and bearers of the traditions—these factors, so it is argued, point to a period considerably later than the time of Paul. Moreover, the heresies against which warning notes are sounded appear to be Gnostic heresies which first became truly menacing in the second century.

In reply, let it be pointed out that from the earliest period of his ministry Paul was concerned for decency and order in the churches which he founded. Luke relates that on his very first missionary journey Paul and Barnabas "ordained . . . elders in every church" (Acts 14:23). In writing to the Philippians his salutation is addressed to "all the saints in Christ Jesus which are at Philippi, with the bishops and deacons" (Phil. 1:1). Moreover, Paul's concern for the several orders of the ministry is made very evident in a passage such as Eph. 4:11-12.

The New Testament thus bears impressive witness to the fact that elders, bishops, and deacons were among the earliest officials of the infant Church. Edwin Hatch indicates that the

[5]"The Pastoral Epistles: First and Second Timothy and Titus," *The Abingdon Bible Commentary,* ed. by F. C. Eiselen, *et al.* (New York: Abingdon-Cokesbury Press, 1929), p. 1275.

organization of the early churches followed patterns which had become familiar in the organization of secular societies. He said: "Every one of the associations, political or religious, with which the Empire swarmed had its committee of officers. It was therefore antecedently probable . . . that when the Gentiles who had embraced Christianity began to be sufficiently numerous in a city to require some kind of organization, that organization would take the prevailing form; that it would be not wholly, if at all, monarchical, nor wholly, though essentially, democratical, but that there should be a permanent executive consisting of a plurality of persons."[6] This trend is evident in Paul's appointment of elders (presbyters) in the churches which he organized. It is evident, furthermore, that the chairman of this group of elders, the financial as well as the spiritual head of the local church, was known in Greek as *episcopos*, in English as "bishop." It was his task, among other duties, to maintain the fiscal integrity of the local church. Since the church had charitable functions as well as religious, including many in its ranks who were in dire need, the custody of the church's benevolent funds was a major responsibility; and this rested on the bishop.

In dispensing these funds to those in need, the bishop had associated with him a group of officials known in Greek as *diakonoi*, in English as "deacons." The diaconate which was established later in the Early Church was clearly anticipated in New Testament times when the apostles in Jerusalem appointed "seven men of honest report, full of the Holy Ghost and wisdom," whose duty it was to care for "the daily ministration" of help for the needy (Acts 6:1-3). Ultimately it was the practice in the Church that the actual distribution of this help was the business of the deacons, while the final responsibility belonged to the bishop, acting as the president and agent of the church's board of elders. It is true, as the Church moved into the second and third centuries these offices underwent significant changes. But the fact remains that they did exist in New Testament times and that the duties attaching to them were essentially the same as in later times. It appears, therefore, that the type of church organization reflected in the Pastorals does not necessarily take us beyond the period of Paul.

c. The third front on which the Pauline authorship is assailed is the doctrinal: Are there such radical doctrinal differ-

[6]*The Organization of the Early Christian Churches* (London: Longmans, Green and Co., 1901), p. 63.

ences between these Epistles and Paul's earlier writings as to make untenable the view that the Pastorals are the work of Paul? Those who would deny the Pauline authorship on this score cite the fact that the apostle's characteristic doctrines such as the "fatherhood of God" and "the believer's mystical union with Christ" or the apostle's unique expression "in Christ," all are missing from the Pastorals. And what, it is asked, has become of the apostle's concept of the Holy Spirit?

In reply it must be pointed out that the purpose of the apostle in writing the Pastorals differs from his purpose in any of his earlier writings. In these earlier Epistles he is writing as an evangelist and teacher and also as a pastor or shepherd of the flock. His method is in some cases theological (as in Romans), corrective (as in the Epistles to Corinth), concerned with removing dangerous misconceptions (as in the Epistles to Thessalonica), and always hortatory. But in the Pastorals he is farther removed than heretofore from the pastoral responsibility. Younger men are leading the combat troops of the faith, and Paul's role lies more in the field of strategy and direction. It is true that he is concerned with soundness of doctrine, as would befit "Paul the aged" writing to younger men. It is true that "the faith" has come to characterize the Christian message and formalized statements of faith appear more conspicuously than in Paul's earlier letters. But these reflect not only the changing situation in the churches and the total Christian enterprise, but also the psychological changes which were accompanying the apostle's advancing years. In view of all these considerations, it seems captious indeed to deny on this score the apostle's authorship of these obviously Pauline letters.

But the question must be faced as to the heresies against which the Pastorals sound a warning: Do these false teachings necessarily belong, as some allege, to the period of the second century rather than the first? Alfred Plummer has made a careful study of the teaching which Paul seeks to refute. He analyzes it thus:

"(1) The heresy is *Jewish* in character. Its promoters 'desire to be teachers of the Law' (1 Tim. 1:7). Some of them are 'they of the circumcision' (Titus 1:10). It consists in 'Jewish fables' (Titus 1:14). The questions it raises are 'fightings about the Law' (Titus 3:9).

"(2) Its *Gnostic* character is also indicated. We are told both in 1 Tim. 1:3, 4 and in the Epistle to Titus (1:14; 3:9) that it deals in 'fables and genealogies.' It is 'empty talking' [KJV:

'vain jangling'] (1 Tim. 1:6), 'disputes of words' (1 Tim. 6:4), and 'profane babblings' (1 Tim. 6:20). It teaches an unscriptural and unnatural asceticism (1 Tim. 4:3, 8). It is 'Gnosis' [KJV: 'science'] falsely so called' (1 Tim. 6:20)."[7]

Plummer furthermore cites Godet, who observes that in the relationship between Judaism and Christianity in the first century there were three distinct phases. First was the period when Judaism was outside the Church and opposed it to the point of blasphemy. Second was the period when Judaism attempted to invade the Church, seeking to foist the Mosaic law upon it. Finally came the period when Judaism became a heresy within the Church. In this third period, says Godet, "pretended revelations are given as to the names and genealogies of angels; absurd ascetic rules are laid down as counsels of perfection, while daring immorality defaces the actual life."[8] It is this final phase which confronts us in the Pastorals, a phase which obviously fell within the lifetime of the apostle. We can only conclude that, whatever changes may have come over the Gnostic heresy in subsequent years, we see that heresy clearly foreshadowed in the final years of the apostle's life and clearly unmasked by him in the Pastoral Epistles.

d. The fourth and final front on which the battle has been carried on is the linguistic: Are the differences in vocabulary which exist between the Pastorals and Paul's letters to the churches sufficient to impair the thesis that the Pastorals are Pauline in origin? Here the issue turns about the appearance of some one hundred seventy-five so-called "hapaxes" (words which appear for the first time in an author's work) in the three Pastoral Epistles. These words, it is alleged, are second-century words; which, if this allegation be sound, points to an authorship later than Paul.

Research has discovered, however, that the language of the Pastorals contains no words which do not appear elsewhere in Christian and secular literature by the middle of the first century; and nearly half of the supposedly "new words" appear in the Septuagint (*ca.* 200 B.C.). These and similar allegations are all based on a view of Paul's mental abilities which does him no credit. His was a vital and imaginative personality, in rapport with the changes incident to the growing influence of Christianity in its invasion of the Gentile world, and fully alive to the perils

[7]*Op. cit.*, p. 33.

[8]Quoted by Plummer, *op. cit.*, p. 34.

to the faith which attended these changes. Speaking to this very point, N. J. D. White observes that "such a man is likely to undergo changes in mental outlook, to become possessed by fresh ideals and conceptions, so as to bewilder less agile minds; and, of course, new thoughts require for their expression words and phrases for which the man had no use before. In the case of St. Paul, this is no imaginary supposition. The difference between the Paul of Philippians and the Paul of I Timothy is not greater than, perhaps not as great as, between the Paul of Thessalonians and the Paul of Ephesians."[9]

This is not to say that the apostle was personally responsible for every word employed in these Epistles, or, for that matter, in any of his Epistles. J. N. D. Kelly[10] has recently suggested that Paul's dependence upon an amanuensis could well have been considerably greater in the circumstances under which the Pastorals were produced, and that this could easily account for whatever variations in style and vocabulary his critics believe they have detected. But to concede this is in no sense to leave the authenticity of these Epistles in doubt.

This hasty review of the evidence relevant to the authorship of the Pastorals points to the conclusion that these letters are indeed the work of Paul. Their author is a Paul stricken in years and facing mortal danger, realizing fully that his own ministry nears its close and that the torch must be passed on to younger and more stalwart hands. But his view of the goal of Christianity is in no wise dimmed and his commitment to the Christian task is undiminished.

C. Destination and Purpose

The fact that the Pastoral Epistles are directed to individuals rather than to a church or a group of churches marks them as unique in the Pauline writings. Timothy and Titus were young men who held a very intimate and tender place in the apostle's trust and affection. Paul had placed them in Ephesus and Crete (see map 1) respectively, where they were bearing the heavy responsibility of leading these Christian churches. In both situations the church was a little island of transformed Christian souls surrounded by a vast ocean of paganism and moral corruption.

[9]"Introduction to the Pastoral Epistles," *The Expositor's Greek Testament,* ed. W. Robertson Nicoll (Grand Rapids: Wm. B. Eerdmans Publishing Co., n.d.), IV, 59.

[10]*A Commentary on the Pastoral Epistles* ("Harper's New Testament Commentaries"; New York: Harper and Row, 1963), pp. 25 ff.

To maintain the integrity of the Christian movement amid such surroundings was a colossal task. Paul could not disengage his mind and heart from the events which were transpiring on these two battlefronts. He was planning a journey which would bring him within reach of these two under-shepherds and he must see them to encourage and advise them. But some questions were too pressing to await personal interviews and on these matters he gives written advice. There are bishops and deacons to be appointed, and they must be men of peculiar integrity. There are false teachings which threaten the unity of the faith, and the apostle is constrained to do what he can to keep his young assistant's vision in sharp focus. In the second letter to Timothy he is facing the fact that little time remains to him. He leaves with Timothy a final confession of his unfaltering trust in Christ and his assurance that, though the state may destroy his body, it cannot impair his vision of the glorious future.

D. Probable Date

These Epistles were written after Paul's release from his first Roman imprisonment, a release which came probably in A.D. 61 or 62. Tradition has it that the apostle suffered martyrdom sometime during 67 or 68. The terminal dates of this final period in Paul's life are thus defined with a fair degree of assurance. During this period the Pastorals were written, and in this order: I Timothy, Titus, and II Timothy. In spite of some disagreement among the experts, this seems the probable sequence. Following his release Paul returned to his campaigning for Christ, though his goings and comings can only be conjectured. It is clear that Timothy and Titus were commissioned to serve as pastors, the one in Ephesus, the other in Crete. Their new responsibilities included the selection and appointment of suitable officials in these churches, and unmasking and rooting out of heretical trends, the direction and disciplining of the faith and conduct of these new Christians. I Timothy and Titus were written during the interval of freedom which Paul enjoyed between his two Roman imprisonments, perhaps as early as 63 and 64 respectively. II Timothy was written during the apostle's final confinement, the outcome of which was becoming increasingly plain, the date thus falling somewhere about 66 or 67. Here then we have what may properly be called the last will and testament of the great apostle, the man whom Deissmann describes as "the first under Christ" in the inception of the Christian Church.

Outline

THE FIRST EPISTLE TO TIMOTHY

I. Salutation, 1:1-2
   A. The Apostle's Authority, 1:1
   B. God Our Saviour . . . Christ . . . Our Hope, 1:1
   C. Unto Timothy, 1:2
   D. Grace, Mercy, and Peace, 1:2

II. Paul and Timothy, 1:3-20
   A. Timothy's Task at Ephesus, 1:3-7
   B. Function of Law in the Christian Life, 1:8-11
   C. Christ's Mercy in the Apostle's Life, 1:12-17
   D. Paul's Charge to Timothy, 1:18-20

III. Concern for Church Order, 2:1-15
   A. The Orderly Worship of God, 2:1-7
   B. Reverence in Public Worship, 2:8-15

IV. Qualifications of Christian Ministers, 3:1-13
   A. The Character of Bishops, 3:1-7
   B. The Character of Deacons, 3:8-13

V. Paul Defines the Church, 3:14-16
   A. The Household of God, 3:14-15
   B. The Mystery of Godliness, 3:15-16

VI. Threats to Integrity of the Church, 4:1-16
   A. Danger of Undue Asceticism, 4:1-5
   B. The Stature of a Good Minister of Christ, 4:6-10
   C. The Minister as an Example, 4:11-16

VII. Church Administration, 5:1-25
   A. Youth Should Respect Age, 5:1-2
   B. Responsibility Toward Dependent Widows, 5:3-16
   C. The Honor Due an Elder, 5:17-25

VIII. Various Instructions, 6:1-19
   A. Christian Slaves and Christian Masters, 6:1-2
   B. Consequences of Unsound Teaching, 6:3-5
   C. The Perils of Wealth, 6:6-10
   D. Aims and Rewards of Godly Living, 6:11-16
   E. The Proper Stewardship of Wealth, 6:17-19

IX. Paul's Concluding Appeal, 6:20-21

Section I Salutation

I Timothy 1:1-2

In common with most Greek letters of the first century, this Epistle begins by identifying the sender—**Paul, an apostle of Jesus Christ**—and the addressee—**Timothy, my own son in the faith.** Despite the fact that the letter is an exchange between the dearest of friends, it adheres to this formal and dignified salutation. As John Wesley remarks, not inappropriately: "Familiarity is to be set aside where the things of God are concerned."[1]

A. The Apostle's Authority, 1:1

In the majority of Paul's letters he identifies himself as **an apostle.** (The only exceptions are I and II Thessalonians, Philippians, and Philemon.) This word was the usual Greek term for a messenger, one charged with the task of conveying important information. The term, once it was taken up by the early Christian Church, came to designate an office of great distinction and importance in the movement's leadership. When we come to the late date of this first letter to Timothy (*ca.* A.D. 63), the term *apostle* had attained "official significance; it indicates status, a position of primary authority in the church. Paul as an apostle has the right to command and to be obeyed. In his own churches he is first, under God."[2]

But this was not an office upon which Paul ventured apart from the clear leading of God. Rather, he declares that he bears this responsibility **by the commandment of God our Saviour, and Lord Jesus Christ.** In other contexts he avows that it is "by the will of God" (II Cor. 1:1) that he is called to bear this burden. It is true, when his apostolate is under fire by his Judaizing enemies in the Church, he defends with utmost vigor

[1]*Explanatory Notes upon the New Testament* (London: Epworth Press, 1950), p. 771.

[2]Fred D. Gealy, "I Timothy" (Exegesis). *The Interpreter's Bible,* ed. George A. Buttrick, *et al,* XI (New York: Abingdon-Cokesbury Press, 1955), 376.

the authenticity of his divine appointment; yet his discharge of its functions is always in a spirit of humility as befits the bond-servant of Christ. It has long been held in the Church that the ministers of the Word are recruited by the call of God, and that a clear sense of this divine appointment is the *sine qua non* of him who would venture to preach the gospel. It is a matter of profound regret that belief in the indispensability of such a call seems now to be considerably less firm than in other days. If indeed this be true, then it should concern us most deeply that the Church recover this all-important faith in the divine vocation. Every man who enters upon the task of the Christian ministry, whether he be pastor, evangelist, district superintendent, or bishop, must be able to say from the heart with Paul, "Woe is unto me, if I preach not the gospel!" (I Cor. 9:16)

B. God Our Saviour . . . Christ . . . Our Hope, 1:1

God our Saviour is a striking variant of our usual manner of speaking of salvation through Christ. It is customary for Christians to speak of "Christ our Saviour." Yet there is considerable authority in the Pauline writings, and particularly in the Pastorals, for this variation (cf. 2:3; 4:10; Titus 1:3; 2:10; 3:4). This does not suggest that Christ is not our Saviour, but it does make emphatic the partnership of the three Persons in the blessed Trinity in the work of human redemption. The Father as well as the Son, and in a very real sense the Holy Spirit, were all engaged in the task which, from a more narrow point of view, was entrusted chiefly to the incarnate Son. We must remember that the divine Trinity is also a holy Unity, and that our human salvation is made possible by the will and infinite sacrifice of the Godhead.

N. J. D. White has suggested that "in the text, there is an antithesis between the offices of God *our Saviour* and of Jesus Christ as *our hope*."[3] The former expression looks to the past, recalling the finished work of God in Christ, when at Calvary our Lord gave himself for us. Paul says of that event that "God was in Christ, reconciling the world unto himself" (II Cor. 5:19). But the expression **Christ, which is our hope** looks to the future, with its fullness and consummation of what is now only partial and incomplete. The apostle had reached the stage in his service for

[3]*Op. cit.*, IV, 90.

Christ when physical strength had begun to abate. He had tasted some of the bitter cost of an uttermost loyalty to Christ. Perhaps there was in his soul an increasing longing for the hour when his race would be finished and the unfading wreath would rest upon his brow. The promise of the future which came to such eloquent expression in II Tim. 4:6-8 was already beginning to possess his spirit. The Saviour was to him and may be to us all indeed **Christ . . . our hope.**

C. Unto Timothy, 1:2

Timothy, my own son in the faith—such is the apostle's characterization of this young man. The RSV renders this "my true child in the faith"; while the NEB puts it movingly as my "trueborn son in the faith." The salutation in II Timothy is even more affectionate: "My dearly beloved son."

Timothy first appears in the New Testament in Acts 16:1. This chapter relates Paul's second visit to Derbe and Lystra on the occasion of his second missionary journey. Timothy was the son of a Greek father and a Jewish mother. We are justified in assuming that Timothy's mother (Eunice) and grandmother (Lois) (II Tim. 1:5) had been reached by the gospel during Paul's first visit to this area. It was at Lystra that Paul suffered such violent persecution; and it is not unreasonable to conjecture that he was cared for in his affliction in the home of Eunice. It is altogether likely that Timothy became a Christian on the occasion of the apostle's first visit. Plummer[4] estimates that that conversion took place in A.D. 45, while the apostle's second visit to Lystra occurred "six or seven years" later. He estimates further that Timothy "was probably not yet thirty-five when Paul wrote the First Epistle to him." Assuming that he was thirty-five years of age in A.D. 63, he must have been around seventeen when converted, and twenty-three or twenty-four on the occasion of Paul's second visit to Lystra. The apostle persuaded this promising young man to "go forth with him" (Acts 16:3) and become the companion of his travels and labors. Paul also had Timothy undergo the rite of circumcision, but only to anticipate and forestall the erection of any barriers to the young man's ministry in the Jewish synagogues of the Dispersion. These synagogues were invaluable "ports of entry" for the gospel into the Jewish communities of the Gentile world. It is probable that the apostle

[4]*Op. cit.*, pp. 21-22.

then proceeded to set Timothy apart for the work of the ministry by some process of ordination which involved the laying on of hands. It would seem that this ceremony is alluded to in I Tim. 4:14: "Neglect not the gift that is in thee, which was given thee by prophecy, with the laying on of the hands of the presbytery."

Paul and his traveling companion Silas, now accompanied by Timothy, continued their travels, coming presently to Troas (see map 1), where Luke joined their company (Acts 16:8-10). The party proceeded on to Philippi, Thessalonica, and Beroea, proclaiming the message that "Jesus is Christ," and encountering mounting opposition. Paul moved to Athens; but Silas and Timothy continued in Beroea to consolidate what gains had been made (Acts 17:14-15). From Athens, Paul proceeded to Corinth, where Silas and Timothy rejoined him. Concern for the work so well begun at Thessalonica prompted the apostle to send Timothy back to them to "establish" and to "comfort" them concerning their faith. The apostle's already high estimate of Timothy's worth is evident in his commendation of him as "our brother, and minister of God, and our fellowlabourer in the gospel of Christ" (I Thess. 3:2).

The two Epistles to the Thessalonians include in their salutations the name of Timothy along with those of Paul and Silas. We find Timothy and Silas in Corinth, holding up the apostle's hands and assisting him in the evangelistic task. For the next few years references to Timothy are meager, though undoubtedly he continued as Paul's faithful helper. In A.D. 55 or 56, when the First Epistle to the Corinthians is probably to be dated, we find the apostle sending Timothy as his representative to the church at Corinth, charged with the task of recalling that difficult church to a renewed loyalty to the truth as Paul had proclaimed it among them. The apostle commends him warmly to them as "my beloved son, and faithful in the Lord, who shall bring you into remembrance of my ways which be in Christ" (I Cor. 4:17). But when the Second Epistle to the Corinthians was written, perhaps a year later, Timothy was again at the apostle's side and shares the salutation with him. In A.D. 56, when Paul wrote his letter to the Romans, Timothy was among those sending greetings to the believers at Rome (Rom. 16:21). And when the apostle made his way through Macedonia en route to Jerusalem, where "bonds and afflictions" awaited him, Timothy is named as a member of his company (Acts 20:4).

During Paul's two years' imprisonment at Caesarea (see map 2) there is a silence in the record concerning Timothy. But during the apostle's first Roman imprisonment we find Timothy again at his side and included in the salutations of Paul's letters to the Philippians, the Colossians, and Philemon—all "Prison Epistles." Indeed, during this period Timothy made a journey on Paul's behalf to the church at Philippi. And here again we have a most appreciative appraisal of the young man's worth: "I hope in the Lord Jesus to send Timothy to you soon, so that I may be cheered by news of you. I have no one like him, who will be genuinely anxious for your welfare. They all look after their own interests, not those of Jesus Christ. But Timothy's worth you know, how as a son with a father he has served with me in the gospel" (Phil. 2:19-22, RSV).

Whatever else we know of Timothy in his relation to Paul must be derived from these two Epistles addressed by the apostle to his esteemed helper. The whole record exhibits the deep, fatherly concern of Paul for his most distinguished convert and assistant in the gospel work. It reflects also the filial devotion which characterized Timothy's selfless loyalty to the apostle who was his spiritual father.

D. Grace, Mercy, and Peace, 1:2

Paul's benediction addressed to Timothy is extraordinary in that **mercy** is added to **grace** and **peace.** Wesley observes that "St. Paul wishes *grace* and *peace* in his epistles to the churches. To Timotheus he adds *mercy,* the most tender grace towards those who stand in need of it." And, adds Wesley, "the experience of this prepares a man to be a minister of the gospel."[5] It is truly a matter of the utmost importance that those who are called to handle the divine mysteries be men who are deeply conscious not only of their need for God's mercy, but of the fact of that mercy. No man is ever worthy of this responsibility, and must be constantly and vividly aware that only "by the grace of God I am what I am."

[5]*Op. cit.,* p. 771.

Section II Paul and Timothy

I Timothy 1:3-20

A. Timothy's Task at Ephesus, 1:3-7

1. *Stay in Ephesus* (1:3)

"Stay where you are"—such, in Moffatt's vigorous translation, is the admonition of Paul to Timothy, rendered in the KJV as **I besought thee to abide still at Ephesus.** The events in Paul's life during these brief concluding years can be deduced only with difficulty from these Pastoral Epistles. It appears that Paul felt urgently drawn toward Macedonia, and that Timothy desired greatly to accompany him. It would be easy to rationalize such a proceeding, for Timothy had been the apostle's strong helper on many such journeys. Paul himself, if he had been in position to consult only his own preferences, would have looked with favor on Timothy's companionship on the journey. But other and more pressing considerations must prevail. Timothy's leadership and direction were needed in Ephesus, and duty must take precedence over personal preferences.

There are many occasions in life when it is far easier to move on than to remain in a difficult situation. The instinct to escape from onerous responsibility, to "run away when the battle gets hot," is present with us all, and must be resisted with firm resolution. The easy way out, following the line of least resistance, the tendency to drift with the current rather than to breast it with courage and fortitude—these possible alternatives become grievous temptations at times. To escape from a galling situation, to make a fresh start elsewhere, where the grass is greener and the prospects more inviting—this is a course of action which the tempter can disguise so completely as to make it appear the will of God. But when God says, "Stay where you are," it is both cowardly and sinful to abandon one's responsibilities for something that appears more winsome. There are times, to be sure, when God's word is, "Go," and not, "Stay." But whichever it may be, one must be sure that his attitude is one of instant obedience.

2. *Timothy's Task* (1:3-4)

Timothy's immediate responsibility was to **charge some that they teach no other doctrine** (3). We are not told whom the apostle had in mind in issuing this warning; probably Timothy already knew full well those who were involved. Moreover, the nature of these heresies is described only vaguely as **fables and endless genealogies, which minister questions, rather than godly edifying which is in faith** (4).

While it is impossible to conclude with complete assurance what were these teachings which the apostle felt were subverting the faith of the Ephesian Christians, it is not farfetched to suggest that an incipient Gnosticism was involved. The heresy known as Gnosticism, which became such a serious menace to the integrity of Christian teaching in the second century, had Jewish as well as Gentile roots. There were three successive phases of Jewish influence in the Early Church (see Introduction). The second was the Judaizing phase which Paul combated so effectively in his Epistle to the Galatians. It is the third phase, where "pretended revelations are given as to the names and genealogies of angels," which the apostle is seeking to warn Timothy against in the passage now before us.

Gnosticism's basic fallacy was the positing of a fundamental dualism between spirit and matter, between good and evil. Admittedly God was good, but the world was essentially evil. Granting this, how can the good God's creation of an evil world be explained? This was accomplished by the concept of a Demiurge —a sort of "half-god" far enough removed from the holy God to be responsible for the creation of the evil world. It can be readily seen how such speculations might be characterized by Paul as **fables,** or "interminable myths" (NEB), and could involve **endless genealogies.** This last expression may refer to the then current emphasis on genealogies in Judaism.

Whatever these teachings were, they were wholly lacking in anything that would edify God's people and, indeed, were very likely to undermine the faith of Christian believers. To **minister questions** (4) would be "to give rise to mere speculation" (NASB). This would offer reason enough for Paul's insistence that such speculative teachings must not be tolerated. The difficult last clause of v. 4 may be rendered "cannot make known God's plan for us, which works through faith" (NEB).

3. *Brotherly Love Must Be Preserved* (1:5-7)

Another factor, equal in seriousness to the first, was this: such teachings tolerated in the church could not fail to destroy the spirit of Christian love which alone identifies unmistakably the company of the redeemed. **The end of the commandment is charity** (love) **out of a pure heart, and of a good conscience, and of faith unfeigned** (5). This emphasis upon love as the very essence of Christian life and experience is not a new note with Paul. Throughout his writings, but especially in Rom. 13:8-10, love becomes for the apostle a summary of the whole of religion. He challenges Christians to "owe no man any thing, but to love one another." Love is a debt which can never be paid in full. He summarizes the social emphasis in the Ten Commandments with the demand, so often stressed by the Master—"Thou shalt love thy neighbour as thyself." He characterizes love and the compassionate attitudes which flow from it as "the fulfilling of the law." And in each case the term employed for love is the Greek word *agape,* or one of its various forms. This is a term which rarely appears in secular Greek, and never in the sense in which it is employed in the New Testament. In the hands of the inspired writers it sets forth uniquely the kind of love which God has lavished on a lost and sinning world. The apostle epitomizes this meaning in his great word in Rom. 5:8: "God commendeth his love [*agape*] toward us, in that, while we were yet sinners, Christ died for us."

But Paul goes further by here using this same unique term to describe the response of love which flows from the hearts of the redeemed, in answer to God's prior love for us. Elsewhere, in I John 4:10-11, both of these uses of the term are illustrated: "Herein is love, not that we loved God, but that he loved us, and sent his Son to be the propitiation for our sins. Beloved, if God so loved us, we ought also to love one another." In each instance where the word "love" appears in this passage from Timothy it is some form of the word *agape.* But let us not assume that this response of *agape* from the hearts of God's people is self-originated. The miracle of grace is such that men who have known only greed and lust may be transformed by the power of God and thus made divinely capable of this *agape* response.

When the apostle deplores the tragic effects which have come about as a result of the activities of these false teachers in Ephesus, it is because this essential climate of the Christian

Church—the climate of *agape* love—has been destroyed. The true atmosphere of the Church of Christ is "love that issues from a pure heart and a good conscience and sincere faith" (RSV).

In John Wesley's early evangelical ministry, the Fetter Lane meeting in London was disrupted by the teaching of quietism by the Moravian leader Molther. Wesley labored long and manfully to bring about peace and understanding. But he finally became convinced that the fomenters of discord had gone so far as to destroy all hope of a restoration of genuine fellowship. Consequently he withdrew his own followers from the Fetter Lane meeting and established a new society in the Foundery, an old building which became famous for forty years as the center of Methodism in London. Wesley made it clear that this division did not come about because of the peculiar views of those who differed with him, but because they insisted that everyone else should hold the same opinions. Wesley was broadly tolerant of differences of theological opinion provided those who held such views kept them to themselves. To attempt to foist such opinions on others could only destroy the climate of love which was so essential to a truly Christian society. The Christian rule must always be: "In essentials, unity; in nonessentials, diversity; in all things, charity."

B. Function of Law in the Christian Life, 1:8-11

Here at Ephesus **some having swerved** had **turned aside unto vain jangling** (6; "a wilderness of words," NEB). They desired **to be teachers of the law** (7) but were utterly ignorant of its Christian interpretation. The essential climate of love cannot hope to survive long in such a situation.

The apostle is carrying forward his indictment of the incipient Gnosticism, which had appeared in Ephesus, in this further appraisal of the function of the law. It is true that the perverters of the Christian way against whom he is warning desire to be teachers of the law—a law whose meaning they distort to serve their evil purposes. We are not justified, however, in repudiating the law because some fail to **use it lawfully** (8). Paul, who in the controversy of "law versus grace" definitely took the side of grace, makes it clear that there is a valid and continuing function to be performed by law, especially the moral law as stated in the Ten Commandments. There is a conscious and obvious reference to the so-called "second table" of the Decalogue in 9 and 10 (cf. Exod. 20:12-17).

What are we to understand by the words: **The law is not made for a righteous man** (9)? It surely does not mean that the righteous man is no longer amenable to the moral law which the Decalogue so clearly and so timelessly enunciates. To believe otherwise would be to commit oneself to antinomianism. This law was our "schoolmaster" to lead us to Christ. But to know Christ as Saviour and Lord is to have that law inscribed on our hearts. Speaking of the days of the new covenant, Jeremiah says: "After these days, saith the Lord, I will put my law in their inward parts, and write it in their hearts; and I will be their God, and they shall be my people" (Jer. 31:33). **But for the lawless and disobedient, for the ungodly and for sinners,** and for all other transgressors in the apostle's list of evildoers, the law thunders its "Thou shalt not." Phillips describes the **unholy and profane** man as one "who has neither scruples nor reverence."

For these and all others who are basically lacking in moral soundness, the law utters its terrible word of judgment. This is the judgment which the apostle clearly indicates as awaiting those who desire to be teachers of the law but who are such strangers to its essential message that they understand "neither what they say, nor whereof they affirm" (7). This note of judgment upon sin, which W. M. Clow calls "the dark line in God's face," is a negative yet essential element in **the glorious gospel of the blessed God** (11) which Paul in his generation, and we in ours, believe is committed to our trust.

It is difficult to imagine a more astounding message than this **glorious gospel.** What it means is faintly suggested by the NEB translation of verse 11: "the gospel which tells of the glory of God in his eternal felicity." This should not be understood to suggest that now, at long last, an affirmative answer has been found to the questions of Zophar, the Naamathite: "Canst thou by searching find out God? Canst thou find out the Almighty unto perfection?" (Job 11:7) Surely the mighty God can never be captured by our definitions. But if "the glory of God in his eternal felicity" is ever to be glimpsed by mortal man, it will be in the context of our redemption through Christ. We shall know Him, if we are to know Him at all, in the proffer of His saving mercy which flows to men from Christ by the revealing and interpreting Spirit. And to be the custodians of such a message is sufficient to stagger the stoutest mind and heart.

C. Christ's Mercy in the Apostle's Life, 1:12-17

1. *A Man Called of God* (1:12)

No man in the history of the Christian ministry has been more clearly conscious than was Paul of divine appointment to this task. In writing to the Galatians he suggests that from his birth and even before, so far as God's will was concerned, he was destined to the work of an apostle (Gal. 1:15). There was little evidence of this divine purpose during the days of his mad assault upon the Church; though even then, as we view it in retrospect, by background and education he was being prepared for this solemn responsibility. Once Christ had won Saul to himself, there could be no further delay; and we read in the Acts (9:20) that "straightway he preached Christ in the synagogues, that he is the Son of God." If Horace Bushnell is right in his great sermon "Every Man's Life a Plan of God" (and I believe he is right), then this was the divine "blueprint" for Saul of Tarsus. And he declares before Agrippa, "I was not disobedient unto the heavenly vision."

But even more forthright is his declaration of faithfulness, mingled with thanksgiving, in the passage now before us: **I thank Christ Jesus our Lord, who hath enabled me, for that he counted me faithful, putting me into the ministry.** Here is the testimony of Christ's servant, grown old in the service of his Lord. And it is no idle boast—indeed, if it be considered in any sense a boast. It is rather the declaration of one who, like the Psalmist, makes his "boast in the Lord" (Ps. 34:2); and it would be entirely proper to add, with the Psalmist, "The humble shall hear thereof, and be glad." It was through the grace and strength of Christ Jesus that the amazing record of Paul's life "in Christ" had been achieved.

2. *The Apostle's Shameful Past* (1:13-14)

Nevertheless the apostle was acutely conscious of his unworthiness of even the least of God's mercy. Though the sins of those years when he had waged his futile war on Christ and His Church had been long since forgiven, yet the memory remained to lacerate his soul and induce a never-ending sense of sorrow. Paul did not spare himself in his allusions to this shameful past. In speaking before King Agrippa he admitted frankly his forthright opposition to Christ, his harrying of Christ's followers, and even tacitly admitted his complicity in their death. In I Cor. 15:9 he confessed with shame: "I am the least of the apostles, that am not meet to be called an apostle, because I persecuted the church of God." In Gal. 1:13 we hear him acknowledging that "beyond measure I persecuted the church of God, and wasted it." But in the passage before us, confession of his continuing remorse goes beyond anything encountered elsewhere in his writings. He describes himself as **before a blasphemer, and a persecutor, and injurious** (13). Plummer points out that "there is . . . an ascending scale in the iniquity which the Apostle confesses. He not only blasphemed the Divine Name himself, but he endeavored to compel others to do the same."[1]

It is the third term in this "ascending scale of self-condemnation" which is the most violent and shameful of all. The word **injurious** does not convey the meaning of the original, though to find an adequate substitute for it is not easy. The RSV uses the term "insulted"; NEB, "outrage"; and Weymouth translates it "insolent in outrage." Such is the forgiven sin which the apostle recalls with shame and regret. It is not to glory in his sinful past that he alludes to these events, but only to magnify the grace of God, which is so much greater than the abounding sin of his youth.

Paul suggests that the ignorance which blinded his eyes and prejudiced his heart was a factor in God's miracle of forgiveness. In fact, it seems likely that in most cases of forgiven sin ignorance is a contributing factor. No man, if he knew fully the sinfulness of his sin, its inevitable and ongoing consequences, would be guilty of the insane folly of defying Almighty God. Men are first deceived by the tempter and then are persuaded to this folly. But the glad truth is that, despite the magnitude of our human sin, God's grace is more than sufficient, and every one who turns to Christ may obtain mercy. As the apostle so clearly witnesses, indeed, **the grace of our Lord was exceeding abundant** (14). The seventeenth-century rhetoric of this passage may be archaic, but the truth to which it bears witness is a glorious reality. It means, in the vigorous contemporary English of the NEB, that "the grace of our Lord was lavished upon me, with the faith and love which are ours in Christ Jesus."

[1]*Op. cit.*, p. 54.

3. *Christ Came to Save* (1:15)

Moved by this deep sense of gratitude to God for His infinite mercy, Paul is constrained to utter one of his most moving declarations of God's saving purpose in the redeeming gift of His Son. The declaration proper is contained in the familiar words: **Christ Jesus came into the world to save sinners.** But it is prefaced with an introductory expression which is designed to point up its importance as a brief summary of the essential Christian message: **This is a faithful saying, and worthy of all acceptation.** Most New Testament scholars see in this declaration concerning the purpose of Christ's coming a quotation from some source which was current in the Church in Paul's day and quite familiar among the Christians to whom Timothy was ministering. The source could have been a creedal statement or baptismal formula, or it could have been a fragment of an early hymn of the Church. But whatever its source, and even though brief, it is so pointed and so definitive as to possess lasting value. The apostle makes clear that this statement of our Lord's unique place in salvation history is an utterly dependable one.

Christ's concern is for the saving of sinners. One is reminded of Jesus' own statement, "I am . . . come to call . . . sinners to repentance" (Matt. 9:13). Couple with this that other saying, uttered on the eve of His suffering, "The Son of man is come to seek and to save that which was lost" (Luke 19:10), and you have from the lips of our Lord a declaration almost identical with St. Paul's.

4. *Chief of Sinners* (1:15-16)

The apostle adds to this a touch which is characteristically Pauline when he follows the word **sinners** with the phrase **of whom I am chief.** Expressions of continuing remorse for past sins are not uncommon on Paul's lips. What does he mean by designating himself as the chief of sinners? It is difficult to believe that, however stained and guilty the record of Saul of Tarsus may have been, he should be regarded in any absolute sense as the worst of all possible sinners. What he is saying is that his offense against God was so great and his sense of guilt so overwhelming that he felt himself to be the number one sinner of all time. And who of us can hope to turn to God in any other spirit than this? Only when we are overwhelmed with a sense of shame for our sins and are utterly speechless, with nothing to plead before the

God we have offended, can we hope for mercy and forgiveness. Each of us must echo with all his heart this cry of the apostle, "of whom I am chief." Thus could Charles Wesley sing,

Depth of mercy! Can there be
Mercy still reserved for me?
Can my God His wrath forbear?
Me, the chief of sinners, spare?

In 16, Paul carries forward a little further his efforts to understand the miracle of mercy which had so greatly changed his life. Earlier (in 13) he had cited the fact of his ignorance as a mitigating circumstance in his sinful opposition to Christ. But now he suggests further that he **obtained mercy, that in me first Jesus Christ might shew forth all longsuffering.** Nothing could be more eloquent of the goodness and grace of God than some outstanding examples of the power of Christ's redemption. And surely no miracle of grace in all of Christian history has spoken more convincingly of the saving and transforming power of Christ than the utterly changed life of Saul of Tarsus. In speaking of the manner in which the news of his conversion to Christ affected the churches in Judea, he says, "They had heard only, That he which persecuted us in times past now preacheth the faith which once he destroyed. And they glorified God in me" (Gal. 1:23-24).

5. *To God Be the Glory* (1:17)

It is small wonder, therefore, that verse 17 is a doxology of praise to God. This is one of two doxologies appearing in the First Epistle to Timothy, the second occurs in 6:15-16. This first doxology wells up spontaneously from the heart of the apostle, moved as he is by the memory of his own marvelous deliverance. **Now unto the King . . . the only wise God, be honour and glory for ever and ever. Amen.** God is described as **the King eternal** (or King of the ages), **immortal** (or, as described in the second doxology, "who only hath immortality"), **invisible** (the invisible God, whose image is seen in Jesus Christ, Col. 1:15), **the only wise God** (or, as most recent versions render it, "the only God"). This is obviously the language of liturgy, and is an attempt to describe the being of God, whose greatness must ever defy our efforts at description.

Thus in 12-17 the great apostle bears his adoring witness to the mercy, grace, and re-creating power of God in his own life. If it be true that preaching is essentially witnessing, then these verses are preaching of a high order.

D. Paul's Charge to Timothy, 1:18-20

1. *Timothy's Ordination* (1:18-19)

In this section the apostle returns once more to the solemn commission which was placed upon the young man Timothy as a result of his ordination to the Christian ministry. Language which anticipates this commission appears in v. 3, while in 5 one of its goals is clearly enunciated. Here the apostle repeats the commission, addressing the young man in tender tones: **This charge I commit unto thee, son Timothy** (18). All the loving concern of a father is implicit in this address. Having repeated the charge, Paul immediately proceeds to amplify its significance by alluding to the circumstances under which Timothy's ministry was launched. **According to the prophecies which went before on thee** may be translated, "the prophecies previously made concerning you" (NASB). A measure of light is cast on this allusion by calling attention to two subsequent references to the young man's ordination. One is in I Tim. 4:14: "Neglect not the gift that is in thee, which was given thee by prophecy, with the laying on of the hands of the presbytery"; the second in II Tim. 1:6: "Wherefore I put thee in remembrance that thou stir up the gift of God, which is in thee by the putting on of my hands."

It seems evident that Timothy had been inducted into the ministry in a solemn ceremony over which the apostle himself presided and in which he was assisted by other ministers of the church. It is not necessary, as some interpreters have attempted, to see in this reference to **prophecies which went before on thee** the special activities of some order of prophets in the Early Church. This type of ministry had its place. But to be set apart for the work of the ministry by the laying on of Paul's hands, and to receive one's ordination charge from his lips, would be a situation which could only be described as "prophetic." Even today no experience compares in solemnity and prophetic grandeur with the moment when one feels the weight of the elders' hands on his head and hears the fateful words: "Take thou authority as an elder in the Church of Christ." Only one who has received such a charge can appreciate the significance of this essentially indescribable experience. No moment can possibly be more prophetic than this.

Such a hallowed moment had come to the young man Timothy, and the apostle would have him regard it as an assignment to leadership in the army of King Jesus. The military figure **war a good warfare** is one that Paul adopts frequently, especially in dealing with Timothy. The young preacher is an officer of the line, fighting in the forefront of the battle for Christ and truth at Ephesus. Paul suggests that he take firm hold on **faith, and a good conscience** (19) as weapons perfectly suited to his purpose. The NEB brings this out most clearly in its rendering: "So fight gallantly, armed with faith and a good conscience."

2. *Faith and Conscience* (1:19)

It would be difficult to exaggerate the importance of this spiritual weaponry, especially the support which **a good conscience** offers to one's **faith** in God. Paul thinks immediately of a tragic example of failure at this point: **which** (good conscience) **some having put away concerning faith have made shipwreck.** In this familiar form the verse sounds archaic. But the RSV renders it in such precise English as to leave no uncertainty: "By rejecting conscience, certain persons have made shipwreck of their faith." Here is a vivid metaphor which renders graphic the spiritual disaster which overtakes one who ignores conscience. One can retain **faith** in Christ only as he maintains **a good conscience.**

Shipwreck suggests the magnitude of the moral tragedy against which Paul warns. Some who are concerned to question the Pauline authorship of this First Epistle to Timothy point out that nowhere else has the apostle employed this metaphor. Yet what would be more likely to occur to him than this picture? He had himself passed through the experience of shipwreck on his first journey to Rome, and the horror of it must have been ineffaceably impressed on his memory. Only by maintaining a good and tender conscience can spiritual tragedy be avoided. This emphasis is most timely for Christians in our momentous days. We need to hear again that wise warning which Susanna Wesley wrote to her son John during his days at Oxford. "Take this rule," she admonishes: "Whatever weakens your reason, impairs the tenderness of your conscience, obscures your sense of God, or takes off the relish of spiritual things; in short, whatever increases the strength and authority of your body over your mind; that thing is sin to you, however innocent it may be in itself."[2]

3. *Two Men Who Failed* (1:20)

In this verse the apostle names two persons—**Hymenaeus and Alexander**—whom he regards as having made the compromise against which he warns. It is virtually impossible to establish the precise identity of these two men. **Alexander** is a name which appears in Acts 19:33 in the story of the early days of the church at Ephesus. He was a man who at that time held an honored place in the Christian community. But we have no assurance that the **Alexander** here named is the same man mentioned in the Acts. It was a common name and there could have been a number of persons so named in the Ephesian church. Moreover, we cannot with complete assurance identify him with "Alexander the coppersmith," who is said to have done the apostle "much evil" (II Tim. 4:14). The other man named in Paul's indictment is **Hymenaeus.** He is named also in II Tim. 2:17, where he is linked with Philetus as advocating the erroneous notion that "the resurrection is past already"—a teaching which had an unsettling effect on some of the believers. Possibly some such teaching was the occasion for the apostle's severe censure here; at least it was some teaching which in his judgment represented blasphemy.

4. *Church Discipline* (1:20)

We are uncertain as to the precise penalty which Paul pronounces on these offenders. What is meant by his word **I have delivered** (them) **unto Satan?** Some see in it the sort of radical exclusion from the Christian fellowship which would be properly described as excommunication, while others contend it was something far more drastic than this. Whatever view we take, this much is clear, the penalty was intended to have remedial effect: **that they may learn not to blaspheme.** Wesley sees in the apostle's judgment this purpose: "That by what they suffer they may be in some measure restrained, if they will not repent."[3]

[2]John Whitehead, *Lives of John and Charles Wesley* (New York: R. Worthington, 1881), p. 222.

[3]*Op. cit.*, p. 774.

There is a profoundly disturbing instruction for us in this spectacle of the apostle exercising discipline in the church at Ephesus. The realization of a need for discipline in the community of faith has all but disappeared from our thought in these days. Our accepted standards of life have undergone no change from their initial rigor, but they are honored too often in the breach rather than the observance. And such flouting of basic Christian conduct goes unrebuked. Yet a part of our divine commission is to "reprove, rebuke, exhort with all longsuffering and doctrine" (II Tim. 4:2). It requires little courage to denounce the sins of our people from the pulpit; but it calls for real fortitude to face the sinner as an individual and rebuke his sin in a spirit of meekness and love. As J. H. Jowett points out, "The fear of *a man* is a much more subtle thing than the fear of *men*."[4]

[4]*The Preacher: His Life and Work* (New York: Harper and Bros., 1912), italics mine.

Section III The Concern for Church Order

I Timothy 2:1-15

A. The Orderly Worship of God, 2:1-7

1. *Importance of Church Order* (2:1)

With the beginning of the second chapter the apostle comes to the question which had prompted him to write to Timothy—his concern for proper church order in Ephesus. The priority that Paul gave this concern is evident from the phrase in his opening sentence: **I exhort therefore . . . first of all.** There is a certain fitness which should characterize the public worship of God. Surely it is not objectionable formalism to be concerned for the fitting and proper sequences which should be observed when Christians gather for worship. The apostle urges therefore the type of prayer which should form a part of every such service. **I exhort . . . that . . . supplications, prayers, intercessions, and giving of thanks, be made for all men.** No Christian duty toward our fellowmen compares in importance with one's duty to pray for them. S. D. Gordon has pointed out that no one can do anything to help another until first of all he has prayed for him. After he has prayed, there are many things he can do; but until he has prayed, there is nothing he can do except pray.

There does not seem to be any particular significance attached to the order in which the terms **supplications, prayers, intercessions, and giving of thanks** appear. Of these four terms the second is the broadest and, in a sense, includes the other three. Paul's meaning seems to be that prayer in all its forms should occupy a central place in the church's service of worship. Moreover, it should be indiscriminate in its outreach, including **all men** in its scope. God's offer of mercy in Christ is extended to all alike. There are no favored few who alone belong to God's elect. He desires and has made provision for the salvation of all who will yield to His saving mercy revealed in Christ. We are to pray in a spirit of intercession, therefore, that the redeeming outreach of the gospel may be as wide as possible.

2. *Those for Whom Prayer Should Be Made* (2:2-4)

The apostle now becomes more explicit, stating expressly that prayer should be made **for kings, and for all that are in authority** (2). This is to be understood as referring to the civil rulers of the ancient world at all levels of authority. When we remember that, at the time Paul was writing, most rulers were enemies of the Christian faith, and that within a decade the apostle himself would forfeit his life at their hands, this exhortation to prayer becomes a splendid example of Christian magnanimity. The first reason for such prayer is that **kings and all that are in authority** are also men—men for whom Christ died—and they are within the outreach of the gospel. But a second reason for such prayer is vaguely hinted in the words: **that we may lead a quiet and peaceable life in all godliness and honesty.** To pray earnestly for those in authority could very well place in God's hands the means for restraining from evil and misguided purposes these men who were in position to harm the Church of Christ.

It would be difficult indeed to overestimate the power of the church's united prayer. E. K. Simpson is surely correct when, in commenting on this verse, he says: "No Bible-taught Christian can dispute the efficacy of believing prayer in regard to public events and their supervisors. More things are wrought thereby than this world dreams of. The supplication of faithful intercessors for the common weal lays invisible restraint on the powers of darkness and their tools and brings reinforcement to honest rulers from the Governor among the nations (Ps. 22:28)."[1]

That the former of these two reasons for such prayer is of major importance is made clear by 3 and 4: **For this is good and acceptable in the sight of God our Saviour; who will have all men to be saved, and to come unto the knowledge of the truth.** Here is clearly stated God's universal desire for mankind, a desire which can be thwarted only by man's resistance in freedom to God's saving purpose. The apostle dared to believe that God's faithful Spirit was at work in the hearts and lives of all men and could save those of high degree quite as readily as those of lower station. This had already been proved to his complete satisfaction during his first Roman imprisonment. In Phil. 1:13, writing from his Roman prison, he says, "My bonds in Christ are manifest

[1]*The Pastoral Epistles* (Grand Rapids: Wm. B. Eerdmans Publishing Co., 1954), p. 40.

in all the palace, and in all other places." His witness, it would appear, was not without effect; for in Phil. 4:22, in his final greetings, he says, "All the saints salute you, chiefly they that are of Caesar's household." It was by no means useless, therefore, to pray for kings and others in positions of authority.

3. *Putting First Things First* (2:4)

We should note, moreover, in v. 4 the order in which appear the two characterizations of God's saving grace. The first is **to be saved,** and the second **to come unto the knowledge of the truth.** There are some who would regard these two expressions as belonging properly in reverse order. But Paul's putting of the matter conforms perfectly to the teaching of the Lord Jesus when, in John 7:17, He said: "If any man's will is to do his [God's] will, he shall know whether the teaching is from God, or whether I am speaking on my own authority" (RSV). In knowing the things of God obedience must always precede further knowledge.

4. *A Magnificent Digression* (2:5-6)

It is frequently pointed out that vv. 3-7 form a digression from the main thrust of this second chapter. Its major emphasis is on the place of prayer in Christian worship; and after interrupting that theme with the digression just mentioned, Paul returns to his central concern in 8. But if this be a digression it is a magnificent one. Indeed, this exploration of inviting vistas is one of the most delightful characteristics of the apostle's literary style. His noble insight concerning the Church in Eph. 5:25-27 is such a digression, as is also the so-called Kenotic Passage in Phil. 2:6-11.

The digression now before us gives a perfect gem of Christological insight: **There is one God, and one mediator between God and men, the man Christ Jesus** (5). It would be difficult to exaggerate the wealth of meaning riding on these words. Their literary form suggests that they were a part of an early creedal statement or baptismal formula, or possibly a portion of an early hymn. The emphasis on **one God** is part of Christianity's inheritance from Judaism, an emphasis which our Lord reaffirmed frequently. The New Testament revelation of plurality within the being of God in no wise diminishes this fundamental understanding of His unity.

The position of Christ as the **one mediator between God and men** is nowhere stated in quite this form in any other of the Pauline writings. There is a hint of this idea in Gal. 3:19-20, though there it is not developed as an office of Christ. And of course the Epistle to the Hebrews deals frequently with this concept. A parallel idea is seen in I John 2:1, where Christ is identified as our "advocate with the Father." Here in the passage before us this unique ministry of our Lord is clearly and forthrightly enunciated. In a book of sermons by G. Campbell Morgan,[2] there is one sermon on the subject: "The Cry for a Daysman." The first of the two texts he employs is Job 9:33: "Neither is there any daysman betwixt us, that might lay his hand upon us both." The second text is the passage now before us: **There is one mediator between God and men, the man Christ Jesus.** A daysman is an umpire, a referee, a go-between, one to make intercession on our behalf; in a word, a mediator. There are many relationships in life where the services of a mediator become at times all-important. What a joy it is to know that in the relationship which matters most in our lives—that between God and us—such a Mediator is graciously provided!

5. *The Essential Manhood of Christ* (2:6)

The apostle stresses one factor which is supremely significant in this mediatorial relationship in which Christ stands to His people—the factor of the essential manhood of Christ Jesus our Lord. From all eternity He was one with the Father, but by His gracious incarnation He has become also one with our sinning race. The mystery of His unique personality we may never be able adequately to define. But the fact of the God-man is clearly taught in the Word of God. It is our tendency to remember His Godhood but to forget or to fail clearly to perceive His essential humanity. We need urgently to recover an understanding of the fact that Jesus was the Son of Man just as surely as He was the Son of God. He is **the man Christ Jesus.**

Verse 6 adds a further important insight: that His present office as Mediator flows out of the fact that He **gave himself a ransom for all, to be testified in due time.** There is a clear continuity between His function as our Advocate on high and His self-giving on the Cross; together they form one unified redemp-

[2]*The Answers of Jesus to Job* (New York: Fleming H. Revell Co., 1935), c. II.

tive enterprise dedicated to the task of "bringing many sons unto glory" (Heb. 2:10). The spectacle of God's mercy which is disclosed in this Christ-event is stated with great cogency by D. M. Baillie when he says: " 'It is *all* of God': the desire to forgive and reconcile, the appointing of means, the provision of the victim as it were from His own bosom at infinite cost. It all takes place within the very life of God Himself: for if we take the Christology of the New Testament at its highest we can only say that 'God was in Christ' in that great atoning sacrifice, and even that the Priest and the Victim both were none other than God."[3] **To be testified in due time** means "the testimony to which was borne at the proper time" (RSV).

6. *Paul's Commission* (2:7)

The apostle next declares that it was to proclaim this message that he was **ordained a preacher, and an apostle.** The Greek word rendered **preacher** is *keryx,* which, as C. H. Dodd defines it, may mean "a town crier, an auctioneer, a herald, or anyone who lifts up his voice and claims public attention to some definite thing he has to announce."[4] This was the original meaning of preaching. Paul's other self-designation—**apostle**—means a messenger, but with authority to act in a particular matter on behalf of the one who sends him forth. St. Paul links with these terms, as a further description of the work to which he felt himself called of God, that of **teacher of the Gentiles in faith and verity.** Phillips interprets the meaning thus: "to teach . . . the gentile world to believe and know the truth." The parenthetical affirmation—**I speak the truth in Christ, and lie not**—is typically Pauline. We see it in Rom. 9:1; II Cor. 11:31; and again in Gal. 1:20. No man ever lived with a more profound sense of mission than did St. Paul.

B. Reverence in Public Worship, 2:8-15

1. *More About Church Order* (2:8)

Returning from the digression of 3-7, the apostle resumes his instruction concerning the orderly worship of God. There is no doubt that he is speaking with the full authority of his apos-

[3] *God Was in Christ* (New York: Charles Scribner's Sons, 1948), p. 188.

[4] *The Apostolic Preaching and Its Developments* (New York: Harper & Bros., n.d.), p. 7.

tolic office. **I will therefore that men pray every where, lifting up holy hands, without wrath and doubting.** The expression **I will** does not carry for modern readers quite the tone of command which invested it in the seventeenth century. The Greek word which it translates (*boulamai*) is a term which, according to J. N. D. Kelly, "in Hellenistic Judaism conveys a note of authoritative command."[5] "This I demand," Paul is saying in effect, "that men pray everywhere."

This entire admonition must be understood in the context of public worship. The apostle is laying down the principle that, wherever Christians gather for worship, the men of the congregation must lead in public prayer. This bears witness to the fact that at this early date the conduct of public worship was not exclusively in the hands of the clergy as distinct from the laity. An appointed ministry there was, and this Epistle is concerned in large part with the establishment of standards which will characterize it. But the conduct of public worship was not delegated exclusively to that ministry. Here in the Early Church is clearly seen full participation by laymen in the work of God. Luther was later to call it "the priesthood of all believers."

It is equally clear, however, that the conduct of public prayer was to be carried on by men rather than women. Verse 12 makes clear the strictures which Paul imposes upon the female members of the congregation. Suffice it to say here that it was the male members of the church who were to lead in public prayer.

The further stipulation is that they lift **up holy hands, without wrath and doubting.** This posture for prayer was a common one for Christians, as it was also for Jews and pagans. But surely the physical posture which is assumed is far less important than the spirit of humility and sincerity in which one approaches God. No case can be made, therefore, for any one prayer posture as against others.

It is important however that we understand and take earnestly to heart the apostle's insistence upon the lifting up of holy hands. Paul is emphasizing not so much the adoption of this physical posture as the condition of mind and heart which is symbolized by **holy hands.** The hand is not inherently holy or unholy. But hands are traditionally the instruments of our spirits.

[5] *Op. cit.*, p. 65.

They are holy only as they are used to implement holy purposes. This is made clear by the further stipulation, **without wrath and doubting.** The intent of this expression is clarified by the NEB: "Excluding angry and quarrelsome thoughts." The apostle here echoes one of our Lord's basic demands. Following Matthew's version of the Lord's Prayer, there is recorded this further word of Jesus: "For if ye forgive men their trespasses, your heavenly Father will also forgive you: but if ye forgive not men their trespasses, neither will your Father forgive your trespasses" (Matt. 6:14-15). Numerous passages in the Gospels having a similar intent might be cited. "Ill-will and misgiving respecting one another," says Plummer, "are incompatible with united prayer to our common Father. The atmosphere of controversy is not congenial to devotion. Christ Himself has told us to be reconciled to our brother before presuming to offer our gift on the altar. In a similar spirit St. Paul directs that those who are to conduct public service in the sanctuary must do so without angry feelings or mutual distrust."[6]

2. *The Christian's Ornamentation* (2:9-10)

The teachings of 9 are linked grammatically with 8: **In like manner also, that women adorn themselves in modest apparel, with shamefacedness and sobriety.** On the face of it, this appears to be a further direction given in the context of public worship. When attending the house of God women should attire themselves with becoming modesty. Guthrie suggests that "*shamefacedness and sobriety* may be rendered 'modesty and self-control,' indicating dignity and seriousness of purpose as opposed to levity and frivolity."[7] But it would be a mistake to restrict this counsel to public worship. Undoubtedly the apostle expected this same modesty to characterize the attire and conduct of Christian women when otherwise employed.

The apostle leaves us in no doubt as to what sort of ornamentation Christian women should avoid: **Not with broided hair** ("elaborate hair styles," NEB), **or gold, or pearls, or costly array** (9). These were conventional practices among non-Christian women, and abstinence from such practices should characterize those who profess faith in Christ. Such is the apostle's judgment.

[6]*Op. cit.*, pp. 98-99.

[7]*The Pastoral Epistles* ("The Tyndale New Testament Commentaries"; Grand Rapids: Wm. B. Eerdmans Publishing Co., 1957), p. 75.

To be sure, every age has its own characteristic marks of worldliness; and it is possible that if Paul were making up a list of "don'ts" today it might differ in some respects from the list which appears here. But his emphasis is not wholly upon prohibitions; he goes on to suggest positively that Christian women should adorn themselves **(which becometh women professing godliness) with good works** (10). Peter points to a similar alternative in worldliness in his famous admonition: "Your beauty should not be dependent upon an elaborate coiffure, or on the wearing of jewelry or fine clothes, but on the inner personality—the unfading loveliness of a calm and gentle spirit, a thing very precious in the eyes of God" (I Pet. 3:3-4, Phillips). Christians should attract notice, not for the manner of their attire, but for the quality of their spirits.

3. *The Place of Women in the Church* (2:11-14)

But the apostle goes further in his prescriptions concerning the conduct of the women who are members of the congregation. Says he: **Let the women learn in silence with all subjection** (11). He makes a similar point in I Cor. 14:34-35: "Let your women keep silence in the churches . . . and if they will learn any thing, let them ask their husbands at home." It is believed that these rigorous strictures were occasioned by the fact that many in the Corinthian church were recent converts from paganism, and that the new freedom which they enjoyed in Christ had led to certain extravagances which were unseemly and irreverent. It is at least possible that a similar reason afforded occasion for these admonitions to Timothy, who pastored a church hewn out of the heathenism of Ephesus.

We cannot accept the idea that even at Corinth the stipulations we have cited were to be applied in every case. Indeed, Paul elsewhere says to them, "Every woman that prayeth or prophesieth with her head uncovered dishonoureth her head" (I Cor. 11:5). This passage is, at the very least, an acknowledgment that in Corinth women did pray in public and in some cases exercised the gift of prophecy; and that this did not meet with the apostle's disapproval, provided the women so engaged were properly attired.

It would ill become us, therefore, to seek to base on Paul's remarks to Timothy a teaching that women are to be excluded from places of leadership in the church. Even v. 12, **But I suffer**

not a woman to teach, nor to usurp authority over the man, but to be in silence, must be regarded as a demand imposed upon the church at Ephesus for reasons unknown to us. No universal teaching which would bind the Church for all time can be properly based upon it. Even the grounds which the apostle cites in 13-14 for laying down this rule seem insufficient to validate it as a policy for all future generations of Christians to follow. The fact that Paul acknowledges freely his debt to a considerable group of women who helped in the work of Christ's Church suggests that he himself was not always bound by such rigid stipulations as those expressed to Timothy.

4. *The Queenly Grace of Motherhood* (2:15)

The apostle adds a final word which is intended to direct Christian women toward their normal and proper area of service: **Notwithstanding she shall be saved in childbearing, if they continue in faith and charity and holiness with sobriety** (15). This appears to say, as Kelly observes, that woman's "faith to salvation . . . consists in accepting the role which was plainly laid down for her in Gen. 3:16 ('in pain you shall bring forth children')."[8] It is not, however, simply by accepting the role of motherhood that she is to be saved; this is the lot of all women, whether Christian or otherwise. The apostle makes it clear that he is thinking of motherhood in the context of Christian faith. A Christian mother who possesses the essential qualities of "faith and love and holiness, with modesty" (RSV) can make a priceless contribution to the work of Christ; and marriage that is sanctified by these hallowed virtues contributes a degree of strength and health to the Church which is absolutely essential to her well-being.

[8]*Op. cit.,* p. 69.

Section IV Qualifications of Christian Ministers

I Timothy 3:1-13

A. The Character of Bishops, 3:1-7

1. *The Office of Bishop* (3:1)

This is a true saying, If a man desire the office of a bishop, he desireth a good work. The apostle's remark which opens this section of his letter—**This is a true saying**—sounds superficially like his earlier statement in 1:15, "This is a faithful saying." But the resemblance is only apparent. That earlier remark introduced a most significant teaching concerning the redeeming work of Christ. But here no such solemn statement of faith is involved. While scholars are not wholly agreed at this point, it seems probable that the NEB has found the correct translation: "There is a popular saying: 'To aspire to leadership is an honourable ambition.'"

The expression **the office of a bishop** is somewhat misleading for modern readers, because with us the office of bishop has ecclesiastical associations. To desire this office would be to seek preferment in the Christian ministry. Such ambition, we properly believe, is unworthy of a man whose life is dedicated to the service of Christ. As has been pointed out in the Introduction, the term "bishop," which translates the word *episkopos*, was derived originally from the organization of secular societies and has the basic meaning of "overseer" or "leader." The apostle is simply saying that it is a worthy ambition to desire a place of responsible service among God's people. The saying that Paul quotes was a familiar adage which he used to introduce the subject with which he proposed to deal.

2. *Qualifications for a Bishop* (3:2)

A bishop then must be blameless, the husband of one wife, vigilant, sober, of good behaviour, given to hospitality, apt to teach. In all there are fifteen qualifications laid down by the apostle, seven of them appearing in 2. It is significant that the first and foremost of these is blamelessness. This means, as some of the other versions suggest, "above reproach," "of blameless reputation," "of irreproachable character." By any test this is the most inclusive virtue that appears in the list. It means that a leader in the Church of Christ must have no obvious defects in his character and must be a person of unsullied reputation. He could hardly be expected to be faultless, but he must be blameless. Indeed, it is only proper that the minister be judged by a higher standard than even the lay members of the church. Laymen may be forgiven for defects and failures which would be utterly fatal for a minister. There are some things which a merciful God will forgive in a man but which the church can never forgive in its ministry. This demand for irreproachableness is one upon which we must insist today, as did Paul in the first century.

Especially in matters relating to sex must a leader of the church be exemplary. This is pointed up in the apostle's second stipulation: **the husband of one wife.** Here is a caution against polygamy, which posed a serious problem for the church whose members must be won to Christ out of a paganism which was easily tolerant of plural marriages. Wherever the Church with its high ethical standards concerning marriage confronts the heathenism of our day, in uncivilized areas and elsewhere, the Christian insistence upon purity must be enunciated clearly and adhered to rigorously.

But we must ask, Does Paul here intend to regard with disapproval all second marriages? Some of the early manuscripts seem to require the translation "married only once," which appears in the footnotes in the NEB. "On this matter, as on many others," notes Kelly, "the attitude of antiquity differed markedly from that prevalent in most circles today, and there is abundant evidence, from both literature and funerary inscriptions, pagan and Jewish, that to remain unmarried after the death of one's spouse or after divorce was considered meritorious, while to marry again was taken as a sign of self-indulgence."[1] It is evident that in some sections of the Early Church this was the view that prevailed, coming to its ultimate extreme in the demand for a celibate ministry.

This, however, is not the understanding of Paul's teaching which prevails today. His own preference for the single life as

[1]*Op. cit.*, p. 75.

opposed to the married state is well known; and there are passages in his writings in which he commends this view to others (e.g., I Cor. 7:39-40). Perhaps for our day the best summary of the apostle's intent is stated by E. F. Scott: "A bishop must show an example of strict morality."[2]

The next three specifications—**vigilant, sober, of good behaviour**—are closely related and describe an orderly Christian life. Moffatt translates these qualities by the words "temperate, master of himself, unruffled." Temperance in this context seems to carry the idea of self-control or self-discipline.

The next quality is set forth by the apostle in the descriptive phrase **given to hospitality.** This same characteristic is detailed in greater fullness in Titus 1:8: "A lover of hospitality, a lover of good men." In those early days of the Church this was a virtue which was most important. There were few hostelries in the first-century world, and Christian apostles and evangelists who went from place to place were dependent upon the hospitality of Christians who had a "prophet's chamber," maintained for the purpose of meeting just such needs. In our day of hotels and motels we often express our Christian hospitality in different ways. But when the Church was young this hospitality was most essential, and the duty and privilege of ministering it naturally devolved upon the pastor or bishop. The essential spirit of the act is as important today as it has ever been.

Equally essential and even more important is the seventh quality which Paul mentions: **apt to teach.** It would seem that not all elders were employed in the teaching ministry. This appears from I Tim. 5:17: "Let the elders that rule well be counted worthy of double honour, especially they who labour in the word and doctrine." But the ability to teach was clear gain for a Christian minister. It was important then and is still important. There will always be some who possess a greater aptitude in this area than others, but some ability to teach is most essential to a full and fruitful ministry.

3. *Men of Sobriety* (3:3)

This verse contains six further specifications which must characterize the Christian leader: **Not given to wine, no striker,**

[2]*The Pastoral Epistles* ("The Moffatt New Testament Commentary"; London: Hodder and Stoughton, 1936), p. 31.

not greedy of filthy lucre; but patient, not a brawler, not covetous. All but one of these are negative, but all are important. The first of them strikes us as somewhat strange, especially when its precise meaning is clearly apprehended. The NEB renders it, "He must not be given to drink," while the RSV translates it by the blunt words, "No drunkard." The thing that puzzles the modern reader is that such a stipulation should be necessary. In the thinking of most evangelical people today, total abstinence from intoxicating liquors is elementary in the Christian life. And it is not difficult to realize that the moral judgment that dictates total abstinence for the Christian—layman or minister—is the *ultimate* insight of Christian ethics. But this idea, like the moral judgment against slavery, was not clearly discerned in the first century. We must bear this in mind if we are to understand the apostle's allusions to the use of wine here and in other places. Kelly remarks that "modern people are sometimes surprised that Paul should have thought it necessary to make such a ruling, but the danger must have been a real one in the uninhibited society in which the Ephesian and Cretan congregations were placed."[3]

No striker is an expression which calls for some interpretation in this context. Literally it means "not a giver of blows," and has been translated by Kelly as "not given to violence." A man of God must be characterized by Christian love and restraint.

There is no obscurity attached to Paul's next stipulation: **not greedy of filthy lucre.** Here is a warning against that love of money which the apostle, later in this same Epistle (6:10), declares to be "the root of all evil." Such an admonition had immediate relevance, for it was the bishop's responsibility to care for the church's funds. Here would be a constant source of temptation for an avaricious man. Only one who gave every evidence of complete deliverance from a spirit of covetousness could safely be set apart for the work of the ministry.

It is quite possible, of course, for ministers as well as laymen to be misled by what our Lord called "the deceitfulness of riches" (Matt. 13:22). The subtle thing about this deception is that one need not possess riches to be deceived by them. To yearn for them, to allow oneself to adopt calculating attitudes in hope of acquiring riches, to become unduly concerned about the rewards

[3]*Op. cit.*, p. 77.

and emoluments of this present world, cannot fail to impoverish and ultimately to destroy the value of one's ministry. All of this is implicit in Paul's warning against the controlling desire for money.

The one positive virtue in 3 is **patience.** This means not so much the ability to keep one's temper under control as the ability to endure when the pressure is on, with an unfailing spirit of gentleness and forbearance. Paul extols this virtue in I Cor. 13:4 when he assures us that love "suffereth long, and is kind"—kind even at the end of the suffering. The further specifications —**not a brawler, not covetous**—are really repetitions for emphasis of the points already made.

4. *A Good Father* (3:4-5)

Here is a point of the gravest importance: **One that ruleth well his own house, having his children in subjection with all gravity** (4). As E. K. Simpson points out, "So utterly foreign to the primitive model is the ideal of sacerdotal celibacy, that it is presumed the candidate for the ministry is already a married man of mature age. Slipshod paternal discipline disqualifies him at once for rule in the church."[4] The Phillips version renders v. 4: "He must have proper authority in his own household, and be able to control and command the respect of his children." It must be admitted that this is one of the most difficult to meet of all Paul's standards. Yet how important it is! Many a minister has had his usefulness impaired or even destroyed by his failure to exercise parental discipline. It is easy to become so involved in saving the children of others that we allow our own to slip out of our control. Admittedly, there comes a time when one's children grow up and must assume the direction of their own lives; and when this time comes, no one can prevent them making whatever choices they may see fit. But firm, loving, and prayerful discipline during the formative years of our children's lives will surely be a mighty determining factor with them when they must finally decide for themselves the course they will follow in life. There is cogency, therefore, in Paul's insistence upon the minister's duty to control his own household. And the basic truth of the parenthesis in 5 cannot be gainsaid: **For if a man know not how to rule his own house, how shall he take care of the church of God?**

[4]*Op. cit.*, p. 52.

5. *A Man of Maturity* (3:6-7)

Verse 6 gives a most interesting insight into the Ephesian situation: **Not a novice, lest being lifted up with pride he fall into the condemnation of the devil.** This is a warning against the too rapid promotion to leadership of "recent converts" or persons "newly baptized." Even though the church at Ephesus had been in existence for a number of years and should have had no dearth of mature leaders, it would appear that there was some likelihood that immature candidates for the ministry were being drawn into service. Paul believed in the maturing and seasoning of candidates for this holy office, and for a good and sufficient reason. There was a danger that, for one inadequately prepared, the temptation to spiritual pride might become too great to be resisted. This could not fail to have tragic result, a result which the apostle describes as falling **into the condemnation of the devil.** C. K. Barrett points out that "judgement is not contrived by the devil but carried out by God in strict accord with truth."[5] Phillips' rendering reflects what appears to be the apostle's meaning: "For fear of his becoming conceited and sharing the devil's downfall."

This warning is reminiscent of a situation in our Lord's dealings with His followers, related in Luke 10:17-20. The seventy had just returned from their assigned mission and were exulting in the fact that "even the devils are subject unto us through thy name." Jesus did not at once rebuke their incipient spiritual pride, but remarked rather cryptically, "I beheld Satan as lightning fall from heaven." Then He continued: "Behold, I give you power . . . over all the power of the enemy. . . . Notwithstanding in this rejoice not, that the spirits are subject unto you; but rather rejoice, because your names are written in heaven." It was pride which cost Lucifer his place in the heavenly host, and this was **the condemnation of the devil.** Let the Christian minister beware lest through pride he be compelled to share this condemnation.

One final specification remains for him who would serve in the office of bishop or leader: **Moreover he must have a good report of them which are without; lest he fall into reproach and the snare of the devil** (7). The Christian minister must command the respect and confidence of the community outside the

[5]*Op. cit.*, p. 60.

church if he is to win others from that community to the church. It is easy to say, "I do not care what people think of me"; and so long as this is properly intended and correctly understood, it is not without justification. But no man should be indifferent toward his reputation in his community. He should desire fervently that others regard him as completely beyond reproach. To view the matter otherwise, says Paul, exposes him to the same snare that awaits the man whose spirit is marred by spiritual pride.

B. The Character of Deacons, 3:8-13

1. *The Office of Deacon* (3:8)

Paul turns next to the order of deacons and delineates the qualifications which should characterize them. It is customary, in seeking to understand the diaconate in the Early Church, to refer its beginnings to the congregation in Jerusalem. There, as recorded in Acts 6:1-6, the church chose seven men who should "serve tables," in order that the apostles would not be required to "leave the word of God." Here was a clear division of responsibility between the apostles, who were the spiritual leaders of the church, and the "seven men" (they are nowhere called deacons) who were responsible for looking after the temporal needs of the believers. It cannot be proved beyond question that the order of deacons which we encounter in the Pauline churches (e.g., Phil. 1:1) is in lineal descent from this action of the Jerusalem church. There can be little doubt, however, that this precedent established in Jerusalem exerted a profound influence on the development of the diaconate in the Later Church.

The earliest function of the deacons was to care for the distribution of the church's charitable funds. As B. S. Easton points out, "While the Greek noun transliterated 'deacon' means 'servant' or 'assistant,' either translation would be misleading, for the deacons were not the assistants of the rulers but the dispensers of the Church's charities; they 'served' the poor and the sick."[6] As the term "deacon" survives in the Church today, it has lost most of its original denotation. In the Episcopal and Methodist churches it is the beginning order of the ordained ministry, leading normally to the priesthood or eldership, while in the Congregational and Baptist churches it is an office held by

[6]*The Pastoral Epistles* (New York, Charles Scribner's Sons, 1947), p. 132.

laymen. But in the Church of the first century, **deacons** held a place of dignity and influence comparable to **bishops,** and the qualifications for this office which Paul spells out are no less demanding.

2. *Discipline Required of Deacons* (3:8)

Likewise must the deacons be grave, not doubletongued, not given to much wine, not greedy of filthy lucre. Here we encounter some of the same expressions the apostle employed in laying down his standard for bishops: the same requirement that they **be grave,** "men of high principle" (NEB); the same demand for a self-disciplined temperance; the same warning against allowing oneself to be corrupted by greed. A new note is sounded, however, in the apostle's warning against permitting oneself to be **doubletongued.** While this is an archaic expression, its meaning is by no means obscure. Kelly renders it, "consistent in what they say"; and he remarks further that this expression has been "taken to mean 'no tale-bearers,' the reference being to the opportunities for malicious tittle-tattle which deacons had in their house-to-house pastoral work. A literal translation, however, would be 'not double-talkers,' and so it is likely that the true sense is either 'not saying one thing while thinking another' or (more probably) 'not saying one thing to one man and a different thing to the next.' "[7]

The evil of "tale-bearing," which so easily becomes malicious gossip, can hardly be exaggerated. In its most extreme form it can become that ugly thing to which in our day the name "character assassination" has been applied. Probably no one who believes himself a follower of Christ would knowingly indulge in conduct which he clearly foresaw would have this result. The desultory sort of gossip which leads to such ghastly results seems harmless and even pleasant. Paul sees it for what it is, however, and warns us solemnly against it. It ill becomes any Christian, not to mention Christian leaders, to indulge this "innocent" yet deadly pastime.

3. *Men of Spiritual Integrity* (3:9)

The apostle then proceeds to name, as a qualification for the office of deacon, a point that goes beyond his requirements for bishops: **Holding the mystery of the faith in a pure conscience.**

[7]*Op. cit.,* p. 81.

In all fairness, it must be pointed out that in Titus 1:9 the apostle does include, in the qualifications for elders or bishops, a specification very similar to the one laid down for deacons in the passage before us. What is meant by the **mystery of the faith?** "Mystery," says Guthrie, "is a common Pauline expression denoting, not what is beyond knowledge, but what, being once hidden, is now revealed to those with spiritual discernment."[8] Later in this same chapter the apostle gives a most interesting summary of the "mystery of godliness" (see comments on 16). This is the central core of Christian teaching, apart from which there can be no distinctive Christian faith. Men who would hold the office of deacon must hold their faith **in a pure conscience.** This means with utter sincerity and without mental reservations.

4. *Men of Proven Worth* (3:10)

Verse 10 carries further this tendency on Paul's part to feel that candidates for the office of deacon must be subjected to an even closer scrutiny than bishops: **And let these also first be proved; then let them use the office of a deacon, being found blameless.** In our day we could easily make too much of the differing degrees of rigor imposed upon candidates for these offices in the Early Church. As a matter of fact, the functions of both categories, whether bishop or deacon, are incorporated in the one work of the ministry for the Church today. All that Paul says in this connection, whether addressed to bishops or deacons, is in effect addressed to every man who feels himself led of the Spirit into the work of the ministry. We today recognize the need for proving by practical tests men who are candidates for ordination. We insist upon spiritual maturity and upon educational qualifications; but we insist equally that a man must have carried on with a promising measure of success in some practical phase of the ministerial office. And no candidate should receive the church's ordination who has not, in the apostle's word, been **found blameless.**

5. *The Deacon's Wife a Fitting Helpmate* (3:11)

Verse 11 presents some difficulty to exact interpretation: **Even so must their wives be grave, not slanderers, sober, faithful in all things.** The word rendered **wives** is the general word for women, used without the article. Is this to be understood as an exhortation addressed generally to the women of the congre-

[8]*The Pastoral Epistles*, p. 84.

gation? If so, it fits strangely into a chapter devoted to the qualifications for special office in the church. Are the women here addressed the wives of the deacons? If so, why does the apostle make a special case of deacons' wives when nothing was said concerning the wives of bishops? Or does Paul have in mind the female counterpart of the deacons, i.e., "deaconesses"? The answer to this perplexity may never be found. The KJV interprets the apostle as meaning the wives of the deacons; and in this judgment the translators of 1611 are supported by the NEB and the Phillips translation, while the RSV neatly straddles the fence. This much may be said: that the wives of both bishops and deacons in the first century and the wives of ministers today carry a burden of responsibility for their husbands' success out of all proportion to the burden carried by the wives of men in other callings. In most cases it is difficult to think of a pastor's wife as a co-pastor with her husband. But the virtues upon which Paul insists in 11 are indispensable if a wife is not to hinder rather than help her husband in his heavy tasks. She must be seriously concerned about the work of God's Church, careful never to lend her tongue to speaking evil, temperate in her self-mastery, and **faithful in all things.**

6. *A Good Husband and Father* (3:12-13)

Verse 12 repeats for deacons the requirements already imposed on bishops, that they be **the husbands of one wife, ruling their children and their own houses well.** Paul believed that virtue of the sort he has been inculcating will not fail of reward. Indeed, 13 seems to suggest in part what that reward will be: **For they that have used the office of a deacon well purchase to themselves a good degree, and great boldness in the faith which is in Christ Jesus.** This cannot mean that a deacon who exemplifies these qualities is likely to be promoted to higher office. Such an interpretation would fly in the face of the principles Paul has been at such pains to lay down. Neither can it mean that faithfulness in these details will give him enhanced standing in God's sight. The only possible meaning is that thereby he will gain the reputation of being a good and faithful man. Simpson summarizes the matter: "Influence is a by-product of character, and the apostle's mind has been dwelling on the elements that contribute to a staunch manhood with godliness at its base."[9]

[9]*Op. cit.*, p. 57.

Said the wise man, "A good name is rather to be chosen than great riches" (Prov. 22:1). It is no mean reward, therefore, for one who has determined at any cost to be true to Christ, to have it said of him, as was said of Barnabas, "He was a good man" (Acts 11:24). **Boldness in the faith** (13) is interpreted as "gaining confidence and freedom in the Christian faith" (Phillips).

Section V *Paul Defines the Church*

I Timothy 3:14-16

The passage now before us is the dividing point in this Epistle, forming a bridge from the apostle's emphasis upon the conduct of public worship and the qualifications for the work of the ministry to the practical instructions and exhortations which follow. But the passage is significant in its own right. Paul reveals his hope of an early meeting with Timothy, if not at Ephesus, then surely at Miletus. But he allows that this plan may not work out; so he resorts to writing an Epistle to make sure his instructions reach the young pastor. **These things write I unto thee, hoping to come unto thee shortly: but if I tarry long, that thou mayest know how thou oughtest to behave thyself in the house of God** (14-15).

It is difficult to believe that the apostle is concerned here simply with what we commonly mean by "behaving oneself in church." The context seems to suggest that it is the seriousness and gravity which should attend the ongoing work of the Church in all its phases which is weighing on his mind. He is concerned about the sort of people who become ministers and leaders in the Church. Particularly important is it that the Church's ministers be men who know and love and deeply reverence the mysteries of our holy faith. The Church came into existence to preserve, interpret, and perpetuate these mysteries. Paul proceeds therefore to give a pungent threefold definition of the Church: **the house** (household) **of God, which is the church of the living God, the pillar and ground of the truth.** We who love the Church would do well to ponder this definition, to discover its continuing validity, and to inquire what it demands of us in our day.

A. The Household of God, 3:14-15

The family idea is implicit in the phrase **the house** (household) **of God** (14). The Church is the family of God. Believers become the children of God and therefore "heirs of God, and joint-heirs with Christ" (Rom. 8:17). The metaphors of birth and adoption are employed in the New Testament to describe the miracle of Christian experience (John 3:3; Gal. 4:5). The idea of a household suggests, further, that this newfound relationship to God through Christ, while individual, is also societal. The Church is a society of the redeemed; the household of God is made up of the twice-born living in Christian fellowship.

Paul next describes this unique fellowship as **the church of the living God.** The term **church** has many meanings, none of which is unimportant. But in its basic meaning it includes all who have heard and responded to the divine vocation, who are the "God-called." In this sense it is made up of all Christians, the Church both militant and triumphant: we who run the race today and the cloud of triumphant witnesses which surrounds us (Heb. 12:1). It is **the church of the living God,** and God's quickening presence animates the whole.

The apostle finally describes the Church as **the pillar and ground** ("bulwark," NEB) **of the truth.** What does Paul mean by **the truth?** It surely refers to the fact that "Christ Jesus came into the world to save sinners." But no doubt the apostle has in mind particularly the "mystery of godliness," which he elaborates in 16: "Without controversy great is the mystery of godliness: God was manifest in the flesh, justified in the Spirit, seen of angels, preached unto the Gentiles, believed on in the world, received up into glory."

B. The Mystery of Godliness, 3:15-16

The expression **mystery of godliness** (15) occurs only here in Paul's writings, though the word "mystery" appears frequently. Why has the apostle used this particular phrase? Guthrie suggests that "the answer may be found in the implied comparison between the practical godliness previously enjoined on church officers and the inner character of its revealed secret described here."[1]

Verse 16 is intended to suggest what is contained in this **mystery of godliness.** Here, as on other occasions, the apostle employs what appears to be a fragment of an early Christian hymn which, in its own way, outlines the drama of the Christ-event. Barrett has analyzed it in six terse propositions which together comprise the wonder of redemption. Says he: "On the

[1]*The Pastoral Epistles,* p. 89.

whole it seems best to recognize a chronological progression in the hymn (if such it is), and to suppose that it refers to (1) the incarnation, (2) the resurrection, (3) the ascension, (4) the preaching of the Gospel, (5) the response to it, and (6) the final victory of Christ."[2] **Justified in the Spirit** has been rendered "vindicated in the Spirit" (RSV), i.e., resurrected by the power of the Spirit.

This then is the **mystery of godliness,** or, as more recent versions put it, "the mystery of our religion." It is this message of which the Church collectively and each Christian individually is the "pillar and bulwark." As individual believers our ultimate witness to this truth must be the lives that we live—lives transformed by the power of Christ. The recovery of this clear witness by the Church is the most urgent need of our times. Lancelot Andrewes' prescription for the Church of his day could well be adopted as the goal of the Church's striving today: "The restoration of the things that are wanting; the strengthening of the things that remain."

[2]*Op. cit.,* p. 66.

Section VI *Threats to Integrity of the Church*

I Timothy 4:1-16

A. Danger of Undue Asceticism, 4:1-5

1. *False Teachings Will Arise* (4:1-2)

The apostle turns now to deal with the false teachings which had been plaguing the church at Ephesus, a difficulty to which he alludes in c. 1. Error is forever opposing itself to the truth of the gospel, a conflict for which God has sought to prepare His Church. **Now the Spirit speaketh expressly, that in the latter times some shall depart from the faith** (1). It is the Holy Spirit, who is the Spirit of prophecy, to whom Paul refers. It is impossible to determine what particular prophecy the writer has in mind. The apostle was himself at times moved by the Spirit to prophesy. One of the numerous instances of such inspiration involved this Ephesian church, where Timothy served: "For I know this, that after my departing shall grievous wolves enter in among you, not sparing the flock. Also of your own selves shall men arise, speaking perverse things, to draw away disciples after them" (Acts 20:29-30). This development, so clearly foreseen some years earlier, is near at hand; indeed, it has already begun. Guthrie suggests that " 'in the latter times' is a phrase which suggests a more imminent future than 'in the last days' (used in II Tim. 3:1). . . . Indeed, as often in prophetical utterances, what is predicted of the future is conceived of as already operative in the present, so the words have a specific contemporary significance."[1]

Not alone tomorrow, but already today, this leaven of error is at work. Some have already departed from the faith, seduced by the "stratagems of Satan and his allies" (Kelly). Such preternatural forces Paul describes as "principalities . . . powers . . . the rulers of the darkness of this world . . . spiritual wickedness in high places" (Eph. 6:12). The word rendered **seducing spirits** actually means a "strolling quack" or "vagabond" (Simpson), suggesting his power to beguile and deceive. Such evil spirits

[1]*The Pastoral Epistles*, pp. 91-92.

employ their victims, in turn, as agents of their nefarious purposes. The apostle describes these agents of error as **speaking lies in hypocrisy; having their conscience seared with a hot iron** (2). The term **hypocrisy** suggests a knowing and deliberate effort to deceive, a moral knowledge that the teachings they propagate are **lies.** Yet so blinded by unbelief are they and so hardened in heart that conscience is no longer capable of performing its appointed task. It is **seared with a hot iron** ("cauterized" would be a transliteration of the Gk. term in the Received Text). In Eph. 4:19 the apostle describes one in this moral condition as "past feeling."

2. *Meaningless Asceticism* (4:3-5)

Paul now defines two details of the teaching he is denouncing: **Forbidding to marry, and commanding to abstain from meats, which God hath created to be received with thanksgiving of them which believe and know the truth** (3). This prohibition of marriage and the eating of certain foods points toward an early type of Gnosticism as the error which had gained a foothold in the church at Ephesus. The main drive of Gnosticism for a place of influence in the Early Church did not occur until the second century. But already an incipient form of this heresy, a form largely Jewish in character, had assumed menacing proportions. All forms of Gnosticism held in common the idea of a fundamental dualism between matter and spirit. This meant that everything pertaining to the body was intrinsically evil. These misguided teachers advocated a strict and essentially false asceticism. Marriage must be avoided and abstention from certain foods must be practiced.

The first of these teachings Paul condemns, but, as Kelly points out, he "does not refute it by argument. The explanation probably is that he had already made his views on the naturalness and propriety of marriage abundantly clear in his treatment of the qualities required in office-bearers."[2] It is true that the apostle preferred celibacy rather than the married state for himself, and that in writing to the Corinthians (I Corinthians 7) he suggests that it would be well for other Christians to follow his example. The reason for this judgment was far removed, however, from the erroneous views he was seeking to counter in Ephesus. In I Cor. 7:26 he points to "the present distress," and

[2]*Op. cit.*, p. 95.

in verse 29 he reminds his readers that "the time is short." Both of these passages seem to be veiled allusions to Paul's expectation of the near return of Christ. In view of the fact that "the fashion of this world passeth away" (I Cor. 7:31), many things that in themselves are right and proper assume a minor importance, and among them the issue of celibacy and marriage. But he could not be tolerant of the prohibition of marriage for the *wrong* reason, as was the case at Ephesus.

Against the second false teaching—that of abstinence from certain foods—the apostle makes out a carefully reasoned case. **For every creature of God is good, and nothing to be refused, if it be received with thanksgiving** (4). Paul here maintains his position of freedom from the prohibitions laid down by the ritual of the Jews. These prohibitions had been clearly abrogated by Peter's vision on the housetop in Joppa (Acts 10:9-16). The one stipulation Paul laid down concerning God's gift of nourishing food was that it be received **with thanksgiving.** And the manner in which such thanksgiving should be expressed is at least suggested: **For it is sanctified** ("consecrated," Berk.; "hallowed," NEB) **by the word of God and prayer** (5). It is evident that grace before meals was one of the earliest customs in the Church. Indeed it appears that, in addition to a prayer of thanksgiving, it was the custom of the early believers to employ excerpts from the Scriptures in their expression of gratitude to God. It would seem that a prayer of thanksgiving before partaking of food, however meagre our fare, is the Christian's minimum obligation. And no such prayer of thanksgiving is more fitting than the one John Wesley and his preachers employed:

Be present at this table, Lord;
Be here and everywhere adored;
These creatures bless, and grant that we
May feast in Paradise with Thee.

B. The Stature of a Good Minister of Christ, 4:6-10

1. *A Good Minister* (4:6)

The apostle now turns to address Timothy personally and define his area of responsibility as a pastor: **If thou put the brethren in remembrance of these things, thou shalt be a good minister of Jesus Christ, nourished up in the words of faith and**

of good doctrine, whereunto thou hast attained. Paul knew full well that the answer to error must not be simply negative denunciation, that evil can best be refuted by the positive proclamation of Christian truth. The brethren are to be reminded, therefore, by having the apostle's instructions placed before them. **If thou put the brethren in remembrance of these things** has been rendered, "By offering such advice to the brotherhood" (NEB). **These things** would refer to the teachings in 4-5 and 7-10. The **brethren** may be the leaders of the Ephesian church or the spiritually responsible membership of that church as a whole. The apostle is not attempting to coerce their thinking, but places his confidence in the convincing character of the Christian answer to the errors which threaten.

To urge these considerations on the church is the part of **a good minister of Jesus Christ.** The word rendered **minister** (*diakonos*) is the word translated "deacon" in 3:8, though its actual meaning is "servant" or "minister." It is a word which was "in the process of becoming specialized," though its more general meaning is found much more frequently in the New Testament than its specialized meaning.[3]

In further description of the **good minister** which he hopes Timothy will prove to be, Paul adds the final clause of this verse: "bred in the precepts of our faith and of the sound instruction which you have followed" (NEB). The richness of Timothy's Christian heritage is suggested in greater detail in II Tim. 1:5: "I am reminded of your sincere faith, a faith that dwelt first in your grandmother Lois and your mother Eunice and now, I am sure, dwells in you" (RSV). Added to this was the young pastor's incomparable instruction in things spiritual at the feet of Paul. In addition to these great Christian influences Timothy had had some decisive moments in his own inner experience, some "Ebenezers" (I Sam. 7:10-12) erected as memorials to God's transforming grace in his life. There is a sense in which one's faith may be inherited; but it must also become a genuine and articulate reality in one's own experience if it is to sustain the soul amid the pressures of life.

It is not enough for us to cry, as did the Jews in John the Baptist's day, "We have Abraham to our father." We are our fathers' sons, to be sure; but the qualities of life and character

[3]Kelly, *op. cit.*, p. 68.

which made these fathers the mighty men they were cannot be transmitted from parent to child. Each generation must achieve for itself, through vital experience of the grace of God, the qualities which made our fathers holy men, men who loved God and the truth, who under God were able to become the founders and builders that they were.

2. *Maintain Sober Judgment* (4:7-8)

But refuse profane and old wives' fables, and exercise thyself rather unto godliness (7). The apostle does not hesitate to stigmatize the false teachings in Ephesus as beneath his contempt. **Old wives' fables** has become a traditional expression describing the sort of superstitious notions which underlay these errors. Moffatt in his translation calls them "drivelling myths." Paul makes the point that such notions are **profane** ("godless," RSV). **Refuse** them, says the apostle, **and exercise thyself rather unto godliness.** This means, as Phillips interprets it, "Take time and trouble to keep yourself spiritually fit." Paul's thought moves on immediately to a contrast between the discipline of the body and the discipline of the soul: **For bodily exercise profiteth little: but godliness is profitable unto all things, having promise of the life that now is, and of that which is to come** (8).

We are not justified in assuming that Paul is here frowning on the idea of bodily well-being. On the contrary, there is evidence that the cult of physical fitness, which was so much a part of life in the ancient Hellenic world, challenged his interest to a considerable degree. He draws on the sports of that first-century world rather freely in seeking to set forth the need for a disciplined spiritual life. But to make the cultivation of a fine physique the chief end of man was wholly foreign to Paul's scale of values. There is a need for a healthy and vigorous body if one is to be at the peak of his effectiveness as a servant of Christ—though amazing results have been achieved by some who throughout life have had to wage an unceasing struggle against ill health. One's great concern in life ought to be the health of the spirit; and here godliness is the all-important factor. In describing the worth of godliness, Paul has produced one of those gems of rhetorical expression for which his writings are justly famous: **having promise of the life that now is, and of that which is to come.** There is no finer description of the value in time and eternity of fellowship with God through Christ. Here is the only value one can carry with him out of this world and into the next.

3. *Sound Teaching* (4:9-10)

This is a faithful saying, and worthy of all acceptation (9). Here again we encounter the formula which Paul employs for emphasis, identical with 1:15. Yet the scholars cannot decide with certainty whether the apostle seeks to emphasize 8, which precedes it, or 10, which follows it. Phillips has chosen the former alternative, while the NEB chooses the latter. But either reference is important and well deserves the emphasis which is intended.

For therefore we both labour and suffer reproach, because we trust in the living God, who is the Saviour of all men, specially of those that believe (10). Paul here continues the metaphor of 8 with its emphasis upon disciplined living. But his thought has now switched to the price he has himself been called upon to pay in order to be faithful to God, **we both labour and suffer reproach.** But amid all the pressures of his apostolic labors he is sustained by his **trust in the living God.**

The final section of 10 presents some difficulties. **The Saviour of all men** suggests superficially some sort of universalism. But of what sort is it? Barrett suggests that "because God is living and the source of life he *is the Saviour . . . of all men,* whom he preserves in life, making the sun to shine and the rain to fall on good and bad alike."[4] Understood in this fashion, the final words of the verse become intelligible: **specially of those that believe.** All men receive God's general mercy, and most of them have no sense of gratitude for it whatever. But the *saving mercies* of God are received only as awakened men make a total response in surrender to and faith in Christ.

C. The Minister as an Example, 4:11-16

1. *Paul Admonishes Timothy* (4:11-13)

In the final paragraph of c. 4 the apostle becomes more directly personal in his address to Timothy. **These things command and teach** (11). The word rendered **command** is one "with military overtones" and must have come to the young pastor with peremptory force. The evidence all points to the

[4]*Op. cit.*, p. 70.

conclusion that Timothy was retiring and diffident, a man whose self-confidence needed constantly to be strengthened. Most of this paragraph suggests such an estimate. He needed to hear this authoritative note from the apostle to give him renewed assurance. It is clearly implied that it is the business of Christian ministers to preach and teach with a properly understood authority. It is not their business to carry on as "lords over God's heritage," to use Peter's appropriate expression (I Pet. 5:3). It is rather a spiritual authority that stems from a daily walk in close fellowship with Christ and a preaching and teaching ministry which bears the evident marks of the Holy Spirit's anointing. The recovery of this peculiar spiritual quality called unction is among the pressing needs of the Church's ministry today.

Concerning **Let no man despise thy youth** (12), Simpson remarks that "no Greek maxim was more familiar than the subordination of youth to age."[5] The probability is that among the leaders or elders of the Ephesian church there were a number who were of more mature years than was Timothy himself. He could easily feel himself at a serious disadvantage in performing the functions of a pastor in such a situation. Youth, of course, is a relative term. N. J. D. White observes that "forty is reckoned old for a captain in the army, young for a bishop, very young for a Prime Minister."[6] Timothy was probably under forty and by the standards of the first-century Hellenic world was youthful. "Let no one despise you on this account," admonishes Paul, "but so conduct yourself as to command the love, respect, and confidence of your people."

In the modern church world youth has come to be regarded as an asset rather than a liability. Of course, if youth is a man's only outstanding quality, he is probably headed for a very brief career. But it is age rather than youth that is in danger of being despised in our day. When a church seeking a pastor automatically disqualifies every man on its list of possibilities who is fifty years of age or older, it has come dangerously near to despising maturity. This in our day is a more deplorable situation than the then prevailing attitude toward youth which Paul here rebukes.

The antidote, the apostle suggests, is, **Be thou an example of**

[5] *Op. cit.*, p. 70.

[6] "The First and Second Epistles to Timothy," *The Expositor's Greek Testament* (Grand Rapids: Wm. B. Eerdmans Publishing Co., n.d.), IV, 126.

the believers, in word, in conversation, in charity, in spirit, in faith, in purity. By a reverent and Christlike demeanor a pastor who may not be a "ten-talent" man can serve so effectively as to overcome numerous handicaps which might otherwise have a crippling effect on his ministry.

The six areas in which Paul suggests that Timothy might serve as an example are reduced to five because the word **spirit** does not appear in the oldest and more dependable manuscripts. The RSV lists them thus: "in speech and conduct, in love, in faith, in purity." The first two of these relate to Timothy's public life and ministry. But the remaining three are inner qualities. "Love" is the term *agape,* which denotes God's kind of love. **Faith** carries the sense of faithfulness or fidelity. **Purity** means not only chastity, but suggests also sincerity and blamelessness.

Till I come, give attendance to reading, to exhortation, to doctrine (13). The expression **Till I come** reminds Timothy of Paul's avowed purpose of paying him a visit in the near future (3:14). Until then, the young man is admonished to "attend to the public reading of scripture, to preaching, to teaching" (RSV). This reminds us that the Old Testament in its Greek translation (the Septuagint) was the Bible of the Early Church. Early Christian services were patterned after the synagogue service at least to the extent that the reading of the Old Testament formed a part of the worship of God. Kelly observes that "this is in fact the earliest reference to the use of Scripture in the Church's liturgy."[7] This would be increasingly supplemented by the reading of Christian documents such as the letters of Paul and of other apostles. It seems probable that the churches were already building up libraries of such documents and were beginning to venerate them as writings inspired by the Holy Spirit. **Exhortation** is commentary on and proclamation of the Word of God, i.e., preaching. **Doctrine** suggests the catechetical instruction in Christian truth. This was particularly important for beginners in the faith, though essential for all believers in whatever stage of maturity.

2. *Cultivate God's Gifts* (4:14-16)

Neglect not the gift that is in thee, which was given thee by prophecy, with the laying on of the hands of the presbytery (14). The apostle is recognizing in this passage that what might

[7]*Op. cit.*, p. 105.

be called the charismatic preparation for the ministry is by all means the most important. He suggests that Timothy had received this gift **by prophecy,** a repetition of the point Paul had made earlier in 1:18. The call of God to those who would serve in the work of the ministry is the prior and principal consideration. It is the Holy Spirit who must instigate a man's choice of this holy vocation. And with His call we have reason to believe there will be the accompanying qualifications of "grace, gifts, and usefulness." There may be exceptional cases where some of these qualities may not be in evidence, though God sees them to be latent; but the rule is as stated above. This means more than that a man has a "gift of gab," or is a "complete extrovert," or "gets on well with people," or is a "natural leader." Some of these qualities may well supplement the essential spiritual equipment, but none are substitutes for it.

It would be a mistake, moreover, to assume that even the church's ordination can supply this mystic quality when it is lacking. The significance of the church's ordination and its relation to the Spirit's prior action is clearly set forth in Acts 13:2-3. Speaking of the church at Antioch in Syria, Luke relates that "the Holy Ghost said, Separate me Barnabas and Saul for the work whereunto I have called them. And when they had fasted and prayed, and laid their hands on them, they sent them away." Mere "digital contact," as someone has called it, the laying on of the elders' hands, has no meaning apart from this antecedent work of the Holy Spirit. Paul's language clearly indicates that, in referring to Timothy's ordination, the action of the **presbytery** (elders) was in recognition and confirmation of the Spirit's prior action.

Meditate upon these things; give thyself wholly to them; that thy profiting may appear to all (15). The word **meditate** has a connotation of passivity today which is far from the apostle's meaning. It means rather the practice of these things with a diligence comparable to that displayed by the athlete who is training for the racecourse. "Make these matters your business and your absorbing interest" (NEB). The practice of the pastoral procedures recommended in this chapter by the apostle must be the major concern of a true minister of Christ. There is no place here for halfheartedness or qualified devotion. **That thy profiting may appear to all** has been translated, "so that your progress may be evident to all" (NASB).

Eternal issues are riding on the manner in which a minister discharges these responsibilities—his own soul's salvation as well as the salvation of those to whom he ministers. Paul therefore admonishes: **Take heed unto thyself, and unto the doctrine; continue in them: for in doing this thou shalt both save thyself, and them that hear thee** (16). For a minister of the gospel this is one of the most sobering verses in the New Testament. It is possible that a man may become inordinately concerned about his own success in the ministry. If he uses as his measuring stick the degree of preferment he enjoys, or his promotion to ever increasing responsibility with its enlarged emolument, he may fail in the end to save himself. Paul confesses this fear in his own heart when he says, "I keep under my body, and bring it into subjection: lest that by any means, when I have preached to others, I myself should be a castaway" (I Cor. 9:27). Let us not forget that, in our efforts to carry forward the work of Christ's Church, our own soul's salvation is hanging in the balance, and that we must take heed to ourselves as well as to our teaching and ministry.

Section VII *Church Administration*

I Timothy 5:1-25

A. Youth Should Respect Age, 5:1-2

With the opening of c. 5, Paul launches into instructions of a more specific nature addressed particularly to Timothy as the pastor and leader of the entire church at Ephesus. Especially is the apostle concerned that Timothy get on happily and in a manner above reproach with all the age-groups under his charge. **Rebuke not an elder, but intreat him as a father** (1). The church then as now was made up of men and women, both older and younger. The success of Timothy's ministry and the well-being of the church rested in large part upon the skill which he displayed in dealing with each of these classes. This was particularly important for a young pastor such as Timothy when problems arose involving senior members of the congregation. The admonition, **Rebuke not an elder,** does not relate to an ordained minister in the church, "not to 'elders' in the ecclesiastical sense, but to the older men in the Christian community."[1]

No ordained minister has the right to invoke this word of Paul in order to escape a proper censure for some folly on his part. The apostle's directive is intended solely for the guidance of a young man in his dealings with persons older than himself. The word rendered **rebuke** is a stronger one than this rather mild translation would suggest. The NEB renders it: "Never be harsh with an elder." This is not to suggest that correction and discipline have no place in the work of a pastor. Rather, it emphasizes the importance of tact in dealing with cases which call for correction and amendment. No one has exhibited this essential quality more splendidly than has Paul himself. For instance, in writing his perfect gem of a letter to Philemon, pleading for mercy and forgiveness for Onesimus, he says, "Though I am bold in Christ to command you to do what is required, yet for love's sake I prefer to appeal to you" (Philem. 8-9, RSV). Paul's advice to Timothy is thus in keeping with his own practice.

[1]Scott, *op. cit.,* p. 55.

Instead of rebuking an older person, entreat him; "appeal to him as if he were your father" (NEB).

The same verb, rendered **intreat** or "appeal to," controls the three remaining clauses in 1 and 2: **the younger men as brethren; the elder women as mothers; the younger as sisters, with all purity.** The analogy of the family is unmistakably present in the apostle's mind as he defines these delicate social relationships. The Church is the family or household of God, and the love which binds each to the other in its fellowship is like the love of parents and children, of brothers and sisters. If this could only be borne in mind and exemplified by all concerned in the Church of Christ, we would see the end of the misunderstanding and strife which so frequently tear the Church asunder.

In speaking of Timothy's relationship to the younger women, the apostle adds the significant phrase **with all purity.** Scott observes appropriately that "the most delicate of all the relations in which . . . [Timothy] was placed, as a spiritual adviser, is exquisitely touched on in a single word, which says everything."[2] How many men over the centuries have ended their ministry in shame and remorse because of their failure to heed this word!

B. Responsibility Toward Dependent Widows, 5:3-16

These verses suggest a serious problem which the Church in its early centuries was compelled to reckon with, viz., the predicament of widows in the ancient world. Early in the Church's history this problem had arisen in Jerusalem. Acts 6:1 relates that "in those days, when the number of the disciples was multiplied, there arose a murmuring of the Grecians against the Hebrews, because their widows were neglected in the daily ministration." The plight of widows was particularly poignant because little economic opportunity existed for them in the Roman world. As Holmes Rolston puts it, "A woman who was left a widow had very little opportunity to enter the labor market and earn a living for herself."[3] It is evident that the church at Ephesus was plagued with this problem, and Paul is seeking to

[2]*Op. cit.*, p. 56.

[3]*1-2 Thessalonians, 1-2 Timothy, Titus, Philemon* ("The Layman's Bible Commentary," ed. by B. H. Kelly, *et al.;* Richmond: John Knox Press, 1963), p. 86.

offer Timothy some guidance in meeting the situation. Parry points out that this portion dealing with widows "falls naturally into two sections, (1) 3-8, (2) 9-16. In the first section the subject is simply the relief of widows in distress; and the object is to insist on the private duty of relations, and the personal character of the widow, both to be considered before the Church gives relief. In the second section, the widow is regarded as in the employment of the Church for certain purposes. A list of such widows is to be kept, and rules are given for the construction of the list. These widows will be supported by the Church, unless they have a relation who can support them and so relieve the Church of the charge."[4]

1. *Duties the Church Owes to Widows* (5:3-8)

Honour widows that are widows indeed (3). By **widows indeed** the apostle means "widows who are really alone in the world" (Phillips). These would be women not only bereft of husband, but without children, grandchildren, or other relatives who could contribute to their support. Widows in this category should be treated "with great consideration" (Phillips). It seems likely that Wesley is correct when he interprets candidly the words **honour** as meaning "maintain out of the public stock."[5] Paul was deeply concerned that those in real need and deserving of the church's help should receive proper support. It is interesting to look in upon a situation in which the church dispenses its own charity. Earlier, such dispensing had been largely delegated to the state or to various relief agencies, as today.

The apostle is equally concerned lest the church be imposed upon by the greedy relatives of such a needy widow who would gladly turn over her support to the church rather than assuming it themselves. To guard against such an eventuality, Paul says, **But if any widow have children or nephews, let them learn first to shew piety at home, and to requite their parents: for that is good and acceptable before God** (4). Here is a standard of family responsibility which in our day frequently is honored more in the breach than in the observance. Indeed, how often do we see the sorry spectacle of elderly parents and

[4]*The Pastoral Epistles* (London: Cambridge University Press, 1920), p. 29.

[5]*Op. cit.*, p. 780.

grandparents compelled to become public charges while children and grandchildren spend their substance for their own selfish ends! It would appear to be the chief concern of many parents to provide well for their children while giving little thought to the privations endured by their own aged parents. The first responsibility for such care must be borne, as Paul insists, by the family of which the widow is a member. **Nephews** is more accurately translated "grandchildren" (cf. RSV). Only when this resource is exhausted does the support of such widows become the responsibility of the church.

The apostle recognizes that there are qualitative differences between persons in the category of **widow,** differences which bear on the church's obligation. **Now she that is a widow indeed, and desolate** (one completely alone in the world), **trusteth in God, and continueth in supplications and prayers night and day** (5). Here is described one who, not only because of her desolate widowhood, but because of her consistent and genuine devotion to Christ and His Church, is deserving of every consideration the church can bestow. But the apostle recognizes that not all widows are thus deserving. He acknowledges that there may be among the church's widows some who, far from setting their hopes upon Christ, are self-indulgent and even sensual in their attitudes and conduct. Of such persons the apostle remarks, **She that liveth in pleasure** ("wanton pleasure," NASB) **is dead while she liveth** (6). The implication is that the church is under no obligation to assume the support of any such worldly-minded widow.

These, then, are the guidelines Timothy must follow in determining the policy of the church in dispensing charity. **These things give in charge** ("command," RSV), **that they may be blameless** (7). The pronoun **they** obviously refers to the widows who are maintained by the church. It is important that the church's support be reserved for those truly worthy of it.

Before leaving the subject of family responsibility, Paul is constrained to add one further observation calculated to stigmatize anyone who neglects this fundamental duty. **But if any provide not for his own, and specially for those of his own house, he hath denied the faith, and is worse than an infidel** (8). We should not construe the apostle as equating such conduct with infidelity, reprehensible though it is. He speaks thus presumably "because even pagans, who do not know the Commandments or the law of Christ, recognize and set store by the obligations of children to parents."[6]

2. *Duties Which Widows Owe to the Church* (5:9-16)

The apostle turns next to a phase of the subject of the relationship of widows to the church concerning which we have most meagre information: **Let not a widow be taken into the number under threescore years old, having been the wife of one man, well reported of for good works; if she have brought up children, if she have lodged strangers, if she have washed the saints' feet, if she have relieved the afflicted, if she have diligently followed every good work** (9-10). The expression **taken into the number** is rendered by the RSV "be enrolled" and by the NEB "put on the roll." This seems to be more than is meant by our expression "relief roll," though on this point scholars are not in agreement. Rolston is probably correct when he says, "It would seem that there was in the Church at the time when Paul wrote, a loosely organized order of older widows who ministered to others in the name of Christ and his Church and who were at least in part supported by the Church."[7]

Superficially it would appear that the order of widows which Paul describes were deaconesses, or were at least doing the work of deaconesses. Wesley identifies these widows as "deaconesses, who attended sick women or traveling preachers."[8] But most interpreters hesitate to go this far. It is clear that these widows were a highly select group. Their minimum age of sixty would guarantee their maturity. To be eligible for this list, a widow must have been **the wife of one man.** This may mean, as Wesley construes it, "having lived in lawful marriage, whether with one or more persons successively."[9] At the very least it means that such a widow must possess a good moral character. However, in view of the requirements imposed upon bishops and deacons, we may be justified in finding here a reflection of the first-century prejudice against second marriages, however legitimate they may be from our point of view. Scott reminds us that "ancient sentiment allowed a special credit to the widow who refrained from second marriage."[10]

[6]Kelly, *op. cit.*, p. 115.
[7]*Op. cit.*, p. 87.
[8]*Op. cit.*, p. 781.
[9]*Ibid.*, p. 781.
[10]*Op. cit.*, p. 60.

Further qualification for inclusion in the roll of widows who served the church was a reputation for **good works** of whatever sort. This would include the ability to care for and rear **children;** a spirit of hospitality, which was a vital matter in the life of the Early Church, when evangelists, apostles, messengers, and ordinary Christians were constantly coming and going; the willingness to stoop to any task, however menial, as, for instance, washing **the saints' feet;** and an eagerness to minister to **the afflicted** whatever their need may have been. This was surely the work of a deaconess, and these "enrolled" widows were expected to practice it diligently.

The apostle next proceeds to justify his requirement that enrolled widows be at least sixty years of age. **But the younger widows refuse: for when they have begun to wax wanton against Christ, they will marry; having damnation, because they have cast off their first faith** (11-12). Apparently enrollment in the order of widows involved a pledge never to remarry, and the apostle felt that widows younger than sixty years might find adherence to such a pledge too difficult. To fail at this point would bring them under condemnation (such is the meaning of **damnation** in the KJV). The NEB greatly clarifies these verses: "Younger widows may not be placed on the roll. For when their passions draw them away from Christ, they hanker after marriage and stand condemned for breaking their troth with him."

Paul also gives a further reason for his conviction that only the older widows should serve the church in this ministry. **And withal they learn to be idle, wandering from house to house; and not only idle, but tattlers also and busybodies, speaking things which they ought not** (13). Here is a familiar pattern of conduct. Most experienced pastors at some time or other have had to deal with the tragic aftermath of gossiping and backbiting. In all candor, let us admit that at times older widows might be quite as guilty of this sort of conduct as the younger, and that men as well as women can engage in this malicious pastime. The apostle hoped apparently that the older widows would have learned from maturity and experience the folly of such behavior.

Paul is clearly convinced that the proper field of service for younger widows is not in this sensitive area of social contacts. He is most forthright in saying: **I will therefore that the younger women marry, bear children, guide the house, give none occa-**

sion to the adversary to speak reproachfully. For some are already turned aside after Satan (14-15). Whatever Paul may have held as the ideal with respect to second marriage for widows, his better judgment recognizes that remarriage, the maintenance of a home, and the rearing of children would be more likely to satisfy their instinctive urges. His warning concerning some who have **already turned aside after Satan** may have been based on the example of some of less mature years who had assumed vows which later they regretted and violated. It could well have been some such experiences which prompted him to adopt the minimum age of sixty for widows employed by the church.

This passage comes to a close with 16: **If any man or woman that believeth have widows** (among his relatives), **let them relieve them, and let not the church be charged; that it may relieve them that are widows indeed.** This is a recapitulation of Paul's argument in 4-8, and lays additional emphasis upon the fact that the resources which the church had available for relief must be expended in ministering to only the most worthy and deserving cases.

C. The Honor Due an Elder, 5:17-25

1. *Proper Reward for Faithful Service* (5:17-18)

It is obvious that the term **elder** carries two meanings in this Epistle, meanings which, though distinct, are related. In 5:1 it clearly means the senior members of the congregation. But here it evidently refers to those set apart for the work of the ministry: **Let the elders that rule well be counted worthy of double honour, especially they who labour in the word and doctrine** (17). There are some commentators who find in this verse an anticipation of the distinction between "ruling elders" and "teaching elders," which is the practice in some Reformed churches. However, this seems unlikely when we recall that Paul states specifically in 3:2 that all elders (or bishops) must be "apt to teach."

The apostle is here reminding Timothy that an elder who combines capability as a leader of the church with faithful and gifted service as a preacher and teacher should receive **double honour.** It is difficult to believe that this means simply "a double stipend," as the NEB renders it. No doubt it did include a monetary consideration, as Paul's further remarks make clear; but it must have included honor along with honorarium. The day had not yet arrived when the Church's ministers would receive full support. It was still customary for the Church's leaders to support themselves, just as the apostle himself did. Yet Paul believed that good service deserves recognition and reward. One whose time was taken up largely by the work of the Church should receive greater compensation.

Paul buttresses his advice with an argument reminiscent of I Cor. 9:9: **For the scripture saith, Thou shalt not muzzle the ox that treadeth out the corn. And, The labourer is worthy of his reward** (18). The first of these passages is an Old Testament precept found in Deut. 15:4, and in its original setting is simply a humanitarian ordinance. But Paul argues elsewhere that it has a deeper meaning: "Doth God take care for oxen? Or saith he it altogether for our sakes?" (I Cor. 9:9-10) The apostle also appeals to another passage to which apparently he attaches equal importance: **The labourer is worthy of his reward.** This is a saying of our Lord found in Luke 10:7. The surprising thing here is that New Testament scholars seem unable to find evidence to prove that Luke's Gospel was generally accessible when these words were written. Some, of course, would leap at once to the conclusion that the Pastorals must have been written much later than the date we have assigned them. But it is more probable that Luke's Gospel was known to Paul and also to Timothy. E. K. Simpson takes the position, along with B. B. Warfield, that "we have here a citation verbally exact from Luke's Gospel, treated as an integral portion of Holy Writ."[11] In this passage the apostle makes clear his opinion that faithful and effective service deserves recognition and suitable reward. It is apparent that the Church was beginning to move in the direction of a salaried ministry.

2. *Discipline Must Be Fair and Impartial* (5:19-21)

From the suitable rewarding of those who have served the church well, Paul now turns to the question of censuring those who have been remiss. Verse 19 is most significant: **Against an elder receive not an accusation, but before two or three witnesses.** Here is invoked one of the most basic principles of

[11]*Op. cit.*, p. 78.

Jewish jurisprudence: "One witness shall not rise up against a man for any iniquity, or for any sin, in any sin that he sinneth: at the mouth of two witnesses, or at the mouth of three witnesses, shall the matter be established" (Deut. 19:15). Our Lord appeals to this legal principle in Matt. 18:16, and Paul in II Cor. 13:1. If the Church were to follow this principle faithfully, no member or minister would ever become the victim of one vengeful individual. It is a principle which every responsible denomination has incorporated in its disciplinary procedures.

The apostle goes further in 20: Them **that sin rebuke before all, that others also may fear.** If and when the fault has been proved by the mouths of two or three independent witnesses, the guilty man must suffer the consequence of his sin, however painful and humiliating it may be. Sin cannot be hushed up but must be exposed and rebuked "in the presence of all" (RSV). Such procedure, Paul believed, would point up the fact that no man, not even a minister of the church, can sin with impunity.

There is an extraordinarily solemn note in 21: **I charge thee before God, and the Lord Jesus Christ, and the elect** ("chosen," NASB; "holy," Phillips) **angels, that thou observe these things without preferring one before another, doing nothing by partiality.** The tone of this passage suggests that scandals may have arisen in the past by reason of preferential treatment of offenders, and the apostle would eradicate once and for all such injustice. Moffatt renders the latter portion of the verse thus: "Be unprejudiced in carrying out these orders; be absolutely impartial." E. F. Scott comments: "The caution is twofold: 'do not pre-judge a case, admitting doubtful charges because you do not like the man; and do not be lenient on any personal grounds, when a case is proved.' "[12]

3. *Avoid Haste in Ordinations* (5:22-25)

Lay hands suddenly on no man, neither be partaker of other men's sins (22). This counsel of the apostle almost certainly relates to the laying on of hands in the ritual of ordination to the Christian ministry. There is excellent reason why a man should prove himself over a period of years until his fitness for the office of elder is clearly apparent. Even when the utmost caution is exercised, mistakes are made at this point in church

[12]*Op. cit.*, p. 66.

administration. Delay in such matters may be irksome and frustrating many times for the candidate, but delay is important. The man who betrays his trust and falls into sin not only brings reproach upon himself, but also upon the church whose confidence he has betrayed. Paul goes so far as to suggest that in a certain sense those who have laid hands on a man who proves unworthy become **partakers of other men's sins.** This surely does not involve guilt on their part, but it cannot fail to cause pain and grief. Paul drives this admonition home with the terse demand: **Keep thyself pure.** Rolston remarks in this connection that "the minister must be very careful not to be compromised in his stand for righteousness by endorsing men who are not worthy of his trust."[13]

The apostle now interrupts his train of thought by injecting a purely personal counsel: **Drink no longer water, but use a little wine for thy stomach's sake and thine often infirmities** (23). The English of the KJV is archaic, but is clarified by the NEB: "Stop drinking nothing but water; take a little wine for your digestion, for your frequent ailments." This is admittedly a difficult verse to interpret in view of our modern Christian emphasis upon total abstinence. No thoughtful reader of the Bible can fail to recognize that the attitude toward the use of wine in both Old and New Testaments differs markedly from present-day Christian conviction. D. Miall Edwards points out that "the drink question is far more complex and acute in modern than in Bible times, and that the conditions of the modern world have given rise to problems which were not within the horizon of New Testament writers."[14] While the practice of abstinence is not formally laid down in the New Testament, there are broad principles of Christian responsibility which in view of modern conditions surely call for abstinence from all intoxicants (cf. Rom. 14:13-21; I Cor. 8:13). As Barclay notes, Paul's advice to Timothy "simply approves the use of wine where wine may be medicinally helpful."[15]

Having thus advised Timothy, Paul now returns to the general subject he has been discussing: **Some men's sins are**

[13]*Op. cit.*, p. 89.

[14]"Drunkenness," *International Standard Bible Encyclopedia*, ed. by James Orr (Chicago: The Howard-Severance Co., 1925), II, 881.

[15]*The Letters to Timothy, Titus and Philemon* ("The Daily Study Bible"; Edinburgh: The Saint Andrew Press, 1960), p. 139.

open beforehand . . . and some men they follow after (24). In rather archaic English this says simply that some men's sins are so open and obvious that no one would dream of making them elders in the church; while with other men, their sins are so secret and subtle that only as one knows them well and intimately does he discover their hidden disqualifications for office. In either case Timothy is advised to move very deliberately in approving men for places of leadership.

In 25 the apostle deals with the converse of 24: **Likewise also the good works of some are manifest beforehand; and they that are otherwise cannot be hid.** The obscurities of this verse are clarified by Phillips thus: "Similarly some virtues are plain to see, while others, though not at all conspicuous, will eventually make themselves felt." Both hidden sins and hidden virtues eventually will come out into the open. These facts add impressiveness to the apostle's advice to move with caution and deliberation in the important business of selecting leaders.

Section VIII Various Instructions

I Timothy 6:1-19

A. Christian Slaves and Christian Masters, 6:1-2

1. *A Standard of Conduct* (6:1)

The institution of slavery was one of the curses of the ancient world. It has been said that the Roman Empire rested on the backs of slaves. When the Christian Church invaded the first-century world it was inevitable that the fact of slavery would pose a multitude of problems. Among those who welcomed the gospel message and eagerly embraced the new faith were many who were in the bonds of involuntary servitude. In the course of time many slave-owning masters embraced the faith, presenting a situation where a master and his slave, though far apart in economic and social realms, were now brothers in Christ in the fellowship of the Church. A number of Paul's Epistles deal with this problem and suggest the patterns of conduct which should guide both masters and slaves. Indeed, the first verse of this chapter is a fair summary of the standard of conduct spelled out in detail elsewhere. **Let as many servants as are under the yoke count their own masters worthy of all honour, that the name of God and his doctrine be not blasphemed.** C. K. Barrett suggests that Paul may have had in mind not only church members who were slaves, but also elders who were slaves.[1] Thus the language of the apostle seems to suggest that this passage may be a further specification within the general subject of the eldership.

It was impossible for the Christian Church to strike overtly in any effective way at the institution of slavery. But indirectly the Church sounded the death knell of this institution by its emphasis upon the dignity of man and the supreme value of personality. Meanwhile, Paul's advice is that masters, even though heathen, must be counted as "worthy of all respect."

2. *Fellow Church Members* (6:2)

This verse deals expressly with the situation where masters and slaves were members of the same Christian church. **And**

[1]*Op. cit.*, p. 82.

they that have believing masters, let them not despise them, because they are brethren; but rather do them service, because they are faithful and beloved, partakers of the benefit (2). The expression **partakers of the benefit** means "because they are thereby benefiting those who have the same faith and love as themselves" (Phillips). It would be a sore temptation to a Christian slave to take advantage of his Christian master simply because they were brethren in Christ and on a basis of equality before God. It must have called for an amazing degree of forbearance on the part of both parties to this relationship to make it work. Paul's frequent mention of the issue suggests that it was a sore problem and one present everywhere throughout the first-century Church. The concluding exhortation, **These things teach and exhort,** suggests the touchiness of the issue.

B. Consequence of Unsound Teaching, 6:3-5

In these verses the apostle returns to his polemic against those who were guilty of corrupting the faith in the Ephesian church. **If any man teach otherwise, and consent not to wholesome words, even the words of our Lord Jesus Christ, and to the doctrine which is according to godliness; he is proud, knowing nothing, but doting about questions and strifes of words** (3-4). Here is a crushing and almost bitter indictment of those described in the first chapter, who are deviating from the Christian position. Doctrinal novelties are departures from that sound teaching which was the Church's heritage from her Lord, a teaching which alone leads to the transforming grace of God. Paul's characterization of such perverters of the faith is picturesque, to say the least. It is variously translated: **knowing nothing** (4); "a conceited idiot" (Phillips); "a pompous ignoramus" (NEB); "a swollen-headed person" (J. N. D. Kelly). This is as close to invective as the apostle ever comes.

Paul goes on to show that out of such teachings and attitudes **cometh envy, strife, railings, evil surmisings, perverse disputings of men of corrupt minds, and destitute of the truth, supposing that gain is godliness: from such withdraw thyself** (4-5). Attitudes such as the apostle is denouncing here cannot fail to produce an evil progeny, such as "jealousy, quarrelling, slander, base suspicions, and endless wrangles" (NEB). These things cannot fail to destroy the Church's unity and fellowship, grieving the Holy Spirit, and destroying the effectiveness of the gospel.

"A sad indictment this, copiously exemplified (alas!) in the annals of the visible Church, and recalling the caustic saying that 'the apostolical succession of Judases has never failed.' "[2]

The words **supposing that gain is godliness** (5) suggest that these traitors to the faith were hoping to make a monetary profit by means of their false teachings. Parry itemizes their offense under three heads: "It is implied (1) that these teachers professed to teach the Gospel, (2) that they claimed on this ground payment for their work, (3) that the thought of money-making was prominent in their motives."[3]

For Timothy there can be only one answer to such an invasion of error into the Church: **From such withdraw thyself.** There can be no toleration of such faithlessness to Christ. Here is a spirit with which there can be no reasoning or persuasion. Paul advises peremptory action against all who are of this unholy temper.

C. The Perils of Wealth, 6:6-10

1. *The True Gain of Godliness* (6:6-8)

The spectacle of false teachers who not only corrupted the Christian faith but also put a price upon their distortions, prompts the apostle to a word of timeless wisdom: **But godliness with contentment is great gain** (6). The Christian faith does indeed pay rich dividends to one who embraces it humbly and completely and discovers for himself the infinite satisfaction that comes of living for Christ. To serve God and accept gladly whatever He sends is the happiest life that can be imagined. Contentment does not arise from having all of our wants and whims supplied, but rather from reducing our desires to the essentials. Surely no truth speaks more directly to the condition of our surfeited generation than this. When Epicurus was asked the secret of contentment, he replied, "Add not to a man's possessions but take away from his desires." Paul himself is bearing witness to this secret when he said, "I have learned in whatsoever state I am, therewith to be content" (Phil. 4:11). It is this independence of circumstances to which the apostle bears witness in his own life that is denoted by the word translated **contentment.**

[2]Simpson, *op. cit.*, p. 84.

[3]*Op. cit.*, p. 39.

Verse 7 is a familiar saying, found elsewhere in Scripture (Job 1:21; Eccles. 5:15) and in other ancient literature: **For we brought nothing into this world, and it is certain we can carry nothing out.** Barrett comments appropriately that "the final nakedness of death demonstrates and underlines the initial nakedness of birth."[4] We may gather much or little between these two events, but in that final hour we must leave it all behind. Only the values that inhere in one's spirit can be carried with him into eternity, and only these will stand on the credit side of his ledger in the day when he renders final account.

The apostle now indicates just how "stripped down" one must be if he is to render full service to Christ: **And having food and raiment let us therewith be content** (8). John Wesley, in his sermon on "The Danger of Riches," asks the question, "What is it to be rich?" and answers: "'Having food and raiment,' (literally *coverings;* for the word includes lodging as well as clothes,) 'let us therewith be content.' 'But they that will be rich' . . . [means those] who will have more than these; more than food and coverings. It plainly follows, whatever is more than these is, in the sense of the Apostle, *riches;* whatever is above the plain necessaries, or at most conveniences, of life. Whoever has sufficient food to eat, and raiment to put on, with a place where to lay his head, and something over, is *rich.*"[5] This is a rigorous standard, and by it many of us would be regarded as rich men. Of course, life is infinitely more complex today than in the eighteenth century, and a reasonable prudence would require a somewhat broader view. Nevertheless we must guard against the tendency to make financial gain the supreme concern in life. Our Lord's warning against the deceitfulness of riches (Matt. 13:22) must be borne in mind constantly.

2. *The Danger of Acquisitiveness* (6:9-10)

The apostle carries his warning even further in these verses. **But they that will be rich fall into temptation and a snare, and into many foolish and hurtful lusts** ("desires," NASB), **which drown men in destruction and perdition.** It is surely true that nothing assails a man with greater violence than the desire for financial gain, once he has given place in his soul to this demon of greed. Men are lured further and further away from their

[4]*Op. cit.*, p. 84.

[5]*Works*, VII, 3.

principles of honesty and honor by the prospect of easy profits. How many a man in public life has found himself powerless to resist the temptation to take illicit gains in violation of his once honored scruples. Paul has not exaggerated the dangers that await one on this path when he says that such a one will be swamped in a morass of iniquity and end in total ruin.

Verse 10 is equally pungent in its putting of this truth: **For the love of money is the root of all evil: which while some coveted after, they have erred from the faith, and pierced themselves through with many sorrows.** The meaning of the apostle seems to be that the love of money is the root of evils of *every sort.* Of course, not all evils spring from this cause. Yet one is justified in saying that this is one of the most prolific sources of evil. This judgment concerning **the love of money** was not original with Paul; it is echoed in much of the Jewish and pagan ethical literature of the first century. But in the apostle's warning its special menace to one's Christian faith is made clear. His whole discussion recalls Jesus' caution: "Ye cannot serve God and mammon" (Luke 16:13).

D. Aims and Rewards of Godly Living, 6:11-16

1. *Follow After* (6:11)

After painting the evils of lust for gain in as lurid colors as he had at his command, the apostle returns to his concern for Timothy's spiritual well-being. **But thou, O man of God, flee these things; and follow after righteousness, godliness, faith, love, patience, meekness.** Paul could not make a more eloquent appeal than one in which he would characterize Timothy as a **man of God.** This was the usual description of God's servants in the Old Testament. By its use the apostle suggests the dignity, the high and solemn responsibility of the office which Timothy held and which is held equally by every Christian leader. Paul's admonition is to **flee these things.** His meaning seems to be not alone the deceit of riches, but all of the evil attitudes which have been exposed from 4 onward. There is an interesting antithesis in the command to **flee these things,** and on the other hand to **follow after** the particular virtues which have been named. It is a striking list of virtues Paul would inculcate. The list begins with **righteousness,** the most comprehensive of the virtues; it means to render to both God and men what is due. The next three form a group, all of which are directed toward God. **Godliness** is a reverent awareness that all of life is lived in the presence and under the eye of God. **Faith** is fidelity which holds one steady, exhibiting loyalty to God in every situation. **Love** (*agape*) is the expression of the soul's gratitude and praise for the wonder of redeeming grace. Finally, Paul would inculcate **patience** and **meekness,** which are rendered in the RSV as "steadfastness" and "gentleness." These are the characteristics of the Christian life as it is lived in contact and fellowship with others. The contrast between these virtues and the evils which Paul has been denouncing could not be more startling.

2. *Fight the Good Fight* (6:12)

One is reminded, when reading this verse, of an athletic coach seeking to instill courage and a fighting spirit in his team on the threshold of a crucial game. **Fight the good fight of faith, lay hold on eternal life, whereunto thou art also called, and hast professed a good profession before many witnesses** (12). The apostle's figure of speech is derived more from the athletic contests of the first century than from military life. The verb **fight** is to be understood as the agonizing struggle required if one is to overcome in a wrestling match. Paul found graphic analogies, of course, both in the life of the soldier and in that of the athlete. Every Christian is called to carry on a personal struggle against evil in all of its forms. And, as Kelly points out, "the imperative is purposely in the present, indicating that the struggle will be a continuous process. On the other hand," continues Kelly, "the aorist imperative 'possess yourself' [KJV, **lay hold**] suggests that Timothy can lay hold on eternal life (here conceived of as the prize for the athletic event) immediately, in a single act."[6] Thus the Christian athlete can enjoy the prize while still engaged in the contest.

To this lifelong campaign Timothy is said to be **called.** Indeed, he possessed a double call: a call to follow Christ, which was sealed in his public confession of faith in baptism; and a call to preach the gospel, to which task he had been ordained by the apostle himself with others assisting. Most interpreters find it difficult to determine which of these callings is referred to in the final clause of the verse. The RSV interprets it "when you made the good confession in the presence of many witnesses." It would seem more fitting, however, to regard this as a further

[6]*Op. cit.,* p. 141.

allusion by the apostle to the ordination event which he frequently mentions (e.g., 4:14).

3. *A Sacred Charge* (6:13-16)

These verses are invested with a high degree of solemnity: **I give thee charge in the sight of God, who quickeneth all things, and before Christ Jesus, who before Pontius Pilate witnessed a good confession; that thou keep this commandment** ("your commission," Phillips) **without spot, unrebukeable, until the appearing of our Lord Jesus Christ** (13-14). Paul seeks to impress Timothy's mind and conscience with the importance of being faithful to the awesome responsibility that rests upon him as a man of God and leader of His holy Church. Here is an obligation which must be held inviolate, in momentary expectation of the return of Christ in judgment and reward. The apostle had all but given up the hope that he himself would live to see that glorious day of the Lord. But he would hold before Timothy the hope that the younger man might live to witness that wondrous consummation. Concerning the certainty of Christ's return Paul never wavered; only his hope of living to see it for himself now seemed unlikely. But Timothy could well witness the coming of that day. To him the apostle says in effect, "I charge you to live and labor with that day clearly in your view."

Additional solemnity is added to the apostle's charge by his pointing out that all of Timothy's labor and service is carried forward under the eyes of God, "who gives life to all things" (13, RSV), and of Christ, who did not waver in His confession when He stood before Pilate. The consciousness that God's eye is upon him and the inspiration of his Lord's stalwart example in the hour of supreme trial should give strength to the young man's heart and hands. There is a certain liturgical sound to these verses. Paul's appeal to the good confession which Christ witnessed before Pontius Pilate sounds very like that clause in the Apostles' Creed, "Suffered under Pontius Pilate." This language sets the proper mood for the doxology which immediately follows.

This doxology comprises 15-16: **Which in his times he shall shew, who is the blessed and only Potentate, the King of kings, and Lord of lords; who only hath immortality, dwelling in the light which no man can approach unto; whom no man hath seen, nor can see: to whom be honour and power everlasting. Amen.** The first clause of 15, **which in his times**, is archaic, but obviously refers to the **appearing of our Lord Jesus Christ** of 14. In modern English it says simply: "That appearance God will bring to pass in his own good time—God who in eternal felicity alone holds sway" (NEB). These great events which shall usher in the final consummation were declared by our Lord to be put in the Father's own power (Acts 1:7). And that is where they must remain.

The doxology which follows is said by Scott to be "more akin to the hymns of praise in Revelation than to the doxologies of Paul. Not improbably it is suggested by a Christian hymn, modelled on the liturgy of the synagogue."[7] But whatever its source, it is magnificent beyond words. **King of kings, and Lord of lords** may have been a subtle attack on the cult of emperor-worship, a part of the growing paganism which the Church was compelled to resist. **Who only hath immortality** "does not deny it to any other, but brings out the uniqueness of the divine immortality in that God alone inherently possesses it, being Himself the source of all life."[8] His eternal transcendence and invisibility are both clearly asserted—"the one who lives in unapproachable light" (Phillips). When we stand in the presence of God, what words can we utter? Paul can only conclude this paean of praise with the ascription of **honour and power,** rather than the more usual "honour and glory" (cf. 1:17).

E. The Proper Stewardship of Wealth, 6:17-19

1. *The Peril of Wealth* (6:17)

On the face of it, these verses seem like a sudden descent from the sublime to the commonplace. Following Paul's magnificent doxology, he turns immediately to practical and mundane problems. **Charge them that are rich in this world, that they be not highminded, nor trust in uncertain riches, but in the living God, who giveth us richly all things to enjoy.** This abrupt lowering of the apostle's tone, this apparent intrusion of earthly things, is really not an intrusion at all. Indeed, verses 11-16 are the intrusion. Paul had been speaking in 10 of worldly wealth and its potential dangers. But in 11-16 he digresses, quite in the Pauline manner, and a splendid digression it is. Now in 17 he

[7]*Op. cit.,* p. 79.

[8]Guthrie, *The Pastoral Epistles,* p. 117.

resumes the theme which his inspired parenthesis had pushed aside.

In handling this subject earlier in the chapter, the apostle had in mind those who aspire after riches. Here he addressed himself to those who are already rich. This is an interesting insight into the economic situation of at least some members of the church in Ephesus. Not all of the early Christians were slaves and humble artisans. There evidently were men of wealth and circumstance among them—and there is peril in the increase of riches. The sobriety, industry, and prudence which the gospel introduces into the believer's life must inevitably lead to increased prosperity; and the prosperity may well undermine the Christian faith which underlies the new disciplines. So does wealth often become the enemy of the soul. And, as Paul clearly sees, the chief danger it presents is that of being **highminded** (proud). There is that about wealth which promotes in one a false sense of security; it is difficult to have great wealth without in some measure trusting in it. Paul refers to wealth most perceptively as **uncertain riches.**

A further reason for the avoidance of pride in respect to one's wealth is suggested in Paul's reminder that **God . . . giveth us richly all things to enjoy.** All is of God, both wealth and the ability to acquire it. In fact, all that any man enjoys of the satisfactions of life, whatever may be the forms which they take, comes from the open-handedness of God.

2. *The True Stewardship of Wealth* (6:18-19)

That they do good, that they be rich in good works, ready to distribute, willing to communicate ("ready to give away and to share," NEB); **laying up in store for themselves a good foundation against the time to come, that they may lay hold on eternal life** (18-19). Here is Christian guidance in the proper uses of wealth. One is reminded of John Wesley's threefold counsel to Methodists who were prospering: "Gain all you can, save all you can, and give all you can."[9] Money can never buy one's salvation; but the proper and Christian use of money can make for Christian character and may enable one the more firmly to lay hold on eternal life. Phillips translates v. 19 clearly: "Their security should be invested in the life to come, so that they may be sure of holding a share in the life which is permanent."

[9]Sermon on "The Use of Money," *Works*, VI, 124 ff.

Section IX *Paul's Concluding Appeal*

I Timothy 6:20-21

O Timothy, keep that which is committed to thy trust, avoiding profane and vain babblings, and oppositions of science falsely so called: which some professing have erred concerning the faith. Grace be with thee. Amen (20-21). The apostle in these words is summarizing the grave concern which prompted him to write this letter, and gives the young man his final exhortation. Kelly suggests that "the strongly personal tone may be a sign that, in his usual manner, Paul added these closing lines in his own hand."[1]

He refers to the trust which has been committed to Timothy, using "a legal term connoting something which is placed on trust in another man's keeping."[2] Undoubtedly he means the Christian faith, that "form of sound words" (II Tim. 1:13) which he had received from his father in God, the apostle. He is urged to "turn a deaf ear to empty and worldly chatter, and the contradictions of so-called 'knowledge' " (NEB). However accurate this use of **science** may have been in the seventeenth century, in our day the word has taken on a highly specialized meaning which makes its use in the context of Paul's warning highly misleading. The apostle is alluding again to the false teachings which he has been denouncing throughout this letter. Concerning these "contradictions of what is falsely called 'Knowledge' " (Moffatt), Scott suggests that "here, perhaps, we have the clearest indication given us in the Epistles that the false teaching was of a gnostic type. Its exponents laid claim to a 'gnosis' or higher knowledge, although, in the writer's view, they were misusing a great word."[3] Those who held these views "had missed the mark as regards the faith" (Kelly's translation).

The letter ends with a word of blessing or benediction: **Grace be with thee. Amen.** The pronoun **thee** is plural in form and has been properly rendered by the NEB: "Grace be with you all!" Though the apostle's letter has been addressed to Timothy, it is evident that he has the entire church at Ephesus in mind when he pens his parting benediction.

[1]*Op. cit.*, p. 150.

[2]*Ibid.*

[3]*Op. cit.*, p. 83.

Outline

THE SECOND EPISTLE TO TIMOTHY

I. Salutation, 1:1-2
   A. The Writer, 1:1
   B. The Addressee, 1:2

II. Tribute to Timothy's Early Faith, 1:3-5
   A. Concern for Timothy's Welfare, 1:3-4
   B. Timothy's Heritage, 1:5

III. Paul Encourages Timothy, 1:6-14
   A. Stir Up God's Gift Within You, 1:6-7
   B. Be Fearless in Your Work, 1:8-10
   C. Paul's Own Appointment, 1:11-12
   D. Importance of Sound Teaching, 1:13-14

IV. Loyalty and Disloyalty, 1:15-18
   A. False Friends, 1:15
   B. A True Friend, 1:16-18

V. Paul Admonishes Timothy, 2:1-26
   A. Be Unfaltering in Devotion to the Truth, 2:1-2
   B. Be a Good Soldier of Jesus Christ, 2:3-4
   C. Rewards Await Fidelity, 2:5-7
   D. Through Death to Life, 2:8-13
   E. How to Deal with False Teachers, 2:14-19
   F. Teach the Truth in Love and Forbearance, 2:20-26

VI. Perilous Times Will Come, 3:1-9
   A. Marks of Impending Moral Decay, 3:1-5
   B. Even Now These Conditions Obtain, 3:6-9

VII. Remember My Example, 3:10-15
   A. Paul's Sufferings for Christ's Sake, 3:10-11
   B. Steadfastness Is Essential, 3:12-15

VIII. Inspiration of God's Word, 3:16-17

IX. Paul's Final Charge, 4:1-18
   A. Preach the Word, 4:1-5
   B. The Apostle's Valedictory, 4:6-8
   C. Personal Requests, 4:9-13
   D. A Particular Warning, 4:14-15
   E. Paul Rejoices in God's Faithfulness, 4:16-18

X. Final Greetings and Benediction, 4:19-22

Section I *Salutation*

II Timothy 1:1-2

We notice a marked difference as we move from I Timothy to II Timothy. Paul's situation has clearly changed for the worse. He is no longer a free man laying plans for the future, his mind filled with high expectation. He is now a prisoner without human hope. There is no prospect of ultimate acquittal, but rather a resignation to an inevitable death sentence. There is no difference in the apostle's spiritual resiliency, however, for his indomitable spirit rises above what must otherwise have become a mood of black despair. Paul's faith is being subjected to its uttermost test and is proving to be completely adequate. There are emotional overtones which can be clearly detected, overtones which his tragic situation could not fail to induce. The letter is a message of farewell from a man who knows that death is very near.

A. The Writer, 1:1

Paul is still a man engaged in a divinely appointed mission. His body is in chains, and freedom of movement is no longer his, but he is still Christ's apostle. **Paul, an apostle of Jesus Christ by the will of God, according to the promise of life which is in Christ Jesus.** The expression **by the will of God** has an authentic Pauline sound, for he so describes his call in II Corinthians, Ephesians, and Colossians. The further clause, **according to the promise of life which is in Christ Jesus,** is noteworthy for two reasons. Paul feels himself to be the bearer of a life-giving message whose significance is in no wise diminished by the fact that its appointed bearer is under sentence of death. Here is a paradox which only the redeemed can understand. Moreover, the message is significant because it bears an unmistakable Pauline signature in the expression **which is in Christ Jesus.** The very keystone of Paul's mysticism is found in his "in Christ" concept, and here is one clear echo of that concept in the Pastoral Epistles. Valiant effort has been expended to prove a totally different meaning here from that which the expression carries in his earlier Epistles, but in vain. According to Kelly, such theories receive "no support from a passage like this, where the mystical sense 'in union with Christ' is fully in place and the alternatives proposed are strained and unnatural."[1]

B. The Addressee, 1:2

To Timothy, my dearly beloved son: Grace, mercy, and peace, from God the Father and Christ Jesus our Lord. The note of affection which is sounded in Paul's reference to **my dearly beloved son** is even deeper and more poignant than the description in I Tim. 1:2. It reveals the warm and tender regard which the apostle felt for his favorite son in the gospel. The triad in Paul's benediction, **Grace, mercy, and peace,** is an exact repetition of that in the First Epistle (1:2). As M. P. Noyes points out, "The words of this verse are often used today as a benediction at the close of a church service or a religious gathering."[2]

[1]*Op. cit.,* p. 154.

[2]"The First and Second Epistles to Timothy and the Epistle to Titus" (Exposition), *The Interpreter's Bible,* ed. George A. Buttrick, *et al.,* XI (New York: Abingdon-Cokesbury Press, 1951), 460.

Section II *Tribute to Timothy's Early Faith*

II Timothy 1:3-5

A. Concern for Timothy's Welfare, 1:3-4

It was customary in ancient letters to follow the salutation immediately with expressions of concern for the addressee's welfare. Paul usually conforms to this convention, though for some reason, only here in the three Pastorals has he done so. **I thank God, whom I serve from my forefathers with pure conscience, that without ceasing I have remembrance of thee night and day (3).** The apostle speaks here of his own background in a manner totally different from that of the First Epistle. There (1:13) he describes himself as one "who was before a blasphemer, and a persecutor, and injurious," while here he speaks of serving God from his forefathers in good conscience. These two attitudes are not mutually exclusive, however. In the first letter he was thinking of his opposition to Christ, whom, until his eyes were opened, he regarded as an impostor. Here he recognizes that there was a certain continuity between Judaism and Christianity in his life. While recognizing the weaknesses which were inherent in Judaism apart from its fulfillment in Christ, he never fails to acknowledge the abiding values of his heritage. This comes out clearly in Rom. 9:3-5 and again in Phil. 3:4-6.

The apostle gives us almost casually a glimpse of the depth and continuousness of his prayer life. Timothy is held up to the throne of grace **night and day.** Paul declares the same thing of his churches and his associates in the gospel. How broad the sympathies and how deep the concern of one who bore so constant a burden! One would think that amid the pressures of prison life he might be tempted to seek respite from this heavy concern. Yet his burden for the work of God seems even heavier than before, now that his preaching voice has been silenced.

The apostle's deep feeling for Timothy and probably the intense loneliness of his situation are here revealed clearly: **Greatly desiring to see thee . . . that I may be filled with joy (4).** Paul was a man who yearned for his friends and who found solace and strength in the sympathy and understanding of his associates in Christ. We encounter the attitude repeatedly in this letter; e.g., in 4:9, "Do thy diligence to come shortly unto me"; and again in 4:21, "Come before winter." His letters to the churches also contain expressions of fondness for individuals whom he names. Surely fellowship of this quality is precious beyond words and can be found only in the context of Christian faith.

Moreover, the apostle recalls Timothy's grief at their last parting—**being mindful of thy tears.** When this occurred is not stated, but it could well have been the time when Paul was taken into custody the second time and transported to Rome for his final imprisonment. To see the young man Timothy again would, as the NEB renders it, "make my happiness complete."

B. Timothy's Heritage, 1:5

Paul is reminded at this point of Timothy's heritage of faith: **When I call to remembrance the unfeigned faith that is in thee, which dwelt first in thy grandmother Lois, and thy mother Eunice; and I am persuaded that in thee also.** In speaking of Timothy's **unfeigned faith** the apostle is not thinking of that faith which "is the gift of God" (Eph. 2:8), but rather the response to God's love in Christ which flowed spontaneously from Timothy's heart. This same response characterized the attitude of the young man's mother and grandmother. This may mean that the grandmother Lois was the first member of the family to find Christ as Saviour and Lord, and was instrumental in leading the younger members to embrace the Christian faith. Or, as seems more likely, Paul is referring to the attitude of piety and religious devotion which had characterized Timothy's family for at least three generations, beginning in Judaism and coming to its fullness and flower in the acknowledgment of Christ Jesus as Messiah and Lord. In 3, Paul had spoken with appreciation of a background similar to this in his own life. Both Paul and Timothy had grown up among those Jews of the Dispersion who were "waiting for the consolation of Israel" (Luke 2:25) and had found it in Jesus.

Section III *Paul Encourages Timothy*

II Timothy 1:6-14

A. Stir Up God's Gift Within You, 1:6-7

Wherefore I put thee in remembrance that thou stir up the gift of God, which is in thee by the putting on of my hands (6). The transitional word **wherefore** is rendered in the Phillips translation "because of this faith." It suggests that it is Paul's unwavering confidence in the reality of Timothy's devotion to Christ which prompts the exhortation to **stir up the gift of God, which is in thee by the putting on of my hands.** In I Tim. 4:14 this same concern is expressed negatively: "Neglect not the gift that is in thee." Here is a perennial need in the hearts of all Christians and especially in those who are cast in the role of leaders of the church. Our constant danger is the lessening of our ardor and the slackening of our pace. Periodically we need to seek renewal of our commitment and to reaffirm our loyalty; "to stir into flame the gift of God" (NEB). This is the basic meaning of revival and it must come periodically to us all.

The allusion to **the putting on of my hands** indicates that it is Timothy's divinely given qualifications for the work of the ministry that Paul has in mind. If these qualifications were not actually bestowed in the service of ordination, they were certainly sharpened and focused in that experience.

In 7, Paul points out at least a part of this spiritual endowment: **For God hath not given us the spirit of fear; but of power, and of love, and of a sound mind.** The NEB rendering of this is good: "For the spirit that God gave us is no craven spirit, but one to inspire strength, love, and self-discipline." We are not justified in assuming, as some would have it, that Timothy had been playing the coward's part in his work at Ephesus, for which he is now being sharply rebuked. Indeed, Paul is gentle in his chiding, not using the pronoun "you," but rather **us** as including himself along with Timothy. The task which Timothy was called upon to perform may have demanded qualities which were not native to one of his gentle disposition, but which must be cultivated if God's work were to prosper. A spirit of holy boldness is the order of the day; a vigorous strength, a love that is divine in its quality and source, and a self-mastery that makes one's spirit under God the master of one's body.

B. Be Fearless in Your Work, 1:8-10

Be not thou therefore ashamed of the testimony of our Lord, nor of me his prisoner (8). This incipient sense of shame concerning the testimony of Christ may be no part of the experience of a typical extrovert. But for people naturally timid, as Timothy evidently was, it can be a sore test of loyalty. Paul exhorts Timothy to put it away from him resolutely. The temptation to be ashamed of Paul, God's prisoner, could very well stem from the fact that the apostle had been thrust into the role of criminal and was now feeling the heavy weight of pagan justice. Moreover, Christianity was existing under new and dangerous conditions. It was no longer tolerated as it had been, but was regarded (mistakenly of course) as the enemy of the state. To bear clear witness to one's faith in Christ might place his life in jeopardy. Fearless witnessing called for courage of a particular kind. Paul bids Timothy not to draw back: **but be thou partaker of the afflictions of the gospel according to the power of God.** This means literally "to take one's share of ill-treatment."[1] And Paul assures him that he shall be able to endure "in the strength that comes from God" (NEB).

Verses 9-10 give a typically Pauline summary of the miracle of divine grace which God has revealed in Christ's redeeming work: (God), **who hath saved us, and called us with an holy calling, not according to our works, but according to his own purpose and grace, which was given us in Christ Jesus before the world began.** It is already an accomplished fact that God **hath saved us.** This is the true Christian's assured position. Salvation in this sense is not deferred to the far distant future, but is the believer's present experience. Nevertheless there is an increasing purpose in God's mercy and a growth in grace which lead to a continuing enrichment of that experience. God has **called us with an holy calling.** This means more than a holiness that exists in name only or is merely imputed to the believer by the supreme holiness of God; it means that the believer is loosed from his sins and delivered from their guilt and power.

[1]Guthrie, *The Pastoral Epistles*, p. 128.

God's call is to an experience and life that involve a complete consecration on the believer's part and a complete inner cleansing on God's part. But Paul cautions immediately that this is **not according to our works,** for these of themselves are utterly unworthy. Rather, it is **according to his own purpose and grace.** The initiative is with God in this matter. It is He who awakens us from our death in sin and calls us unto holiness; and it is through His intercessions by His Spirit that we are able to respond, a response made possible only by His enabling grace. Thus the miracle of human transformation is all of God, though our consent to it in full freedom is essential to its accomplishment. And all of this belongs in the eternal counsels and purposes of God, a mercy **given us in Christ Jesus before the world began.**

Verse 10 suggests that God's purpose of human redemption and salvation from sin **is now made manifest by the appearing of our Saviour Jesus Christ.** God's plan of salvation is not a divine afterthought, a plan hit upon by the Creator after other plans had failed. The coming into history of God in Christ is a fulfillment in time of the great design of Almighty God conceived in eternity.

Christ's coming represents an invasion of time by eternity, a realized eschatology, as C. H. Dodd[2] has conceived it: an enjoyment in this present life of "the powers of the world to come" (Heb. 6:5). Paul asserts consequently that Christ **hath abolished death, and hath brought life and immortality to light through the gospel.** Here is an amazing claim, and passing strange it is on the lips of a man who is about to die! (Cf. 4:6-9.) In what sense dare we believe that Christ **hath abolished death?** Simpson suggests that the word rendered **abolished,** as Paul employs it, "means to render nugatory, frustrate, quash, dismantle."[3] The NEB puts it thus: "He has broken the power of death." Our Lord's own victory over death has robbed it of whatever terror it had, a fact of which Paul's own triumphant testimony in this letter is clear evidence. Because Christ has gone this way before us, we need not fear to follow. Not only is death done away, but life and immortality are brought into full view and placed within

[2]*The Parables of the Kingdom* (New York: Charles Scribner's Sons, 1936), pp. 197-206.

[3]*Op. cit.*, p. 125.

the reach of faith. There is a strange yet sublime commingling of two worlds here. **Life** pertains to time while **immortality** pertains to eternity; yet through Christ they are both placed within our grasp here and now.

C. Paul's Own Appointment, 1:11-12

We must admit that grammatically 11 belongs with 10. Yet in 11 the direction of Paul's thought changes from a sublime estimate of the work of God's grace to his own responsibility toward it: **Whereunto I am appointed a preacher, and an apostle, and a teacher of the Gentiles** (11). The terms **preacher, apostle,** and **teacher** may have been clearly distinguished in the Early Church, but Paul evidently is not thinking of such distinctions when he piles up these terms in an effort to display the magnitude of his task as a herald of the gospel of Christ. His confidence in the divine appointment to this task never wavered. In one passage indeed he goes so far as to assert that even before his birth he was chosen of God for this ministry (Gal. 1:15). If ever his sense of mission were to waver, it would surely be amidst his present circumstances, in prison and doomed to almost certain death. Yet his consciousness of vocation is as radiantly clear in these circumstances as in more propitious times.

He admits frankly that it is his uncompromising loyalty to God's call which has brought upon him his present difficulties: **For the which cause I also suffer these things** (12). The real secret of his fortitude is found in his magnificent confession of assurance which follows immediately: **I know whom I have believed, and am persuaded that he is able to keep that which I have committed unto him against that day.** It is noteworthy that Paul uses **whom** rather than "what" in this witness. It was not mere subscription to a proposition, but love for and loyalty to a Person, that he confesses. Here is an essential characteristic of the Christian faith. It is not enough that we hold a personal *credo* concerning Christ, however important in its proper place that may be. There must be a love fellowship with a Person—none other than Christ—if our faith is to be truly Christian.

Concerning the apostle's persuasion that Christ is able to keep that which is committed to Him, we encounter some obscurity in the original. The words **what I have committed** mean literally "my deposit"; and this is a frequently used term in the

Pastorals. Always (except here) it refers to the Christian message with which Paul and Timothy have been entrusted. This "deposit" may mean "what I have committed unto him" or "what he has put into my charge" (NEB). The KJV takes the former position while other versions prefer the latter. The original could mean either. Since either view is correct, the reader can make his own choice between them.

However this uncertainty of interpretation may be resolved, it is probable that the devout hearts of Christians in all ages will find their greatest comfort and assurance in the more familiar rendering—**he is able to keep that which I have committed unto him against that day.** In those crises of our experience of God's grace when one is placing his unknown future at the disposal of the will of God, it gives strength and comfort to the soul to be assured of the keeping power of God. And in the hours when obedience is difficult and the way ahead is shrouded in darkness and uncertainty, one finds in this assurance the fortitude to carry on without compromise or faltering. Paul's great witness thus becomes a rallying cry to the sorely tried spirit and one of the most dearly loved of New Testament texts.

D. Importance of Sound Teaching, 1:13-14

Paul turns now to exhortation concerning the integrity of the Christian message which Timothy has received. **Hold fast the form of sound words, which thou hast heard of me, in faith and love which is in Christ Jesus** (13). Here is a passage which is seized upon avidly by proponents of a late dating of these letters and their non-Pauline authorship. Superficially this admonition *sounds* vaguely like a later day when creedal formulas had become matters of greatest importance. But the apostle is not demanding slavish adherence to any set and accepted form of words, in which words alone the orthodox faith may find expression. As Kelly points out, "Paul is not saying that Timothy should reproduce his teaching word for word. . . . The word rendered 'model' [KJV: **form**] denotes an outline sketch or ground-plan used by an artist or, in literature, a rough draft forming the basis of a fuller exposition."[4] It was not Timothy's responsibility to "parrot" the message of his apostolic mentor, but to speak God's word in full freedom while maintaining a concern that the

[4]*Op. cit.*, p. 166.

authentic emphasis of the Christian message should undergo no change.

The same point is made even more fully in 14: **That good thing which was committed unto thee keep by the Holy Ghost which dwelleth in us.** Moffatt renders this verse: "Keep the great securities of your faith intact, by aid of the Holy Spirit that dwells within us." The apostle in speaking thus is recognizing one of the great truths of Christian experience: that the Holy Spirit abiding in the heart is the great Conservator of orthodoxy. Those periods in the life of the Church when the Holy Spirit has been most evidently present in mighty quickening power have also been the periods when the truth has been preached in purity and power. These two are inseparable and must ever remain so.

Section IV *Loyalty and Disloyalty*

II Timothy 1:15-18

A. False Friends, 1:15

The assured confidence in God of which the apostle has been speaking, and the devotion to Christ and the Church which he and Timothy have in common, suggest to Paul poignant and unhappy memories of what he has suffered from false friends. **This thou knowest, that all they which are in Asia be turned away from me; of whom are Phygellus and Hermogenes.** The **Asia** here mentioned is the Roman province of Asia, whose capital city was Ephesus (see map 1). It is evident that in the time of the apostle's dire need, probably when he was taken into custody by the Roman authorities, many from whom he had reason to expect friendship and assistance were content cravenly to abandon him to his fate. This is not to be construed as a general repudiation of Paul's apostolic authority by these churches, nor does the apostle's use of the word **all** suggest that he had no courageous friends. Two men from whom he had reason to expect some measure of help were **Phygellus and Hermogenes,** and both turned away from him. Paul is not reproaching them, but is only reporting what must already have been a notorious fact. Kelly translates the opening words of verse 15: "You must be aware." If Timothy was well informed about this failure of nerve on the part of the two men named, it was probably a matter of general knowledge.

B. A True Friend, 1:16-18

Against this background the loyalty and concern of **Onesiphorus** stood out in bold and vivid colors and Paul expresses undying gratitude for it. **The Lord give mercy unto the house of Onesiphorus; for he oft refreshed me, and was not ashamed of my chain** (16). The fact that the apostle speaks of **the house** (household) **of Onesiphorus** has suggested that when Paul was writing this letter Onesiphorus was already dead. Some go so far as to believe that his life was forfeited because of his befriending Paul. At any rate, the apostle was **oft refreshed** (Moffatt renders it: "he braced me up") by the faithful friendship and Christian brotherhood of this man.

The length to which Onesiphorus was willing to go in befriending Paul is clarified further in 17: **But, when he was in Rome, he sought me out very diligently, and found me.**

We can only imagine what the sight of that familiar and friendly face must have meant to the apostle as he languished in his prison. Indeed, a bit of high drama is implied in Paul's statement that **he sought me out very diligently, and found me.** P. N. Harrison writes that "there is a great story behind Paul's brief but suggestive record of that search through Rome. We seem to catch glimpses of one purposeful face in a drifting crowd, and follow with quickening interest this stranger from far coasts of the Aegean, as he threads the maze of unfamiliar streets, knocking at many doors, following up every clue, warned of the risks he is taking but not to be turned from his quest; till in some obscure prisonhouse a known voice greets him, and he discovers Paul chained to a Roman soldier."[1] No wonder is it that Paul felt such a profound gratitude for such an example of Christian brotherhood!

Verse 18 carries the apostle's benediction even further: **The Lord grant unto him that he may find mercy of the Lord in that day: and in how many things he ministered unto me at Ephesus, thou knowest very well.** The expression **that day** evidently refers to the Judgment Day.

This verse presents a problem for many interpreters because, on the assumption that Onesiphorus had died before the writing of the letter, the apostle's language sounds like a prayer for the dead. This issue does not really deserve the amount of attention it has received. As Kelly points out, "The prayer in question . . . is an exceedingly general one, amounting only to the commendation of the dead man to the divine mercy."[2] This problem disappears completely if we take the view of E. K. Simpson that Onesiphorus was not dead at all, but away from his family and probably still at Rome, delayed in his return home by concern for the beloved apostle.[3]

[1]*The Problem of the Pastoral Epistles* (London: Oxford University Press, 1921), p. 127.

[2]*Op. cit.*, p. 171.

[3]*Op. cit.*, p. 129.

Section V *Paul Admonishes Timothy*

II Timothy 2:1-26

A. Be Unfaltering in Devotion to the Truth, 2:1-2

In chapter 1, Paul has noted the failure of some men in their devotion to the gospel and, in contrast, the unfailing loyalty of Onesiphorus. Against this background he now directs his exhortation to Timothy. **Thou therefore, my son, be strong in the grace that is in Christ Jesus** (1). The tone of his opening address is emphatic to a degree scarcely suggested by the KJV. Kelly translates it by the phrase, "It is for you, then, my son, to be strong." Paul has reminded Timothy of his ordination and the vows he has assumed, and of the example of uttermost devotion which the apostle himself is displaying before him. It is now for the young man to show the mettle that is in him and exhibit in his turn a similar example of selfless consecration to the Christian task. The apostle's day is almost done; but to Timothy belongs the present hour, and the Christian message rests, for good or ill, in his hands. Not in himself however nor in his own strength will he be able to carry on. Only by the grace of God can he hope to be true to his commission.

Moreover, Paul is looking ahead even beyond the day when Timothy is the custodian of the salvation message. The young man must also have an eye to the future integrity of this mighty deposit of truth: **And the things that thou hast heard of me among many witnesses, the same commit thou to faithful men, who shall be able to teach others also** (2). In a literal sense Timothy received his message from the apostle. It was he who first declared the truth concerning Jesus to Timothy's family, with the result that three generations became followers of Christ. But Timothy had also witnessed Paul's missionary preaching in scores of situations—an experience which must greatly have enhanced his knowledge of the gospel. Moreover, it appears that the apostle, aided by other elders of the Church, ordained Timothy to the work of the ministry. On this occasion undoubtedly a sobering charge had been laid on the young man's heart. None of this was done in a corner, but came to him **among many witnesses.** There seems every reason to conclude that the apostle had all of this communication in mind when he spoke of **the**

things that thou hast heard of me. And now Paul admonishes him that he commit what he has received **to faithful men** who, in their turn, will be able to hand it on to others in all of its original purity and power.

It is a serious and sobering truth that the saving message which has brought such spiritual riches to our lives has come down to us from innumerable generations of Christian believers who have preceded us. It is our responsibility to assure ourselves of its authenticity, to hold it inviolate, and to pass it on to those who follow after us, with its richness and purity and power undiminished. Needless to say, this ideal has not been achieved in every instance. The result is that the Christian message becomes at times diluted or polluted, and there arises in every generation the need for a recovery of the pristine glory and power of the gospel. This amazing power of self-renewal in the Christian message is one of the wonders and glories of the gospel.

B. Be a Good Soldier of Jesus Christ, 2:3-4

How may a Christian leader condition himself for this task? Paul's answer is in these verses. **Thou therefore endure hardness, as a good soldier of Jesus Christ** (3). The apostle turns here and in the following verses to three analogies: the soldier, the contender in the games, and the tiller of the soil. The military analogy is a favorite one for Paul, not because he was military-minded, but because in the Roman Empire soldiers were a familiar sight, and even more so because the soldier's life was such a splendid analogy for Christian living. Unfortunately, we too are familiar with the demands imposed upon the soldier. To serve in this rigorous activity requires an extensive conditioning of one's body. Everyone who has gone through "boot camp" knows how difficult it is to toughen one's body to the point where his strength will be equal to the demands made upon it. But something comparable to this is necessary for the Christian, and especially the Christian minister. **Endure hardness**, says Paul. Take difficulty and privation and danger in an uncomplaining spirit as part of the task of soldiering in Christ's army.

The apostle extends this analogy in 4: **No man that warreth entangleth himself with the affairs of this life; that he may please him who hath chosen him to be a soldier.** It would be difficult to find a more apt analogy than this for the consecration demanded of the Christian. When one becomes a soldier, he is separated from the society with which he has been familiar all his life and introduced into a new and highly specialized community. He is stripped of his own clothing and attired in an outfit provided by his government. He goes and comes only under orders or with express permission. He sleeps where he is told to sleep and eats what is provided for him. Indeed his very life is at the disposal of his government, and if occasion arises he may be considered as expendable. Such is the consecration of one **chosen . . . to be a soldier;** and every detail of it is paralleled by the life of one wholly yielded to Christ. The soldier cannot put down roots at any point, however desirable it may seem to be. He is not his own, but belongs to another.

C. Rewards Await Fidelity, 2:5-7

In 5, Paul moves to the analogy of the contender in the games: **And if a man also strive for masteries, yet is he not crowned, except he strive lawfully.** This statement reveals graphically a second of Paul's interests, that of physical prowess. The Olympic games of ancient Greece were probably in the apostle's mind. This was something of an obsession in the ancient world, where every city had its stadium and physical competition was the order of the day. The RSV translation of this verse makes its meaning clearer: "An athlete is not crowned unless he competes according to the rules." This could mean the rules laid down for some particular game or athletic event. But it seems likely that a broader meaning is intended. As Scott points out, "It is the preparation for the contest which is in question and not the contest itself. An athlete has no chance of victory unless he has complied with certain previous conditions; he must have undergone the necessary training and limited himself to a given diet. Like the soldier he must give up everything with the one object of winning the game."[1]

The third of Paul's analogies is that of the hardworking farmer. **The husbandman that laboureth must be first partaker of the fruits** (6). If he hopes for a crop, the farmer must expend his labor, preparing the soil, sowing the seed, guarding against drought and blight, until at last he enjoys the fruit of his labor.

There is one point which Paul is seeking to make in all of

[1]*Op. cit.*, p. 102.

these analogies. Whether it be the soldier's expectation of ultimate victory, the athlete's vision of the crown, or the farmer's hope of a harvest: "each of them submits to the discipline and the toil for the sake of the glory which shall be."[2]

The apostle is concerned that Timothy grasp the point upon which he is insisting: **Consider what I say; and the Lord give thee understanding in all things** (7). By admonition, warning, and exhortation, and now by analogy, Paul has spelled out the type of dedication which he expects of his young assistant. "Think over what I say," says the apostle, "and trust in God for His wisdom and guidance."

D. Through Death to Life, 2:8-13

1. *The Example of Our Lord* (2:8-10)

In the apostle's efforts to hearten and inspire Timothy to give himself without reservation to the task of Christian leadership, Paul climaxes his appeal by pointing to the Lord Jesus: **Remember that Jesus Christ of the seed of David was raised from the dead, according to my gospel** (8). Here is the supreme example of devotion, and Timothy is urged to emulate His blessed Master. **The seed of David** is an expression pointing to the real identity of Christ Jesus with our human race. The emphasis here is upon "the man Christ Jesus." But linked with the recognition of our Lord's humanity is the glorious fact of His resurrection. As Barclay points out, "The tense of the Greek verb which Paul uses does not imply one definite act in time, but a continued state which lasts forever. Paul is not so much saying to Timothy: 'Remember the actual resurrection of Jesus'; rather he is saying: 'Remember Jesus for ever risen and for ever present; remember your risen and ever-present Lord.' "[3]

The apostle's words here are reminiscent of that earlier passage in Rom. 1:3-4: "Jesus Christ our Lord, which was made of the seed of David according to the flesh; and declared to be the Son of God with power, according to the spirit of holiness, by the resurrection from the dead." C. H. Dodd believes that in this passage "Paul is citing more or less exactly a common confession of faith."[4] Here in II Timothy the verse we are consider-

[2]Barclay, *op. cit.*, p. 188.

[3]*Ibid.*, p. 189.

[4]*The Epistle to the Romans* ("The Moffatt New Testament Commentary"; London: Hodder and Stoughton, 1949), p. 5.

ing could likewise be a portion of an ancient and familiar creed. The additional phrase—**according to my gospel**—gives an authentic Pauline tone to the sentence.

It was the apostle's unflinching loyalty to this gospel which had brought him into his present predicament: **Wherein I suffer trouble, as an evil doer, even unto bonds; but the word of God is not bound** (9). The word rendered **evil doer** means literally a common criminal. It is the word used in Luke 23:32-33, 39 to describe the malefactors who were crucified alongside of Jesus. Phillips' translation puts it clearly: "For preaching this I am having to endure being chained in prison as if I were some sort of criminal." But though the apostle is in chains, **the word of God is not bound.** Paul had discovered this glorious truth in his earlier imprisonment and reports that "the things which happened unto me have fallen out rather unto the furtherance of the gospel" (Phil. 1:12). No doubt his later confinement was more severe than the earlier one, yet the gospel was still free. As Moffatt puts it, "There is no prison for the word of God."

The apostle has reached the point where he is willing to bear without repining whatever suffering may come to him for Christ's sake: **Therefore I endure all things for the elect's sakes, that they may also obtain the salvation which is in Christ Jesus with eternal glory** (10). It is "for the sake of God's chosen ones" (NEB) that Paul is enabled to carry on with courage and fortitude. From 11 and 12 it is clear that **the elect** may maintain their standing with God only on the conditions laid down. In his earlier imprisonment, writing to the Philippians, Paul said, "I have learned in whatsoever state I am, therewith to be content" (Phil. 4:11). Now he is in a position to put to an even sterner test his total submission to the will of God. He is able, moreover, to see in the triumphant suffering of Christ's followers a certain extension of our Lord's redemptive suffering. His example of uttermost devotion could contribute something to the salvation of others.

2. *Christ Is Completely Trustworthy* (2:11-13)

It is a faithful saying (11). These words appear repeatedly in the Pastorals (cf. I Tim. 1:15; 3:1; 4:9; Titus 3:8). They usually introduce a fragment of a creed, a bit of liturgical prayer, or a snatch from a hymn. Verses 11*b*-13 appear to be taken from a hymn which undoubtedly was familiar to both Timothy and the Ephesian church. **For if we be dead with him, we shall also**

live with him. It is surely not physical death in martyrdom of which the apostle is thinking here. Elsewhere, and particularly in Rom. 6:1-11, Paul develops a mystical doctrine of dying with Christ in a death to self and sin which leads to new life in Christ. Indeed, "Now if we be dead with Christ, we believe that we shall also live with him" (Rom. 6:8) is almost exactly reflected in II Tim. 2:11. Such a death is symbolized in the rite of Christian baptism (Rom. 6:3); but it leads to such a mystical and spiritual identification with our Lord that in a sense we share His sufferings. This consequence Paul echoes in 12, **If we suffer, we shall also reign with him.** By suffering Paul was probably thinking of enduring for Christ's sake sufferings such as were his present lot. But the prospect of reigning with Christ more than compensates for the pain one must bear. Some interpreters view the prospect of reigning with Christ as a reflection of "the primitive Christian hope that, when Christ returns in glory to reign (I Cor. 15:24 f.), the saints who have endured will sit on thrones alongside him (Rev. 5:10)."[5] But it could mean quite as appropriately that we shall have the rare joy of sharing His kingdom.

There is a tragic note in this hymn which must not be overlooked: **If we deny him, he also will deny us: if we believe not, yet he abideth faithful: he cannot deny himself** (12-13). If under the pressure of persecution a man disowns Christ, his faithlessness can only result in his being himself disowned. Our Lord said as much in Matt. 10:33: "Whosoever shall deny me before men, him will I also deny before my Father which is in heaven." But a note of hope is injected into this passage dealing with warning and judgment. **If we believe not** should be rendered "If we are faithless," suggesting a failure, not in belief, but rather in fidelity. Even for such a one there is still a remaining hope; for Christ **abideth faithful: he cannot deny himself.** There is no limit to the divine compassion, and there is no sin too deep-dyed for the Blood to cover. Such is the magnitude of God's mercy.

E. How to Deal with False Teachers, 2:14-19

1. *What to Promote* (2:14-15)

Of these things put them in remembrance (14). People need constantly to be reminded of the things they already know but are in danger of forgetting or overlooking. Paul evidently is

[5]Kelly, *op. cit.*, p. 180.

thinking of the truth which it has been his mission in life to proclaim, the responsibility for which now is largely in Timothy's hands. A faithful pastor will of necessity be somewhat repetitious in the emphases of his ministry. There are many important truths which can be inculcated only by the "line-upon-line, precept-upon-precept" procedure. Paul has previously exhorted the young man along this line, and what he is now saying is, "Go on reminding people of this" (NEB); keep up the good work.

Paul then becomes more explicit, reverting to a theme with which he had dealt in I Timothy 1. **Charging them before the Lord that they strive not about words to no profit, but to the subverting of the hearers.** The apostle is again expressing his concern about the conduct of the self-appointed teachers in the church at Ephesus, whose tactics were promoting only controversy, bitterness, and division. Such conduct would have the effect of sowing discord among brethren (cf. Prov. 6:19). This "only demoralizes the listeners," as Kelly renders it.

Paul then addresses Timothy directly concerning his own ministry: **Study to shew thyself approved unto God, a workman that needeth not to be ashamed, rightly dividing the word of truth** (15). The verb **study** does not refer to the work which a minister does with his books in his place of study, important as that is. Its true meaning is captured by the NEB: "Try hard to show yourself worthy of God's approval." This has to do in part with the hours spent in the sort of intellectual labor which is indispensable to real success in the ministry; but it includes besides the whole posture of "dead-in-earnestness" which must characterize a minister's attitude toward his responsibility. Scott sees in the words **approved unto God** a veiled reference to the final judgment seat before which Timothy must ultimately render his account. The word rendered **workman** means basically an agricultural worker; and so the NEB renders **rightly dividing** by the expression "driving a straight furrow." But whatever the precise imagery in the passage, it seems clear that the apostle is concerned that God's Word be subjected to sound exegesis and its correct meaning be properly ascertained. Nothing is more essential than this for the reverent handling of biblical truth.

2. *What to Shun* (2:16-18)

But shun profane ("worldly," NASB) **and vain** ("empty," NASB) **babblings: for they will increase unto more ungodliness** (16). Here is language identical with that of I Tim. 6:20.

(See comments on that passage.) Paul again denounces the false teachers who had been promoting dissension in the Ephesian church. They were doing Satan's work and their pretended familiarity with hidden truth had the effect of desecrating it. Timothy's course of action should be one that shuns such teachings. No compromise can be made with error.

These **babblings** "will lead to further ungodliness" (NASB); that is, wicked living. The virulence of such teachings is emphasized in 17: **And their word will eat as doth a canker: of whom is Hymenaeus and Philetus. Their word** would be the teachings of these false leaders. The term rendered **canker** is translated in both RSV and NEB by the term "gangrene," while Phillips employs the clause, "Their teachings are as dangerous as blood poisoning to the body." Here is a deadly danger whose menace must not be misjudged. Paul names in particular two who were busy spreading this moral and spiritual infection: **Hymenaeus** we have met before, in I Tim. 1:20, though beyond these references nothing is known of him. **Philetus** meets us here for the first and only time.

Verse 18 gives us our only hint as to the nature of the error associated with these names: **who concerning the faith have erred, saying that the resurrection is past already; and overthrow the faith of some.** Scott suggests two possible meanings for this reference. "The idea," he says, "may have been that this life itself, in which the soul was reborn out of some previous life and death, was the true resurrection. Or more probably the Christian doctrine was interpreted in a purely spiritual sense; since by faith in Christ men enter into immortal life, the resurrection will not come after death but has already taken place."[6] The doctrine of the Resurrection was the most sensitive point in Christian teaching. It denoted Christ's triumph over death, and by analogy stood for the new life in Christ which baptized Christian believers enjoy. And it was the symbol of the Christian's hope of eternal life. There must be no tampering with any truth so vital as this; hence the extreme denunciation to which the apostle subjects the erroneous teaching.

3. *Truth's Sure Foundation* (2:19)

The apostle has no qualms about the stability and security of Christ's Church, as 19 makes clear: **Nevertheless the foundation**

[6] *Op. cit.*, p. 111.

of God standeth sure, having this seal, The Lord knoweth them that are his. And, Let every one that nameth the name of Christ depart from iniquity. The analogy of a building or temple had long been a favorite with Paul in setting forth his doctrine of the Church. **The foundation** may be variously construed as referring to the Church as a whole or to the tried and true members of the Ephesian congregation. In comparison with this rugged foundation, the false teachers were an unstable minority.

In line with the analogy of a building with its foundation and cornerstone suitably inscribed, the apostle sees God's foundation as bearing two seals. One, taken from Num. 16:5, reads: **The Lord knoweth them that are his.** In these words Moses proclaimed, in the face of the rebellion of Korah, that God knows and will identify those who are His and thereby Moses' leadership would be vindicated. Paul may have had in mind that similarly God would vindicate His apostle's leadership in this Ephesian situation. The second seal—**Let every one that nameth the name of Christ depart from iniquity**—is not an exact quotation of any Old Testament passage. However it bears so close a resemblance to Num. 16:26 that we are justified in the view that Paul has this ancient situation in mind as he deals with the Ephesian problem. The significance of these seals is well summarized by Rolston as follows: "The first mark of the approved workman is purity of doctrine, the handling aright of the word of truth; the second mark is purity of life."[7] These two tests of genuineness must never be separated.

F. Teach the Truth in Love and Forbearance, 2:20-26

1. *Vessels unto Honor* (2:20-21)

The apostle evidently is still thinking of the mixed situation which obtains in Ephesus. There was the fine, solid core of dedicated persons whose devotion is only set in fairer colors by the defection of the few dissidents. **But in a great house there are not only vessels of gold and of silver, but also of wood and of earth; and some to honour, and some to dishonour** (20). The analogy here is not a building but a household equipped with vessels both honorable and dishonorable, or "valued" and "cheap" (NEB). The analogy is far from perfect; for there was a place in **a great house** for both valued and cheap utensils; but in the

[7]*Op. cit.*, p. 105.

Church, as Paul saw the issue, there was no place for these vain and profane babblers. Nevertheless the apostle's intention is clear, and is made unmistakable by 21: **If a man therefore purge himself from these, he shall be a vessel unto honour, sanctified, and meet for the master's use, and prepared unto every good work.** An element of uncertainty turns about the meaning of the term **these.** It would seem to refer to the cheap and unworthy utensils in the great houses, though Paul still undoubtedly has in mind the false teachers whom Timothy is admonished to shun.

To be purged from these is to be **a vessel unto honour, sanctified, and meet for the master's use, and prepared unto every good work.** Here is a series of phrases which have a noble history and hold a secure place in the Church's treasury of devotion. To be **sanctified** is to be dedicated to holy uses and to be cleansed from defilement. **Meet for the master's use** is a phrase which emphasizes the amazing privilege of God's faithful ones being employed in holy tasks. **Prepared unto every good work** seems to be an almost extravagant expression. The apostle, speaking under the Spirit's inspiration, holds aloft for our viewing the glorious possibility that, through a miracle of grace, God's people may be readied for any task He may appoint them. The prospect thus set forth is almost breath-catching in its wonder!

2. *The Conduct of a Teacher* (2:22-26)

We are reminded in 22 that Timothy is still a young man, with the vast potentialities of youth, but also facing the perils of youth, against which he must be fortified: **Flee also youthful lusts: but follow righteousness, faith, charity, peace, with them that call on the Lord out of a pure heart** (22). The term **lusts** has a specialized meaning today with which it was not restricted in the seventeenth century when the KJV was published. The NEB renders it: "Turn from the wayward impulses of youth," while Barclay translates it: "Flee from youthful passions." It might seem that Timothy, now approaching forty years of age, would be beyond the need for such an admonition. Yet Satan is no respecter of persons, any more than God is. God's leaders in the Church, occupying as they do such a conspicuous position, are bound to be the targets of Satan and need to redouble their vigilance against the wiles of the devil. The apostle knew that the best defense against such demonic assaults is to be eagerly on the stretch for God's best. **Follow righteousness, faith, charity, peace;** or, as Moffatt renders it, "aim at integrity, faithfulness, love and peace." And in this earnest Christian quest we are to count ourselves one with God's faithful people wherever they may be found—one **with them that call on the Lord out of a pure heart.**

In these verses (22-26) Paul returns to his constructive admonitions concerning Timothy's personal conduct. In 23 he emphasizes the tact and restraint which should characterize the younger man's leadership: **But foolish and unlearned questions avoid, knowing that they do gender strifes.** While refusing to compromise with error, he must nevertheless avoid an unwarranted degree of rigor in his denunciation of it. In Christian leadership one must not allow his zeal for the truth to betray him into a quarrelsome spirit. There is no substitute for a spirit of kindness and love in dealing with those who are one's opponents. This point is clearly made in 24: **And the servant of the Lord must not strive; but be gentle unto all men, apt to teach, patient.** What a lovely cluster of Christian virtues this is! And the list is augmented by 25: **In meekness instructing those that oppose themselves;** that is, those who place themselves in opposition to his message. The real purpose of disciplinary action is not alone the vindicating of the truth, but also the recovery to Christ's fellowship of those who are led astray by false teaching: **If God peradventure will give them repentance to the acknowledging of the truth; and that they may recover themselves out of the snare of the devil, who are taken captive by him at his will (25-26).** The misfortune which has befallen these false teachers is not alone ignorance and a headstrong determination to propagate falsehood; it is equally true that they have been deceived and duped by Satan. They are entrapped in his snare and are his captives. Yet God hopes to recover and save them; He yearns to grant them **repentance to the acknowledging of the truth.** Christ's minister must keep the door of penitence and hope open for their return to the Father's house.

Section VI *Perilous Times Will Come*

II Timothy 3:1-9

A. Marks of Impending Moral Decay, 3:1-5

Up to this point Paul has been dealing with the demands imposed upon Timothy by his task as a pastor. But now in prophetic spirit he turns to the society which surrounds the infant church and discovers in it factors which could exert a tragic influence upon God's people. **This know also, that in the last days perilous times shall come** (1). The expression **the last days** refers usually to the period at the end of the present age and immediately preceding the return of Christ; and there is no reason to believe that the apostle had anything other than this in mind. Paul believed in the nearness of Christ's return, even though he would not himself live to see it. The period Paul is describing could therefore well be the times immediately ahead of Timothy. And he calls them **perilous.**

He then details a list of the sinful attitudes of men which will characterize this period: **Men shall be lovers of their own selves, covetous, boasters, proud, blasphemers, disobedient to parents, unthankful, unholy, without natural affection, trucebreakers, false accusers, incontinent, fierce, despisers of those that are good, traitors, heady, highminded, lovers of pleasures more than lovers of God** (2-4). This entire list constitutes one sentence. It is a sordid and depressing delineation of human sins. The ethical literature of the first century frequently contained such lists, and Paul himself had resorted previously to this device (Rom. 1:30-31). Sins of various degrees of gravity are brought together more or less indiscriminately, with the idea possibly of pointing out that in God's sight all sins are equally grave, whether they are sins of the flesh or the spirit, whether committed against God or our fellowman. These sins, common in the first century, are flourishing also in alarming measure today. Here are vivid indications of the last days.

Perhaps v. 5 is the most disturbing thought in this paragraph. **Having a form of godliness, but denying the power thereof: from such turn away.** Kelly says that 5 is a "stinging clause," which the apostle "thrusts in, by way of climax . . . the Ephesian errorists . . . make a great parade of Christianity."[1] It is astonishing indeed that men guilty of such flagrant sins may still find in formal religion a salve for their consciences. This is not intended to suggest that true religion is formless. Indeed form and power are not natural enemies or mutually exclusive. In fact there must be a marriage between form and power if the worship of God is to be the thing of grace and beauty that God desires. There are probably many ways of **denying the power** of religion. But the most subtle and deadly of these is simply the willingness to live day by day without the presence of God's power in one's religious life. This is a hazard that faces many a person who would blush even to read the sordid list of sins which Paul enumerates.

B. Even Now These Conditions Obtain, 3:6-9

When we come to this section it is apparent that Paul believed these evils were not only future but even then such conditions were present. **For of this sort are they which creep into houses, and lead captive silly women laden with sins, led away with divers lusts, ever learning, and never able to come to the knowledge of the truth** (6-7). The apostle would seem here to have changed the tense from the future to the present and to be addressing the situation Timothy is facing in Ephesus. The subtle methods employed by such depraved persons is suggested by the expression **creep into,** which may be rendered, "worm their way into." **Silly women** is translated "weak women" in the RSV. Such persons are easily seduced and led into a multiplicity of sins. Paul "has just as little sympathy for the dissolute women who cultivate religion along with their other excitements as he has for the dishonest teachers who prey upon them."[2]

It is an interesting analogy which Paul draws in 8: **Now as Jannes and Jambres withstood Moses, so do these also resist the truth: men of corrupt minds, reprobate concerning the faith.** The two men here named were among Pharaoh's magicians who attempted to duplicate the wonderful works of God and thus **withstood Moses** (Exod. 7:11; 9:11). Their names are not given in the Exodus account but appear in Jewish tradition.

[1]*Op. cit.,* p. 195.

[2]Scott, *op. cit.,* p. 121.

From this source they found their way into early Christian literature. It is evident that these names were well known to Timothy, for the apostle's reference to them carries no explanation. At this period the Old Testament narratives were frequently interpreted typologically. Israel's experience at the time of the great deliverance from Egypt was regarded as an anticipation of experiences which befell the Early Church and its leaders. Paul may have seen a parallel between Moses' experience in Egypt and the opposition which he had himself endured at the hands of men like Hymenaeus and Philetus.

The apostle is grandly confident that these subverters of the faith will not be able to inflict lasting harm on the Church. **But they shall proceed no further: for their folly shall be manifest unto all men, as theirs also was.** God is able to confound by His truth every effort made against the progress of the Church.

Section VII *Remember My Example*

II Timothy 3:10-15

A. Paul's Sufferings for Christ's Sake, 3:10-11

The apostle now turns to the example of endurance which he himself has set: **But thou hast fully known my doctrine, manner of life, purpose, faith, longsuffering, charity, patience, persecutions, afflictions, which came to me at Antioch, at Iconium, at Lystra; what persecutions I endured: but out of them all the Lord delivered me** (10-11). The phrase rendered **thou hast fully known** is much stronger than a casual reading of the KJV would suggest. It probably means that Timothy had accompanied Paul, and so had firsthand knowledge of these experiences. As Kelly points out, "it is also a technical term defining the relation of a disciple to his master, and can be paraphrased 'study at close quarters,' 'follow in spirit,' 'carefully note with a view to reproducing,' and so 'take as an example.' "[1] Phillips renders the passage, "But you . . . have known intimately both what I have taught and how I have lived."

These examples of the persecutions which Paul endured were all taken from the apostle's first missionary journey and in the area of Asia Minor (see map 1), where Timothy had made his home. The young man could well have been an eyewitness of some of them, even though they may have occurred before his conversion. Indeed, this series of events in Paul's life may have been the deciding factor in the winning of Timothy's family to Christ. Barclay observes that "it may well be a proof of Timothy's courage and consecration that he had seen very clearly what could and did happen to an apostle, and had yet not hesitated to cast in his lot with Paul."[2]

The thing that the apostle magnifies, however, is God's faithfulness to deliver His servant. He did not seek persecution or glory in it for its own sake; he recalls it only to praise God for the strength and grace that brought him through.

[1]*Op. cit.*, p. 198.

[2]*Op. cit.*, p. 227.

B. STEADFASTNESS IS ESSENTIAL, 3:12-15

Paul is convinced that there is no easy road for the children of God: **Yea, and all that will live godly in Christ Jesus shall suffer persecution** (12). Jesus declared the cross would be inescapable for those who followed Him, and so has it always been. One can be a nominal Christian without suffering much inconvenience. But those who would be genuine Christians must pay an inevitable price of suffering, though assured of God's delivering power.

To live in defiance of God's will and to give oneself to the propagation of errors will in the end bring a deepening shame: **Evil men and seducers shall wax worse and worse, deceiving, and being deceived** (13). One who allows himself to be seduced by the errors of the Ephesian deviationists must expect his condition to worsen; not only will he deceive others, but his condition will proceed from bad to worse until total spiritual blindness will be his portion. Human experience surely bears witness that this is the ultimate fate of one who rejects Christ.

With Timothy the case is different. The apostle exhorts him: **But continue thou in the things which thou hast learned and hast been assured of, knowing of whom thou hast learned them** (14). Undoubtedly the young man had had the benefit of many Christian teachers, chief of whom was Paul himself. This was an extraordinary privilege and one of which we could well be envious. Continue in this heritage of truth, urges the apostle. But Paul knows full well that the structure of truth in Timothy's life rested on a foundation which others had laid: **From a child thou hast known the holy scriptures, which are able to make thee wise unto salvation through faith which is in Christ Jesus** (15). This is a tribute to the faithful instruction he had received from his godly mother and grandmother. Instruction in the Scriptures was regarded as a sacred responsibility in every orthodox Jewish home and should be regarded with equal seriousness in every truly Christian home. Nothing could do more than this to enrich the lives of our children.

Section VIII *Inspiration of God's Word*

II Timothy 3:16-17

Here is a passage which has become a principal proof text for the Christian doctrine of the inspiration of the Bible. **All scripture is given by inspiration of God, and is profitable for doctrine, for reproof, for correction, for instruction in righteousness** (16). It seems clear that Paul has in mind the Old Testament, for at the time he was writing, these writings were the Scriptures of the Early Church. Here, as Scott points out, "the crucial word [**inspiration**] means literally 'breathed into by God'—i.e. a Divine quality is present in Scripture, distinguishing it from all human utterance."[1] With the development of the New Testament canon alongside the canon of the Old Testament, it was easy and highly proper for this concept of inspiration to be attributed to these newer writings which developed in the context of the Christian Church. Concerning the Scripture, John Wesley calls our attention to the fact that "the Spirit of God not only once inspired those who wrote it, but continually inspires, supernaturally assists, those who read it with earnest prayer. Hence it is so profitable for doctrine, for instruction of the ignorant, for the reproof or conviction of them that are in error or sin, for the correction or amendment of whatever is amiss, and for instructing or training up the children of God in all righteousness."[2]

The real purpose of the understanding of Scripture is made clear in 17: **That the man of God may be perfect, throughly furnished unto all good works.** Paul is saying in effect that no man is prepared to serve God adequately in the work of the ministry without a thorough knowledge of the Word of God. Whatever other qualifications he may possess, he must have this preeminent one, that he is a careful and conscientious student of God's inspired Word. Only thus may **the man of God . . . be perfect,** in the sense of complete in his preparation for his holy task, i.e., **furnished unto all good works.**

[1]*Op. cit.*, p. 127.

[2]*Explanatory Notes upon the New Testament*, p. 794.

Section IX *Paul's Final Charge*

II Timothy 4:1-18

A. Preach the Word, 4:1-5

There is an extraordinary degree of solemnity attaching to these concluding words of the apostle. He writes in full realization of the fact that time is running out and this is in all likelihood his farewell to his "beloved son."

I charge thee therefore before God, and the Lord Jesus Christ, who shall judge the quick (living) **and the dead at his appearing and his kingdom** (1). The word **charge** carries more emphasis than this translation would suggest, and "should be rendered *adjure,* for it has the weight of a legal affirmation."[1] The apostle had elaborated in great detail the responsibility which rests upon a Christian minister. Now he lays upon Timothy the demand that he assume this burden in full realization that for the discharge of his obligation he is answerable finally to **God, and the Lord Jesus Christ.** Both living and dead must stand finally before the Judge of all the earth. All that ultimately matters is what will matter **at his appearing and his kingdom.** After the thrones and dominions of earth have passed from the scene, and all the sovereignties of the nations are no more, God will still reign. Before Christ Jesus, whom He hath appointed the Judge of all the earth, all men shall render their account. No one among the myriads of earth will find that day more solemn than those who have served as Christ's ministers.

It is in the presence of these sobering considerations that Paul utters his charge: **Preach the word; be instant** (urgent) **in season, out of season; reprove, rebuke, exhort with all longsuffering and doctrine** (2). By **the word** the apostle means the message concerning Christ as Redeemer, Saviour, and Lord. This is what the New Testament means by the *kerygma* or proclamation.[2] This is to be the substance of Christian preaching. No sermon is really a sermon unless it makes explicit some biblical truth. **Be instant in season, out of season** is rendered in the NEB, "press it home on all occasions, convenient or incon-

[1]Simpson, *op. cit.*, p. 152.

[2]Cf. C. H. Dodd, *The Apostolic Preaching and Its Development* (New York: Harper and Bros., n.d.), pp. 7-35.

venient." Here is set forth the sense of urgency which should characterize our preaching. This must necessarily involve the responsibility to **reprove** and **rebuke,** and the more positive duty to **exhort.** We must seek to provoke in all who hear us the disposition to respond in full obedience to the Word of God. Above all should God's servant cultivate the grace of patience in his efforts to lead others to Christ and train them in Christian truth.

Verses 3-4 point out what Paul sees to be a growing tendency on the part of those who reject the rigors of the Christian way: **For the time will come when they will not endure sound doctrine; but after their own lusts shall they heap to themselves teachers, having itching ears; and they shall turn away their ears from the truth, and shall be turned unto fables.** These words must have been descriptive of the situation which already obtained in Timothy's day. But godless men have always displayed a preference for the prophet who prophesies "smooth things." One is reminded of the story of King Jehoshaphat's unholy alliance with King Ahab. When the king of Judah was uneasy about the rosy predictions of Ahab's prophets and called for the opinion of at least one more prophet, Ahab grudgingly admitted that "there is yet one man, by whom we may enquire of the Lord: but I hate him; for he never prophesied good unto me, but always evil" (II Chron. 18:6-7). So men today have ears that "itch" for the smooth and comfortable word and are willing to reward handsomely the man who is sufficiently compromising to speak it. Hearers of this type have rejected the truth and prefer to hear the lie.

In the face of such a situation, Timothy's duty is clear: **But watch thou in all things, endure afflictions, do the work of an evangelist, make full proof of thy ministry** (5). "Keep calm and sane at all times"—thus does the NEB render this first clause. The younger man is admonished to be constantly alert, serving Christ with his brain as well as his heart. **The work of an evangelist** may suggest a special order of the ministry in the Early Church, an order to which the apostle thought of Timothy as belonging. This charge seems to suggest that in the gospel war it is well to apply the military principle that the best defense is to attack. Proclaim the message of salvation in all of its purity, power, and rigor, and thus confuse and defeat the enemies of the Lord. Thus, as Phillips renders it, you will "carry out to the full the commission that God gave you."

B. The Apostle's Valedictory, 4:6-8

The kind of courageous loyalty which the apostle seeks to inculcate becomes the more necessary in view of his own impending fate: **For I am now ready to be offered, and the time of my departure is at hand** (6). Paul knew full well that he was facing the supreme sacrifice. A literal rendering of his words would be: "I am already being poured out as a libation, or drink offering, on the altar." There is infinite pathos in his words, and a certain sense of human sorrow at the fact of the impending separation from those he loved. The words **the time of my departure** have in them the imagery of the ship weighing anchor or the soldier striking camp.

But Paul is not overwhelmed or even abashed by the prospect before him. In view of it, he calmly reviews the course he has pursued and pronounces it good: **I have fought a good fight, I have finished my course, I have kept the faith** (7). The figure of speech is not taken from warfare but from the athletic contest. In keeping with this idea, Kelly translates the first clause: "I have fought in the noble match."[3] The NEB goes even further, making the first clause agree more fully with the second: "I have run the great race, I have finished the course." There are no regrets in such a testimony. The toils and sorrows and suffering are now forgotten in the assurance of a task well done. And the highest testimony of all is the clause **I have kept the faith.**

This relates wholly to the past; and if the apostle's witness were to end here it would be valiant but hopeless. There is, however, a future tense: **Henceforth there is laid up for me a crown of righteousness, which the Lord, the righteous judge, shall give me at that day: and not to me only, but unto all them also that love his appearing** (8). The word **henceforth,** which means literally "for the rest," is a term which draws "attention to what remains to be realized as contrasted with those things already accomplished."[4] **The crown of righteousness** continues the imagery of the racecourse, where the prize would be a garland of olive leaves. Here it is a **crown of righteousness,** which, as White points out, is "the crown which belongs to, or is the due reward of, righteousness."[5] Paul's expression **on that day** obviously

[3]*Op. cit.*, p. 208.

[4]Guthrie, *The Pastoral Epistles*, p. 170.

[5]*Op. cit.*, p. 178.

refers to the day of final judgment and reward, the day of which he reminded Timothy in the first verse of this chapter.

The comfort which these verses bring to Christian hearts is not to be found alone in the spectacle of the apostle's own triumphant spirit, but also in the assurance that all of Christ's followers may enjoy an equally abundant entrance into our Lord's glorious presence. **All them also that love his appearing** can know this comforting prospect.

C. Personal Requests, 4:9-13

The main portion of Paul's letter is now complete, and the conclusion is taken up with personal matters. **Do thy diligence** ("make every effort," NASB) **to come shortly unto me** (9). Here is expressed the fond yearning of the apostle's heart for one more visit with his beloved protégé. This would be a difficult request to fulfill. The time factor was a serious one, for communication and travel both were slow. There would be a serious question whether enough time remained for Timothy to receive Paul's request and comply with it. Then, too, it might involve Timothy in personal danger, though it is not likely that he would be deterred by this consideration. But the yearning of Paul's heart is understandable. In 1:4 he had declared himself as "greatly desiring to see thee," and now he returns to this theme.

No doubt Paul's hunger to see Timothy was rendered the more poignant by the departure of a number of friends who had been boon companions. **For Demas hath forsaken me, having loved this present world, and is departed unto Thessalonica; Crescens to Galatia, Titus unto Dalmatia** (10). Concerning Demas little is known beyond the information contained in this passage. In Col. 4:14 and in Philem. 24 he is named among the apostle's trusted companions. Had Demas backslidden and became an apostate from the faith? Most of the translations and the early traditions support this opinion but we are not justified in an unqualified judgment at this point. Paul does not say that Demas forsook Christ—only that he had forsaken the apostle. Men may disassociate themselves from us without being cut off from Christ. Demas' love of **this present world** is circumstantial evidence but not conclusive proof. Phillips introduces an appropriate element of reserved judgment into his rendering of the passage: "Demas, loving this present world, I fear, has left me and gone to Thessalonica." Though we may be charitable in our judgment, two major question marks raise grave doubts about a man's Christian faithfulness. Demas gave evidence of a love for the **world**, and he broke with one of God's great leaders of the Church. It is evident that he fell short of the high expectations which Paul entertained for him and had chosen an easier road. We cannot escape the feeling that somehow Demas lacked "the power to see it through."

Crescens is mentioned only here in the New Testament, and nothing more is known of him except some references in the early traditions. His destination—**Galatia**—could have been Galatia in Asia Minor, to which area Paul addressed one of his letters, or it could have been a district in western Europe known in the first century by the name of Gaul. Both RSV and NEB suggest "Gaul" as an alternative reading. But lacking clear evidence, we are safer in concluding that Galatia in Asia is intended (see map 1). **Dalmatia,** for which **Titus** had departed, is, as Kelly reminds us, "the southern portion of the imperial province of Illyricum, on the western shores of the Adriatic (the present Yugoslavia). We learn from Rom. 15:9 that Paul's missionary activity had extended there."[6] Unlike Demas, probably these two men had been sent by Paul on missions to the churches in the areas named.

Paul's loneliness was relieved only by the presence of one of his most faithful friends: **Only Luke is with me** (11). The "beloved physician" was the one remaining member of Paul's intimate circle to be at his side. So he pleads with Timothy, **Take Mark, and bring him with thee: for he is profitable to me for the ministry.** Mark had been a controversial figure in the apostle's earlier ministry, when the second missionary journey was about to begin. Paul and Barnabas had differed so sharply about the propriety of taking Mark with them that they had separated. Apparently Mark had atoned for his earlier failure and would now be gladly welcomed to the apostle's companionship.

Another of Paul's friends had been entrusted with a new mission: **Tychicus have I sent to Ephesus** (12; see map 1). Here was a trusted friend who had accompanied Paul on his final

[6]*Op. cit.*, p. 213.

visit to Jerusalem (Acts 20:4). Paul's letters to the Colossians and the Ephesians had been delivered by his hand (Col. 4:7-8; Eph. 6:21-22). Now he was off on another mission for the apostle, perhaps to convey this letter to Timothy, perhaps to replace Timothy at Ephesus in order to make possible his longed-for visit to the apostle in his prison.

If there is any unmistakable mark of authenticity in this letter, it is found in 13: **The cloke that I left at Troas** (see map 1) **with Carpus, when thou comest, bring with thee, and the books, but especially the parchments. The cloke** was a very simple garment, made of a blanket with a hole in the middle for the wearer's head. In many parts of the world cloaks of a similar type are still worn. **The books** were probably papyrus rolls that made up a small traveling library which the apostle usually carried with him. **The parchments** were probably skins or vellum, prepared for writing. On the other hand, Moffatt translates **the parchments** by the expression "my papers," believing that the reference is to official documents which Paul needed, possibly to establish the fact of his Roman citizenship. But this we can only conjecture.

D. A Particular Warning, 4:14-15

There is one situation concerning which Paul is sufficiently exercised to utter a a word of caution: **Alexander the coppersmith did me much evil: the Lord reward him according to his works** (14). The latter clause is better rendered, "the Lord will repay him according to his deeds" (NASB). Here there is no vindictive spirit, but rather a leaving of judgment in the hands of God, to whom it belongs. We have no certain identification of this man, for **Alexander** was one of the most common names of the time and coppersmithing was one of the most common trades. It could well be that this man is to be identified with the Alexander mentioned in I Tim. 1:20, for it would be unusual for the apostle to have had serious difficulty with two men so named within a relatively brief space of time. But here, too, we can only conjecture. At any rate, Paul warns Timothy solemnly against him: **Of whom be thou ware also** ("Beware of him yourself," RSV); **for he hath greatly withstood our words** (15). Here was a dangerous man, and Timothy should be on his guard against him.

E. Paul Rejoices in God's Faithfulness, 4:16-18

The apostle now recalls how, when forsaken by all others, God demonstrated His faithfulness: **At my first answer no man stood with me, but all men forsook me: I pray God that it may not be laid to their charge** (16). The reference here is to the first hearing of his case, and the NEB so translates it. Does this mean, as some contend, his arraignment after his first arrest? Verse 17 would seem to lend support to this view. But the more probable reference is to his second arrest, for he speaks as though this were a relatively recent event. At any rate he was completely forsaken by his friends in the hour of his supreme need. Nevertheless he refused to become embittered by this experience. Indeed, his prayer for those who thus forsook him is almost identical with Stephen's prayer for his murderers: "Lord, lay not this sin to their charge" (Acts 7:60).

But God remained faithful: **Notwithstanding the Lord stood with me, and strengthened me; that by me the preaching might be fully known, and that all the Gentiles might hear: and I was delivered out of the mouth of the lion** (17). The apostle is alluding to the influence of his courageous facing of his enemies and the faithful witness to the gospel of Christ which he was enabled to bear at the time of his arraignment. His deliverance from **the mouth of the lion** was an inner and spiritual triumph over all that Satan's minions were able to do against him.

He concludes this victorious recital with a confession of faith for the future and a shout of praise: **The Lord shall deliver me from every evil work, and will preserve me unto his heavenly kingdom: to whom be glory for ever and ever. Amen** (18). It is clear that the apostle is not referring to a physical deliverance from death and the clutches of his enemies. On the contrary, his moving valedictory in 6-8 indicates that he expects and is prepared for the worst. For years he had cherished the desire that he might live to see the fulfillment of his blessed hope of Christ's return. But he is now ready to concede that this will be denied him. Nevertheless, he is far from hopeless. If he were writing I Thess. 4:15 now, he might change the pronouns, but the assurance would still stand, to wit: "*You* which are alive and remain unto the coming of the Lord shall not prevent *us* which are asleep." He is still radiantly confident of that glorious coming and of the **heavenly kingdom** which it will usher in.

Section X *Final Greetings and Benediction*

II Timothy 4:19-22

No matter how tragic the apostle's own circumstances might be, he remained gratefully mindful of his friends. **Salute Prisca and Aquila, and the household of Onesiphorus** (19). **Prisca,** otherwise known as Priscilla (Acts 18:2), and her husband, **Aquila,** were among Paul's oldest friends in the gospel. They were Romans and had come to Corinth (see map 1), where the apostle met them. Later they moved on to Ephesus and were influential in the establishment of the church there. The apostle's greeting suggests that they stayed on in Ephesus. The greeting to **the household of Onesiphorus** implies that this noble Christian to whom tribute is paid earlier (1:16), was indeed dead; otherwise he would have been included in the salute.

Information concerning two other of the apostle's erstwhile companions is contained in 20: **Erastus abode at Corinth: but Trophimus have I left at Miletum sick** (see map 1). Two men named **Erastus** appear in the New Testament. One is mentioned by Paul in Rom. 16:23 and is described as "the chamberlain of the city" (of Corinth). Another appears in Acts 19:22 as the companion of Timothy on a mission to Macedonia. It is probably this latter Erastus concerning whose whereabouts Paul is sending words to his old friend Timothy. The note concerning **Trophimus** is obscure. This man had been a traveling companion of the apostle on several important journeys. But we are not told the occasion of his falling ill in Miletum.

Paul now returns to his earlier plea for a visit from Timothy before it is too late: **Do thy diligence to come before winter** (21). Here again appears the sense of urgency which pervades all of this Epistle. Winter storms will, before long, make sailing hazardous and he urges Timothy to make the trip soon.

There were some of the Christians in Rome whose names have been immortalized by their being included in Paul's letter: **Eubulus greeteth thee, and Pudens, and Linus, and Claudia, and all the brethren.** Nothing more than their names is known of these believers. Mention of these Roman friends of the apostle should not be construed as in violation of his statement in 16 that "all men forsook me," for there he is speaking of his arraignment. There were some Christians in Rome who, though timorous, still loved the apostle.

The final benediction is a moving one, constituting as it does Paul's last words for posterity. They are addressed to Timothy, but they include us all as well: **The Lord Jesus Christ be with thy spirit. Grace be with you. Amen** (22).

Outline

THE EPISTLE TO TITUS

I. Salutation, 1:1-4

II. Qualifications of Elders and Bishops, 1:5-9

III. False Teachers Must Be Refuted, 1:10-16

IV. Standards of Christian Conduct, 2:1-10
- A. Standards for the Aged, 2:1-3
- B. Standards for Younger People, 2:4-8
- C. Standards for Those Who Are Slaves, 2:9-10

V. Readiness for Christ's Coming, 2:11-15

VI. Christians in a Pagan World, 3:1-7
- A. Be Good Citizens, 3:1-2
- B. Christians Are Transformed by Grace, 3:3-7

VII. Closing Admonitions, 3:8-11
- A. Keep Busy for Christ, 3:8
- B. Avoid Futile Controversies, 3:9-11

VIII. Conclusion, 3:12-15

Section I *Salutation*

Titus 1:1-4

The Epistle to Titus is of a type similar to the letters to Timothy, with its principal concern advice to a young pastor by his senior supervisor. But pastoral concerns are jostled by personal matters in this letter, as in those to Timothy. Though its position in the New Testament follows II Timothy, its chronological position probably should be between the two letters to Timothy. We are sure it preceded II Timothy, for the apostle was still a free man when he wrote it. But whether it precedes or follows I Timothy is difficult to say.

The opening sentence in the KJV takes up the first four verses, a sentence which the NEB breaks into three sentences. The salutation is distinguished by its length, which exceeds considerably the salutations of the other pastorals. **Paul, a servant of God, and an apostle of Jesus Christ, according to the faith of God's elect, and the acknowledging of the truth which is after godliness** (1). The apostle characterizes himself as the *doulos* of God, a term which means literally "slave." Perhaps some softer translation, such as "bondservant," would be a more fitting rendering of Paul's meaning. Elsewhere he has described himself as the slave or bondservant of Jesus Christ (e.g., Rom. 1:1), but only here as **a servant of God.**

Linked with this menial self-description is the further characterization **an apostle of Jesus Christ,** a term which means "envoy" or "messenger." The clauses which follow this designation are difficult and involved, both in the original Greek and the King James translation. **According to the faith of God's elect, and the acknowledging of the truth which is after godliness**— these are the problem clauses. Are they intended to modify the term **apostle?** Or are they designed to suggest the direction and thrust of the apostle's ministry? The NEB adopts the former interpretation and consequently renders it thus: "marked as such by faith and knowledge and hope." But the RSV favors the latter and translates the passage: "to further the faith of God's elect and their knowledge of the truth which accords with godliness." We favor the latter interpretation. Paul's apostolate is not demonstrated or verified by **the faith of God's elect;** on the contrary, that faith is encouraged, nourished, and sustained by the apostle's ministry.

This faith, however, and the truth which it acknowledges, are never an end in themselves. They look toward a glorious fulfillment: **In hope of eternal life, which God, that cannot lie, promised before the world began** (2). The **hope of eternal life,** as the phrase is employed here, does not mean simply that the apostle is sustained in his labor by this hope: it means further that the hope of eternal life is an essential part of the message which the apostle is propagating. Here is a promise God made **before the world began.** Just as Christ is "the Lamb slain from the foundation of the world" (Rev. 13:8), so is this promise made to all men who receive new life through Christ. This is unshakable truth, spoken by the God of truth, a God **that cannot lie.**

This eternal purpose and will of God is now made known: **But hath in due times manifested his word through preaching, which is committed unto me according to the commandment of God our Saviour** (3). Here again, as in every New Testament reference to his divine commission, the apostle reveals his overwhelming wonder that he should be entrusted with such a responsibility. We who follow in his train are not apostles as Paul was, but ours is a task of such magnitude and importance that beside it every other business on earth becomes secondary. Let no minister of Christ ever allow himself to think meanly or disparagingly of the commission his Lord has laid upon him.

To Titus, mine own son after the common faith: Grace, mercy, and peace, from God the Father and the Lord Jesus Christ our Saviour (4). Titus is not mentioned in the Acts of the Apostles among Paul's assistants, though he is mentioned a number of times in II Corinthians, and in Galatians and II Timothy. He was a Greek and was probably won to Christ by the apostle's ministry. When the Judaizing controversy arose, Acts 15:2 tells us that the brethren determined that "Paul and Barnabas, and certain other of them, should go up to Jerusalem unto the apostles and elders about this question." Paul tells us (Gal. 2:3) that among these "certain other of them" was Titus (assuming that this was the same visit to Jerusalem). This young man appears later in Paul's second letter to the Corinthians, where there are eight references to him, which reveal him as a trusted helper of the apostle. In II Tim. 4:10 we read that Titus was engaged in a mission to Dalmatia. At the time of Paul's letter to Titus, the younger man is the apostle's representative in Crete (see map 1), where he was evidently pastor of the Christian church.

Paul addresses Titus as **mine own son after the common faith,** an expression which is rendered even more precise by the NEB: "my true-born son in the faith which we share." The benediction which follows is typically Pauline in its character, conferring an additional note of authenticity on this Epistle. **Grace, mercy, and peace, from God the Father and the Lord Jesus Christ our Saviour.**

Section II *Qualifications of Elders and Bishops*

Titus 1:5-9

The apostle launches abruptly into the concern which prompted him to write this letter. Missing is any expression of appreciation or thanksgiving for Titus such as appears in II Tim. 1:3-5 (though this is missing also from I Timothy). **For this cause I left thee in Crete, that thou shouldest set in order the things that are wanting, and ordain elders in every city, as I had appointed thee** (5). It seems evident that Paul had lately been in Crete himself, with Titus serving as his assistant. There is no historical record in the Acts of the Apostles covering this Cretan campaign. The Acts terminates abruptly with the concluding events of Paul's first imprisonment in Rome. Our thesis, which makes possible the Pauline authorship of the Pastoral Epistles, is that the apostle was set free and allowed to continue his work. Although there is no account of these final years of the apostle's life, they could well have made possible the extensive evangelization of the island of Crete. How extensive that activity was is suggested by the fact that Titus was charged to **ordain elders in every city.** Paul's ministry in Crete had recently ended; but Titus, his assistant, was left behind by the apostle to complete the task of organizing the churches. Paul's language suggests that not all was well in the Cretan churches and that part of Titus' task was to correct what was amiss.

Titus was instructed to appoint and ordain elders for the churches. This was in keeping with the apostle's custom. As early as his first missionary journey, Luke tells us that "when they had ordained them elders in every church, and had prayed with fasting, they commended them to the Lord, on whom they believed" (Acts 14:23). There is a difference in the apostle's instruction in I Timothy and Titus. In the former the existence of elders is assumed, while in the latter, due probably to the newness of the Cretan church, elders are to be designated for the first time.

The sort of men to be selected for this important office are then described: **If any be blameless, the husband of one wife, having faithful children not accused of riot or unruly** (6). These qualifications which elders must possess are similar to the list of qualifications of a bishop in I Timothy 3. **Blameless** means having "unimpeachable character" (NEB). This is a quality of great importance. The Christian minister must be one who not only avoids evil, but who avoids the very appearance of evil. In every respect his conduct must be above reproach. Moreover, his marital relationships must be unsullied by any breath of scandal. **The husband of one wife** was taken by many in the Early Church to be a prohibition against second marriages for any reason. The obvious reference here would seem to be to dual marriages. The Christian mores of our day certainly do not frown on the second marriage of one whose first wife has died. Yet this is an area in which discretion should be observed. The scandal of divorce has so thoroughly poisoned the stream of the social order in our day that the utmost wisdom and caution should be employed in this matter of second marriages, "that the ministry be not blamed" (II Cor. 6:3).

Having faithful children is an expression calling for some consideration. Its real meaning is captured by the NEB: "the father of children who are believers." The stipulation laid down in I Tim. 3:4 says only: "having his children in subjection with all gravity." But Paul goes beyond this in insisting that in Crete men who are set apart for the office of elder must have been successful in commending the Christian faith to their children. It is true, of course, that no parent can control or determine the moral and spiritual decisions of his children. Sometimes, despite our best and most sincere efforts, our children in their freedom make choices which are heartbreaking for their parents. But nothing does more to commend the sincerity and devotion of a godly minister than the fact that his children are following him as he follows Christ.

Not accused of riot or unruly is, in a sense, the alternative to **faithful**. The RSV clarifies the phrase by rendering it "not open to the charge of being profligate or insubordinate."

For a bishop must be blameless, as the steward of God; not selfwilled, not soon angry, not given to wine, no striker, not given to filthy lucre (7). The subject of this additional list of qualifications is the singular **bishop**, rather than the plural "elders." Barrett observes that "the change from plural (elders) to singular (bishop) is best accounted for not by supposing that in each town there was a group of elders but only one bishop, but by the view . . . that whereas *elder* describes an official, *bishop* describes his function: The elders you appoint must have certain qualifications, for a man who exercises oversight must be"[1] **not selfwilled, not soon angry,** etc.

The quality of blamelessness—"unimpeachable character"—appears again because the responsibility of the bishop is to serve **as the steward of God.** The term **steward** means literally "the manager of a household or family" (Kelly). The bishop was the chief financial officer of the local church and for this, if for no other reason, he should be a man of the utmost integrity.

The apostle then lists five vices from which a bishop must be conspicuously free. They are all character flaws which, if tolerated in a church leader, would be certain to accomplish his ruin. A man **selfwilled** is bound to be arrogant, opinionated, and stubborn. A characteristic such as this would be a complete betrayal of the spirit of the Master. A man **soon angry** would be hot-tempered, vindictive, and totally lacking in the patience which is so essential to a servant of Christ. **Not given to wine** is an expression which continually surprises us in a context such as this. Yet it was a very real problem in the first-century Church. The production of wine was carried on everywhere throughout the Mediterranean basin, and the temptation to use it, and that to excess, abounded on every hand. **No striker** suggests the temptation to violent or high-handed action, which must certainly have been presented occasionally to local leaders in the Early Church. **Not given to filthy lucre** is another earthy characteristic against which Paul warns. As the custodian of the church's funds this could become a source of temptation to a man.

To offset this list of five vices to be avoided, Paul follows with a list of six virtues to be cultivated by church leaders: **A lover of hospitality, a lover of good men, sober, just, holy, temperate** (8). The duty of hospitality is named in Paul's list of qualifications of a bishop in I Tim. 3:2, and is repeated here. As the leader of the church it became the bishop's responsibility to entertain the visiting apostles and evangelists who came by in their travels. Only in modern times has the "spare room" in the home been replaced by hotels and motels for the housing of guests. In first-century Crete hospitality was an important asset for the church leader.

[1]*Op. cit.*, p. 129.

A lover of good men is a rather forced translation. Its literal meaning is "good-loving" or "right-minded." The RSV renders it "a lover of goodness." One is reminded of Paul's admonition in Phil. 4:8, "Finally, brethren, whatsoever things are just, whatsoever things are pure, whatsoever things are lovely, whatsoever things are of good report; if there be any virtue, and if there be any praise, think on these things." To follow this instruction is to be a lover of goodness, a characteristic which in a minister of Christ's Church should be outstanding.

The term translated by the word **sober** is very close in meaning to the word **temperate,** which appears in this same list of virtues. Both terms suggest self-mastery or self-control, the ability to deal objectively with difficult situations without being swayed by prejudice. Barclay in his translation prefers the word "prudence," and quotes Trench's definition of the term as "entire command over the passions and desires, so that they receive no further allowance than that which the law and right reason admit and approve."[2] The qualities denoted by the terms **just** and **holy** suggest strictly religious ideas. But it seems likely that the former should be understood, not as referring to the man's standing before God, as one justified by faith through grace, but rather to his ability to deal justly with his fellowmen, to administer his office with scrupulous fairness and unimpeachable integrity. The term **holy** is rendered by "devout" in the NEB, and suggests the quality of godliness, the quality of warm, loving personal relationship to Christ. But Barclay tells us that even more is suggested by this term; "for it describes the man who reverences the fundamental decencies of life, the things which go back beyond any man-made law or regulation."[3]

The apostle introduces in 9 a further requirement: **Holding fast the faithful word as he hath been taught, that he may be able by sound doctrine both to exhort and to convince the gainsayers.** Here is a theme which appears in I Timothy, though not with quite this degree of emphasis. In I Tim. 5:17, Paul singles out those elders "who labour in the word and doctrine" as "worthy of double honour." But here in the Epistle to Titus competence in this area is expected of all elders. It is surely a ministry such as this to which God calls men when He issues to them the divine summons to go and preach. It is the preacher's

[2]*Op. cit.*, p. 273.
[3]*Ibid.*

business to "offer men Christ," as Charles Wesley loved to put it. This central task of preaching is described lyrically in his lines:

> *O let me commend my Saviour to you;*
> *The publican's Friend, and Advocate too:*
> *For you he is pleading his merits and death;*
> *With God interceding for sinners beneath.*

But to preach Christ and commend Him to others is to know the sure Word of God concerning Him, to hold it in reverent regard, and to declare its truth to others. In these pastoral letters Paul is interested vitally in **sound doctrine.** The Church's message had by this time taken shape in creeds and baptismal formulas. We see fragments of such credal statements cropping out in the letters to Timothy. Each new generation of Christian leaders faces the necessity for declaring anew the basic tenets of the Christian faith and justifying them in the minds and consciences of their hearers. But sound doctrine includes also ethical precepts, indicating how all Christians, male and female, younger and older, bond and free, should live in a Christ-rejecting world. All of this is involved in the task of exhorting and convincing the **gainsayers**—those who deny and contradict the truth.

Section III *False Teachers Must Be Refuted*

Titus 1:10-16

This portion of the chapter suggests the reason for the sense of urgency which pervades the apostle's exhortation to Titus to get busy setting up a qualified leadership in the Cretan churches. There was much work for such leaders to do. **For there are many unruly and vain talkers and deceivers, specially they of the circumcision** (10). The NEB renders this verse in a form that gives a somewhat more pointed meaning: "There are all too many, especially among Jewish converts, who are out of all control." The phrase **they of the circumcision** is not here to be understood as an allusion to the old Judaizing controversy, with which Paul's letter to the Galatians is concerned. It is rather to be regarded as a reference to the Jews who were converts to the Christian faith. It is evident that many such persons were refusing to accept the standards of conduct prescribed for Christians. The apostle describes these persons as "empty-headed," futile in their talk. Such practices are far from being harmless, for those indulging in them are both self-deceived and deceivers of others.

The apostle's warning continues in 11: **Whose mouths must be stopped, who subvert whole houses, teaching things which they ought not, for filthy lucre's sake.** Up to this point no real hint is given as to the precise nature of this false teaching, though later in the chapter some intimations begin to emerge. But the dangerous extent of the defection from the faith is clearly implied in the observation that **whole houses** were being led astray. These proponents of falsehood were, as the RSV puts it, "teaching . . . what they have no right to teach." Any teaching that leaves one worse than it finds him is false. Of course, truth should grapple with men's minds and make them rethink some of their basic ideas. As Barclay puts it, "Christianity does not run away from doubts and questions, but faces them fairly and squarely. It is true that the truth often mentally takes a man by the scruff of the neck and shakes him; but it is also true that teaching which ends in nothing but doubts and questionings is bad teaching."[1]

[1]*Ibid.*, p. 276.

Evidently it was teaching of this character against which Paul warns. And to add further to the apostle's condemnation is the motive which underlay these reprehensible activities: it was being done **for filthy lucre's sake.** Such deceivers were actuated solely by the profit motive. No wonder the apostle declares that their **mouths must be stopped!** Kelly points out that this translation "preserves the vigorous metaphor of the Greek . . . which means to put a muzzle, not simply a bridle, on an animal's mouth."[2]

The mood of 12 is frankly astonishing, even though the apostle is speaking under strong provocation. **One of themselves, even a prophet of their own, said, The Cretians are always liars, evil beasts, slow bellies** ("lazy and greedy," Phillips). There is some uncertainty as to the identity of this **prophet of their own.** Clement of Alexandria says that he was Epimenides of Cnossus, in Crete, who lived in the sixth century B.C. Whether the line is his or not, the judgment concerning the Cretans was, rightly or wrongly, the commonly held opinion of the first century. Kelly points out concerning "the shocking reputation for mendacity which the Cretans had in the ancient world" that "so prevalent was this that the verb 'to Cretize' (Gk. *Kretizein*) was a slang word for lying or cheating."[3] It is indicative of the apostle's strong feeling concerning the threat to the existence and integrity of the Cretan churches that he went to the length of citing this quotation. On its face this verse would appear more likely to give offence than to make friends. Perhaps the people who really were essential to the future of the church in Crete would be willing to agree that the poet's judgment was a fair one.

At any rate Paul agreed with it and says so bluntly: **This witness is true. Wherefore rebuke them sharply, that they may be sound in the faith; not giving heed to Jewish fables, and commandments of men, that turn from the truth** (13-14). Barclay suggests the unsettling emphasis which **Jewish fables, and commandments of men** might exert when he says: "The great characteristic of the Jewish faith was its thousands of rules and regulations. This, that and the next thing was branded and listed as unclean; this, that and the next food was held to be tabu; when Judaism and Gnosticism joined hands even the body became unclean, and marriage and the natural instincts of the body

[2]*Op. cit.*, p. 234.

[3]*Ibid.*, p. 235.

were held to be evil. The inevitable result of this was that long lists of sins were constantly being created. It became a sin to touch this or that; it became a sin to marry and to beget children. Things which were either good in themselves or quite natural became defiled and polluted."[4] Such was the ascetic legalism to which the false teachers in the Cretan churches would reduce Christianity. It was a heresy markedly similar to that which Paul denounced in his Epistle to the Colossians.

The truth of this diagnosis of the Cretan problem is confirmed by the apostle's next words: **Unto the pure all things are pure: but unto them that are defiled and unbelieving is nothing pure; but even their mind and conscience is defiled** (15). Paul is affirming a vitally important principle in this passage, but it is a generalization which it is quite possible to misuse. "Have we not all heard these words misapplied?" asks G. H. Morrison, and he continues: "The commonest misuse of them is this. Something offensive has been spoken, something coarse or allusively indecent, and one of the company with a hot heart has protested against the evil utterance; whereon immediately, sometimes with a smile, oftener with the suspicion of a sneer, he is told that unto the pure all things are pure. The devil can cite Scripture for his purpose, and such a citation is the devil's handiwork. . . . There are things that are everywhere and always right, and there are things that are everywhere and always wrong, and there is little hope for any man who has learned to tamper with these fixities."[5] Paul's words may be, as some contend, a popular proverb. But they must be understood here in the context of the Jewish **commandments of men** which he is denouncing. They have the same meaning here as appears in the saying of Jesus recorded in Mark 7:15: "There is nothing from without a man, that entering into him can defile him: but the things which come out of him, those are they that defile the man."

The apostle is equally emphatic in stating the negative of this principle, and with particular application to the false teachers in Crete. To those who are **defiled and unbelieving**—the order in which these terms appear is significant—everything is defiled. Such a man "can take the loveliest things and cover them with a smutted uncleanness. He can see an unclean jest where there is no uncleanness. But the man whose mind is pure

[4]*Op. cit.*, p. 279.

[5]*The Afterglow of God* (London: Hodder and Stoughton, 1912), p. 27.

finds all things pure. It is a terrible thing to have that film of uncleanness and impurity in the mind."[6] When the **mind** is depraved and the **conscience** is seared, little hope of recovery to the truth remains.

The apostle carries his denunciation one stage further: **They profess that they know God; but in works they deny him, being abominable, and disobedient, and unto every good work reprobate** (16). This is as strong language as Paul ever employs, and the fact that he speaks so forcefully here reveals the depth of his feeling about these dissemblers who were subverting the work of Christ in Crete. Yet, though their evil influence was so profound and far-reaching, they claimed for themselves that they (and probably they only) knew God. There are some interpreters who see in this prideful claim evidence of the typical Gnostic self-assertiveness. And it is true that central to Gnosticism was the claim to a special knowledge of God which was denied to those less fortunate. But the evidence in 14 suggests that the false teachings in Crete were Jewish in origin rather than Gnostic, though not without some admixture of Gnostic influence. Kelly is probably correct when he observes that "it was the special boast of the Jews that, unlike the pagan world, they knew God as he had revealed himself to men" (cf. Gal. 4:8; I Thess. 4:5; II Thess. 1:8). As the Cretan heretics were Judaizers, it is therefore possible that the Apostle is criticizing the complacent assumption that they were an elite possessing privileged knowledge of God."[7] Indeed, their false assurance may have stemmed from a mingling of these two factors.

But as the apostle sees it, theirs is a confidence utterly without foundation. The palpable fact that **in works they deny him** is conclusive evidence of their falsity. I John 2:6 lays down a rule which must guide all who profess to know Christ: "He that saith he abideth in him ought himself also so to walk, even as he walked." In the pungent English of the Phillips translation this becomes even stronger: "The life of a man who professes to be living in God must bear the stamp of Christ." This mark, this brand of identity and ownership was totally lacking in these self-assured teachers. Indeed, as Paul describes them they appear to be utterly loathsome. The first adjective—translated **abominable**—comes from "a noun which denotes what causes

[6]Barclay, *op. cit.*, p. 280.

[7]*Op. cit.*, p. 237.

horror and disgust to God."[8] The term **disobedient** suggests an attitude of insubordination toward the leadership of the apostle and hence toward the way of God's truth as taught by him. Finally, the expression **unto every good work reprobate** should be set in contrast with Paul's phrase in II Tim. 3:17 where he describes the perfect man of God as "throughly furnished unto all good works." The vast ethical distance between these two extremes needs no further comment.

[8]*Ibid.*, p. 238.

Section IV *Standards of Christian Conduct*

Titus 2:1-10

A. Standards for the Aged, 2:1-3

From the laying down of the standards of life to which Christian leaders should conform, and the castigation of the evil obstructionists who were imperiling the integrity of the churches, Paul turns now to a pastoral concern for the Cretan believers. He addresses Titus pointedly: **But speak thou the things which become sound doctrine** (1). The word rendered **thou** is emphatic. As over against the falsity of the opponents' position, it becomes the duty of Titus to stand forth boldly for the truth. Here again is evident Paul's concern for the deposit of **sound doctrine** which is the Church's precious heritage. But it is not doctrine in the sense of dogma, the verbal formulation of Christian truth, which he has in mind. It is rather the proper ethical consequences which must ever flow from Christian truth. This is made abundantly clear in the verses immediately following.

That the aged men be sober, grave, temperate, sound in faith, in charity, in patience (2). The gospel of Christ must not only change one's mode of thinking, but must bear fruit in transformed living. It was this mighty transformation which made the Early Church invincible. How did the Christian Church overthrow the entrenched paganisms of the Roman Empire? T. R. Glover's answer is that "the Christian 'out-lived' the pagan, 'out-died' him, and 'out-thought' him."[1] At every point the Christian exceeded by far the highest standards the pagan world knew. This is here illustrated clearly. The first three character marks enjoined upon **the aged men** are stated thus: **be sober, grave, temperate.** The term **sober** is to be understood in the sense of "temperate"—temperance in the use of wine, to be sure, but also an attitude of moderation in all of the indulgences of life. The term rendered **grave** in the KJV appears in I Tim. 3:8, 11, where it is applied to deacons and their wives. It suggests a seriousness of purpose which, as Guthrie points out, "particularly

[1] *The Jesus of History* (New York: George H. Doran Co., 1917), pp. 200-201.

suits the dignity of seniors, yet," he cautions, "gravity must never be confused with gloominess."[2] The third term, **temperate,** means properly self-disciplined; Moffatt translates it "masters of themselves."

Thus far it might have been possible for the Stoic ethical teachers of the first century to go. But Paul does not end his list of character marks here. He adds three more, each of which is pronouncedly Christian: **That the aged men be . . . sound in faith, in charity** (love), **in patience** (2). E. F. Scott reminds us that "for Paul the cardinal Christian virtues are faith, hope, and love," as I Cor. 13:13 makes abundantly clear. But concerning the substitution of patience for hope, Scott further observes that "perhaps he thinks of hope as included in the faith which lays hold of the life to come. Or perhaps he sets patience in the place of hope because he is thinking specially of old men, whose attitude to life is now one of resignation."[3]

The soundness in faith of which Paul speaks is not to be understood here as soundness in doctrine, however important such soundness may be. It is rather that vigorous, healthy faith which binds a man savingly to Christ which Paul is stressing. Linked with it is that divine love (*agape*) which is so graciously shed abroad in the hearts of those who are yielded to the sway of Christ. **Patience,** the third virtue of this second triad, is the strength and purpose of heart to see the Christian life through to the end. It is rendered in the RSV by "steadfastness," and in the NEB by "endurance." These are the spiritual qualities which enrich the mature years of life.

The aged women likewise, that they be in behaviour as becometh holiness, not false accusers, not given to much wine, teachers of good things (3). The apostle admonishes the elderly women in the Church that they cultivate virtues similar to those insisted upon for the older men. The term **likewise** suggests this parallel. But he is most specific in his demands upon them. The phrase **in behaviour as becometh holiness** is rendered in the modern versions by the expression "reverent in behavior." The term translated "reverent" literally means "to demean oneself as a priestess in discharge of her duties." Here is pictured the mature woman who is dedicated to godliness. The figure of the

[2]*The Pastoral Epistles,* p. 191.
[3]*Op. cit.,* p. 163.

"mother in Israel" (Judg. 5:7) has all but disappeared from the Modern Church. The saintly women of other days are in desperately short supply today. Women who know Christ and love Him, women for whom the privilege of ministering to the Lord is life's highest joy, women such as graced the Bethany household of Mary and Martha—such women are needed in the Church today—and tomorrow.

It hardly need be added that such godly women would not need the apostle's next stipulation: **not false accusers, not given to much wine**—which, when translated into the earthy language of the NEB, becomes: "not scandal-mongers or slaves to strong drink."

The further specification—**teachers of good things**—is not to be understood in any sense which would violate the apostle's rule as laid down in I Tim. 2:12. Paul's insistence that women must not teach publicly in the churches is presumed to be as valid for the Cretan churches as for the church in Ephesus. The teaching which the apostle has in mind is probably that which emanates from a godly example, supplemented by advice and encouragement given privately. This duty laid upon the elderly women forms the transition to the apostle's exhortation to younger women.

B. Standards for Younger People, 2:4-8

It is the duty of older women to **teach the young women to be sober, to love their husbands, to love their children** (4). Here surely is one of the essential ingredients in a happy and Christian home. Love of husband and children was a virtue celebrated among pagans and Christians alike. Kelly quotes from a gravestone found in Pergamum, in Mysia (see map 1), the following fragment of an inscription: "Julius Bassus . . . to his most sweet wife, devoted to her husband and devoted to her children."[4] However ideal such virtues may be, it is a melancholy fact they are too often honored in the breach rather than the observance.

But the apostle's standard imposed upon young women continues: **To be discreet, chaste, keepers at home, good, obedient to their own husbands, that the word of God be not blasphemed** (5). This entire passage, to be understood, must be seen against

[4] *Op. cit.*, pp. 240 ff.

the background of Greek custom. Barclay points out that "in the ancient Greek world the respectable woman lived a completely secluded life. In the house she had her own quarters, and she seldom left them, not even to sit at meals with the menfolk of the family; and into them came no man, except only her husband. She never attended any public assemblies or meetings; she seldom appeared on the streets, and if she did . . . she never appeared alone."[5] To women thus cloistered the Christian faith came with a marvelous liberating power. Indeed, it would be an easy thing for such an emancipation to go to scandalous extremes when viewed against the background of this traditional seclusion. If the standard Paul lays down seems narrow and circumscribed, it must be understood against the background of the standards of the first century.

The term **discreet** is rendered by Moffatt "mistress of themselves." This same virtue is reflected in the term **chaste,** which in its New Testament use always denotes purity. **Keepers at home** is the down-to-earth quality of good housekeeping. Moffatt's word for this virtue is "domestic." The term rendered **good** has the meaning of kind, sympathetic, and understanding. **Obedient to their own husbands** is an attitude which the apostle seeks frequently to inculcate (Eph. 5:22; Col. 3:18). It is an old-fashioned virtue and one definitely out of favor with the modern young woman. But it does suggest an attitude of deference toward the husband she loves. In turn it calls for a kindness and understanding and reasonableness on the part of the husband which would go far toward making this virtue commendable in our day.

Paul makes these demands for a very basic Christian reason: **that the word of God be not blasphemed.** It would be fatal for the Church if it were laid open to the accusation that the freedoms it bestowed on its members were subversive of the ideals of homelife. Moffatt's putting of this point is fully justified: "Otherwise it will be a scandal to the gospel."

The apostle then turns to the younger men: **Young men likewise exhort to be sober minded** (6). The responsibility to be **sober minded** is not only laid upon the young men, but also upon Titus, whose task it is to **exhort** them to this end. This term in the Greek is considerably stronger than the verb rendered

[5]*Op. cit.*, p. 286.

"speak" in the first verse of this chapter. Many of the modern versions use the term "urge." The virtue to which Titus is expected to urge them, rendered **sober minded** in the KJV, is the Stoic virtue of self-control. Phillips puts it thus: "The young men, too, you should urge to take life seriously." And 7 continues in the same vein: **In all things shewing thyself a pattern of good works.** There is some uncertainty as to whether the phrase **in all things** goes with the admonition to Titus or belongs rather to the sober-mindedness of 6. Either opinion is feasible, for it is purely a matter of punctuation. Whichever is the correct view, the phrase emphasizes the wide scope of this virtue. Titus is advised not only to inculcate it, but also to exhibit it in his own conduct. Example is far more potent than advice, and men are going to follow us as we follow Christ, whether we follow closely or afar off.

The apostle's exhortation to Titus continues: **In doctrine shewing uncorruptness, gravity, sincerity, sound speech, that cannot be condemned; that he that is of the contrary part may be ashamed, having no evil thing to say of you** (7-8). It is evident that Paul is fully as concerned with Titus' teaching as with his conduct. The NEB renders 7*b* thus: "In your teaching, you must show integrity and high principle." Titus is urged to use **sound speech, that cannot be condemned.** Phillips construes this passage: "Your speech should be unaffected and logical, so that your opponent may feel ashamed at finding nothing in which to pick holes." Titus was expected to be an apologist for the Christian faith in Crete (using "apology" in its correct theological sense as proclaiming and supporting).

C. Standards for Those Who Are Slaves, 2:9-10

Again, as in I Tim. 6:1, we encounter the fact of human slavery. This curse of the ancient world existed in Crete as elsewhere throughout the Roman Empire. In the churches in Crete it is evident that slaves as well as masters were obedient to the faith. The apostle adds to his admonitions, therefore, some that relate to the Christian conduct of slaves. **Exhort servants to be obedient unto their own masters, and to please them in all things** (9). It is probable that Paul is thinking here of Christian slaves who were the property of Christian masters, and of whom no activity inconsistent with their Christian profession would be required. It is probable that those Christian slaves who had heathen masters were faced by many difficult decisions. It is not likely that Paul would require unquestioning obedience in such a case. But in Christian households slaves should maintain an attitude of submission; as the NEB puts it, "Tell slaves to respect their masters' authority in everything." It would be a real temptation to such slaves, who realized their complete equality with their masters in God's sight, to presume upon this Christian relationship in business and domestic matters.

The apostle spells out in detail the sort of conduct which should characterize slaves under these conditions: **Not answering again; not purloining, but shewing all good fidelity; that they may adorn the doctrine of God our Saviour in all things** (9-10). **Not answering again** means obedience to masters without any back talk. To accept orders and instruction in a submissive and cooperative spirit would be a convincing mark of Christian behavior. **Purloining** means petty thievery, a practice which could be easily carried on by a slave who had access to his master's possessions. Honesty and trustworthiness must be marks of a Christian character in every conceivable life situation. The standard of life for the Christian slave must be one that, in Paul's phrase, will **adorn the doctrine of God our Saviour.** Moffatt uses the expression "an ornament to the doctrine," while the NEB renders this passage: "they will add lustre to the doctrine." Paul's phrase has become a familiar and frequently used characterization of outstanding Christian conduct. We employ it often in describing behavior that is conspicuously Christian. But we do not often reflect that in its original setting it is addressed to Christian slaves.

Section V *Readiness for Christ's Coming*

Titus 2:11-15

The mention of "God our Saviour" (10) suggests to the apostle the thought of the next few verses, a passage that is indeed sublime. **For the grace of God that bringeth salvation hath appeared to all men** (11). Here begins the apostle's statement of the theological grounds for all that has gone before in this Epistle. By **the grace of God** Paul means the free, unmerited favor of God which is made available to all men through the redeeming office of Jesus Christ and the faithful ministry of the Holy Spirit. In one sense, of course, this grace may not have as yet appeared to all men. Not all men have yet heard, even at this late hour, that God has given His only begotten Son to redeem and save us. And insofar as this is true, it is to the shame of the Church, whose Lord laid upon it centuries ago the commission, "Go ye therefore, and teach all nations" (Matt. 28: 19). In another sense, though some may have never heard of Christ, yet the prevenient grace of God is flowing to all men everywhere. This grace is unconditioned and not dependent upon the individual's faith, but ministered freely to the whole human race as a universal benefit of the atonement. Speaking of the fact of universal human responsibility before God, John Wesley writes:

> Allowing that all the souls of men are dead in sin by *nature,* this excuses none, seeing there is no man that is in a state of mere nature; there is no man, unless he has quenched the Spirit, that is wholly void of the grace of God. No man living is entirely destitute of what is vulgarly called *natural conscience.* But this is not natural: It is more properly termed, *preventing* [prevenient] *grace.* Every man has a greater or less measure of this, which waiteth not for the call of man. Every one has, sooner or later, good desires; although the generality of men stifle them before they can strike deep root, or produce any considerable fruit. Every one has some measure of that light, some faint glimmering ray, which, sooner or later, more or less, enlightens every man that cometh into the world. And every one, unless he be one of the small number whose conscience is seared as with a hot iron, feels more or less uneasy when he acts contrary to the light of his own conscience. So that no man sins because he has not grace, but because he does not use the grace which he hath.[1]

[1]"On Working Out Our Own Salvation," *Works* (Jackson ed., Kansas City: Nazarene Publishing House, n.d.), VI, 512.

By the same token, it is true that, as the NEB puts it, "the grace of God has dawned upon the world with healing for all mankind." Here is universal provision for our universal need. Though some may reject this grace and refuse to have any part in Christ, yet provision has been made for their salvation and they may claim it if they will.

Paul continues: **Teaching us that, denying ungodliness and worldly lusts, we should live soberly, righteously, and godly, in this present world** (12). This verse could well serve as a summary of the ethical demands imposed upon men by the Christian message which Paul preached. It has both a negative and a positive emphasis. Its first demand is that we deny **ungodliness and worldly lusts.** This does not mean that one must strike off his own chains, which is something that no man can do. It is our task, as we are helped by the Spirit, to renounce "godless ways and worldly desires," and by Christian discipline to live above such sordid and selfish things; but it is by the grace and power of God that our deliverance is wrought.

The positive demand of God's grace is the converse of this negative requirement. **We should live soberly, righteously, and godly, in this present world.** Moffatt's rendering speaks in contemporary terms: "To live a life of self-mastery, of integrity and of godliness."

Scott points out that these three words describe man's life in its threefold relation—(1) To himself; (2) To his fellowmen; and (3) To God. He must learn to control his own passions, to deal justly with his neighbors, to worship God and obey Him.[2]

Moreover, this is the Christian prescription for living **in this present world.** No quarter is ever given by the apostle to the idea of sin in the lives of Christians in the first-century Church.

Looking for that blessed hope, and the glorious appearing of the great God and our Saviour Jesus Christ (13). Our Lord's second appearing was still Paul's blessed hope, even though he stood very close to martyrdom himself. Plummer points out concerning this entire paragraph that in it Paul "once more insists upon the inseparable connexion between creed and character, doctrine and life, and intimates the close relations between the past, the present, and the future in the Christian scheme of salvation. There are certain facts in the past, which must be be-

[2]*Op. cit.*, p. 168.

lieved; and there is a kind of life in the present, which must be lived; and there are things in store for us in the future, which must be looked for. Thus the three great virtues of faith, charity, and hope are inculcated."[3]

Paul's term, the **blessed hope,** has become one of the most familiar of our designations for the Church's expectation of the return of Christ. This hope has been a radiant one in every era of the Church's life. Some, who are compelled to recognize that in the apostle's earlier writings the belief that Christ Jesus would come again was a central idea, would have us believe that he had come to recognize this earlier view as a mistaken one. It is true, of course, that Paul's earnest hope that this event would take place during his lifetime had to be relinquished as certain death drew near. But this letter to Titus dates from that very period. The testimony of 13 bears eloquent witness to the apostle's continuing confidence that God would yet bring to pass this glorious consummation. Kelly, who suggests that this verse "is perhaps an excerpt from a Christian hymn or liturgical formula," remarks further that it "contains a glowing expression of the eschatological expectation of the primitive Church, which impatiently awaited the Lord's second coming at the right hand of God."[4]

A difficulty of some magnitude for Bible scholars arises in our attempt properly to construe Paul's language here. There are two possible renderings of 13; one is that of the KJV: **the glorious appearing of the great God and our Saviour Jesus Christ.** The second is suggested in the margin of the ASV of 1901 and adopted by the RSV: "the appearing of the glory of our great God and Savior Jesus Christ." The earliest versions favor the first of these renderings, while the Greek fathers quite uniformly prefer the latter. The former seems to draw a distinction between God and Christ in speaking of the **glorious appearing.** The latter identifies Christ with God—and proclaims His essential deity, or identity, with God, in announcing His imminent appearing. Guthrie points out further that "the use of the word *appearing,* which is never used of God, further supports the ascription of the entire phrase to Christ."[5] The bulk of evidence seems to favor the latter of these two views.

[3]*Op. cit.,* p. 260.

[4]*Op. cit.,* p. 246.

[5]*The Pastoral Epistles,* p. 200.

Paul links with this reaffirmation of his faith in the Second Coming a further analysis of the redemptive significance of the work of Christ. **Who gave himself for us, that he might redeem us from all iniquity, and purify unto himself a peculiar people, zealous of good works** (14). In a typical Pauline expression the apostle is declaring here the substitutionary character of our Lord's sacrifice of himself on the Cross. This self-giving is "on our behalf" or "instead of us"; the idea of "proxyship" is definitely present in the preposition rendered **for** (*hyper*). And the purpose of this self-giving of Christ is declared to be our redemption. Here is an echo of our Lord's own designation of himself as "a ransom" (Mark 10:45). It would be quite beside the point to invest this idea of ransom with all of the extravagances which came to characterize it in the Early Church. Nevertheless the ransom idea is too precious for us ever to relinquish it; for it says something about the cross of Christ which can be expressed in no other terms.

Our redemption is a redemption **from all iniquity**, which the apostle contends is ours through Christ's suffering. Barrett points out that "the meaning of this liberation is given in the positive clause that follows; it is a release not so much from guilt, as from actual sin, a cleansing and an impetus towards good works."[6] Here again we see that Paul was no apologist for sin, but believed in a real deliverance from it.

It is evident that Christ is concerned to have a people for himself; a people cleansed and purified, and belonging to Him in a unique sense. The adjective **peculiar** does not refer to oddities which might characterize such a people. Rather, the meaning is set forth clearly in the rendering of the NEB: "a pure people marked out for his own." Paul further emphasizes the ethical thrust of such a life in the words **zealous of good works**, or "eager to do good" (NEB).

The chapter ends on the same note with which it begins: **These things speak, and exhort, and rebuke with all authority** (15). Titus' ministry must be marked by a firm, courageous, uncompromising adherence to this message. And, adds Paul, **let no man despise thee.** Something of a similar nature was said to Timothy on account of his youth (I Tim. 4:12). This admonition to Titus may have been for a similar reason.

[6]*Op. cit.*, p. 138.

Section VI *Christians in a Pagan World*

Titus 3:1-7

A. Be Good Citizens, 3:1-2

The apostle now moves into a new area of Christian living of which the Cretan believers must be continuously aware. In the earlier chapters of his letter he has been dealing with the believers' relationships with each other and the problem of Christian order among the churches. Now he turns to their relationships with the "powers that be." **Put them in mind to be subject to principalities and powers, to obey magistrates, to be ready to every good work (1).**

Paul's philosophy of government is rather clearly stated in Rom. 13:1-7, beginning with the words: "Let every soul be subject unto the higher powers. For there is no power but of God: and the powers that be are ordained of God." In this view, the state derives its authority from God. This is not to say that those powers are never exercised by the consent of the governed. It declares simply that, other things being equal, one should reverence and obey the civil authorities. It does not really matter that those who occupy positions of authority are not themselves Christian, or that many times they are pagan, as in the first century. Nor does this attitude foreclose a Christian's right to resist oppression or an official attempt to destroy freedom of worship. The time came when the heavy hand of governmental oppression fell upon the Church and the only Christian course was one of civil disobedience. But that time was not yet. In Crete the duty of Christians was **to be subject to principalities and powers, to obey magistrates.**

Paul's further admonition, **to be ready to every good work,** is not to be understood as a general exhortation to Christian service, but belongs rather in the context of good citizenship. A Christian must be prepared to serve his community in whatever constructive ways he can. This could well mean running for and serving in political office, or taking an active part in worthy projects for the promotion of charity and the welfare of children. No man should withdraw from the performance of his civic responsibilities under the pretext that, while he is *in* the world, he is not *of* it. Whatever Jesus meant in His high priestly prayer in John 17:16, He did not mean this. In civic affairs, Christians must "be prepared to render whatever good service they can" (Phillips).

The apostle continues in 2 his delineation of the Christian's civic behavior: **To speak evil of no man, to be no brawlers, but gentle, shewing all meekness unto all men.** The first of these reminders is one we need to hear and heed in the context of the church as well as in that of the civic community. There are three tests to which we should put every derogatory speech we are tempted to make about others: (1) Is it true? (2) Is it kind? and (3) Is it necessary? How many times the application of these three tests would effectively seal our lips!

No brawlers, but gentle. This means simply to avoid quarreling and the quarrelsome spirit out of which quarrels are born. On the contrary, urges Paul, be **gentle.** Some of the connotations of **gentle** are quietness, kindness, tenderness, refinement—all of them qualities distinctively Christian. **Showing all meekness** is a phrase which lends itself to misunderstanding. The RSV has captured its meaning precisely: "Show perfect courtesy toward all men."

B. Christians Are Transformed by Grace, 3:3-7

As a reason for such kindly and considerate treatment of others who are lost from God, Paul reminds the Cretan Christians of the pit from which they had been digged: **For we ourselves also were sometime foolish, disobedient, deceived, serving divers lusts and pleasures, living in malice and envy, hateful, and hating one another** (3). This is a dark and forbidding picture, yet who would question its truth? And with characteristic modesty the apostle includes himself among those who had once been thus deceived. The utter folly of sinful living, the defiance of God's way and will for one's life, the terrible lostness of one who is alienated from God in the midst of God's universe, the slavery to one's bestial nature which sin necessarily involves, a godless life aflame with envy and hatred—all this is gathered up in the apostle's portrayal of the slimy pit from which these believers in Crete had but lately been recovered.

For that glorious recovery he proceeds immediately to give God praise. **But after that the kindness and love of God our Saviour toward man appeared** (4). The apostle is thinking here of the miracle of justification by faith, the gracious pardon of past sins, which has been brought into the realm of human experience by the coming of God's Son into the world. Paul sees in the incarnation of God's Son the dawning of a new day in human affairs. This dawning or "appearing," to use the term employed by the KJV, is really an "epiphany" or divine disclosure; and the things revealed are the **kindness and love of God our Saviour.** This Greek word *chrestotes* literally means benignity. "Used of God," notes Kelly, "it connotes his kindness and pitying concern."[1] It is frequently linked, as here, with the Greek word *philanthropia,* which means affection for man as man. Obviously "philanthropy" is a term derived from this root. These are the qualities in the character of God which are particularly revealed in this appearing of **God our Saviour.** God is so described because it was in fulfillment of His saving purpose that Christ came to our world.

That God's redeeming intervention on our behalf is wholly a matter of divine grace, and in no sense the result of human merit, is made clear by verse 5: **Not by works of righteousness which we have done, but according to his mercy he saved us, by the washing of regeneration, and renewing of the Holy Ghost.** The utter impossibility of man's performing **works of righteousness** is a frequent theme of the apostle, set forth with particular cogency in the opening chapters of the Epistle to the Romans. Paul is talking about the vanity of any hope of man that he might merit the grace of God. Nothing we can do can place Almighty God under obligation to us. Salvation is "not of works" but wholly of grace. Our only hope lies in the response of our awakened spirits to the prior arousing ministry of the Holy Spirit, a response which prompts us to sincere repentance and to sue for God's mercy. But the initiative is always with God, and our response is an enabled one, made possible by the Holy Spirit. So then **according to his mercy he saved us.** There is no other explanation possible. And yet this really does not explain, for no man can comprehend the mercy of God.

Paul's understanding of the divine method in accomplishing our salvation is a twofold one. In the first place he speaks of **the washing of regeneration,** which employs the language of the rite of baptism. Baptism is not to be understood as the actual means by which men are saved, but is rather to be regarded, here at least, as symbolical of the experience of death to sin and

[1]*Op. cit.,* p. 251.

spiritual resurrection in newness of life. The apostle elsewhere invests the baptismal symbol with this meaning when he says: "Therefore we are buried with him by baptism into death: that like as Christ was raised from the dead by the glory of the Father, even so we also should walk in newness of life" (Rom. 6:4). To be saved is to be thus made alive, risen from the death of trespasses and sins.

The second aspect of the salvation experience is **the renewing of the Holy Ghost.** The Holy Spirit, in the language of the Church's ancient creeds, is "the Lord and Giver of life." This involves all of life in all of its manifestations. But in a particular sense is the forgiven and renewed sinner made alive by the Holy Spirit. This life is the Spirit's unique work—in its inception, its growth and increase, and its fullness.

The present reality of the Spirit's outpouring is proclaimed in 6: **Which he shed on us abundantly through Jesus Christ our Saviour.** The Holy Spirit's life-giving function is related intimately to the redeeming and intercessory work of the Lord Jesus. He himself proclaimed that the gift of the Spirit would be bestowed by both the Father and himself (John 14:26; 16:7). It is this teaching which is set forth in the doctrine of the "double procession" of the Holy Spirit; He proceedeth both from the Father and from the Son. His coming is related to our Lord's return to the Father's right hand (John 7:39). The coming of the Holy Spirit at Pentecost was regarded as a bestowal by the glorified Saviour (Acts 2:33). And every regenerated soul is made alive by this same quickening Spirit.

The apostle now carries his survey of the miracle of spiritual transformation to its logical and inevitable conclusion: **That being justified by his grace, we should be made heirs according to the hope of eternal life** (7). Justification is one of the authentic emphases of Pauline thought. He taught that by casting oneself in surrender and faith upon Christ, the forgiveness of sins is assured and the sinner himself, whatever the past may have been, is received into God's grace and favor. But there is more here than the promise of the life that now is: for **the hope of eternal life** is likewise bestowed on every sinner who turns to God through Christ. What the apostle is giving us in verses 4-7 is the whole scheme of the divine mercy and the plan of salvation. Few summaries of the saving grace of God are more luminous than this.

Section VII *Closing Admonitions*

Titus 3:8-11

A. Keep Busy for Christ, 3:8

Paul now, as he nears the conclusion of his letter, turns to exhortation once again. **This is a faithful saying, and these things I will that thou affirm constantly, that they which have believed in God might be careful to maintain good works.** The first clause of this verse we encounter frequently in the Pastorals (I Tim. 1:15; II Tim. 2:11). Kelly points out that "it looks back [to verses 3-7] rather than forward." He holds the view that "all or part of 3-7 is a quotation, probably from some hymn or liturgical piece connected with baptism."[1] If it be a quotation, it is clear that the apostle gives it his complete approval and urges it upon the attention of Titus as the message which he should preach. The suggestion is obvious that to hold this faith and to be totally committed to it will result in the careful maintenance of **good works.** It is important to distinguish clearly between those "works of righteousness" which, in 5, are declared to be useless as a means of commending oneself to the favor of God and these **good works** which are the inevitable outflow of the life transformed by grace. These are the works which James regarded as the sure mark of a truly Christian life (Jas. 2:18). And, as Paul clearly sees, it is only those who greatly believe who faithfully serve.

The apostle's judgment on this point is tersely put in the concluding statement: **These things are good and profitable unto men.**

B. Avoid Futile Controversies, 3:9-11

The apostle now returns to the heresies which had plagued the Cretan churches and restates his warning of 1:10-16: **But avoid foolish questions, and genealogies, and contentions, and strivings about the law; for they are unprofitable and vain (9).** This repeated caution reveals how deeply the apostle felt about

[1]*Op. cit.*, p. 254.

the disruptive effect of such teachings, and his concern that Titus be fully aware of them and well armed against them. The description included in this final reference makes clearer than in the earlier discussion the Jewish character of these heresies.

Scott insists to the end that the Cretan heresies were predominantly Gnostic in character. But he is proceeding on the assumption that the Pastorals are post-Pauline in authorship, to be dated at a time when the Church's battle against Gnosticism was at its height. As we have contended throughout our discussion of the Pastoral Epistles, the heresies which threatened the integrity and life of the churches in both Ephesus and Crete represented the earlier phase of Gnosticism when it was predominantly Jewish in character. Indeed, the evidence for this point of view goes far toward establishing the earlier dating of these letters and their authentic Pauline authorship.

The apostle next suggests the appropriate disciplinary action which should be taken against those who reject his admonition: **A man that is an heretick after the first and second admonition reject; knowing that he that is such is subverted** ("perverted," RSV; "has a moral twist," Phillips), **and sinneth, being condemned of himself** (10-11). The word **heretick** is derived from the Greek word *hairetikos.* Not until the second century did this term come to mean one who holds false doctrine. Here in 10 it means a noisy and opinionated person who will not give up until he has brought everyone else around to his point of view. The RSV renders it "a man who is factious," while Phillips translates the passage: "If a man is still argumentative after the second warning you should reject him." Barclay is helpful at this point. "A heretic," says he, "is simply a man who has decided that he is right and everybody else is wrong. Paul's warning is a warning against the man who has made his own ideas the test and standard of all truth. A man should always be very careful of any opinion which separates him from the fellowship of his fellow believers. True faith does not divide men; it unites them."[2] The apostle stands firmly by his judgment here. The man who refuses to hear and heed the warnings of God's ministers against his divisive attitude and persists in attempting to make his own notions the norm of Christian truth has indeed fallen into sin—the sin of pride of opinion—and stands self-condemned.

[2]*Op. cit.,* p. 304.

Section VIII *Conclusion*

Titus 3:12-15

In customary Pauline fashion, the letter concludes with some purely personal items. **When I shall send Artemas unto thee, or Tychicus, be diligent to come unto me to Nicopolis: for I have determined there to winter** (12). One or the other of the men here named, the apostle intended to send to Crete to replace Titus so that he could leave for the trip to Nicopolis. Just which of them it was to be was yet to be determined. **Artemas** is mentioned nowhere else in Paul's letters, but **Tychicus** is a fairly well-known figure. He was a traveling companion of the apostle (Acts 20:4), and served as his messenger in bearing Paul's Ephesian letter to Ephesus (Eph. 6:21). He performed a similar service in respect to the Colossian letter. Later on, when Paul was suffering his final imprisonment, Tychicus was sent on a mission to Timothy in Ephesus (II Tim. 4:12).

There were a number of cities in the ancient world bearing the name **Nicopolis.** The one Paul has in mind would appear to be Nicopolis on the Greek mainland (see map 1). The note in II Tim. 4:10, written two or three years later, that Titus had gone to Dalmatia would place Titus at this later date in the general vicinity of Nicopolis.

Bring Zenas the lawyer and Apollos on their journey diligently, that nothing be wanting unto them (13). The name of **Zenas** is another of the friends of Paul whom we meet nowhere else in the apostle's writings. The designation **the lawyer** is added probably to distinguish him from some other person bearing the same name. **Apollos** is well known to us, appearing both in the Acts (18:24) and in I Corinthians. These two Christian leaders were evidently coming to visit Crete and perhaps were even the bearers of Paul's letter to Titus. The apostle is concerned that appropriate hospitality be extended them.

On the face of it, 14 is somewhat obscure: **And let ours also learn to maintain good works for necessary uses, that they be not unfruitful.** This seems to be an exhortation to be industrious. The RSV (marg.) suggests the reading: "Let our people learn to enter honorable occupations." But it could well be that the reference in 13 to the hospitality to be accorded Zenas and Apollos suggests to the apostle's mind the need for inculcating this virtue of hospitality among the generality of Christians in Crete.

The Epistle ends with a general greeting. **All that are with me salute thee. Greet them that love us in the faith. Grace be with you all. Amen** (15). The apostle does not name all of his present company, but includes them all in his greetings to Titus. Paul had some dear personal friends in Crete, perhaps his children in the gospel; and to **them that love us in the faith** he sends affectionate regards. The final benediction is completely in character, and includes the whole church of Christ in Crete: **Grace be with you all. Amen.**

Bibliography

TIMOTHY AND TITUS

I. COMMENTARIES

BARCLAY, WILLIAM *The Letters to Timothy, Titus, Philemon.* "The Daily Study Bible." Edinburgh: The Saint Andrew Press, 1956.

BARRETT, C. K. *The Pastoral Epistles.* "The New Clarendon Bible." Edited by H. F. D. SPARKS. London: Oxford University Press, 1963.

DODD, C. H. *The Epistle of Paul to the Romans.* "The Moffatt New Testament Commentary." London: Hodder and Stoughton, 1949.

EASTON, B. S. *The Pastoral Epistles.* New York: Charles Scribner's Sons, 1947.

GEALY, F. D. "The First and Second Epistles to Timothy and the Epistle to Titus" (Exegesis). *The Interpreter's Bible.* Edited by G. A. BUTTRICK, *et al.*, Vol. XI. New York: Abingdon Press, 1952.

GUTHRIE, DONALD. *The Pastoral Epistles.* "The Tyndale New Testament Commentaries." Edited by R. V. G. TASKER. Grand Rapids: Wm. B. Eerdmans Publishing Co., 1957.

KELLY, J. N. D. A *Commentary on the Pastoral Epistles.* "Harper's New Testament Commentaries." Edited by HENRY CHADWICK. New York: Harper & Row, 1963.

LOWSTUTER, W. J. "The Pastoral Epistles: First and Second Timothy and Titus." *The Abingdon Bible Commentary.* Edited by F. C. EISELEN, *et al.* New York: Abingdon-Cokesbury Press, 1929.

NOYES, M. P. "The First and Second Epistles to Timothy and the Epistle to Titus" (Exposition). *The Interpreter's Bible.* Edited by G. A. BUTTRICK, *et al.*, Vol. XI. New York: Abingdon Press, 1951.

PARRY, R. ST. JOHN. *The Pastoral Epistles.* London: Cambridge University Press, 1920.

PLUMMER, ALFRED. *The Pastoral Epistles.* "The Expositor's Bible." Edited by W. R. NICOLL. New York: A. C. Armstrong & Son, 1898.

ROLSTON, HOLMES. *1-2 Thessalonians—1-2 Timothy—Titus—Philemon.* "The Layman's Bible Commentary." Edited by B. H. KELLY, *et al.*, Vol. 23. Richmond: John Knox Press, 1963.

SCOTT, E. F. *The Pastoral Epistles.* "The Moffatt New Testament Commentary." London: Hodder and Stoughton, 1936.

SIMPSON, E. K. *The Pastoral Epistles.* Grand Rapids: Wm. B. Eerdmans Publishing Co., 1954.

WESLEY, JOHN. *Explanatory Notes upon the New Testament.* London: The Epworth Press, 1950.

WHITE, N. J. D. "The First and Second Epistles to Timothy and the Epistle to Titus." *The Expositor's Greek Testament.* Edited by W. R. NICOLL, Vol. IV. Grand Rapids: Wm. B. Eerdmans Publishing Co., n.d.

II. OTHER BOOKS

BAILLIE, D. M. *God Was in Christ.* New York: Charles Scribner's Sons, 1948.

DODD, C. H. *The Apostolic Preaching and Its Developments.* New York: Harper and Bros., n.d.

———. *The Parables of the Kingdom.* New York: Charles Scribner's Sons, 1936.

GLOVER, T. R. *The Jesus of History.* New York: George H. Doran Co., 1917.

GUTHRIE, DONALD. *New Testament Introduction: The Pauline Epistles.* Chicago: Inter-Varsity Press, 1961.

HARRISON, P. N. *The Problem of the Pastoral Epistles.* London: Oxford University Press, 1921.

HATCH, EDWIN. *The Organization of the Early Christian Churches.* London: Longmans, Green and Co., 1901.

JOWETT, J. H. *The Preacher: His Life and Work.* New York: Harper and Bros., 1912.

MORGAN, G. C. *The Answers of Jesus to Job.* New York: Fleming H. Revell Co., 1935.

WESLEY, JOHN. *Works.* Edited by THOMAS JACKSON, Vols. VI and VII. Kansas City: Nazarene Publishing House, n.d.

WHITEHEAD, JOHN. *Lives of John and Charles Wesley.* New York: R. Worthington, 1881.

III. ARTICLES

EDWARDS, D. MIALL. "Drunkenness." *International Standard Bible Encyclopaedia.* Edited by JAMES ORR, *et al.*, Vol. II. Chicago: The Howard-Severance Co., 1925.

The Epistle to

PHILEMON

John B. Nielson

Introduction

A. Time

The letter to Philemon appears to be a twin to the Colossian Epistle. It is addressed to the same city (Col. 4:8-9), and it is written by the same Apostle Paul.[1] It was also probably written at the same time as Colossians, about A.D. 62 (Col. 4:7-9).[2]

That it was written from a Roman prison has been held until modern times.[3] It has been suggested, however, that the request, "Prepare me also a lodging" (22), suggests the Caesarean imprisonment from which Paul expected to be released to preach (Acts 23:33—26:32; Phil. 2:24). It is argued that Paul would not likely ask for a lodging from so distant a place as Rome.[4] However, the Lycus Valley believer, Philemon, appears to have been very dear to the apostle (19, 21-22). Paul would naturally seek out such a congenial lodging as the home of so intimate a friend if he were permitted to visit the area again.

B. Destination

John Knox suggests with Goodspeed that this letter is the "epistle" to Laodicea (Col. 4:16-17). It is further suggested that the charge to Archippus (Col. 4:17) is the request of the Philemon letter, that is, to receive and restore Onesimus (10).[5] However, this view has little support. Most commentators accept the traditional view that this was a personal letter written to Philemon of Colossae by Paul (Col. 4:8-9).[6]

Though he is not named in the letter, Tychicus, in the company of Onesimus, is the bearer of it (Col. 4:7-9).

[1]Herbert M. Carson, *The Epistle of Paul to the Colossians and Philemon.* "Tyndale New Testament Commentaries" (Grand Rapids: Wm. B. Eerdmans Publishing Co., 1960), pp. 12-13.

[2]See Introduction to Colossians, BBC.

[3]C. F. D. Moule, *The Epistle of Paul the Apostle to the Colossians and to Philemon,* "The Cambridge Greek Testament Commentary" (Cambridge: University Press, 1957), p. 22.

[4]See Carson on this question, *op. cit.,* pp. 13-15.

[5]Moule, *op. cit.,* pp. 15-16.

[6]*Ibid.,* p. 16. See Moule on the reconstruction of the interpretation of Philemon as proposed by Goodspeed and Knox. See also Carson, *op. cit.,* pp. 18-20.

C. Purpose

The letter is addressed to an individual, Philemon, primarily, but it is also sent to the church that meets in his house (2).

The problem concerns the institution of slavery, traffic in human lives, and what the Christian's response must be. The problem is not only personal and private as in this case; it is a public problem which the whole Christian community and the world at large must face and solve (Col. 3:22—4:1).[7]

What will Paul say and do in the face of such a dilemma? He pits his faith against a whole culture and system of government that condones and protects trade in human lives.

Paul does not attack slavery directly. He does not counsel rebellion or defiance of prevailing law and order. On the contrary he counsels obedience to government (Rom. 13:1 ff.). What he does is to lift the whole issue to a high spiritual plane. He solves the question of slavery, not by compulsion, but by redemption. Paul shows that the believing slave is as truly a Christian brother and as really "in Christ" as the believing master (Rom. 12:4-5). All believers are equally in Christ and are therefore members of the body of Christ. Though each member may have a different function and though there may be distinctions among the members, yet each is a necessary member of the *body* (Eph. 4:11-16). Further, there is no schism in that *body* (I Cor. 12: 25 ff.). No one member or function of the body of believers (the body of Christ) has any inherent authority over any other member or function. All are shown to be equally responsible to their *Head,* who is Christ (I Cor. 12:12-14; Eph. 1:22-23). Further, all the members are to be "subject to one another out of reverence for Christ" (Eph. 5:21, RSV).

What Paul does, therefore, is to inject the Christian solution into the prevailing culture. The leaven of that concept continues to permeate society for its ultimate betterment and correction (Matt. 13:33). The full weight of Paul's teaching, however, has immediate application in the Christian context; all *believers* are brothers—they are one body in Christ (John 17:19 ff.) and therefore are to be treated under the rule of Christian love.

[7]See comments there, BBC.

Outline

A. Prelude, 1-3
   1. The Writer, 1
   2. The Recipients, 1-2
   3. The Greetings, 3

B. Prayer, 4-7
   1. The Prompting of the Prayer, 4-5
   2. The Purpose of the Prayer, 6-7

C. Problem, 8-14
   1. The Appeal Made, 8-12
   2. The Answer Expected, 13-14

D. Proposals, 15-22
   1. Restoration, 15
   2. Elevation, 16-17
   3. Substitution, 18-19
   4. Trust, 20-22

E. Postlude, 23-25

Section I *Slavery and the Christian Response*

Philemon 1-25

A. Prelude, 1-3

1. *The Writer* (1).

In Colossians, Paul calls himself a "servant" (Col. 1:1). Here he states that he is **a prisoner of Jesus Christ.** He is both bound *to* Christ through faith and commitment, and also bound *in* a Roman prison because of his faith in Christ Jesus and his loyalty to Him (Acts 28:30). **Prisoner** indicates what adverse conditions he works under. In the light of the purpose of the letter—to inspire grace and forgiveness in Philemon toward Onesimus—the deplorable circumstances of Paul make the difficulties of Philemon as nothing.

Timothy, as in Colossians, is included as one of the senders of these sentiments and requests. He is Paul's **brother,** spiritually speaking.

2. *The Recipients* (1-2).

The letter is sent primarily to **Philemon our dearly beloved** (1). This gracious word is reserved for Paul's closest companions (cf. II Tim. 1:2). This man is also one of Paul's fellow laborers in the preaching and promotion of the work of Christ. Though the letter is personal and addressed to Philemon, it is also directed to the whole **church** (2), because the problem is public as well as private. Among those addressed is **Apphia,** actually "sister," not **beloved.**[1] It is suggested that she may have been the wife of Philemon. At least she is a "sister" in Christ. Roberts[2] reminds us, as does the italics in KJV, that **our** is not in the Greek text. **Archippus** is called **fellowsoldier,** a companion or associate in the service of Christ. Knox suggests that he rather than Philemon was pastor of the church (Col. 4:16-17).[3]

And to the church in thy house would indicate that the home of Philemon was the meeting place for worship by the Colossian believers (Col. 4:8-9). The church in Laodicea met in the house of Nymphas (Col. 4:15). Very little is said of Hierap-

[1]Alexander Roberts, *Companion to the Revised Version of the New Testament* (New York: Cassell, Petter, Galpin & Co., 1881), p. 56.

[2]*Ibid.*

[3]Quoted in Carson, *op. cit.*, pp. 19-20.

olis, the third town in the Lycus Valley. It is probable that there was no organized church, although its mention suggests that some believers lived there.

3. ***The Greetings*** **(3)**

The familiar Pauline salutation, grace . . . and peace,[4] is here. They are declared to be divinely bestowed from the Father and the Son, the Lord Jesus Christ. The Holy Spirit is not mentioned in this short Epistle.

B. Prayer, 4-7

1. ***The Prompting of the Prayer*** **(4-5)**

Paul is a master in psychology. Characteristically he prepares the ground thoroughly before he plants his seed (Acts 26:2 ff.). He notices and commends the good before he applies words of correction or rebuke.

Praise is characteristically on his lips with the words, I thank my God (4). According to the grammar Paul thanks God always (not, ***prays*** **always).[5] NEB translates it, "I thank my God always." The reason for Paul's praise is Philemon's love and faith (5).[6] These Christian graces are manifested first toward the Lord Jesus (vertical) and then toward all saints (horizontal). The sequence is especially significant for this Epistle because there is no proper human relationship unless there is first a right relationship to God.**

2. ***The Purpose of the Prayer*** **(6-7)**

The purpose of Paul's prayers is the communication (sharing) of Philemon's faith (6). The word ***koinonia,*** **here translated communication, signifies the fellowship of believers (I Cor. 1:9; Gal. 2:9; Phil. 1:5). In I Cor. 10:16 it is used in connection with the Lord's Supper, the Communion meal. Paul's object in praying for Philemon is that his faith may become effectual; i.e., that it may have the power to accomplish the end Paul has in view (Col. 3:17). This end is the admission that all good must be in Christ Jesus. Jesus is omitted in some manuscripts.[7] The**

[4]See comments on Col. 1:2, BBC.

[5]D. Eberhard Nestle, *Novum Testamentum Graece* (Stuttgart: Privilegierte Wurttembergische Bibelanstalt, 1936), in loco.

[6]See comments on Col. 1:4, BBC.

[7]Nestle, *op. cit.,* in loco.

phrasing of this verse calls to mind the spring and end of all ethical conduct as revealed in Col. 3:17 and 23.[8]

The fruit of such experience in Philemon is that wherever he goes his presence and spirit have a salutary effect (7). Read "I had" for **we have.**[9] Some students substitute "grace" for **joy** (*charan*). One Greek letter makes the difference.[10] **Consolation** is from *parakeleo* (John 14:16), and signifies strengthening.[11] **Bowels** (*splangkna*) means heart or emotions, the inner being of man.[12] **Are refreshed** (lit., come to a pause) suggests that all worries and tensions seem to subside by his presence and spirit (cf. 20). Paul calls him **brother** because both are related to the same "elder brother," Christ (Rom. 8:16-17). The wonderful Christlike spirit of Philemon is cause for praise and prayer in Paul.

C. Problem, 8-14

A slave has been converted under Paul's ministry in Rome. The apostle has no right to retain him or to direct him anywhere but to his rightful owner. He must return. What shall Paul do? His problem is at least threefold: (1) Paul is holding property that belongs to another and he must dispose of it in accordance with Christian principles. In this instance the property is a human being, a slave (16). (2) Paul is guided by the culture of his times. He is responsible to the civil law which recognizes and protects the institution of slavery. (3) On the other hand, he lives by and teaches a higher Christian way that rejects and eliminates all prejudices in the Christian *koinonia* (Eph. 6:8; Col. 3:11).

1. *The Appeal Made* (8-12)

Paul, therefore, requests Philemon to receive Onesimus as a member of the fellowship, for he by faith in Christ (10; Col. 4:9) has become a Christian brother.

[8]*Ibid.* See comments on the "pronoun problem" at Col. 1:8, BBC.

[9]Roberts, *op. cit.*, p. 56. ,

[10]H. C. G. Moule, *The Epistles to the Colossians and to Philemon,* "The Cambridge Bible for Schools and Colleges," ed. J. J. S. Perowne (Cambridge: University Press, 1893), p. 170.

[11]Liddell and Scott, *Greek-English Lexicon* (New York: American Book Company, 1882), in loco.

[12]*Ibid.*

Wherefore (8) indicates that Paul believes Philemon will take his request rightly. He has complimented him on his wonderful spirit, and now expects a continuation of that same attitude. Paul could be bold and **enjoin** (command) because of his apostleship, but he does not appeal to this authority (cf. 1). He would rather **beseech** (9; entreat). The apostle uses his rank cautiously. Paul operates from the base of love, **for love's sake,** rather than coercion. He must persuade rather than command. (How many times men turn to force and coercion to achieve their ends when they become too weak to persuade!) **Convenient** signifies that which is fitting or proper. The RSV has "required."

a. Seniority (9*b*). Paul is **aged** (*presbutes,* an old man).[13] The RSV has "ambassador." However, it seems that **aged** fits the mood of this letter more appropriately in the light of the previous verse, where he disclaims the use of his authority as an apostle (Eph. 6:20). Paul was probably sixty years of age at this time.[14]

b. Imprisonment (9*c*-10). Paul is **a prisoner** because of his faith in **Jesus Christ** (9). While in prison he has **begotten** a **son** (10), a metaphor indicating that he had won a convert (cf. Gal. 4:19). God also is said to beget (I Pet. 13:3). Paul asks for sympathy for his **son** on the part of Philemon, seeing he himself cannot release him to the Lord's service. **My** is omitted in some manuscripts in reference to **bonds.**[15]

c. Transformation (11). Onesimus (10) means "profitable," "beneficial" (cf. 14, 20).[16] He is **now profitable** for the first time. The meaning of his name is now his own character. Col. 3:22-23 shows why he will be **profitable** to both Paul and Philemon.

d. Intimacy (12). **Whom I have sent again** (*anapempsa*) is an epistolary aorist and is to be rendered in the present tense, "I am sending" (NEB). It means to refer back, as a prisoner is returned to another tribunal (Luke 23:7, 11; Acts 25:21). Paul would thus be faithful to his duty. **Receive him . . . mine own**

[13]See footnotes, RSV; Liddell and Scott, *op. cit.,* in loco. See also H. C. G. Moule, *op. cit.,* p. 172.

[14]Alexander Maclaren, *The Epistles of St. Paul to the Colossians and Philemon.* "The Expositor's Bible," ed. W. Robertson Nicoll (New York: A. C. Armstrong and Son, 1903), p. 451.

[15]Nestle, *op. cit.,* in loco.

[16]Carson, *op. cit.,* p. 109.

bowels is the same as saying, Receive him as me, as my offspring. The relationship is tender and intimate. Have they not prayed together, suffered, wept, and sung together? The RSV translates it, "I am sending him back to you, sending my very heart."

2. *The Answer Expected* (13-14)

Paul expects in Philemon that higher goodness which springs from free will. **Whom I would have retained** (13) is imperfect, indicating half-purpose,[17] self-counseling. With the words **in thy stead** Paul implies a debt owed him on the part of Philemon (cf. 19*b*). **In the bonds of the gospel** equals the "bonds of Christ."[18]

Mind (14) equals "consent." The benefits are reciprocal, toward Paul as well as toward Philemon, and Onesimus also. But Paul would have Philemon's decision to do right spring from within himself, **willingly**, rather than from **necessity.**

D. Proposals, 15-22

Paul's solution to the problem with which he is faced is fourfold.

1. *Restoration* (15).

Departed is really passive and should be "was parted." Stated in this fashion the word suggests a divine providence in the departure of Onesimus (Rom. 8:28).[19] **Season** is literally an "hour," meaning a short time. **For ever** (*aionion*) means "for good" or permanently. Paul therefore requests Philemon to restore Onesimus to personal, permanent fellowship.

2. *Elevation* (16-17).

Paul does not deny the fact of slavery nor seek to destroy it overtly, but he does lift it to a new dimension of free and responsible relationship.[20] He suggests that Onesimus be considered **a brother beloved** (16); that is, a Christian (Rom. 8:29; I Cor. 5:11). Though the curse of slavery might one day be removed, the law of service and work must never be abrogated (Eph. 5:21; II Thess. 3:8-10). Many want the law of work repealed and look to welfare and handouts, but the Scriptures teach the law of responsible service. Christianity really solves the

[17]Moule, *op. cit.*, p. 174.
[18]See comments on v. 1.
[19]Maclaren, *op. cit.*, p. 470.
[20]Carson, *op. cit.*, pp. 23-24.

slavery problem, where it solves the oppression problem.[21] The benefits flow both ways—**to me . . . unto thee,** and to the slave as well (cf. 11). **In the flesh** should not be taken literally. It signifies material blessings as **in the Lord** signifies spiritual blessings.

How significant the phrase **in the Lord!** Slavery, degradation of women, infanticide, war, immorality—all are destroyed by union with Christ.

Partner (17) comes from the same word as Christian fellowship (*koinonia*). Paul declares that his role and that of Onesimus could be exchanged, so intimately associated in Christ's service are they. The apostle sees also the potential in Onesimus. He is called a bishop by Ignatius, which fact could be a "spectacular sequel to Paul's letter many years later."[22] It seems in the light of Col. 4:1 that Paul is hinting at the release of the slave.

3. *Substitution* (18-19).

Restitution for wrongs done is a necessary requirement for right relations with God and man. The beautiful thing here is the utterly Christian attitude in the apostle (Exod. 32:32). Paul is the Good Samaritan (Luke 10:33 ff.). He offers to pay the bills owed. **Put** (18; *elloga*) equals "impute." The apostle assumes the same spirit that Christ takes toward sinners (Col. 2:14). **I Paul have written it with mine own hand** (19) makes the promise a bond.[23] However, Paul gently implies that, if the debt is put to his account, then it is already cancelled by what Philemon owes to him as his spiritual father.

4. *Trust* (20-22).

"Let me have this benefit [*onaimen*] of you" could be an allusion to the name of Onesimus.[24] **Refresh** (20) means to encourage and parallels v. 7. **In the Lord** signifies that the joy Paul desires is spiritual satisfaction.

His proposal is a continuation of the **confidence** (21; trust) that he has had in Philemon through the years. He is confident of his **obedience** (Rom. 5:19), i.e., of his loyalty to the Lord. It is literally that he will "hearken unto him."[25] **Do more than I say** suggests the possible freeing of the slave.

[21]See Introduction, "Purpose."
[22]Moule, *op. cit.*, p. 21.
[23]Maclaren, *op. cit.*, p. 479.
[24]See footnote 16.
[25]Liddell and Scott, *op. cit.*, in loco.

Paul is confident of continued friendship, for he asks for a **lodging** (22; guest room), probably in Philemon's home, although he does not say so specifically.[26] Paul also states confidence in Philemon's **prayers,** for he expects through them to **be given unto you,** i.e., released from prison. To be in adverse circumstances by the permissive will of God does not require abject resignation. The Christian in such circumstances intercedes with God for better times and greater opportunity, whatever that may be.

E. Postlude, 23-25

There follows a greeting from some of Paul's companions. These associates are the same as those mentioned in Colossians, with the exception of Justus (see comments on Col. 4:7-14). Here **Epaphras** is called a **fellowprisoner** (23). The reference may be to physical imprisonment or it may mean captured by Christ. In Colossians he is called a "fellowservant" (1:7; 4:12).

The familiar benediction of **grace** (25) is bestowed upon Philemon and his friends. **Your spirit** should be plural.[27] Here the **grace** is from **our Lord Jesus Christ** (cf. 3).

Paul is a master of argumentation and persuasion. He understands the psychology of human relations. Note how he approaches leadership and the exercise of authority. He has learned from his Lord (9) that the morality that counts springs not from compulsion but from free will. True fellowship exists where free men serve each other to the glory of Christ (Rom. 12:1-8; Eph. 5:21). If Paul seems at times authoritarian and dogmatic, this attitude springs, not from a feeling of superiority (I Cor. 15:9; Eph. 3:8), but from the firm conviction of the trustworthiness of his report of the meaning and significance of the gospel (Gal. 1:8-9).

It should be held in mind also that Paul's principles apply primarily to the Christian community, the *koinonia.* The world of unbelieving, unconverted men can never live on this level of human relationship until changed by divine grace (II Cor. 5:17). Therefore the work of the Christian community—if it is to see the kingdom of God come on earth—is to persuade the world to enter the new life in Christ. Our task is to "make all men see what is the fellowship of the mystery" of this new way. To such a vision Paul and the Christian Church are committed.

[26]Moule, *op. cit.*, p. 177.

[27]Nestle, *op. cit.*, in loco.

Bibliography

I. COMMENTARIES

BARRY, ALFRED. *The Epistle to the Ephesians, Philippians, and Colossians.* "Bible Commentary." Edited by CHARLES JOHN ELLICOTT. London: Cassell and Co., Ltd., n.d.

CALVIN, JOHN. *Commentary on the Epistles of Paul the Apostle to the Philippians, Colossians, and Thessalonians.* Translated by JOHN PRINGLE. Edinburgh: 1851.

CARSON, HERBERT M. *The Epistles of Paul to the Colossians and Philemon.* "Tyndale New Testament Commentaries." Grand Rapids: Wm. B. Eerdmans Publishing Co., 1960.

CLARKE, ADAM. *The New Testament of Our Lord and Saviour Jesus Christ,* Vol. II. New York: Abingdon Cokesbury Press, n.d.

HENRY, MATTHEW. *Commentary on the Whole Bible,* Vol. VI. New York: Fleming H. Revell Co., n.d.

JAMIESON, ROBERT, FAUSSET, S. R., BROWN, DAVID. *A Bible Commentary,* Vol. II. New York: Fleming H. Revell Co., n.d.

LIGHTFOOT, J. B. *St. Paul's Epistles to the Colossians and to Philemon,* Revised. London: The Macmillan Co., 1900.

MACLAREN, ALEXANDER. *The Epistles of St. Paul to the Colossians and Philemon.* "The Expositor's Bible." Edited by W. ROBERTSON NICOLL. New York: A. C. Armstrong and Son, 1903.

MOULE, C. F. D. *The Epistles of Paul the Apostle to the Colossians and to Philemon.* "The Cambridge Greek Testament Commentary." Cambridge: University Press, 1957.

MOULE, H. C. G. *The Epistles to the Colossians and to Philemon.* "The Cambridge Bible for Schools and Colleges." Cambridge: University Press, 1893.

II. OTHER BOOKS

GOODSPEED, EDGAR J. *New Solutions of New Testament Problems.* Chicago: University of Chicago, 1927.

———. *The Story of the New Testament.* Chicago: University of Chicago Press, 1916.

HICKIE, W. J. *Greek-English Lexicon.* New York: The Macmillan Co., 1934.

LIDDELL AND SCOTT. *Greek-English Lexicon.* New York: American Book Company, 1882.

NESTLE, E. EBERHARD. *Novum Testamentum Graece.* Stuttgart: Privilegierte Wurttembergische Bibelanstalt, 1936.

ROBERTS, ALEXANDER. *Companion to the Revised Version.* New York: Cassell, Petter, Galpin and Co., 1881.

III. ARTICLES

GOODENOUGH, E. R. "Paul and Onesimus." *Harvard Theological Review,* Vol. XXII. Cambridge: Harvard University Press, 1929.

Map 1

THE MEDITERRANEAN WORLD
in the Time of Paul
SCALE OF MILES
EUROPE
MACEDONIA
ACHAIA
ITALY
SICILY
MELITA
Black Sea
Adriatic Sea
Aegean Sea
MEDITERRANEAN SEA
ASIA
BITHYNIA
GALATIA
CAPPADOCIA
PONTUS
ARMENIA
CILICIA
SYRIA
PISIDIA
PAMPHYLIA
LYCIA
CYPRUS
CRETE
CLAUDA
LIBYA
RHODES
SAMOTHRACIA
PATMOS
SAMOS
CHIOS
Rome
Three Taverns
Appii Forum
Puteoli
Rhegium
Syracuse
Nicopolis
Thessalonica
Berea
Amphipolis
Apollonia
Philippi
Neapolis
Corinth
Cenchreae
Athens
Troas
Assos
Mitylene
Adramyttium
Pergamum
Thyatira
Sardis
Smyrna
Ephesus
Philadelphia
Laodicea
Hierapolis
Colosse
Miletus
Cnidus
Rhodes
Patara
Myra
Attalia
Perga
Antioch
Iconium
Lystra
Derbe
Tarsus
Seleucia
Antioch
Salamis
Paphos
Phenice
Lasea
Fair Havens
C. Salmone
Cyrene
Alexandria
Sidon
Tyre
Ptolemais
Caesarea
Samaria
Joppa
Jericho
Jerusalem
Gaza
Damascus
N
E
S
W

Map 2

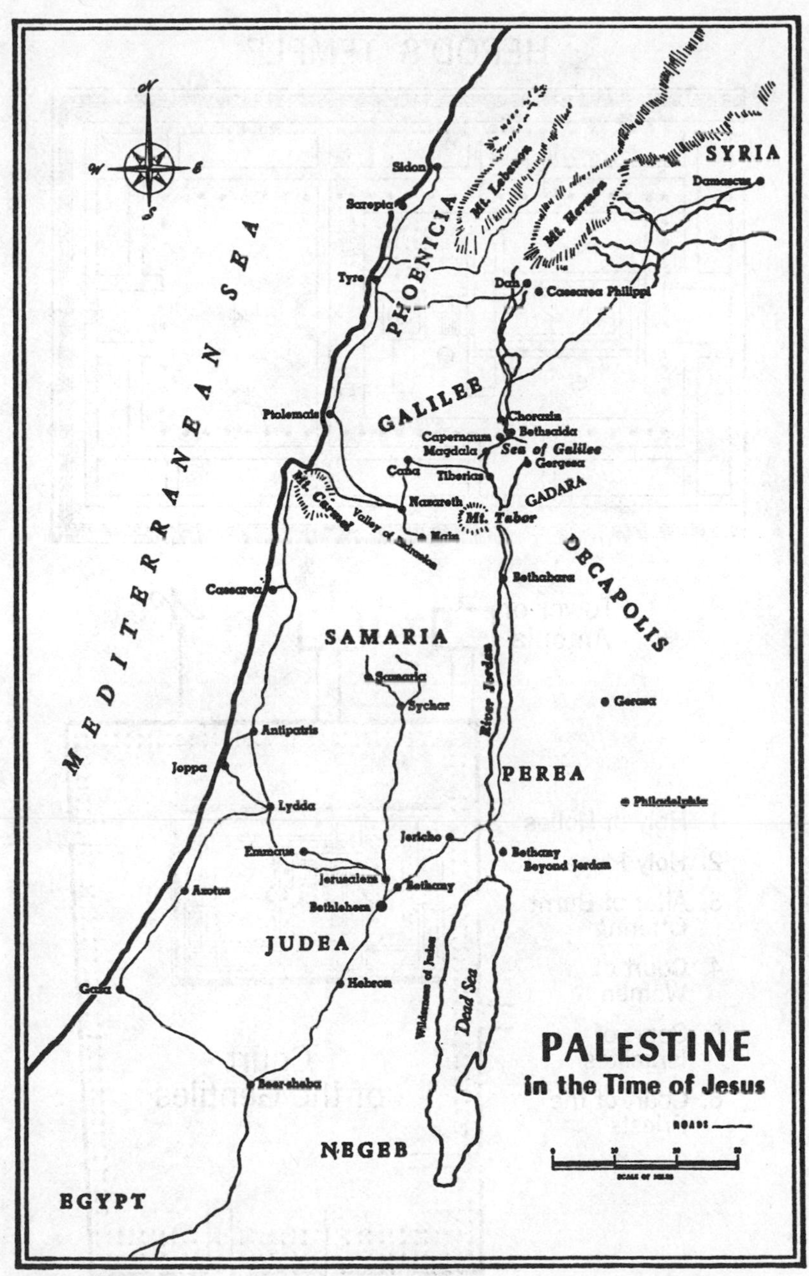
SYRIA
Damascus
Sidon
Sarepta
Mt. Lebanon
Mt. Hermon
PHOENICIA
Tyre
Dan
Caesarea Philippi
MEDITERRANEAN SEA
GALILEE
Ptolemais
Chorazin
Bethsaida
Capernaum
Magdala
Sea of Galilee
Gergesa
Cana
Tiberias
GADARA
Mt. Carmel
Nazareth
Mt. Tabor
Valley of Esdraelon
Nain
DECAPOLIS
Bethabara
Caesarea
SAMARIA
Samaria
Sychar
Gerasa
River Jordan
Antipatris
Joppa
PEREA
Lydda
Philadelphia
Jericho
Emmaus
Bethany
Beyond Jordan
Jerusalem
Bethany
Azotus
Bethlehem
JUDEA
Hebron
Gaza
Wilderness of Judea
Dead Sea
PALESTINE
in the Time of Jesus
ROADS
Beer-sheba
NEGEB
EGYPT

Chart A

HEROD'S TEMPLE

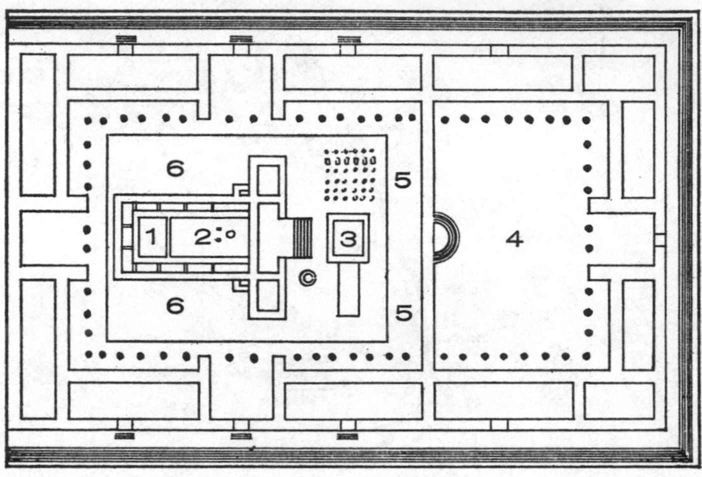

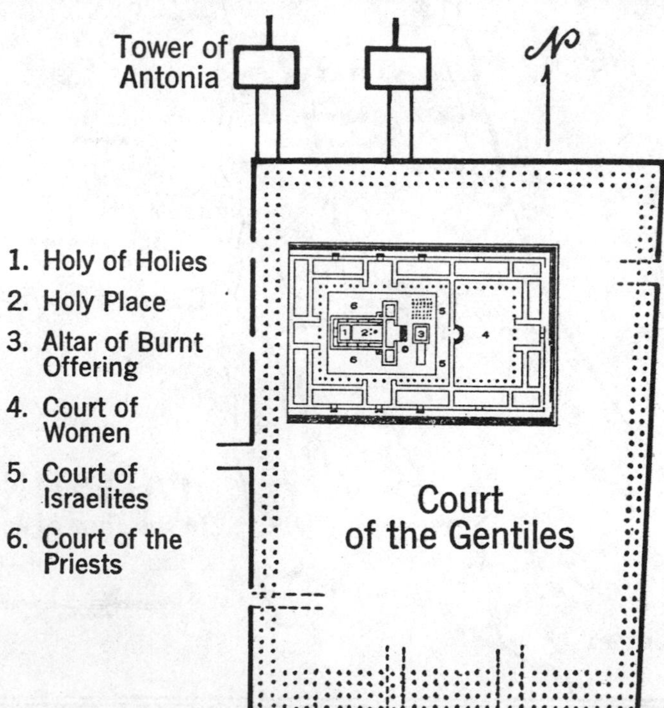